SHADES OF GREENE

Jeremy Lewis worked in publishing for much of his life after leaving Trinity College, Dublin, in 1965, and was a director of Chatto & Windus for ten years. He has been a freelance writer and editor since 1989. The deputy editor of the *London Magazine* from 1990 to 1994, he has been commissioning editor of the *Oldie* since 1997, and editor-at-large of the *Literary Review* since 2004. He has written three volumes of autobiography, *Playing for Time*, *Kindred Spirits* and *Grub Street Irregular*, and edited an anthology, *The Chatto Book of Office Life*. His authorised biography of Cyril Connolly was published by Jonathan Cape in 1997, and a life of Tobias Smollett in 2003; *Penguin Special: The Life and Times of Allen Lane* was published by Viking in 2005. A committee member of the R.S. Surtees Society and a Fellow of the Royal Society of Literature, he is currently researching a biography of David Astor of the *Observer*, to be published by Jonathan Cape. He is married with two daughters and lives near Richmond Park.

JEREMY LEWIS

Shades of Greene

One Generation of an English Family

VINTAGE BOOKS
London

Published by Vintage 2011

2 4 6 8 10 9 7 5 3 1

First published in Great Britain in 2010 by
Jonathan Cape

Vintage
Random House, 20 Vauxhall Bridge Road,
London SW1V 2SA

www.vintage-books.co.uk

Addresses for companies within The Random House Group Limited
can be found at: www.randomhouse.co.uk/offices.htm

The Random House Group Limited Reg. No. 954009

A CIP catalogue record for this book
is available from the British Library

ISBN 9780099551881

The Random House Group Limited supports The Forest Stewardship
Council (FSC), the leading international forest certification organisation.
All our titles that are printed on Greenpeace approved FSC certified
paper carry the FSC logo. Our paper procurement policy can be found
at www.rbooks.co.uk/environment

Mixed Sources
Product group from well-managed
forests and other controlled sources
www.fsc.org Cert no. TT-COC-2139
© 1996 Forest Stewardship Council

Typeset by Palimpsest Book Production Limited, Falkirk, Stirlingshire
Printed and bound in Great Britain by
CPI Cox & Wyman, Reading RG1 8EX

To my sister, Julia,
and in memory of my parents,
George ('Mo') and Janet Lewis

CONTENTS

Preamble

In the early years of the last century two brothers found themselves living in a small country town some thirty miles north-west of London. Neither was a native of the town: both were middle-aged, and both had been successful in their careers, albeit in very different ways. The older of the two had led a quieter, more conventional life: after taking his degree at Oxford, he had become a schoolmaster, and was now the headmaster of the public school which dominated the town, and took its name from it. His brother, less academically inclined, had left school in his teens to work in France and Germany before settling in Brazil, where he had made a fortune as a coffee merchant. There had long been money in the family, but whereas the headmaster and his family lived modestly on school premises, the coffee merchant bought a handsome Georgian mansion at the other end of the town, and employed a large contingent of servants to look after the house, its inhabitants and its extensive grounds.

Both the brothers had six children apiece, and it is they who form the subject of this book. They all knew each other while they were growing up, in varying degrees of intimacy and friendship, and of the twelve, at least eight led lives of distinction or of interest to the world at large. Taking in part after their mother, the headmaster's children were tall, lean, elegant and clever, with round heads like cannonballs and bulbous blue eyes. A natural reserve was attributed by some to an innate coldness of disposition, by others to shyness. Of the four boys, one became one of the best-known writers of the century, one the Director-General of the BBC, one an Everest mountaineer and pioneer endocrinologist, and one, the black sheep of the family, a fantasist and amateur spy. Spying, it was said, ran in the family, and the second daughter worked for many years for MI6.

The coffee merchant's children were equally tall and, like their cousins, spoke in clipped, almost staccato tones; their mother was German, and some of them had grown up speaking German as their first language. They were warmer, less cerebral and less alarming than their cousins; both families grew up with leftwards-leaning inclinations, but the coffee merchant's offspring tended to be more idealistic and less down-to-earth than their harder-headed cousins down the road. Three of them led quiet and seemingly unremarkable lives, but one son was active in the pre-war Labour Party before being interned in May 1940 at the same time as Oswald Mosley; another was the BBC's first North-American correspondent and went on to write admiring books about Communist China; and a daughter wrote a book about travelling around Liberia with her novelist cousin, and spent the war years in Nazi Germany.

This is not intended to be a family history – such books are boring to read, and equally boring to write and research – but ancestors and descendants will play their parts, albeit in supporting roles. The siblings and first cousins who grew up together in that small country town went on to lead varied and often colourful lives, but had certain traits in common, inherited from and shared with a large cast of uncles, aunts and forebears: literacy, and an ability to put pen to paper; a melancholic streak, which had descended into madness in earlier generations; initiative, independence and an ability to make their own ways in the world with the self-confidence that was once so typical of the English upper middle classes. The Greenes were, and still are, a remarkable tribe, and the activities of that generation which forms the subject of this book are not only fascinating in themselves, but illuminate and embody many of the political, cultural, literary and social complexities of the times they lived in.

Much to my relief, the book has proved less lop-sided than I feared. It was suggested to me by Graham C. Greene, the son of Hugh Carleton and the nephew of Graham, and although I accepted with alacrity, I was uneasily aware that I knew next to nothing about the Greenes. Graham Greene was, of course, a familiar name; I remembered reading about Hugh Greene when he was running the BBC, and the name Felix Greene rang faint bells as an authority on China; but that was as far as it went. I worried that Graham would dominate the proceedings, and that I would end up writing yet another biography of Graham Greene, with Hugh playing second fiddle and other members of the family reduced to spear-carrying roles. My fears proved unfounded. Not only had the other Greenes led, as often as not, unconventional lives, but because they belonged to a literate and articulate family, some of them left such voluminous archives that, in moments of panic, I had to remind myself that I was writing a group biography, rather than the life of any single Greene.

Graham Greene has been badly served by his biographers, but the facts of his life have been well covered in the various lives that have been written, as well as in his own memoirs and his published letters; and whereas his siblings and cousins are, for the most part, *terra incognita*, I have assumed a degree of prior knowledge of his life and work on the part of my readers. To have included every known detail of his life would have destroyed the balance of the book, and made it intolerably long, so I have concentrated on those aspects of his life – publishing, the literary world, espionage – which, to a greater or lesser extent, involved other members of the family as well. (The Greenes' involvement in the book trade has enabled me to indulge my own interest in publishing history.) I have made no attempt to summarise the plots of his novels, let alone indulge in any form of literary criticism: partly because I am not qualified to do so, and partly because it has been undertaken at length elsewhere.

My book is chronologically unbalanced in that I have concentrated my fire on the period between 1920 and the 1940s, when my subjects were full of hope and promise, and their lives were more interlaced than they later became: although Raymond was revered by his medical colleagues, he was never a public figure as such, and Graham, Hugh and Felix are the only Greenes whose lives were of interest to the world at large from the cradle to the grave. Eager to evoke a society as well as a family, I have provided detailed accounts of particular incidents or aspects of my subjects' lives, from the Everest expedition of 1933, the activities of British fascists in the thirties and the hazards of the journalistic life in pre-war Germany to the mysterious workings of MI6 when Kim Philby was its rising star, office politics in the upper echelons of the BBC, and the machinations of London publishers. As a biographer, I enjoy building up subsidiary characters, and they proliferate in these pages. Certain names recur – Sefton Delmer, Claud Cockburn, Malcolm Muggeridge, Alexander Korda, Lord Reith, Robert Vansittart, Count Bernstorff, Ivone Kirkpatrick, Gerald Heard, Maxwell Knight, Richard Stokes MP, Clare Hollingworth, Richard Crossman – and I dwell on them at length, partly because they are no longer household names, and partly because they weave in and out of the story, sometimes flitting between one Greene life and another. On the other hand, those siblings and first cousins who led quiet, domesticated lives of little interest to the general public – Molly, Ave, Edward ('Tooter') and Katharine – make few appearances in these pages; and since I have no desire to invade their privacy more than is strictly necessary, the Greenes of a younger generation are only mentioned where they intrude on the activities of their elders.

I have never been happy about calling people I have never met by their first names, in print or in person, and in earlier biographies I insisted on referring to my subjects as 'Connolly', 'Lane' or 'Smollett'. In this case, I have been forced to break my own rules, and I apologise to the shades of long-dead Greenes for an unwonted familiarity.

I

Ancestral Voices

Towards the end of 1974 Hugh Greene wrote to his brother Graham to say that the journalist Susan Barnes wanted to write a book about the Greene family, and had been discussing the idea with his eldest son, also a Graham, and the managing director of the publishers Jonathan Cape. The idea, Graham replied, 'fills me with distaste': such a book should be written 'after all our deaths', and 'I feel there is a nasty air of Greene self-congratulation about it. This won't deter Raymond, but I wonder how Elisabeth will feel' – Raymond was his medical brother, an authority on Greene family history and genealogy, Elisabeth their youngest sister and his part-time secretary. 'I must admit that the attraction of the Susan Barnes project for me came partly from my own laziness,' Hugh replied. 'I am always being pressed to write an autobiography, and this would provide an alibi.'

Hugh Greene never completed or published his memoirs, but as he neared the end of his life he became increasingly intrigued by his family's history and connections; and, for all his fastidious disdain, Graham himself was not immune to his siblings' obsession with genealogy, and was particularly proud of the fact that his branch of the Greenes were cousins of Robert Louis Stevenson, whom he thought of as 'one of the family', sharing his own restlessness and melancholia as well as his literary bent. Raymond Greene was convinced that the Greenes were related to Henry VIII's sixth wife, Catherine Parr, and spent part of his retirement trying to prove the connection. He also wrote an unpublished history of the Greenes, which has subsequently been amended and expanded by other members of the family; and this, in part, provides the basis for this introductory chapter. Readers who, like myself, are easily bored or baffled by family trees should be warned that the Greenes are not only numerous but confusing, in that, out of family piety, they are prone to recycling the same Christian names among the boys in particular, with Benjamin, Raymond, Graham and Edward recurring again and again. They should bear in mind that, as far as this particular book is concerned, all paths lead to the hapless figure of William Greene, whose sons were the head-master and the coffee merchant, and whose grandchildren will eventu-ally occupy centre stage.

Although some members of the family would become, in due course, extremely rich and grand, the Greenes were descended from a long line of Bedfordshire and Northamptonshire tradesmen and drapers. The first Greene to make his mark in the wider world was Benjamin, who grew up in Oundle and trained as a brewer with Whitbread's in London in the 1790s before moving to the Suffolk town of Bury St Edmunds, where he set up on his own account and went on to prove the point of Dr Johnson's observation that brewing provided 'the potentiality of growing rich beyond the dreams of avarice'. The early years of the nineteenth century were particularly beneficial to brewers; home-brewing was in decline, and commercial brewers both supplied and bought up public houses. In 1806 Benjamin Greene and his partner William Buck bought the Westgate site in Bury St Edmunds, where the brewery that bears the family name still has its headquarters.

A year earlier, Benjamin had married one Catharine Smith. Her father was a close friend of John Howard, the prison reformer, and Sam Whit-bread, the brewer, and her mother was the daughter and heiress of Zachariah Carleton, a London banker. Carleton was to become another recurrent family name; and although Benjamin exchanged the family's Dissenting tradition for adherence to the Church of England, and became increasingly High Tory as the years went by, his wife's family provided a connection with, and a sympathy for, high-minded liberalism that was to become a recurrent motif among the Greenes, along with a subversive streak and a salutary sense of mischief. Such views are perfectly compatible with business acumen and the accumulation of wealth, and Benjamin and some at least of his thirteen children continued to expand and diversify the family interests.

The initiative that loomed largest in the imaginations of his great-grandchildren, and of Graham and Hugh in particular, was the acquisition in 1825 of large sugar estates on the West Indian island of St Kitts. This was not, as it turned out, the shrewdest of investments: the abolition of the slave trade, which Benjamin fiercely opposed, meant that after 1833 plantation owners could no longer rely on free labour, and during the course of the nineteenth century West Indian sugar suffered not only from competition from Cuba, Brazil and Mauritius, but from the increasing dependence of Europeans on sugar beet rather than sugar cane. Greedy and inattentive absentee landlords were another serious problem, and to remedy this Benjamin sent out his eldest son, Benjamin Buck Greene, to manage the St Kitts estates. The younger Benjamin was shrewd, hard-working, entrepreneurial and single minded, and during his eight years on the island he reduced costs and increased output, not least by using steam engines to power the sugar mills. His father, in the meantime, had moved to London, where he set up as a West Indian merchant, with offices in Mincing Lane and a house in Russell Square – it was said that he rode to work every day, followed by a groom in livery – while his third son, Edward, remained in Bury St Edmunds to run the brewery. Benjamin Buck returned to London in 1837, and was replaced in St Kitts by his sixteen-year-old brother Charles, who was joined there two years later by William, a mere fifteen when he arrived. Charles was blessed with a 'very affectionate nature', but in 1840 he died of yellow fever, leaving behind him – or so it was said – thirteen illegitimate children: both Hugh and Graham were fascinated by these distant cousins, and after a visit to the island Graham claimed that at least one of the 'black Greenes' bore a distinct resemblance to his uncle Graham, an austere and dedicated civil servant who never visited the island and, as far as we know, led a chaste and exemplary life.

A dreamy, melancholy figure, with no aptitude for business, William proved an ineffectual steward on St Kitts: West Indian sugar prices steadily declined during the 1840s, and the last family property in St Kitts was sold in 1898. Benjamin Buck, on the other hand, would soon become the grandest of all the Greenes. His wife had sugar and shipping interests in Mauritius, so he concentrated on these instead, and his firm of Greene & Blyth also traded in coal, fertilisers, textiles and machinery. Benjamin Buck was a Director of the Bank of England for over fifty years, and an innovative Governor for three years in the 1870s. A formidable figure, 'Uncle Benjamin' acquired an enormous white stuccoed house in Kensington Palace Gardens, familiarly known as 'Millionaires' Row', and a model farm at Midgham, near Reading. His niece Alice visited him there when he was well into his eighties, and he proudly showed her round the farm and the dairy, village school and church, all of which he had built. 'He is king and reigns supreme,' she told a friend, adding, apropos the village, that 'he is very proud because there is not a single pauper in it.' He had, she continued, 'the same keen glance, the same almost fierce decision, the same exceedingly rapid, springy step' as his brother William: but there, it may be, the similarities ended.

Brother Edward, in the meantime, was running the family brewery.

Like his older brother before him, he had been educated at Bury Grammar School, and had gone straight to work after leaving. Brewing was becoming ever more profitable, and Edward's own diligence, honesty and attention to detail soon bore fruit. The removal of beer duties in 1830 led to lower prices and increased consumption, and the expansion of the railways enabled brewers to market their wares over a far wider area. Like the best kind of old-fashioned businessman, Edward lived opposite the brewery, and was the first to arrive at work in the morning. He expanded the workforce, and, as a benign paternalist, housed them in brewery cottages at a low rent. In due course he became a magistrate, a Tory MP, the Master of the Suffolk Hunt, and a popular figure in Suffolk society. He bought himself a farm, which he ran on up-to-date lines, pioneering the use of steam power and trying out new crops and breeds of animals; and in 1874 he acquired and rebuilt a grand country house called Nether Hall, with 850 acres attached. His first wife Emily was a clergyman's daughter, and their daughter was the grandmother of the writer Christopher Isherwood; another daughter, Julia, married a Dr Fry, later to become the Headmaster of Berkhamsted School, and one of Graham Greene's *bêtes noires*. Edward became a benefactor, paying for the building of its red-brick Victorian Gothic chapel, and initiating a long association between the Greenes and the school.

In 1860 Edward's son Walter left Rugby and went to work in the brewery. A convivial, pleasure-loving individual, a keen yachtsman and huntsman, he was idler and less driven than his father and devoted much of his time and energy to the social and sporting life: Christopher Isherwood's mother Kathleen wrote in her diary in 1883 that Nether Hall, by then in Walter's possession, was 'the scene of continuous hospitality; dances, shoots, hunt breakfasts, house parties', and recalled the anti-climax of having to go 'back from Paradise to earth, in other words Nether Hall to Bury', where her father, Frederick Machell-Smith, worked as a wine merchant. By now the brewing trade was going through momentous changes. Small breweries were being swallowed up by larger rivals in the 'Brewers' Wars' of the 1880s, and in 1887 the Greene brewery was merged with that of Frederick King, a rival who had started brewing in Biggleswade in 1867, and was rather more dynamic than his high-living rival.

By the 1900s, Walter had become the quintessential Edwardian plutocrat. Though ineffectual as an MP, he was knighted in 1900, and spent as much time as he could on the grouse moor or in Monte Carlo, Cowes or Newmarket. Like other Greenes, including his great-nephews Raymond and Graham, he had a weakness for elaborate and wearisome practical jokes: house guests were handed exploding cigars, their shotguns were loaded with fireworks instead of cartridges, they were encouraged to blast away at stuffed rabbits rather than the real thing, and his wife was unduly alarmed when their son Raymond, under the guise of being the victim of a shooting accident, was carried past the window on a dismantled door. Though affable enough on the whole, he was also – like other Greenes – prone to sudden fits of rage, and once beat a farmer with his riding crop for poisoning a fox. Although the Liberal government of the time favoured the temperance movement, the Greene King brewery was so profitable and so well run that Walter could afford to pay himself £18,000 a year. Raymond was educated at Eton and Oriel, and in due course inherited the baronetcy: he had no interest in the day-to-day running of the brewery or Suffolk life, far preferring to spend his time in London, and sold Nether Hall on Walter's death in 1920. He was decorated during the Boer War, fought with the 9th Lancers during the First World War, hunted with the Cottesmore, and was painted by Alfred Munnings, famed for his portrayals of horsey and hunting scenes.

Restless readers with no taste for family trees will be relieved to learn that we have almost done with the sons of the original Benjamin Greene, and that only two others need to be mentioned here: John, and the luckless William, recently returned from St Kitts. John, the second son, is, in genealogical terms, more mind-boggling than most. One of his sons married into the Wollaston family: A. F. R. Wollaston was the Medical Officer on the 1921 Everest expedition – Everest will loom large in a later chapter of this book – and was eventually murdered by a demented Cambridge undergraduate; his son was the travel writer and novelist Nicholas Wollaston, who was encouraged in his early days as a writer by Graham Greene, always a generous supporter of young writers who seemed to show promise. More relevant to this particular story was John's fifth son, Carleton Greene. His wife, Jane, was the daughter of the Reverend Lewis Balfour of Pilrig: her first cousin was Robert Louis Stevenson, her second cousin Whyte Melville, the long-forgotten Victorian hunting novelist. (Raymond Greene, with his interest in family history and Greene connections, once noted that Balfour blood ran in the veins of the Dukes of Sutherland, the Earls of Rosslyn, Viscounts Lyttelton and Cobham, and the Begum Aga Khan.) Carleton suffered from extreme melancholia, verging – it was thought by some – on lunacy: since melancholy was a family trait, it seems appropriate that an ancestor of the Greenes, Dr Robert Whytt of Edinburgh, the physician to George III, should have published in 1765 the first textbook of neurology,

Observations on the Nature, Causes, and Cures of Those Disorders Which Have Been Commonly Called Nervous, Hyperchondriac or Hysteric, in which he recommended claret, travel, 'agreeable company', exercise and 'a variety of amusements' as the best antidotes to 'low spirits'. In 1875 Carleton Greene was presented with the living of Great Barford, near Cambridge, by his old college, Trinity: he remained in post till 1913, despite having ceremoniously defrocked himself in a field near his church, declaring that he could no longer continue as the vicar, and spent the last eleven years of his life in a mental home in Northampton. Though suffering from what his grandson Raymond retrospectively diagnosed as arteriosclerosis – by 1900 he had 'difficulty in locomotion' – the Reverend Carleton Greene fathered five children. One of them, Francis Carleton Greene, married the daughter of the Irish poet, John Todhunter; a daughter, Marion, married the future headmaster of Berkhamsted, Charles Greene (her first cousin once removed), and was the mother of, among others, Raymond, Graham, Hugh and Elisabeth Greene.

And so to William, the paternal grandfather of the twelve Greenes on whom this book will, eventually, focus its attention. A sad, sympathetic figure with 'hair like spun gold and turquoise blue eyes', he was unable to settle to anything, and was haunted by restlessness, melancholy and a sense of failure. His grandson Graham, the novelist, felt him to be a kindred spirit, and remarked on his 'frustrated romantic nature'. His daughter-in-law remembered him as a 'nervous, highly-strung man with no real occupation' who enjoyed walking and 'spent whole days wandering about the countryside with a volume of Plutarch or Bacon's *Essays* in his pocket, reading from time to time in the shade of trees or hedges'; another grandson, Raymond, once again exercising his powers of retrospective diagnosis, suggested that he suffered from 'recurrent endogenous depression'. He qualified as a solicitor, but never practised; he dabbled in scientific farming, but was unable to retain his interest. His wife, Charlotte, was the daughter of a coal merchant from Lincolnshire, and with their nine children they lived, at various times, in Essex, Twickenham, Henley, Grantchester and Bedford. His daughters in particular were of an arty disposition, much given to writing poems and plays, and in the 1860s, when the family lived in Grantchester, they staged pageants and *tableaux vivants* to raise funds for the church, while their brother Graham, the future civil servant, rode to school in Cambridge on a donkey.

From Grantchester they moved to a large square stone house in Bedford, with long narrow corridors, steep stairs, innumerable bedrooms, a huge drawing-room which had been expanded by a previous mayor of

Bedford to host official receptions, and an ice house in the garden, which sloped down to the river. By now William had abandoned full-time employment, and the family lived off the £750 a year left to him by his father, and what little money came his way from the remaining proper-ties in St Kitts. A remote if kindly figure, he spent long hours brooding in his study, but joined the rest of the family in the evenings to read Dickens, Scott and Thackeray aloud. At one stage he interested himself in a scheme to turn peat from Dartmoor into fuel, and was made a director of the company involved. He spent weeks on end camping out on Dartmoor with a book in his pocket: he described the hovel in which he stayed as 'Bleak House, the Plains of Desolation', and was under-standably upset when one of his fellow-directors committed suicide. Given William's air of distraction and frequent absences from home, Charlotte assumed the role of head of the family. Great Barford, the home of the equally melancholic Carleton Greene, was only six miles from Bedford, and the two Greene families got to know one another.

In 1881 William decided to revisit St Kitts. His son Graham met him in London the day before his departure. 'I left him at 1 a.m. at the Charing Cross Hotel, endeavouring to finish a large cigar,' Graham wrote to his mother. 'He told me that he intended to take very little rest that night, as he wished to be very sleepy on the following, the first night on board. I hope this plan succeeded, but I have strong misgivings thereon . . .' 'Like Mama, I do not like the thought of you being all alone; it seems so dreary for you,' his daughter Alice wrote to him after his arrival. 'But as Mama, I suppose, has written to you all the pros and cons for your projects, I think we need not say any more, except to hope that we shall all meet again somewhere or other.' Alas, this was not to be: William contracted a 'low fever', emerged with an 'altered appearance' after taking a cold bath, died the following day, and was buried next to his brother Charles. He had not been the most helpful of husbands or fathers, and from now on the family in Bedford would have to look after themselves.

★

Three years after William's death, Charlotte and her children moved from Bedford to a tall white house in Stanley Gardens in Belsize Park. Life became bleaker still when Charlotte's allowance from Benjamin Buck and Edward the brewer was gradually reduced from £60 a month in 1881 to £15 a month by 1890. Her son Graham, now aged twenty-three, assumed the role of *paterfamilias*. Because he was to loom large in the minds of a younger generation of Greenes, be looked to as a source of wisdom and advice, achieving such distinction as an *eminence grise*, and living to such a great age, he deserves a paragraph or two at this stage.

Whereas his younger brothers Charles and Edward – the future headmaster, and the future coffee merchant – attended Bedford Grammar School, William Graham was sent away as a boarder, to Cheltenham. Though extremely clever and well-read, he never went to university: years later, after a visit to Cambridge, he told his sister Alice that he felt 'as if there had been a leaf out of my life, which I had ignorantly lost, and which is all-important to one's inner life. I felt like a rude Roman among the marbles of Athens.' After leaving school he was sent to Brunswick to learn German, and worked for some years in the family brewery before training as an engineer in Bedford. He gave this up for reasons of ill health, took the Civil Service exams and joined the Inland Revenue as an assistant surveyor of taxes. 'There's nothing like healthy occupation and preoccupation in the affairs of others to keep at a distance the phantom of melancholia,' he wrote to Alice, who worried that he might succumb to the family malaise, and from now on the demands of his career and his position as head of the family would leave little or no room for private life of any kind. 'Macaulay made a somewhat similar mistake when he devoted himself to his sisters, never thinking of the time when they would marry and he would be left, a solitary bachelor, to his own resources,' he told Alice. As it turned out, his sisters were not of the marrying kind; and when, some years later, her eldest son took a set of rooms in Park Lane, his mother remarked that 'It seems his intention is to remain a bachelor, and I am glad.' It is hard not to think of 'Uncle Graham' as a wizened, desiccated figure, bowed down by his responsibilities, but he was a dapper, good-looking man with a sleek round head, not unlike his nephews Raymond and Graham in build and appearance, though not as tall. According to his niece Barbara, to whom he gave tea in Bond Street on Tuesdays whenever she was in London, he had wanted to marry, but 'felt he must wait till his duties towards his family were settled – unfortunately the girl did not see it that way, and married someone else.'

In 1881 Graham Greene moved from the Inland Revenue to the Admiralty, where he soon proved an indispensable and increasingly influential figure. He joined its Foreign Intelligence Department four years later, and in 1887 was appointed Assistant Private Secretary to the First Sea Lord. In 1907 he was made the Assistant Secretary at the Admiralty, working closely with 'Jackie' Fisher and Prince Louis of Battenburg; four years later he was knighted, and promoted to Permanent Secretary. When war broke out in 1914 Winston Churchill, the First Lord of the Admiralty, made him one of his inner circle of advisers. Once described as 'the octopus of Whitehall', he was renowned for his mastery of detail and for his diligence, often remaining in his office until two in the morning before returning home to his flat in Park Lane. Churchill thought very highly of him, but others were less well-disposed. 'He holds in his hands all the strings of the Admiralty and it is not too much to say that he exercises more power than any of the Sea Lords, including possibly the First Sea Lord himself,' the *Daily Mail* declared. 'Sir Graham Greene [as he now was] is no doubt a well-meaning and zealous official, but his activity has magnified the importance of the civilian secretariat at the Admiralty.' Admiral Beatty called him 'one of those half-dead men'; a colleague apostrophised him as a 'dry old stick, experienced, prudent and precise', and his nephew Graham recalled him as being 'very remote' and remarkable for 'his dryness and his taciturnity and the glasses which dangled over his waistcoat on a broad black ribbon . . . His speech was all "ehs" and "ahs". Perhaps he felt ill-at-ease with anyone but a civil servant.' Churchill's successors, Arthur Balfour and Edward Carson, were happy to take his advice, but Hankey, the Secretary of the War Cabinet, complained that he had been slow to implement reforms necessitated by the submarine crisis of 1917, and Lloyd George insisted on his retirement that year at the age of sixty. Sir Graham may have arranged for the fleet to be on manoeuvres and ready for action in August 1914, and been at Churchill's side throughout the Dardanelles campaign, but his departure was unmourned by the *Evening Standard*, for whom he had been 'a fine type of the red-tape bureaucrat, out of touch with the service, unacquainted with the sea or the temperamental qualities of naval commanders, with little imagination and an extravagant addiction to routine.' He spent the rest of the war with Churchill at the Ministry of Munitions and, though well past retirement age, he served on the Committee of Imperial Defence from 1920 until 1940.

When not in London, Sir Graham lived in Harston House, a long, low wisteria-covered William-and-Mary house in the village of Harston, near Cambridge, which he rented in 1891, bought in 1893, and shared in later years with various unmarried sisters. He had initially rented it as a home for his mother. 'The place looked very cold and miserable,' Charlotte Greene wrote at the time. 'It is a very old house, pretty outside, red brick. The late tenant has left it in a wretched condition but I think we could make it homelike and comfortable. But at present it is damp owing to the rooms being lower than the ground outside.' It had eight bedrooms, a walled garden, a lily pond, a paddock, some barns and plenty of room for her daughter Helen's chickens to run about: the drains were a problem, but Sir Graham had, as a temporary measure, installed an earth-closet in the box room. Harston was to loom large in the memories of his nieces and nephews as a centre of Greene family life, visited as often as not in summer holidays; in later years there would be much debate about who should inherit it, with Graham and Hugh as prime contenders. Sir Graham himself was regarded as a well-connected fount of wisdom and advice. Worried about what his nephew Graham should do next in terms of a formal career – he had recently left *The Times* – Sir Graham wrote to Eddie Marsh, Churchill's secretary and patron of the Georgian poets, to see if Churchill could help in any way ('Nothing doing,' the great man scrawled in the margin of Sir Graham's letter); ten years later, when Christopher Isherwood's boyfriend was threatened with deportation back to Nazi Germany, his family turned to Sir Graham for advice, even though Isherwood and Heinz were living in Portugal at the time and an eighty-year-old former civil servant was unlikely to cut much ice in Berlin; when his nephew Ben was interned in Brixton in May 1940, his family immediately turned to Sir Graham for advice. While in his eighties, Sir Graham fell under a tube train and, with due presence of mind, lay rigidly to attention next to the electric rail ('It was most interesting. I had never before seen the underside of an electric train,' he told his rescuers); he prowled the garden at Harston with secateurs in hand, went blind and had *The Times* read to him by his sister Polly, and quizzed his nephew Raymond about scientific matters. He died at the age of ninety-three after falling out of an apple tree, the branches of which he was trimming; his ashes were scattered at sea, and warships at anchor in the Solent lowered their flags as the destroyer *Finisterre* steamed past with his urn on board. He had been, his *Times* obituarist declared, 'a conscientious, zealous and greatly experienced officer, but his modest nature deprived him of the strong personality which might have given him a greater influence in the conduct of affairs.'

Readers of Graham Greene's *A Sort of Life* will remember that he and his siblings were well endowed with aunts, particularly on his father's side. Florence, the eldest, emigrated to British Columbia and was referred to rather than encountered in the flesh, but Alice, Polly and Helen were all familiar figures in the lives of the younger generation. Alice went to teach in a girls' school in South Africa, where she met the great love of her life, Elizabeth Molteno: she befriended Olive Schreiner and Gandhi, then a young lawyer working in South Africa, disapproved of Cecil Rhodes, supported the Boers when war broke out, much to Sir Graham's dismay, and helped Emily Hobhouse write her controversial report about the camps in which Boer women and children were held. Polly was a painter, and wrote a number of plays, some of which were performed locally. She studied art at the St John's Wood School of Art, at the Royal Academy and in Paris. In 1891 she opened an art school in Cambridge. Gwen Raverat was her most celebrated pupil, and in *Period Piece* she wrote that Polly's Wednesday drawing class was 'the centre of my youthful existence' and that 'Miss Greene's warm, generous, appreciative nature was a great release and encouragement to me.' In later years she went to live with Sir Graham: her nephew Graham remembered her as 'dear muddle-headed Polly who lived at Harston and painted bad pictures and taught Gwen Raverat to draw and wrote ambitious plays for the village institute.' Helen, the youngest sister, was an early enthusiast for Swedish gymnastics, worked as a physiotherapist in Cambridge, and ran a convalescent home for soldiers during the First World War. Despite suffering from ill health for much of her life, she lived to the age of ninety.

Sir Graham was one of five boys. The youngest, Benjamin, was thought to be self-absorbed and impractical, and an attack of diphtheria had left him an invalid for many years; he went to live with his sister Florence and her husband in British Columbia, and was drowned in 1906 while swimming in Lake Geneva. Fred was an even sadder case. In 1891, at the age of twenty-three, he was admitted to St Andrew's mental hospital, diagnosed as suffering from 'mania' (his father, William, it was noted, had also been 'afflicted with insanity'). He had suffered an earlier attack: 'It would have been better, as you said at the time, both for himself and others, that the first attack should have taken the form of a fatal illness. His life must be a burden to himself and his relations,' Sir Graham wrote to Alice in South Africa. He died in 1897, still a private patient in St Andrew's: his condition, according to Sir Graham, was unchanged, and his death came as 'a merciful end to a life which was only an increasing burden to him.'

'It is sad, but the Greene family is not a marrying one, at least among our contemporaries,' Sir Graham told Alice in January 1890. He was about to be proved wrong: his brothers Charles and Edward were very much of the marrying kind, and would, in terms of progeny, make up for the childlessness of Sir Graham and their other siblings.

2

Two Brothers

Charles Greene, the future headmaster, was born in 1865, and his brother Edward ('Eppy'), the coffee merchant, was eighteen months younger. Charles was cautious, conscientious, high-minded, idealistic and academically inclined, and his career was more conventional and a good deal less dashing than that of his brother. Edward was, as a young man, impatient of academia, enterprising, restless and eager to make his own way in the world through the accumulation of experience rather than book-learning. Both attended Bedford Grammar School; Charles went on as an Exhibitioner to Wadham College, Oxford, where he rowed in the college boat and was thought to be something of a dandy, but Edward couldn't wait to leave school, and far preferred swimming and climbing trees to staring at a blackboard. After leaving Oxford, Charles considered reading for the Bar but was offered, and accepted, a temporary teaching post at Berkhamsted School by its then headmaster, Charles Fry, who – as we have seen – was himself married to a Greene. 'Of course you have heard that I have entered the noble army of pedagogues,' an embarrassed-sounding Charles wrote to his sister Alice in May 1889, after the temporary post had become a permanent position; and although a year late he was still eating dinners at the Inner Temple, he had already been made a housemaster, and was to spend the rest of his working life at Berkhamsted. Since the school will occupy the whole of the next chapter, and the concluding part of this, we will leave him there *pro tem*, and concentrate instead on his more feckless-seeming brother.

Eppy – the nickname suits his youthful insouciance, and distinguishes him from his brewing uncle, Edward – left school at sixteen, and was sent to Essex as a farm pupil, acquiring thereby a lifelong love of farming. When, after his father William's defection to St Kitts and subsequent death, the family moved to Belsize Park, Eppy took up various positions in the City, learning shorthand, bookkeeping and the rudiments of commerce. Eager to improve his qualifications with a knowledge of languages, he decided to work in France for a time. 'I am looking forward to going abroad tremendously,' he told Alice. 'I shall live in abject poverty for a while, but I shall not mind that. It will be grand to be out of London.' Two years later he wrote again from Nantes, where he was working for a British firm of 'coal-heavers and anything-you-like merchants', and doubling up as a clerk at the British Consulate. His French was now excellent, and he wanted to learn German, and possibly Spanish and Italian as well. 'The only thing that gives superiority is a wide experience and a knowledge of languages, and this one can only get by knocking about', he told Alice. 'I have enjoyed my stay in France enormously, and though green enough I do not think I am such an idiot as I was when I left England.' Writing from Berlin a year later, he reported that 'after lurching around a bit looking for work, I found a job in Stettin at a herring merchant's office.' He had no desire to return to England, and was considering a job in Zanzibar, but on a visit to London he had seen an advertisement for a post with Edward Johnston Ltd, coffee merchants and traders. It had a good salary attached, and he decided to take things further.

The family firm of Edward Johnston had been founded in 1842, and was well established in Brazil (a scion of the family was Brian 'Johnners' Johnston, the much-loved cricket commentator). Eppy worked for a time in their City headquarters, and was then shipped out to the Rio de Janeiro office. 'Dear old Eppy is now going out to Rio,' his mother informed Alice. 'I do feel anxious about his going so far and I do not believe it is a healthy place. He will have to take great care about his food.' 'I can't tell you how dreadful it was parting from the dear boy,' Helen wrote to her sister in South Africa. 'It seemed as if all the family was dwindling away.' Charlotte Greene's anxieties were all too well-founded, since yellow fever was raging when Eppy arrived in May 1891. He commuted into Rio from Petropolis, a town in the hills, and a three-hour journey each way by boat and train. 'I am glad to say that our firm is specially noted for its upright dealing and what I saw of the Johnstons in London pleased me very much, in fact I think I am very fortunate in having got among such people,' Eppy reported. 'I do not think I shall care to go back to England till I am quite rich,' he added. 'Rio itself is the foulest city on earth, I should say,' and it became still more unpleasant when he went down with a bout of yellow fever. But he was not to remain there long; the following year he was moved to Santos, sixty miles south of Sao Paulo, and the main port for the export of Brazilian coffee.

In later years Eppy's wife Eva was to look back on Santos as a paradise lost, a prelapsarian Eden of flowers and sea and sunlight in which she had dwelt with her husband and their white-clad, laughing children; but when Eppy first went to work there it seemed like a hell on earth. Built on an island, the port was low-lying and stiflingly hot. Once again, yellow fever was raging when Eppy arrived: it seemed like a 'town of the dead', with huge cauldrons of tar simmering to clear the air; low tide revealed raw sewage and dead dogs and mules stranded in the mud. Yellow fever was finally eliminated in 1894, but three years earlier the rotting hulks of ships whose crews had died could still be seen offshore, and when the fever raged visiting seamen were ordered to keep their distance while skeleton crews took their ships into Santos harbour.

British firms with offices in South America liked to employ former public schoolboys: because of the long hours, the frequent absences up-country, and a climate considered unsuitable for women – or for English women at least – they were often forbidden to marry under the age of thirty, and sometimes had to obtain permission thereafter. Edward Johnston Ltd was no exception; their Brazil offices were staffed by expats, who were expected to become fluent in Portuguese. The English were not great coffee-drinkers, and the major markets for Brazilian coffee were in Germany, Austria, the Low Countries, Scandinavia and the United States; quite apart from which, as Eppy would soon discover, there was a sizeable German population in Brazil itself. On his arrival, he decided to share a *chacara* or bungalow with other expats, some of whom worked for the firm: it was separated from the sea by a lawn, a hibiscus hedge and miles of silver sand, and from other bungalows by high bamboo hedges; he commuted to work every day on the *bonde*, a little wooden tram which was pulled by mules and took forty minutes to reach the centre of Santos.

Coffee was big business in Brazil, and when Sao Paulo state replaced Rio as the major area of production, Santos became the epicentre of the trade. Coffee accounted for 70 per cent of the country's exports, and 75 per cent of the world's production still originated in Brazil. It was a disconcertingly volatile business, vulnerable to the weather and to five-yearly cycles of scarcity and over-production, with bumper crops being followed by lean years and alarming fluctuations of supply and demand: high prices invariably led to over-production of new crops, which led to lower prices until demand resumed once again and prices began to creep up. Eppy's arrival coincided with a period of over-production and falling prices, with farmers planting more coffee than the market could bear: in due course the Brazilian government intervened with 'valorisation' schemes whereby, in order to modify the damaging fluctuations in price and supply and increase the incomes of coffee farmers, it bought up huge reserves of coffee when the prices were low and stored them until demand had risen again: the net result of which was further over-production, and the subsidising of inefficient farmers.

Eppy himself was far from inefficient, and was determined to alter and improve the workings of the trade in the face of increasing competition from German and American coffee merchants. He cut out middlemen and dealt directly with farmers, advancing them money when times were lean. He invested in model estates, improved warehousing up-country and in Santos itself, kept a close eye on fluctuating exchange rates, diversified into the milling and cleaning of the coffee beans, and insisted on the overriding importance of quality. On his return from a visit to London in 1894 he took over the running of Santos House: in due course he built a three-storeyed, granite-clad office in the centre of the city, reflecting the effective running of the business and emphasising to the Brazilians themselves that 'they are dealing with people who have a greater stake in the country than an office table and a chair.' By now the Santos office was far more profitable than its rival in Rio, and in 1895 Eppy was admitted to a partnership in E. J. Johnston Ltd. He was unable to raise the required sum of £2500, but he put up half the amount, asked his brother Graham to sell securities on his behalf, and borrowed the balance from the other partners. In 1900 the partnership was renegotiated to give him a larger share of the profits.

When not attending to business, he ordered provisions from the Civil Service Supply Association in London – including marmalade, Pear's Soap and a selection of Crosse & Blackwell's jams – and shirts, collars and a white flannel suit from his tailor, on the understanding that 'Miss Sewell, a lady friend, would bring them out for him', and that 'Mr W. G. Greene, of the Admiralty, would pay the account as usual'. Quite who Miss Sewell was remains obscure, but in 1901 Eppy got the approval of his partners to marry a seventeen-year-old German girl called Eva Stutzer, who had been born in Goslar in 1883 and was descended from a mixture of Lutheran, Huguenot and Jewish intellectuals, several of whom had been writers and actively involved in German politics. Although she never lived in Germany after the age of eight, and was to spend most of her life in England, Eva retained a lifelong interest in German affairs, and kept in touch with an assortment of German relations. Her father, Gustav Stutzer, a former Lutheran pastor, had served as a nurse in the Franco-Prussian War and founded a mental home in Germany before emigrating with his family to Brazil in 1885. There he joined his brother, managing property belonging to his son-in-law, Wilhelm Richers, in Ribeirao Pires, a hill resort in the mountains between Santos and Sao Paulo. The family returned to Germany the following year but made their way back to Brazil in 1891. Stutzer went back to his homeland in 1909 at the age of seventy; there he published *Meine Therese*, a much-admired book about his wife. The youngest in a family of girls, Eva inherited her father's literary gifts, and grew up speaking German and French: at the age of twelve she was sent to a boarding school which catered for smart Brazilian girls, and acquired fluent Portuguese as a result. Good-looking with fair hair, big blue eyes and a Grecian nose, she was only fourteen when she first met Eppy in Ribeirao Pires. Eva, Eppy told Alice, 'is much older than most girls of her age, her family have been through burning fiery troubles and they have left their mark on her young soul but left pure gold behind. Only one thing troubles my mind. Ought I not to have allowed one of her own nationality to have tried his luck before I, a foreigner, claimed her for ever?'

Such compunctions were soon set aside, and the fact that her husband-to-be could speak German, French and Portuguese proved invaluable to Eva, whose English 'did not go much beyond "the cat sat on the mat"'. As soon as they were married, Eppy asked the London partners to lend him the money to buy the Chacara Americana, the house on the beach which he had shared with other expatriates in his bachelor days, and set about transforming it into a family home. French windows opened onto a verandah looking out at the sea; he planted flowers and fruit trees in the garden, which attracted humming birds and butter-flies; the rooms were separated from one another with strings of glass beads, which tinkled in the breeze; the great stretch of white beach was, for much of the time, almost deserted except for a few fisherman, Turkish or Syrian vendors hawking their wares from house to house, and cows cooling their heels in the shallows. The intense heat in summer made an early start advisable: Eppy would go for a ride or a swim at 6.30 every morning, and leave for the office twenty minutes later. Eppy and Eva – and, in due course, their children – were invariably dressed in white, and a black washerwoman spread out their washing to dry on adjacent orange trees.

Early in 1901 Eppy took his young wife to England to meet his family. 'Poor Eva came in looking blooming and excited meeting us all,' his mother told Alice. 'She looked older than eighteen, as all German girls do. I suppose she is rather nice-looking, with large speaking eyes. She is a very nice girl. I feel I shall love her.' This must have come as a relief to Eppy, who told Alice that 'even mother, who is difficult, was contented' with her new daughter-in-law. Graham was equally taken with her, reporting to his sister in South Africa that 'what I have seen of Eva in no way lessens the favourable impression she has made on us.' The newly-weds spent much of that summer in Harston House, which Eva remembered years later as 'a gracious William and Mary building of soft pink brick, covered in roses and clematis'. It was, in Eva's recollection, an idyllic spot. 'The old garden, enclosed by a high wall, was gay with flowers, turtle doves cooed in the Wellingtonia trees, the splash of the fountain made a cool sound on the lawn where we had afternoon tea in the shade of old lime trees . . . On long peaceful afternoons we drifted down the river in our boat under willow trees and past flowering meadows, and I picked tall yellow irises growing near the water's edge.' But 'ordinary daily life in England seemed complicated by a great many unwritten laws and customs and regulations. There seemed to be so many things an "English lady" should or could not do, or knew without being told, how to do things like eating asparagus with one's fingers and how many cards to leave at a house after paying a call.' It was not done, she discovered, for a lady to leave the house without putting on a hat, and if Charlotte Greene spotted her daughter-in-law bare-headed in the garden she would tap on the window to remind her to take a hat from a pile by the back door. Sundays proved 'very serious and strangely heavy days', involving three church services, sausage and bacon for breakfast, roast beef and Yorkshire pudding for lunch, and hymn-singing after supper. Eppy was amazed at how much more easy-going Sundays had become since his childhood, when all toys and books were locked away on Saturday night. 'Only when I brought down a little piece of embroidery did my mother-in-law gently chide me: "Not on a Sunday, my dear. You must never, never do such a thing again,"' Eva recalled.

They took tea with Sir Walter Greene MP on the terrace of the House of Commons, and they were summoned to lunch by the ninety-three-year-old Benjamin Buck Greene – something Eppy dreaded, and had hoped to avoid. It was a brilliant sunny day, and coming into the enormous white house in Kensington Palace Gardens was like entering a cave, with all the blinds down and the curtains drawn to keep out the sunlight. The rooms were filled with gigantic items of furniture, and the walls covered with gold-framed paintings. Cousin Isabel, Uncle Benjamin's daughter, hurried forward to greet them. She was clad in a plain grey dress, 'giving her an almost nun-like appearance', and her grey hair was

pinned up in a bun; years earlier she had fallen in love with an impoverished curate, but her parents had forbidden them from writing or meeting,
and she had devoted the rest of her life to good works and to looking
after her father. A few minutes later Uncle Benjamin appeared, and proved
to be 'a most impressive old gentleman, portly and tall, very courteous
but in a short dictatorial way, and obviously expecting and used to being
obeyed'. Served by three footmen and a butler, they ate a seven-course
meal in semi-darkness. Eva sat next to their host: 'his voice was like the
rumble of a distant thunderstorm in my ears, and his words were lost
in his great white beard as he bent over his plate.' When lunch was over
Uncle Benjamin ordered Eppy to follow him into his study to discuss
some Brazilian shares, while the two women read extracts from devo-
tional works. They were then taken for a ride in Uncle Benjamin's carriage,
drawn by two black horses. A footman with folded arms sat beside the
coachman on the box, both wearing 'dark green liveries with silver
buttons bearing the family crest', and two specially trained Dalmatians
trotted along on either side. The heat, the heavy lunch and the strain of
trying to make conversation with Uncle Benjamin made Eva sleepy, 'and
the seat was so narrow and slippery that I was afraid of falling out.'
Whenever they passed another carriage, they bowed and smiled in its
direction. Eventually they returned to Kensington Palace Gardens for an
enormous tea of scones, sponge cakes and biscuits. Eva's heart 'leapt
with joy' when she heard Eppy make their excuses to leave on the grounds
that they were going to the theatre that evening. She never met Uncle
Benjamin again, and he died the following year. He left nothing to his
nieces, but £50 each to his nephews and great-nephews: Eva's and Eppy's
son Ben was born just in time to enter into his inheritance. The balance
of his enormous fortune was left to Cousin Isabel; it was said that she
left half of what she received to a missionary society on the understanding that staff going into the field should not receive any medical
training which might dilute their adherence to the 'pure word' of God,
and the other half to a home for lost cats.

Ben, their first child, was born in December 1901, shortly after their
return to Brazil. He was followed fifteen months later by Eva (known
as Ave, to differentiate her from her mother) and by Edward (known as
'Tooter') in November 1904; Barbara followed three years later, and Felix
was born in Berkhamsted in May 1909. Katharine, the youngest, did not
make an appearance until 1914, by which time the family had been back
in England for a good four years. As they grew up, the children played
on the beach when the sun was not too hot; their parents called in at

the Athletic Club, where British expats amused themselves playing tennis, cricket and cards; and roller skating proved popular with the long-skirted ladies. Wives were expected to take turns in providing tea on Sundays, and Eva wasn't always best pleased at this. 'The condescending way of the men nearly drives me wild,' she wrote. 'I can read their thoughts quite plainly on their faces: oh bother, there is that stupid Mrs Greene, she hasn't a word to say for herself, can't amuse a chap at all, but I suppose one has to go up & talk to her . . .' Eppy provided superior amusement in the evenings at home, reading her Tennyson and Dickens when not discussing his all-consuming business interests. 'He could not live without business now,' Eva had come to realise after finding him in the dining room in the middle of the night, writing up his ideas for expanding and improving the company, fending off the competition, and somehow mitigating the notorious volatility of the coffee trade: he had a dread of failure and a passion for setting up new businesses, and Eva worried that his health could pack up under the strain. He had expanded into areas like warehousing, and appointed buying agents in the interior to further reduce his dependence on middlemen; in 1905 the Companhia Registradora de Santos was founded, and this and other companies were bought by the Brazilian Warrant Company, founded in 1909 as the holding company. Mr Barham, the manager of the Santos branch of the London & Brazilian Bank, was a close friend, and his son Jack would, in due course, marry Eppy's eldest daughter, Ave. 'I do wish you had asked me more about my father,' Eppy's daughter Barbara wrote to her cousin Graham after publication of *A Sort of Life*. 'He was more than just rich and worldly, though I have only realised it during the last years. We knew him so little and, to our eternal shame, we were little interested in what he was really doing in Brazil. I know now that he had a vision and also a romantic strain which he suppressed, perhaps because he got so little response.'

Wearing a stiff collar, a starched shirt and a tie even in the hottest weather, Eppy worked six days a week, including Saturdays; on Sundays the family ate lunch together, and the German cook prepared roast beef and floating island pudding. Light relief was provided by Manuel, the Portuguese gardener, who amused the children by tying the ends of his moustache under his chin: he was devoted but dim, planting gladioli bulbs imported from Europe upside down, watering the cabbages in the wake of a tropical storm, and interrupting one of Eva's dainty tea parties in order to ask whether he had added enough manure to the soil, a large sample of which was dripping from his hands.

With Eppy at work for so much of the time, German was the first language of the four eldest children. Thekla, the Polish nanny – 'middle-aged, small, very plain and of an absolutely unpredictable temperament' – had poor German but no English; Miss Koch, the children's tutor, was German, and Eva's letters to Alice are replete with references to Tooter 'forgetting all his English', or an excited Barbara shouting 'Mein Burstag, mein Burstag!' – meaning 'Mein Geburtstag', 'my birthday' – or how 'Ben will soon be able to write you a little letter in English', or how the children gathered round the Christmas tree to sing 'Vom Himmel hoch fa komm' ich her' while Ben strummed the piano. Ave spoke 'impeccable' German all her life, and although Barbara prided herself on her Englishness, she spoke with a very slight German inflection (and vice-versa when speaking German).

Super-sensitive and, from very early on, too tall for his own comfort – in due course he would reach a height of six-foot eight, and be fondly referred to as a 'gentle giant' – Ben was, in some ways, the most worrying of Eva's and Eppy's children. 'A beautiful little boy, with his clear skin, golden fair hair and blue eyes', very fond of flowers, he was, his mother wrote, 'the sunniest, gentlest little boy, always ready to share all he had with others and give even his most treasured possessions away' – including a new pair of shoes, which he thrust on an impoverished urchin. Somewhat literal-minded when young, he felt the sufferings of others to a far greater extent than most small boys. 'He takes all the little sentences quite seriously & when he has to read "the cat may not sit on the mat" he gets quite angry and wants to know why it shouldn't,' Eva reported of her eight-year-old son, already displaying that concern for the oppressed that would, in due course, lead him to undertake famine relief in Russia after the First World War and to become an idealistic irritant on the far left of the Labour Party. Reading with Ben proved a harrowing business. He became very upset when he misread 'shod' as 'shot' in a story about an ass that needed a new set of shoes, 'wailing in piteous tones "Mama, Mama, do tell them not to shoot the ass, it will hurt him so dreadfully"', and flinched away when he read about Benjamin Bunny being beaten by his father. He was, Eva noted, 'rather slow in his movements and liked to ponder over things and take his time'; Miss Koch reported that 'of course Ben is slow, nobody denies that, but he gets on all right in spite of it.' A kindly, benign figure, he couldn't stand up to the 'whirlwind' Ave, 'like a little live doll, so dainty and so small but full of mischief'. 'In spite of being so exceptionally tall and big for his age, our Ben has a fine little soul and is very sensitive',

Eva wrote. 'He needs so much love and gentle handling. I am afraid that life will often hurt him very much.'

The family spent a year in England in the summer of 1908. Eppy was preparing the ground for their return to England, and after visiting Helen in Norwich and Polly in Harston, he rented a house in Berkhamsted to be near his brother Charles. He returned to Santos ahead of the family, and was in Brazil when Felix was born. Eppy may have been a shy and rather distant father, but Barbara looked for him everywhere after he left, and 'when she could not find you she got so angry that she stamped her little foot and would not be comforted.' Eva struck up a close friendship with Alice, and after her return to Brazil in the summer of 1909, the two women engaged in a fulsome and rather glutinous correspondence about the children, whom they referred to variously as 'fairies', 'elves', 'dormice' and the like. 'I do miss you, dear Eva, badly. I cannot tell you, & you do not need to be told, the joy that my life with you has been,' Alice wrote. 'To think that I must do without Ben's sunny joy & Tooter's sparkling rapture & Barbara's grand exuberant *joie de vivre* . . . Why must children grow into stupid, anxious & irritable grown-up people? Imagine Tooter *ein mensch!*' On board the *Asturias*, poor Ben continued to find life a stressful business. 'I found him a few days ago looking out of the porthole in our cabin with such a miserable face & such big eyes,' Eva reported to the anxious Alice. 'I asked him what was the matter. Ben had to swallow down a little sob before he could answer. "I threw a rotten apple into the sea & it looked so lonely there . . ."'

They docked in Rio, and 'as soon as we dropped anchor people began to swarm on the ship, & looking down I suddenly caught sight of dear old Eppy! It was a joy. He looks very well, but a little tired, & his hair has gone very grey.' Some local dealers felt threatened by the activities of the Companhia, and there was talk of a boycott: 'He eats so little, almost nothing, but tells me he really feels quite well. I hope it will not be necessary for him to go up-country for a little while, it never does him any good.' As for the children, 'they were very calm until we got to the house, but then their excitement knew no bounds, they rushed about through the house & garden, & welcomed with shrieks of delight every tree or flower or old toy.' But their days in Santos were numbered, and Eva's letters reflect the reluctant recognition that before long they would have to exchange their sunlit Arcadia for the cool, grey shores of England. Alice wrote of Eva's children as 'half angels, half fairies, who live in an enchanted garden full of birds & flowers & sunshine & laughter,' and was happy to know that 'your Elves of Paradise will be safe in Santos for another eight months or so. I fear it is England where elves can scarcely be allowed to live!' Despite worries about money and Eppy's health, Eva was 'so happy here, quite ridiculously happy. I love this place too much, how shall I ever be able to leave it? I want to make the most of every hour, every minute that I am still here. The beauty & charm of nature here grip my heart afresh every day.'

The children had lessons every day from 12.30 to 2.30, after which Eva had a bath and prepared to receive lady visitors. Tooter was proving to be 'a charming little fellow, he is such a cavalier to ladies & kisses Barbara's hand in a very courtly fashion.' He had been frail as a baby, and had not been expected to live. Small, neat and tidy, unlike Ben, he hoped to be an ogre when he grew up: nicknamed the *gallo brigador* or fighting cock, he 'fights with all and everybody, and it is hard lines on good old Ben, who will never defend himself.' 'Ben must go to school,' Eva decided. He spent too much time with girls, and needed to mix more with boys, but she was reluctant to send him to a big school 'until he speaks English properly.' In the meantime, escape was to hand in the form of a pony called Billy Malone, which was 'as gentle as an old cow'. Ben and Eppy went riding together, and 'it looks awfully nice to see the two trotting off together, they are such good friends.' Ben remained as unworldly as ever, living 'in a wonderland where enchanted princesses are quite a common thing and where a talking frog or fish is nothing to be wondered at.' By contrast, Barbara was 'a very wide awake little lady', 'very strong-minded and independent', and 'it is wonderful how well she still understands English, much better than Tooter.' Felix was fine-featured even as a baby, and Ave called him the 'little Jap'. 'He is a queer little fellow,' Eva told Alice. 'He is either in a raging fury, screaming and stamping with his feet, or he is wildly happy, shouting with delight and laughing aloud.' Both temperamentally and physically he was unlike his siblings, boasting 'black hair'.

'Eppy begins to talk more definitely about our going to England,' Eva told Alice in December 1909. 'My heart aches a little. Shall I ever return here? I never loved this place as I do now. My whole heart is here; to go away for a few days is misery & to live anywhere else is banishment.' In her last letters from Santos she evoked a paradise lost. 'A few white-clad Englishmen are driving a golf ball along the beach, three or four cows are standing up to their knees in water, a little further out to sea a canoe glides through the water – six men are standing in it rowing, they look like black silhouettes against the sky. Thekla and the children are in front of the gate to the beach; I can hear their voices, but the hibiscus hedge hides them.' One evening she sat on the verandah watching her children playing football on the beach with 'several Barhams and various other little friends'. 'The ball is flying high through the air. The whole sky is a golden pink, reflected in the calm blue sea, and the mountains are almost black against the glowing background . . . I want to keep it in my mind's eye when we leave this land of sun and colour.' They sailed for England in July, leaving behind a heartbroken Manuel.

★

'Alas, I have given up my idea of the Bar,' Charles Greene wrote to Alice from Oxford in December 1887. He was not yet wholly committed to teaching, and would give the Ceylon Civil Service a whirl: but if that failed 'I shall then go in for schoolmastery. Charles Fry says that my prospects would be good and he promised to shove me on as much as possible.' Four years later he was still contemplating a possible alternative – he had, rather improbably, been asked to write a 'history of commerce' – but by 1894 he was so well established at Berkhamsted that he had been made a housemaster, and there was no turning back. More will be said about the school in the next chapter: in the meantime, Charlie (as he was known in the family) needed a housekeeper, and who better – in those days – than an unmarried sister? Alice was still in South Africa, Polly was busy painting and writing plays, and was living with her mother ('Mater') in Harston, so, Graham informed Alice, 'Helen is to go.' Poor Helen longed to lead a life of her own, and to achieve a degree of independence – ideally as a nurse – but her duty lay elsewhere, and she reluctantly submitted. 'It is rather amusing to see one's younger brother in the position of paterfamilias and head of house, reading prayers, prescribing litanies etc, while I am still living en garcon!' reported a rueful Graham.

But Charlie, uxorious by nature, needed a wife, and he fell in love with his willowy cousin, Marion Greene. It's not hard to see why: she was tall and elegant, with an almost swan-like beauty and the kind of figure that was shown to perfection in the close-clinging long white dresses worn by late-Victorian and Edwardian upper-middle-class ladies. She was thought by some to be rather cool and distant, and her detractors have attributed to her the coldness sometimes associated with her offspring: but she comes across, in her letters at least, as a warm and affectionate mother, and her remoteness may well have reflected shyness rather than an inherently chilly nature. Charlie was thick-set with a heavy moustache, and he and Marion must have looked, at times, an incongruous couple. The revelation that they wanted to get married caused consternation among other members of the family: not because Marion was considered unpleasant or unsuitable, but because there was a history of madness, or near-madness, in her family as well as his, and for two Greene first cousins-once-removed to marry and have children could intensify the strain. 'Charlie spoke to me about Marion & said it was the only thing in the world to make him happy,' Charlotte Greene told Alice. 'I then told him I did not think it right for him to marry, & the reasons. Poor boy, he did not know the nature of your father's illness, & Carleton too has suffered from nervous attacks.' Alice was equally concerned. 'I have been very far from happy about this love affair of Charlie's all along,' she wrote to Graham, though she recognised that 'this is no slight boy's affection on Charlie's part but the one great love of his life.' Ever the anxious and responsible head of the family, Graham consulted doctors and family friends, and was suitably concerned. 'I have no doubt it was very stupid of me not to notice the direction in which things were tending . . . I did not notice anything more than a cousinly liking for each other,' he told Alice. 'It placed me in a very difficult and unfortunate position, as I was obliged to tell Charlie my own views upon the question of cousins marrying, and also the particular reason which in the case of our two families makes such a marriage particularly undesirable. Charlie behaved exceedingly well. He told me that if he had known eighteen months ago what I put before him, he would not have felt justified in proceeding further in his suit.'

But by now it was too late – and, whatever their reservations, Charlie's family seemed well disposed to his wife-to-be. 'Marion is a good and very beautiful girl and she and Charlie have such a perfect understanding together that it does seem as if a very beautiful married life might be the result,' Alice decided. His mother and Graham had utilitarian reservations. 'I do hope Marion will enter into the life & make a useful wife,' Charlotte Greene declared. 'No doubt Charlie thinks she is perfect almost. She is pretty & intellectual but I hope she will be practical too.' Graham, though lacking immediate experience of such things, pronounced her to be 'a fine example of a healthy, right-minded girl'. Marion *was* practical, but unlikely to match the 'managing powers' of Helen. Be that as it may, Helen's days as a housemaster's housekeeper were numbered. 'To Helen this marriage means the prospect of being placed on the shelf, a thing she does not at all like,' Graham informed Alice – who, having escaped to South Africa, was happily immune to the fate that then awaited so many unmarried daughters. Having tasted freedom of a kind, Helen would now have to look after her mother at Harston, and Graham urged Alice to write to her and 'point out to her that her duty is at home'. Aunt Helen eventually went to live with her companion, Marie Hall, in a cottage opposite the gates of Harston: Sir Graham, as he had now become, disapproved of their ménage, and Marie was barred from Harston Hall.

The wedding 'went off capitally', Graham reported in January 1896: 'the bride was lovely' and the 'bridegroom was modest and manly.' 'Charlie is purchasing his boarding-house . . . it will be an inducement to him to save and devote himself to the school,' Graham wrote some nine months later, adding that 'Charlie has none of the restlessness which he had before. Marion makes him a good wife, and they ought to have a prosperous future.'

Hall and School House Greenes

Berkhamsted was, and still is, a small country town in Hertfordshire. It lies in a fold of the Chilterns; Peter Quennell, whose family came to live in a suburb of Berkhamsted in 1917, thought it a 'drab, prosaic town', but although its brickwork looks pale and washed-out when compared with that on display further south in Amersham or Gerrard's Cross, the overall effect is pleasant if low-key. Then as now, the remains of the castle loom up on one's right as the train comes into the station from London; low, plain-fronted late Georgian and early Victorian buildings prevail, and green hills rise up on either side. The handsome red-brick Venetian gothic town hall still stands in the High Street, almost opposite an old coaching inn; the school still dominates the town, but the site of the Hall – the huge, early nineteenth-century house to which Eppy brought his family in 1910, when they finally left Brazil – has long been a housing estate.

Despite the misery of his schooldays there, Graham Greene returned to the town again and again in his writings, and became fond of the place with the passing of time. 'I walked down towards my old home, down the dim drab high street, between the estate agents, the two cinemas, the cafés; there existed still faint signs of the old market town – there was a crusader's helmet in the church. People are made by places, I thought; I called this "home", and sentiment moved in the winter evening, but it had no real hold,' he wrote in The Lawless Roads. (A recurrent motif in Graham's autobiographical writings, the crusader's helmet in the parish church seems to be a figment of his imagination.) A story called 'The Innocent', published two years earlier in 1937, strikes a kinder note. Walking up from the station, its narrator passes some 'ugly almshouses, little grey stone boxes', yet 'I knew them as I knew nothing else. It was like listening to music, all that walk,' and had he not been accompanied by a now unwanted girl friend, 'I could have been very happy that night in a melancholy autumnal way, wandering about the little town, picking up clues to that time of life when, however miserable we are, we have expectations.' Years later, in *A Sort of Life*, he recalled 'the Grand Junction canal with slow-moving painted barges and remote gypsy children, the watercress beds, the hillocks of the old castle surrounded by a dry moat full of cow parsley,' and how 'the faint agreeable smell of coal dust blew up from the railway.'

To one side of the town stretched an enormous common on which, more than once, Graham sought refuge from the miseries of school. 'The long secret trek through the heather by Alan Breck and David Balfour always for me took place on Berkhamsted Common; it almost seemed a personal adventure, perhaps because my mother was kin to the Balfours of Pilrig, and indeed first cousin to Stevenson himself,' Graham wrote of *Kidnapped*, one of his favourite books; and towards the end of his schooldays he 'began to develop a love for the landscape around Berkhamsted which never left me . . . Chenies, Ivinghoe, Aldbury have always meant more to me than Dartmoor or the fells of Yorkshire, and the hidden spots of the Chilterns were all the dearer because they were on the very borders of Metroland. They had the excitement of a frontier.' Unlike Graham or his contemporary W. H. Auden, the denizens of Berkhamsted had no desire to see themselves as frontiersmen. A good many commuted into London every day, like Eppy en route to the Brazil Warrant Company's headquarters in the City, or, half a lifetime later, Castle, the MI6 double agent in *The Human Factor*, who bicycled home from the station every evening 'across the canal bridge, past the Tudor school, into the High Street, past the grey flint parish church, then up the slope of the Chilterns to this small semi-detached house in King's Road.' Literary types and left-wing intellectuals lived in the town or thereabouts, among them the short story writer W. W. Jacobs, best remembered for 'The Monkey's Paw', and a friend of Charles Greene; the historian G. M. Trevelyan, who owned large stretches of land near the town; R. H. Tawney, the Fabian sage; the left-wing economic historians J. L. and Barbara Hammond; and Peter Quennell's parents, well known for their books on domestic architecture and artefacts. And, of course, a good many Berkhamstedians were employed by the school, as masters, matrons, handymen, maids, groundsmen and gardeners.

Berkhamsted School had been founded in 1543, and still boasted a red-brick hall, like that of a small Cambridge college, from the walls of which generations of headmasters glowered down in gowns and mortar boards. 'Part rosy Tudor, part hideous modern brick the colour of dolls'-house plaster hams', as its most famous son once put it, the school consisted of two quadrangles, with outbuildings and playing fields beyond. Peter Quennell, a school contemporary of Graham's, described it as a 'humdrum institution', but he yearned for grander company, and once ensconced at Balliol, consorted almost exclusively with Old Etonians. Unlike some of the better-known schools, Berkhamsted was poorly endowed in terms of land or the backing of City livery corporations, and its staff were paid less than they might have earned elsewhere. In 1887, after centuries of somnolent mediocrity, the school was revitalised by the arrival of Dr Charles Fry. A stocky, bald, heavily bearded character with bright blue eyes, Dr Fry was, like Charles and Eppy Greene, a product of Bedford Grammar School; but whereas Charles, his successor as Headmaster, had been awarded a third at Oxford, Fry had been a scholar of Pembroke, Cambridge, and narrowly missed a first. He was also, albeit indirectly, a member of the Greene family: in 1876 he had married Julia, a daughter of Edward Greene the brewer, and was never short of funds thereafter. After teaching at Cheltenham he had been appointed Headmaster of Oundle, but was taken ill and only survived four terms. He took a keen interest in drainage, and commissioned a detailed report on the Berkhamsted drains before taking up his new post.

Once installed, he set about the place with phenomenal energy. He increased the number of masters from nine to twenty-one, and the number of boys from 170 to 470; he opened a new boarding house, St John's, in 1890, and this was followed in due course by Incent's, named after an eminent sixteenth-century Anglican divine associated with the school; he and his wife paid for what Peter Quennell described as 'a repulsive red-brick chapel approached by a range of ill-proportioned cloisters' to replace its cast-iron predecessor. In 1910, shortly after he had moved on to become the Dean of Lincoln, Deans' Hall was opened for school meetings, named after Dean Fry and Dean Incent. He was keen on games, started the school Cadet Corps, emphasised discipline and hard work, built labs and a gym, wielded the cane *con brio* and, as a keen mountaineer who had scaled the Matterhorn, introduced a benign virus into the Berkhamstedian bloodstream that manifested itself in such first-rate mountaineers as Frank Smythe, H. W. Tilman and Raymond Greene. Graham detested the very idea of his father's 'sinister sadistic predecessor', whom he described as a 'Manichean figure in black gaiters with a long white St Peter's beard'. He particularly disapproved of the fact that when Dr Fry came to stay the hall outside the dining room had to be cleared of maids and children after breakfast 'so that the Dean could go to the lavatory unobserved and emerge again unseen by anyone'.

Years later, after the publication of *A Sort of Life*, Greene found himself corresponding with various contemporaries from school, not all of whom shared his view of the Dean. One of them questioned whether what Greene had said about Fry was really his 'considered opinion'; as far as he remembered, the boys were 'proud of the stern old Doctor' who had 'dedicated his life and his wealth' to the school; he always seemed 'the personification of dignity and strength, and we always gave him credit for having made a great school of Berkhamsted.' Graham remained unmoved. He told his correspondent that his mother had found Fry 'a great pest' when he came to stay, and that he was 'hated by Kenneth Bell' – Kenneth Bell being an Old Berkhamstedian who was later Greene's tutor at Balliol, and seems not to have held the views attributed to him. 'The end of his life was an absurd one,' and 'a man who cannot be seen coming out of a lavatory by children or servants had something intrinsically wrong with his character,' Graham concluded: and with that the great Dean vanishes from our story.

In the meantime, Charles Greene was proving a capable and conscientious housemaster of St John's, paid all of £150 a year and worn out by his labours. 'I remember your tall, beautiful mother, and your father as a tired-looking, bowed, moustached figure, rather short,' another Old Berkhamstedian recalled, and in Graham's recollection his father seemed far removed from 'the young dandyish man who appeared in a tinted Oxford photograph on their bathroom wall, with a well-trimmed moustache, wearing evening dress with a blue waistcoat.' The arrival of six children in fourteen years put strains on the family finances. Molly, the eldest, was born in 1896, and was followed two years later by Herbert, generally regarded as the black sheep of the family; by Raymond in 1901; and by Graham in 1904. The babies of the family were Hugh, born in 1910, and Elisabeth, born the year in which the First World War broke out. According to one of her nieces, Marion, their mother, was 'very beautiful, very dignified, but she always knew best. She was a bit cold and we were all a bit frightened of her, I guess. She never doubted that she was in the right and I think that made a wall between her and her children. She was also very cool, very aloof, even with her own children, even with the two youngest, Hugh and Elisabeth.' 'I never thought of it, but she *had* a Plantagenet look,' a former pupil, Eric Guest, recalled, adding that 'I always liked and felt comfortable with her detachment,' and in *A Sort of Life* Graham wrote of how 'I associate my mother with a remoteness, which I did not at all resent, and with a smell of eau de cologne. If I could have tasted her I am sure she would have tasted of

wheaten biscuits,' possessed as they were of 'a very pale pure unsweet-
ened flavour'. When, in due course, he was promoted to Headmaster,
Charles Greene seemed 'even more distant than our aloof mother'. 'I
think my only real moments of affection for my father were when he
made frog-noises with his palms, or played Fly Away, Jack, Fly Away, Jill,
with a piece of sticking plaster, or made me blow open the lid of his
watch,' Greene confessed in late middle age. 'Only when I had children
of my own did I realise how his interest in my doings had been genuine,
and only then I discovered a buried love and sorrow for him, which
emerges today from time to time in dreams.'

    Graham Greene's first memory may have been of 'sitting in a pram
at the top of a hill with a dead dog lying at my feet', but despite this
inauspicious beginning and cool or abstracted parents, life at St John's
was pleasant enough. There were unmarried aunts in abundance who
read poems, played party games and fussed over nephews and nieces;
there were seaside holidays at Littlehampton and Overstrand in Norfolk
and outings to see Uncle Graham at Harston House, where the three-
year-old Raymond fell into the fountain on the front lawn and, when
asked how he had extricated himself, reported that he had 'struck out
for the shore'. Staff came with the job of housemaster, and 'my mother's
remoteness, her wonderful lack of the possessive instinct, was made
much easier for her to achieve by the presence of Nanny.' And in 1910, the
same year in which Charles Greene became the Headmaster, the number
of Greenes in Berkhamsted was suddenly doubled. After a brief sojourn
in 'Elvyne', a house on Chesham Road, Eppy and Eva Greene bought a
large property at the far end of Berkhamsted, and a small army of exotic-
seeming cousins took up residence the following year. The new arrivals
were to be known henceforth as the 'rich' or 'Hall' Greenes, as opposed
to the 'intellectual', 'poor' or 'School House' Greenes.

    According to a prospectus produced seventeen years later by Knight,
Frank & Rutley's Hanover Square office, the Hall was set in twenty-five
acres of parkland and boasted seventeen bedrooms, three bathrooms, a
billiards room, a 'Tudor-style dairy', a vegetable garden, a 'garage for
three large cars', an orchard, a walled garden, tennis courts (two grass
and one hard), stables, a home farm producing milk, cream and eggs
and three cottages for members of staff. The house itself was 'of brick
with slated roof, the walls being roughcast and covered with wisteria
and other creepers'. Eppy must have been gratified to learn that Euston
was forty minutes away on the train, that if the mood took him he could
play golf on Berkhamsted Common or hunt with the Hertfordshire and

Old Berkeley Fox Hounds; and that, when it came to his children's education, 'the famous Berkhamsted Grammar School is within ten minutes' walk' of the house. Eppy was by now a very rich man, and the Hall Greenes lived in style. They employed eleven indoor servants, as well as a carpenter, several gardeners, a chauffeur called Collins who, according to Barbara, had been brought up on a farm and 'was far more used to animals and never understood the workings of a car', and a very old man, the chauffeur's father, whose sole job was to mow the lawns with a horse-drawn mowing-machine and remove every weed in the process. The housemaids carried boiling water about the house in huge brass kettles, and were expected to empty the chamber pots every morning; according to Barbara, when they arrived there was only one bathroom for the whole family plus nurses and governesses, so those referred to in the prospectus must have been added by the Greenes. Thekla, the Polish nurse, had come with them from Brazil, but although Barbara and Felix adored her, she had never got on as well with the older children, and with Ben in particular. She was eventually dismissed: it was, for Barbara, 'my life's first tragedy', and 'I can feel the misery still.'

According to Barbara, life in the Hall was unusually free and easy-going. 'There were few rules except good manners, church on Sundays and punctuality,' she recalled, but 'woe betide any of us who were even a moment late for breakfast at eight o'clock – and that went on even after we were grown up and had been to dances the night before.' Breakfast was of the old-fashioned variety, with kippers, kidneys, scrambled eggs and bacon waiting under silver salvers. The children were expected to amuse themselves and invent their own games: much emphasis was placed on self-discipline – 'Pull yourself together or leave the room', 'Don't fuss' and 'What can't be cured must be endured' were family mottoes – and Eva only became irritated on those rare occasions when they said they didn't know what to do. They were punished if they were rude to their mother, or told a lie, when 'we heard the dreaded words from my father: "I want to see you in my office in half an hour." The half hour waiting was agony, and then we were given a solemn talk – nothing more – which usually ended in tears. Once that was over, every-thing was forgotten and never referred to again.' Eva loved to spend time with her children and, because she was still so young herself, she was very much on their wavelength; she encouraged them to read, to enjoy music, poetry and plays, with or without the enthusiastic support of the aunts. Only the grapes and the peaches in the greenhouses were out of bounds, being reserved for grown-ups' dinner parties.

Although, as the youngest boy, and a very good-looking one at that, Felix was very much his mother's pet, his memories of life at the Hall were far less rosy. Years later, when Felix talked to his prospective biographers about his parents and his childhood, Barbara was outraged by what he told them: he may have been the most naturally gifted of his generation of Greenes, but Felix was haunted by a sense of his own worthlessness and inadequacy, by a notion that he was both unloved and unlovable, and – in retrospect at least – he put much of the blame on his parents, and his mother in particular. 'We lived in an atmosphere of total hypocrisy,' he claimed: his parents' marriage was a wretched business, and Eva made up for it by being over-fond of her adored Felix. Matters were made worse by the war, since, according to Felix, 'Mama felt horribly torn between her feelings for her own country and the sufferings of her relatives, and her loyalty to Papa; and she felt Papa was totally incapable of understanding this conflict.' Eppy, it seems, was not only 'a strong disciplinarian and remote' but, for all his wealth, a bit of a miser: if Felix asked him for sixpence to go to the cinema, Eppy would say 'Well, what do you want it for? Aren't you happy here? We've given you everything, you've got a horse, you've got a farm, you've got everything . . .' Ave, his eldest daughter, claimed that if one of Eppy's children asked for a shilling endless questions were asked, but larger sums were more easily agreed to.

Felix's claim that the Hall Greenes felt intellectually inferior to the School House Greenes, and were rather despised by their more cerebral cousins, has the ring of truth. On the other hand, Barbara recalled, 'our cousins at the School House were far more strictly and conventionally brought up and envied us our free and easy life. I suppose this was due to my mother having been brought up in Brazil and she found many English customs unnecessarily restricting. They loved to escape to the more free and easy atmosphere of the Hall. Their parents were strict about them doing well at school, while my parents didn't seem to mind too much as long as we got along.' For the young Graham, the new arrivals had 'an intimidatingly exotic air'. In terms of age, his cousins 'were inserted between us, our family starting first, as though my uncle, who was the younger brother, had suffered from a competitive spirit and wanted to catch my father up.' The unmusical and buttoned-up School House Greenes particularly dreaded visiting the Hall on Christmas Eve to inspect the tree. 'I used to be embarrassed by the carols in German round the tree because I was afraid I might be expected to sing too,' Graham remembered. 'The whole affair in our eyes seemed rather Teutonic.' Although he was never close to Ben or Felix, Graham always had a soft spot for his cousin Edward, known as 'Tooter', and as adolescents both he and Herbert fell in love with their cousin Ave (who, for her part, liked Raymond the best of all). Graham had fond memories of sitting on the roof of the Hall with Tooter on warm summer afternoons, eating stolen currants and sultanas. But, for all its grandeur, the Hall was being eaten away by dry rot, and after the Greenes had moved away it had to be demolished; and 'no stone of it now remains, a building estate has swallowed all – the lawns, the trees, the stables and the meadows, which were to be the scenery of my calf-love.'

★

With Charles now the Headmaster of Berkhamsted, the intellectual Greenes moved out of St John's into School House. Their new home formed part of the main school buildings, on the northernmost of the two quadrangles. Graham's famous green baize door, the divide between barbarism and civilisation, separated their living quarters from the boarders of School House itself, and from the old Tudor hall with its permanent display of previous Headmasters. Light, airy, white-painted rooms, some of them still boasting grey sixteenth-century fireplaces, looked over a graveyard to the flint-built parish church, with or without its crusader's helmet; a steeply turning staircase led to bedrooms above and, on the second floor, School House dormitories and the dark and fearful spot where the young Graham was 'terrified by a witch who would lurk at night on the nursery landing by the linen cupboard'. In the high-walled gardens were greenhouses, a croquet lawn, an apple orchard, and a tennis court surrounded by pear trees; loganberries and raspberries were grown in a kitchen garden. Reminders of mortality were seldom far away: the boys were paid a penny per hundred to massacre cabbage whites with tennis racquets or sprinkle snails with salt, and, or so Hugh remembered, the prevailing peace was 'occasionally disturbed by the dying shrieks of animals from a neighbouring slaughterhouse'.

'Two countries just here lay side by side. From the croquet lawn, from the raspberry canes, from the greenhouse and the tennis lawn you could always see – dominatingly – the great square Victorian buildings of garish brick,' Graham wrote in *The Lawless Roads*.

From my mother's bedroom window – where she had borne the youngest of us to the sound of school chatter and the disciplinary bell – you looked straight down into the quad, where the hall and the chapel and the classrooms stood. If you pushed open a green baize door in a passage by my father's study, you entered another passage deceptively similar, but none the less you were on alien ground. There would be a slight smell of iodine from the matron's room, of damp towels from the changing rooms, of ink every-where. Shut the door behind you again, and the world smelt differ-ently: books and fruit and eau de cologne.

Raymond and Hugh were happy, successful schoolboys, but for Graham what lay beyond the green baize door was an initiation into a world of cruelty, terror and deception. 'In the land of the skyscrapers, of stone stairs and cracked bells ringing early, one was aware of fear and hate, a kind of lawlessness – appalling cruelties could be practised without a second thought; one met for the first time characters, adult and adolescent, who bore about them the genuine quality of evil,' he wrote some fifteen years after leaving school. But with the fear and the sense of evil came an aware-ness of God: 'And so faith came to one – shapelessly, without dogma, a presence above a croquet lawn, something associated with violence, cruelty, evil across the way. One began to believe in heaven because one believed in hell, but for a long while it was only hell one could picture with a certain intimacy – the pitch-pine partitions of dormitories where everybody was never quiet at the same time; lavatories without locks; walks in pairs up the suburban roads; no solitude anywhere, at any time.'

The children's memories of life in School House were, inevitably, frag-mentary and impressionistic. Raymond and Graham shared a room for a time, and had violent quarrels, one of which ended with Graham hitting his older brother on the head with a croquet mallet; Herbert won a baby pig at a fair, and brought it home briefly; every afternoon, between half-past five and half-past six, they were allowed into the dining room after tea to play with their mother, and in return 'she paid occasional state visits to the nursery in the School House, a large confused room which looked out onto the flint church and the old cemetery, with toy cupboards and bookshelves and a big wooden rocking horse.'

Hugh and Elisabeth were by far the youngest members of the family, and in later life would become particularly close to Graham. Hugh's first memory was, like Graham's, of life in his pram, though in his case he busied himself unscrewing the brass screws of its hood and hurling them into the grass. 'I am alone, unobserved and happy,' he later wrote of this interesting occurrence. 'The year must be 1913, and I am between two and three years old.' Pink-and-white, chubby and endowed with golden curls, he was 'a rather nervous child, reserved and shy with no taste for rough games'. At the age of four he appeared unannounced at a grown-up party and ordered the eminent novelist Mrs Humphry Ward to remove herself from a chair normally occupied by his mother; he was prone to biting people, once sinking his teeth into the 'succulent calf' of a house-maid, and to dissuade him Marion bit him in the arm, drawing blood in the process. She had wanted another daughter, which may explain why the infant Hugh tended to be togged out in white smocks, and why he was sent as Charles I's daughter to a fancy-dress party ('my trailing skirts saved me from active participation in the games the other children played'). Both Hugh and Elisabeth were given to bawling at night: Hugh later claimed that they suffered under a sadistic nurse, but never told their parents about her. 'My father and mother were remote figures, kind but in a world apart,' Hugh wrote in an unpublished memoir. 'With both my parents the close relationship which would have provided the tenderness one needs in child-hood only came later in life, a very common experience, I should imagine, with that nurse-ridden generation.' Only once was Hugh chastised by his father, and that came about through a misunderstanding. One day at break-fast Hugh refused to eat his porridge; Charles, clad in gown and hood, and about to go into morning assembly, told him to be a 'good boy'; Hugh mistook this for an instruction to do what was referred to in those days as 'Number Two', and, not feeling the urge at that moment, dug his heels in. It was, he tells us, 'the only occasion on which my father, a kind and liberal though often, I think, bewildered man, ever beat me.'

Despite the differences in their ages, Hugh and Graham came to share a room, and Graham was kept awake by his brother's cries at night. Hugh's first memory of Graham was of their lying side by side on a sofa in the day nursery, while Graham read him Rider Haggard. 'Those hours of listening to Graham reading left me with a lasting love for adventure stories,' Hugh recalled. Together they read Captain Marryat and G. A. Henty and Stanley Weyman and Robert Louis Stevenson and Rider Haggard, and invented an elaborate war game based on H. G. Wells's *Little Wars*, played on long tables in the School House dining room ('Graham was the better general: he always won'). Their shared passion for late-Victorian and Edwardian adventure and detective stories remained with them for the rest of their lives, prompting them to jointly edit *The Spy's Bedside Book* for Rupert Hart-Davis in 1957 and to scour second-hand bookshops for forgotten thrillers which might be reissued by The Bodley Head or, in the case of short stories, included in Hugh's antholo-gies of turn-of-the-century detective stories.

The Greenes have produced more than their fair share of writers, journalists, publishers and broadcasters, early manifestations of which appeared in an in-house family magazine, the *School House Gazette*. Herbert, soon to be sent away to school at Marlborough, was its editor, and Raymond the office boy, later promoted to assistant editor; Aunt Nora – Marion Greene's sister, familiarly known as 'Nono' – and Aunt Helen were at various times on the staff. According to Graham, Herbert was 'always of an adventurous character until he was changed by the continual and sometimes shameful failures of his adult life.' 'I hated every minute at Marlborough, and when my form master Mr Fisher gave me a good caning I ran away,' Herbert told Olga Franklin of the *Daily Mail* many years later: he claimed to have knocked the future Archbishop of Canterbury off his horse and into a gorse bush – accidentally, of course – and left Marlborough at the age of sixteen without having made any contribution to the academic or sporting life of the school. Though most admired in the family as a cricketer, he shared its literary leanings and, in due course, wrote a book about his alleged adventures as a secret agent during the Spanish Civil War and a good deal of doggerel, proudly proclaiming himself a 'journalist' when asked his occupation. Raymond was his polar opposite, being diligent, academic, upright and successful both academically and on the games field.

Molly – for whom, at that stage, the young Graham 'had a good deal of undeserved contempt', of a kind he reserved for girls in general – was also a regular contributor to the family magazine. She is best remembered for falling down a 'vertical chimney' while mountaineering with Raymond in the Lake District in 1920: she struck a grass ledge fifty feet down, bounced off again, and was eventually hauled up by her brother on the end of a rope, suffering only 'minor cuts and bruises'. The episode was witnessed from below by the fourth member of the party, the lovesick Lionel Walker, who was later emboldened to ask her for her hand, and duly became her husband. The first handmade issue of the *School House Gazette*, published in 1911, revealed how Molly had been 'severely bitten' by her dog Bikki, 'who in consequence received eight strokes of the cane'; she contributed an article entitled 'How I Saw a Ghost' ('Oh how frightened I was! I trembled all over . . .'), and reference was made to a poem, allegedly written by the Dean of Lincoln, which described how he had fallen over and injured his nose while visiting Berkhamsted the previous summer. Regular items in forthcoming issues included limericks by Herbert, schoolboy jokes ('Q: Why is your eye like a schoolmaster using corporal punishment? A: Because it has a pupil under the lash'), puzzles and small ads: Herbert provided a piece on 'Our Motor Drive to Berkhamsted' and an account of the Marlborough vs Rugby cricket match; Raymond contributed articles on 'Antiquities of Berkhamsted' and 'Our Day in London' – he and Graham went up for the Coronation of George V – and a classified ad read 'Lost: Graham's temper on Sunday evening between 4.30 and 5.30. Finder taking it to WHG [Herbert] shall be rewarded.'

Rather more revealing was a survey in which contributors were asked about their likes and ambitions. Molly's 'greatest aim in life' was 'to ride as much as I can', Raymond's 'to have a submarine', Graham's 'to go up in an aeroplane' and Herbert's 'to be a Field Marshal'. Raymond's 'idea of happiness' was 'to be finding fossils all day', Graham's 'going to London', Herbert's 'to be happy'; Molly nominated Sir Graham Greene as England's 'greatest living statesman', Raymond opted for 'Mr Asquith' and Herbert for 'Mr Balfour', while Graham 'didn't know any'. Raymond's 'favourite pastime' was carpentry, Graham's 'playing Red Indians', and Herbert's 'playing cricket and collecting autographs' (he once asked Graham to collect players' autographs for him at a county cricket match, and in reply to Question 7 – 'the cricketer most admired' – the sports-loathing Graham dutifully replied 'Herbert Greene', while Herbert himself chose 'Plum Warner'). Pathetic as he became in later life, it's hard not to sense a bully in Herbert, as older brother, editor and games player, and the dislike he aroused in his siblings – and Graham's hatred for organised games – may have reflected this.

One by one the boys followed each other into Berkhamsted's prep school. Graham tells us little of his experiences there, 'except that once I teased my cousin Tooter, who ran home from the playing fields, crying. I felt a great shame at this, I knew already in my heart that I belonged on the side of the victims, not the torturers, and this was a betrayal of all those sunlit afternoons on the roof of the Hall.' Despite such momentary lapses, life in School House seems to have been almost idyllic, a self-contained world of games in the garden or the nursery, kindly, absent-minded aunts putting on plays for their nieces and nephews, and occasional forays to the Hall when a change of scene was called for. 'The clouds of unknowing were still luminous with happiness,' Graham wrote in A Sort of Life. 'There was no loneliness to be experienced, however preoccupied the parents might be, in a family of six children, a nanny, a nursemaid, a gardener, a fat and cheerful cook, a beloved head house-maid, a platoon of assistant maids, a whole battalion of aunts and uncles, all of them called Greene.'

4

A Country Under Occupation

Looking back on his schooldays at Berkhamsted from the vantage point of middle age, Peter Quennell remembered how, in Deans' Hall, 'we often sighted a short but dominant personage, fixing us with sternly watchful eyes as we went about our business, and sometimes lifting his voice to deliver a sonorous reprimand, bidding us remove our hands from our pockets or objecting to the colour of a pair of socks.' Suitably clad in hood, gown and mortar board, his hands firmly clasped behind his back, Charles Greene was, to his pupils at least, an awe-inspiring figure. At daily assemblies in the hall, Quennell continued, the Headmaster would occasionally deliver 'a fine specimen of Ciceronian invective', and never more so than when some sexual peccadillo – masturbation in the dorms, or homosexual tendencies – had been suspected or unearthed: in which case 'he would rather, he cried, that the school should cease to exist than that it should become – as might well happen unless the evil were promptly scotched – a hotbed of unmentionable vice; and later we learned of the various expulsions that had resulted from the scandal.'

Claud Cockburn, later to become a subversive and inventive left-wing journalist, best-known for his evocation of a 'Cliveden Set' of socialites and politicians well-disposed to Hitler and in favour of appeasement, was a contemporary of both Quennell and Graham Greene; and he too provided vivid memories of his old Headmaster. In order to keep the boys from mischief, 'efforts were made to fill every interstice of every day with public and communal activities – many of them conducted, like the drill of the Italian *bersaglieri*, at the double,' and 'as a direct result of all this supervision and ordering about, one of the most valuable lessons my school taught me was how to break other people's rules.' Cockburn shared the Headmaster's passion for chess, and they would play for hours on end by the fire in Charles Greene's study, 'listening contentedly for the imperious, but temporarily innocuous, jangle of bells summoning people to get on with something or other, and the shouts of prefects driving others along cold corridors without.' Greene, Cockburn recalled,

> gave the impression of conducting the affairs of the school and viewing life in general with the same smouldering, sometimes explosive intensity which he brought to the chessboard. He was a man of powerful and vivid reactions. Certain events, sometimes major, sometimes quite trivial, seemed to strike his mind with the heart and force of a branding-iron, and for a long time would remain in the forefront of consciousness, to be referred to, commented on, brooded upon aloud in a singularly sonorous voice, and with occasionally florid eloquence.

And yet, for all his grandeur, Greene was liked as well as respected, even by the acidic Quennell. 'In my youth I failed to recognise his virtues,' Quennell admitted. 'What I noticed were the portentous mannerisms behind which he hid his true face. I suspect that he was really a shy man: short himself, and latterly a little stout, he had married a tall slender wife, and begotten a family of tall children; and perhaps it was his own comparative shortness that had encouraged him to develop at school so majestic a persona.' 'I liked your portrait of your father,' he told Graham after reading *A Sort of Life*. 'Until I had left the school, I never knew how much I had owed to his kindness, or to the benevolent conspiracies that he and my father organised on my behalf, allowing me to pretend that I had a weak heart and an over-sensitive nervous system; with the result that I was let off not only the Corps, but every form of games and any scholastic system to which I didn't take a fancy.' 'I'd forgotten that your father used to lie on his back while talking,' he added; and Graham himself recalled how his father 'was never during school hours without gown and mortar board and it was a shock sometimes to encounter him in his uniform on the home side of the green baize door: it was like a breach of neutrality.'

Cecil Parrott, a future diplomat and translator of *The Good Soldier Švejk*, recalled the 'gentle' atmosphere of Berkhamsted, and how 'the tone of the school was extremely good compared with other public schools.' Martyn Skinner remembered the Headmaster as 'a dear old man who give me my first caning, three gentle taps which misled me into believing that that was all caning was.' 'I had a great respect for him,' a former pupil told Graham. 'He spoke to me once or twice, I daresay because I had only one leg.' But Charles Greene's charity was not restricted to the maimed or the crippled. 'Although he had to give me some thorough swishings, my memories of your husband are not only of kindness but of justice: and that is the highest praise that can be given to a headmaster,' an Old Berkhamstedian wrote to Marion Greene after her husband's death in 1942. 'Through his learning, taste, insight and enthusiasm he opened doors to us, and invited, not compelled us, to pass through,' another recalled. 'His conception of government in a school was to reduce regulations to a minimum – and to rule by personality, example and the creation of "tone", by which I mean freely accepted standards of conduct which were not to be transgressed.'

The Headmaster taught history and, according to Claud Cockburn, his lessons 'were not so much history lessons as comments on a state of affairs in which history had taken a turn for the worse . . . Charles Greene was, in the widest as well as the party-political sense of the word, a Liberal, and in the crack-up of Liberalism he saw the mark of doom.' The First World War saw his liberal principles put to the test. Returning to Berkhamsted in the autumn of 1914, the future mountaineer Frank Smythe found 'that sleepy little town in the throes of war's alarms and excitements'. German spies were thought to be ubiquitous, so much so that 'even our inoffensive little German master was arrested, but to everyone's surprise he was found to be innocent of spying and released.' H. W. Tilman, another mountaineer in the making, took a more hard-boiled view of the proceedings. 'Well, the little squit was arrested' he told his parents. 'Charles Greene like an idiot bailed him out for £100 and he is now put under the five-mile limit. We have got a new man in his place. He will probably be arrested again and sent to a concentration camp.' A committee of public safety was set up by elderly town dignitaries and, according to Smythe, the school's Officers' Training Corps armoury was placed under nightly guard 'in case the "enemy" should appropriate the antiquated Mauser rifles, relics of the Boer War, housed there'. 'A dachshund was stoned in the High Street, and once my uncle Eppy was summoned by night to the police station and asked to lend his motor car to help block the Great North Road down which a German armoured car was said to be advancing towards London,' Graham recalled in *A Sort of Life*. Towards the end of the war Herbert was made a lance corporal in the Honourable Artillery Company: he was put in charge of a German spy awaiting execution in the Tower of London, but – or so Graham claimed – lost his stripe after letting him out of his cell to watch an air raid. Nor, with their German connections, were the rich Greenes immune from prejudice. 'I actually met your German aunt going up to London one morning and felt that her position in England during the First World War was awkward, to say the least,' a former resident of the town told Graham Greene over half a century later. 'She seemed to me grateful to meet someone who was friendly and forthcoming.' As an enemy alien, she had to report to the police on a regular basis, and – as the son of a German mother – Felix once claimed that, as a very small boy, he got into trouble for flying a kite as a signal to passing German aircraft.

Chaos erupted in the town on Armistice Day: drunken soldiers broke into the school, incited the boys to riot, and threatened to throw the Headmaster into the canal, or so Claud Cockburn recalled. 'Next day, from the platform of the new hall, Dr Greene delivered one of his loudest and longest and most condemnatory speeches,' Peter Quennell remembered. In Cockburn's opinion, the drunken soldiery – like prefects neglecting their duties, or the pacifist French master, or pupils attempting to wear blue serge suits for chapel rather than black coats, or death-watch beetles in the Tudor hall – came to embody, in the Headmaster's mind, 'manifest indications of the Bolshevistic way things were tending', and since 'he said all these things with a vivid sincerity, and these extravagances were the product of genuine and agonised beliefs, the effect was not at all grotesque, but as vividly impressive as a revivalist meeting.' When, in due course, Charles Greene contemplated the terms of the Treaty of Versailles,

> his slightly bulbous grey eyes rolled, shone and started from his head, and his yellow moustache bristled. It reminded him of every disaster in the history of treaty-making since the errors committed by Pericles. As he spoke of it he sank back in his chair, pulling the mortar board farther and farther down on his forehead as though to shield his eyes from the sight of so much folly and horror . . . The spirit of Bolshevism, he said, was permeating everywhere, and the most ordinary events and contretemps of everyday life confirmed this view.

Amidst all these excitements, various members of the Greene family, both rich and intellectual, were passing through the school, with differing degrees of liking, loathing and success. Raymond was briefly at Marlborough, where he was bullied and very unhappy, but was then transferred to Berkhamsted; Graham and Hugh were at Berkhamsted throughout. Of the Hall Greenes, Ben spent his school career at Berkhamsted, Tooter was there for a time before transferring to Bedales, and Felix was sent to Sidcot, a Quaker school in Somerset, as was his sister Barbara. Raymond was the most successful of them all, triumphing in the classroom and on the games field and pulling his weight in extra-curricular affairs; Graham hated it the most, and made his feelings plain in later life; Hugh was a successful schoolboy; Ben and Tooter were never more than average.

As Peter Quennell ruefully remarked, Berkhamsted was 'not at all fashionable', but to keep their ends up 'my contemporaries pretended to regard the Etonians and Harrovians they met on field days as a crowd of dissipated snobs.' Be that as it may, the school was riven with its own forms of snobbery. Boarders made up the aristocracy, day boys like Quennell the middle class, and the 'train boys' who commuted in from the country round about were looked down on as the proletariat: 'we derided both their rough accents and their old, unsightly clothes, and even credited them with a rank, distinctive odour.' Whatever their ranking in the hierarchy, 'we were constantly hungry,' Claud Cockburn remem-bered. 'It was the fag end of the First World War, and we lived on three slices of bread and margarine for breakfast, a suet pudding with mince in it for lunch, six slices of bread and margarine for tea, and at bedtime two small biscuits.' Life in the classroom was equally austere. According to Frank Smythe, 'the system of education then in vogue was primarily competitive, and devil take the hindmost. I was among the hindmost.' Whether a boy moved up a class at the end of term depended on the aggregate of his marks in all subjects: Smythe got as far as the Remove, a haven for boys who were more proficient with their hands than their brains.

Graham famously detested his time at public school, and since he was more vocal on the subject than his siblings or cousins, it makes sense to deal with him first. His life became a torment when, at the age of thir-teen, he moved on from prep to public school, and exchanged the comforts of home at School House for the bleakness of life as a boarder at St John's, the boarding house in which he had lived as a small child when his father was its housemaster. 'There was a schoolroom with ink-stained nibbled desks insufficiently warmed by one cast-iron stove, a changing room smelling of sweat and stale clothes, stone stairs, worn by genera-tions of feet, leading to a dormitory divided by pitch-pine partitions that gave inadequate privacy – no moment of the night was free from noise, a cough, a snore, a fart,' he wrote in *A Sort of Life*. But his loathing for St John's was not simply a matter of physical discomfort or revulsion.

I had left civilisation behind and entered a savage country of strange customs and inexplicable cruelties: a country in which I was a foreigner and a suspect, quite literally a hunted creature, known to have dubious associates. Was not my father the headmaster? I was like the son of a quisling in a country under occupation. My elder brother Raymond was a school prefect and head of the house – in other words, one of Quisling's collaborators. I was surrounded by forces of the resistance, and yet I couldn't join them without betraying my father and my brother. My cousin Ben, a junior prefect, one of the rich Greenes, had no such scruples and worked covertly against my brother, gaining much popularity in consequence, so that I felt the less sympathy for him when he was later imprisoned, without warrant or reason.

To make matters worse, he was hopeless at games, hated the Corps, and was persecuted by a terrible boy called Carter who, a contemporary recalled, had 'pale red hair' and a 'snake-like skull', and took a particular delight in persecuting 'train boys'.

Years later, Raymond Greene was sceptical about Graham's miseries in general, and his position as the headmaster's son in particular. 'I cannot imagine why he appeared to have suffered such torment,' he told a countryside magazine. 'I think he imagined the problem.' Nor was Hugh entirely convinced. Years later, he and Graham revisited Berkhamsted with Yvonne Cloetta, Graham's close friend for the last thirty years of his life. Hugh said he couldn't understand why Graham had been so unhappy at school, when he and Raymond had enjoyed it so much. 'Well, there must have been something wrong with me at that time,' Graham replied, 'as if emerging from a nightmare'. Others were more sympathetic. 'I had not realised how unhappy you were, and felt that I ought to have,' Greene was told by Eric Guest, who had gone on to become a distinguished Bow Street magistrate. 'But I think much of it was due to your individual position which of course I was not imaginative enough to appreciate. As far as I was concerned my reaction to the place was boredom (not your intense kind) but an absolute acceptance that that was what life was like when you were young, and that it had to be got through.'

Not only was Graham bad at games, but he was bullied mercilessly by Carter and his sidekick, Wheeler. 'What a lot began with Wheeler and Carter – suspicion, mental pain, loneliness, this damned desire to be successful that came from a sense of inferiority,' he wrote in *The Lawless*

Roads. So relentless was their bullying that Graham attempted suicide rather than endure further persecution. He tried to cut open his knee with a penknife, and to poison himself with a bottle of eye drops. According to Marion Greene, Graham had a slight temperature and a sore eye on the day he should have returned to St John's, so she decided to keep him in bed. She put her head round the door to see how he was getting on, only to find his bed empty and a note to the effect that he couldn't face going back to school: he had drunk some eye drops, and they would not be seeing him again. They decided against involving the police, but Eppy asked his bailiff to search the canal, and their doctor drove Marion round the golf course in his car looking for the escapee. After lunch Molly announced that she thought she knew where he was, and set off for Berkhamsted Common, taking some food with her. She found him sitting in a little wood, and two hours later she brought him home.

'Graham was a very sensitive child, he hated to be taken notice of or favoured in any way,' Marion Greene recalled. Back home, he had a long talk with his father, leading to a 'whole comedy of errors': 'I suppose I complained of the general filth of my life at St John's, meaning the unlocked lavatories, the continual farting of my companions, but he misunderstood me and believed I had been the victim of some ring of masturbation . . .' Graham lived at home for the rest of his school career, but in the meantime he needed therapy of some kind. Raymond, who was by then in his first year of reading medicine at Oxford and 'felt great pride in the trust reposed in him', suggested psychoanalysis and recommended a course of treatment with an eccentric and unqualified practitioner called Kenneth Richmond. Worried that the family's strain of madness might be reasserting itself, Charles Greene agreed that the sixteen-year-old Graham should be taken out of school for six months, and sent to live with the Richmonds in their house off the Bayswater Road. Richmond was a great believer in the curative value of his patients recounting their dreams: Graham, who developed a lifelong interest in dreams – in old age he put together an anthology of his own, almost all of which were as tedious as other people's dreams invariably are – was happy to co-operate: one of his dreams, or so he informed his psychotherapist, involved Richmond's beautiful wife Zoe leaning naked over him and dangling her bosoms in his face. Richmond liked to consort with literary types, including Walter de la Mare, J. D. Beresford (years later Graham reissued his novel *The Hampdenshire Wonder* at Eyre & Spottiswoode), and Naomi Royde-Smith, the editor of the *Weekly*

Westminster, who had published the early work of Rupert Brooke, and would soon do the same for young Graham. According to Marion Greene, Richmond felt that for Graham 'to express himself in writing would help so much', so his time in Devonshire Terrace may well have had potent and long-term side effects. Years later, Graham told Zoe Richmond that 'the six months I spent in the house with you and Kenneth were among the happiest in my life': no doubt he had half fallen in love with the lovely Zoe, but she faced stiff competition when Eppy, 'who perhaps did not wish to be outdone by his intellectual brother', arranged for his oldest daughter, Ave, to be treated by the Richmonds. Both Herbert and Graham were smitten by Ave, and jostled for her favours – so much so that 'there were moments when my German aunt became worried: another first-cousin marriage in the Greene family would have been a disaster.' Years later, Ave revealed that her cousin wanted to marry her, 'but then he said no, we're cousins, my father and mother wouldn't have it . . . I was fond of him, but I wouldn't have married Graham. I wouldn't have known from one day to the next what would happen.' To clear the air, perhaps, Aunt Eva took Graham with her by boat to Lisbon. There they met Eppy, who was on his way home from a business trip to Brazil, and visited the grave in Corunna of Sir John Moore, a distant relation of the Greenes. Kenneth Richmond, a man of parts, eventually abandoned psychotherapy in favour of a system of shorthand, invented by himself and designed to break Pitman's near monopoly: he also became the secretary of the Society for Psychical Research, and edited its journal.

School life was altogether more tolerable for Graham after six months away. He was no longer a boarder, he was in the sixth form, he could study the subjects he liked and be taught by congenial masters, and he consorted with kindred spirits like Peter Quennell and Claud Cockburn. His time in London had give him an aura of worldliness and sophistication, made all the more impressive when he invited Walter de la Mare to visit Berkhamsted. Arthur Mayo, a contemporary, remembered Graham as 'a quiet withdrawn boy with few friends', but Peter Quennell evoked a more confident figure who kept himself aloof from school life and observed the goings-on around him with a cool, sardonic eye. 'His talk had an exuberantly sceptical and blithely pessimistic turn; and his contemplation of the horrors of human life appeared to cause him unaffected pleasure,' he recalled in his memoirs. 'At each fresh insight he obtained into human absurdity or wickedness, his pallid, faintly woe-begone face would assume an air of solemn glee.' Claud Cockburn remembered Graham's interest in dreams, some of which, he claimed, coincided with or even anticipated events in the world at large, including the sinking of the *Titanic*. Dreams would be discussed over breakfast, and 'he would leave the bacon cooling on his plate as he listened with the fascination of a secret detective. When necessary he would lure them on to provide more and more details which to them were amusing or meaningless but to him of thrilling and of usually scandalous significance. "It's amazing," he said to me once, "what those dreams disclose . . ." and at the thought of it gave a low whistle.'

What was undeniable, however, was his ineptitude at, and indifference towards, games of any kind, or indeed, any manifestations of team spirit. The St John's house record book spells this out, while shedding light on the achievements of other members of the family. Points were awarded every year for prowess on the games field and on the parade ground. In 1918–19, Raymond got 6 for rugger, 3 for cricket, 21 for swimming and 4 for his activities in the school Corps; Ben, a rather less successful all-round schoolboy, got 8 for rugger, 18 for swimming, and 3 for the Corps; Graham and Tooter got 2 each for Corps, and nothing more. The following year Raymond notched up 12 for rugger, 5 for cricket, and 19 for swimming; Graham and Tooter got no points whatsoever. Like Graham, Tooter was academically undistinguished: at Bedales, never the most sporting of schools, he made his mark as a sprinter, swimmer and fast bowler, before going up to St John's, Cambridge, to read history. It is wrongly assumed that large boys make useful and enthusiastic rugger players, and poor Ben was no exception. 'The heaviest forward in our scrum,' he was also 'rather clumsy, chiefly on account of his awkward shape,' but 'being tall his speciality was the line-out, and he often gained us a lot of ground here.' As a swimmer, he specialised in something called the 'lunge', and 'with a little more practice Greene should succeed in breaking the record.'

Whereas Ave and Barbara were driven to their day schools in Berkhamsted by Collins the chauffeur, Ben and Tooter walked to school every morning from the Hall. Asked what he would like do after he left, the thirteen-year-old Ben said he'd like to become 'an engineer in a railway workshop' or, failing that, to join the Royal Engineeers ('one gets good pay and gets food free'), while Tooter opted for becoming a 'coffee merchant', like his father. As such, 'I will go to London nearly every day, sometimes I will bring things for my children and my wife': an accurate enough prediction, though he would never become a father.

Apart from his time at Marlborough, Raymond's childhood had been 'happy and free from incident'. Always self-disciplined, he learned to master his shyness; as a schoolboy he far outstripped his brothers and cousins, excelling as a sportsman, keeping order as a house and then a school prefect, editing the school magazine, playing a key role in the Debating Society, winning a prize for drawing, sharing the Arnold Medal for Verse with Peter Quennell, and crowning his career by being awarded a Theodore Williams Medical Scholarship at Pembroke College, Oxford, worth £100 a year for the following five years. Unlike curly-haired, short-sighted, broad-headed Hugh, Raymond was dark and good-looking as well as tall and slim, with more regular, less rounded features than Graham, and less of that slightly pop-eyed look associated with some of the Greenes. As a busy member of the Debating Society, he opposed the motion that 'the Government are justified in adopting reprisals in their air policy against the Germans', denied the existence of ghosts ('In closing the debate, C. R. Greene tried not to be scornful'), opposed the nation-alisation of the railways, opposed the setting up of a League of Nations ('one nation would make use of the credulity of the rest and prepare in secret for a world catastrophe'), and proposed that 'there is no new thing under the sun,' ('He exhorted the house to take a wide view and study the evidence of history', the minutes reveal, adding that Cockburn C. 'must learn that offensiveness to one's opponents is not a good form of argument'). More relevant to his later development was his introduction to mountaineering while still a schoolboy. Charles Greene had 'loved mountains and walking in them, but was never a climber in the sense of frequenting places where a rope round the waist was necessary': he 'encouraged the itch in his children', but only Molly and Raymond responded. When Raymond was sixteen, Ashley Abrahams, 'the great pioneer of English rock climbing', lectured at the school, and invited Raymond to visit him in the Lake District. Raymond took up his offer the following year, and a passion was born.

In December 1919 Raymond took over as editor of the *Berkhamstedian*, and set about transforming a tedious collation of sporting reports, debating society minutes and news of Old Boys into something of more general interest. 'We want contributions,' he thundered in his opening editorial. 'Complaints have reached us that the *Berkhamstedian* is but a dry-as-dust production. But what else can you expect when *you yourself* do not assist us? Rumours have reached us of wits, of poets, of novel-ists, of journalists, all at hand within the School itself: yet seldom have their effusions been sent for our approval.' His first issue included a sixteen-page article entitled 'France to Egypt by Aeroplane', 'Impressions of Syria', and parodies of Tennyson and Wordsworth; subsequent editions included early work by Graham, and Raymond's own prize-winning poem ('Thou art lone in the midst of the mountains / Thou art holy and mighty of power, Midst the roar of the torrents and fountains / When the clouds of the Hell Gates lower . . .'). But his final editorial strikes a melancholy note, that is all too familiar to editors and publishers. He was only too well aware that the last two editions had not been up to scratch, but 'Believe us, reader, it is not our fault. The prices of paper and printing have enormously increased, and where'er we go, there is one who follows and whispers "Economy" in our ears . . .' One wonders what Graham made of his concluding appeal: 'When the mantle of Editorship has fallen on other shoulders, remember, please, that your debt to the old School is greater than you can ever repay.' In later issues of the magazine, published after Raymond's departure, we learn that Graham 'spoke at some length and somewhat off the point' at a meeting of the Debating Society, that Raymond had presented 'a quantity of fossils and minerals' to the school's Natural History museum (gifts from other Old Boys included 'some well preserved snakes' heads' and an elephant's tooth), and that Miss A. M. Greene – Molly – and Mr F. L. Walker had been married in the school chapel in October 1922, and enjoyed a honeymoon in the Lake District. The Walkers had two children and an army of grandchildren; and with that the eldest of the School House children fades from the scene.

Molly's schooling has left no trace, but Elisabeth was sent to away to Downe House in Kent. Hugh remembered her trying to make herself sick by drinking salt and water at the end of one holidays in order to postpone the awful moment of departure. Hugh and Elisabeth were very much the junior members of the family, and Hugh suffered from an extreme form of Greene shyness which made him seem, in later years, a remote and chilly figure. (Both Hugh and Graham were short-sighted, and this may have contributed to their shyness: Hugh could not manage without his spectacles, but Graham, who could, whipped them off in public, or in the presence of a photographer.) Shyness, Hugh once wrote, 'was like a great wave of hot water through which one struggled to the surface, sweating and breathless, in a strange blue light – like the light of the school swimming baths, which I hated.' Though not as tall as his cousin Ben, he became, in due course, the tallest of all the School House Greenes, with a round, rather squashed-looking face adorned with a pair of bottle-end spectacles; but as a small child he had looked too angelic for his own good, with pink-and-white cheeks, blue eyes and fair yellow curls, and 'when the time came to leave the world of the nursery and the garden and go to school I left behind a sheltered, if not particularly happy, period of my life. I had never had a bicycle or a dog, I had not had much to do with other children, and my shyness was overwhelming.'

Hugh was, and would remain, less of a loner and more of a team-player than Graham, and he proved both academically bright and, in school terms, a responsible citizen. He was a day boy until his father retired, when he moved into the old family home as a boarder, 'so for all those years I had the precious privilege of privacy.' 'I suppose it was a combination of shyness and being the headmaster's son that made happiness impossible,' he wrote in his unpublished memoir, which both stylistically and in its subject matter echoes and counterpoints *A Sort of Life*. 'One moved among one's fellows as a sort of quisling in daily touch with the occupying power. But I am not sure it is a bad thing to be unhappy at school. Life afterwards is a constant relief.' Although Hugh enjoyed his schooldays, his version of Berkhamsted is even more alarming than Graham's. It may not have been as bad as some public schools, 'but even in the outer circles of hell the flames could be hot enough.' He recalled in particular a 'murky cavern' where, in the winter, school bullies held small boys against the blazingly hot radiators: years later, Hugh could 'still hear the screams of the victims and the laughter of the torturers, and smell burned flesh', but he never told his father about it. He remembered only two masters with any affection: one of them, who helped him through School Certificate maths, was sent to prison for obtaining money under false pretences and ended his days as a golf club caddy, and 'I can still smell the whisky on his breath as he leant over, patiently, kindly and lucidly explaining what was so clear to others but so difficult to me.' Claud Cockburn, then at the end of his time at Oxford, stood in for an absent master, teaching the classics and ancient history, and proved to be 'the most brilliant teacher I have ever experienced.'

Hugh was to become, years later, a radical and subversive Director-General of the BBC, but as a schoolboy he was, according to one contemporary at least, clever, distant and conformist, 'completely docile, completely dedicated to doing the right thing'; another recalled him as a 'tall, remote intellectual.' Whereas Graham never rose from the ranks, Hugh became head of his house and a school prefect, as well as winning a Foundation Scholarship in 1924 and an Incents Scholarship in 1926. As head of Uppers, 'I learned for the first time the heady joys of exercising authority and also, at times, of behaving with complete irresponsibility.' 'His position has not been altogether an easy one but I, for one, have very greatly appreciated the way he has behaved in the house and to me personally,' his housemaster reported in 1927, the year in which Charles Greene retired due to ill health. Hugh took an instant dislike to his father's successor, the brother of the poet James Elroy Flecker and a 'revolting oily man' who had previously taught at Marlborough. Charles Greene had abolished flogging except for major offences, and then only by the headmaster or housemasters: Flecker reintroduced flogging by prefects. As head of house, Hugh once beat a rugger player who 'had behaved in a particularly disgusting way in the dormitory'.

During his last term, in the summer of 1929, Hugh won a classical postmastership at Merton College, Oxford, and 'enjoyed the fact that no master could any longer exercise any authority over me or require me to do anything I did not want to do, like parading with the school OTC' (in which he had never risen above the rank of lance-corporal). As the editor of the *Berkhamstedian*, he provoked an infuriated Flecker into accusing him of having 'the mind of a *Daily Mail* reporter' and expressing 'grave fears about your future', and he wrote a poem about a girl, a friend of Raymond's, which was returned to him by the Sixth Form master with a note that read 'Too intimate for criticism'. The Greene sense of mischief, a quality Hugh shared with Graham in particular, was already making itself felt.

Two years earlier, Charles and Marion Greene had moved into a rambling red-brick Edwardian house in Crowborough, in the Sussex Weald, which they named Incents as a tribute to the school. That same year the Hall was put on the market: the rich Greenes had already moved away to a farmhouse at Little Wittenham in Oxfordshire, and to a house in Montagu Square. Berkhamsted would become, for most of the Greenes, no more than a memory: it was time to be moving on.

Oxford Adventures

Ben was the first of the Greene cousins to come up to Oxford, but he made little impression, and left without taking a degree. Following in the footsteps of his uncle Charles, he arrived at Wadham in the autumn of 1920 to read history. According to the college records, he rowed in the 'torpid' boat the following spring – the 'torpids' being inter-collegiate races – and a group photograph, taken in the college quad, shows him looming head and shoulders over his fellow oarsmen. Thereafter he vanishes from view, but he must have still been in Oxford in the autumn term of 1922: Graham, newly arrived in Balliol, wrote home to say that he had visited Ben in Wadham for drinks and dinner in college, and reported that he would be bringing some of Ben's luggage home with him at the end of term so that his cousin could bicycle back from Oxford to Berkhamsted.

Ben's indifference to Oxford and undergraduate life reflected the fact that he was more taken up with the problems of the world at large. He was in touch with the Labour Party as represented in the university by Ruskin College; he disliked what he condemned as 'doctrinaire socialism', and found 'my spiritual home in the Independent Labour Party with its parliamentary traditions going back to the early Chartist movement, including the Christian Socialism of Charles Kingsley and Ruskin and Morris, and its close links with the Christian non-conformist movement.' He also joined the Quakers, accepting 'their freedom of theological doctrine with their testimony of pacifism'; from now on his life was to be dominated – and, it could be argued, destroyed – by an idealistic and overriding commitment to pacifism. This, he later suggested, was partly inherited from his German mother. 'Her attitude towards her native land was governed by a deep repulsion to [sic] the arrogant militarism of which the Kaiser was the symbol. From her I acquired a deep and perma-nent detestation of militarism in all its forms.' As a schoolboy he had been profoundly affected by the deaths of school-fellows and younger masters serving with the forces. He had felt enormous relief when the fighting came to an end, but 'dominating all thought was the conviction that if this immense effort directed to death and destruction was possible, what could not be achieved if such an effort were directed to the construction of a new and just society.' He was outraged by the 'total failure of organised Christianity to face up to the moral issues which the murderous war had produced', but despite his detestation of militarism, 'my first great disillusionment with the new age came when I realised with what brutal sneering and cold ingratitude the ex-servicemen were being treated' – sentiments shared to the full by his future colleague John Beckett, who would also join the ILP in due course.

Ben made his first visit to Germany during one of his vacations from Oxford. Fridtjof Nansen, the Norwegian polar explorer, was a passionate advocate of the League of Nations, and involved in organising relief work in Central and Eastern Europe; Ben went to a talk Nansen gave in Oxford and, fired with enthusiasm, went out to do relief work for the Quakers at Berlin University. While in Germany, he was struck, for the first time, by 'the full force of the treachery of the Peace Treaty.' Like many other Englishmen from both the left and the right of the political spectrum, including his uncle Charles, he became convinced that the terms of the Treaty of Versailles – including reparations, the notion of Germany's sole and exclusive war guilt, the loss of territory to Poland and Czechoslovakia – were grossly unfair; and this sense of outrage, combined with his pacifism, was to shape his political thinking over the next twenty years. 'I realised the outraged bitterness of every German in every walk of life at the duplicity of which they were the victims,' he wrote. 'I could not escape the conviction that in the Peace Treaties, unless revised, we had the sure causation of another war.'

While still nominally at Oxford, Ben went on to do relief work in Warsaw, Kraków and in the contentious Polish Corridor that now separated Germany from its outpost in East Prussia. Co-ordinating the activities of the Friends – the Quakers – and the Save the Children Fund, he found himself taking a train from Berlin to Konigsberg in East Prussia, during the course of which 'I experienced some of the humiliating hardships to which the German people had to submit.' At the Polish frontier 'we all had to get out with all our luggage and were herded into wire cages on the platform offering no protection from wind and rain.' A long and detailed examination of luggage and passports then ensued; once back on the train, Polish guards with fixed bayonets occupied every corner seat. On another mission to the free city of Danzig, Ben went to investigate the plight of a German village on the Vistula which should have had access to the river and its fish and water supplies, but was separated from it by a barbed-wire fence. There was only one narrow point of access, to visit which called for a passport or permit; fishing was virtually impossible for the German villagers, nor could they get their cattle down to the river. Ben reported all this to the League of Nations Commissioner in Danzig. Back in England, he was more convinced than ever that 'the academic life at Oxford was too remote from the realities of the world.'

Raymond and Graham, by contrast, flung themselves into the life of undergraduates. Raymond was regarded as a grand and impressive figure, with fingers in several Oxford pies; Graham was active in undergraduate literary life, as well as indulging in colourful extra-mural activities. 'C. R. Greene is in majestic seclusion at Pembroke, and in a special interview gave us to understand that he intended to work,' the *Berkhamstedian*'s Old Boys' News reported in December 1922: but although Raymond almost certainly worked hard, he was also active as a mountaineer, a part-time poet and literary man, a practical joker and an oarsman; and if he later claimed to have discovered at Oxford 'the hatred of institutional life that has remained with me always', this proved no bar to his being the President of the Pembroke JCR, and an active member of various college clubs. He regarded the scientist J. S. Haldane as his Oxford 'paterfamilias', taking note of Haldane's celebrated experiments on atmospheric pressure on the human body, and later putting them to good use as a medical mountaineer attached to Himalayan expeditions. He met Einstein at a meeting of the Alembic Club, during the course of which – or so he claimed – the great man put his hand on his knee and said 'I didn't know you kept sharks at Parson's Pleasure'. Kenneth Richmond had introduced him to various well-known writers, and during his time in Oxford he visited W. B. Yeats in the Broad – he and Richard Hughes tried, without success, to introduce him to Graham – and attended gatherings in a pub called The Jolly Farmers in St Ebbe's at which A. E. Coppard, Roy Campbell, Louis Golding and others met to carouse and read their works aloud. (Nearly fifty years later, Raymond persuaded his nephew Graham, then the managing director of Jonathan Cape, to reissue Coppard's short stories, which had fallen into neglect.) 'I have looked upon literature as an escape from education, as a sane refuge from the exacter pleasures of the laboratory and the dissecting room, as an excuse for idleness,' he once declared. As befits a literary dilettante, he was a competent practitioner of light verse, and in the years to come he would produce amusing and well-made *vers d'occa-sion*. He became fascinated by the doomed figure of Thomas Beddoes, the drug-addicted Victorian doctor-cum-poet, and tried to track down portraits of him. He read learned papers to the Beaumont Society on poisoning and on Florence Nightingale, and since he shared Graham's penchant for elaborate and long-winded practical jokes, he once gave a lecture to the Johnson Society about an imaginary poet named John Allen Barker, and spoke of him with such conviction and enthusiasm that he found it hard to persuade dons and undergraduates alike that Barker was a figment of his imagination. (Graham, for his part – or so Walter Allen would have us believe – turned up at Highgate School while still an undergraduate to give a lecture to the boys, disguised as an army officer, wearing breeches and a false moustache, and carrying a box of slides bought in the Charing Cross Road.)

Young Raymond must have seemed, at times, too good to be true, but he had a raffish side which manifested itself in visits to the Caves of Harmony, a drinking club in Seven Dials run by Charles Laughton and Elsa Lanchester, and – more spectacularly – in his trip to Sicily to seek out the notorious Aleister Crowley, variously referred to as 'the Beast' and 'the Wickedest Man in the World'. A balding, portly figure who wrote self-conscious *fin de siècle* poetry and was also an intrepid moun-taineer, Crowley was notorious for his interest in satanism and black magic, and was said to mastermind horrific orgies in his so-called 'abbey' in Sicily, involving naked maidens and the ritual slaughter of goats. He had supported the Irish rebels in 1916, proclaiming himself King of Ireland, renouncing his British citizenship and disseminating anti-British propa-ganda in the United States. James Douglas, an irascible Scottish journalist who loved to whip himself and his readers into a frenzy of righteous rage over matters of sexual depravity and threats to the nation's morals, was leading a campaign against Crowley in the pages of the *Sunday Express*: 'A Cannibal at Large', 'In the Drug Fiend's Abbey' and 'A Man We'd Like to Hang' were among the headlines provoked by the Beast. A few years later Douglas turned his wrath on Radclyffe Hall's lesbian novel, *The Well of Loneliness*, forcing Jonathan Cape to withdraw it from publication. (Some thirty years later, his successor, John Gordon, another apoplectic Scot employed by the *Sunday Express*, led a similar campaign against Vladmir Nabokov's *Lolita*, provoking Graham, in pranksterish mood, to found the John Gordon Society in his honour.)

One day in February 1923 Raymond spotted a copy of the *Sunday Express* in the porter's lodge in Pembroke. 'MORE SINISTER REVELATIONS

OF ALEISTER CROWLEY. VARSITY LAD'S DEATH. DREADFUL ORDEAL OF YOUNG WIFE' ran the headline. He might not have paid much attention were it not for the fact that he was acquainted with the 'varsity lad' in question. Raoul Loveday had been a small, fair-haired undergraduate at St John's who claimed that his father was a naval officer and a King's Messenger rather than a petty officer who had occasionally run errands for Sir Graham Greene. While still an undergraduate, Loveday had developed an interest in black magic, and after graduating he had gone out to Sicily to be Aleister Crowley's secretary, taking with him his wife Betty May, an artist's model, cocaine addict and denizen of bohemia who was a fair bit older than her husband and had posed for Jacob Epstein. Crowley had decided that Loveday 'possessed every qualification for becoming a Magician of the first rank', and had appointed him his 'magical heir'. According to the Sunday Express, Betty May had returned to England in a terrible state, 'unable to give more than a hint of the horrors from which she had escaped': not only had her husband died under mysterious circumstances, but she had been 'left alone to fight the Beast 666' and had witnessed behaviour 'too unutterably filthy to be detailed in a newspaper, for they have to do with sexual orgies that touch the lowest depths of depravity.'

Oxford was electrified by Raoul Loveday's death, and Raymond found himself at the centre of a plan to find out exactly what had happened and, if necessary, exact some kind of revenge on the Beast. He learned that Betty May was holding court at the Golden Cross Hotel, and hurried round to make her acquaintance. She was lying in bed, and he found her 'very attractive in a rare Mongolian way'. She showed no signs of being in a state of shock, but told him how she and Raoul had made their way uphill to Thelema, Crowley's infamous Abbey in Cefalù, where they had been exposed to 'terrible rites and orgies'. Raoul had been taken ill – she thought he might have been persuaded against his will to experiment with drugs, but Crowley claimed that both he and Loveday had been struck down by an 'inexplicable illness', which he diagnosed as 'Mediterranean fever' – and after his death she had wandered the bare Sicilian hills all night before eventually making her escape. Betty May's undergraduate admirers were duly outraged, and Peter Rodd – later to become Nancy Mitford's feckless and unsatisfactory husband and the model for Evelyn Waugh's Basil Seal – suggested to Raymond that he should go out to Cefalù in the Easter vacation, shoot the atrocious Beast, and make his way to the south coast of Sicily, where Rodd would be waiting with a boat to spirit him away to North Africa. Richard Hughes, later to become a well-known novelist, best remembered for *A High Wind in Jamaica*, heard of Rodd's plan, and wrote to Raymond, urging him to desist. 'Naturally one's first impulse was to assume that Aleister Crowley had murdered him, and want to retaliate,' Hughes wrote. 'I heard from various sources that you were conspiring: I'm afraid your secret is not particularly well guarded. As for my co-operation, I'm afraid it will be of very little use to you. Kidnapping, of course, is not merely impossible, it is ridiculous. The only thing of any possible use would be to confront the man and shoot him outright. That I am not prepared to do; and nor are you.' Hughes's cautionary words were uncalled for, since Raymond never had any intention of putting Rodd's half-baked plan into operation, but he decided to go to Sicily all the same and find out what he could about the death of his friend. As if by magic, Crowley heard of his plans, and wrote to Raymond to say that Loveday's death had been 'a terrible blow', and that he had been training him up to continue his work.

The only faintly sinister moment of Raymond's Sicilian adventure occurred at a puppet show in Palermo, when he felt that he was being crowded out by a gang of evil-looking heavies and was advised to make his escape – an incident later recycled by his Oxford acquaintance Louis Golding in his novel *The Camberwell Beauty*. From Palermo Raymond made his way to Cefalu and its dreadful secrets. Far from being a sinister, rock-hewn fortress perched on the brim of a gorge, the Abbey turned out to be a whitewashed bungalow surrounded by olive trees: three normal and cheerful-seeming children were playing in the garden, and a Frenchwoman called 'Chummy' explained that the Beast was feeling unwell and had gone into Palermo to see the doctor. Raymond was shown into a sunny, untidy sitting room: pentacles and triangles painted on the floor and a collection of books about black magic suggested its owner's interests, but the only obscene note was struck by a tripod brazier incorporating three men with gigantic erections. Back in Palermo, Raymond was joined by Peter Quennell, Peter Rodd and Richard Hughes. There was still no sign of the Beast, but Raymond met his secretary Alostrael (the Swiss-American Leah Hirsig), whose flushed cheeks, excitable manner and enlarged pupils suggested, in retrospect at least, that she was on amphetamines, and he returned with her to the Abbey. Crowley's children were once again playing in the garden and, disappointed not to see their father, raised a plaintive cry of 'Where's Beastie, why haven't you brought back Beastie?' Alostrael then showed Raymond the notorious *chambre des cauchemars*, the walls of which were decorated with obscene murals painted by Crowley: one of them depicted a man having a violent attack of diarrhoea, and Raymond found it hard to control his laughter. By now he was convinced that Loveday had met a natural death, and this was confirmed by a local doctor, who suggested that he had been brought down by a combination of malaria and enteritis. Years later Raymond told John Symonds, who was editing the *Confessions of Aleister Crowley* for publication by Jonathan Cape, that although the denizens of the Abbey were 'a bunch of very queer self-deluders', he had quickly realised that 'they were guiltless of Raoul's death. They were silly, not sinister.'

Disappointed at not having met the Beast in person but aware that there was nothing more he could usefully do in Cefalù, Raymond made his way slowly home to England. A few days later, in Naples, a voice behind him chanted 'Do What Thou Wilt Shall Be the Whole of the Law', and, turning round, he found himself face to face with Aleister Crowley, whose antinomian catchphrase this was. 'He was a big man of forty-seven, inclined to be corpulent, with a bald head, grey hair and a sallow complexion. His manner was peevish and he had a slight cockney accent,' Raymond recalled, adding that he was also 'disappointingly unsinister'. Over the next twenty years Raymond bumped into Crowley from time to time, but he continued to think of him as a 'very silly man'; and, years after the Beast's death, Raymond asked his nephew Graham to remove any references to him from the *Confessions*.

But mountaineering was Raymond's great passion, to be indulged at any opportunity. He had arrived in Oxford with his arm in a sling, the result of a climbing accident, and before long he had revived the Oxford University Mountaineering Club, together with John Wolfenden (best remembered for the report into prostitution and homosexuality which bore his name) and Herbert Carr, a First World War veteran who was also at Pembroke and became 'the architect of my mountain career'. Club members climbed in Wales in January, in the Lake District over Easter and, if possible, in the Swiss Alps in the summer. They also mounted an expedition to Cambridge: this proved to be 'the most terrifying weekend of my life', involving as it did an assault on the chapel at King's. But Raymond really longed to join the Alpine Club in South Audley Street, the members of which were the best mountaineers in Britain. To qualify for membership he needed a third Alpine season under his belt, so to fund this he took a job tutoring a small boy in Bavaria for three months in the summer of 1923. After spending three weeks climbing in the Swiss Alps, he moved on to what was to prove the first of three visits to the small town of Garmisch: it lay in a valley, one end of which opened out onto the Bavarian plain, while the other led up to the Wetterstein peaks on the Austrian border. He struck up a friendship with a well-known guide and climber called Georg Scheurrer, who taught him to ski: together they climbed the steep eastern approach of the Dreitorspitze, which had only been scaled once before – and that had been discounted by purists, on the grounds that the climbers had used pitons – and smoked their pipes on the summit.

The Villa Lutzenchirchen was owned by a Frau Mayer, the Irish-born widow of a German-Jewish army officer. A family friend, and regular visitor, was General Karl Haushofer. Best remembered as a proponent of geopolitics, the general was never a member of the Nazi Party and, because his wife was of partly Jewish ancestry, he had no time for anti-semitism. He was a friend of Rudolf Hess, who acted as his assistant and was later to introduce Hitler to some of the central tenets of Haushofer's geopolitics, including 'autarky', or economic self-sufficiency, the notion of the 'organic' state, and lebensraum – albeit, Haushofer claimed, in a distorted and more radical form. Hitler had recently been imprisoned at Landsberg following the unsuccessful Beer Hall Putsch, and the general visited him there. It was rumoured – falsely – that he had contributed to the writing of Mein Kampf. According to other rumours – again inaccurate – Hess had taken refuge with the Haushofers, but Raymond had no memories of meeting him. After the general had been overheard telling Frau Mayer that 'I didn't think I could ever like an Englishman, but I like that young tutor of yours,' Raymond struck up a friendship with the Haushofers' son, Albrecht and they often went climbing together. 'When I knew many years later of the stand he had made against the domination of the Nazis' – Albrecht Haushofer was executed for his involvement with the wartime opposition to Hitler – 'my sadness at his death was partially eased by gladness that he had not deceived me; that he was the man I thought he was.'

Raymond was not immune from the simmering violence of German politics. One evening he found himself strolling down a sunlit street in Munich. The street was empty apart from a tall, fair young man, who was walking ahead of him. A shot rang out, and the young man collapsed, a pool of blood forming around his head. Raymond dodged into a doorway; the young man was obviously dead, and there was no sign of the gunman. Back in the Villa Lutzenchirchen, the Haushofers told him not to go to the police, and to forget all about it. On his way home from a visit the following year, he was briefly incarcerated in a mediaeval dungeon: there was a strong separatist movement in Bavaria, and Raymond had a visa to visit Germany but not Bavaria, so he spent the night on a stone floor, reading a work entitled *Oxidations and Reductions in the Animal Body*. He did not return to Garmisch until 1936, by which time 'rumours had reached me and I did not try to find the Haushofers.' But his climbs in the Bavarian Alps had stood him in good stead: in 1924 he was elected to the Alpine Club, where he could rub shoulders with George Mallory, Sir Francis Younghusband, Sir Aurel Stein and other legendary explorers and mountaineers, and partake of tea with buttered toast and Dundee cake, the only meal on offer at the club. He left Oxford with a scholarship in anatomy and physiology at Westminster Hospital: great things lay ahead, on the mountains as well as in the laboratory and the consulting room.

Graham's Oxford career was as colourful as Raymond's, and equally devoted to extramural activities. Thanks to Kenneth Bell's intervention, he had been awarded an exhibition to read history at Balliol but, if the *Berkhamstedian*'s reporter could be relied upon, Graham combined his studies with an unexpected and short-lived interest in sport. 'Cockburn and G. Greene pursue golf balls at Cowley with admirable persistency, which argues an optimistic spirit and unlimited wealth,' the *Berkhamstedian* informed its readers. 'When carrying a full complement of ammunition they have been known to play as many as nine holes. Cockburn's rooms in Keble have definitely been located, but investigation has utterly failed to discover Greene's abode in Beechcroft Road, from where he gives us to understand that he makes periodic visits to Oxford.' ('I guessed you was one of them long Mr Greenes,' his landlady had informed him when he turned up at his digs.) Described by his distant cousin Evelyn Waugh as a 'tall, spectacled young man with an air of Budapest rather than Berkhamsted', Cockburn remained a kindred spirit: years later, Richard Ingrams remembered how he retained his 'schoolboyish zest for life', and how in 'a deep bass voice he spoke in staccato bursts in the manner of Mr Jingle in *The Pickwick Papers*'. For Peter Quennell, on the other hand, meeting Graham again in Oxford proved a 'disappointing' business. He found Graham's circle of friends 'rather tedious; and after a week or two of sharing their honest fun, I wandered off into a different milieu.' Like Evelyn Waugh, Quennell attached himself to the Oxford later associated with *Brideshead Revisited*, a 'showy, expensive world' of Old Etonian aesthetes, socialites and poseurs: in later life Graham both liked and revered Evelyn Waugh, but he kept his distance as an undergraduate. In his autobiography, Waugh wrote that he only knew Graham 'very slightly' at Oxford, and that he remained a 'very private' figure: he had 'the impression that he looked down on us (and perhaps all undergraduates) as childish and ostentatious. He certainly shared in none of our revelry.' 'I was not suffering from any adult superiority at Oxford to explain our paths not crossing, but I belonged to a rather rigorously Balliol group of perhaps boisterous heterosexuals, while your path temporarily took you into the other camp,' Graham told Waugh after reading *A Little Learning*, adding that 'for a considerable period of my time at Oxford I lived in a general haze of drink', as had Waugh himself. 'For nearly one term I went to bed drunk every night and began drinking again immediately I woke,' he explained in his own memoirs, and 'it left me with a strong head and a tough liver', attributes that would come in hand in the hard-drinking years ahead.

'Why Graham at Oxford should have so carefully avoided notice is a question which I cannot answer,' Quennell went on to wonder. He must have been looking in the wrong direction, for although Graham was not seen consorting with Brian Howard or Cyril Connolly or Alfred Duggan, he soon made his mark on the Oxford literary scene. 'There was also in the last two years a would-be Oxford *Horizon* called the *Oxford Outlook* to keep me occupied. Harold [Acton] used to contribute to this, and Eddy Sackville-West, and Edith Sitwell. Alas, I had no chance of printing anything by you,' he explained to an equally puzzled Evelyn Waugh. The *Oxford Outlook* had been founded by Beverley Nichols, and under Graham's editorship it published poetry by Peter Quennell and Edmund Blunden as well as those mentioned in his letter to Waugh. As its editor, Graham displayed the professionalism that he would later display as author, literary editor, journalist and publisher. He drummed up advertising, sought out sponsors, made sure the latest issue was reviewed in *Isis* and *Cherwell*, wondered whether 'Da' could persuade G. M. Trevelyan to contribute a piece, and enrolled the Berkhamsted aunts as subscribers. He accepted a subsidy of £200 from the Liberal candidate in the 1923 election, in exchange for which Claud Cockburn, then a Liberal, wrote a partisan piece.

Nor did he forget to advance his own claims as a poet – so much so that Basil Blackwell, who eventually took over the *Oxford Outlook*, published a short book of his poems entitled *Babbling April*. In later life Graham was understandably embarrassed by this work and sought to buy up any copies that might find their way onto the second-hand market, but in the autumn of 1923 he was 'overwhelmed for the moment with excitement', and upset when Harold Acton gave his book a withering review. Blackwell had agreed to publish *Babbling April* on the under-standing that he had an option on Graham's next two books: Graham got in touch with A. D. Peters, who had just started his own firm and would eventually become the most distinguished literary agent of his generation, and persuaded him to read his first attempts at writing a novel. He hoped, too, that Peters would show another collection of poems to J. B. Priestley, the reader for The Bodley Head, in the hope that this might gain him an *entrée* to a distinguished if somnolent London publishing house. Many years later the two writers, who had never got on, were to become directors of The Bodley Head, differing widely in their views but sharing space on the same letterhead. In the meantime, Graham sent a copy of *Babbling April* to Walter de la Mare – 'I hope it will not be too presumptuous of me to send you this, my first book. I expect you've forgotten who I am, unless you remember our strawberry tea at Berkhamsted,' he wrote in an accompanying letter – and, at a less elevated level, looked keenly out for a review in the *Berkhamstedian*.

Nor was this the end of his activities as an Oxford poet and man of letters. He persuaded Naomi Royde-Smith, the owner of the *Weekly Westminster Gazette*, to send him to Ireland with his cousin Tooter during a vacation, and to publish his 'Impressions of Dublin'; he put on plays with Claud Cockburn, including an adaptation of W. W. Jacobs's 'The Monkey's Paw', and asked his mother to raid the dressing-up box at home for suitable costumes; he met Robert Graves, and J. C. 'Jack' Squire, the influential editor and Georgian poet, and an 'extraordinarily nice' John Buchan ('Hugh will be glad to know that he's just finished another novel,' he reported home). He also ran the Contemporary Poetry and Drama Society, inviting leading London figures down to Oxford to discuss contemporary trends in the theatre: they included Clifford Bax, who introduced him to A. D. Peters. Edith Sitwell wrote to say how much she had appreciated an article he wrote about her poetry in the *Weekly Westminster*: most people didn't understand her poetry, but 'your comprehension appears to be absolutely complete' and she was anxious to invite him round for tea ('Do remember me to your aunt, whom I knew when young,' she told him in another letter, but which aunt she was referring to remains a mystery). Most famously of all, he arranged for a group of Oxford poets including A. L. Rowse, Brian Howard, Joseph Macleod and T. O. Beachcroft to read their poems live over the air on the BBC. 'I enjoyed the broadcasting very much, though I felt extremely nervous,' he told Hugh, still a schoolboy at Berkhamsted. 'We sat in a kind of sumptuous drawing room, with beautiful armchairs & sofas, & each had to get up & recite in front of a beautiful blue draped box on a table.'

A. L. Rowse remembered Graham for his 'extraordinarily youthful appearance with the curly flax-gold hair and the odd strangulated voice, speaking from his Adam's apple, as if he had difficulty in producing the voice. Most of all one was struck by those staring, china-blue eyes, wide open to the world. Later on, those eyes came to have an expression as if they had looked on some nameless horror . . .' No doubt the youthful appearance and the strangulated voice were combined with the shyness that he shared with other members of his family, but there was never any doubt about his steely determination to follow a literary career, and a successful one at that. Unlike some of his more precocious or naturally gifted contemporaries, Graham was not, perhaps, a natural writer. His letters home – indeed many of the letters he wrote during his lifetime – were awkward, dull, clumsily written and showed no great feel for language; his early attempts at fiction seem amateur and inept compared with those of Evelyn Waugh, while his poems were mawkish and saccharine. One has the sense of a man who had an intuitive love of literature, was well and widely read, and was set upon making his way in the literary world through diligence and application, learning his craft as he went along. He was the polar opposite, perhaps, of his Balliol contemporary Cyril Connolly, who as a schoolboy at Eton wrote a far more sophisticated and 'literary' prose than anything Graham managed before *Stamboul Train*, but was undone by sloth and self-doubt, and spent his life wishing that he too had been a novelist rather than an essayist and aphorist, albeit of the most brilliant kind. Graham's ambition was complemented by his professionalism, while his shyness could all too easily be seen as a chilly hauteur: both led him to develop a hard-boiled public persona, which manifested itself most obviously in his dealings with agents, publishers, newspaper men and other business associates, and seemed at variance with his generosity towards many of his fellow-writers and the melancholic sweetness of expression evident in his photographs. By nature a gentle, kindly man, he could seem callous and cold-hearted in his private life as well, and never more so than when he felt guilty towards those who were closest to him.

He was equally determined to lead a varied and adventurous life. In this he succeeded to a greater extent than any of his contemporaries, with the possible exception of Arthur Koestler, and set about realising his ambition while still an undergraduate. Under the terms of the Treaty of Versailles, the French occupied the Rhineland Palatinate and the

Saarland, areas of heavy industry which had previously formed part of Germany. Influenced, perhaps, by his father's diatribes against the Versailles peace settlement, Graham's sympathies were on the side of the Germans, and in the spring of 1924 he wrote to the German Embassy in London to say that although opinion in Oxford as a whole favoured the French, he was keen to write a series of articles about the Rhineland for the *Oxford Outlook* and for a local paper, the *Oxford Chronicle*, and to ask whether they would be able to provide him with accommodation. A few days later he returned to his rooms in Balliol to find Count Albrecht von Bernstorff, a German Embassy official, happily ensconced and drinking his brandy. Enid Bagnold, who was in love with Bernstorff, remembered him as 'nearly a giant, perhaps six-foot six, certainly at one time weighing twenty stone, blond as a baby, bald, but with the remains of curling tendrils above his ear'. Her passion was unrequited since, as Graham recalled, 'he was such a complete homosexual and haunter of homosexual clubs that it is difficult to believe that a woman would take to him.' One of the first German Rhodes Scholars at Oxford, he was a popular figure in London society – he once declared, apropos the English, that 'Once we Germans learn to laugh as they do, we shall inherit the earth' – and had already made Raymond's acquaintance. After the Nazis came to power he was dismissed from his post, and during the war he helped to run an escape route for Jews to Switzerland before being arrested by the Gestapo and executed in Ravensbrück ('I thought in those days that Hitler was a new God and Albrecht a donkey not to see it. And he has paid by being swung on his poor huge neck,' a chastened Enid Bagnold confessed on hearing the news). After Bernstorff had offered Graham £25 towards his expenses, Graham set out for the Ruhr with Claud Cockburn and, since neither of them spoke any German, Tooter joined the party. 'I can remember still the menace of Essen where most of the factory workers were on strike: the badly lit streets, the brooding groups. We flirted with fear and began to plan a thriller rather in Buchan's manner,' Graham remembered. They met a director of Krupps, and noted the behaviour of arrogant French officers and the presence of Senegalese troops, both of whom were resented by the Germans, and Graham wrote home to say that because they were often assumed to be French, 'everybody glowered at us, and there was a very delightful sensation of being hated by everybody.'

Back in Oxford, Graham wrote an article for the *Oxford Outlook* in which he described French repression, and singled out the use of black troops by the French as 'a deliberate insult against a defenceless people'.

He suggested to Bernstorff that he should act as a courier between the German government and its agents in the occupied zone; Bernstorff, for his part, proposed that Graham should contact the French-backed separatists – who favoured the establishment of a 'revolver republic', and were widely regarded as collaborators – and report back on their activities. Graham got in touch with the French Embassy in the hope of obtaining introductions to separatist leaders, and – as if his life wasn't complicated enough already – he approached a right-wing magazine called *The Patriot*, which was owned by the Duke of Northumberland and supported both the French and the separatists. He had plans of becoming a double agent, or posing as a supporter of the separatists while reporting back to the Germans, but the French and the German governments came to an agreement, a separatist Palatinate was no longer contemplated, and 'one insignificant recruit to the rank of espionage was told to fall out – his services no longer required. All the lessons in German I had been taking from a maiden lady in North Oxford had been wasted time.'

As a child, Graham had loved reading about spies and double agents and men on the run in the novels of William le Queux and John Buchan and Robert Louis Stevenson, and now he was sampling that world for himself: it would later bear fruit in his novels and in his involvement with MI6. In the autumn of 1924, he and Cockburn briefly joined the Communist Party, and visited Paris the following year to attend a French Communist Party conference in Menilmontant: the street riots that accompanied the conference gave him a flavour of European politics, but his membership of the Party, so lightly entered into, would have long-term consequences when it came to visiting the United States during and after the McCarthyite witch-hunts against Communists and Communist sympathisers.

Adventures like these not only helped to keep boredom and melancholia at bay – it was during his time at Oxford that Graham claimed to have played Russian roulette on Berkhamsted Common with a tiny revolver belonging to Raymond – but provided raw material for future fiction; as did the activities of his oldest brother, Herbert. 'Seedy' is the epithet most frequently employed to describe Graham Greene's imaginary worlds, but Herbert was, in person, a far seedier figure than his dapper, elegant brother, and his seedy characteristics provided first-hand insights into the ways of *rentiers* and con men, and a model for the shabby, disreputable figures who flit through Graham's fiction – the most obvious of whom, Anthony Ferrant in *England Made Me*, was explicitly based on Herbert. Unlike his brothers, Herbert never went to university, but – like an old-fashioned remittance man – he moved from job to job, borrowing money off his long-suffering parents, invariably getting the sack, and leaving a trail of debts in his wake. As Graham later put it, unemployment was to Herbert 'like a recurring flu'. 'How miserable about Herbert,' an anxious Graham wrote home from Balliol after learning of yet another doomed endeavour. 'Has he any job in sight? A pity he couldn't have a spell at a school, games-mastering through the summer. Then he'd have open air and get physically tired out, which would probably be a good thing for him . . .' 'He has never tried to borrow money from me,' he added, but in later years, outraged by Herbert's raids on his parents' slender means, he would find himself acting as his brother's reluctant paymaster.

Herbert's cousin Barbara was rather more sympathetic than his immediate family. 'I can't help now feeling a bit sorry for him' she declared in later years. 'He was not brilliant, not very good at school and all the brothers were so brilliant, and he was just good-looking, keen on cricket and was really a very average sort of person in a brilliant family. He's always been a bit looked down on. They didn't like him. Yet actually he was the most harmless creature except for making debts at times, and I think he was probably spoilt by the girls because he was very, very good-looking.' Vivien, Graham's future wife, put some of the blame on Marion Greene. She was, Vivien told the novelist Gabriel Fielding, 'totally rational, cold, just, kind, unloving perhaps, with that pathetic trait, sad and dreadful to both, of totally disliking and rejecting the failure son (the oldest)' – so much so that if Herbert came into the room, his mother would immediately walk out. Poor Herbert was, by all accounts, a pathetic creature, and his future exploits, comical as they often were, were to prove a source of endless embarrassment to his branch of the family – to such an extent that many of his nieces and nephews were never allowed to meet him, for fear of contamination. Nor did he improve his standing with his beer-loving brothers by – or so it was claimed – watering the beer in a club of which he was briefly the secretary.

Ben's future exploits were to land him in far hotter water than the feckless Herbert; but whereas Herbert was to become a shifty fantasist, Ben was – and would remain – an idealist, busily engaged in the world around him yet far too unworldly for his own good. In 1921 a fearful famine had scoured southern Russia, exacerbated by years of civil war and a blockade by the Western powers. A Russian Famine Relief Fund was set up by the journalist H. N. Brailsford, and an All British Appeal, backed by the Quakers and the Save the Children Fund, had been signed by, among others, George Bernard Shaw and David Lloyd George. As a League of Nations High Commissioner, Fridtjof Nansen, the Norwegian polar explorer whose lecture had inspired Ben to travel to Berlin, was responsible for co-ordinating the various national campaigns and negotiating with the Soviet government. Two years later, the famine was still taking its toll, and in the early spring of 1923 Ben set out on a three-day train journey from Moscow to the famine-stricken region round the Volga basin. Instead of enjoying his final year at Wadham, he had offered his services to the Friends' Famine Relief Fund, working in conjunction with Herbert Hoover's American Relief Administration. The train ride was, he reported home, 'a miserable affair, what with smells, thick air etc. All was dirty and gloomy, and huge grease spots everywhere': at one stage the heating exploded, and rats invaded the compartment. Nor were conditions any better when they reached Alexievska, near the southern city of Samara. The whole area had been devastated by fighting between the Red Army and the anti-Bolshevik Czech Legion. 'Houses stand open, either bombarded in the civil war or famine has removed the inhabitants', and samovars, icons and pianos lay among the ruins. Children with swollen bellies were too weak and too cold to move from their mud-floored huts; *babushkas* lay on unlit stoves; all the livestock, including cats and dogs, had long ago been eaten, and the survivors lived off flour made from bones mixed with corn and 'horrible bread made from pumpkin seeds and rinds'; people begged from door to door, or 'sit freezing till they die'; the air was foetid, and the stench so appalling that Ben couldn't face eating his supplies of bully beef. A year earlier, in the spring of 1922, the Quaker Ruth Fry had undertaken famine relief in the nearby town of Buzuluk, where supplies of flour, beans, rice, cocoa and tinned meat were unloaded from trucks marked with the Quaker star, and taken away on sledges pulled by cattle or Bactrian camels. 'We found ourselves in a land where death seemed more real than life,' she recalled. She reported cases of cannibalism, of bread made from grass and twigs: one of the few cheerful photographs in the relevant albums in the Friends' Library shows Ben, three smiling ladies and two goats standing outside a wooden hut in the snow; others are of ruined cottages – the turf on the roof had been eaten, the timbers burned as firewood – and a pile of naked, emaciated bodies, like those encountered at Belsen in 1945, waiting to be buried in the frozen earth.

The Quakers ran – or tried to run – the local hospital. Laid out round a courtyard, it had been built on a hill alongside three creaking windmills, and the wind whistled through the buildings. Broken medicine bottles, mouldy straw, used cotton wool and unwashed crockery were piled up outside the doors, and the smell was 'sickening'. There was a dark and stuffy consulting room, with cobweb-strewn icons on the walls. Ben asked to see a ward, and was shown into a room 'as big as Tooter's bedroom' containing twelve beds, all of them askew on a floor that was damp underfoot; in one corner of the room, a samovar was bubbling on a charcoal-burning stove. Ben, taking command, told one of the doctors to remove the samovar, get the patients back into bed, and open the windows to let some fresh air in. From there he went on to a children's home, populated mostly by orphans. 'They are all jolly kinds with huge eyes, and very polite,' Ben told his parents, and 'they make my height no butt of amusement.'

One of Ben's first jobs was to convert a cinema into a warehouse for relief supplies. To make sure that light-fingered delivery-men hadn't secreted provisions in their fur hats or voluminous trousers, he weighed and inspected all the tins and boxes. He visited the local soviet, and found it a 'priceless sort of place'. Its officials 'have no uniforms and apparently only have one blunt razor among them.' Most of them were unpaid, so there was no shame attached to pilfering food from relief organisations: a favourite trick was to steam the labels off tins, siphon out the contents, and paste back the labels. It was so cold that the Friends' typewriter froze solid, but Ben was 'very comfortable' in his accommodation. 'Lucy Sampson is the housekeeper and she turns bully beef into various forms of food with fair success,' he reported home, and 'we are a jolly party.' Another colleague, Jessica Smith of the American Mission, wrote an account of how she and Ben had set out in three sleighs – 'Ben almost fills one of them' – to visit a feeding station serving 20,000 people. They stayed in a peasant's house on the way, and it proved a 'revelation' to Ben: 'his eyes grew wider and wider, the atmosphere thicker and thicker, the snores louder and louder. Ben was in such a hurry to get away that he would not even stop to wash his face in the kitchen. He thinks he has had all the thrills that Russia can give.' On another sleigh trip to Pugachev – the ninety-mile journey took two days – they called at a famine-ridden town where ashen faces stared out from grubby windows, wolves prowled the side streets and, Ben noted, the icons were made from flattened-out Tate & Lyle golden syrup tins.

With the arrival of spring the snow began to melt, and they had to deal with flooding and an outbreak of malaria brought in from Turkestan; the trains broke down and Ben and his colleagues were cut off for weeks on end. He asked Eva to post him his rowing shorts, as 'they will be very useful in the mud.' In a PS he added 'Please don't put "Esq" on the envelopes. It is not appreciated in this country a bit. Being a Friend, the usual "Comrade" need not be used.' Reports about Russia in the British Press made Ben's blood boil. 'The Bolsheviks are the slandered men in Christendom today,' he told his father, and 'the *Times* you have sent me is one mass of lies when it comes to Russia.' But although the 'Bolsheviks were not half as bad as the thoroughly comfortable people make out at home', he assured Uncle Graham that 'there is certainly no fear that I am going to turn Communist. Though I belong to the Labour Party in England, I am not reactionary enough to go further than I have. Communism is usually considered to belong to a very extreme progressive wing – but it is not really progressive. When it comes to power it either has to cease to exist or ruin the people and itself with it. It can destroy but it cannot build up, and in the destruction that it causes it destroys itself.' 'A 100 per cent Communist is an undesirable creature, but not more undesirable than a 100 per cent Englishman,' he declared, and after listening to some children singing the 'Internationale' he decided that he preferred it to 'God Save the King'. On a visit to Moscow, he found the theatre 'wonderful', and was particularly struck by the fact that the audience wore informal dress ('one goes to the theatre to see the play and not partake of snobbery'). Lenin's New Economic Policy, he decided, 'has lifted Russia out of the slough into which she sank and is now making her one of the great powers in Europe. In Russia one feels not that one is at the end of a civilisation, as one does in Germany, but that one is at the beginning of one ... Moscow with its bullet-marked façades and gutted windows, its ruined houses and shell-pitted parks, is a living centre.' Lenin, he observed, 'is loved and venerated by all', and 'no drones can live in the Russian honeycomb.'

Ben never learned much Russian, and was pleased to be able to speak in their own language to the long-established German settlers in the Volga basin, some of whom provided him with a breakfast of eggs and honey, such 'as only a German can give'. He walked twenty-seven miles across the interminable steppe, the telegraph poles stretching on and on into the distance; he slept under a hayrick, fought off the flies, read his Bible during rest breaks, was gratified to note that the railway lines were made in Sheffield, and wrote how the inhabitants of a particular town were 'inclined to giggle at my height'. Back home in Berkhamsted, Eppy chaired a meeting at the YMCA devoted to 'Relief Work in Stricken Europe' at which extracts from Ben's letters were read aloud. Ben's thoughts were turning to home. 'I am getting keener and keener on politics from the Labour Party point of view. Would like to start at the bottom in a shipping firm in a Labour City like Glasgow,' he announced, and he fulminated against the 'High and Mighty Ones that dwell in Downing Street and sit in editorial chairs', and the way in which the British ruling classes spent huge sums of money on defence and armaments rather than education. He revisited Moscow on his way home: he went to the Bolshoi, where he approved the Cubist sets and Futurist costumes, and the informal clothes and behaviour of the audience (a woman on one side of him munched a pear, a man on the other did a crossword throughout the proceedings). At an international trade fair he admired the 'proud flag of Italian fascism', but had less time for that flown by 'that parody of the German republic'. He came home via St Petersburg, Helsinki, Bergen and Newcastle idealistic as ever, scarred by what he had seen but ready to do battle for the poor and disadvantaged of the earth.

Climbing Ahead

By the end of the 1920s Raymond and Graham must have seemed the two Greenes most likely to make their names in the world. Herbert was already regarded as a hopeless case, to be bailed out with frequent injections of cash and job opportunities that came to nothing. Ben was active in left-wing politics, and yearned to make the world a better place, but he had to combine that with earning a living. After his return from Russia he worked as a researcher for the ILP, and for Clement Attlee in his Limehouse constituency; he became one of Ramsay MacDonald's part-time secretaries, and stood unsuccessfully as a Labour Party candidate for Basingstoke in the 1924 General Election. The following year he married Leslie Campbell, whose parents had been active in setting up the co-operative movement with Keir Hardie, and were friends of Ramsay MacDonald. The ceremony took place in St Botolph's Church in the City of London: Eppy generously agreed to pay for their honeymoon in North Africa, but although they travelled there and back in the greatest possible luxury, he insisted on buying third-class tickets for the train journey from Fenchurch Street to Tilbury.

Marriage concentrates the mind, and Ben briefly joined the family coffee business, travelling widely on its behalf in the United States, and living for a while in New Orleans: Eppy had hoped to send him to Brazil, but nothing came of it. He worked for an insurance company in London and as the sales manager of a subsidiary of the Hudson's Bay Company before taking charge of Kepston's, a small firm in Berkhamsted owned by his father which specialised in making the wooden pulleys then used in mechanical power transmission, as well as chair legs and other mass-produced items which involved the turning of wood. As for his siblings and cousins, Tooter had dutifully joined the Brazilian Warrant Company, and would spend most of his working life in the coffee trade; Hugh and Felix were at school or university; Molly and Ave were married, and the other girls were too young or, in Barbara's case, too devoted to social life to bend their minds to more serious matters.

Both Raymond and Graham were tall, lean, good-looking and ambitious, but whereas Raymond had the natural superiority that comes to those who excel in many different spheres of life, Graham was driven on by 'this damned desire to be successful that came from a sense of inferiority' – inflamed by feelings of inadequacy when, as a schoolboy, he compared his own inglorious career with that of his dashing older brother. In later years Raymond would become a respected elder statesman of the Greene family, and one of the few points of contact between the 'rich' and the 'intellectual' Greenes, but although Graham would often consult him about medical details for his novels, fondness and respect were combined with a slight reserve, a sense that for all his qualities, both personal and professional, Raymond was rather an Establishment figure, anxious to help and an authority on family history and genealogy, but liable to pontificate on matters which – or so Graham thought – fell outside his areas of expertise. Both men would achieve fame in their late twenties, Raymond as a mountaineer, Graham as a novelist, and both would reach the top of their professions, but whereas Graham would become world-famous as a writer, Raymond's equal eminence as an endocrinologist would earn him the respect and admiration of his peers but would never make him a household name. In those early years, however, they often found themselves running on parallel lines. They had many friends in common in London and Oxford, and when Graham went up to Balliol, Raymond introduced him to the writers who hung round the Oxford pubs, and – as an *habitué* of Kate Merrick's raffish 43 Club in Gerrard Street and Rosa Lewis's notorious Cavendish Hotel – to the nightclubs and low life of Soho, Seven Dials and Jermyn Street.

Raymond went from Oxford to train as a doctor at the Westminster Hospital; after qualifying in 1927, he worked there as a house surgeon, house physician for children and obstetric assistant. He studied for a time in Edinburgh, did a locum in Wisbech (where 'I learned more than in the previous many years of study'), and was offered a registrarship in pediatrics back at the Westminster Hospital. He was tempted to accept, but his father had recently retired from the headmastership of Berkhamsted and was in poor health, and Raymond felt that the time had come to earn his living as a general practitioner. He joined a prosperous and successful practice in Oxford, run by a Dr Counsell, borrowing heavily to buy his half share in the business. After failing an anatomy exam he had, at one stage, contemplated abandoning medicine for the law: he retained an interest in forensic medicine, and was always happy to be called as an expert witness in criminal cases. As a GP, he liked looking after the slum-dwellers of St Ebbe's, and was intrigued by their way of life. At the other end of the social spectrum, he drove Tallulah Bankhead round the Oxford countryside and enjoyed a brief friendship with Evelyn Waugh. They had not liked each other as undergraduates – at the Union 'we made snide remarks about each other, his being far more clever than mine' – but now they briefly struck it off. Waugh, who was making his name as a novelist, was trying to finish a travel book, *Labels*, and Raymond was working flat-out to obtain another medical qualification; they stayed for some days at John Fothergill's Spread Eagle pub in Thame, a place much patronised by worldly undergraduates, and spent long hours walking in the surrounding countryside. Raymond also found time to get married for the first time, though no mention is made of this in his memoirs or obituaries. 'I've been let into the secret about Raymond. I met her yesterday. Very pleasant, I thought, and extremely pretty,' Graham told his parents: as well as being good to look at, Raymond's fiancée, Charlotte Mackenzie, had contributed poems to the *Oxford Outlook*.

Raymond's meeting Charlotte coincided with Graham's falling in love. Vivien Dayrell-Browning was also a fine-looking girl, a year or so older than Graham, with a round, sweet face, a good Grecian nose and a tiresome-sounding mother. Her father had been kicked out of the family home after starting an affair; her mother, Muriel, comes across as a neurotic, affected, embittered woman with literary pretensions, who regarded men in general with deep suspicion, and sought to infect her beautiful daughter with her own feelings of repugnance vis-à-vis sex and all that it entailed. She addressed Vivien in a saccharine baby talk, in which cats took the place of humdrum and untrustworthy human beings – 'My precious baby sugar-kitten . . . I always did mean to keep you as a *great* friend from the moment I saw your chubby pink face and heard your cheerful gurgle,' she once informed her – and the habit proved contagious. At a more elevated level, Vivien had been received into the Roman Catholic church by the Dominican Bede Jarrett, a well-known figure in Catholic circles who had founded the Blackfriars community in Oxford; urged on by her mother and by her uncle R. N. Green-Armytage, a bibliophile who later helped Eric Gill set up the Ditchling Press, Basil Blackwell agreed to publish a collection of Vivien's verse and prose, dutifully dedicated to 'Mummydar, who has shown me beauty everywhere' and carrying a foreword by G. K. Chesterton. Blackwell also published the *Blackfriars* magazine, and when Graham met her Vivien was working for him in the children's books and poetry departments.

One day in the spring of 1925 Graham found a note waiting for him at the porter's lodge in Balliol. Its sender, Vivien Dayrell-Browning, had written to object to his referring to the 'worship' of the Virgin Mary in a film review published in the *Oxford Outlook*: the correct term, she informed him, was 'hyperdulia'. 'I was interested that anyone took these subtle distinctions of an unbelievable theology seriously, and we became acquainted,' Graham remembered years later. He wrote back an apologetic note, explaining that he had written the review in a great hurry and that 'I was feeling intensely fed up with things, & wanted to be as offensive all round as I could', and inviting her out to tea. They must have made a fine-looking couple and, unsurprisingly, they fell in love. 'I've never really been in love before, only suggested myself into a state of mild excitement in which I could draw fifteen bob out of the *Westminster* for a piece of verse,' Graham told his sweetheart, but now everything had changed. Love letters are, more often than not, repetitive, mawkish and of interest only to the sender and the recipient, and Graham's were no exception to the rule. Read in cold blood, his letters to Vivien seem both embarrassing and, for a would-be writer, semi-literate, crammed as they are with ecstatic cries of 'Ooo!', drawings of stars symbolising love and reciprocated baby talk. Towards the end of his life Graham told his official biographer, Norman Sherry, that he had included 'an excess of sentimental love letters' in his opening volume 'when one would have been sufficient', and one knows how he felt.

They eventually announced their engagement, and Graham took his fiancée to Berkhamsted to meet his parents. 'I am so glad you and Graham are fond of each other,' Marion told her future daughter-in-law. 'I did not say anything to you as I really did not know what your mother thought about it. I hope she approves of Graham. We feel you are just the person for *him*. He is so good and considerate always to me . . . I hope you feel that he will really make a name.' Vivien had indeed told her mother about Graham, exciting a further flurry of baby talk – 'Darling pusskin, I not only feel flattered but honoured. I purr, being intensely gratified and rewarded . . . your own Whiskerpuss.' 'I always feel I ought to call on your mother. Aunt Nono thinks it very wrong I have not done so but perhaps she would not want me to do so,' Marion wrote on another occasion, but she would not have appreciated pussy-cat talk, and wisely kept her distance.

Falling in love was all very well, but Graham's time at Oxford had come to an end – he left with a second-class degree in history and over a hundred pounds' worth of debts, the bulk of which his father paid off 'with hardly a complaint' – and he had to bend his mind to the matter of gainful employment. His overriding ambition was to become a writer, but his first novel, *Anthony Sant*, had been rejected by Basil Blackwell. A. D. Peters liked it well enough, but had no luck in placing it with The Bodley Head; as 'the months passed the tone of his letters changed from enthusiasm to cold second thoughts' and when Graham completed his second novel, also unpublished, Peters refused to handle it. A more humdrum occupation was needed to pay the bills, and during his last year at Oxford Graham began, rather half-heartedly, to test the waters. He had given up his early ambition of joining the Nigerian navy, and although he passed the viva for the Consular Service, he seems not to have taken things further. Armed with a reference from Kenneth Bell, which declared him to be a 'good mixer', he was interviewed by the Lancashire General Insurance Agency's Oxford office, after which he made his way to Little Wittenham, some fifteen miles from Oxford, to seek advice from Uncle Eppy. 'Uncle E was rather surprised at my wanting to go into business! . . . I only hope he keeps my 'orrible literary past a secret!' Graham told his mother. Eppy had a word with one of the directors of the Asiatic Petroleum Company, but although Graham went along for an interview, the directors took a dim view of *Babbling April*, and nothing came of it. He worked for a fortnight for the British American Tobacco Company, with a view to being sent out to China, but, realising that it wasn't for him, he handed in his notice.

Herbert, in the meantime, was proving as unsatisfactory as ever, and a drain on the straitened family resources. He had been sent to Santos in 1919 to work for the Brazilian Warrant – it was rumoured that Ave had become too keen on him, and that Eppy had shipped him out to Brazil to lower the temperature – but that had come to nought; he had contemplated a job in Calcutta, and tried his hand as a tobacco farmer in Southern Rhodesia, but his family's hopes were invariably dashed. Graham suggested that he too should apply to the British American Tobacco Company, but one of the conditions of the China job was that successful applicants should refrain from getting married for at least four years, 'so it would put a very indefinite stopper on his marrying Audrey' – Audrey Nutting was the future Mrs Herbert Greene. Graham resented the way in which Herbert sponged off his parents, and was all in favour of taking a tough line. 'I'm awfully sorry about Herbert,' he told his mother. 'I should think Da's done all he can, and more. I should feel inclined to allow him enough a week to live on, only to be drawn from the bank by the week, and not enough to come home on, for six months, with a warning that all money was going to stop at the end of that time, and he'd either got to get a job & stick it, or starve. Herbert would certainly never do the last . . .'

Like many of his contemporaries with literary aspirations, including John Betjeman, Evelyn Waugh and W. H. Auden, Graham applied to one of the agencies that specialised in supplying seemingly unemployable graduates with temporary teaching jobs – Gabbitas & Thring in his case – and worked for a time tutoring a small boy in the Pennines, writing his novels in the evenings; and, like many another literary aspirant, he persuaded Bruce Richmond, the editor of the *Times Literary Supplement*, to send him the occasional book to review. On a visit to London, he was granted an interview by the editor of *The Times*, Geoffrey Dawson, later to be execrated for his appeasement of Hitler. He was, Graham reported home, 'an awfully nice man . . . he could promise me a job, if I took a year on a provincial paper first.' Salvation was to hand in the form of Sir Charles Starmer, who owned several provincial papers as well as the *Weekly Westminster Gazette*, and in the autumn of 1925 Graham went to work as an unpaid editorial dogsbody on the *Nottingham Journal*, accompanied by his labrador Paddy and subsisting in digs off a modest allowance from his father and a diet of tinned salmon, much of which he fed to the dog.

'When I read Dickens on Victorian London I think of Nottingham in the twenties,' he wrote in *A Sort of Life*. 'There was an elderly "boots" still employed at the Black Dog Inn, there were girls suffering from unemployment in the lace trade who would, so it was said, sleep with you in return for a high tea with muffins, and a haggard blue-haired prostitute, ruined by amateur competition, haunted the corner by WH Smith's bookshop. Trams rattled downhill through the goose market and on to the blackened castle . . .' Grim as it was, he became very fond of Nottingham, and recalled it later in a novel, *A Gun for Sale*, and his most famous play, *The Potting Shed*. 'I had found a town as haunting as Berkhamsted,' he continued, 'the focal point of failure, a place undisturbed by ambition, a place to be resigned to, a home from home.' One day he was granted an audience by 'Nottingham's Tin God', a successful middlebrow novelist called Cecil Roberts, who had also served time on the *Nottingham Journal*. 'Everyone hates him, and everyone is under his yoke,' Graham informed his mother, but he took with him a copy of *Babbling April*: 'As he's a

Heinemann man, and I want an introduction, I'm going to sell my soul for the hope of pottage, & pander to his conceit, which everyone tells me is monstrous.' Graham found Roberts insufferably pompous and patronising, and wrote about their meeting years later in *A Sort of Life*. Roberts was outraged when he read a set of proofs: not only did Graham wrongly claim that he was 'the illegitimate child of one of the Dukes in the Dukeries', but, his lawyers warned The Bodley Head, their client had never 'suffered from, or been threatened by, creeping paralysis: Mr Greene could not in any case have witnessed his increasing decline from this disease, as he reported in a letter to his mother, as he only saw Mr Roberts once for one hour.' The Bodley Head wrote to literary editors and others begging them not to quote from or refer to the offending passages, which were promptly excised, and no more was heard on the matter.

More importantly, Graham decided, while in Nottingham, to learn more about the Catholic faith, for Vivien's sake if not his own. 'It was only fair, since she knew what I believed – in nothing supernatural,' he wrote years after the event. 'Besides, I thought, it would kill the time.' He went along to the gloomy Victorian gothic cathedral, explained what he had in mind, and was introduced to Father Trollope, 'a very tall and very fat man with big smooth jowls which looked as though they had never needed a razor.' 'I was not struck by him. He was a little gross in appearance, and there was also a most trashy novel from Boot's library, lying in his room,' he told Vivien. But first appearances were misleading: Father Trollope may have looked like one of those corrupt, hard-drinking, worldly, secretly lecherous Catholic priests who haunted the English Protestant imagination, but he was, in fact, the most saintly and self-effacing of men. He had been, in an earlier incarnation, a successful West End actor who had loved 'the smell of greasepaint and the applause at a curtain-fall', and still pined for that world: he too had been a convert – a conversion, Graham learned, which had been fiercely opposed by Dr Fry, 'that former ogre of Berkhamsted'. For all his regrets for the world he had left behind, Trollope devoted himself to his new life with a sad and single-minded dedication that Graham found immensely attractive. The two men battled for Graham's soul – 'It was on the ground of a dogmatic atheism that I fought and fought hard', Graham later recalled – and eventually Father Trollope prevailed. In due course Graham would become, with Evelyn Waugh, the most celebrated English Catholic novelist of the twentieth century: but whereas Waugh adhered to every particular of the faith, and revered the authoritarian, dogmatic creed into which he too had converted as a young man, Greene had a much more agonised relationship with the Church, delighting in doubt and, by the end of his life, seeming half in and half out of the fold.

Graham was now in a position to marry Vivien, and his experience at the *Nottingham Journal* had qualified him for work on a national newspaper. In March 1926 he joined *The Times* as a sub-editor, and he remained with the paper for the next three years. 'I can think of no better career for a young novelist than to be for some years a sub-editor on a rather conservative newspaper,' he wrote in his memoirs: not only were his colleagues literate and well-informed – they included a Fellow of All Souls and a future Labour Cabinet Minister, Douglas Jay, who sat at the next desk – but the sub-editorial labour of chopping redundant verbiage, removing clichés and tidying up grammar and punctuation provided, for Graham at least, invaluable training in the virtues of brevity, clarity and writing to the point. He was very happy in the old *Times* offices near Blackfriars Bridge, the wood-panelled rooms of which were more reminiscent of a club in Pall Mall than a modern newspaper office: 'I remember with pleasure – it was a symbol of the peaceful life – the slow burning fire in the sub-editors' room, the gentle thud of coals as they dropped one by one in the old black grate.' The hours were ideal: disciplined as he would always be, he wrote 500 words of a novel in the morning – like Anthony Trollope, he was a firm believer in getting so many words written per day, come what may – before clocking into work at four in the afternoon, continuing until the final edition had been put to bed at midnight. He worked on the letters page, which brought him into regular contact with Geoffrey Dawson, before being promoted to the Court Circular. In this capacity he found himself having to deal with an offering by Herbert. 'I've been through Herbert's stuff,' he told his mother in the spring of 1928. 'It's too long as it stands for any newspaper. If you think I could have a free hand to chop and sub-edit, I think I might be able to get the part about the servants onto the Court page . . .' But he couldn't persuade his colleagues, and some weeks later he wrote to say that 'I'm afraid Herbert's article must be no go . . .'

Two years earlier, Graham had found himself caught up in the General Strike of 1926. *The Times* was the only national newspaper to continue publication throughout the strike, albeit in attenuated form, and it attracted the wrath of the strikers, who tried to set fire to its offices by stuffing petrol-soaked rags through the letterbox. Graham enlisted as a Special Constable, as did Raymond: he referred to his fellow-Constables as 'stormtroops', ready to do battle with strikers massed on the far side of the river. After the strike had ended he and his colleagues were given a silver matchbox, two weeks' extra pay and an album of commemorative photographs. It was, he confessed later, 'a memory of which I am not very proud', nor did it chime with his having recently joined the ILP, of which Ben was already a member. Although Graham's sympathies and politics would always be to the left, he was never a joiner or a conformist or a follower of party lines and, as writers often do, he would sometimes find himself working for, and writing for, publications and companies with very different political views from his own.

Like many young men, Graham worried about his health. One day he went to see a seedy local doctor in Battersea to complain of stomach pains: the doctor issued him with a bottle of medicine, but when that proved ineffectual he consulted Raymond, then at the Westminster Hospital. Raymond instantly diagnosed appendicitis, and hurried him off for an operation. While recuperating in the public ward, Graham witnessed two deaths: one of an old man, and the other – altogether more harrowing – of a little boy. His fellow-patients drowned out the cries of the little boy's relatives by clamping earphones to their heads and tuning in to *Children's Hour*, but Graham listened with a terrible fascination. 'Are people who write entirely & absolutely selfish, darling?' he asked Vivien. 'Even though in a way I hated it yesterday evening – one half of me was saying how lucky it was – added experience – & I kept on catching myself trying to memorise details – Sister's face, the faces of the other men in the ward. And I felt quite excited aesthetically. It made one rather disgusted with oneself.' 'There is a splinter of ice in the heart of a writer,' he later declared, looking back at the incident from the eminence of old age. Rather more worrying were the implications of a fainting attack in *The Times*'s offices: Graham now learned, for the first time, that Kenneth Richmond – who had no medical training – had earlier attributed a fainting attack at Berkhamsted to possible epilepsy, and had warned that, if Graham were epileptic, he should perhaps refrain from getting married. Raymond declared that Richmond had been talking nonsense, and had unduly alarmed Charles and Marion Greene, who had been hugging Graham's secret to themselves all these years. John McNair Wilson, *The Times*'s medical correspondent and a world authority on Napoleon, agreed with Raymond; and although he may, in fact, have suffered from mild epilepsy when young, Graham was cleared to marry Vivien, on medical as well as religious grounds.

This in itself promised to be an unorthodox affair. Although Graham was extremely highly sexed, Vivien had been imbued with a dread of the whole business by her mother; it had been agreed between them that they should enjoy what amounted to a *mariage blanc*, and live together as the best of friends rather than as lovers. 'I've never met so complete a companion as you . . . It's companionship with you that I want,' Graham had assured her when they were still both living in Oxford, far removed from the realities of everyday life and free to indulge the most whimsical fantasies. 'What I long for is a quite original marriage with you, companionship & companionship only.' Vivien, he had declared, would be free to see her mother as much and as often as she liked: 'There'd be no domestic tying down, & you'd always keep your ideal of celibacy, & you could help me to keep the same ideal.' As for companionship, 'I shouldn't grumble if it was a less share than your mother had.' Quite how keen he still was on the notion of a 'monastic marriage' remains unclear, but the baby talk and the cries of 'Ooo!' and the stars denoting eternal love still peppered their correspondence. 'Ooo darling, let me try to put "To my wife" in a book once – to try to convince myself that it's true,' he suggested in the spring of 1927. 'I'm going to marry in a fortnight the most wonderful person ever,' he informed her six months later, signing off as 'Your lover for all eternity'. They were married on 15 October 1927 in St Mary's Catholic Church, Holly Place, Hampstead – those in attendance included Claud Cockburn, and his distant cousin Christopher Isherwood – and went to live not far away, between Hampstead and Golders Green.

Vivien's mother lived close by; this can't have made life easy, for Graham at least, but no mother-in-law jokes or grumbles surface in his correspondence. In later years, when the marriage was on the verge of collapsing altogether, the supposedly icy Marion Greene would write anxious, affectionate and comforting letters to her unhappy daughter-in-law, but in the meantime Vivien may have felt *de trop* on visits to Crowborough. 'My mother-in-law used to say "And this is my other daughter-in-law. She's very artistic, you know." It wasn't a compliment. It meant one was dreamy and liable to forget things,' she informed one of Graham's biographers many years later. Graham himself had no such reservations. 'I haven't had a moment to write before, and being of a terribly undemonstrative nature I shan't say so on Saturday,' he wrote to his mother, apropos an impending visit. 'I love seeing you and Da. I'm very happy at present, & I realise the huge proportion of it I owe to you both. I hope I become a success, if only so that all you've both done for me isn't wasted. There comes a time when gratitude wells up to a height above flood level, & as it's hard, owing to some kink in my nature, to speak it, I have to write it.' Monastic or not, married life was, for the time being, all that he could have wished for. 'I could never have imagined that I could love you as much as I do now – or so worship you or so adore you,' he told Vivien on their first anniversary. Two years later he was 'wildly happy . . . because I'm married to you, beautiful miracle.' 'I'm simply parched for the sight of your cat face. The thought of it makes me go all wuzzy and despairing and achy,' he told her on another occasion.

A seemingly happy marriage was combined with literary success when Charles Evans, the managing director of William Heinemann, rang to say that they would like to publish *The Man Within*. 'Nothing in a novelist's later life can equal that moment,' Graham recalled. 'Triumph is unalloyed by any doubt of the future.' As if that weren't enough, Doubleday, the New York publishers, had also made an offer, and would be contributing an advance of £50 to Heinemann's £30 against royalties of 12.5 per cent; by a pleasing irony, The Bodley Head – who would, years later, supplant Heinemann as Graham Greene's publishers – also came up with an offer, prompted by an enthusiastic report from J. B. Priestley. 'It could only have been written by a Greene,' a proud Uncle Eppy declared and, flushed with excitement, Graham hurried round to Heinemann's offices in Great Russell Street to meet Mr Evans.

William Heinemann founded his publishing company in 1890, and it had rapidly established a reputation as a firm that was both literary and highly commercial. Heinemann himself had published Robert Louis Stevenson, Rudyard Kipling, H. G. Wells, Henry James, Joseph Conrad and Max Beerbohm, and more recent recruits to the list had included D. H. Lawrence, Somerset Maugham and John Galsworthy. Charles Evans had, like many of the best publishers, left school in his teens, and had worked as a schoolmaster before joining Heinemann. He had a nose for bestselling books: he encouraged J. B. Priestley to write *The Good Companions* and spotted the huge sales potential of Margaret Kennedy's *The Constant Nymph*. 'With his bald head and skinny form he looked like a family solicitor lean with anxieties, but a solicitor who had taken an over-dose of some invigorating vitamin,' Graham recalled. 'His hands and legs were never still. He did everything, from shaking hands to ringing a bell, in quick jerks.' Alan Hill, who was to become one of Graham's closest allies in the firm, remembered Evans as 'trembling with pent-up energy, like taut elastic . . . small, nervous and quick in all his reactions', while the literary agent David Higham recalled that 'he had the air of a child almost, a certain simplicity, a naïvety of which he was never ashamed;

and beneath all that a warm and genuine heart, a generous one too.'
Unusually for a publisher at that time, most of whom regarded agents as
interlopers and wide-boys, Evans's generosity extended to recommending
his new author to David Higham, a heavily whiskered young agent whose
clients would eventually include Anthony Powell, Dylan Thomas, A. J. P
Taylor, Malcolm Muggeridge and Edith Sitwell. Agenting is a fissiparous
business, and Higham and two colleagues, Nancy Pearn and Laurence
Pollinger, had recently split off from Curtis Brown to form Pearn, Pollinger
& Higham. Graham appeared in his office one day carrying a note from
Evans which read 'The bearer of this note is a young author I have just
taken on and who has, I believe, a considerable future.'

Despite a fearful moment when, at proof stage, Graham discovered
that his name had been given as 'Green' on the title page, *The Man Within*
enjoyed a phenomenal success, selling 12,594 copies for Heinemann alone.
Graham found himself a literary celebrity, rubbing shoulders with
grandees like Arnold Bennett, Hugh Walpole, J. B. Priestley, Maurice
Baring and Michael Arlen. 'We went to a terribly grand party at the
American publishers the day before publication, with people like the
Duchess of Devonshire, Rudyard Kipling etc floating about. We drank
a lot of champaign [*sic*] and felt happy,' he told Hugh, who was by then
up at Oxford. A 'painted old woman I used to see wandering about
Oxford, rather a revolting spectacle' turned out to be the celebrated
literary hostess Ottoline Morrell, who promptly invited him and Vivien
to tea at Garsington Manor, the Jacobean house outside Oxford where
she entertained writers such as Lytton Strachey, Bertrand Russell, D. H.
Lawrence and Aldous Huxley, who had urged her to read *The Man Within*.
Being a published author was, Graham told Raymond, 'great fun' and
gave one a 'great sense of importance', but 'the funniest part of the
absurd, joyful situation is that the book is quite terribly second-rate.'

Second-rate or not, Heinemann and Doubleday had such faith in their
new author that they offered him the enormous sum of £600 a year for
three years to write more novels for them. He could now, or so he
thought, live off his writing, and – much as he liked it – give up his job
at *The Times*. Very sensibly, as it turned out, his colleagues urged him
not to resign. George Anderson, the chief sub, who translated Verlaine
in his spare time, told him that he had a great future on the paper – he
might even become the correspondence editor one day – and 'foresaw
a time might come when novel-writing would fail me and I would need,
like himself, a quiet and secure life with the pubs opening at half-past
five and the coal settling in the grate'; Geoffrey Dawson himself observed

that several *Times* employees combined working on the paper with writing novels, and pointed to Charles Morgan, the drama critic, as an eminent example. But Graham had made up his mind, and offered his resignation. It was, he later declared, a decision he came to bitterly regret. 'I thought I was a writer already, and that the world was at my feet,' he wrote in *A Sort of Life*.

Proof to the contrary was provided the following year when his second novel, *The Name of Action*, was published. It drew on his Rhineland adventures with Claud Cockburn, but although Aunt Eva enjoyed it, Barbara got stuck halfway through and abandoned ship; the reviews were uncomplimentary, and it sold a quarter as many copies as *The Man Within*. Charles Evans had sent Graham a complimentary telegram after first reading the new novel, but 'it was a thoroughly bad book. That telegram was not helpful. What I should have had was severe criticism', ideally from his kinsman and literary hero Robert Louis Stevenson: as he told a correspondent many years later: 'I think it was Stevenson's method of describing action without adjectives or adverbs which taught me a good deal. The reader may think that action in a novel is easier than dialogue, but the contrary is true, and many writers get their action with the help of adjectives. Even the most violent action in *Treasure Island* is conveyed, as I remember, without the use of adjectives.' But whatever his later reservations, he stoutly defended his new novel, within the family at least. 'I'm glad that you at least prefer *The Name of Action* to *The Man Within*, a view which seems confined in the family to we three and in the Press to *The Times*,' he told Hugh, while to his mother he wrote that '*The Man Within* is, I'm convinced, a moderately bad book, while this, I'm equally certain, is a moderately good one.' The commercial success of his first novel may well have been a fluke or good luck – it seems, in retrospect, a fairly undistinguished piece of work – and despite increasing critical acclaim it took years before sales of his novels matched those of *The Man Within*: but it had been, for this most professional of authors, a salutary lesson in the workings of the literary world.

★

Herbert would, before long, assume fictional form in *England Made Me*, and in the real world he continued to be a source of anxiety to his family despite having married the long-suffering Audrey. 'Herbert is again very much on the warpath,' Eva Greene reported in the spring of 1931. 'Did I tell you that he drifted to South America on some absolutely

mad scheme and then got stranded in Buenos Aires?' The 'rich'
Greenes had more time for their errant cousin than his siblings –
Barbara felt sorry for him, and Felix always found him a sympathetic
figure – and Eva and Eppy called on his parents to discuss 'the eternal
Herbert problem'. As a result, Eppy paid for Herbert and Audrey to
be shipped home from Argentina, and 'Uncle Charlie was terribly cut
up about it all, and very ill.' Before long the errant couple were back in
Crowborough, sponging off his parents and plotting their next move.

Whatever their feelings about Herbert, his parents and siblings were
united in finding Audrey a good egg, and admired her for putting up
with so much for so long. They were regarded as a devoted couple, and
they remained together to the very end, whereas Herbert's brothers
had chequered marital careers. Raymond's first marriage proved a very
short-lived affair. They were a good-looking, fashionable couple, but
Charlotte was not popular with the rest of the family. 'Raymond and
Charlotte motored over for tennis,' Eva wrote from Little Wittenham
in the summer of 1930. 'Charlotte more distant and superior than ever,
and only showed interest when the talk turned to her latest pet, a
monkey': exotic pets were a modish accessory between the wars, but
whereas Cyril Connolly and his first wife, Jeannie, owned a lemur, the
Greenes had opted for a marmoset. No doubt the marmoset was given
the run of their house in Denbigh Street in Pimlico, but Raymond, for
his part, confessed to 'caged feelings' despite his love for Charlotte: he
used to go for long solitary walks on Sundays, pretending to himself
that he was still a free man and a bachelor, and Charlotte his mistress.
But for all that, he admitted a few years later, 'I know that till the end
of my days I would not have left her, nor, while she loved me, been
unfaithful.' The choice was not his to make: Charlotte left him for
another man. Eva was astonished that the 'Raymond ménage went on
as long as it did,' and reported 'Charles and Marion surprised and upset',
and that 'in true School House fashion [they] had to vow secrecy, as
if such a thing could be kept secret.'

Graham, on the other hand, was sympathetic to both sides. 'What a
pity they both couldn't have fallen out of love at the same time,' he told
his mother. 'He has, I think, been badly warped by his last years at
school, and it has made him extraordinarily difficult.' After Charlotte's
departure, Graham had accompanied his brother to Burgundy, where 'I
had never liked him so well – defences down . . .' Reinforcing the notion
of Raymond and Charlotte as a thoroughly modern couple, he pointed
out that 'they had both founded their marriage on theories, and it is

unfair really to blame her for following the line to which they had both agreed years ago.' As for Charlotte, 'Oxford wasn't her milieu. I know that I couldn't live in a man's club where everybody played and talked cricket and golf, and she couldn't live in a town of knitting gossips . . . It's rotten for him to have his bones picked by them and listen to the obscene whispers.' However tiresome she may have been, Charlotte came to a sad end: she eventually committed suicide, and was never mentioned in Raymond's entries in *Who's Who*. 'It is strange how Raymond has suddenly become "one of us" again,' Eva declared, with obvious relief, after Charlotte had vanished from the scene. But he would not be with them for long. To take his mind off his misery he was preparing to indulge an old passion, and on a scale that would make him, like Graham, a figure of national renown.

The Canadian novelist Robertson Davies studied in Oxford in the 1930s, and was recommended to see Raymond for a 'ferocious cold and cough'. He was impressed by the book-lined consulting-room – 'because I can read the title of a book at forty yards, I knew at once they were not books about medicine' – and found Raymond 'most agreeable', and a 'first-rate' if unconventional doctor. It soon became apparent that Robertson Davies was working far too hard, and Raymond advised him 'not to put so much emphasis on your work'. 'My work would eat me up, but I keep it in place by climbing mountains,' Raymond continued. 'And, do you know, climbing mountains makes me a better doctor.' He put theory into practice when, in 1931, Frank Smythe invited him to join an expedition to attempt Kamet, an unclimbed peak in the Garwhal Himalayas. Reaching the summit would be a great achievement, since no mountain of over 25,000 feet had ever been climbed before.

Although they had not known each other well at Berkhamsted – they were in different houses, and whereas Raymond was a schoolboy success, Smythe never got beyond the Remove – Raymond remembered Smythe as 'a rather frail fair-headed boy who was said to have a weak heart and was not allowed to play football because of a murmur in the chest': he still looked frail and had a heart murmur when Raymond gave him a medical in the Himalayas, and was only forty-eight when he died. At school he had spent his days dreaming of becoming a mountaineer; he was, according to Raymond, 'more highly strung than his rather shy and reserved manner might suggest . . . he had an innate dislike for the mechanical world, and fled to the mountain solitudes for a respite.' After leaving Berkhamsted he had trained as an engineer and worked for a time in Egypt. He was invalided out of the RAF in 1927, yet despite his apparent poor health he was beginning to make his name as a mountaineer, famed for his frequent ascents of Mont Blanc. Raymond used to meet him climbing in Wales and the Lake District, and was impressed by his determination to prove himself, both intellectually and physically, and by the way he 'tried always to reach heights which were just a little beyond his powers, great though these were.' At ground level he could be irritable, tactless and swift to take offence, but 'at great altitudes a new force seemed to enter into Frank. His body, still apparently frail as it had been in boyhood, was capable of astonishing feats of sudden strength and prolonged endurance.' He became self-confident and serene on the mountains: Raymond remembered the Kamet Expedition as 'a period of calm unbroken by more than a rare small ripple of disagreement, and the calm was the result of Frank's confident but always modest and unassuming leadership.'

In 1930 Smythe had taken part in a large international expedition to Kanchenjunga, and he was determined that his new expedition should be small in terms of the manpower involved – six Europeans, and ten locally enlisted porters – and that since none of those whom he planned to approach had large private means, it should also be comparatively inexpensive. It would cost between £400 and £500 per member, and be financed in part by gathering rare seeds in the foothills of the Himalayas to sell to well-heeled collectors back home, by making a film of their exploits, and by writing and sending home regular reports to *The Times*. Choosing the right men for the job was a tricky business. As Smythe wrote in his account of the expedition, 'Your friend in civilisation may become your enemy on a mountain; his very snore assumes a new and repellent note; his tricks at the mess table, the sound of his mastication, the scarcely concealed triumph with which he appropriates the choicest tit-bits, the absurd manner in which he walks, even the cut of his clothes and the colour of the patch on the seat of his trousers, may induce an irritation and loathing almost beyond endurance.' Raymond, who had equally strong views on the matter, noted that 'the man who is a professional self-acclaimed tough, ever trying to prove himself to himself, seldom makes the grade. It is nearly always the quietly, politely self-confident man, going because he likes it, just for the fun of it, with no psychologically complicated ulterior motives, fitting in best with the party and working the hardest, who pushes the party to the top on his shoulders, not caring greatly whether he gets there himself.' As a keen member of the Alpine Club, Raymond was well aware that the 'upper middle classes' still dominated the mountaineering world, and would provide Smythe with the members of his expedition. (They did not include Evelyn Waugh, who asked Raymond whether he could come along as an observer, but was ruled out of court.)

The two best mountaineers in the party were Smythe and its youngest member, Eric Shipton, a coffee farmer in Kenya who had climbed Kilimanjaro and Mount Kenya, and would become the most famous mountaineer of his generation. The transport officer, E. St J. Birnie, was a captain in Sam Browne's Cavalry, a dashing Indian Army regiment, a polo-player and big-game hunter who spoke fluent Hindustani and, according to Smythe, 'thoroughly understood the simple, childlike psychology of the hill people from whom we had to draw our porters'. Wing Commander E. J. Beauman was an experienced Alpine skier and mountaineer; R. E. Holdsworth, the expedition's botanist, taught classics at Harrow and had blues in both cricket and soccer. As for Raymond, 'I was never a first-class climber on rock or snow, but I was a moderate on both, and sometimes a reliable second-rater in all circumstances is more desirable as a companion than a man who is a tiger on the one and a rabbit on the other. I had two other advantages: I was a doctor and I was physically very strong.' The doctor on such an expedition, he later declared, 'must be something of a physician, something of a surgeon, especially an orthopaedic surgeon, with a little knowledge of every speciality and a lot of knowledge of psychology – not the school psychology of Freud and Jung and Adler and the rest, but the sort of common-sense knowledge of human nature which seems to be beyond the scope of these masters and most of their hidebound disciples.' Raymond's own contribution went well beyond the purely medical: both on Kamet and, later, on Everest, he was regarded by other members of the party as the resident intellectual-cum-entertainer, better read and better educated than his fellows, and adept at keeping them entertained with jokes, readings and 'horrific' ghost stories.

Shortly before he left for India, Raymond had briefly encountered a world with which both School House and Hall Greenes would have dealings over the years. Dining one evening in St Edmund Hall, Oxford, he found himself talking about the expedition with a man who would later be known as General Sir Bernard Paget. Paget asked him whether he had thought of returning home via Afghanistan and Russia. It hadn't occurred to him to do so, but a week later he received a letter addressed to Lieutenant C. R. Greene R.A.M.C. – he held a commission in the Territorial Army – asking him to call at the War Office next time he was in London. He dutifully did so, and a Colonel Murray told him that he was looking for a mountaineer with some military training to find out whether the Russians could invade India through Afghanistan via Merv or Mazar-i-Sharif. Raymond was excited by the idea, and they spent the rest of the morning poring over a map of the area. He was told that although the War Office might be able to arrange some kind of *ex gratia* payment, it was essential that he should go as a tourist and make his own travel arrangements, and that his dealings with the India Office and the Russian Embassy should not involve the War Office in any way. The India Office was happy to help, as were the Russians, though they warned him that it might take time for the necessary paperwork to be processed in Moscow. It was agreed that permission would be posted to Simla, and that Raymond would pick it up on his way back from Kamet. In the event, the Russians refused permission. Raymond cabled the War Office, who replied 'On no account go', and that was the end of Raymond's career in espionage.

No records remain of the journey out from England by a P&O liner, but the party assembled at Ranikhet in the foothills of the Himalayas, just over a hundred miles, and a fortnight's march, from their destination. As they made their way through a lush landscape of gorges and torrents – initially in a decrepit lorry, and then by foot – Raymond found himself called upon to treat those they met on the way, as well as the Sherpas and Bhotias, beneath whose 'ragged and odorous exteriors', Smythe assured his readers, 'are hearts of gold': he removed a boy's tonsils, treated septic legs and cases of VD, and stitched up the head of a porter who had been knocked down by a flying boulder. The most valuable drugs he took with him were 'analgesics and hypnotics, quinine, alkali for digestive disturbances, cascara against constipation and opium against diarrhoea', and he made frequent resort to the Epsom Salts. Dysentery and malaria were endemic in the foothills, and conditions were insanitary by European standards. The Sherpas 'look on the boiling of milk as an insane whim', and their notion of washing-up consisted of spitting on the plates and wiping them dry with a shirt tail. Nor were his colleagues much better: Raymond noted 'the way they look over their shoulders to see where the doctor is before drinking from an obviously suspect stream', and how they took a 'childish pleasure' in not imbibing their daily dose of quinine. Smythe remembered Raymond's 'stentorian bellows' of indignation, and how 'the volume of his voice is commensurate with the inches of his frame.' And, since they were all quintessentially English, they adopted a baby musk deer, which Raymond fed from a syringe.

Raymond's medical equipment was carried by porters, as were bedding, tents, food, clothing, collapsible furniture, scientific equipment, the cine camera and food supplies. One porter carried a treasure chest stuffed with rupees, while another was bowed down by a gramophone and records provided by HMV: Beauman sat on and broke many of the records, but those which survived were enjoyed by the locals, who preferred Gracie Fields to Brahms. They augmented their own rations with local delicacies, including cuckoo soup; cigarettes were lit whenever they paused for a break, though both Raymond and Holdsworth preferred a pipe, and Smythe immediately looked up the cricket scores when messengers arrived bearing post and out-of-date newspapers. Eventually, at 11,000 feet, they reached the pass which separated the foothills from the Himalayas proper – only to find an intrepid English spinster, Miss Gertrude Benham, already installed and sketching the view. They were joined by some Garwhal Bhotia coolies, who, according to Smythe, 'exuded strong odours of yak' and were 'simple and childlike in disposition'. Raymond's servant, Passang, 'lumbered along with an ungainly gait', but 'what he lacked in grey matter was more than compensated by his prodigious strength.'

Plodding steadily uphill, they established Base Camp at the foot of the Raikana Glacier: at 15,500 feet, they were already almost as high as Mont Blanc. By now it was mid-June, and they were anxious to attempt the summit before the monsoon broke, bringing heavy snow and making an ascent impossible. For the time being at least, 'even Greene's presumptuous announcement that any party he accompanied was always favoured with fine weather failed to arouse the wrath of the gods.' The plan was to establish a series of camps up the side of the mountain until they reached a shallow depression called Meade's Col, from which they would attempt the summit. At Camp 3 they were caught in a blizzard, but when it cleared 'we saw Kamet, looking terribly cold and forbidding in a sky of cruel feline green.' After climbing up a steep rock face to Camp 4, Smythe remarked on how 'after my own heavings and struggles it was somewhat disconcerting to see Greene ascend after a few minutes' pause with leisurely elegance,' and how 'Greene's six-and-a-half feet of height, combined with a proportionately long reach, enables him to grasp holds far beyond the reach of normal mortals.' No sooner had they arrived at Camp 4 than Smythe, not to be outdone, was spotted 'tapping out on his typewriter with the greatest energy and concentration a long despatch for *The Times.*'

Raymond, for his part, was investigating two aspects of mountaineering on which he would become an authority: frostbite, a subject on which he would advise the armed forces during the Second World War; and the effects of lack of oxygen, or anoxia, on the human mind and body. Lack of oxygen not only led to breathlessness, lassitude, headaches, blue lips and mountain sickness, but affected the memory and often resulted in irritability, insomnia and forgetfulness. His Oxford mentor, J. S. Haldane, had studied the effects of oxygen deprivation and experimented on himself and on volunteers with a giant metal cylinder from which the oxygen was gradually withdrawn. Raymond had taken part in Haldane's experiments with low-pressure chambers, and he was to become a passionate advocate of acclimatisation, of allowing the body to adapt slowly to higher altitudes. He would make his views felt two years later on the slopes of Everest, but in the meantime, in the spirit of Haldane, he experimented on himself with doses of ammonium chloride.

Smythe, Shipton, Holdsworth and a Sherpa called Lewa were the first to reach the summit: whereas earlier expeditions had employed Swiss guides, and used local people simply as porters, the tendency now was to encourage selected Sherpas to climb as well as carry. Holdsworth smoked his pipe on the summit, and they enjoyed a view which took in the dusty yellow Tibetan plateau to the north, and the Karakorams to the west. Two days later, Raymond, Birnie and a bearer, Kesat Singh, made their own, separate, attempt – and, unlike their predecessors, they were not burdened with a cine camera. According to Birnie's report in *The Times*, Raymond led initially, 'at a rhythmical pace which kept us going for long periods without a rest'. After two hours they changed leaders: Raymond felt breathless and exhausted, and sent the others on ahead. After admiring the view, he slept for an hour before making his way up to the summit to join his companions. Raymond had a narrow escape on the way down – left dangling on the end of a rope over a vertical drop, he scrabbled his way to safety – and they were met at Camp 4 with welcome supplies of rum and chocolate. The weather broke as the party made its way down to Base Camp, and they were exposed to blizzards, freezing winds and frostbite. As they descended into lower altitudes, Raymond noticed how, as the oxygen supply improved, his senses became sharper, and the world a brighter place. Back at Base Camp, they had a celebratory party; brandy and cigars were produced, and Shipton wound up the gramophone and played records of Paul Robeson and Caruso singing 'O Sole Mio'. Miss Benham was still behind her easel as they made their way down to the Dhauli Valley. Lewa was suffering dreadfully from frostbite and, according to Frank Smythe, 'we could not help but perceive in his moral breakdown and distress the essential difference between the European and the native. Had one of us been seriously frostbitten he would at least have *tried* to bear his misfortune with stoical calm and fortitude. But a native cannot control his feelings; he is a child; his mind cannot master pain or mental depression.'

Climbing Kamet was not the only aim of the expedition: they also wanted to explore the Badrinath range of mountains, which was poorly mapped and virtually unexplored by Europeans, and to find the source of the Alaknanda river, itself the source of the Ganges. Smythe and his companions decided to take a difficult overland route to the holy city of Badrinath, and sent most of their provisions via the easier pilgrim route. This proved unfortunate when Smythe was suddenly seized by an agonising toothache, and asked Raymond to remove the offending tooth. '"Certainly" replied Greene with a broad grin and offensive cheerfulness. "But I'm afraid I've no cocaine or chloroform. It's gone round to Badrinath with the heavy luggage."' Smythe downed three-quarters of a bottle of brandy and carved himself a 'dental prop' out of a juniper branch; Raymond gave him a gigantic dose of morphine and, to a terrible cry from his patient, the tooth was yanked out.

Three fortune-tellers had told Raymond that he would die at the age of thirty, and on his thirtieth birthday he was almost killed by a falling rock. He survived that, and being carried through a raging torrent by his servant – 'it was amusing to stand on the bank and watch Greene, almost completely enveloping the squat Passang,' Smythe recalled. They joined the pilgrim way, meeting as they went a steady stream of beggars and fakirs, and an Indian in Oxford bags whom they assumed to be a 'Congress wallah'; in Mana they were received by the Rawal Sahib, had garlands draped around their necks, and were presented with gifts of mangoes, nuts and onions. They reached the watershed of the Alaknanda and Gangotri rivers, previously unvisited, by Europeans at least, and celebrated by opening a tin of sardines. Smythe and Raymond went on alone to reach the source of the Alaknanda, picking their way along great gorges, with huge, mist-strewn boulders to either side and torrents raging down the middle. It proved a 'scene of utter desolation', with the great river emerging as a grey trickle from the 'dirty snout' of a glacier. Back in Mana, the Rawal Singh bestowed upon them the title of 'Mahatma', in recognition of their having splashed water over themselves at the source of the Ganges. The ceremonies over, they made their way back on ponies to Ranikhet before setting off for England.

Shortly after their return, Raymond received a letter from Harold Raymond of Chatto & Windus, asking him if he would like to write a book about his experiences. He declined, 'partly because I am too busy, partly because I doubt my ability, and partly because Smythe is writing one. He, alas, has already a contract with Gollancz.' Raymond's divorce went through while he was climbing Kamet, and he was now a free man. He was also, like Graham, a public figure – he may not have written a book about his experiences on Kamet, but a film of the climb was released in due course – and before long he would once again be summoned to the Himalayas to tackle the greatest challenge of them all.

No Love Lost

Each set of Greene parents tried hard to show an interest in the other branch of the family, but there was little real contact between the cousins themselves; and, where Hugh and Felix were concerned, indifference turned into positive dislike. But although they kept well apart in their private as well as professional lives, and had very different personalities, their careers had much in common. Both led public lives, as journalists or commentators on the political and social scene; both were exceptionally competent organisation men, adept not just at running businesses and public bodies, but providing the innovations and ideas they needed; both had meteoric careers in the BBC, albeit at different times. But whereas Hugh, as befitted a School House Greene, had a cool, unillusioned and generally hard-headed view of human nature in general, Felix was always, like Ben, an idealist, for ever searching for a heaven on earth and an all-explaining system of belief, for ever disappointed and for ever moving on; he was amazingly efficient, yet he combined this with a kind of innocence and naïvety that made him, in political terms, a willing and gullible 'useful idiot'. They embodied very different views of human nature, and whereas Hugh rose steadily to the top of the tree, Felix flitted from one passion to another, quickly making his mark wherever he went yet never staying in one place for long enough to make a deep impression.

Unlike Hugh, Felix was prone to endless self-analysis, most of which had to do with his own feelings of inadequacy and general hopelessness, and his relations with his family, and his mother in particular. He once wrote, in note form, of how he had endured 'a restrictive upbringing, in which there was little security and very little affection. Great competitiveness between the children. No warm influence from my father. Emotionally starved mother who derived her emotional satisfaction from her children, especially her youngest son who was me. Falsity and pretence pervaded the entire family atmosphere. I had to become self-reliant and self-resourceful, and be ready for any attack. Evasion, lying and subterfuge had to be resorted to in order to "keep in" with my mother and prevent my being a total outcast. Her main weapon over her children was to make them think of her as an infinitely unselfish being whom we were ill-treating. In other words, she was always able to make me feel guilty, unworthy, thoughtless and despicable.' He was, he claimed, 'not a love-able person, nor even a likeable one', and 'my immediate family – brothers and sisters – certainly didn't like me. We were constantly at war, spoken or unspoken.'

Felix was, and would remain, unusually good-looking, with black hair and eyebrows, and blue eyes that were not pale, like those of his cousin Graham, but a deep cerulean. But for all his charm and good looks, he felt lonely and 'emotionally starved', incapable of becoming close to other people, and always keeping them at arm's length: 'friendless at school and college, this sense of being an outsider has remained with me constantly, a kind of unworthiness to be a friend.' 'I revolted as best I might,' he recalled, 'by being perpetually dirty and untidy, by stealing small things and lying, by using my gift for appearing loving to inveigle what I wanted.' As a small child he was 'either wildly happy or in a terrible rage', and was – or so he claimed – severely punished by Eppy for his 'violent fits of temper'.

After a spell in Berkhamsted prep school, Felix was sent off to Sidcot, a Quaker co-educational boarding school in Somerset where Barbara was already installed. Barbara loved her time there but was an utterly undistinguished pupil, chalking up a single School Certificate (in Spoken French) and failing to move fast enough about the tennis court. Felix wrote that he loathed every minute – he hated the cold showers, the filthy food and the cult of games – but seems to have hurled himself into every aspect of school life with typical energy and resilience. He stopped speaking German when he went away to school, but that didn't stop him from being teased for having a German mother, and when in 1926 he won the Dymont Elocution Prize, those responsible noted that although his pronunciation of some words was unconventional – 'peas' for 'peace', 'covetjus' for 'covetous' – his readings had 'real dramatic power'. That same year he played de Stogumber in a school production of Bernard Shaw's *St Joan*, and was singled out for a 'performance of quite exceptional merit': as the school magazine recorded, 'there must have been few, among the crowded audience of parents and others, who were not deeply moved by the sincerity of his acting.' He edited the school magazine, proved a competent batsman and a reliable fielder, became head prefect in due course, and, in an early manifestation of his unfailing practicality, did all the cooking on a school camp, catering for more than thirty boys and serving up 'luxuriant stews and a splendiferous salmon pie'.

Felix was also called upon – or so he tells us – to masturbate a homosexual master, who left his bedroom window open at night to allow him easy access. Although innumerable women were to fall in love with Felix over the next sixty years, his sex life and his love life were always complicated and unsatisfactory, with Felix invariably backing off and unable to match action to rhetoric. He found it impossible to separate sex from guilt, and claimed that he was paralysed by a fear of being somehow disloyal to his mother. Despite his much-discussed 'affairs' with women, Felix sometimes wondered whether he was not, in fact, homosexual, and recalled how the gardener's boy at the Hall not only told him the facts of life, much to Eppy's relief, but had taken Felix's hand and placed it on his groin. This was not the kind of information his parents would have welcomed, but it was while he was at Sidcot that he began his lifelong habit of writing regular letters home, crammed with advice, consolation and ruminations on the human condition, and his own in particular.

In the spring of 1928 Felix was chosen to join a party of fifty public school boys on an Empire Tour of South Africa. Eppy paid £150 for the privilege, and the tour was conducted by a master from Rugby, a former adjutant of the Eton Corps, and a scholar of New College who had been 'the late captain of the Winchester eleven'. 'I am getting to know a species of boy entirely different to what I have been used to. I listen in silent awe to learned discussions on the technicalities of rugger, of boxing, of OTC camps, and feel how very sadly my education has been neglected,' Felix told his parents as the party steamed south on board the *Balmoral Castle*. The Etonians and the Wykehamists kept themselves to themselves, but even so, 'if you saw me now you would think I'd been at Eton or Harrow, for I've grown into a perfect "public school boy".' As they crossed the line, the men in first-class challenged the Empire Tour boys to a rugger scrum. 'Thank goodness we mix with the first-class for most things,' Felix reported. 'The first-class are a topping set, and don't seem to mind us, mere second-classers, joining in.' Journalists and photographers swarmed onto the ship as it docked in Cape Town harbour, and the *Cape Times* headline read 'PUBLIC SCHOOLBOYS WELCOMED.' They met the Earl of Athlone and the tycoon Sir Abe Bailey, attended innumerable mayoral banquets, visited gold and diamond mines, watched endless displays of tribal dancing, toured the battlefields of Ladysmith and Spion Kop, and admired the Victoria Falls; a member of the party was attacked by a leopard, and Felix noted how, on a visit to Zulu *kraals*, the natives 'only talk to one grovelling on the ground, for they look up to the white man as a god.' 'Personally I have the highest respect for them,' Felix noted, apropos the Zulus. 'They are dirty, I admit. They have no sense of gratitude, but they are honest, hard-working, very tender with women and children, and above all they have a keen sense of humour.' Not surprisingly, perhaps, 'the colour question has not affected us, but the racial antagonism between the Dutch and English most certainly has.' It was a relief to get back to Cape Town, where 'everyone is English – jolly, hopeful, never disheartened.'

The tour had lasted nine weeks, but Felix stayed on after the rest of the party had returned home. He travelled up to Southern Rhodesia, where he met the Governor and spent two days with Herbert and Audrey on their farm at Sinoia, 120 miles north of Salisbury. 'I looked over their farm critically and took many notes, so I can tell Uncle Charlie a lot when I get home,' he told his parents. 'Herbert is putting tremendous energy into his work and if only he can tide over this first year he will be on his feet.' He was growing maize as well as tobacco, and his farm looked better-run and more prosperous than most. Audrey loved the life, but Herbert had become stick-thin, and they 'both gave me rather a start when I first saw them – they looked so ill.' The settlers in Rhodesia tended to live above their means and bought everything 'on tick', and no doubt Herbert happily followed their example. As Felix finally headed home, the Secretary of the 1820 Memorial Settlers' Association wrote to Eppy to say that he had read some of his letters about South Africa, 'and extraordinarily interesting they are. You should be proud of your boy, for he has the gift of observation and descriptive ability much beyond his years.' This must have come as balm to Eva in particular: she had literary ambitions for Felix, and was confident that 'at some time or other you will take to the pen'.

Nor was that the end of his travels. In the late summer of 1928 he and Barbara travelled out to Brazil via New York and the West Indies. 'She is the most inconsiderate creature, and I have to get away alone to get over my exasperation,' he complained to his parents: she irritated him beyond bearing with her cries of 'Just too divine', but 'we have spasms of great friendliness. You can't imagine how nice she can be when there happens to be a lack of dancing partners.' Back on *terra firma*, he enrolled as an undergraduate at Clare College, Cambridge. Despite being overpowered by feelings of social and intellectual inadequacy, he soon began to make his mark, acting in plays, becoming college secretary of

the League of Nations Union as well as the Conservative Association,
editing a pamphlet grandly entitled 'A Declaration of Tory Principles',
and taking tea with Geoffrey Crowther, the President of the Union and
a future editor of the *Economist*, to discuss how best to raise money for
distressed miners. He flirted with Eleanor Gamble, a rich American friend
of Barbara's who later became the second Mrs Raymond Greene, dreamed
of becoming an orator like Disraeli, and spent one vacation working on
The Times. He started out in the advertising department before moving
on to the sub-editors' room. 'There are eight sub-editors, all with bald
heads and grey hair,' he told his parents. They proved very pleasant, and
'they are all very fond of Graham, and I was introduced to them as "a
cousin of that other Greene".' According to Felix, Graham 'disowned
me. He wouldn't even acknowledge me. It was rather infra dig for him.
He'd got himself a good status on *The Times*, and here was this squirt
of a cousin with no intellectual or literary pretensions sitting at the same
table night after night. At the end of the night's work we'd all walk to
the Blackfriars underground, but he'd never walk with me.' Being cold-
shouldered in this way made him feel more useless and inadequate than
ever, but his sufferings left little mark on their perpetrator. 'I have
completely forgotten that Felix came to *The Times* while I was there',
Graham wrote years later, but 'if I behaved like that I can't help feeling
both ashamed and surprised.' Like Hugh, he rather despised and disliked
Felix, and no doubt he resented him for invading his domain. Be that as
it may, Felix was urged to reapply to *The Times* once he had finished at
Cambridge, albeit on the managerial rather than the editorial side.

Felix's days at Cambridge were over sooner than expected: after
eighteen months he decided that he wanted to make his way in the wider
world, and abandoned his studies. Eppy, who was not best pleased, wrote
out a cheque for over £1000 to cover his university debts. 'Well, never
mention this again,' he said as Felix mumbled his thanks. Tooter was in
Brazil learning about the coffee trade, and Felix was keen to be on his
travels once again. 'I want to leave my mark on the world, as a man who
has got to the top of something,' he declared, and where better to start
than the States, hovering as it was on the brink of the Great Depression.
The ever-patient Eppy agreed to finance a three-month foray, and Felix
was on his way. He headed for New York, and an unpaid job in Brazilian
Warrant's Manhattan office: 'There is no feeling of "pep" here,' he
informed his father. 'Too many cigars are smoked, too many newspapers
read.' When not remarking on the indolence of his colleagues, he busied
himself on Ben's behalf, trying to drum up orders for Kepston's pulleys,

garden chairs and ironing boards. He then joined a party of Oxford and Cambridge Commonwealth Scholars which included Geoffrey Crowther and Launcelot Fleming, a future Church of England bishop, and they spent the next few months travelling round America together. Felix had an introduction to a Vice-President of General Motors, as a result of which he was able to buy a Buick Convertible for a handsome discount; they visited Hollywood, and Felix, suddenly taken with the notion of a career in films, made himself known to the bosses of United Pictures and MGM. Years later he would become a brilliant maker of documentary films, but back in 1930 he was thinking along very different lines.

All this time he was writing home at length, and receiving equally long and effusive letters in reply. 'It seems like a dream that you are so far away,' Eva wrote from their house in Montagu Square. 'I still listen for your voice, your dear voice, and for your step on the stairs – I find it very hard to adjust to a world in which you are not near me . . . I love you more than I can say.' And a month later she told him how 'When I get your letters perhaps that constant little pain in my chest will stop, that never ceasing longing for the tone of your voice, the touch of your hand, that sweet close companionship.' 'Up to now you have walked in the golden mists of youth, free of burdens as only youth can be,' she wrote on the eve of his twenty-first birthday. 'I long to take you in my arms, to feel you as my baby boy whom I can shelter and protect, and it almost hurts to know that the hour has come irrevocably when you must step into the ranks of men.'

Life was not easy for the older Greenes, and Eva and Eppy longed to have their youngest son back with them, dispensing advice and radiating efficiency and practicality. The coffee trade remained as volatile as ever, and although the Brazilian Warrant Company had expanded its business in the post-war years, buying estates and plantations, opening branches in New York and New Orleans, opening the Cambuhy estate, a model *fazenda*, diversifying into cotton, cereals, shipping, insurance and – a speciality of Eppy's – trading in futures, it remained as vulnerable as ever to the cycles of shortage and over-production. Eppy had been made the managing director of BW in 1914 – his other directorships included the British Bank of South America – and he was appointed the chairman of both BW and Edward Johnston Ltd in 1920, after the retirement of the Earl of Bessborough. Ave's brother-in-law, Robert Barham, was appointed manager of the export department in Santos in 1926, and Tooter went to work in Brazil the following year. Two years later the Brazilian government withdrew its policy of federal support for the price of coffee, and in October 1929 reduced demand around the world coincided with the collapse of coffee prices. By 1931 these were a third of what they had been two years earlier, but although demand had begun to rise again, a bumper crop led to fearful over-production, with millions of bags of coffee being burned or thrown into the sea, and farmers surrendering up to a third of their output to the government to be destroyed. Edward Johnston was active in exploiting the markets in Holland, Scandinavia and Germany, but BW's results were poor throughout the 1930s: funds were withheld from Brazil, dividends were passed, and a capital reconstruction of the firm led to massive losses for shareholders.

Eppy had been the leading shareholder since 1920, with 4148 preference shares and 150,000 ordinary shares, and he suffered accordingly, both financially and in terms of health and morale. In 1932 he resigned, following a boardroom coup. He remained a very rich man, and a leading figure in the world of Anglo-Brazilian business, but, much to Eva's regret, he had to sell Montagu Square. Poor health and money worries had, he told Felix, 'deprived me of my old powers of rapid decision and prompt action'. Kepston was a permanent worry, and the farm at Little Wittenham was being mismanaged – though this proved no bar to his adding a billiards room and a 'belvedere' near the tennis courts. 'If only Papa did not look so sad and old,' Eva told Felix; he had become very deaf, suffered dizzy attacks, and grew thinner by the day. She wished, for their peace of mind, that he would sell his remaining properties in Berkhamsted and some of the Little Wittenham farmland. Felix's upbeat and exuberant letters were like balm to his embattled parents. 'They always make the whole world shine,' Eva told him. She read them aloud to Eppy before tucking them under her pillow at night, and 'I wish you could see the happy expression on Papa's face.' She longed to see Felix's 'clear blue truthful eyes', and loved his 'clear brain, practical hands, loving heart and, thank God, healthy body.'

After the Commonwealth Scholars had returned home, Felix found himself a job with N. W. Ayer, an advertising agency based in Philadelphia, initially checking invoices before moving on to higher things. Eppy was glad to hear that he was gainfully employed, still more so since at Ayer's 'you will not be known as the son of a rich man.' 'It will be an enormous relief to me if you can now earn your own living', he wrote, and he urged Felix to 'learn, learn, learn' all he could about business, and 'to make a million as the family wants someone who is successful.' This was, no doubt, a reference to Ben, who was still trying to combine left-wing politics with a reluctant career as a businessman. When his wife Leslie first met him he was, according to their eldest daughter Margaret, 'terribly ashamed of the fact that his parents were terribly rich. He'd become a socialist and a Quaker.' He had given evidence to a Royal Commission on unemployment insurance, describing himself as an employer 'in a small way' who was 'keenly interested' in the subject, and had written a pamphlet which he had sent to leading politicians; Ramsay MacDonald had written to him about it, promising to show it to the relevant experts, and there was some talk of its being published by Faber. On holiday by the seaside Ben spent much of the time reading Hansard, though 'when he plunges into the sea it is like the launching of a battle-ship.' 'Ramsay MacDonald said to Ben that politics mean a whole time job, and that it was no good trying to do it as a sideshow,' Eva reported to Felix, but so long as he was running Kepston's, a sideshow it would have to be. From the far side of the Atlantic, Felix shared his parents' anxieties. 'Ben has never had the strength to grind away at a job that didn't appeal to him. He could never face routine work, with the result that he never learned his job, and the outcome of it all is the Kepston muddle,' he declared. Eppy reluctantly agreed: Ben 'failed at Kepston's because he had never learned business and thought he could learn through the light of his own intelligence.' His oldest son was 'no real businessman. His heart is in politics and there he may do something great one day.' Felix thought so too. 'Dear, magnificent, great old Ben,' he wrote home. 'How I wish one could help him. I am sure one day he will do great things. There is a streak of genius about him.'

Barbara was proving another source of transatlantic worrying. She had briefly contemplated life as an actress, and after enrolling at Fay Compton's studio she had been given a walk-on part in a play at the Fulham Rep, but had done little more than giggle in the wings. Felix worried about her relapsing into 'that old hopeless melancholy', while Eva wished she had more sense of direction, and that she didn't lead such a boring and empty life; back home at Little Wittenham, she did nothing but read novels and play tennis, while her relations with her parents were those of 'polite strangers'. Raymond had, by now, returned from Kamet, and was divorced from Charlotte. 'There are strange threads between him and Barbara which I don't understand, and which half frighten me,' Eva reported. Nothing came of that, but at some point Barbara became un-happily infatuated with a married man. 'Heard the full story of the end of Barbara's infatuation for the married and crooked artist,' Graham noted in his diary, 'and rejoiced at the unashamed melodrama of his final ignominious visit to Little Wittenham, his signature to a paper declaring that he had deceived Barbara, and his departure gratefully clutching a pound note.' But, he added, 'one deplores the older gener- ation being proved right, for they press it home so hardly, and have Barbara, now quite broken, in their power.' Tooter was back from Brazil: he hated having to work in London, and spent most of his spare time on the golf course. 'Ave and Jack seem as happy as can be. Positive unhap- piness doesn't come their way, only that sense of incompleteness which comes from a limited scope of life,' Felix reported of Ave and her husband Jack Barham after their return to England, adding that 'They have been most charming and friendly towards me, quite different from their normal on-the-defensive attitude which it is usually my lot to receive.' (Eva Greene was equally dismissive of cousin Molly's domestic arrange- ments: 'Lionel [Walker] is a queer fish but harmless, one just feeds him and sees that he has *The Times*, and otherwise he seems to prefer to wander about on his own and help Molly with Janet.') It was not hard to see why Eppy and Eva were pinning their hopes on their youngest son.

Far removed from this dispiriting scene, Felix was combining his work at Ayer's with two unpaid jobs: working on the literary pages of the Philadelphia *Public Ledger*, and helping out at a Quaker-run soup kitchen catering for black orphaned children. One of the soup kitchen's backers was a very wealthy woman called Peggy Bok. She was married with three children, one of whom went on to become the President of Harvard, and her husband, Curtis Bok, was a lawyer; his family owned the Curtis Publishing Company, whose publications included the *Saturday Evening Post* and the *Ladies' Home Journal* as well as the *Public Ledger*. Years later, Felix couldn't remember when 'I first knew for certain that Peggy had become helplessly, feverishly enamoured of me': either way, his relation- ship with her was 'complex, contradictory and very ambivalent on my side, though extraordinarily passionate and demanding on hers.' Felix's affair – if such it was – with Peggy Bok was to prove long-lasting and, from her point of view at least, extremely destructive, and it was to be the first of many such relationships in which Felix worked up the women to a frenzy of adoration but failed to provide the emotional or, one suspects, physical response expected of him. Slim, laughing, not conven- tionally good-looking – Felix ungallantly observed that her head was too big for her body – always dressed in white, and quite a few years older than her paramour, Peggy bought him clothes, took him to the opera and drove him around in her Rolls-Royce. 'I had fled without realising it the suffocating influence of a too adoring mother, only to find an equally suffocating and adoring substitute,' Felix recalled, adding that 'we had some happy times together – at least I suppose we did, though I cannot remember them.'

Felix was eventually sacked from Ayer's after they had lost the Ford Motor Company account, and he took the opportunity to escape from Peggy's suffocating embrace. Curtis Bok, a seemingly complaisant husband, lent him $100 to buy an old car, and he headed out west to the San Joaquin Valley in California. Always well-connected thanks to Eppy's business contacts, he went to stay with the Guthries, who owned a fruit-picking business. Like the other pickers, he earned a mere 25 cents an hour, but 'I knew full well that if ever I was in real trouble I need only cable my father and he would bail me out.' He was shocked by the way perfectly good fruit was dumped in order to keep up the price, and tried to stand up for his fellow-workers. Like a voice from a distant and very different world, Peggy bombarded him with desperate letters ('You are my very life, my every hope. You are my GOD'). But the time had come to head back home. The Guthries provided him with a free ticket to New York via the Panama Canal, and from there he returned to England. Working in the soup kitchen and with the fruit pickers had pricked what proved to be a tender social conscience, and before long he would be making his name and reputation as a radical and – in the eyes of the Establishment – subversive public figure.

★

Hugh's apotheosis as a radical and subversive figure would occur a good thirty years later, albeit in the same organisation that would soon be employing Felix; but before he could embark on a career, he had to complete his education. His parents decided that he should learn German before going on to Oxford – a shrewd decision with huge implications for his future – and he was despatched to the small university town of Marburg. It was his first trip abroad, and 'I can see myself, a very thin and shy youth of eighteen, in a corner of a third-class carriage, trying on a very hot day to keep a window open against the protests of my fellow-travellers.' He lodged with an old-fashioned, very formal family, much given to bowing and the shaking of hands, and was taught German by a Fraulein Dietzen, who had the 'long, thin, bearded face of an ancient and dyspeptic goat.' When not learning German he wandered through the surrounding woods, visited unaltered mediaeval villages, and translated

Catullus for 'a beautiful and wanton (though unfortunately not with me) English girl with whom I was very much in love.'

Usefully equipped with a good grounding in German, he returned home to take up his classical postmastership (i.e. scholarship) at Merton College, Oxford. The college was 'noted for its ancient dons, smelling of dust and cheese, for gaiety, for hard drinking and gentlemanly homosexuality', and Hugh took to the drinking at least with huge enthusiasm. 'Mr Greene, sir, up the pole again last night,' his scout once reported after Hugh had enjoyed a night on the tiles. 'Had to clear up a terrible mess in the fireplace.' He made more noise than most when climbing into college, and was once spotted waving a sabre. On one occasion he and Raymond drove over to Little Wittenham to visit Eva and Eppy: Hugh, suffering no doubt from the night before, was violently sick on arrival, and Eva told Felix that 'he looked the strangest sight, half lying on the couch in the hall with his endless legs, snow-white face, very pink nose and all those incredible curls.' Because of his great height, he had a special bed delivered to his rooms in college; unlike Raymond and Graham, he was never good-looking: he had a penchant for German girls in particular, and a taste for the risqué and the avant-garde.

Hugh started out reading classics, but after deciding against German on the grounds that he couldn't face having to read Kant, he switched to English for his last two years. He studied Anglo-Saxon under Neville Coghill, but became particularly friendly with the gnome-like poet Edmund Blunden, best known as the author of *Undertones of War*, who had recently been appointed a tutor in English at Merton, and took him to visit Graham and Vivien, who had recently moved to a cottage in the Cotswolds. He enjoyed *Beowulf* and *Sir Gawaine and the Green Knight*, and became an expert on the seventeenth century, and Dryden in particular: 'If I was able as a journalist to express myself with clarity, I would give credit to Dryden's "Essays" coming on top of Latin and Anglo-Saxon,' he declared in later life. He wrote his weekly essays in the bath while heartier contemporaries were playing games; early on in his time at Oxford he tried his hand at rowing, but gave it up after getting a boil on his buttocks, and dismissed it thereafter as 'a sport fit only for galley slaves'.

He involved himself in university journalism and, like Graham before him, tried to persuade well-known names to contribute. 'Beware of university journalism, fatal to firsts,' Graham warned him. 'I don't think I can be much use to you. I no longer know Edith Sitwell – have not seen or heard from her since I went down. De la Mare the same. One has to know somebody very well to ask him or her to contribute for nothing to somebody else's magazine.' And, like Graham, he also contributed to non-university newspapers. In 1959 the *Oxford Mail* finally paid him the three shillings it owed him for covering a fire in Finstock thirty years before, half-a-crown of which was the fee for eighteen lines, and sixpence the cost of phoning them through. But his real passion was for films. He reviewed them for *Cherwell*, and founded the Oxford University Film Society. He took over a cinema in Headington for a season of silent films, and, as President of OUFS, made frequent trips to Soho to pick up new releases and the occasional gift of a cigar from distributors in Wardour Street. These expeditions to London had to be authorised by Dr Bowman, the Warden of Merton, a reclusive character who only went into college for the annual Boar's Head dinner and end of term collections. Hugh would dutifully knock on the door of the Warden's lodgings and be greeted by an ancient butler who, appropriately enough, looked exactly like Boris Karloff. The ancient butler would set off, very slowly, up a steep flight of stairs to consult the Warden, and reappear some ten minutes later to announce that 'The Warden says you may go, Sir.' Hugh was convinced that he never delivered the message: it was the ritual that mattered.

The Electra Cinema, where OUFS films were shown, was run by a Mr Roberts, who boasted a blond moustache. Hugh was smitten by Mrs Roberts, and on more than one occasion he was duly embarrassed when the commissionaire boomed out 'Mrs Roberts will be twenty minutes late, sir.' Mr Roberts, for his part, was rather taken with the actress Hermione Baddeley, a frequent visitor to Oxford, and would chase her round the foyer shouting 'I want Hermione badly'. (On a visit to Oxford, Graham recorded having 'obnoxious cocktails at Hugh's till dinner. Barbara was there, also Hermione Baddeley, looking like the vulgarest little street woman.') When not pining after Mrs Roberts or reading Dryden, Hugh would sometimes see two films a day, noting their titles, directors and stars in his diary and marking them 'alpha minus', 'beta plus' or worse. He had a particular liking for German films – after seeing Fritz Lang's *The Spy* in Tunbridge Wells while on vacation with his parents in Crowborough, he declared that 'three of the main interests of my life immediately coalesced: Germany, films, espionage' – but he was not above showing his members Walt Disney's 'Silly Symphonies'.

Despite this ardent film watching, Hugh was 'mildly disappointed' not to get a first. Blunden told him he almost made it, but the examiners were 'shocked by my excessive quotations from indecent poems', in particular from Lord Rochester, a poet both Hugh and Graham greatly admired. 'It would have been a superhuman feat to have got a first as well as run the Film Society, but that doesn't make it less maddening,' Graham told him by way of consolation, after reading the results in *The Times*. Brooding on the matter many years later, Hugh reckoned that, with a first under his belt, he could easily have slipped into academic life: he had wanted to write a thesis on a virtually unknown seventeenth-century writer called Katherine Phillips, 'stressing her lesbian characteristics', and had he remained in Oxford 'perhaps I should have produced some learned editions of forgotten seventeenth-century poets.' But it was not to be. Away from academia, Graham promised to have a word with Rupert Hart-Davis about jobs in publishing. Ian Parsons of Chatto & Windus had offered Graham a position, which he turned down 'very reluctantly, because I've always wanted to be in a publishing office . . . if I had been living in London, I could have gone gently on with my own work of an evening, but as it is my evening would be spent in getting home.' Parsons then mentioned an 'apprentice job' in the firm, suitable for someone who had just left university, but he couldn't pay more than £300 a year. Both Graham and Hugh would work in publishing at various times, as would other members of the Greene family, but for the time being Hugh would have to look elsewhere. He wondered about going into the film business, on the production side rather than as an aspiring director, and wangled introductions to Michael Balcon and to Sam Eckman, the cigar-puffing head of MGM's London office, but nothing came of them, while Alan Cameron, Elizabeth Bowen's husband, told Graham that there was 'nothing doing' at the Film Institute (lacking, as yet, its 'British' prefix). As it turned out it was Graham, rather than Hugh, who would make his mark in the cinema – as a prolific and outspoken film critic, as a scriptwriter and as a novelist and short-story writer, many of whose works were made into films. But then Edmund Blunden, who took a paternal interest in his students, put Hugh on to Kingsley Martin, the editor of the *New Statesman*, and thereafter he never looked back.

Aspects of England

Not long after he'd handed in his resignation at *The Times*, Graham, Vivien and a highly-strung Pekinese went to live in a tiny thatched cottage at the end of a muddy lane on the outskirts of Chipping Campden in Gloucestershire. It had no electric lights, rats scuttled about in the roof, there were apple trees in the garden, and they paid a pound a week in rent. Graham's arrangement with Heinemann and Doubleday had, in theory, enabled him to try his luck as a full-time writer and bought him the time to work on his novels. Like many young couples before or since, they may well have had fantasies about the bucolic life, far removed from the strain and aggravation of the city. Hugh was still at Oxford and was a frequent visitor: he and Graham went for enormous walks together, stopping off at pubs for lunches of beer, bread, cheese and – a particular Greene favourite – sausages. When not writing or reading – he worked his way through a prodigious quantity of books in his country incarnation – Graham grew lettuces, gathered blackberries, played chess, brewed parsnip wine and, when necessary, wormed the Pekinese. Hugh was sick out of a window after an excess of cider; their visitors included Eppy, Eva, Raymond, Edmund Blunden and Sir Graham Greene, by now in his late seventies. They visited Little Wittenham, where Hugh played tennis with Barbara while Graham read a book. His physical self-consciousness and sense of inadequacy about any form of games or sport were as evident as ever. He refused to join in when David Higham and his wife insisted on swimming in a nearby pool, and attributed this to 'what I suffered in the baths at school, not physical suffering but mental, when I was alone in being unable to swim.'

If Graham's ailments were anything to go by, country life was far from idyllic. He suffered at various times from asthma, hay fever and a twitching eyelid, and despite Raymond's reassurances he still worried that his occasional fainting fits were evidence of epilepsy. 'My faintings are preceded always by physical revulsion,' he noted in his diary: he claimed that his 'last medically recognised fit' had been in 1929, when he had a steel splinter removed from his eye, and that he had fainted while watching the film version of *All Quiet on the Western Front*. 'My nerves horribly on edge,' he noted after spending a day waiting for Vivien in a rainswept Oxford: 'that feeling of lurking madness, of something swelling in the brain and wanting to burst; every sound, however small, made by anyone else, the clink of a fork on a plate, piercing the brain like a knife.' He suffered from insomnia as well, recording how 'the noise of mice in the thatch, the flutter of moths against the glass, are enough to keep me awake, terrified.' Years later, long after he and Vivien had gone their separate ways, he paid tribute to 'the courage and understanding of my wife who never complained of this dangerous cul-de-sac into which I had led her from the safe easy high road we had been travelling while I remained on *The Times*.'

And, like most freelance writers, he was always worried about money. He told Hugh that they'd love to have him to stay, but 'we are on the verge of bankruptcy', so much so that they would have to charge guests, including family members, half-a-crown a night to cover the costs. He even pawned a bust of Shakespeare for £2. On learning that Raymond had been awarded a Schorstein research fellowship at Oxford to investigate the effects of extreme cold and high altitudes on the human body, worth £200 a year on top of his earnings as a GP, he wrote 'I felt great and genuine pleasure at the news. Was it quite disinterested, or did I take it as a sign that good fortune had not quite deserted the family?' An obvious solution to their problems was for him to find a job. He answered an advertisement for an assistant editor on the *Observer*, but nothing came of it; he was treated with such condescension by the editor of the *Catholic Herald*, which had advertised for a sub-editor, that 'since then I have taken a biased view of Catholic journalism and Catholic humanity.' Robin Barrington-Ward, the deputy editor of *The Times*, refused to have him back, and nothing came of an approach to a university in Bangkok, where an Oxford friend was teaching. A new friend, Rupert Hart-Davis, now entered the picture. Graham had talked to Hart-Davis, then an editor at Heinemann, about a possible biography of Lord Rochester, and they immediately got on: 'Graham is very unattractive, but I like something about him,' Hart-Davis confided to his diary. Hart-Davis had found Charles Evans a difficult and ungenerous employer, jealously guarding his patch and unwilling to advance the careers of younger colleagues, and had resigned from Heinemann. Hamish Hamilton then wangled him a job with Jonathan Cape, but in the meantime he had been offered a temporary job at the Book Society, and Graham, still employing the feline phraseology associated with letters to and from Vivien, decided to sound him out. 'I want to approach you, on padded feet, with whiskers tentatively advanced, ready to retreat at the first sign,' he declared. 'If for some reason you decide not to apply for, or if, more unaccountably, you fail to get appointed by the Book Society, could you at once let me know and I shall try for the job?' Hart-Davis decided to take up the Book Society's offer, but could help in other ways. One of his closest friends was Peter Fleming, then on the staff of the *Spectator*. Fleming asked Graham to review novels on a regular basis, and the raffish Derek Verschoyle, a future literary editor of the magazine, accepted 'Death in the Cotswolds', a piece about Charley Sykes, a tramp-like figure who had been found frozen to death in his cottage and was revealed to have been, in an earlier incarnation, a well-heeled graduate of St John's College, Oxford.

The *Spectator* was to loom large in Graham's journalistic career, but book reviewing has never been a well-paid business, and Graham found it hard to avoid a sense that 'my three guaranteed years of security had been squandered.' *The Name of Action* and *Rumour at Nightfall* had been commercial disasters – *Rumour at Nightfall* sold a mere 1200 copies – but because the annual salary paid him by Heinemann and Doubleday was advanced against royalties on all the titles published by them, he could find himself, if the novels continued to sell so badly, writing books for no return. It was not surprising, given his early experiences, that he later became such a hard bargainer with publishers, keeping a keen eye on every aspect of the business from blurbs and jackets to publicity photo-graphs and foreign rights, or that he came to set such store on selling the film rights in his work, converting his long-standing interest in the cinema into a useful source of income. But his dissatisfaction with the two novels he wrote in the Cotswolds was literary as well as financial. In later years he refused to allow either book to be reprinted. 'There is no spark of life in *The Name of Action* or *Rumour at Nightfall* because there was nothing of myself in them,' he wrote in his autobiography. Not only had he tried too hard to avoid writing covert autobiography, but both books were, he confessed, horribly overwritten and far too much under the influence of Joseph Conrad. 'An unfavourable criticism by Frank Swinnerton opened my eyes to the defects of what I believed to be true art, and so reality, blessed reality, broke through,' but by then it was too late, in monetary terms at least. Nor were his finances or his morale improved when Heinemann rejected as obscene *Mr Rochester's Monkey*, his biography of the lewd seventeenth-century Restoration poet. John Hayward, who was confined to a wheelchair and was a close friend of T. S. Eliot, had earlier edited a privately published collection of Rochester's poems, and gave Graham help and advice; they remained friends, and Graham's biography was eventually published, in a lavishly illustrated edition, in 1974.

In 1931, the year in which *Rumour at Nightfall* was published, Graham 'deliberately set out to write a book to please, one which with luck might be made into a film'. He decided to set it on the Orient Express: although, in the interests of research, he took a train to the German border, and on to Cologne free of charge, he couldn't afford to take the Orient Express all the way to Istanbul. 'The best I could do was to buy a record of Honegger's *Pacific 231* which I hoped, when I played it daily, would take me far enough away from my thatched cottage, a Pekinese dog which suffered from hysteria, some barren apple trees, the muddy lane and a row of Cos lettuces.' The novel was completed the following summer, and delivered to the publishers. Graham opened a letter from Heinemann with 'trembling hands', and was delighted to learn that Charles Evans liked it. *Stamboul Train* was to become, rightly, one of Graham's most popular novels, but in later years he found it impossible to read, since 'the pages are too laden by the anxieties of the time and the sense of failure.' Nor would it necessarily solve his money problems. It was the third in a three-book contract, and would have to do exceptionally well to make up for the low royalties earned by its predecessors. Although Heinemann agreed to pay him a further £300 by way of an annual salary, Doubleday were only prepared to stump up two months' worth, and not a penny more, and as far as Heinemann were concerned, 'any losses were to be made up on future books, so that if *Stamboul Train* fails, I may have to write two books for no payment whatever. I found myself close to tears.' Rupert Hart-Davis paid a visit to Chipping Campden and, 'under the influence of sun and parsnip wine', told Graham that, in his new role as assistant to Alan Bott, the boss of the Book Society, he would do his best to advance the cause of *Stamboul Train*. He wasn't on the panel of selectors, so he couldn't vote on the matter, but he was, even then, famed for his charm and his powers of persuasion, and their mutual friend Edmund Blunden, who had just replaced J. B. Priestley on the panel, had promised to do what he could to help. The Book Society had been founded three years earlier in 1929: unlike the book clubs which sprang up later in the thirties, it did not sell books to its members at a discount – they were expected to pay the full price – but its imprimatur carried great weight with the middlebrow reading public and could add a substantial number of copies to the original publisher's print run, and convert what might have been a modest loss into a welcome profit. But Heinemann 'offered little hope of the Book Society' because of a lesbian character in the novel, allegedly modelled on Graham's friend Clemence Dane, whom he had met through Kenneth Richmond and who was on the Society's panel of selectors. They were wrong, as it turned out: of the five selectors, Hart-Davis reported, Hugh Walpole was 'delighted' with the book, Robert Lynd agreed with him, Clemence Dane was reluctantly opposed, George Gordon, the President of Magdalen, was extremely hostile, and Blunden, for all his warm words, was feebly in favour. The print run was increased by a further 10,000 copies, and Doubleday agreed to join Heinemann in funding Graham for another full year. Graham presented Hart-Davis with the corrected typescript of the book, and many years later, when funds were low, Hart-Davis sold it for £500, with its author's blessing.

J. B. Priestley may have left the selection panel, but he was not done with *Stamboul Train*. There was no love lost between him and Graham: Graham had been outraged by Priestley's affair with Hart-Davis's first wife, Peggy Ashcroft, and 'Jolly Jack' may have scented his disapproval. Derek Verschoyle then asked Graham to review Priestley's new novel, *Faraway*, in the *Spectator*. Graham thought it 'a piece of sheer impertinence even to his public, so padded and slackly written and childishly constructed', but was dissuaded from putting his thoughts into print by the worldly David Higham, who pointed out that Priestley was one of Heinemann's best-selling authors, and that for Graham to attack him in public would do him no good with his publishers, who had not yet given him a contract for his next novel. But although that particular hazard had been avoided, Priestley and Graham were doomed to do battle. Priestley wrote to Charles Evans after reading a proof of *Stamboul Train* to say that he would sue them and Graham for libel if they published the book as it stood. He objected to the figure of Quin Savory, a blunt, pipe-smoking, man-of-the-people best-selling novelist, and insisted that he would press ahead unless Graham agreed to remove all references to Dickens (with whom Priestley had been compared), pipe-smoking and blunt fingers. 'His family had all recognised him in it,' Graham told his mother, 'and the fact that neither his publishers nor his friends at the Book Society seem to have spotted him did not make him waver.' Graham suggested that he and Heinemann should counter-sue, but Heinemann would have none of it. In purely commercial terms, Graham was a lightweight in comparison to Priestley, and might would prevail. 13,000 copies of the novel had already been printed and bound, so urgent action had to be taken. Graham spent the large part of a day in a phonebox, ringing through changes and corrections; the bound copies were then unstitched and dismantled so that the revised material could be inserted. Priestley and Compton Mackenzie gave *Stamboul Train* hostile reviews, and Graham himself told Mrs Belloc Lowndes that he had 'never been more uncertain of a book', but most of the reviews were enthusiastic, and were reflected in its sales. Not surprisingly, perhaps, Graham had a nightmare in which he murdered Priestley 'and was arrested at the Times Book Club and taken away in a Black Maria'.

One welcome by-product of *Stamboul Train* was an improvement in the family finances. The film rights had been sold to MGM, and in the spring of 1933 Graham received a cheque for £1738. He sent Molly £35 so she could take her brood on holiday, but he and Vivien had need of every penny: for all their talk of a chaste marriage, Vivien was pregnant, and Graham was appalled at the idea. 'Wrote to Raymond about it. I know so little about such things,' he confided to his diary after an earlier intimation of pregnancy. 'It may be nothing at all, but it represents to me the most horrible possibilities.' Children didn't fit in with his way of life or his cast of mind, then or later, nor would he ever claim to have been more than a remote and largely absent father, happy to write out cheques when called for but shying away from any emotional or practical involvement: a familiar pattern, perhaps, with writers in particular, who are self-absorbed, think of little else but their work, and are essentially loners, combining kindness and generosity to friends and acquaintances with an inability, or reluctance, to assume the responsibilities of a parent. 'I can't bear her suffering, and any child will be an intrusion. I'm trying to resign myself to it,' he noted in his diary. Halfway through Vivien's pregnancy her mother died, unexpectedly, of an embolism. They were in Wales at the time: Vivien, Graham reported, was 'terribly broken', letting out a 'horrible high cry' when the news came through. Writing to Vivien's uncle to explain her absence from the funeral – a doctor had advised her not to make the long journey to London – Graham admitted that 'her mother and I did not care for one another.' A month or two later, Felix and Kate, his youngest sister, drove them over to Little Wittenham, where 'Aunt Eva was lavishingly gushing and sentimentalising about Vivien's pregnancy.' Lucy Caroline was born four days after Christmas 1933: Vivien had hoped for a son but, Graham told his mother, 'I don't care a brass farthing either way, perhaps I incline a little towards a girl, but I don't like to see her disappointed.' Vivien's wish would be granted three years later when their son Francis was born.

Vivien may or may not have imbibed some of her mother's disgust about sex, but like many Englishmen of the time, Graham may well have regarded sex and marriage as incompatible, and from early on in their marriage he sought relief elsewhere. After a visit to Heinemann he 'went up and down Bond Street looking at the whores', and seems to have established a regular relationship with a girl called A., with rooms in Warren Street. In *Ways of Escape* he suggests that he met A – the 'Annette' of *England Made Me* – through Herbert, and Tooter may also have availed himself of her services. Whether Vivien suspected what Graham got up to on his visits to London is something we may never know, but she would be dreadfully hurt in the years ahead by his repeated infidelities, and withdrew, to some extent, into a make-believe world manifested in her love of Victoriana – flushed with cash from the success of *Stamboul Train*, Graham bought her an intricate Victorian needle-case, and her famous collection of dolls' houses. Graham became convinced at one point that Fred Hart, a neighbour in the village, had fallen in love with Vivien, and suggested that this would have proved 'a trying position for an elderly, old-fashioned and terribly upright man'. For Vivien to be involved with someone else might have made him feel better about his own increasingly frequent affairs, but she was to remain faithful to him, and married to him, for the rest of his life.

On a visit to Chipping Campden, Hugh told Graham things about their family which he had never known before, including Benjamin Buck Greene's governorship of the Bank of England, their great-uncle Charles's amorous escapades on St Kitts, and their paternal grandfather's sad and hopeless life. 'One sees his blood coming out in Herbert,' Graham noted, apropos the way in which William Greene had frittered away such money as came his way; the fact that Herbert still expected to be funded and bailed out by his parents remained a source of worry and aggravation. 'I'm terribly sorry to hear that Herbert's returning,' Graham wrote to his mother. 'I hope you won't let him settle for long at Incents on a permanent invitation. It's painful to think of the comparative peace you've had at Crowborough being disturbed. A cottage sufficiently far away for you both to be able to forget him, for at any rate hours at a time . . . It does seem preposterous that Da should have to go on paying out in order to allow Herbert to play tennis and cricket. I can't help hoping that your feelings are sufficiently chilled to confine relations with him to purely business ones at a distance.' His parents were nothing like as well off as Eppy and Eva, and although he was to outlive his younger brother, Charles's health was none too good. He had diabetes, and Marion had to keep him on a strict diet and make sure she injected him with insulin every day. 'Marion was the driving force,' Vivien remembered. 'I think she was fonder of [Charles] and her two daughters than of anybody. It was everything for Charlie. He smoked very much and everything smelt of pipe tobacco. He played chess by himself or by correspondence. He sort of mumbled about. He was a sweet old thing, but I don't think he had much to say for himself.' 'The more I see him the more I admire his great uncomplaining spirit,' Eva told Felix, and in Herbert he had plenty to complain about. Graham felt, very strongly, that his parents should not be left to deal with Herbert's monetary demands, and that the younger generation should help out. He offered to pay £10 a month towards his brother's expenses, and as he became increasingly prosperous and successful in the years ahead, he took over the role of paymaster general, not only subsidising Herbert but, when times were hard or school fees had to be met, writing cheques with the same self-effacing generosity with which he provided moral and financial support to young writers starting out on their careers.

His own career, in the meantime, was beginning to take flight. The *Spectator* asked him to review a biography of Ivan Kreuger, the Swedish match tycoon who had built up an empire and eventually committed suicide. It provided a germ of inspiration for *England Made Me*, the novel in which a lightly disguised Herbert loomed large, and Graham and Hugh travelled to Sweden together to soak up the atmosphere of Stockholm. That same summer of 1933, Graham and Vivien exchanged their cottage in the Cotswolds for a flat in North Oxford, off the Woodstock Road. Vivien began to make friends among Oxford academics and their wives – her friends included John Sparrow and Lord David Cecil – while Graham, as a member of the ILP, agitated on behalf of poorly paid college servants. He flew, for the first time, to Paris, and told Hugh that he had become 'passionately addicted' to air travel – an addiction he would indulge to the full in the years ahead. The success of *Stamboul Train* enabled him to make the transition from a young writer of promise to a familiar figure on the literary scene. 'I seem to have gatecrashed into the highbrow citadels,' he wrote after being asked to review T. S. Eliot's *After Strange Gods* for Desmond MacCarthy's well-regarded literary magazine, *Life and Letters*. Rupert Hart-Davis, now an editor at Jonathan Cape, commissioned him to edit *The Old School*, an anthology of essays in which writers looked back on their schooldays with varying degrees of nostalgia or disdain. Graham himself wrote about Berkhamsted, and Derek Verschoyle tried to recall his time at Malvern: other contributors included W. H. Auden, Anthony Powell, Elizabeth Bowen, Harold Nicolson, Antonia White, H. E. Bates, William Plomer, Stephen Spender and Seán Ó'Faoláin. Graham had been grounded for three years after leaving *The Times*, but now he was airborne at last.

★

One evening, while still living in Chipping Campden, Graham spent an evening in London with Tooter, Barbara and Felix. 'How extraordinarily nice Barbara is!' Graham told his mother, but fond as he always was of Tooter, he found Felix 'rather trying'. A couple of years later he paid a visit to Broadcasting House: he met, among others, the writer and future editor of the *Listener*, J. R. Ackerley, but 'of course the ubiquitous Felix tried to push his way to the fore.' Felix's cousins may have found him irritating, even bumptious, but he had reason to feel pleased with himself. Like Graham, he was making his name in a highly competitive world: since his return from America he had established himself as one of the rising stars of the BBC while still in his early twenties.

Felix had set his sights, initially, on a career in politics, and, like Ben before him, he came into the orbit of the former Labour leader, Ramsay MacDonald. The Great Depression was at its nadir, and in 1931 MacDonald, as Prime Minister, had lost the support of most of his colleagues in the Labour Party by sticking to the gold standard and cutting pay to the unemployed. He had been expelled from the Party, and had disgraced himself further in the eyes of his former colleagues by agreeing to lead a National Government which included Conservatives, headed by Stanley Baldwin, as well as a beleaguered rump of National Labour MPs. Felix had become very friendly with MacDonald's daughter Sheila, a shy, sweet-natured girl; she was almost certainly very keen on him, so much so that mutual friends expected them to announce their engagement at any moment. Felix lunched once a week at No.10 and was allowed to wander into the house and make his way up to Sheila's room whenever he liked. Security was lax in those days, and in the early months of his premiership MacDonald, who was reluctant to move into Downing Street, had travelled to work by Tube from his home in Belsize Park. Both Ben and Felix stood for Parliament in the 1931 general election, and both were unsuccessful. Ben stood for the Labour Party in Gravesend, and described himself in his nomination papers as a 'works manager', which sounded more proletarian than 'managing director'. Felix, who firmly endorsed his girlfriend's father – 'I stand firmly behind the Prime Minister's manifesto to the nation,' he told the electorate – stood for the South-East Essex constituency. 'We used to be rather embarrassed when little boys ran after him in the street singing the then-popular Felix the Cat song "Felix kept on walking, kept on walking . . .",' Barbara recalled, adding that 'when heckled he used to simply answer "My dear man, you don't know what you're talking about" and left the questions unanswered.' Despite his failure to be elected, Felix continued for a time to be involved in National Labour politics. He was put on the National Labour Committee in February 1932, editing a fortnightly newsletter with Clifford Allen and attending the Geneva Disarmament Conference. Nothing came of his romance with Sheila – no doubt Felix, as ever, found it hard to match words with action and backed away – but although he remained friends with the MacDonalds, he became increasingly disillusioned with party politics. He told his parents that he found it increasingly hard to defend Ramsay MacDonald; National Labour had become 'a futile body, and I hate to be associated with a futile body.'

He was still in touch with Peggy Bok and her husband, and in 1932 he visited the Soviet Union with Curtis Bok. Like Shaw, the Webbs and countless other well-disposed idealists, he was bowled over by what he saw. Kulaks were being starved and murdered in their thousands, and their farms forcibly collectivised, but, Felix told his parents, 'It astonishes me that a country as strong and alive and vital as this one should have been for so long the subject of such consistent misrepresentation throughout the world. Here industry is steaming full-speed ahead, the country is humming like a busy factory, and behind it all is a spirit of enthusiasm which carries the people beyond their privation, even beyond their hunger, and which will in the end be undefeatable . . . I wish you could be here with me: the spirit of enterprise and courage and stupendous enthusiasm would appeal to you as much as it does to myself.' Thirty years later, Felix would be even more rapturous about Chairman Mao and Communist China, but in the meantime, the Russian secret police, hoping that Curtis Bok could influence his family newspapers to take a more pro-Soviet line, arranged a 'honeytrap' in the form of an agent named Tania, who seduced him on a cruise down the Volga. Curtis declared himself in love; he decided to stay on in Moscow with Tania, and Felix returned home alone. A year later he received an urgent message from Peggy to say that Curtis was keen to return. Felix flew out to Moscow, but was unable to find his friend. By pure chance he bumped into Curtis on the street: he had lost his papers, but somehow Felix spirited him out of Russia on a British passport. Despite Felix's mercy dash, the Boks' marriage was over, and in due course Tania made her own way out, and was reunited with her lover.

Felix, for his part, became briefly involved in prison reform, and gave a series of lectures in Wormwood Scrubs. He was shocked to discover that his well-meaning, kindly parents rented out poor-quality property in Abingdon, and could be described as slum landlords. Eager to put such thoughts behind him, he made the first of many visits to Dartington Hall, the progressive school in Devon, which he came to see as a 'spiritual home'. Its founders, the Elmhirsts, were friends of the Boks: Mrs Elmhirst had been earlier married to Willard Straight, the American railroad millionaire; their son, Michael, would be involved with the notorious Cambridge spies and, years later, play a critical role in the exposure of Anthony Blunt as the 'fourth man'. Like Sheila MacDonald before her, the Straights' daughter fell for Felix. Nothing came of it, but in due course Felix persuaded Ben and Leslie Greene to send their daughters to Dartington. A frequent visitor to Dartington was the writer and mystic Gerald Heard, who worked at the BBC, and was to play an important part in Felix's life. Short, with bright blue eyes and a jutting beard, he was thought by E. M. Forster to have 'one of the most penetrating minds in England', while Evelyn Waugh rated him 'the cleverest man in England'. According to Forster's biographer, P. N. Furbank, 'He was reported to read two thousand books a year and had an extraordinary flow of information about hygiene, sex, paranormal phenomena and the probable destiny of mankind. He was a dress-fetishist, favouring purple suede shoes and leather jackets with leopard-skin collars, and he had his eyelids painted with what looked like mascara (actually a specific against conjunctivitis). Strangers thought of him, nervously, as a sort of Wellsian super-mind or "man of the future".' Felix met him through the Elmhirsts, and he in turn introduced Felix to Sir John Reith, the Director-General of the BBC, and to Lionel Fielden and Charles Siepmann of the BBC's Talks Department. Felix was bright, ambitious and personable, and before long he was offered a job.

The Talks Department had been set up in 1927, and had soon established a reputation as the most exciting and innovative branch of the BBC. Hilda Matheson, its founder and presiding genius, was a firm believer in socialism, feminism and modernism, commissioning talks from Bernard Shaw, H. G. Wells, Julian Huxley, John Maynard Keynes, Beatrice and Sidney Webb and other luminaries of a liberal and leftwards-leaning persuasion. In 1932 she was replaced by her deputy, Charles Siepmann, who enjoyed stirring up controversy, shared her concern with social questions, and increased the size of the department. His assistants included Felix, Lionel Fielden and Peter Fleming . The BBC was anxious to investigate the 'condition of England' in the early 1930s, and its findings both complemented and preceded the revelations made later in the decade by socially aware institutions and individuals such as Mass Observation, *Picture Post*, the film-makers John Grierson, Paul Rotha and Humphrey Jennings, and the photographer Humphrey Spender, as well as by writers like George Orwell, J. B. Priestley and Walter Greenwood. In 1931 William Beveridge gave a series of talks on unemployment, and afterwards he told Siepmann that he 'should have liked the leisure to make them a little more human', interlacing statistics and economics with accounts of what it was like to be unemployed and on the dole in the worst-hit areas of South Wales and North-East England. The following year A. D. Lindsay, the leftwards-leaning Master of Balliol, gave a talk on 'Helping the Unemployed to Help Themselves' in which he touched on the psychological damage inflicted on those who found themselves out of work. Unemployment reached a high point of three million in the winter of 1932–3, and Lindsay reminded his listeners that its casualties included skilled workers, craftsmen, office workers and professional people as well as the feckless and the unemployable. In December the National Council for Social Services organised a giant rally at which the Prince of Wales called for voluntary efforts to help the unemployed; in a broadcast that same month Ramsay MacDonald said that 'never before has the mass of the poverty-stricken contained so large a proportion of the really deserving,' and appealed for 'the discovery of the community of friendship'. At the same time he tried to placate trade unionists and those on the Left who were calling for state action, and dismissed the emphasis on charitable and voluntary work – as advocated by Reith and the Prince of Wales – as mere middle-class condescension.

With Reith's encouragement, the Talks Department began to devote more time to the unemployed and their problems. In 1933 S. P. B. Mais, a former headmaster and a prolific author, inaugurated a series of talks entitled 'SOS'. The first of the eleven reports was introduced by the Prince of Wales. 'Here is an SOS message, probably the most important you will ever hear, and it vitally concerns you,' he declared, before going on to inform his listeners that they were 'called upon to create an entirely new social order'. Howard Marshall talked to slum-dwellers for his programmes on 'Other People's Houses'. Both series adopted an apolitical tone, stressing good neighbourliness and voluntary schemes, with Mais in particular requesting help from vicars, schoolmasters and other embodiments of the middle-class social conscience, and urging his listeners to get in touch with unemployed families, donate money and clothes, and even pay the occasional milk bill. Both were denounced by right-wingers for inciting Bolshevism, and by the left wing – in particular Wal Hannington, the organiser of the National Hunger March – as embodying a middle-class conspiracy to keep the lower orders in their place, and neutralise any political threat to the established order.

Taking up the cause of the unemployed appealed to all Felix's frustrated idealism. After the *Listener* had published a series of articles entitled 'Memoirs of the Unemployed', in which a miner, a factory worker and others described their experiences of being out of work, it was decided that the Talks Department should do something along the same lines. Felix was put in charge of the operation, and visited the most afflicted areas, calling at pubs, clubs and labour exchanges. He was appalled by what he saw. 'I remember the shock I received on my first visit to the north,' he recalled. 'I had come by train from London to one of the smaller Lancashire towns. It was raining when I left the station, and it was dark, and down the street hundreds of mill girls were passing on their way from home to work. Watching them I realised that I was in a country quite new to me. These girls, with shawls on their heads and wooden clogs on their feet, and speaking a language I could hardly understand, were (I had to remind myself) English.' In Gateshead he visited a row of 'diseased and rotting cottages', and 'groping my way up the dark flight of stairs I could feel the uneven boarding give beneath each step. The very bricks stank of damp and decay. In one of the upper flats I found that the roof had fallen in and the family sat huddled in the remaining room. Downstairs a woman said, "Come and look in here. This is how we have to live." There were eight or nine people in the room. A man was cooking potatoes over a stove which made the atmosphere hot and foetid. Two or three children were playing on the floor which was covered with dirt, and on the bed lay a young mother with a newborn child.' In a two-roomed flat, 'the ceiling was damp and the plaster leaking, and the damp was also coming through the walls. A broken windowpane was covered with paper and the floorboards were rotting . . . I saw no tap and asked where she got her water. She pointed down a long flight of steps to the back yard.'

Felix was a pioneer of what came to be known as 'social action broadcasting'. Asking members of the public to describe their experiences over the air is something we take for granted, but he was venturing into unknown territory: it was one thing to invite academics, writers and public figures to ventilate their views through carefully scripted radio talks, but persuading working-class housewives and unemployed miners to talk about their lives was a very different matter. Later in the decade, innovative radio journalists like Richard Dimbleby would adopt more familiar broadcasting techniques, thrusting a microphone forward and recording what was said, but Felix was more cautious and less direct. He interviewed his subjects as informally as possible in advance of any broadcast: a secretary took down what was said in shorthand, and once this had been agreed with the subjects, they would be invited down to Broadcasting House, where they would say their pieces as per the script. Felix's 'Time to Spare' programmes were broadcast on Saturday evenings – the peak listening time – between April and June 1934. Each programme lasted twenty-five minutes: a fifteen-minute statement by an unemployed man or woman was followed by an expert giving advice. Felix's timing could not have been better: the series began shortly before the third and final reading of an Unemployment Bill, and immediately provoked the kind of nationwide controversy that any journalist dreams of. Labour MPs referred to the programme's findings when attacking the National Government over the notorious and widely resented means test; an MP used the talks to ridicule Government claims that the unemployed were better off than they were because of a fall in the cost of living, citing a family of four living off dole payments of eight shillings a week; the Ministry of Labour did battle with the BBC hierarchy, claiming that the figures quoted in the programme were incomplete and unrepresentative. The *Daily Herald* reported that the Cabinet was thinking of stopping the talks – '"Time to Spare" is shattering too many illusions. Millions are being turned against the Government' – and Sir John Reith, the Director-General, was summoned to Downing Street and told to discontinue the series. He informed the Prime Minister that if that was the case, he would order announcers to tell the listening public that a half-hour silence was about to follow because the Government had refused to allow the unemployed to express their opinions. MacDonald caved in, and Reith agreed that, in the final programme, the Government should be given some credit, and time to put forward its point of view. As it turned out, the final talk was given by A. D. Lindsay: Siepmann was anxious that it should not seem to reflect Government policy, and Lindsay made little use of the official material provided by the Ministry of Labour.

Writing in the *Radio Times*, Felix told his listeners that agreeing to take part in his programme called for a degree of courage, since 'there are neighbours who will gossip, and the Press who will worry one, and the Public Assistance Officers who will make enquiries.' R. S. Hudson, the Parliamentary Secretary to the Ministry of Labour, was determined to discredit those who had participated in the programmes. He claimed that the BBC had failed to check its facts, had omitted essential details, and had chosen to interview men and women who were both unreliable and unrepresentative. Hudson's especial ire was directed at a Mrs Pallis in Jarrow and a Mr Evans in South Wales, and – much to his annoyance – both cases attracted massive publicity. He disputed Mrs Pallis's claim that, as a left-handed riveter, her husband found it particularly hard to find work in the shipyards, and her complaint about the lack of birth control facilities in the neighbourhood, and dismissed Mr Evans's claim that his daughter only earned seven shillings a week. Felix infuriated Hudson by asking how he could justify statements made in the House of Commons, and received a letter from MacDonald's private secretary referring to his request as 'a piece of impertinence which has given great offence.' Charles Siepmann leapt to Felix's defence, and started a thorough investigation into the claims and counter-claims: both Mrs Pallis and Mr Evans were vindicated, and Mr Hudson was forced to beat a retreat. Reith told the Prime Minister of Siepmann's findings; the BBC received a tidal wave of letters objecting to birth control being mentioned on the airwaves, with the result that the subject remained out of bounds till the 1950s; and the *Evening Standard* declared that 'whatever the political implications of this series may have been, Mr Greene showed that he has a gift for making people talk naturally before the mike.'

None of this was allowed to interrupt Felix's busy social life. Peggy Bok invited him to the South of France to join her on her yacht, and Felix informed his parents that 'the idleness, exquisiteness and irresponsibility of these dear people who are our hosts, and the life on the beautifully equipped boat, suspend one very effectively from any consideration of unemployment, the BBC and what is wrong with the world.' Years later, Sheila MacDonald recalled how Felix agonised about the unemployed, 'and then had to go and have cocktails', and how although 'he couldn't quite reconcile his principles and his behaviour, he didn't allow his high-minded principles to destroy his enjoyment of life.' Those who met Felix were impressed by 'his looks, which were very remarkable, and his ability to express himself. People loved to listen to him. We used to find ourselves in quite high company, and he distinguished himself very much with older people. He didn't mince his words at all. He was direct. He didn't smarm up to anybody.' For all Graham's and Hugh's reservations, Felix was an extremely bright and competent young man, and 'Time to Spare' had marked him out as one of the BBC's rising stars.

Back in London, Felix continued to involve himself with the unemployed and their problems. He was instrumental in setting up Unemployed Clubs in the distressed areas, equipped, if possible, with a library, billiards room, woodwork shop and canteen, and a radio provided by the BBC. By 1935 there were some 400 such clubs in existence, providing community centres for 250,000 members. He edited a book based on the series: *Time to Spare: What Unemployment Means by Eleven Unemployed* was published by Allen & Unwin, and carried contributions by, among others, S. P. B. Mais and A. D. Lindsay. 'No man or woman worth the name of "citizen" can have passed by unemployed fellow-citizens in the streets without the thought "There, but for the grace of God, go I,"' Felix wrote in his introduction. He sent a copy to G. K. Chesterton, who wrote in the *Listener* that 'it will make you shake, and you want shaking. So do I, and I was shaken all right.' Fired by missionary zeal, Felix wrote a memo to G. N. Pocock, the head of the new General Talks Department, in which he said that 'there exists among the poor a growing and urgent need for information in regard to legal questions, elucidation of new regulations and an explanation of their rights', and suggested that a new programme should give advice on such matters as rent restrictions, health insurance, the hated means test, the implications of the 1934 Unemployment Act and old age pensions. 'I can vouch for everything Felix Greene says in this memorandum and I believe that the proposal Felix Greene puts forward would be of real national importance,' Pocock informed his immediate superior, the Controller of Programmes. He was also involved in plans for a new series entitled 'What Price Freedom?', the participants in which were to include Stanley Baldwin, H. G. Wells, Oswald Mosley and the left-wing writer John Strachey, though Felix thought Strachey too academic, and suggested that he should be replaced by Harry Pollitt, the General Secretary of the Communist Party of Great Britain. 'There is no getting away from the fact that countless numbers of unemployed and working-class listeners are still suspicious and unfriendly towards us, and I can think of nothing that we could do that would alter this more effectively than a decision to allow Pollitt for once to have his say,' he told Siepmann. Siepmann agreed, but had to refer the matter to Reith and the Governors of the BBC: in the end Mosley was dropped from the programme, and no approach was made to Harry Pollitt.

But changes were imminent, both at the BBC and in Felix's own career. Documentary programmes like 'Time to Spare', 'Other People's Houses' and 'Crisis in Spain' had attracted the angry attention of conservative papers like the *Daily Mail* and the *Morning Post*; the BBC's charter was due for renewal, and the Corporation was under scrutiny from a Parliamentary Committee of Enquiry. Much as he sympathised with the aims of the Talks Department, Reith was anxious to keep out of trouble and avoid controversy, for the time being at least. In 1935 the Talks Department was reorganised: Siepmann was moved to the provinces, Howard Marshall was 'banished' to Manchester and Lionel Fielden was sent out to India. Felix had kept on good terms with Ramsay MacDonald throughout it all, but in May 1935, after dining at Downing Street, he told his parents that the Prime Minister was 'deplorably lacking in grip', and his Quaker conscience was outraged by the fact that 'he and his lovely government have just issued a most deplorable White Paper justifying increases of £10 million in the fighting services – making Germany the excuse.' Germany would soon loom large in the lives of Hugh and Ben in particular; in the meantime, Felix's future with the BBC seemed assured and, still in his mid-twenties, he was about to reach new heights in his career.

9

Everest Unbeaten

Mount Everest is the highest mountain in the world and it was, until the middle of the last century, one of the most inaccessible. The people who lived in its foothills – Tibetans to the north, Nepalese to the south – regarded it as an abode of the gods, a sacred place, and were unwilling to allow outsiders to profane it. Sir John Hunt's successful expedition of 1953 was allowed to approach Everest from the Nepalese side, but from 1815 until 1945 access through Nepal was strictly forbidden, and expeditions had to make the long journey through Tibet and attempt it from the north, where climbers were exposed to bitter north-easterly winds. The Tibetans were suspicious of all foreign travellers, and geologists in particular, but in 1920 Sir Charles Bell visited Lhasa and got permission from the Dalai Lama for attempts to be made on Everest. Expeditions were mounted in 1920, 1922 and 1924. The 1924 expedition is best remembered for the deaths of Mallory and Irvine, last seen heading purposefully for the summit, but one of its by-products, known as the affair of the 'dancing lamas', proved disastrous in terms of Anglo-Tibetan relations and, for a time, made it impossible to mount further expeditions. John Noel, the cameraman on the 1922 and 1924 expeditions, made a documentary film called *The Roof of the World*, in which he not only showed lamas performing religious rituals and dancing on stage, but included a scene in which a Tibetan was shown looking for fleas in a child's hair and cracking them with his teeth. The Tibetan authorities, already incensed by some members of Colonel Norton's party having strayed across the border from Nepal without permission, were outraged by the film, and banned all future attempts on Everest.

Mounting expeditions to Everest had been a British monopoly, but in 1931 the Government of India, worried by rumours that the Americans, the Germans and the Swiss had plans of their own, began to put pressure on the Dalai Lama to change his mind, and the following year he agreed to lift the ban. Plans were immediately set in motion from the British end. The Everest Committee in London, the body charged with organising an expedition, had been impressed by the climbing of Kamet, and wanted its veterans, Raymond among them, to form the nucleus of the team. 'Smythe, Birnie and Shipton are coming too, so we shall have a Kamet clique,' Raymond wrote home from Oxford. But Smythe would not be leading this particular expedition. Howard Somervell, a highly regarded veteran of earlier Everest expeditions, had reported him to the Committee as being 'a bad mountaineer, always slipping and kicking stones down, and an intolerable companion. No one in our party could stick him for more than a few days, owing to his irritating self-sufficiency [and] his incessant conversation makes others tired.' This was far removed from Raymond's experience of Smythe on Kamet, or on Everest, as it turned out: he too found Smythe irritable, tactless and easily offended at ground level, but once in the mountains he became the perfect companion and leader. However, the Committee's mind was made up: Smythe had been critical of their activities in the past, and they disapproved of his writing books about his adventures, which, since he was paid for his labours, made him into a professional mountaineer. They chose instead Hugh Ruttledge, a modest, self-effacing, forty-eight-year-old official in the Indian Civil Service: he was not a seasoned mountaineer, but had made trips to the Himalayas with his wife and spoke several native languages, and walked with a limp as a result of an accident while pigsticking. He turned out to be an amiable if ineffectual leader, hovering in the background rather than leading the charge. 'He tends to worry, and this affects his health,' Raymond noted later in his diary. 'But on the march [through Tibet] his cares fell away from him and he became a different man.' As for Frank Smythe, 'he was equally good as a follower. Under Ruttledge on Everest he was as imperturbable, reliable and good-tempered under circumstances far harder [than Kamet]. Whatever winds of disagreement might disturb the surface of our companionship, Frank was unruffled, his mind perhaps too concentrated on our great enterprise for petty squabbling.'

Every member of the expedition had to be, in Raymond's words, 'morally and physically fit, for Everest will accentuate his smallest imperfections of mind and body, and bring into prominence his secret failings.' As its chief medical officer and an authority on the effects of altitude and oxygen deprivation on the human body, he was involved in vetting candidates at the RAF's Central Medical Establishment. The fourteen men selected were drawn from the professional middle classes, with army officers and Oxbridge graduates predominating. Colin Crawford and

E. O. Shebbeare were 'Everesters', veterans of earlier expeditions. Shebbeare, known as 'Shebby' was, at forty-nine, the oldest member of the expedition, and a member of the Indian Forestry Service. Raymond thought him 'the most delightful of men, who wears kindness like an aura', but soon discovered him to be 'the most inefficient transport officer any expedition has ever had.' Percy Wyn Harris had a Cambridge blue in cross-country running and, while a member of the Kenya Civil Service, had climbed Mount Kenya with Eric Shipton. He was used to climbing with one or two companions at most, thought the party far too large for its own good, and later wrote that he could 'think casually of at least four whom the expedition would have been better without'. Tom Brocklebank was, like Irvine before him, a Cambridge rowing blue, had taught at Eton, and had climbed in the Alps. Laurence Wager had travelled in Greenland with Gino Watkins, the celebrated Arctic explorer: he was, according to Raymond, a 'small, powerful, level-headed scientist', and 'after Frank and Eric, our best man'. Willie McLean was the other doctor in the party, and had recently given up his London practice to join the Mission to the Jews in Jerusalem; Raymond found him 'bone idle'. Jack Longland was widely admired as a rock climber, had a Cambridge blue in pole-vaulting, taught English at Durham University, and was in charge of the expedition's travelling library. The most exotic member of the party was Hugh Boustead. He had joined the Navy after leaving school, but had deserted ship in Simonstown harbour to fight on the Western Front. He had been a champion boxer while in the army, captained the British pentathlon team in the 1920 Olympics, and was now serving as an officer in the Camel Corps of the Sudan Defence Force. He had climbed in the Alps and the Himalayas, and Colonel Norton, the leader of the 1924 Everest expedition, had been sufficiently impressed to recommend him for the 'next Everest show'. He was also, Raymond noted, the only other Oxford graduate in the team.

The Everest Committee needed to raise £7000 to mount the expedition. J. M. Scott, a writer and another former colleague of Gino Watkins, was employed as a full-time organiser, and a sub-committee which included the great Himalayan explorer Sir Francis Younghusband and Leo Amery, a future Colonial Secretary and a passionate mountaineer, appointed a literary agent who, in turn, sold the book rights to Hodder & Stoughton for £3000, and persuaded the *Daily Telegraph* – rather than *The Times* – to pay £3500 for exclusive rights to up-to-the-minute reports from the mountaineers. To make this possible, a radio and telephone network would be taken to Everest for the first time, operated by two full-time wireless operators. The transmitters were extremely heavy, but they would enable the party to keep in regular touch with London, listen to the BBC, and – most importantly of all – receive regular weather reports; and a field telephone would make it possible for those in Base Camp to keep in touch with their colleagues higher up the mountain. Offers of support came in from all sides. Three sixty-foot rope ladders were presented by the Yorkshire Ramblers Club; a man offered to lay gas piping up the side of Everest to provide oxygen to the climbers, while another suggested a man-lifting kite carrying the inscription 'Buy New Zealand Butter'; a Mr Lawrie of Burnley supplied the boots, the soles of which included a layer of asbestos between two layers of leather, designed to keep frostbite at bay.

Food was always a vexed issue, in terms of both quantity and quality, and a Dr Zilva was commissioned to work out a high-altitude diet which would provide the mountaineers with all the vitamins and calories they needed. Bovril provided pemmican, the concentrated beef essence used by Scott's expedition to the Antarctic twenty years before; Raymond was keen to supply his men with fresh fruit and vegetables, but these proved impossible to obtain in the wastes of Tibet, and they had to make do with concentrated lemon juice provided by Lyons: it also acted as an anti-scorbutic. Toffee, Kendal Mint Cake, Ovaltine and Huntley & Palmer's biscuits proved to be popular items. Raymond particularly asked for Marmite to be included, but none was sent and he had to buy up as much as he could as they wended their way to the Himalayas. A tender from Fortnum & Mason to supply the bulk of the food was rejected in favour of an offer from the Army & Navy Stores for what were generally agreed to be otherwise 'unsaleable goods'. According to Percy Wyn Harris, 'the rations were absolutely revolting. The tins were not of the best quality, and the diet was extremely monotonous,' while Raymond had to admit that 'it was not Dr Zilva's fault that a diet which looked well on paper tasted less well in the mouth.'

An equally controversial subject was that of oxygen masks and oxygen cylinders: extreme opponents claimed that they were, by definition, unsporting (in Hugh Boustead's words, they were 'looked on as offside'); more moderate opponents thought that carrying heavy metal cylinders at great heights hampered the movement of climbers and impaired their balance, and that the equipment was likely to break down at critical moments. The 1924 expedition had used oxygen, but Wyn Harris was convinced that either Mallory or Irvine had toppled onto his back and that his oxygen cylinders had acted like a sledge, plummeting both men

to their deaths. Although Raymond had spent a great deal of time simpli-
fying and improving the existing apparatus so that it only weighed twelve
and three-quarter pounds, a third of the weight of that used in 1924, he
was, like his mentor J. S. Haldane, a great believer in acclimatisation, in
allowing men time to adjust to altitude over a period of time, and he
shared Haldane's belief that 'the highest points in the world could be
reached without the help of oxygen provided they had the right men in
the right weather.' It was agreed that they would take oxygen with them,
but only use it if a first attempt without it failed. As it was, Raymond's
new apparatus was never used for the purpose for which it was intended,
but he used the oxygen to treat the sick, and porters' frostbitten hands
in particular. Although the breathing apparatus was abandoned somewhere on the lower slopes of Everest, that taken on the 1953 expedition
was identical in every way. As for more conventional medical equipment,
Raymond recorded how 'MacLean and I, with howls of laughter, have
been through the list of medical stores . . . It reads like the sale list of a
practitioner who has at the age of ninety-seven decided at last to retire',
though elsewhere he wrote that the equipment was adequate except for
a shortage of throat lozenges to combat the appalling dust-storms of
Tibet. Wyn Harris ridiculed a 'nerve tonic', which he eventually fed to
the yaks. A new 'Everest carrier', designed to manhandle ill or disabled
climbers from the scene of action, collapsed ignominiously under the
weight of a porter with a broken leg. Raymond thought it a ludicrous
and ill-conceived contraption, and years later he came up with his own
superior alternative, designed to carry wounded soldiers back to base.

The climbers left home in February 1933. Eric Shipton was on his farm
when he received his summons, 'peacefully occupied with problems of
manure, soil erosion and farm politics', and he left Kenya, never to return.
Hugh Boustead was on exercises in Darfur when an RAF plane arrived
bearing iced beer, mail and an invitation to join the expedition, and he
sent a message via the pilot to say that he was 'both keen and delighted'.
He was flown to Port Sudan, and travelled on by ship to Aden and
Bombay. Raymond and Frank Smythe took the Bombay Express from
Victoria to Marseilles, where they boarded the P&O *Viceroy of India*,
travelling first class. A day later they steamed past Cefalù, the former
haunt of Aleister Crowley, 'and all the memories of that ridiculous saga
returned to me.' They donned tropical suits in Port Said, and Raymond
indulged in 'the difficult analysis of my feelings for E. G.' (Eleanor
Gamble, the American girl with whom Felix had briefly flirted in
Cambridge); he decided to be vaccinated against a reported smallpox

epidemic in Bombay, since 'my return to England with a pock-marked face might resolve my conflict rather over-suddenly.' The rest of the party had left on an earlier boat, and to keep themselves entertained they tried to learn Nepali: Shipton was completely baffled, but consoled himself by noting how Wyn Harris 'conversed happily in Swahili, which seemed to be as effective as anything else'.

Raymond and Frank Smythe were met in Bombay by Lall, a servant from Kamet days. They watched Royal Navy gunboats on exercise in the harbour, and Raymond 'felt again that delightful easing of the inferiority complex which the white man feels when surrounded by a subject race'. That evening they caught the Calcutta Mail. One of their fellow passengers was an Old Berkhamstedian, and 'it was curious to hear again my old school nickname, Rayee. I wonder how long has passed since last he heard himself called Mucky G?' They enjoyed some brisk social life in Calcutta before setting off for Darjeeling, the expedition's assembly point. By now it was well into March, and timing was all important. An attempt on Everest had to be made in the brief, windless interval from May to June, between the spring gales and the monsoon, when the north face of the mountain was as clear as it could ever be: the dreaded monsoon brought with it fine powdery snow, which obscured hand- and footholds and made marching and climbing almost impossible, and warmer weather triggered off avalanches. Once assembled, they moved north to Kalimpong, where they were joined by Hugh Boustead. Raymond noted in his diary that he seemed to be 'a quiet and exceptionally pleasant person with a record of adventure behind him enough to makes one's hair curl and an intimate knowledge of literature hardly consistent with his job of commander of the Sudan Camel Corps.'

It took six weeks to march from Kalimpong to the Rongbuk Valley, at the foot of Everest. Crossing Sikkim alone involved a two hundred-mile trek through lush semi-tropical valleys. Doubling up as a part-time vet, Raymond operated on an elephant with an abcess on its back, belonging to a Mrs Wrangham-Hardy. In Gangtok, the capital of Sikkim, they were received by the Maharajah, an insignificant-seeming character: his brother, who had been at Pembroke with Raymond, had recently been murdered by upstart lamas, and his palace resembled a 'cheap seaside hotel'. From there they began to climb towards the Tibetan border, the vegetation grew sparser; the landscape bleaker and less hospitable, the air thinner and much colder. They went over a pass at 14,000 feet, and were in Tibet at last, a world of iced-up rivers, yellow snow-topped cliffs, frozen waterfalls, grey skies and interminable, howling winds. 'My most vivid memories are of monasteries perched on the flanks of great hills rising out of the plain, of the monks and their butter-tea, a taste not easy to acquire,' Hugh Boustead recalled, adding that 'the expedition must have looked like the retreat from Kabul to Kandahar in the first Afghan War.' The European contingent rode ponies; their provisions – food, tents, clothing, books, a gramophone, chairs and tables, a telescope, wireless and oxygen equipment, whisky and cigarettes ('neither in moderation ever harmed a healthy man,' Raymond declared) – were mounted on 300 yaks, mules and donkeys, escorted by 170 porters. Vetting the porters had been, Raymond admitted, a comparatively cursory affair, 'for though collectively of the greatest possible importance, individually they are of less importance than the Europeans', while Hugh Ruttledge had to admit that 'we spent much time trying to distinguish one flat face from another.' Some of the porters were Sherpas, described by Ruttledge as 'fine, free movers on a hillside, with the bold, open manners of the true hill man,' others Bhutias, 'splendid load-bearers, hardy and amenable to discipline'. Lewa, the head *sirda*, had been on Kamet, where he had lost his toes to frostbite. Runners took photographs back for despatch to the *Daily Telegraph*, and returned with out-of-date copies of *Punch*. Like Wyn Harris, Smythe thought the expedition too large for its own good, and lacking in homogeneity. 'These hordes of animals and hundreds of packing cases separated us from the simplicity of travel,' he wrote in *Camp Six*. 'Somehow this vast transport made Everest into an inexorable and rather dull duty. The companionship of the campfire was absent and in its place was a rowdy mess tent.'

Raymond enjoyed racing his pony across the endless yellow plains. He extracted a porter's rotten tooth and, when another porter's heart stopped working, started it up again with an injection. 'I am only tonight beginning to feel that contentment which came upon me so early in the Kamet expedition. This may be Eleanor's fault in part, and in part because I was happy in England before this show, not miserable to suicide as I was before Kamet,' he confided to his diary on 23 March. Earlier that day they had visited the fort, or *dzong*, of Phari, said to be the dirtiest village in Asia. The inhabitants' faces and clothes were covered with dirt, the roofs of the houses were covered with rotting turf, and the alleyways were ankle-deep in raw sewage. A nearby nunnery reeked of faeces and rancid yak butter; the blackened faces of its inhabitants were topped by huge, elaborate wigs and, as always in Tibet, 'a wind blew continuously from every direction, blowing into the tents, the cooking pots, one's eyes and mouth, a fine irritating dust, consisting partly of the sands of the desert and partly of the excreta of generations of constipated nuns.' At Tengyke Dzong they visited the palace or *dzongpen*, where the ceilings were black from smoke and the pillars which supported them decorated with pages from the *Illustrated Sporting and Dramatic News*. Hugh Ruttledge wore a top hat for the occasion; they were served a mildly alcoholic drink, and treated to a display by dancing girls. Some climbing boots, whisky and equipment were stolen by three muleteers; the matter was referred to the local district commissioner, and the culprits received a hundred lashes each, administered with a rawhide whip.

The dust and the wind led Raymond to install a 'daily nose and throat toilet' routine. Porters saw no point in washing pots and pans and dishcloths, or in boiling milk or water, and he noted 'it is impossible to deny the danger to health of the filthy habit of native cooks in a country where dysentery is endemic.' He was outraged to discover that the advance guard had set up the mess tent downwind from the monastery of Shekar Dzong: from a distance the huge white monastery perched on a cliff face looked like 'the fairy palace of my childish dreams', but it did not bear closer inspection. Despite the squalor, a degree of lethargy set in, and it proved hard to get away: Boustead sat reading Montaigne, while the Cambridge contingent practised bodyline bowling with a mangel wurzel. At Kampa Dzong they caught their first glimpse of Everest: it was, Raymond remembered, 'the most beautiful and the most appalling thing I had ever seen.' 'I have cast off England again. I think the sight of Everest made the change,' Raymond wrote in his diary. 'On Kamet it took a fortnight only for me to feel "settled" in the nomad life, with no cords binding me to home or pulling me back. The party was smaller and more intimate, the march perhaps less beautiful but less strange. For the six weeks of this expedition, though I have liked my companions and been interested and aesthetically thrilled by my surroundings, I have found myself repeatedly thinking of the joy of going home again. I have not, as I used to put it in my lost Kamet diary, lain and "gloated" in my tent at the perfection of life.'

They passed a cairn erected to the memory of Alexander Kellas, who had written an influential paper describing the symptoms of mountain sickness, emphasising the need for good diet, rest, training and acclimatisation, and querying whether Everest could ever be climbed without oxygen; he had taken part in the 1921 expedition, and had died on the approaches to Everest. They finally reached the Rongbuk Valley on 16 April. It presented a dismal scene – low grey hills to either side, grey skies overhead, grey rocks underfoot and, ahead, the dirty grey ice of the Rongbuk Glacier, inching its way out of the side of Everest itself. The following day was Raymond's birthday, and after setting up their Base Camp they visited the Rongbuk Monastery, home to 300 monks, and, at 16,000 feet, said to be the highest inhabited spot on earth. The abbot was a 'fat and jovial old man with twinkling eyes who laughed loudly with pleasure at the presents we brought him, a leather attaché case, plastic cups and saucers, some cloth of gold'. They were all tapped on the head with a prayer wheel and given a white packet containing seeds before returning to Base Camp for a slap-up dinner. Two days were employed sorting out stores and testing the oxygen equipment; according to Shipton, a great deal of the day was spent in bed, since it was dark by four in the afternoon, and it was too cold to sit around. Raymond occupied much of his time sorting out minor ailments, from throat troubles to diarrhoea, flu and bronchitis. One member of the party was already affected by anoxia or oxygen deprivation, which in his case took the form of extreme lassitude and loss of interest, and an inability to pull his weight thereafter. 'Greene, himself a hard worker, found these so-called invalids a pretty handful,' Ruttledge later remembered, but anoxia was a real problem, only overcome, in Raymond's opinion, by gradual acclimatisation. Symptoms of oxygen deprivation included lethargy, sleeplessness, irritability, sickness, blue face and hands, anxiety, slower reactions, a lack of concentration, persecution mania and losing one's sense of time. To offset them he recommended that, ideally, no one should climb more than 1000 feet a day, and that they should spend four days in each camp, giving their bodies the time to adjust. Or, as Raymond put it in his diary, 'Every expedition has taught us that "he-man stuff" will not work. We must climb this mountain in the most comfortable possible way or not at all. The attainment of the virgin must be by seduction and not by rape.'

Although Raymond was to break his own rules, and suffer thereby, the 1933 expedition acclimatised far better than its predecessors: people slept better, and mental deterioration occurred only among those who reached great heights. In the meantime, at Base Camp, Shipton noted how they all became 'ridiculously self-conscious' about acclimatisation, counting their heartbeats, monitoring their breathing and indulging in hypochondria. But, he went on, 'We had not yet had time to become irritable or irascible with each other, and with the wide diversity of professions in the party, the talk was good and varied. This was spoilt at times by a natural tendency to talk shop. To a layman it would have seemed amazing that, in a simple matter like the climbing of a mountain, we could have found so much to argue about. Each of us had his own pet theory on every aspect of the problem and aired it with monotonous regularity and lamentable disregard for opposing points of view.' But 'Crawford's acute sense of the ridiculous kept us from taking ourselves too seriously', and 'Greene's remarkable gift for anecdote was always fresh – I never grew tired of listening to him.' As on Kamet, Raymond found himself called upon to entertain the troops with his 'rolling Gibbonian prose'. 'In Greene we discovered a raconteur of unrivalled capacity,' Ruttledge recalled, while Boustead remembered him as 'a great raconteur'. 'I seem to have been pushed into a position of Scheherezade,' Raymond confided to his diary. 'Every night the mess screams for a story. My stories are getting slowly exhausted, but they say they will kill me when the 1001 nights come to an end.' When not telling yarns, he read *South Wind* in his tent and dreamed of being whisked away to Quaglino's or a cocktail bar in Jermyn Street, where Eleanor would be waiting, 'dressed as usual in the perfect frock'.

Climbing Everest involved elaborate logistics as well as endurance, courage, will-power and mountaineering skill. The two wireless operators remained in Base Camp throughout, together with those who were injured or unwell. The rest of the party, accompanied by porters carrying equipment and provisions, then established a series of camps at ever-increasing heights up the side of the mountain, and from then on there was a constant coming and going of men and provisions between them. Some members of the expedition – those with less experience of mountaineering at great heights, or older members like Shebbeare, the transport officer, or Ruttledge himself – seldom or never ventured above Camp III. Only the most experienced mountaineers – Shipton, Smythe, Birnie, Wager, Longland, Wyn Harris, Boustead and Raymond – would attempt the steep and dangerous climb up to the North Col, the saddle-shaped ridge from which the summit itself would be attempted.

Raymond was involved at every stage, and although he had never thought of himself as a 'first-rate mountaineer' – as opposed to a 'first-rate traveller', and 'the kind of doctor who can do his job in a snowdrift or in a tropical forest without the conveniences of an operating theatre and a crowd of nurses' – he felt a surge of confidence: he was very fit, and was regarded as a fully-fledged member of the assault team. Camp II was established in the upper basin of the Rongbuk Glacier, at 21,000 feet. A storm blew up, and Raymond quickly realised that the Meade tents with which they had been supplied were utterly inadequate – snow crystals blew through the fabric – and better suited for a Mediterranean holiday than the slopes of Everest. Moving up the glacier to set up Camp III, they passed the seracs, 'giant pine trees of ice [which] cluster about the way, white and pale blue and pale sea green, the creation of an insane Lalique.' Despite his insistence on acclimatisation, all was not well. Boustead was 'showing signs of slight altitude irritability', and 'must be watched'; at Camp III Bill Birnie – the polo-playing Indian Army officer who had been with them on Kamet – suddenly picked an argument with Frank Smythe, accusing him of profiting unduly from the earlier expedition by writing a book about it. Raymond was outraged: 'At lower altitudes I must tackle him about it. Bill is one of the best people in the world, and it annoys me to see him suffering from what looks like a petty, vulgar and selfish jealousy.' As for Shebbeare, 'he seems to me to be a dear old man who ought to be sitting in front of his club fire with a tankard of ale in his hand, not toiling up Himalayan glaciers under conditions which are a test for the youngest and strongest of us,' and his 'mind has apparently ceased to function under the influence of altitude, old age and diarrhoea.'

The weather was atrocious, so losing them valuable time. 'None of us had been in such continuously bad weather in the Himalayas,' Frank Smythe recalled. They were battered by a 'ceaseless, relentless, bullying wind', and 'there was something implacably hostile about the great mountain, and in the absence of sun, with a wind-driven smother of flying snow and a smooth, slate-grey cloud oiling along with extraordinary speed, yet ever forming so quickly as to remain clinging to the summit, it was possible to imagine a vengeful and terrible personality.' An 'appalling row' broke out between Birnie and Boustead on the one hand, and Harris and Wager on the other. 'Bill has begun to behave like a shit,' Raymond noted. 'He ought to be sent down or he will damage our morale.' Raymond 'once again entertained us with some of his stories, which not even an altitude of 22,000 feet could dull in telling', but all was not well. Smythe, Shipton, Longland and Raymond established Camp IIIa at the foot of the North Col. On their way down, Raymond glissaded down an icy slope, performed a cartwheel in mid-air, and strained his stomach muscles. Earlier, returning to Base Camp from Camp II, he had felt a 'pre-cordial' pain and been uneasily aware of a racing pulse; he was the tallest man on the expedition and, like many tall men, he may have given more easily exhausted than his stockier colleagues.

On 13 May Camp IV was established on an ice ledge just below the

Graham and Vivien Dayrell-Browning
on their wedding day

Felix during his early career

Ben in Buzuluk, Southern Russia

Ben, Eppy and Aunt Polly (ringing the bell)
at Little Wittenham

Graham and Barbara en route to Liberia

Graham in travelling attire,
minus the falling socks, Liberia

The Everest Expedition in Sikkim: (*standing*) Smijth-Windham, Raymond Greene, Wood-Johnson, Brocklebank, the Political Agent, Shipton, McLean, Smythe, Thompson, Wyn-Harris; (*sitting*) Longland, Ruttledge, Birnie, Wager, Shebbeare, Crawford (in hat), Boustead

crest of the North Col. Smythe had led the way, at one point hacking steps in a forty-foot high wall of ice, vertical for most of the way with an overhang at the top. Before long the slopes of the North Col would be festooned with ropes and ladders, making possible a constant traffic of men and supplies. The storm was still raging, and his group were confined to their sleeping bags for several days. Nor did morale improve when they learned over the radio that the monsoon had reached Ceylon, and was between ten days and a fortnight from the Himalayas. 'Life on Mount Everest,' Raymond wrote later, 'is an alternation of monotony with periods of great strain', and both the strain and the altitude were taking their toll. One source of irritation was the food. 'Unlike our forebears, we were not prepared to live on condensed milk, jam and acid drops,' Raymond recalled. 'We wanted meat, cut off the joint, and two veg. Urgent messages were sent daily to the harassed party at Camp III, and by them passed on by wireless to the base, demanding mutton and ham and eggs. At Camp IV men dreamed, with childlike blissful smiles on their brown and hairy faces, of steaks and onions and roly-poly puddings, while the more fiery spirits emptied into the crevasse tin after tin of a particularly loathsome tinned meat ration, unpalatable at any height and inedible when great altitudes had made gourmets of us all.' Tempers flared and nightmares interrupted sleep, but Smythe remained aloof. 'It seemed that chronic anoxia increased his placidity,' Raymond remembered. 'At low altitudes a little inclined to take offence, at great heights he emanated serenity and an infectious happiness.'

But not all Smythe's colleagues were as easy-going. A week after Camp IV had been set up, Wyn Harris, Birnie, Boustead and ten porters set out to establish Camp V at 25,700 feet. A blizzard was blowing, and before they reached their destination Birnie decided that the porters had had enough, and that they should withdraw. Boustead agreed, but Wyn Harris wanted to press on. They all returned to Camp IV, where a blazing row broke out, with Harris berating the 'bloody army officers'. Ruttledge came up from Camp III: he told Birnie and Boustead that their behaviour amounted to 'the most disgraceful day in the annals of Everest', and said that a team consisting of Harris, Wager, Longland and Raymond should now 'attempt to overcome the previous day's "disgrace" by putting Camp V as high as possible'. Two days had been lost and, in retrospect, Raymond reckoned that, with the monsoon approaching at speed, the delay proved fatal to the expedition's chances of success.

Camp V was duly established, but Raymond was unhappily aware that his heart was feeling the strain, and that – in defiance of his own rules

– he had not given himself enough time to acclimatise at Camp IV. The plan was that Raymond and Wyn Harris should then press on, establish Camp VI, and from there make the first attempt on the summit, but Raymond had found it increasingly hard to keep up with Wager, then leading the party and climbing at the rate of 600 feet an hour in fifty-minute stretches, with ten-minute pauses in between. On the way up they came across frozen remnants of the 1922 expedition: the tents were in tatters, but the labels on the tins were still readable, and a canister of oxygen was lying in the snow. Raymond gave himself a whiff of oxygen, and suddenly the world seemed brighter than before: momentarily refreshed, he decided to carry on, but by the time they reached Camp V he knew he would have to give up. His pulse was irregular, 'and when I felt for my heart beat I found it two inches out of place,' he recalled in *Moments of Being*. 'Completely exhausted, I lay and thought. The burden of my thoughts was heavy,' he wrote in his diary. 'The place of the MO is at the base, yet I had been given the opportunity of the first assault on the summit, without any wangling on my part.' He felt he should step aside for Wager, 'and this, with the literal tears of altitude emotionalism in my eyes, I did. I stripped off my spare weathers and, with a real lump in my throat I left Camp V in the menial occupation of porter escort for Camp IV. That, with the possible exception of the return from Kamet, was the worst journey of my life.' On the way down he had what he later diagnosed as a 'near-death experience': utterly worn out, he found a sheltered spot, out of the wind, and began to doze off, but luckily he came to, and made himself carry on down the mountain. His pulse was still racing wildly when he reached Camp IV, and Frank Smythe remembered that he looked 'very done in'.

'By establishing Camp V 3000 feet above IV and 500 feet higher than it had ever been put before, I felt I had done my job,' Raymond scribbled in his diary. 'I was content to lie in the sun at Camp III for a day and then descend to the Base, doing what small jobs I could on the way, and there laze awhile and attend to the wants of the casualties from above.' Boustead came with him. His leave from the Camel Corps could be extended no longer, and he had to make his way back to the Sudan. He had frostbitten feet – 'each time I put my foot on the ground it was like treading on red-hot bricks' – and Raymond tried to mitigate the pain with sporadic doses of oxygen. At Camp II Lachman Singh had a tent ready and waiting, with tea on the boil, magazines laid out and a jar of tobacco at the ready; at Camp I they tucked into a meal of pea soup, galantine of chicken, dried figs and a Stilton. Back at Base Camp,

Raymond expelled some local spongers who were making inroads into their rations, consumed 'copious draughts' of poor-quality Army & Navy Stores rum, and had his first bath for six weeks: he was astonished at how wasted his muscles had become, and by the spots all over his body, the result of too much sweating. 'I cannot give you any idea of the marvellous happiness which comes to one when one gets back from the High Camps to Base,' he told Eleanor. 'The warmth and thickness of the air, which passes over one with a glossy feeling after the thin air above; the joy of being able to move without panting, of taking off one's clothes for the first time in six long weeks; of the sound and smell and sight of living things . . .' After a welcome change of clothes, he attended a farewell dinner for Hugh Boustead. With his beard shaved off, Boustead 'looked a rather pathetic little man, for all his adventurous life – very like RLS in his last days on Samoa. Given his proper supply of oxygen he had recovered all his former charm, and although there were times at Camp IV when I had difficulty in suppressing my dislike for his know-all and grumbling ways, I shall look forward to seeing him again.'

By now the monsoon had reached the Bay of Bengal: the snow was melting, the weather was balmy, birds sang, butterflies fluttered to and fro, and, with oxygen in more adequate supply, the world looked brighter and clearer than higher up the slopes of Everest, and 'I use my dilated heart (which I am sure is no longer dilated) as an excuse for an idle-ness as prodigious as my appetite.' Raymond lay about in the sun in his shorts, smoking or reading a book, bathed in a makeshift swim-ming pool and, remembering how 'in the arctic tent at Camp IV the floor was covered always by a horrid melange of sleeping bags, boots, dirty underclothes, paper, dirty plates, knives, forks and spilt food, the whole stuck together by ancient lumps of Kendal Mint Cake or over-turned tins of condensed milk,' he enjoyed the luxury of having a clean, uncluttered tent all to himself. It was a relief, too, to be able to eat his meals sitting at a table, and he soon forgot 'the recurring frightfulness of cooking for oneself on a diseased Primus the nearly inedible tinned filth of the Army & Navy Stores, which somehow always got spilt on one's sleeping bag.' He wrote home to say how 'frightfully pleased' he was about Graham's success with *Stamboul Train* – 'You omit the most interesting news. How much money has Graham made?' – and how sorry he was to hear about the demise of Graham's dog Paddy ('Being a snob about dogs I never really appreciated him, but I know you will miss him a lot'). He also received a radio message from Eleanor, who was helping to prepare their despatches for the *Daily Telegraph*:

'Anxiously waiting your return August wish you success but do be careful all my love.'

Several thousand feet above him, Wager and Wyn Harris were making the first attempt on the summit from Camp VI. Frank Smythe and Eric Shipton had come up to Camp VI, and sent a wireless message to say that the two climbers had been seen making good progress until cloud obscured them from view. By the time they had decided to approach the summit via Norton's Traverse rather than Mallory's Ridge – where Harris found an ice axe which Raymond later believed had belonged to Mallory – time was running out and, and a thousand feet from the summit, they had to turn back. Shipton and Smythe were left alone in Camp VI, preparing their own assault. A blizzard was blowing, it took an hour to melt a saucepan of snow over a solid fuel stove, and they rolled on top of one another in their sleeping bags. A whole day was wasted, during which time the route to the summit had been covered with a fine, powdery snow that made the going even harder than it might otherwise have been. Shipton had slept badly and had stomach cramps, possibly brought about by some meat essence eaten the night before. 'Anyone leaving Camp VI would have said, "There go two crocks who ought to be in hospital,"' Smythe recalled. Both men were suffering from altitude sickness, albeit in different ways. After a while, Shipton collapsed. He urged Smythe to press on alone, and headed back down the mountain. He got lost on the way down, and when Tom Brocklebank eventually met him on the North Col, 'he just gazed at me with those blue eyes, beaming a wide smile, but was unable to speak for twenty-four hours.' Smythe was known to suffer visual illusions at great heights, referred to by his fellow climbers as 'Frank's pulsating teapots', and as he plodded on alone he became convinced that he was accompanied by a friendly spirit for whom, in a companionable way, he snapped off a piece of Kendal Mint Cake. It was a beautiful bright day but, a thousand feet from the summit, he decided that the condition of the snow made it impossible to continue. He took a last look at 'the brown Rongbuk Valley, and the sandy plateau of Tibet checkered with blue cloud shadows stretching endlessly northwards into the vastnesses of the Gobi Desert and Central Asia,' and began the long climb down the slopes of Everest.

'With the exception of Hugo [Boustead] and Bill, whose temper on the mountain became ungovernable and who was the origin of every "unpleasantness", I had come to like each one of the party more and more. The greater the discomfort and mental strain, the more I came to respect them,' Raymond noted in his diary. Bill Birnie was still causing trouble, barking out orders, being insufferably rude, calling Raymond 'the laziest bloody doctor he had ever known', and threatening to report him to the Everest Committee for keeping him waiting for a medical. 'When he came up for air I remarked that I was not worried by that sort of thing as I had worked in a lunatic asylum for six months,' Raymond observed. Birnie was suffering from frostbite and altitude sickness and, to the relief of all, he sulked in his tent. McLean had pneumonia, Longland was suffering from diarrhoea, and Shipton was still incapable of speech, though when a crate of champagne was opened to celebrate someone's birthday, he became extremely drunk – 'a smile of infantile beatitude illuminating his face, his beard more frizzy than ever' – and had to be carried back to his tent. When not tending the sick, Raymond busied himself collecting plants and insects to take back to England, pondered the possibility of writing a book about his experiences, and took care not to damage the twelve glass ampoules containing alveolar gas expelled by his colleagues at Camps III, IV and V, which would be used to further his pioneering research into acclimatisation.

Despite the arrival of the monsoon, there was talk of some members of the party staying on to make another attempt when the weather improved, or later in the year. The Political Officer in Sikkim had reported – wrongly, as it turned out – that the Tibetan Government would not give permission for another expedition to be mounted in 1934, so Ruttledge sent a message to suggest that he, Raymond, Smythe, Shipton and two others should remain at Base Camp, possibly until the early autumn. Raymond was sceptical: Smythe was suffering from frostbite, the avalanche season was upon them, and he saw himself sitting about 'longing for home, though my return would mean a fateful decision (which in my heart I had already made) and conscious of the gradual ruin of my practice.' But 'now that we are free of the "fucking soldiery" we are a very friendly and happy party,' and he dutifully took part in some preliminary forays up the mountain. To his relief, the Everest Committee ordered them home. The party, he recorded in his diary, 'resigned itself without undue depression to a defeat which had been obvious to many members for some weeks . . . We were less affected by that hatred of Everest which seems to have affected former defeated parties, and conversation was all of "next time".' Raymond shaved off his beard, leaving only a small moustache, and having packed their provisions, they set off down the Rongbuk Valley, now bright with flowers. 'Greene, Crawford and I were among the last to go,' Ruttledge recalled. 'As we turned the corner of the moraine we had one more look at

Mount Everest. Then the clouds came down for good. We had done with it all.' They made the long trek back to Darjeeling, a high point of which saw Raymond and Jack Longland, stark naked, racing their ponies across the windswept Tibetan plateau. George Wood-Johnson suffered from a gastric ulcer, and because the Army & Navy stretcher had broken in pieces, he had to ride in agony. The 'damned mountain' had taken 'heavy casualties' both physically and mentally – so much so that 'of the fourteen of us, six have definitely been a bit batty at some time or other.' 'I love you as I have never loved before,' Raymond had written to Eleanor from the slopes of Everest some weeks earlier, adding the proviso that 'still I feel that the bachelor life is so very much preferable to the married.' Back in India, Raymond wrote again to say that he would leave the ship at Marseilles, take the train through France, enjoy a Turkish bath on arrival in London and take her out dancing in the West End. He and Ruttledge stayed with the Viceroy, Lord Willingdon, before boarding the boat for the long voyage home.

The following February Raymond read a paper to the Royal Geographical Society on 'The Food and Health of the Mount Everest Expedition', a meeting attended by, among others, J. S. Haldane, and over the next few months the Secretary of the RGS pestered him for an article for the Society's magazine. In the years to come Raymond would write innumerable learned articles about frostbite and oxygen deprivation, but despite having told his mother from Base Camp that he had 'got so much clinical material that I think I shall have to write a book', he was too busy to get down to it. 'I have been hideously overworked for the last few months – hence probably my collapse with the first cold I've had for about ten years,' he told the RGS, and 'earning my living takes up too much time.' 'Would that you could be a GP for a little!' he wrote some three months later. 'But I will keep your letter on my desk and perhaps one day (when we are both bald and grey) something may get written.' Nor were they alone in seeking Raymond's words or company. 'Why the devil aren't you here? You would enjoy the show. It's Kamet over again and even pleasanter,' Frank Smythe cabled him from Mount Everest in 1936. Raymond had proved an invaluable member of the Kamet and Everest expeditions, as medic, climber and raconteur, and though his Himalayan adventures were over, he still had much to contribute to the welfare and well-being of his fellow-mountaineers.

Foreign Correspondent

Hugh had various reasons for wanting to go to Germany in the winter of 1933. Hitler had come to power the previous January, and however unpleasant and unnerving life in Germany might be, it was the place to be for an ambitious young journalist. He already spoke German, and a German girlfriend from Oxford was back in Berlin; he had been fascinated by a letter from Barbara's former maid, Friedel, singing the praises of the Nazis and blaming Germany's woes on the Jews. His godfather, a successful QC, had urged him to read for the Bar, while his father thought he should try for the Civil Service, but he couldn't face the idea of any more exams, and wanted to get away. In later years, though, he put it all down to a reading of *The Revolver Republic* by G. E. R. Gedye, claiming that 'if one book decided my future, this was it.' Gedye was an outspoken and highly regarded foreign correspondent, who was to represent the *Daily Telegraph* in Vienna until his expulsion in the spring of 1939, and in his book he described the political machinations involved in trying to set up a separatist state in the Rhineland in the 1920s. It was the world that had so fascinated Graham at Oxford, and Hugh recalled how 'slimy and shady characters like von Papen and General von Schleicher appealed to my imagination.' Kingsley Martin said that he was prepared to consider anything Hugh sent from Germany for the *New Statesman*, and his father agreed to subsidise him with £200 a year. He would earn a crust by teaching English, initially in Munich, and at the same time try to get a foothold on the journalistic ladder.

Hugh was horribly seasick on the boat to Ostend, and always travelled by air thereafter. He took a slow train to Berlin, where he said goodbye to his Oxford girlfriend and went to see the Berlin correspondent of the *Daily Herald*, to whom Kingsley Martin had provided an introduction. 'A venerable figure, or so it seemed to me then, with long grey hair hanging down on both sides of his face and a waistcoat stained by the droppings of innumerable cigars', the *Herald*'s man told him that he wouldn't get far in Munich as the correspondent of a socialist magazine like the *New Statesman*: he fished from his waistcoat pocket a grubby visiting card which read 'Correspondent of the *Detroit Daily News*' and presented it to Hugh, telling him that it would grant him 'a degree of immunity'. Armed with this alter ego and introductions from Graham to useful Jesuit connections ('No need to feign with these people an interest in Catholicism,' his brother assured him), Hugh travelled on to Munich in a wooden-seated fourth-class carriage. He took a room in the middle of the city, paid 70 pfennigs for a huge bowl of soup, meat and two vegetables ('more than I should have in two helpings in Crowborough'), listened to a sermon by Cardinal Faulhaber on the Jewish question, and earned himself 4 Reichsmarks an hour giving English lessons. He visited the Braunes Haus, where the Nazi Party had socialised since its earliest days, and 'everybody was very charming'; on another occasion he spotted Hitler in a corner with Goebbels, 'a tiny little man with a limp, but most attractive-looking, with a charming smile.'

Hugh's journalistic coups included an interview with Grock, a well-known clown, but 'above all I caught the true reporter's fever, the conviction that just round the corner something horrible or important was bound to be going on. And in Nazi Germany there really was something horrible going on just round the corner. Terror had become a part of ordinary respectable bourgeois daily life.' The family with whom he lodged taught him the cautionary verse:

> *Lieber Gott, mach mich stumm,*
> *Das ich nicht nach Dachau kumm!*

He claimed that from that moment on he never believed those who pleaded ignorance of what had gone on in Nazi Germany: 'the littlest of men knew and buried the horror, as far as they could, deep in their subconscious.' Eager to see the worst for himself, he visited Dachau in January 1934. His *Detroit Daily News* visiting card worked its magic, but when he was asked to hand over his passport to the SA, he realised, too late, that tucked inside was an unsealed envelope containing a pamphlet given to him by a member of the Communist underground. No mention was made of it, but it taught him a lesson. Dachau had been set up in March 1933, and its 3000 inmates were, for the most part, political prisoners. 'All I can remember is a hutted camp, prisoners who obviously wanted to talk to me but did not dare to do so because of my escort, an atmosphere of hopelessness,' he recalled years later. 'This was evil in broad daylight, not in the shadow of nightmares.' To 'Mumma' he wrote that 'the guards were quite the most brutal and criminal-looking collection of men I've ever seen, quite different from the prisoners. One is no longer allowed to speak to the prisoners because in the past, the commandant told me, foreign journalists who came used to tell lies about what the prisoners had told them.' He saw no evidence of cruelty, but 'the eyes of the prisoners were horrible.'

Rather than commit it to the post, Hugh gave the letter in which he described his visit to a friend who was returning to England. 'Please make no comment on its contents, except to let me know if you've received it, as all my correspondence is tampered with,' he told his mother. The fact that his mail was intercepted, in much the same way as his phone was sporadically tapped, explains why so many of his letters from Berlin were tedious affairs, devoted to tennis and gardening rather than the turbulent and terrifying times through which he was living. There was plenty to report from Munich itself – Catholic priests were being arrested every day ('I don't think the Catholic Church will sit down under this much longer'), there had been a surge in Monarchist sympathies, storm troopers were being moved into the city – but his articles, committed to the post rather than phoned through as they would be from Berlin, were 'inevitably destroyed by the censors here'. 'I am now a marked man and I don't think much is getting through,' he informed his mother, no doubt with a frisson of pride.

The British Consul in Munich, Donald Gainer, an admirer of Graham's novels, introduced Hugh to two people who were to loom large in his life: Helga Guinness, then aged seventeen, who had recently left school and was learning German in Munich; and Eustace B. Wareing, the *Daily Telegraph*'s chief correspondent in Berlin. Helga's father, Samuel Guinness, was a member of the banking branch of the Guinness family, and had made his own fortune as a merchant banker; her mother was Norwegian. Auburn-haired, pale-skinned and short-sighted, Helga was on uneasy terms with her parents, who tended to bring her out in a rash, and she was keen not to return home to their huge house in Cheyne Walk. For all his single-mindedness and determination, Hugh was as shy and as awkward as ever, and the two of them got on extremely well: she was impressed by his brain and amused by his versifying gifts ('Chocolates are brown./ Sardines are grey;/ Chocolates don't have children,/ Sardines may'). Wareing had the 'large, grey-moustached ruddy face of an army major, a short body and legs with a shambling, flat-footed walk.' He was a pill-gulping hypochondriac, kept himself in shape by means of spinal pads and body belts, and was extremely randy – Hugh remembered how, 'groaning at the exertion and risks to health entailed, he made a somewhat shaky way from bed to bed.' He advised Hugh to move to Berlin, and offered him a month's trial without pay. Hugh had yet to settle his Oxford 'battels', but 'in a moment of clarity I decided to go (the spectre of the Civil Service examination still grinned over my shoulder), and everything that has happened in my life since was somehow a natural progression from that decision.'

The *Daily Telegraph* had been bought by Sir William Berry – later Lord Camrose – in 1927, since when it had been transformed. Berry had cut the price to a penny and concentrated on news above all else, with the result that the circulation had soared. By 1932 it was selling 300,000 a day, 100,000 more than *The Times*; two years later it had passed the 500,000 mark, and it reached 750,000 by the outbreak of war. Although Camrose supported the National Government of Ramsay MacDonald and his successors Stanley Baldwin and Neville Chamberlain, he was far more critical of Germany itself, and of what was to become the British Government's policy of appeasement, than his competitors on *The Times*, still edited by Graham's old boss, Geoffrey Dawson – let alone Lord Rothermere's *Daily Mail*, which was unashamed in its admiration of Hitler and was once described by the American journalist William Shirer as 'a wonderful Nazi mouthpiece and sounding-board'. Hugh could never understand why British politicians and opinion-makers did not read *Mein Kampf* rather than the reports emanating from the British Embassy, after Nevile Henderson had replaced Eric Phipps as the Ambassador in 1937, and he never thought of Hitler and the Nazis as anything but evil and dangerous, both to their fellow-Germans and the world at large. Wareing felt much the same way – Goebbels was frequently infuriated by his reports – while 'the News Editor, Robert Skelton, was completely at one with the views of his man in Berlin, the Editor, A. E. Watson, was massively imperturbable, and the lead writers understood Hitler's aims very well.' But the conventional wisdom liked to think that, for all his brutality and his excesses, Hitler was amenable to reason and would stick to his word, that he was doing good things for the German people in terms of reducing unemployment and improving their self-esteem, and that Britain's nominal allies, the French, were duplicitous, vindictive and not to be relied upon. These views were combined with the belief that war must be avoided at any cost, and that Hitler's territorial claims in the Rhineland, Austria and even in Eastern Europe were justified by the grossly unfair terms of the Treaty of Versailles, which had not only subjected the defeated Germans to monetary reparations and humiliating military restrictions, but surrendered German territory and people to be ruled over by newly invented or resurrected states like Poland and Czechoslovakia.

Hugh moved to Berlin in February 1934, and immediately started work in the *Telegraph's* office, opposite that of *The Times* in Unter den Linden, the great boulevard that stretches away to the east from the Brandenburg Gate. He soon settled into a routine, shared by other foreign correspondents, whereby the early morning was spent scouring through the German newspapers, the mid-morning and early afternoon travelling around Berlin by train to follow up leads and talk to useful contacts, and the late afternoon and early evening writing up stories and phoning them through to London. The Berrys owned the *Sunday Times* as well as the *Telegraph*, and Wareing and Hugh filed copy for both papers – an arrangement that continued after Lords Camrose and Kemsley went their separate ways in 1937. Hugh's contacts included bankers (introduced to him by Sam Guinness), Catholic priests and Evangelical pastors ('never since I left school have I been such a regular church-goer'), underground Communists and Trotskyites, and the anti-Nazi Rote Kapelle group in the Air Ministry. He got to know Hitler's adjutant and former commanding officer, Captain Fritz Weidemann, who courted Helga with flowers after glimpsing her in a café, and became increasingly disillusioned with the regime and sympathetic to the opposition to Hitler. Weidemann in turn introduced Hugh to Bernard 'Fatty' Lescrinier, who had direct access to Goering and useful contacts in the Reichskanzlei: 'a likeable figure, honest, no Nazi and extremely useful', he kept Goering informed about the views of the foreign Press, and provided coups in return, particularly for the *Daily Telegraph*. And he would certainly have had dealings with Ernst 'Putzi' Hanfstaengel, Hitler's half-American, Harvard-educated foreign press chief: widely regarded as an amiable ass as well as a brilliant pianist, he once told a gathering of foreign correspondents, William Shirer among them, that they should 'report on affairs in Germany without attempting to interpret them. History alone can evaluate the events now taking place here under Hitler.' 'I fear Putzi's words fell on deaf, if good-humored, ears among the British and American correspondents, who rather like him despite his clownish stupidity,' Shirer recorded in his diary; as it turned out, Hanfstaengel fell foul of Hitler, and spent much of the war in America, advising his old friend President Roosevelt about the likely behaviour of his former comrades in Berlin. Every now and then Nazi leaders summoned foreign journalists to *Bierabends*, or beer evenings – Alfred Rosenberg's were held

in the sumptuous Adlon Hotel – and Goebbels held regular press conferences at the Ministry of Propaganda: but Shirer found it hard to establish
a working relation with them, partly because few of them had been out
of Germany, and they had little knowledge of foreign countries.

The thirties was the great age of the foreign correspondent, and many
of the best – William Shirer, Sefton Delmer, Norman Ebbutt, Douglas
Reed, Edgar Mowrer, H. R. Knickerbocker – were based in Berlin. Every
evening some or all of them would gather in an Italian restaurant called
the Taverne, the owner of which, Willi Lehman, was, according to Shirer,
'a big bluff German with nothing Italian about him'. In *Goodbye to Berlin*,
Christopher Isherwood described how 'the foreign correspondents dine
every night at the same little Italian restaurant, at a big round table in the
corner. Everyone else in the restaurant is watching them and trying to
overhear what they are saying. If you have a piece of news to bring them
– the detail of an arrest, or the address of a victim whose relatives might
be interviewed – then one of the journalists walks up and down with you
in the street.' For Shirer, who arrived in Berlin in August 1934 as the correspondent of the Hearst newspaper group, the Taverne was 'a momentary
haven from the daily strains of living and working in the topsy-turvy, ugly
Nazi world. It was a quiet, friendly place in which to gather after another
day of battling against the insufferable Nazi hacks and feeling battered and
drained by what we had to see and write. It drew us together and gave us
a collective spirit from which to draw encouragement and the strength to
face another uncertain day.' A *Stammtisch* or club table was reserved for
British, American and French journalists, plus the odd outsider like George
Kennan, a young diplomat from the American Embassy, Elizabeth Wiske-
mann, a former Cambridge don, and John Wheeler-Bennett, later to
become a well-known historian, who had access to sources denied to most
journalists and 'was able, on occasion, to confirm somebody's story or
indicate when I thought somebody else had been given what in American
slang is known as a "bum steer".' From time to time they were joined by
German colleagues, who provided tips or explained the infighting in the
Nazi party, but were treated with caution as potential spies or agents provocateurs: subversive material was offered up in a whisper or in the street,
out of range of Nazi eavesdroppers. According to Wheeler-Bennett, in the
early days of the Nazi regime the Gestapo always sent the same man to
sit at the next table to the *Stammtisch*, 'and when he showed up we would
talk spectacularly ridiculous nonsense in loud voices', and ask him to join
them for a drink, though 'life was soon to be far more realistic and much
less pleasant.'

At the head of the table sat Norman Ebbutt, *The Times*'s Berlin correspondent, a stocky figure in rimless glasses who 'sat in a corner puffing
an old pipe, holding forth in his rather high-pitched voice about the
news of the day and how little of it his distinguished newspaper was
publishing for fear of offending Hitler.' Hugh soon became friendly with
Ebbutt, whom John Wheeler-Bennett remembered as 'a benign, roly-
poly figure with a brilliant mind and a fine sense of journalistic morality',
and they spent much of their spare time playing tennis and *vingt-et-un*
together. Ebbutt had been *The Times*'s Berlin correspondent since 1927,
and Claud Cockburn had briefly worked as his assistant: it was generally agreed that he had better contacts in the Nazi hierarchy than any
of his rivals apart from the *Daily Express*'s Sefton Delmer, and knew
more about what was going on than anyone else, but was frustrated by
Geoffrey Dawson's reluctance to print material that might offend
Hitler or damage the Government's policy of appeasement. 'I do my
utmost, night after night, to keep out anything that might hurt their
susceptibilities,' Dawson once told his newspaper's chief European
correspondent. 'I really can think of nothing that has been printed for
many months past which they could possibly take exception to as unfair
comment.' Dawson's defenders claim that he valued, and agreed with,
much of what Ebbutt submitted, but had to cut heavily simply because
he invariably wrote over length. Dawson's reputation has been blackened by his association with appeasement: he detested the Nazi regime
but, according to Iverach Macdonald, who eventually replaced Ebbutt
as *The Times*'s man in Berlin, he was a firm believer in the hallowed
separation of news and comment, as well as believing that war should
be avoided at almost any cost. Either way, Ebbutt's colleagues benefited,
since he was happy to pass on to them information which, he claimed,
had been spurned or spiked by his editor.

According to Shirer, foreign correspondents' work was not censored
by the regime, nor were they expected to submit pieces for approval,
but those who went too far – like Sinclair Lewis's girlfriend Dorothy
Thompson in her book *I Saw Hitler* – might find themselves expelled.
'Over the next few years many of my colleagues – and they were usually
the brightest and the best – would get the axe,' Shirer recalled in his
memoirs, adding that 'I soon learned to watch my step. All through my
years in Berlin I was conscious of walking a real, if ill-defined, line. If
you strayed too far off it you risked expulsion. One soon got the feeling
how far one could go. I made up my own mind from the very beginning that as long as I could tell the essential story of Hitler's Germany,

I would stay, if I were allowed to. Once that became impossible, I would go.' All foreign correspondents were visited at some stage by the Gestapo, who grilled them about their informants: Shirer learned early on the importance of protecting his sources, who could all too easily be arrested, charged with treason and sentenced to death. Life in Berlin was a hazardous business, for journalists as well as natives. Shirer recalled walking round the city with Darsie Gillie, soon to be relocated to Paris as the correspondent of the *Morning Post*, and a future colleague of Hugh at the wartime BBC, and how every now and then they had to 'duck into stores to keep from either having to salute the standards of some passing SA or SS battalion or face the probability of getting beaten up for not doing so.' Hugh remembered how, when occasion demanded, Ward Price, the *Daily Mail*'s correspondent, gave the Hitler salute 'while the rest of his colleagues would stand around, with rather ostentatious nonchalance, with their hands in their pockets.' To Hugh's surprise, not all the police were Nazi sympathisers: walking home early one morning with Count Yorck von Wartenburg, who would later be involved in the 20 July 1944 bomb plot against Hitler, they passed a police post by the Brandenburg Gate: the Graf raised his arm in a Communist salute and shouted 'Rot Front', and a policeman returned his greeting. But life as a foreign correspondent was, inevitably, a nerve-wracking business: a month after his expulsion from Nazi Germany in August 1937, Norman Ebbutt suffered a severe stroke which left him paralysed and unable to speak, and he never worked again.

Hugh's first story for the *Telegraph* concerned two storm troopers who had flown to London in pursuit of girls, still wearing their SA uniforms, and had been sent home in disgrace by the German Embassy. Karl Robson of the *Morning Post* thought Hugh and his boss an odd couple – Wareing was 'a rather pedantic ex-schoolmaster', while Hugh was 'very much the undergraduate, the personification of an egg-head, very thin and languorous' – but Wareing seemed happy to let Hugh find his feet; every now and then he would pat Hugh on the shoulder in an avuncular way, remind him to put his name on half the stories he sent to London, and 'toddle off in search of girls and patent medicines'. Hugh, for his part, liked Wareing well enough, 'though he's not entirely easy to get on with'. Robson thought Hugh 'much too lackadaisical', was irritated by what he regarded as affectations of weariness and boredom, and was shocked to find him still in bed when he rang him at mid-morning in his furnished flat near the Brandenburg Gate. He found him rather remote: since Berlin was 'an unpleasant place to be', journalists tended to stick together, but

Hugh was not a clubbable figure, and 'he wasn't a bird for staying up late drinking when I first met him.' Ernst Albert of the Austrian News Agency thought him 'a pretty cold fish, but I don't think deliberately so. When you worked with him you had the feeling that there was a barrier . . . It was nothing positive to put you off but a lack of warmth.' 'Reading Hugh's stuff I used to think he was a little too restrained and cautious. He wasn't interpretive – I was much more interpretive,' Robson recalled. Most foreign correspondents were passionately anti-Nazi, but 'he didn't show any great passion for politics. I presume he had orders from the *Telegraph* to play it easy, not to get involved.'

In fact, Hugh never had any illusions about the Nazis, while his remoteness was a by-product of his extreme shyness and great height, as well as an innate coolness: but whatever his colleagues' personal and professional reservations, he was accepted as a full-time member of the Berlin bureau in March 1934, working alongside Anthony Mann as Wareing's assistant. This came as a great relief – in a moment of despondency, he had asked Gabbitas & Thring to send him details of teaching jobs back in England – and he celebrated with beer and goulash, a change from sardines eaten from the tin. Helga was still in Munich, but with 500 reichsmarks a month in his pocket, Hugh felt in a stronger position to advance his cause. 'Though I do like talking to you on the telephone, I'm not sufficiently mechanically minded to find it satisfactory or to be able to say "I love you" to a black mouthpiece with any conviction. And I do love you,' he told her, adding that he was about to cover a speech by Hitler, 'and as I can never understand what he says it's going to be rather difficult.' 'My own dearest darling Helga,' he wrote in more rhapsodic vein. 'I am no good at writing how much I love you. I prefer to kiss you very hard and tell you that way . . . It's easier to write about the limitation of armaments than about my love for you . . . That you love me as you do is something I never dreamed of before you came.' Declarations of undying love – 'I love you exceedingly, tempestuously' – were combined with hard-headed pragmatism: she could put him in touch with 'people who act as informants', and help him to get hold of 'the sort of stuff which does not appear in the paper, or what is behind what appears in the paper'. On her trips to England she could usefully scour the British papers, and come up with suggestions for background reading. Though very quick-witted, Helga was all too well aware of how badly educated she was by comparison with Hugh. 'I only feel sorry that I have not made the most of my opportunities,' she told him. 'There are so many different things in which one can be interested in this life and

I am so young that I am ashamed to admit it. I hope you will not expect too much from me at first. I mean not only for politics and such things but for marriage in general.'

In due course Hugh wrote to his parents to tell them that he was 'following my brother [Raymond] down the primrose path – in other words, I am engaged.' Luckily, he informed them, Helga was 'a Continental seventeen rather than an English seventeen! Otherwise she would be rather young to plunge into the general schemozzle of life out here, and the pretty tough and hard-boiled society of foreign correspondents.' His fiancée, it seemed, was 'not dark but, as you imagined, rather fair' and 'unless her father goes broke, she will have some money of her own.' Helga's parents were planning a visit to Berlin, and 'I'll let you know what I think of the parents before you need think of communicating with them.' He rather dreaded meeting the Guinnesses. 'I am really painfully ignorant of what I believe are called the proprieties,' he warned Helga. 'You know my argumentative nature and I should just love – but don't be afraid that I shall – to dispute the question of the so-called proprieties with people who believe in them . . . I have no patience with anything irrational – like fascism.' Likening his rather conventional future in-laws to fascists was hardly a promising start, and although Hugh told 'Mumma', after their first meeting, that they seemed 'fairly pleasant people', his view of them steadily worsened. Mrs Guinness, 'for someone exceptionally silly, has a curious amount of intelligence' and 'I like her faintly' but he didn't think he'd ever come round to Sam Guinness: 'There was something about him which vaguely repelled me, from the first moment I heard his voice.' He had useful connections in the banking world, but he soon proved 'a terribly uninteresting man with no idea of minding his own business' and a 'complete money snob'. For all his cleverness, Hugh was, like many young men, both callow and self-absorbed, and his dismissive remarks showed little sympathy for a couple who had recently lost their only son at the age of fifteen.

News of Hugh's engagement reached his family on the day of Raymond's wedding to Eleanor Gamble. 'The church on Monday was noisy with the news,' Graham told him. Their mother was pleased and proud, and 'there seemed to be a general impression that you had done something very clever if, like my novels, rather risqué' – presumably because Helga was so young. As for Raymond's wedding, it proved 'very successful: that is to say, the champagne was good and apparently endless.' Two years earlier, Graham had asked the editor of the *Graphic* whether he could write a piece about a Nazi demonstration in Munich:

nothing had come of it, but visiting Hugh in Berlin gave Graham the opportunity to indulge his new passion for flying, sample Nazi Germany at first-hand, and to renew his acquaintance with old friends like Count Bernstorff. In the summer of 1934 he passed through Berlin on his way to Estonia – Moura Budberg, the erstwhile mistress of Maxim Gorky, H. G. Wells and Hugh's future colleague Robert Bruce Lockhart, had told him it was very cheap, and urged him to visit 'a brothel in Talinn which had been kept in the same house by the same family for 700 years' – and on his return he wrote to his brother to say that he had 'liked Helga immensely'.

Sam Guinness appalled his future son-in-law by insisting on a very grand wedding in Chelsea Old Church with eight bridesmaids in attendance. Hugh insisted that he loved Helga 'both physically and mentally', and that 'with both we have the absolutely necessary foundation for a happy marriage', but – like Graham before him – dreaded the whole business of having children. 'I feel that the Christian view of marriage regarding children as a "primary purpose" is very degrading. I marry you because I believe that I can only get the greatest happiness possible for me living with you,' he told her. He longed to make love to her 'entirely for the pleasure and exaltation of the moment, and not in the least for results, which we shall anyhow be trying to prevent. The only reason why I should wish to have children at all – after some years – is because I know it would make you happier and therefore by derivation probably myself.'

But there was work to be done before the Greenes and the Guinnesses could foregather in Chelsea Old Church. In June 1934 Wareing went on an extended holiday to Italy, and Hugh was left holding the fort. He enjoyed being in charge, since 'it's my own responsibility if I drop a brick and not somebody else's, and though there's an awful lot of work there's no fussing.' Wareing's absence coincided with high drama in German domestic politics. Hitler's passing of the Enabling Act in 1933 may have ushered in a monolithic dictatorship in which all opposition would be ruthlessly crushed, and no hint of dissent allowed, but Hugh's *Telegraph* reports suggested that the Nazi hierarchy was bitterly divided, and that the regime was more vulnerable than it seemed. On 20 June he reported that Franz von Papen, the Vice-Chancellor, was in hot water for defending the right to criticise the regime, and that he was voicing the view of 'a great section of the German nation'. Goebbels had started a 'grandiose campaign' against critics and 'grousers' which was arousing both mirth and irritation, and Hugh revealed that 'the greeting "Good morning, you old grouser" has become a serious rival to the customary "Heil Hitler" even among the brownshirts. It is being asked everywhere how strong a government can be when it feels itself menaced by the grumbling of "beer-table politicians".' The following day von Papen attacked Goebbels and the left-wing of the Party. It was rumoured that Hitler and Goering sided with von Papen: posters advertising foreign newspapers in the Unter den Linden announced 'Storms in the Nazi Party', but had been taken down by the early afternoon. According to Sefton Delmer, von Papen was planning to overthrow Hitler with the help of the army and the aged Field-Marshal Paul von Hindenburg, a hero of the last war and the President of the Reich, and reinstate the Hohenzollerns. On the 25th Hugh reported that a shot had been fired at the car carrying Heinrich Himmler, the head of the SS, and that 'differences among the leaders are giving fresh encouragement to enemies of the Nazi regime of every political faction, including anarchists and Communists'; the following day he revealed that von Papen and Goebbels had both attended the Hamburg Derby, but whereas von Papen had been warmly applauded, the Minister of Propaganda had been received in silence. When not informing *Telegraph* readers about these internecine feuds – and the fact that the film *Tarzan and His Mate* had been banned on the grounds that both parties were too lightly clad – Hugh was enjoying the blazing summer weather. He told Helga that he was taking lessons in dancing and fencing, and had lost weight as a result, and that he and Wareing had spent a day sailing on the lakes near Berlin: 'Wareing was looking rather wild and piratical, and I must have been a fearsome sight with the rather nautical striped top of my bathing dress above my trousers, and my face foaming with the grease which Wareing had insisted I should apply.'

Earlier that month, Hugh had reported that Ernst Röhm, the head of the brown-shirted SA, had been granted sick leave, ostensibly on grounds of 'neuralgia of the left arm'. A hardened street-fighter, Röhm had been a close associate of Hitler from the early days in Munich. Sefton Delmer, who knew the Nazi leaders better than most, had a soft spot for 'this gay and expansive old gangster despite his thuggery and his outrageous private life', but according to the *Telegraph* 'his display of luxury has been frowned upon by Herr Hitler, a teetotaller and vegetarian, whose frugal way of life is renowned.' But there was more to it than Röhm's taste for 'sumptuous banquets' and boys in lederhosen. He wanted his storm troopers to be incorporated into, and eventually take over, the regular army, who despised and resented them as a brutish and undisciplined rabble. Hitler may have depended on them in the early days, but now he needed the support of the army in his planned bid to replace the ailing Hindenburg as President; he feared that Röhm planned a 'Second Revolution', and decided to take action. On the morning of 30 June, Hugh and Norman Ebbutt were playing tennis in the Tiergarten. 'We knew something was in the wind, and we played nervously,' so eventually they abandoned their game and wandered down to the Tiergartenstrasse, where they found brown-shirted SA men emerging from their Berlin headquarters with their hands above their heads before being rounded up and driven away by grey-clad members of Goering's Prussian State Police. Sefton Delmer, who was among the other journalists present, later wrote of how the Berlin public reacted to the news with 'grim satisfaction', since 'no one loved Röhm and his parvenu officers, the ex-waiters, ex-hotel porters and ex-plumbers.'

In a few years' time Delmer and Hugh would be colleagues and competitors, each deeply disapproving of the other. A tall, burly, genial character, 'Tom' Delmer had been born and brought up in Berlin; he spoke fluent German, and English with a slight German accent. After leaving Oxford he had returned to Berlin, where his Australian father, a former professor of English at Berlin University, acted as stringer for various newspapers. He met Lord Beaverbrook, who was visiting Berlin with Arnold Bennett, Viscount Castlerosse and Lady Diana Cooper, and 'the Beaver' made him the *Express*'s bureau chief at the age of twenty-four. He was the first British journalist to visit the Brown House in Munich, and Hitler invited him to accompany him on his 1932 election campaign, travelling by air from one German city to another. His most celebrated scoop to date had been to accompany Hitler around the smouldering remains of the Reichstag the previous year. He had deliberately set out to cultivate the Nazi hierarchy, as a result of which, according to Wheeler-Bennett, he had 'an entrée to their headquarters which was unequalled'. But he was regarded as a 'lone wolf' by his colleagues and rivals, 'and was somewhat suspect in the Taverne circle, who were to a man openly anti-Nazi'. Unlike them, he liked to have a whole suite at his disposal: 'I can only think clearly in a five-star hotel,' he once declared.

'I remember that I had a sinking feeling in my stomach. I had only been engaged by the *Daily Telegraph* four months before, my boss was away, and with all my inexperience, I had to cover one of the biggest stories of the decade,' Hugh recalled of his role in covering what came to be known as the Night of the Long Knives. Back in the office, he learned that all telephone lines abroad had been temporarily suspended, and that Goering – rather than Goebbels – was about to hold a meeting for foreign journalists in the Ministry of Propaganda. Goering had masterminded the rounding-up and shooting of SA men in Berlin, while Hitler had hurried down to Munich where, earlier that morning, he had burst into Röhm's bedroom in Bad Wiessee on the Tergensee, found him in bed with a good-looking youth, and ordered his immediate arrest. 'Goering, in his air force uniform, came in jauntily swinging his paunch,' Hugh remembered: '"Some journalists," concluded General Goering with a twinkle in his eye, "like to make a story [he used the English word] out of very little things. You need not make a story out of this; it is there all right."' Hugh went on to reveal how Frau von Schleicher had been shot dead by SS men when she tried to stop them gunning down her husband in the middle of lunch. Ghastly as it had all been, he found it hard not to ridicule the Nazi leaders. 'There is a feeling of horror over the way in which some of the victims were hurried out of life,' he reported three days later, but although 'the dramatic picture by Dr Goebbels of Herr Hitler bearding the lions in their den in Munich made a great impression, some of the glamour is wearing off as it dawns on people that the lions were fast asleep. Inevitably the question is put: what kind of dangerous conspirators were these who, unguarded and unsuspecting, slept peacefully through the night of revolt?' On 11 July all copies of the *Daily Telegraph* in Germany were confiscated, and Goebbels denounced foreign correspondents, and the *Telegraph*'s man in particular, for indulging in 'revolver journalism'. Three days later Hugh was forbidden from entering the Reichstag, which now met at the Kroll Opera House, to hear Hitler justify his purges. He was told that his press card was no longer valid: he was eventually let in after pointing out that his card was identical to those of his colleagues, but that day the *Telegraph* was banned again, this time for a fortnight, by Dr Wilhelm Frick, the Minister of the Interior. Hugh was unconcerned. Journalism, he told Helga, 'has got into my blood too much for me to be happy at any other job. In fact I've got much more of the journalist's instinct than Wareing. He's glad to be away while exciting things are happening and there's a lot to do, whereas I should be mad if I was out of the country during any really big story. I've fallen under the drug all right.'

Ever the professional, Hugh – following up Hitler's claim that full details of the purge would be made available – set out to draw up a complete list of those who had been murdered or committed suicide, but although he 'rang the Propaganda Ministry and asked if they could admit or deny the names on this list, the reply was that no information could be given.' Delmer published his own 'Death List' in the *Express*, and was told that he was to be expelled from Germany as a result: after consulting Beaverbrook he rang the Propaganda Ministry and threatened to reveal all he knew unless his expulsion was revoked, and 'that was the end of my beautiful friendship with Hitler.'

Good journalists are writers as well as sleuths, and a fortnight later Hugh produced one of the finest pieces he ever wrote about Nazi Germany. 'I wonder if I shall get the story tonight or if he will hold out a bit longer,' Hugh told Helga after learning that Hindenburg was dying. A week later he attended a ceremony of mourning at the Reichstag – 'to make my dirty tweed suit look a little more like mourning I wore a black armband and a black tie with a white cricket shirt' – before going on to the old man's funeral, along with 80,000 mourners. It was, he told *Telegraph* readers, 'one of the most extraordinary displays of military pomp and grandeur Germany has ever seen'. Lasting for four hours, it was held at the Tannenberg Memorial, built on the flat Prussian plains to commemorate a First World War victory over the Russians. Fires had been lit on top of each of its eight towers, all of which had been draped in black streamers: it was a blazing hot day, the smoke could be seen for miles around, and 'the whole building appeared like some sinister dream city of the future.' The walls of the Memorial had been covered with black crêpe, and were lined with soldiers and sailors with their rifles reversed: 'the black of the Nazi guards, the grey of the Reichswehr, the green of the Goering police, the steel blue of the "air sportsmen", the olive green of the Labour Corps, and the brown of the Storm Troops united with the exotic uniforms of aged generals and foreign military attachés to form a picture of uniformed strength.' Hitler made a speech which ended 'Dead warrior, go now into the Valhalla. There the German spirit of yore now meets you,' and the singing of 'Deutschland über alles' was followed by the 'Horst Wessel Lied'. According to Hugh's report, at the first note of the Eroica Symphony 'a huge hawk which had been hovering above the ceremony uttered a shrill cry and soared into the sky', but he later admitted that this was pure invention, and had been added to please the acting foreign editor in London, who had a passion for birds and liked them to be smuggled into every story where possible. The seats were unbearably hard and Hugh had a boil on his bottom, and after writing his report in a field he phoned his story through to the Berlin office 'from a hotel that stank to high heaven. The line was so bad that the call took an hour. The phonebox was very small. You can imagine the condition of heat and rage in which I emerged.' The result was a triumph, both entertaining and an evocation of Nazi neo-paganism at its most sinister and seductive.

After holding the fort with such aplomb, Hugh was gratified to learn from Wareing that his name 'breathed forth a sweet odour' in the London office. Back-handed compliments to Hugh and his fellow correspondents were provided by Goebbels, who attacked foreign journalists as 'well-poisoners', who 'should not come here with such slogans as intellectual freedom, which means no more than freedom to lie.' Unabashed, Hugh followed Goebbels's suggestion that he and his colleagues should spend more time talking to the man in the street, with particular reference to a forthcoming plebiscite on whether or not Hitler should succeed Hindenburg as President. 'The answers foreign journalists obtain from German workers are not usually such as would please the Minister of Propaganda,' Hugh reported. 'I discussed the plebiscite with a taxi driver. "Plebiscite," he said scathingly, "it's no plebiscite. If one votes 'yes', well and good; if one votes 'no'" – he stopped and drew his hand across his throat . . .' Life as a foreign correspondent was becoming an ever more hazardous affair, but Hugh told his mother that Elisabeth, who was planning a walking holiday in Germany, should be safe enough provided they steered clear of Franconia, 'Julius Streicher's territory'.

Hugh and Helga were married in Chelsea Old Church that October, just after Helga's eighteenth birthday. The wedding was conducted by George Bell, the Bishop of Chichester, who was to become a contro-versial figure during the war on account of his vocal support for the resistance movement in Germany, including those involved in the 20 July 1944 attempt on Hitler's life, and was described by the Foreign Secretary Anthony Eden as a 'pestilent priest'. 'Tell Da that neither of us enjoyed the wedding,' Hugh wrote to Mumma afterwards. Sam Guinness had refused to allow Hugh to describe himself as a 'journalist' on the marriage certificate, insisting on 'Bachelor of Arts' instead, and relations between them deteriorated rapidly thereafter. 'I know no people I dislike more,' Hugh told Mumma. Sam Guinness hated to see Helga opening a door for herself, and thought the newly-weds should employ more servants, including a chauffeur. 'If one met such an impossible nouveau riche character in a book one would say "How far-fetched,"' Hugh declared, adding that his father-in-law's suggestions were 'sickening nonsense'. But although Helga often sided with Hugh against her parents, she soon discovered that he was neither mature nor responsible enough for marriage, as well as sharing Graham's views on fatherhood. 'One sensed that their hearts weren't in it,' Karl Robson recalled, and that they were 'very different temperamentally', while from Hugh's point of view, 'one couldn't live the life of a married man, that didn't go with being a journalist.' 'He neither considered other people, nor did he need other people much,' Helga recalled. The two people he felt closest to were his mother and Graham: 'he liked his drinking companions . . . Otherwise he liked to read or relax or go to the theatre or a film.' They drifted further apart after the births of Graham in June 1936, and James some eighteen months later. Helga spent the Christmas of 1936 in New York, leaving Graham to be looked after by a nanny. 'I actually went to see how the baby was last Monday,' Hugh reported to Crowborough. 'He seemed very well. I didn't give him his present, I'm afraid.' As for the newborn James, 'it looks exactly like Graham did, not red which is something, though all babies seem to me rather disgusting.' According to Helga, Hugh 'opted out of fatherhood, but I made the mistake of not forcing him back in.' As for his two eldest sons, 'he always said he felt about them as if they were rather nice nephews.' Marriage made him restless in other ways as well: despite the fascination of his work, he briefly contemplated having another crack at the film business, and the Film Institute in particular, and sounded out Graham about possible jobs. Graham, who sometimes considered giving up writing novels for a career in films, was seeing a good deal of film-makers like Alberto Cavalcanti, Basil Wright and John Grierson of the GPO Film Unit. He wrote back expressing surprise at Hugh's revival of interest – 'I thought you were permanently wedded to journalism' – and no more was heard on the matter.

Every now and then members of the Greene family would appear in Berlin: Graham and Barbara en route to Estonia, albeit at different times, and Vivien, who proved 'blessedly independent after the Guinness family'. In February 1935 Ben loomed up for a visit, and Hugh 'felt smaller than ever beside him'. Heavily industrialised, the Saar was, according to Sefton Delmer, 'the most dangerously explosive area of Europe': it shared a border with France, and was adjacent to the Palatinate, which Graham had visited while at Oxford. Under the terms of the Treaty of Versailles, it had been administered by the French on behalf of the League of Nations, on the understanding that after fifteen years a plebiscite would be held in which the Saarlanders would be asked whether they wanted to be reunited with Germany. Rioting was expected between local Nazis and French-backed anti-Nazis: British, French and Italian troops had been sent in to keep the peace, and the League of Nations provided a team of observers under 'the motherly Miss Sara Wambaugh' to ensure fair play. Ben had been asked by the League of Nations to be the Deputy

Chief Returning Officer and, as a fluent German-speaker, he was well equipped to keep an eye on the proceedings. In the event, over 90 per cent of the population voted in favour. 'The Saar was a good tonic for Ben,' Felix told Eppy and Eva. 'He has found some of his buoyancy again. He must not be allowed to slip back into the dreariness of the Kepston-garage routine. When he's alive and keen, Ben is *grand*: when sunk in details about which he does not care, he gets sullen.'

A year later Ben was back in the Saarland to investigate, on behalf of the Quakers, the alleged intimidation of Jews and anti-Nazis since re-unification with the Reich. According to a Society of Friends minute, he had been 'approved as an acceptable neutral by National Socialist and United Front Germans', and was suited for the job by 'his concern, his personal experience, his objectivity and his quiet manner': Ben later learned that the police had watched him throughout the plebiscite proceedings, 'and were quite satisfied of my harmless intentions'. On his arrival at Saarbrücken railway station he was amazed to see two former Communists working there, and he soon discovered that half the former Social Democrats he had met on his earlier visit were now 'enthu-siastic Nazis'. Most of the Jewish population had left for France or Belgium, taking advantage of a clause in the Rome Agreement whereby they could, for the first year after reunification, take their money with them when they left. He spoke to a Jewish shopkeeper, who denied that she had been arrested or maltreated: hers was the only Jewish-owned shop left in Saarbrücken, but the police had come to her aid when the SA had tried to cause trouble outside it. All in all, Ben was favourably impressed. The head of police told him that Communists had been sent to concentration camps, and that the French were fomenting trouble. 'I am not happy about the conditions in the villages, where some of the Party leaders have run amok,' Ben declared, but he was pleased by plans for slum clearance, new housing estates and improved working condi-tions, and 'I have come away with the belief that the populace have in no way regretted their decision to return to Germany and are well satis-fied with the workings of the new regime.' He met Herr Bürckell, the Gauleiter for the Saarland, and 'was impressed by his sincerity and his obvious wish to maintain the spirit of the Rome Agreement'. The Mayor of Saarbrücken told him that Communists had been spreading rumours about a reign of terror, and 'on investigation on the spot I came to the conclusion that there was little if any foundation for these reports of political and racial maltreatment, and I traced them to a German exile living in Lorraine.' Before long Ben's involvement in the Saar was to have unfortunate side effects, in that it 'was used to support a frequent suggestion that I was a Nazi agent'.

Ben was back in Berlin at the time of the 1936 Olympics, but there is no record of his seeing Hugh again. Some years later he claimed he was there because John Wheeler-Bennett had asked him to provide authoritative translations of Hitler's speeches for the Royal Institute for International Affairs at Chatham House, and that through the Anglo-German Fellowship he had been introduced to a source in Berlin. But Ben was not the only member of his family to visit Germany. Barbara's former maid, Friedel, a keen admirer of Hitler, kept in touch with the Greenes at Little Wittenham, and various members of the Stutzer family were still living in Germany. After Ben had returned from his first trip to the Saarland full of enthusiasm, Felix decided to take a look for himself. He went to stay with Aunt Ille in Huchting: both her sons were in the Hitler Youth, and his cousin Claus was off to camp, 'knife in his belt and with shoulder strap, the complete soldier of tomorrow.' A week later he visited a prison camp in Nordfriesland, not far from the Dutch border. 'It was a shock to me,' he told his parents. 'My complacent preconceptions gathered from the general currency of thought in England were very effectively shattered. I began to think – what *did* I know of Germany? Our papers tell us of brutality (I dare say there is plenty of that) and bullying, of conscription, of rapid rearmament, of restriction of the freedom of speech, of June 30th 1934, of that awful talk about "racial destiny" which makes Englishmen feel quite sick, of militarism and aggressiveness, Now I'm quite seriously asking myself whether that is a fair picture . . . There is hardship, but there is constructive enterprise.'

The six camps in the area formed part of the Emsland group, which had been recently reorganised by Theodor Eicke, a former commandant of Dachau. Each contained about a thousand prisoners who, Felix was told, spent their days improving the barren soil and growing corn, vegetables and apples. 'I cannot help feeling that is symbolic of the new Germany,' he declared, and 'watching these prisoners work – they looked healthy and, judging by the diet sheets, were well treated – I thought of our own prisoners wasting their lives in idleness.' Elsewhere he was shown how the previously unemployed were being put to work digging canals and building houses. Remembering his earlier visits to Tyneside and South Wales, 'I could not but think of our own standing at street corners or playing darts at the nearest pub. We boast of our sense of freedom which prevents us putting men to work for so little money, but I cannot think what freedom we give our unemployed except the freedom to rot.' He visited a camp for old and injured people, and years later he recalled that 'as I went round the camp – it was an open place, no guards, no soldiers – I remember feeling "Well, they are looking after these poor wrecks pretty well." The place was neat and clean, there were flowers in the gardens, the attendants appeared to be gentle and caring . . . I gave a report about this visit (I don't know to whom) and later I was accused of having been fooled – that this was one of the "extermination" camps which we began to hear about much later.'

Felix was shown round the camps by a commandant called Georg Schafer, who momentarily froze with horror at his guest's indiscretions. 'Laughingly I said to a group at one of the camps, "You see, what we don't like is not being allowed to say what we think. If I said what a frightful man Hitler is you'd pop me in there" – pointing to inside the barbed wire. This was met with dead silence. Then Georg said, "But you don't understand – no one *can* say anything against Hitler." "That's just what I mean. No one can say anything, but you can't help them thinking it." "Ah," somebody else said, "that shows how little you know. No one is able even to *think* bad things about the Leader. He is above that." Well, I mean to say . . .'

Schafer's brother was 'highly influential in Nazi HQ in Berlin', and 'everywhere men quivered to attention as we walked or swept by in our enormous car.' Schafer listened carefully while Felix elaborated his views on Anglo-German friendship. 'For far too long she has been inferior with a smarting sense of impotence. Power she needs, and power she will get,' Felix declared. 'Germany's need for power and equality can be largely satisfied by a close and reliable understanding with Britain,' and she was 'ready, willing and anxious to give her friendship to England.' Warming to his subject, he went on to say that German propaganda and representation in Britain were quite hopeless: Hitler's speeches were made to sound unduly 'insulting or ridiculous', and he would never have dismissed the popular Count Bernstorff from the Embassy had he anticipated its 'profoundly shocking' effect on London society. 'Berlin must know of this,' Schafer gravely informed his new friend, and promised to arrange for Felix to meet officials from the Ministry of Propaganda, including 'perhaps Goebbels himself'. Felix hoped to meet both Ribbentrop and Hess in Berlin': nothing came of these projected meetings, but through Sheila MacDonald he was introduced to Jochen Bennemann, a senior figure in the Hitler Youth movement. With Bennemann, he arranged for a Hitler Youth party to visit England, camping in the fields at Little Wittenham and visiting the House of Commons. 'Some of them looked darlings, quite loveable and fresh,' he told his parents. 'They'll be black and dirty by the time they get to you, but they're grand stuff underneath.' Sheila MacDonald also introduced Bennemann to Ben, and through the Anglo-German Circle they arranged exchange visits between Boy Scouts from Berkhamsted and members of the Hitler Youth.

'He has this marvellous quality of believing in human nature. Without that he wouldn't have got where he did, but it did make him very unrealistic at times,' Sheila MacDonald once said of Felix, but while his cousins found things to admire in Nazi Germany, and sympathised with German grievances, Hugh became increasingly convinced of the inevitability of war. A visit to Memel, a German enclave which had been ceded to Lithuania and was agitating to be reunited with the Reich, provided a timely reminder of the problems inherent in the postwar settlement of Europe. 'It was rather a nice change to be regarded by the population as something approaching St George,' he told his mother. Hugh and other journalists found themselves jostled by cheering villagers thrusting flowers in their faces and shouting 'You are our deliverers!' while 'the Lithuanian police looked on sourly.'

In March 1936 Hitler marched his troops into the demilitarised Rhineland. According to Hugh, although 'most journalistic and some diplomatic observers in Berlin understood with complete clarity that this was the last chance to stop Hitler in his tracks,' Hitler had sensed the 'blindness, weakness and cowardice of the French and British governments', and exploited their combination of fear and guilt to maximum effect. Hugh went along to the Kroll Opera House to hear Hitler justify his acts. After a 'long boring preamble about world politics and National Socialist philosophy', the Führer announced that the recent Franco-Soviet treaty had annulled the provisions of the Treaty of Locarno, so justifying the occupation. Hugh kept his 'eye on General Werner von Fritzsch, the commander-in-chief of the German army, only two years later to be dismissed by Hitler on trumped-up charges of sexual relations with a male prostitute. The general, I noticed, was not on this occasion the very model of a calm, poker-faced Prussian officer. He fidgeted, he sweated, he kept polishing his monocle.' William Shirer noted that General von Blomberg, the War Minister, was 'as white as a sheet', and that 'he kept fumbling the tip of the bench with his fingers.' Both men knew that Hitler was bluffing, yet *The Times*, 'with its usual fatuity', ignored Norman Ebbutt's reports and hailed Hitler's coup as 'A Chance to Rebuild'. Wareing and Hugh together wrote a long piece for the *Telegraph* in which they said that the Rhineland would now be fortified, to the detriment of

France, that Austria would soon be swallowed up, that Czechoslovakia would be unable to resist German territorial claims, and that Poland would be bullied into giving up Danzig and the Polish Corridor. To their frustration, the article was never used. Ribbentrop, who was in London at the time, persuaded Lord Camrose that their article was nonsense, and it was spiked. Back in Berlin, Ribbentrop took Hugh out to lunch, but 'neither Wareing nor I, after the failure to do anything about the Rhineland, expected any action by Britain or France at any point to interfere with Hitler's plans.' A referendum was held to endorse Nazi policies, with 98.8 per cent voting in favour. Hugh visited former Communist strongholds in Berlin on voting day, and reported that although the streets were less decorated than elsewhere, 'the main impression was one of apathy.'

These were, Hugh told his mother, 'depressing times, but there'll be worse soon.' Most of the other inhabitants of the block of flats in which he and Helga lived had been arrested and taken away; food was in such short supply that Hugh anticipated ration cards ('already there is no beef or pork, and there'll soon be no eggs or butter'); life in Germany was 'rather like living in a lunatic asylum where everybody's got megalo-mania and persecution complex combined. One can never escape a feeling of being in an enemy country.' He sought solace in his roof garden, and asked his father for gardening tips and advice. Light relief of a kind was also provided by a visit from the Duke and Duchess of Windsor. 'After Benito we've had the Windsors, and I've been going round everywhere with them,' Hugh told his parents. The Duke was 'nice and easy to get on with,' the Duchess 'very charming and much better in the flesh than in photographs,' and Hugh had his photograph taken with them at a Nazi training school in Pomerania. He also visited the headquarters of the Austrian Legion in Bad Godesberg, and noted the Nazi banners already inscribed with the names of all the main Austrian towns and cities. In July a pact was signed with Austria, and two Nazis were offered places in Dr Kurt von Schuschnigg's Cabinet. The Spanish Civil War broke out, and Hitler authorised the supply of men and arms to Franco's rebels; Goering announced a Four Year Plan, with no limits on rearmament; belatedly taking the advice of Raymond's former acquaintance, General Haushofer, a passionate Japanophile, Hitler signed an Anti-Comintern Pact with Japan, and visits were exchanged between Hitler and Mussolini. Worse was to come, and Hugh had no illusions on that score.

Real and Imaginary Adventures

A great deal of champagne was drunk at Hugh's and Helga's wedding reception, during the course of which Graham, who had downed his fair share, buttonholed the younger and fitter-looking guests with an unusual request. Heinemann, he explained, had commissioned him to write a book about Liberia, the poverty-stricken West African republic created as a refuge for former American slaves who wanted to return to their continent of origin. He hadn't been out of Europe before, didn't want to go alone, and since Vivien, with a small child to look after, was hardly in a position to go tramping through the bush, he wondered whether any one present would like to come with him. Tooter was among those who declined his offer, but then, as a last resort, he turned to his cousin Barbara – who, to his amazement, agreed at once. No sooner had they sobered up than they both had second thoughts. Liberia had been racked by civil wars, largely between the descendants of American slaves and the indigenous peoples of the interior, so Graham sent Barbara a Foreign Office document which spelled out in detail how the American-born Colonel Davis had waged brutal war against Kru tribesmen, and how President King had shipped his fellow-citizens into slavery in Fernando Po, in the hope that it would put her off the idea: but 'luckily for me my cousin appeared unmoved by the reading material I sent her, for she proved as good a companion as the circumstances allowed, and I shudder to think of the quarrels I would have had with a companion of the same sex.' Barbara asked her father for his views. '"Papa," I said timidly, "I've done a very silly thing. I've told Graham I'd go to Liberia with him." My father, after only a moment's pause, answered quietly but firmly: "At *last* one of my daughters is showing a little initiative."'

Barbara's life so far had been rather unsatisfactory. After leaving school she had amazed her family by insisting on training as a nurse at the Truby King Infants' Hospital. Her real reason for doing so was that she wanted to get away from home and live in London, but she soon discovered that hospital life was less fun than she'd hoped: the hours were long, the discipline stern, and she was far too exhausted for a busy social life. After six months she begged her parents to allow her to give it up, but Eva told her that, having made such a fuss in the first place, she must see it through to the end. Years later she made good use of her training when bringing up two small children in a remote and primitive corner of the Argentine, but that was as far as it went. Nor had her love life come up trumps, lively and attractive though she was. On a trip to Brazil she had met and fallen in love with a banker a good many years her senior. They had dinner together the night before she took the boat back to England, he waved her off from the quayside, and they never saw each other again. A few weeks later, devastated to learn that he had died of yellow fever, she moped about the house at Little Wittenham, casting a pall of gloom, until Eppy eventually summoned her into his study and told her to get a grip on herself. As for her cousin Graham, 'we had never had a great deal to do with one another before Fate and champagne decided to link our lives.'

Graham and family were planning to leave Oxford, which they would do the following year, moving to a handsome red-brick Queen Anne house on Clapham Common recommended by Derek Verschoyle. Restless and claustrophobic by nature, he was eager to broaden his horizons, spurred on perhaps by feelings of rivalry and admiration for Raymond's Himalayan achievements, and a desire to escape the demands of domesticity. This was, he wrote years later, 'a period when "young authors" were inclined to make uncomfortable journeys in search of bizarre material – Peter Fleming to Brazil and Manchuria, Evelyn Waugh to British Guiana and Ethiopia. Europe seemed to have the whole future; Europe could wait.' The itch to travel had been further aggravated by reading a biography of H. M. Stanley, the mid-Victorian explorer of Africa, as well as Gide's *Voyage au Congo* and Conrad's *Heart of Darkness*. Uncle Graham put him in touch with Sir John Harris at The Anti-Slavery and Aborigines Protection Society, who offered him advice and useful contacts in return for his giving a speech on his return. 'You will, I am sure, understand how difficult it is to give advice with regard to a lady going to the tropics; so much depends on her own state of health, but given good health I see no reason why your cousin should not go with you,' Sir John suggested apropos Graham's travelling companion. He recommended that Barbara should be chaperoned, and felt sure that the Church Missionary Society could find a 'suitable missionary-trained woman who would take the journey with you'. 'Do you know anyone in England who owns a revolver?' Graham asked Hugh. He'd been strongly advised to take one with him, though 'my own feeling is that it would be more dangerous to me than to anyone else, and I certainly can't afford to buy one.' He'd been reading books on Liberia, one of which revealed that no European rash enough to venture over the border from Sierra Leone had ever returned, but 'this, of course, is not to be repeated to the family.' Frustratingly, *The Times* refused to commission him to write about the adventure, or appoint him their special correspondent, though they did give him a letter of accreditation.

'I wept a little, and boasted a lot, and tried very hard to look like an explorer as I left London in a thick mackintosh and a "sensible" hat,' Barbara recalled of their departure. They took a cargo boat to Freetown, where Barbara had herself made a pair of pink taffeta shorts: they were both baggy and brief, and 'somehow managed to look like a ballet skirt. I am tall and hefty and later, as we got tired towards the end of our trip, these shorts were to get so much on my cousin's nerves that he was ready to scream every time he saw them.' They hired four 'boys' to look after them and a team of twenty-six porters, all of whom Graham addressed in 'rather literary English'. They had been told that the natives only responded to shouts, and that they would steal, mutiny or desert at the slightest provocation, but Graham spoke to them in exactly the same way as he spoke to anyone else, and even if 'his method of conversation was far from simple, and he used long complicated phrases', they seemed to enjoy his jokes and came to see him as a 'benevolent father'. After consulting their maps of Liberia, which were full of blank spaces marked 'wild animals' or 'cannibals', they set out for the north-western frontier with Sierra Leone: from there they would make their way in a southerly direction to the capital, Monrovia, where another cargo ship would take them home. Now that they were deep in the African bush, 'it seemed rather unreal' to Barbara. 'Any moment, I thought, I will wake up and find myself in London. I will look out of the window and see the usual damp and dreary January morning. My ancient maid will come in with some tea, and the bath water will probably be cold. I will open the paper and read that Europe is again on the verge of a crisis, that there has been another strike, that unemployment figures are going up, that there have been a few more murders most foul . . .'

Originally published as *Land Benighted* but reissued years later with the more anodyne title of *Too Late to Turn Back*, Barbara's account of their adventures is a masterpiece of modest self-deprecation and comic observation, but 'should the reader of this book lean towards the roaring lion type of adventure, let him cast this volume from him. The beasts of the forest kept away from us, the natives were friendly, our adventures were more amusing than frightening, and good luck dogged our footsteps for most of the time.' The countryside was flat and uninteresting, and they plodded single-file along narrow, dusty paths for hours on end, starting at 5.30 every morning, while it was still comparatively cool. The bush on either side was too high to allow views of any kind: 'I was far too stolid in my nature to be able to imagine beauties and excitements where my eye did not see them', and although Barbara had been told about the beauties of the African jungle, 'here it seemed dead, untidy, endlessly big but without any vitality. There was nothing but a ghastly monotony and dreariness.' With nothing to look at, she became obsessed by the way in which Graham's knee-length socks inched their way down his legs to concertina over his boots, before being snagged up again with a grunt of irritation ('"I wish he would pull up his socks," I said to myself, as we were striding along, for by this time I had got well into the way of talking to myself as if I were two people').

They made no use of their tents, but spent nights in villages along the way, where they were offered the use of a hut thatched with palm, banana leaves or rushes. 'I expect you have often seen native huts in Brazil and thought, "How can people live like that!" Well, that's how we have been living, and we have another fortnight or three weeks of it,' Barbara told her parents in a letter which probably reached home after its sender. Rats swarmed everywhere, forcing their way into her suitcase, chewing holes in her clothes and munching the bristles of her hairbrush. Graham had been told he'd get used to them, but 'I had never got used to mice in the wainscot, I was afraid of moths. It was an inherited fear, I shared my mother's terror of birds, couldn't touch them, couldn't bear the feel of their hearts beating in my palm. I avoided them as I avoided ideas I didn't like, the idea of eternal life and damnation. But in Africa one couldn't avoid them any more than one could avoid the supernatural.' When not being bitten by rats – they found her far tastier than Graham – Barbara fought off armies of ants and prised jiggers from the soles of her feet. As for the fleas and lice, 'I've never had such faithful friends in my life.' The food was vile, consisting for the most part of stringy chickens, eggs and 'enormous bowls of rice covered with an evil-smelling, bright yellow sauce, with odd lumps of meat or fish thrown on the top', and despite the bearers' hearty cries of 'Plenty fine chop', she could seldom face a second helping.

Negotiating terms for food and lodgings usually proved 'a long and irritating business', which Graham conducted 'with unfailing patience'; despite appearing 'vague and impractical', Barbara was 'continually astonished at the efficiency and the care which he devoted to every little detail'. He was not the most communicative of travelling companions, and although in later life they became very fond of each other, Barbara found him fairly alarming. 'His brain frightened me. It was sharp and clear and cruel,' she recalled, and 'apart from the three or four people he was really fond of, I felt that the rest of humanity was to him like a heap of insects that he liked to examine, as a scientist might examine his specimens, coldly and clearly. He had a remarkable sense of humour and held few things to be too sacred to be laughed at. I suppose at that time I had a very conventional little mind, for I remember he was always tearing down ideas I had always believed in, and I was left to build them up anew.' But he was 'stimulating and exciting', and 'the best kind of companion one could have for a trip of this kind'. Apart from his ever-descending socks, she became gripped by a twitching nerve over his right eye, and noted that 'for some reason he had a permanently shaky hand, so I hoped that we would not meet any wild beasts on our trip.' As Graham's account of their journey makes plain, Graham was more introspective and more philosophically inclined than his travelling companion, anxious to find in primitive Africa that 'primal memory' that is common to us all, and those 'ancestral threads' which lead back to the heart of darkness. He compared travelling in Africa to a psychoanalyst confronting a patient with something long repressed, 'a long journey backwards without maps', at the end of which 'one has to face the general idea, the pain or the memory. This is what you have feared, Africa may be imagined as saying, you can't avoid it, there it is creeping round the wall, flying in at the door, rustling the grass, you can't turn your back, you can't forget it, so you may as well take a long look.' Appropriately enough, Graham's only reading matter consisted of Richard Burton's *Anatomy of Melancholy*, whereas Barbara tried to relax with the short stories of Saki and Somerset Maugham.

'It is strange, and perhaps rather horrible, how quickly we adapt ourselves to our surroundings,' Barbara wrote some three years after their return. 'My life in England had been led in pleasant places. All my life I had been used to well-cooked food and beautiful clothes, a lovely house filled with people who smoothed out for me as far as possible the rough patches on my road through life. I was taken care of and spoilt both by my family and my friends, and the little, dull, tiresome everyday things were automatically done for me. I had liked to find my evening clothes spread out for me ready pressed on my bed, my bath ready for me, and then to come down to a dinner lit by candle-light. Beauty, comfort and a good deal of luxury had been part of my life.' Quite apart from the 'stupefying boredom' of traipsing through the bush, she was now 'surrounded by rats, disease, dirt, and foul smells, and yet in a very few days I had sunk to that level and did not mind at all.' On a more positive note, 'I began to see the beauty of this strange land: the women rhythmically pounding the rice; the naked babies playing in the dust; the little villages with their mud huts painted white and thatched with palm leaves, set high on a hill like some mediaeval fortress; the magical moonlit nights, and weird music.' For all the filth and exhaustion, 'the beauty of the villages, the courtesy of the natives, the music, the dancing, the warm moonlit nights were things that gladdened the heart anew every day.'

Nor was life entirely lacking in variety or excitements. They called on a German mission doctor, and were disconcerted to see, pinned to the wall of his mud hut, a portrait of Hitler, 'whose stern eyes stared at one accusingly across the room'. In a remote village they encountered the President of Liberia, a bustling, nattily dressed figure 'looking as if he had just left the Fifty Shilling Tailors'. Asked by Graham about his constitutional role, he answered 'Once elected and in charge of the machine, I'm boss of the whole show.' They were introduced to the notorious Dictator of Grand Bassa, Colonel Davis, said to have masterminded the massacre of Kru tribesmen, and Graham felt very grubby as he 'followed the sentry into the wide clean compound and rather absurd, with my stockings over my ankles, my stained shorts, my too, too British khaki sun helmet.' The Colonel assured them that, as a keen Ovaltine drinker and head of the Boy Scouts movement in Liberia, there was no way he could have murdered children, and told them how Russian cigarettes were served as a course at fashionable dinner parties in Monrovia: 'after the fish and before the salad, the lights are lowered and each guest quietly smokes one cigarette.' Mr Prosser, a village schoolmaster, taught his pupils to sing 'Onward Christian Soldiers' as well as the Liberian national anthem ('In joy and gladness with our hearts united, / We'll shout the freedom of a land benighted'), and they tried to explain to him the workings of the London Underground. 'It all sounded horrible, and I almost felt that I did not want to go back – till, of course, I remembered Elizabeth Arden, my flat, and the Savoy Grill.' Food loomed increasingly large in their thoughts: Graham dreamed of steak and kidney pudding and Barbara of smoked salmon, but for all their disagreements they never quarrelled, and were far too exhausted even to squabble over the taffeta shorts.

Some villages were more agreeable than others, and one particularly hospitable chieftain was lavish with the palm wine. Wandering round the village, rather the worse for wear, Graham rediscovered 'a kind of hope in human nature. If one could get back to this bareness, simplicity, instinctive friendliness, feeling rather than thought, and start again . . .' As always on his travels, he found himself looking back to his childhood: it seemed inevitable that 'the moments of extraordinary happiness, the sense that one was nearer than one had ever been to the racial source, to satisfying the desire for an instinctive way of life, the sense of release, as when in the course of psychoanalysis one uncovers by one's own effort a root, a primal memory, should have been counterbalanced by the boredom of childhood too, that agonising boredom of "apartness" which came before one had learnt the fatal trick of transferring emotion . . .'

Graham went down with a fever after visiting a particularly dirty and evil-seeming village where a sinister masked devil performed a ritual dance, and he remained unwell for the rest of the trip. He 'looked ghastly, and was shivering. He had a strange, stupid expression on his face, and sometimes he stumbled slightly as though he could not see very well,' Barbara recalled: his face was ashen, and 'his hand shaking even more than it usually did as he poured the Epsom Salts into his tea.' She packed him off to bed, and ate a lonely supper while thunder rumbled overhead. 'During these last few weeks I had discovered that I liked Graham, and I had learned to look up to him and respect him,' and now, she felt sure, he was about to die. 'I felt quite calm at the thought of Graham's death,' she remembered. 'To my own horror I felt unemotional about it. My mind kept telling me that I was really very upset, but actually I was so tired that although I could concentrate easily on the practical side of it all, I was incapable of feeling anything.' She wondered how and where to bury him, and, since he was a Catholic, worried about the shortage of candles, but next morning, after the storm had broken, 'I went into his room expecting to find him either delirious or gasping out his last few breaths, and I found him up and dressed. He looked terrible. A kind of horrid death's head grinned at me. His cheeks had sunk in, there were thick black smudges under his eyes, and his scrubby beard added nothing of beauty to the general rather seedy effect.' Graham, for his part, 'had discovered in myself a passionate interest in living. I had always assumed before, as a matter of course, that death was desirable . . . It was like a conversion, and I had never experienced a conversion before.'

By now they were nearing the end of their journey, and illness and exhaustion were taking their toll. A German missionary and his wife gave them iced drinks and gingerbread, and 'suddenly she nearly made me weep, for she put her hand softly on my head and said, "Mein armes Kind", exactly as my mother used to say to me when as a child I was feeling sad'. They spotted a lorry for the first time in weeks, and Graham 'wanted to laugh and shout and cry; it was the end, the end of the worst boredom I have ever experienced, the worst fear and the worst exhaustion.' They took care not to bicker although, according to Graham, by then they 'were capable of quarrelling over the merits of tea. The only thing was to remain silent, but there was always the danger that silence might strike one of us as sullenness. My nerves were the worst affected and it was to my cousin's credit that we never let our irritation with each other out into words.' They arrived in Monrovia in a tiny boat heavily laden with drunken politicians, and soon discovered that there was nothing to do in the capital but drink gin. Graham hated being back in partially Europeanised Africa, 'because its people have been touched by civilisation, have learned to steal and lie and kill'. The interior may have been boring, exhausting and squalid, but 'after a trek of more than three hundred miles through dense deserted forest, after the little villages and the communal ember, the great silver anklets, the masked devil swaying between the huts, it was less easy to appreciate this civilisation of the coast. It seemed to me that they, almost as much as oneself, had lost touch with the true primitive source.' He never lost his love of West Africa: it somehow embodied the seedy, which was itself 'nearer the beginning', to the childhood of man in general and his own in particular, where 'the sense of taste was finer, the sense of pleasure keener, the sense of terror deeper and purer' than their more sophisticated embodiments, and hadn't 'reached so far away as the smart, the chic, the new, the cerebral.'

Back in England, Barbara published a short account of their adventures which so irritated a Mr Yapp from the British Legation in Monrovia that he mentioned it in his regular despatch to Sir Samuel Hoare, the Foreign Secretary: her article, he reported, ended with 'a stupid and unnecessary reference to the President's clothes being aired on the balcony of the Mansion House (we are all obliged to do this here).' Graham gave his promised speech to The Anti-Slavery Society, and settled down to write *Journey Without Maps,* which he dedicated to Vivien. It was not an easy business. His strongest memories of Liberia were of rats, boredom and frustration, there had been no scenery or buildings to describe, and 'if this was an adventure, it was only a subjective adventure, three months of virtual silence, of "being out of touch".' The result was, in essence, an interior journey, in which poor Barbara was barely mentioned, and never by name (at least in the first edition). What he hadn't realised was that Barbara too had been making notes as they went along – so much so that 'only in one thing did she disappoint me – she wrote a book.' By the time *Land Benighted* appeared, Graham's own book had been withdrawn after a doctor referred to in it had threatened to sue for libel. Dedicated to Uncle Graham, Barbara's book was favourably reviewed by Peter Fleming in the *Spectator*; Hugh wrote home from Berlin to say that he thought it 'surprisingly good', though 'it could have been still better if she had not been so rushed', and several members of the family thought it a better book than *Journey Without Maps*.

★

Herbert too was back in England and, as ever, proving a source of anxiety to his family, and an irritation to the world at large. Helga wrote to her father about possibly finding him a job, but nothing came of it, while Hugh wondered whether 'Da is worried about Herbert because he has to help him financially, or if it's just because he's at a loose end and without a job. I had always hoped that Audrey has just enough for both.' Graham found himself having to sort out a dispute with Herbert's neighbour over the gravel space in front of his brother's garage. A cabinetmaker in Hornsey wrote an angry letter, accusing Herbert of assaulting a young girl and threatening legal action over his 'disgraceful behaviour', and the manager of the Westminster Bank in Haymarket, momentarily mollified, wrote to thank Herbert for a box of cigars and noted that a temporary overdraft had been paid off.

Herbert and Audrey were now living in Baron's Court, west London. When not in the pub or the pawn shop, Herbert spent as much time as he could in the nearby Queen's Club, best known for its tennis courts. Despite subventions from his family – it had been agreed that Mumma would deduct a pound a week from Hugh's allowance, to be diverted to his oldest brother – funds were running low, so Herbert, anxious, perhaps, to emulate Graham's activities in the Palatinate some years earlier, decided to try his luck as a spy. After consulting the phone book, he got in touch with a Captain Oka, the naval attaché at the Japanese Embassy, and suggested a game of squash at Queen's Club. He had, he explained, considerable experience of the Japanese steamers that plied between Cape Town and South America, and he wanted to recommend to the attaché's attention a particularly efficient steamboat captain. 'The club, as usual in the morning, was practically deserted with the exception of Mr Sutton writing vigorously in a corner of the lounge and Miss Toblin waiting for a partner,' he recalled. To his disappointment, Captain Oka never materialised, but they eventually met, and got on well together. As a patriotic Englishman, Herbert had no desire to spy on his fellow-citizens, and did his best to persuade Captain Oka that he was already working for British Naval Intelligence: but, the Captain assured his superiors in Tokyo, Herbert manifested a 'violent dislike' for the United States and a commensurate admiration for the Japanese, and would like to be employed as 'unofficial staff' to spy on the activities of the US Navy.

Unfortunately for Herbert, Captain Oka's letter of 1 February 1934 was intercepted by British Intelligence, and a copy sent on to Sir Vernon Kell, the head of MI5. From now on Herbert was a marked man. He had evidently boasted of being a nephew of Sir Graham Greene, for the letter reported that 'a nephew of Sir Greene has expressed an ardent wish that he would be delighted to take up intelligence duties on behalf of Japan against any country other than Britain', and that through 'Sir Greene' he had connections with powerful and influential figures in British society. Quite why the naval attaché chose to write home in a variety of pidgin English rather than in Japanese remains unclear, but he went on to say of Herbert that 'at present he is out of work and does not particularly like money-making employment. He has considerable property and is not embarrassed through unemployment but desires work rather than money.' Tokyo wrote back to say that Herbert should be put on six months' trial, and £1000 should be set aside for his costs. He was given the code name of 'Midorikawa' (Green River) – Captain Oka was referred to as 'Arthur' – and it was agreed that, for a start, he should try to ascertain the views of top people in Britain on the highly topical subject of disarmament. Captain Oka was suitably impressed when Herbert mentioned that his brother worked for the *Daily Telegraph* and suggested that he should try to place articles with the paper, as well as exerting influence at the BBC. Despite his alleged dislike of the Americans, Herbert had also volunteered to spy for the United States, to no avail; and the information he provided for Captain Oka was 'worth nothing and chiefly culled from common sense or newspapers', with a retired naval commander adding occasional gobbets, all of them made up.

That same month a letter from 'one of His Majesty's Principal Secretaries of State' authorised the Postmaster General to 'open and produce for inspection' all letters, packets and telegrams addressed to Herbert, as he was 'known to be engaging in intelligence work on behalf of a foreign power.' His passport details were provided: he was just over six-feet two, with blue-grey eyes; he still gave School House, Berkhamsted, as his home address, and described himself as a journalist writing for South American newspapers. From now on little was hidden from MI5. They learned how a solicitor in the Strand had expected to receive a 'substantial' cheque for services rendered, but was surprised to be paid a mere 11s 1d; they opened a letter from Da enclosing a cheque for £35 with a covering note in which he said that he couldn't afford it but would run the risk if Herbert promised to repay him by October; mollified no longer, the manager of the Westminster Bank pointed out that his customer was overdrawn by £40, and demanded immediate payment. And, like a character in one of Graham's seedier novels, Herbert found himself being trailed by MI5 men in mackintoshes, all of whom submitted detailed, laboriously typed-up reports on his day-to-day movements. He was followed on his regular trips on the Piccadilly Line from Baron's Court to Leicester Square, from where he made his way to a Japanese restaurant in Denmark Street for his meetings with Captain Oka: a good deal of 'loitering' was reported, usually involving pubs and 'auction houses' (i.e. pawn shops). At some point Herbert and Audrey moved from Baron's Court to Plumpton in Sussex, but old haunts retained their allure. 'I saw Greene yesterday evening,' one agent reported. 'He is such a vague sort of chap that it is hard to find out what he is up to. He seems to spend a lot of time in Queen's Club, and entertains his Japanese friends there.' One bonus of having moved to the country was staying two nights at Claridge's, courtesy of Japanese Naval Intelligence and conveniently timed to coincide with Hugh's and Helga's wedding. An American naval delegation was in the hotel at the time, and although Herbert was more intrigued to learn that Johnny Weismuller, the current Tarzan, was staying in the room next door, he tried to earn his keep by passing on the news that the Second Battalion of the Royal Welch Fusiliers was about to move from Gibraltar to Hong Kong.

Herbert must have felt uneasy about his role as spy and possible double agent, since he mentioned his activities to Uncle Graham, who urged him to confess all to the Admiralty. They in turn told MI5 that it had been 'pointed out to Greene that he was embarking on a course of action which might land him in very grave and serious difficulties, and in the circumstances he was strongly advised to sever the connection.' When Mr Harker of MI5 learned that Captain Oka had invited Herbert to lunch at Scott's in Panton Street – a smarter restaurant than usual – he decided that he would 'like the meeting covered' and suggested that his Mr Hunter should seat himself at an adjacent table. Herbert was spotted passing over his usual selection of crumpled press cuttings, though he later stated that he had learned important things at the meeting, and that he had wanted to ring the US Embassy as soon as the meal was over, but felt he couldn't trust the telephone operators. He claimed that he had reported his findings to the Admiralty, and that despite his dislike of Americans he had arranged to meet an official from US Naval Intelligence at Queen's and tell him all.

Not surprisingly, Captain Oka and his masters in Tokyo were becoming increasingly disillusioned with Herbert, and questioned whether he was worth his retainer, now £50 a month. Captain Oka's intercepted messages to Tokyo discussed matters of topical concern, such as British worries about retaining naval supremacy in the Far East and the value of Singapore in the event of a war with Japan, but although Herbert claimed that he had received early warning of the forthcoming Anti-Comintern Pact between Germany and Japan, it's unlikely that the Japanese or the British learned much from him. The Admiralty evidently found him a pest and an irritant. 'I am warning you, Greene, that if you are not more careful you will find yourself in the Thames,' an exasperated Admiralty official told him, or so he recalled. More reliably, MI5 reported how he had visited the Admiralty, and became 'very abusive' when told that they disapproved of his actions, and wanted to have nothing to do with him. 'I understand that a final warning was issued to Greene on 21 January [1935],' Sir Vernon Kell was informed. After Herbert had complained to the postmaster in Lewes about interception of his mail, MI5 temporarily suspended their activities, but they had already discovered that a summons had been taken out against him for non-payment of debts, including his rent, and when, despairing of Captain Oka and desperate for funds, he applied to the Russian Embassy to ask if he could spy for them instead, his letter was immediately forwarded to MI5.

That same year in which Herbert and Captain Oka finally parted company, Graham produced what he later described as 'an idealised portrait' of his brother as the feckless Anthony Farrant in *England Made Me*, a novel based on the activities of Ivar Kreuger, the Swedish match millionaire. Graham had visited Stockholm to get the atmosphere of the city; Hugh had joined him from Berlin, and no doubt they despaired about Herbert's activities as they trudged around the streets. Like John Betjeman, Farrant wears an Old Harrovian tie to which he is not entitled, albeit for nefarious rather than jocular reasons. Like Graham's great admirer, Julian Maclaren-Ross, he has been a vacuum-cleaner salesman in his time, and like Herbert, he moves from one country to another, part-remittance man, part-confidence trickster, forever thinking up dodgy schemes that will make his fortune, forever getting the sack, and making his father's life a misery in the process. He was 'tall and broad and thin and a little worn: his round face 'had lost its freshness, like a worn child's', and exuded a 'bonhomie which even a stranger would not trust', while 'his humorous friendly shifty eyes' resembled 'the headlamps of a second-hand car which had been painted and polished to deceive.' His devoted sister Kate ponders his money-making schemes, which 'had always sounded plausible when he described them; they had no obvious faults, except the one fatal flaw that he was concerned in them. "I only want capital," he would explain with a brightness that was never dulled by the knowledge that no one would ever trust him with more than five pounds. Then he would embark on them without capital; strange visitors would appear at weekends, men older than himself with the same school ties, the same air of bright vigour . . .'

Farrant is a veteran of cheap digs and pawnbrokers' shops and, like Herbert, he has spent time in South America. 'All the scoundrels in the world went to the Argentine,' Graham was told before he set out to Liberia. Tooter remembered how his father had found Herbert a job in Santos: he had not only proved drunken and irresponsible but may well have got a local girl 'in the family way', and had turned up again in Santos en route to a job in Buenos Aires. He had invited his fellow-passengers to the Brazilian Warrant's offices to be entertained free of charge, and 'signed chits around the town to show that he was a big man', for which Eppy had to foot the bill. Even the well-disposed Felix conceded that Herbert was 'financially utterly untrustworthy', a gambler who 'got everyone else gambling'. Sir Cecil Parrott remembered him as a drunk who 'often had to be carried home every night'; in *Journey Without Maps* Graham wrote of how, at the mere mention of Rhodesia, where Herbert had failed as a farmer, he immediately thought of '"failure, Empire Tobacco", and "failure" again.'

Graham's anger and resentment had been building up for years. 'I wish he wouldn't choose me as his confidant,' he had told Vivien, after receiving an importunate letter from Herbert. 'The man's an utter bounder. The fact that he's been practically living on his people for the last nearly thirty years doesn't seem to prey on him in the least . . . I thought and genuinely hoped (I think he's driven most of his family that far) that something might finish him in Argentina. I know it's a horrid thing to say, but if he had the self-respect of a louse he'd have done himself in by now.' 'I wish to goodness he'd shoot himself,' he wrote after learning that another overseas job had fallen through, 'but I suppose he hasn't the pluck for that.' Graham hated the fact that Herbert was such a trial to their parents: 'If I was my father, I should simply send him nothing and let him get something or starve. Only I suppose he'd borrow enough money from some fool and get home. Killing would be no murder in his case!' 'It's knocked my father up physically,' he wrote after more bad news had come through. 'He's got to see a specialist on Saturday. I shall do my best to give him [Herbert] a thin time if he ever gets back to England. It makes one feel positively murderous to see a useless idiot like him killing someone who's worth a million times more than him.' In *England Made Me*, Farrant's long-suffering father has been brought to an early grave, but Charles Greene, though 'anxious and in poor health' lived on for another eight years; and Graham was kinder to Herbert in person than his angry words might have suggested.

Herbert resurfaced in fictional form as 'Hands' in 'The Other Side of the Border', a tantalising remnant from a discarded novel by Graham. He makes his first appearance travelling first-class on a third-class ticket – 'the mouth weakened, the handsome too boyish face turned sullen' when he catches sight of a ticket inspector – on a visit to his patient, liberal-minded old father in what is self-evidently Berkhamsted. Later on, he is interviewed for yet another job, this time in West Africa. In real life, Herbert was still flitting round the fringes of the Intelligence world, albeit in a different and more hazardous environment. The Spanish Civil War had broken out, and in January 1937 MI5 reported that he had left Newhaven for Dieppe on a Southern Rhodesian passport, claiming to be in charge of a convoy of motor coaches commissioned by the National Joint Committee for Spanish Relief to move Republican refugees out of Madrid, which was under siege from Franco's forces. A month later MI5 revealed that the mission had been rendered futile by a shortage of petrol, and that the NJCSR party was back in London. In April Herbert was once again spotted leaving Newhaven, this time at the wheel of a Bedford van to be used in relief work. No more is heard of him until September, when a Mr Garratt of the NJCSR confirmed that Herbert and one Frank Rodgers had indeed been employed by the Committee as ambulance-drivers. Both men had proved unsatisfactory, and had been returned to the UK. They had embezzled large sums of money by claiming, mislead-ingly, to be collecting on behalf of the Committee, and the matter was now in the hands of solicitors. They had planned to commit a similar fraud in America, timing their visit to coincide with a tour of the States by the famous 'Red' Duchess of Atholl, a well-known supporter of the Republican cause.

Graham instinctively supported the Republicans, but as a Catholic he deplored the murder of priests and nuns and the destruction of churches. Unlike Evelyn Waugh, who outraged his literary contemporaries by supporting Franco, Graham was ambivalent – according to Raymond Heppenstall, Graham 'somewhat reluctantly supported Franco' – and, like Orwell, he refused to contribute to a widely publicised booklet entitled *Authors Take Sides*, most of the contributors to which were ardently Republican. His own sympathies were with the Basques, and still more so after the bombing of Guernica by the Condor Legion in April 1937, but his hopes of being flown to Bilbao in a two-seater plane were dashed, and he got no further than Toulouse. Herbert had hardly covered himself in glory in Spain, but he was determined to set out his side of the story, and persuaded Robert Hale to publish his memoir, *Secret Agent in Spain*. Hale was a small firm specialising in topographical books, and thrillers and romances designed for the public libraries: in the same month that the Second World War broke out they published T. C. Worsley's *Behind the Battle*, one of the finest and most unjustly neglected memoirs of the Spanish Civil War, but Herbert's book, entertaining and readable as it usually is, has more in common with their fiction list. Graham wrote to offer 'a thousand congratulations on placing your book with Robert Hale', and in a defiant introduction Herbert insisted that 'this is not a story of violent adventure; it happens to be true', and warned the reader that 'there are certain to be charges of "double-crossing" levelled against me.' This was hardly surprising, since throughout the book he inhabits a hazy, half-lit world of meaningful hints and innuendoes, in which neither the narrator nor the reader has any firm idea of what side anyone is on, or what they are really up to. We are told that in January 1937 Herbert received a mysterious phone call from 'Y', whom he had met in Claridge's while monitoring the Naval Disarmament Conference. He is told to come to an office near the Monument to receive his instructions. He never discovers anything about Y, including his nationality and his political sympathies, but he appears to have been a supporter of Franco. Herbert is asked to take a letter to 'X' in Madrid and, making good use of the Spanish he has learned in South America, to report back on the attitude of the Catalonians to the war, the state of morale in Madrid, the condition of a particular viaduct, and how closely the Government forces supervise the French border at Port Bou. 'I do not wish you to come, or be seen near, these offices again. Goodbye and good luck,'

Y tells him. Next morning a thick wodge of pesetas is pushed under the front door of Herbert's cottage in Plumpton, and he is on his way to Spain.

At Newhaven a porter draws him aside and tells him, in a low whisper, to report to a garage in the Boulevard Aristide Briand in the outskirts of Paris, where he will receive further instructions. No mention is made of a fleet of lorries or relief work on behalf of the NJCSR, but Herbert's Studebaker breaks down incessantly on the road to Paris, belching clouds of smoke before grinding to a halt. He is convinced that his hotel room has been searched in Orléans, a beautiful girl in Tarragona asks him to take a letter back to Britain, cars continue to 'conk out', and he warns us that 'conscience is a troublesome possession for work in espionage'. In Republican-held Valencia he meets the Deans of Rochester and Chichester: mutual friends include 'Charlie' Fry, the Canon of St Luke's, Maidenhead and the overweight son of the former headmaster of Berkhamsted, as well as the Bishop of Chichester, who had officiated at Hugh's and Helga's wedding. He offers the Deans a lift to Madrid, and just as they are about to leave a girl called Kitty Bowler rushes over and hands him his toothbrush, which he had left on the hall table of the hotel. Kitty Bowler was a left-wing American journalist, who, while covering the war in Spain, had met and later married Tom Wintringham, a well-known Communist journalist fighting for the International Brigade, and best remembered for having founded the Home Guard Training School at Osterley soon after the outbreak of war. Herbert thanks Kitty Bowler for 'shepherding me round Valencia at night': according to Paul Preston's definitive account of the activities of foreign correspondents during the Civil War, Herbert's references to Kitty Bowler in his book were used by the Communist Party of Great Britain to try to persuade Wintringham to abandon his affair with her (she became his second wife, and he eventually left the Communist Party).

Madrid was full of English journalists 'patiently waiting for the day's ration of beer' – among them Sefton Delmer, who had been on holiday in Spain with his wife when Franco's rebellion broke out in July 1936. He had covered the war since then for the *Daily Express*, and had recently been holed up in the Hotel Florida during the siege of the city by the Nationalists, together with Ernest Hemingway, Martha Gellhorn, John dos Passos and Virginia Cowles. Herbert encounters an arms salesman he had known in Brazil, hands over the letter to X – who, as agreed, makes himself known by dropping his cigarette on the ground – and heads back to Newhaven, where the same porter gives him a meaningful wink. At some stage in the story Claud Cockburn, who was covering the war on behalf of the Communist *Daily Worker* under the *nom de plume* of Frank Pitcairn, is said to have prevented Hemingway from taking a potshot at a tall Englishman in a tweed jacket and flannel trousers – 'Don't shoot him, he's my headmaster's eldest son' – but, like most of Herbert's adventures in Spain, it doesn't quite ring true.

Herbert is once again summoned to meet Y, this time at the Tower of London. By now his sympathies have switched from Franco to the embattled Republican Government. Referring to the Bedford van he will be driving to Spain, he tells Y that 'lending this lorry to help the Spanish people will offset in my mind the work I do for you'. Unfazed by this switch of allegiance, Y begs him 'not to get too fond of them and let me down'. He tells Herbert that 'there is a document at present in Madrid of such importance that it must be in our hands as soon as possible. If you are caught with the document on you, all the might of the British Navy could not help you. You will be shot, and rightly so, but more important than your life will be the fatal results of this list falling into the wrong hands.' Herbert's mission is to pick up this document and bring it back to England; in the meantime, Y asks him to let him know at once if he spots anyone he remembers from the train from Barcelona to Port Bou hanging around the city. Back in Spain, Herbert bumps into his old friend Frank Rodgers, and they travel on together. In Valencia they meet a Mrs Haden-Guest, and Herbert offers her a lift to Madrid in his Bedford van: they are taking a consignment of milk for children in the besieged city, and Mrs Haden-Guest sits in the cab between the driver and a Republican soldier. In Madrid, they encounter Sefton Delmer once again, and Herbert masterminds a cricket match for the visiting journalists. He meets Y's contact – another 'X' – who unravels a roll of lavatory paper to reveal the all-important message which is to be taken back to London, and stitches it into the lining of Herbert's suitcase. Back in Valencia, a stranger creeps into Herbert's hotel bedroom one night, presumably in search of the message. They set off home in a car which explodes *en route*, but somehow make their way back to England, despite the combustible car and Herbert being drugged in Perpignan.

Herbert's third and final journey to Spain begins when Y interrupts a cricket match in Sussex and orders him to report for duty at the Grosvenor Hotel. He is to carry a message to Valencia, and this time he decides to take with him Audrey and her sister Kathleen, who will travel as far as the Franco-Spanish border, and an old army friend called Stanley Carr. They put their Kerry Blue into kennels in Ditchling, squeeze into

Herbert's Morris 8, and set out for France. The ladies are keen to do
some sightseeing but although Herbert insists on flashing along at speeds
of up to sixty miles an hour, he agrees to a delay while they go shopping, and valuable time is lost. By now he is fully converted to the
Republican cause, so he tears up Y's message. His room is bugged in
Barcelona – 'on the top of my wardrobe was a peculiar gadget with a
thin wire which ran into the next room' – and in Toulouse, on the way
home, he recognises a man he had noticed earlier on the train, and met
again on the boat from Dieppe to Newhaven. Back in Sussex, he promises Audrey that he will 'dabble no further in Spanish affairs', and tells
Y that he is no longer at his disposal. What Y had paid him had barely
covered his expenses, but 'my reward was experience and the thanks of
someone who must necessarily remain unmentioned', and 'I have still
occasionally been of service to this man from whom one word of thanks
meant more to me than the criticism of the rest of the world.'

From now on Herbert's career as an amateur spy lurched from bad to
worse. He turned up at the Admiralty in November 1937, 'in a state of
considerable agitation, and poured forth an incoherent story' to the effect
that he was almost bankrupt and was being chased by his creditors: he
had given up spying for Captain Oka at the request of the Admiralty, and
although his trips to Spain had convinced him that all Admiralty men
were 'fools', they had an obligation to find him work of some kind, prefer-
ably in Intelligence. He was given short shrift, and to add insult to injury
MI5 memoed the Foreign Office to say that 'Mr W. Herbert Greene is
known to us and is a most undesirable person. I strongly advise your
having no dealings with him.' While Secret Agent in Spain was edging its
way into print, Herbert momentarily switched from espionage to journalism in order to stave off penury and promote his forthcoming memoir.
'I hear Herbert's been contributing to the Daily Worker,' Hugh wrote
home from Berlin. Under the headline 'I Was in the Pay of Japan . . . A
Secret Agent Tells His Story', Herbert claimed that he was writing for
the Communist Daily Worker because his experiences in Spain had
converted him from Right to Left: as for the Japanese, 'let the Empire of
the Rising Sun be warned to keep her grasping hands off Princess Elizabeth's heritage.' The following day he revealed that he had 'been warned
by the Japanese that they would take drastic action if I published the facts
about my relations with Captain Oka.' According to Graham, Claud Cockburn wrote the articles for Herbert, paid him nothing for them and
borrowed five shillings off him; the general drift of the piece was that
'this story must be true, because Mr Greene is a real "pukka sahib"!, not

a mere worker like you, dear reader.' Be that as it may, the paper insisted that Herbert's articles had caused 'profound sensations' on both sides of the Atlantic, and he wrote to Claud Cockburn to say that he had a 'lot of further stuff to reveal'. Cockburn combined his duties as the *Daily Worker*'s diplomatic correspondent with editing *The Week*, a scurrilous and often extremely well-informed cyclostyled magazine devoured by opinion- and policy-makers: he was not amused to discover that, on a visit to *The Week*'s notoriously chaotic and paper-strewn office, Herbert had stolen a letter from Gerald Hamilton, Christopher Isherwood's louche friend from his Berlin days, recently immortalised in *Mr Norris Changes Trains*; it touched on the pro-Franco views of the British Consul in Tangiers, and Herbert whipped it round to the Admiralty in the vain hope of currying favour.

Herbert's alcoholic intake did little to advance his career. In March 1938 an MI5 agent reported from a barber's shop in the Grosvenor Hotel that 'a man, who appeared to be somewhat the worse for drink, came in and started a conversation with the barber on the situation in Japan.' The barber later told the agent that Herbert was employed by the War Office as a 'double cross agent', supplying disinformation to the Japanese. And a couple of months earlier Herbert had written to Cockburn to say that he had been in a car crash: an incident included many years later, *verbatim*, in Hugh and Graham's anthology *The Spy's Bedside Book*. According to Herbert:

I think it advisable to state that I have no documents of any importance in my possession in connection with any other country or work I have undertaken. I am making this statement as, on January 4th 1938, a friend and I left a certain Embassy in London. We were followed to Victoria Station, where I caught the 5.35 train. From then on my memory is a blank until I found myself in hospital the following morning. Some papers of mine were missing. I will let the *Mid-Sussex Times* complete the story:

ACCIDENT IN MID-SUSSEX
Mr W. H. Greene, of Oak Cottage, Plumpton, is in the Haywards Heath Hospital suffering from head injuries sustained in a motor accident at Plumpton last week. He was found lying unconscious near his damaged car.

By now *Secret Agent in Spain* had been published. Malcolm Muggeridge reviewed it for the *Daily Telegraph*: he found it hard to work out which side Herbert was working for, but 'these journeys led Mr Greene into a variety of adventures (being poisoned, for instance) which he describes with zest.' A former Reuters correspondent in Madrid wrote to say that he had read a good many books about the Civil War, and wanted to thank Herbert for 'the only civil mention of myself – among various uncivil – in these works'. But Mrs Haden-Guest declared herself disillusioned. 'I went to Spain with the idea of assisting the people of Republican Spain and was of course unaware that you were working for Franco,' she wrote to Herbert while *Secret Agent* was still in the pipeline. 'Under the circumstances I would much prefer you to take my name out of your book. Please send me a line to say whether you are willing to do so. If you are leaving my name in the book please publish the enclosed letter in the Appendix.' Herbert dutifully obliged, adding that 'Mrs Guest may have more information than I have myself. I have had no direct contact *to my knowledge* with any agents of Franco.'

Whatever the truth of the matter, Herbert's career as a master spy was almost over. MI5 continued to keep an eye on him all the same. In July they reported that a man had been seen showing his fellow-imbibers in a pub in Plumpton the blueprints of a top-secret fighter aircraft which could take off in seven yards. Herbert then rang in from the bar of the Wellington Hotel in Seaford to say that he had seen the blueprints, which had also been shown to the proprietor of the Sun Hotel in Plumpton. As befitted the occasion he referred to himself throughout as 'C', and gave initials to the other characters involved. Sir Vernon Kell referred the matter to the Chief Constable of Sussex, and asked him to keep tabs on Herbert. Sir Vernon had, in the meantime, been warned by the Foreign Office about Herbert's application to spy for the Soviet Union. 'I could be of use in connection with Japan, as for a year I worked for Captain Oka, the Japanese Naval Attaché, and I am on excellent terms with many Japanese,' Herbert had assured the Russians, adding that he was 'in a special position for obtaining valuable information and am at the same time prepared to do anything or go anywhere required.' Once again, he suggested meeting in the Queen's Club, since 'as a nephew of a late Permanent Secretary of the Admiralty, Sir Graham Greene, you will understand that I have to be careful, which is why I wish to meet your representative away from the embassy.' But Herbert's luck had run out. He would have to turn his mind to other ways of earning his keep.

We've cut the prices at over 500 hotels across the UK.

We've got more hotels than any other UK hotel chain and you can take advantage of our Premier Offers and low prices at over 500 of them.

Here are just some of the hotels with Premier Offer rooms

from £29	from £39	from £49
Birmingham	Bristol City Centre	London Kensington
Cheltenham	Edinburgh	London Putney Bridge
Gatwick Airport	Isle of Wight	London Wimbledon
Heathrow Airport	Liverpool City Centre	London Kew
Glasgow		London Docklands
Manchester		

Other great city locations available from £59

For a full list of locations or to book, visit premierinn.com

PI263PTI9P0B

£29

Take comfort with our £29* Premier Offers

With rooms from just £29 a night, you can afford to stay more often with Premier Inn.

Book at **premierinn.com**

See overleaf for details.

Everything's Premier but the Price

premierinn.com

Westward Look

Towards the end of his visit to Germany in the summer of 1935, Felix drove to the north of the country before making a brief visit to Denmark. He was impressed by the way young people in Germany walked or bicycled huge distances, and as he drove along he picked up two boys striding along the road with rucksacks on their backs. They all slept together in a field, and 'most attractive boys they were'. In Hamburg he met a beautiful half-Norwegian girl called Renate Krieg. Like many women before and after, she fell in love with Felix, but although he claimed to reciprocate her feelings, he eventually wrote to say that they had no future together. Like Peggy Bok, Renate kept in touch with his mother, if not with Felix himself, and many years later Tooter noticed a photograph of his brother prominently displayed on the piano in her Hamburg flat.

In Copenhagen Felix found a letter waiting for him from Sir John Reith informing him that he had been appointed the BBC's first North American Representative, responsible for looking after the Corporation's interests in the USA and Canada as well as producing programmes. Before leaving for New York he had a meeting with Robert Vansittart, the Permanent Under-Secretary at the Foreign Office, an early and persistent opponent of Nazi Germany, an advocate of rearmament to meet the German threat, and an ally and informant of those politicians who opposed the National Government's policy of appeasement, among them Winston Churchill and the Labour Party's Hugh Dalton. (He also provided information for Claud Cockburn's *The Week*.) 'I know Felix Greene well, and am very glad to hear of his appointment,' Vansittart told Reith. 'I think Greene will do well there.' With Reith and Vansittart providing welcome support, Felix arrived in New York in late November. It had been a rough crossing, and the liner was a day late arriving, but Peggy Bok was waiting loyally on the quayside, with a limousine to hand. Felix booked into the St Regis Hotel: since the BBC had, as yet, no base in New York, his bedroom doubled as an office, 'with books stacked on dressing tables and newspapers on the floor. Letters and collars have to share the same space, and often at night my bed has to be cleared of books and papers before I can get into it.'

Within two days of his arrival Felix left for Toronto to reorganise Canadian broadcasting along 'Public Corporation lines'. Reith had provided him with introductions to Mackenzie King, the Dominion's Prime Minister, and the Governor-General, Lord Tweedsmuir, better remembered as John Buchan. 'The authority of broadcasting is at a low ebb. As a force in the life of the community, it is negligible,' Felix reported back to London. A national news service was urgently needed, and broadcasting should be under the control of a single authority, similar to the BBC. In the face of a hostile civil service and interfering politicians, Felix set about reorganising and revitalising the system under the aegis of the Canadian Broadcasting Corporation with his customary efficiency and practicality.

Back in New York, he set about making useful contacts, including the bosses of the two great broadcasting networks, David Sarnoff of NBC and William Paley of CBS: he was particularly taken with CBS's Talks Director, Ed Murrow, who later made his name with his wartime reports from London. But Felix was largely unimpressed by the American radio programmes he listened to from his hotel bedroom. In a memo to C. G. Graves, his Controller in London, he referred to the 'immense potentialities of broadcasting which so pitiably few people here seem yet to have grasped,' but he was worried by the way in which broadcasting was being exploited, for foreign as well as domestic listeners, by the fascist powers, and by Dr Goebbels in particular. Speaking at a lunch given in his honour at the Bankers' Club not long after his arrival in the States, he assured his audience that he was not involved in any kind of 'propagandist mission'. 'Propaganda is becoming a rather ugly word, and where broadcasting is concerned it spells a sinister danger,' he declared 'A terrible disservice is being done to the authority and true development of broadcasting by its use in several countries as a potent means of political propaganda and mass suggestion. Its use should surely be for the very *reverse* of mass suggestion – to stimulate men's minds to free and individual thought. To use its great powers otherwise is a prostitution of its rightful purpose.' Walter Lippmann, the leading political pundit and commentator of the day, asked him for his views on political broadcasts on the BBC; he fielded endless phone calls from people anxious to learn more about the organisation, and was amused by the widespread notion that its broadcasts were devoted almost exclusively to chamber music and similar manifestations of high culture. He was, he told his parents, 'obsessed increasingly with a sense of impending calamity' in Europe, and urged his colleagues in London to agree to closer co-operation with CBS and NBC since, should war break out, 'the availability of the networks here in time of crisis might be invaluable to Britain.' Renting offices in the Rockefeller Center and moving into a basement flat off Fifth Avenue made for a tidier domestic life, but with the international situation as fraught as it was, 'to marry and have a family seems almost to act like rabbits making a burrow while a forest fire is creeping forward' – which let him off the hook as far as Renate was concerned.

Felix's staff consisted of a secretary, a typist and part-time assistants, but before long they were contributing what he later described as a 'prodigious amount of radio time to the BBC', including as many as six or seven programmes a week. Felix himself contributed 'documentary features': a series entitled 'America Speaks' led to meetings with Hoover and Roosevelt, while the first transatlantic coverage of a Presidential inauguration involved Felix being perched alone in a booth in the pouring rain, unable to see anything other than raised umbrellas, and – since FDR was running three-quarters of an hour late – ad-libbing into the microphone. One of his closest colleagues was Raymond Gram Swing, the son of an Ohio preacher and a veteran of the Taverne in Berlin, who went on to produce a weekly 'American Commentary' for the BBC: according to Alistair Cooke, Swing could 'take a subject like agricultural appropriation and make it sound as if the world was coming to an end – all the drama of Lady Macbeth.' Cooke himself moved to New York in 1937. He had been providing a weekly broadcast for the NBC from London, and Graves suggested that Felix should make use of his gifts. 'Don't you think he would be able to work up the "America Listens" feature?' he wondered, providing talks which gave 'a true picture of things that happen in America'. Before long Cooke was deluging Felix with ideas. Felix encouraged him to front a series on American folk song ('I Hear America Swinging'), persuaded London to put up his rates of pay, and gave enthusiastic support for the idea of a weekly letter from America. A year after his arrival, Cooke compèred a jam session from the roof of the St Regis Hotel, broadcast by the BBC, and the ensuing bar bill was viewed askance in London. Cooke, Felix, Gram Swing and Ed Murrow became close friends, often playing table tennis together when not behind the microphone.

Felix never liked New York, and in the spring of 1936 he persuaded his controller to allow him to set out in his Packard convertible on a tour of the States. He was very impressed by the great public works projects being undertaken as part of Roosevelt's New Deal, and by the work of the Tennesseee Valley Authority in particular. 'Why cannot we have our TVA in South Wales or on Tyneside?' he declared, after inspecting the giant Wilson Dam. 'We talk of allotments and clubs for the unemployed, while our people sink into irretrievable desolation.' He went on to visit New Orleans, Mexico City, Denver, Los Angeles and San Francisco before returning to New York after a two-month absence. 'I love them for their gaiety and enormous courage and absurd childishness,' he told his mother. 'They hold the world's future in their hands.' Be that as it may, he sailed for England on the *Queen Mary* in July – the family was increasingly worried about Eppy's health, and Felix had promised to organise a joint birthday party for his parents at Claridge's – and, as it turned out, he was reluctant to return.

The Spanish Civil War had broken out, and Felix was keen to find out what was going on. The BBC, he wrote later, had agreed to pursue a broadcasting equivalent of the British government's controversial policy of 'non-intervention': this involved taking a neutral line, and not using its own reporters to cover the war. Felix was told that he could go as an 'unofficial' reporter rather than an accredited correspondent, but that they would be willing to consider any reports he might send. In August 1936 he set out from Paris to Biarritz in a four-seater plane, together with a reporter from NBC. Felix tried to open the window, which fell off its hinges, and he had to hold it in place for the rest of the flight. He was in Spain for less than three weeks, but experienced rather more than his cousin Herbert. He crossed into the Basque country with a group of foreign journalists, and they were machine-gunned from the air by a fighter-plane: they tried to take cover behind some rocks, and Felix never forgot how a tough-seeming journalist from Chicago was so terrified that he clawed at the ground and tried to cover himself with leaves and twigs. In San Sebastian, still under Republican control but soon to be captured by the Carlists, 'they showed us where on the seafront there had recently been a bloody battle – bits of flesh and much blood lying around the pavilions where previously the rich used to idle away their holidays.' After being sniped at on the road to Burgos, Franco's centre of operations throughout the Civil War, they were captured by Nationalist forces under General Mola and escorted to the Guadarrama Mountains, where fierce fighting was taking place. They watched as fascist soldiers rounded up and machine-gunned a group of twelve-year-old children, after which an officer walked among the twitching bodies, finishing off any survivors with his revolver. 'These were little kids crying for their mothers. It had a terrible effect on me,' Felix recalled years later. Despite having told the officer in charge that he was 'going to let the whole world know this', he 'didn't report it' in the articles he wrote about his experiences in Spain for the *Listener*, a magazine owned and published by the BBC. Back in London, Felix offered to resign from his role as the BBC's North American Representative, begged in vain to be allowed to return to Spain, and urged his colleagues to cover the war as fully and as objectively as possible.

Spain confirmed Felix in his pacifism and his hatred of war, and reinforced his belief that Europe would soon be engulfed by a conflict in which he would play no part. Although he did his work as efficiently as ever, and spoke of the BBC as 'exemplary' and considerate employers, he became increasingly disillusioned with, and detached from, the business of broadcasting, and began to cast around for other ways in which to ventilate his idealism. Nearly fifty years later, he told his prospective biographers that he had come to realise how dishonest his radio reports were, and how a correspondent would 'quite unconsciously bias his reports to meet the expectations of those who employed him.' His work for the BBC remained first-rate – 'I wish all people wrote as well as you do,' Charles Graves told him, after reading his second annual report. 'I didn't feel like reading it in bed, but I hadn't read more than two or three pages before I was just as happy as when reading the novel I usually do at night' – but, like a proto-hippy, Felix professed himself disgusted by the rat race, and longed to find his 'true self'. In his diary he confessed to feeling 'a hopeless misfit', who 'does not *belong* anywhere'. 'New York and I will never agree – this particular kind of civilisation has become repellent to me,' he told his parents. He suffered from a 'Greene grass complex' – a family variant on the 'grass is greener' syndrome – and although 'I think I shall go on being homesick all my life,' this was more a yearning for an imaginary Utopia than a yearning to return to the bosom of his family. 'I long to be in company in which I can be myself, neither feeling out of place nor hypocritical,' he informed Sheila MacDonald. 'I long to free myself both from my despising of the human race and from my dependence on it.' He sold his Packard to salve his conscience, and made programmes about hill-billies in the Appalachians, living off boiled potatoes and cabbage as he did so. He contemplated moving into a luxurious apartment on Park

Avenue, employing a butler and a chauffeur, and spending his week-ends on Long Island, but another part of him pined to live in the slums and do social work. He told his parents that he loved simplicity and simple folk above all else, 'yet here I am, believing in it more strongly than in almost anything, driving a Packard and proposing to live in Park Avenue. The thing is laughable and shameful, or humiliating. I can so burningly see the kind of person I want to be, and yet am apparently unable to go but in the reverse direction. I think it springs from a longing for either the best or nothing. Mediocrity is repellent to me.' Two months after his return from Spain, he moved into an artists' colony in Henry Street, the inmates of which were devoted to play-readings, reading groups and making pottery. 'My uptown friends think I'm crazy or communistic,' he declared, 'but I had got tired to desperation of seeing sham around me.'

Felix's private life was equally confused. He had resumed his inter-mittent affair with Peggy Bok, and it continued after she had divorced Curtis Bok and married Henwar Rodakicwicz, a Polish anthropologist and film-maker, and moved to California, from where Felix wrote to say that he hated having to return to New York, 'that godforsaken city, diseased and decadent'. Through the photographer and gallery-owner Alfred Stieglitz, he met the painter Georgia O'Keeffe: she was twenty-two years older than Felix, and although it's unlikely that they had a fully-fledged affair, she became extremely attached to him and, like Peggy Bok, came to regret and resent her involvement with such an unsatisfactory and elusive admirer. 'We've been fond of each other, but you haven't really ever given me anything,' she told him after he had visited her in New Mexico. 'Nothing has come back from you. I think you'd better go . . .' He had also become involved with a beautiful girl called Betsy Barton, whose father, a Congressman named Bruce Barton, had written a best-selling book entitled *The Man Nobody Knows*, the premise of which was that were Jesus to return to earth, it would be in the form of a Manhattan advertising man. Betsy had been crip-pled in a car accident and was unable to move from the waist down, and, Felix told his mother, 'my heart went out to this beautiful injured creature.' Betsy too was smitten by this good-looking and charming young Englishman: her suicide a few days after Felix had left her in the middle of lunch on BBC business remained one of the 'dark corners' of his life.

But the person he admired above all others was Gerald Heard, the Irish writer and mystic who had first introduced Felix to the BBC, and had now moved to California on his single-minded search for God. Though ridiculed by Arthur Koestler and George Orwell, he counted Aldous Huxley and Christopher Isherwood among his friends and disciples. 'My friendship with him means more each day,' Felix confided to his diary after visiting Heard at home in Hollywood. 'In no man have I ever seen more of God, more gentleness, more selflessness, more humility, more audacity in following his principles wherever they may lead.' Felix found Aldous Huxley rather alarming – 'I'm a little frightened of him, though Gerald assures me that he is in fact a humble man. He appears to eye us muddlers with such a lucidly cynical eye,' he reported after visiting the great man in New Mexico, while a 'highbrow' New Year spent with the Huxleys 'gave me an inferiority complex, and I returned to New York in a gloomy mood' – but Heard was a very different matter. He was, Felix told his parents, 'the world's most delightful companion'. He had come to stay with Felix in New York, and 'we cook our meals and wash our socks, and lie naked, trying to get cool. He's so gay and cheerful and completely uncomplaining. His wisdom and power of human understanding are equalled only by his modesty. He is a great man. I wonder why I have been given the privilege of a great man's friendship. It was meant for something.' His growing friendship with Heard coincided with a restless longing to strike out in new directions. He joined Victor Gollancz's Left Book Club: he found the BBC increasingly 'puerile, ineffective and effeminate', but possible alternatives lay 'in the field of unemployment, re-housing, politics, Huxley's pacifist group – all I know is that it will have to be identified with the improving of conditions for our fellow-men.'

Although Felix's work for the BBC was much appreciated by his superiors in London – in February 1937 Graves wrote to congratulate him on his coverage of flooding in the Mississippi, and said how much better the British did this kind of thing than the Americans – his relations with British officialdom, and the Embassy in particular, were not always harmonious. After he had fallen out with the British Library of Information in Washington, the Ambassador complained to Vansittart that Felix had been both wrong-headed and disrespectful. For all his restlessness, Felix was worried by rumours that he was about to be replaced, and was greatly relieved to hear that Vansittart had taken his side – as had Reith, while conceding that his *protégé* had been impolite to the Ambassador. 'We certainly had doubts on account of his youth, and therefore with respect to some of the more normal faults of youth,' Graves wrote in a memo to Reith, and he reassured Felix that 'there has never been any adverse comment from the FO on your work or behaviour – in fact I happen to know that you have been given a good character!' To complicate matters, it turned out that Lady Reading had complained that Felix had been rude to her, and wasn't fit to represent the BBC, but since he had never met her in his life, she must have mistaken him for someone else.

As it happened, Felix was about to enjoy a closer relationship with the Foreign Office, and with Vansittart in particular, on the contentious matter of the BBC's overseas broadcasts. In 1932 the BBC's Empire Service had been set up, broadcasting to foreign countries in English from Daventry. Since then, both the Germans and the Italians had begun to broadcast to overseas listeners, making effective use of short-wave transmitters and producing programmes which were essentially political propaganda, and were broadcast in a variety of languages, including English. This was a worrying trend, best countered, in Reith's opinion, by exploiting the BBC's reputation for truthfulness and accuracy: he favoured broadcasting in languages other than English, and it was important to 'help in stifling rumour and sensation by the presentation of fully authoritative and carefully reported news'. Felix had mixed views on the matter. Shortly after his arrival in New York he had tuned into the Empire Service, and had been shocked by what he heard. 'I could hardly believe we could sink to such fatuity,' he wrote to Graves. '*Why* do we lower our reputation by putting on shows like that?' The following year he complained that Empire Service programmes were 'flabby and uninspired', and that they bore 'no relation whatever with the needs and tastes of listeners in distant lands'– views that were echoed by his former colleague Lionel Fielden, now working for the BBC in Delhi. 'This is serious, isn't it – even discounting Fielden's pessimism and Greene's desire for a new job', Reith noted. Felix continued to be extremely critical of the Empire Service, but although he agreed about the need to ginger up the BBC's English-language overseas broadcasting along Reithian lines, he was not as yet convinced that the BBC should emulate its rivals in Germany and Italy and venture into foreign-language broadcasting. He wrote Graves an anxious and impassioned memo on the matter after the *New York Herald Tribune* had reported that the BBC was about to move into this area. The Americans, he said, regarded the short-wave broadcasting put out by the Germans and the Italians in particular as so much propaganda, but made an exception of that put out by the BBC. 'They do not lump us with the other Europeans and the reason, I think, is that we are content to use our own language and our own only. That is a great asset which I would be sorry to lose.'

Three years later Hugh would be doing his best to combine the BBC's reputation for truth and reliability with foreign-language broadcasting, and, despite his initial reservations, Felix found himself paving the way for his cousin, albeit unwittingly. Neville Chamberlain, who had succeeded Baldwin as Prime Minister in May 1937, had little time for Robert Vansittart, and had moved him upstairs to a newly invented but powerless post as the Foreign Office's Chief Diplomatic Adviser. One of his new responsibilities was co-ordinating British propaganda and publicity abroad. He was increasingly worried about the effectiveness of German and Italian broadcasts to Latin America, and it was agreed that Felix should make a tour of the major countries of South America, many of which had sizeable German and Italian minorities, and report back to London.

Felix was appalled by what he found. Neither the BBC nor the embassies were doing enough to promote British interests or counteract rival propaganda. 'We are facing damaging propaganda in all its forms, propaganda concerted, skilful, highly organised and presented with resourcefulness, energy and infinite diligence. Countless Brazilians, Argentinians and Chileans, in positions of influence and friendly towards our country, have told me how difficult it is to stand by and watch the effects of these activities and see Britain lift no finger to protect her name and interests,' he declared. 'It will be disastrous to have our programmes compared unfavourably with those already established by Germany and Italy,' he wrote to Graves from Lima: he referred to the 'incalculable importance of our short-wave service', adding that 'now it is to be expanded I am anxious for it to be known as the best service in the world. It will *never* get known as such without a change to more imaginative and less pedestrian programmes.' He met his parents in Rio, on what must have been Eppy's last trip to his old stomping-grounds, and, back in London, reported to Vansittart and a Cabinet sub-committee headed by Sir Kingsley Wood. He also talked to influential figures in the Labour Party, including Hugh Dalton and Clement Attlee. After Attlee had referred to Britain's poor image in South America in a speech to the Commons, Graves wondered how he'd come by this information, and Felix had to explain that Attlee was an old friend of Ben, and that 'my brother, Attlee and myself met informally one day.'

In January 1938 the BBC took the plunge into foreign-language broadcasting with an Arabic Service, designed to counteract German and Italian propaganda in the Middle East, and, prompted in part by Felix's report, it began broadcasting in Spanish and Portuguese to Latin America two months later. Back in the States, Felix remained as critical as ever of the Empire Service. 'There are occasions on which, in my view, we fail lamentably to provide our Empire listeners with an adequate service. They are the occasions when some serious international crisis occurs in Europe,' he declared in one of his formal reports. An egregious example was provided by the *Anschluss*, as a result of which Austria was forcibly incorporated into the Third Reich. 'On March 14th, at the time when America was listening to an account of Hitler's arrival in Vienna, we were presenting to our listeners in the empire "Stars of the Cabaret World". When, later, Americans listened to a very informative and dispassionate account of the day's momentous events from Berlin, our transmitters were sending to the ends of the earth "Old Folks at Home – a Series of Popular Melodies",' Felix reported to his Controller in London. Both NBC and CBS had provided detailed reports from Berlin, Vienna, London and Paris: the BBC's coverage had been 'incomprehensible and a shattering disappointment' to listeners in the States and Canada.

All this coincided with grim news from home. Eppy's health had continued to deteriorate, and the family finances were in a poor way. The Brazilian coffee trade had recovered slightly from the early years of the Depression, when tons of unsaleable coffee were burned or hurled into the sea, but although Tooter had been assiduous in cultivating European buyers, and Germany and the Netherlands in particular, Kenya and Colombia were now competing with Brazil. Brazilian Warrant Company shares had a nominal value of ten shillings, but were now worth a mere threepence a share. Although at the time of Eppy's death the value of his investments was only about a quarter of their par value, for probate purposes these, together with his other assets, would exceed his debts of £60,000 by about £28,000. Felix had been a great source of comfort and advice to his parents despite being on the far side of the Atlantic. He was, he declared, homesick for 'the one place on earth that gives me a sense of complete and affectionate support.' 'The dominating centre of our thoughts and affections is not business or our immediate activities but the family. We are all the same, Ben and Tooter as much as myself,' he told his parents. 'No member of the family will ever feel that he is left on his own. It's a kind of mutual security association, and that means a good deal in an uncertain world . . . Your financial affairs, thanks to Brazil, may be in a rotten condition, but there's one thing our family need never feel, and that's real anxiety.' Little Wittenham may

have been one of the 'fixed points' of Felix's life, but it would have to
be sold, and he comforted his father over the loss, as well as providing
financial advice. 'Your words, if only half true, make me feel as if my life
has not been all in vain,' his father told him.

In July Eppy lapsed into a coma, and Felix and Tooter were with him
when he died, 'in high summer, in his own garden, among his own roses,
with his family near him'. 'My respect and love for him have always been
impersonal,' and he had never felt 'emotionally attached' to his father,
Felix confessed: Eva had always been the family's driving force and
emotional centre. Eppy died owing the bank nearly £70,000. He left Eva
a lump sum of £1000 and an income of £2000 a year, a respectable income
in the 1930s, but little to live on in her old age in the 1970s. Felix found
himself having to subvent his mother as well as paying the Dartington
Hall school fees for Ben's daughters. Convinced that war was about to
break out, he urged Eva to return to Brazil, or to move to the States,
where there was little or no anti-German feeling. In the meantime, she
went to stay at Harston with Uncle Graham. 'I have been thinking of
you at Harston pulling up chairs a little closer to the fire, with a damp
darkness already fallen and those cold sheets still ahead,' Felix wrote
from Jamaica on Christmas Day 1938. He was on his way back from a
Pan-American Conference in Lima, and had been asked to reorganise
the Jamaican broadcasting system along BBC lines. 'You've had your
turkey, and your church in the morning, and Aunt Polly's decorations
hang around the house,' he continued. 'And all the while your heart aches
with the memory of other Christmas days.'

'The work of the BBC in America is now so varied that the New
York office has, in a sense, become a microcosm of Broadcasting House,'
Felix announced in his July 1939 report. The number of programmes
originating in the States for listeners at home had increased by 96 per
cent since he started in his job: sometimes as many as three programmes
a day were broadcast to Britain from New York; regular items included
Raymond Gram Swing's 'American Commentary' and Alistair Cooke's
'Mainly About Manhattan', though 'Letters from America' were still the
preserve of the critic and *New Yorker* writer Alexander Woolcott. Feature
programmes were increasingly popular, evidence of how 'the speed and
fluency of American production methods can very effectively be wedded
to BBC standards of authentic and accurate documentation.' He had
covered the royal tour of Canada with Richard Dimbleby, and, unlike
the State Department, the British Embassy was as unhelpful as ever. In
March 1939, Hitler invaded Czechoslovakia, and the Empire Service was

once again found wanting: 'extracts from the German, Italian, French, Spanish and Russian news bulletins were being broadcast, but no news broadcast by the BBC was heard by American listeners.'

With war apparently inevitable, Felix felt that his days with the BBC were numbered. 'I shall remain here – doing my work if they allow me to do it with no semblance whatever of using this office as a means of persuading this country to come to Britain's support, or propaganda of any form' he told Eva, adding that 'if they ask me to return home to take part in the war, I shall refuse.' When war broke out, he might find himself out of a job, 'but that concerns me very little.' In a speech to the Philadelphia Foreign Policy Association he claimed that punitive Allied policies against Germany after the First World War had been responsible for the rise of Hitler, and that it was essential to understand and accommodate the 'legitimate grievances of the German people'. 'Ed, you and I know that there will be a war. Take it!' he told Ed Murrow, who had been offered the post of CBS's London correspondent, but was reluctant to leave New York: but his own position was more problematic. 'My convictions as a pacifist put me so clearly out of step with the mass of my fellow-countrymen that I am wondering what use I could be to the BBC if I returned to England. On the other hand, the thought of resigning from the BBC is terribly painful to me,' he declared in a memo to Graves. 'At present my pacifist convictions are being no embarrassment to me in regard to my position at NAR. Nor, I think, are they sufficiently widely known to be harming the BBC.' His successor, he added, should be adaptable enough to consort with grandees and politicians, but 'not mind licking his own stamps or waiting at 3 a.m. on the docks to despatch a parcel of recordings.' He should be a good mixer, and avoid the rather supercilious airs and tone of voice which irritated the Americans; and although, for his part, he had arrived with little experience as a producer in London, 'I was lucky in having had some earlier experience in stage production, which I have found invaluable to me here.'

Tooter was in New York on business when war broke out, 'and the prospect of returning fills him with despair.' Programmes from America were temporarily suspended, but Felix cabled London to say that, given the strength of American isolationism, it was 'of the utmost importance that the British people should not be misled by false hopes and that they be frankly informed week by week as to the course of American opinion.' He felt increasingly removed from it all, affecting a lofty, philosophical detachment. 'What heights and depths we reach these days,' he told Eva. They were living through 'some of the strangest days in the whole history of mankind', and 'the only security is security in oneself and the belief that ultimately this world will see goodness and gentleness.' 'I'm keeping very detached from world affairs,' he wrote some six weeks after the German invasion of Poland. 'Alistair Cooke and his wife and Betsy and others feel as I do about the war . . . the less one talks and discusses and argues, the more inner peace one achieves.' He concentrated on making programmes about music and apolitical matters and, as if to emphasise his growing detachment from the BBC, he joined Heard, Huxley and Henwar Rodakiewicz in setting up Film Associates, a short-lived production company. 'Men are fighting for illusions and it is only those who are far away who can understand that,' he informed Sheila MacDonald, but he was not quite free to soar into the empyrean. He had been enlisted for 'unofficial' intelligence work when in London to report on his South American trip, and the head of Naval Intelligence had taken him out to lunch to suggest that he should talk to David Sarnoff, the head of RCA, about the feasibility of the Royal Navy acquiring a new decoding system without infringing American neutrality. Felix never heard back from Sarnoff, but he now received a coded message to the effect that he should, as a matter of course, try to find out as much as possible about the movements and whereabouts of the Nazi hierarchy from the CBS and NBC correspondents in Berlin. Felix had to admit that this made him feel rather important, but he still refused to become 'part of the war effort – in that I will *not* take part.' In February 1940 he finally resigned from the BBC. 'It means terrible risks, and possibly years of uncertainty and hardship, but it's got to be done,' he told Eva. 'I want to keep myself clean and undirtied by taking no part whatever in the present fearful and destructive activities. In that way I *may* be of some use when it is over and a new world requires to be built.'

★

Graham, in the meantime, was leading the life of a well-regarded but only moderately successful literary man. His novels sold in modest quantities, and, like many inhabitants of Grub Street before and since, he had to keep himself and his family by writing articles and reviews, and was often tempted to abandon the hazardous life of a writer in favour of a career in publishing or films. For a time he worked as a scout for Bobbs Merrill, an undistinguished New York firm of publishers; generous as always in the help and encouragement he gave to unknown or struggling writers, he had recommended R. K. Narayan's first novel to Rupert Hart-Davis's friend Hamish Hamilton, who was now running his own firm, and for a time he acted as a reader and proofreader for 'Jamie' Hamilton, 'my eventual aim being a job and then a directorship there'. He got to know his contemporaries, many of whom he had invited to contribute to *The Old School*. He met Geoffrey Grigson, a 'fierce and dangerous creature' who had given *Journey Without Maps* a good review in the *Morning Post*, and claimed to be a distant cousin. He had, he told Hugh, 'a painful purgatorial lunch' with Grigson, Rosamond Lehmann and Stephen Spender, who 'struck me as having too much human kindness. A little soft.'

Few novelists have had as detailed an understanding of the film business as Graham: he worked as a scriptwriter and as a film critic, and many adaptations were made of his novels and short stories, most of which are best forgotten, though a few – Cavalcanti's wartime masterpiece *Went the Day Well?* and Carol Reed's *The Third Man* – are among the finest films ever made. Like Hugh, Graham was a tireless film-goer, and before long he was reviewing films for the *Spectator* – 'the job I once tried to get for Hugh' – and making his name as an entertaining, opinionated and well-informed critic, with a liking for documentaries and little time for costume dramas. Among those whose work he derided was the Hungarian-born director and producer Alexander Korda, who had settled in England in 1931 after working in Budapest, Berlin and Paris, and made his British reputation with *The Secret Life of Henry VIII* and other lavish historical dramas. Graham may have been introduced to Korda by his well-heeled Oxford contemporary John Sutro, whose father had been one of Korda's backers. Despite his unkind remarks in the *Spectator*, Graham became extremely fond of Korda, who not only commissioned him to write the script for *The Green Cockatoo* – the subject matter of which, racetrack gangs, resurfaced in Graham's most successful pre-war novel, *Brighton Rock* – but, after the war, produced *The Third Man* and *The Fallen Idol*, based on Graham's short story 'The Basement Room'. Graham, for his part, evoked Korda as Dreuther, the central character of his novella *Loser Takes All* – the only time, he maintained, that he 'drew a principal character from the life'.

Graham's friendship with Korda may have involved him in another, more elusive world. In the early thirties, before Hitler came to power, Robert Vansittart had combined his work as Permanent Under-Secretary at the Foreign Office with running an organisation, familiarly referred to as 'Vansittart's Private Detective Agency', designed to gather information on the Nazi Party. Vansittart's network of informants continued to provide

him with information even after he had been moved upstairs to become
the Chief Diplomatic Adviser, and complemented the activities of the 'Z'
organisation, run by Claude Dansey of the SIS (better known as MI6),
who employed businessmen working under commercial cover – travel
agents, wine merchants, art dealers and others – to report back on their
visits to, and dealings with, Nazi Germany. Korda was actively involved
in the 'Z' organisation: both Vansittart and Dansey backed his production company, London Films, and Vansittart wrote film scripts for Korda,
including *The Four Feathers*, as well as introducing him to Winston
Churchill, who was employed as a scriptwriter and adviser during his long
years in the political wilderness. Nor was Korda Graham's only connection with the world of spies and secret agents: his youngest sister, Elisabeth, had gone to work for MI6 – 'Elisabeth's job sounds very hush-hush,'
Hugh wrote home from Berlin – and would, in due course, be responsible for enlisting Graham into the secret service. Graham's fascination
with the shady world of spies and informers is reflected in his pre-war
novels. *A Gun for Sale* deals with the topical subject of international arms
dealers, and is set against the background of an imminent European war,
while the central figure of *The Confidential Agent* is on the run from a
nameless civil war, and finds himself adrift in a shadowy world in which
no one can be trusted.

Like many writers, Graham longed to combine the flexibility and
freedom of the freelance with the routine and regular income that goes
with a part-time job, and still more so now that he had two children to
look after. The sale of the film rights in *A Gun for Sale* to Paramount for
$12,000 was a welcome boost to the family funds, and there was talk of
his being commissioned to write a book about the persecution of the
Roman Catholic clergy in Mexico. He was keen to press ahead, but in
the meantime, he told Hugh in December 1936, 'I've been offered the
literary editorship of a new weekly Chatto are starting in the spring.'
Published by Chatto & Windus, and mostly owned by the Chatto partners and their printers, *Night and Day* may well be the most elegant (if
short-lived) magazine ever published in this country, and it boasted an
incomparable contingent of contributors. 'The world may be divided
into those who enjoy *Punch* and those who enjoy the *New Yorker*,' Graham
had declared in *The Old School*, and *Night and Day* was unashamedly
modelled on the latter: its format was almost identical, it combined distinguished prose with first-rate cartoons, and it strove to be entertaining,
worldly and, above all, self-consciously sophisticated. Ian Parsons of
Chatto was its managing director, and the staff of four included John

Marks, who had been at Cambridge with Ian Parsons and Alistair Cooke, translated the works of Celine, and edited the 'front' half of the magazine, which covered current affairs and topical matters; Graham, as the literary editor, looked after the review pages. 'We worked in an ideal partnership, and I don't remember any differences between us,' Graham later recorded. His team of regular critics included Evelyn Waugh on books, Elizabeth Bowen on theatre, Osbert Lancaster on art, Hugh Casson on architecture, A. J. A. Symons on restaurants and his great friend Herbert Read on detective stories. Peter Fleming, writing as 'Slingsby', contributed the gossipy 'Minutes' at the front of the magazine; William Plomer contributed a piece on all-in wrestling and Louis MacNeice covered the activities of the Kennel Club. Occasional contributors included Cyril Connolly, V. S. Pritchett, William Empson, Anthony Powell, Alistair Cooke, Stevie Smith and Hugh Kingsmill. Feliks Topolski's drawings first appeared in *Night and Day*, and he became a regular contributor: Graham was particularly proud of the magazine's cartoonists, who included Nicolas Bentley and the marvellous Paul Crum, who was killed on the Dieppe Raid in 1942.

The magazine was launched with a party at the Dorchester, attended by 800 people and addressed by A. P. Herbert. The first issue appeared on 1 July 1937, and Graham found himself agreeably involved in the day-to-day business of editing a magazine: accepting and rejecting pieces offered to him, haggling over fees, finding new contributors. 'Yes, the pay is rather disappointing, but I'm getting spliced and want as many regular jobs as I can get,' Evelyn Waugh told him on learning that he would be paid six guineas a week for his page of book reviews. 'Supercharger', the motoring correspondent, soon handed in his notice, and Selwyn Powell, the art editor, was asked to hold the fort: 'No matter. You can drive, can't you? And write?' the non-driving Graham declared when Powell confessed that he knew next to nothing about cars. Contributions by Jocelyn Brooke, Marghanita Laski, H. E. Bates and Henry Miller were declined, as was Nancy Mitford's 'I Am a Sailing Widow' ('My God no. And why be so worried about Peter Rodd?' Graham scribbled on her covering letter, apropos her feckless husband). Suggesting that the serious–minded Herbert Read, then editing *Art Now*, should review detective stories proved to be a stroke of genius, uncovering an unsuspected gift for comic prose. And, like innumerable literary editors before and since, Graham found himself having to chivvy publishers for review copies, his own among them. 'One doesn't want to be driven to review nothing but Gollancz or other publishers who send their books regularly,' he told Charles Evans.

Walter Allen, who had contributed a piece on Aston Villa Football Club, recalled visiting Graham in the Chatto offices in William IV Street in the autumn of 1937. 'He was very tall and thin; one felt a gust of wind would blow him over,' he wrote in *As I Walked Down New Grub Street*. 'His face was lined, as though he were under strain or perhaps in some pain, and his smile seemed somewhat reluctant, as though he were using facial muscles not much exercised. His voice, which was a lightish tenor, was not so much high-pitched as curiously strangled.' Whenever Walter asked Graham how he was, he invariably replied 'middling' or 'mediocre': he pictured him always in an 'anonymous raincoat', and he 'embodied the notion of someone walking ahead, as I had imagined him doing in Sierra Leone and Liberia.' One day Graham took Allen to lunch at Rules, the red-plush Edwardian restaurant in Maiden Lane famed for its steak and kidney puddings. Allen, a Midlands man brought up as a Non-Conformist, was shocked when Graham revealed that he would like to live in a seedy South American republic where everyone took bribes and haunted the local brothels.

It is generally assumed that *Night and Day* was closed down after MGM had sued for libel after Graham had made some unkind remarks about Shirley Temple: in fact the magazine was in financial difficulties by the autumn of 1937 – sales never matched expectations – and it closed down three months before the case came to court the following March. Graham had already taken a swipe at the pouting child star in his *Spectator* review of *The Littlest Rebel*, referring to her 'coquetry quite as mature as Miss Colbert's and an oddly precocious body quite as voluptuous in grey flannel trousers as Miss Dietrich's', and *Wee Willie Winkie* provoked him to fresh heights of derision. 'Watch her swaggering stride across the India barrack square: hear the gasp of excited expectation from her antique audience when the sergeant's palm is raised: watch the way she measures a man with agile studio eyes, with dimpled depravity,' he declared in the 18 October issue. 'Her admirers – middle-aged men and clergymen – respond to her dubious coquetry, to the sight of her well-shaped and desirable little body, packed with enormous vitality, only because the safety curtain of story and dialogue drops between their intelligence and their desire.' Years later, when Shirley Temple was the American Ambassador in Ghana, she and Graham entered into an amused and affectionate correspondence; in the meantime, WH Smith's refused to touch the offending issue, and when a letter was received from MGM threatening to sue, Ian Parsons decided to seek legal advice. D. N. Pritt, a well-known Communist MP and a highly regarded KC, reported that Graham's review was in no way libellous, so extra copies of that issue were printed to meet the demand. Graham was not so confident – 'that little bitch is going to cost me about £250 if I'm lucky,' he told Hugh three weeks after *Night and Day*'s demise – but in the meantime he joined his colleagues in trying to keep the magazine afloat. 'Greene rang to say that *Night and Day* is on its last legs; would I put them in touch with Evan Tredegar, whom I barely know, to help them raise capital. They must indeed be in a bad way', Evelyn Waugh noted in his diary in November – Tredegar being a rich socialite whose fortune was based on coal mines in South Wales. But no further capital was forthcoming, and the last issue was published on 23 December.

By the time *Wee Willie Winkie* came to court, Graham was several thousand miles away. Someone suggested that he should write a book about Palestine with Malcolm Muggeridge, a contributor to *Night and Day*, but after much shilly-shallying on the part of various publishers, the suggestion that he should write a book about Mexico at last came good despite Graham's editor at Heinemann, A. S. Frere, having admitted that he hadn't the faintest idea how to sell a religious book, and put himself out of the running. A former journalist on the *Evening News* who had served in the Royal Flying Corps in World War I and was a nimble tap dancer, Frere had joined Heinemann in 1923, became its managing director nine years later, and was to become one of Graham's closest friends and confidants, and the publisher whose taste and advice he always respected. Sheed & Ward, the Roman Catholic publishers who had first suggested the idea, had lost interest, but help was to hand in the convivial form of Tom Burns, who was to become another lifelong friend of Graham's. A saturnine, good-looking man, Burns had met Graham in 1929. 'Graham leapt into my landscape like a leprechaun: witty, evasive, nervous and sardonic, by turns. He stood out in the company we both kept in those days, which was mainly of publishers and authors, and joyfully joined in plans and projects,' he later recalled. Born in Chile and educated at Stonyhurst, Burns was a right-wing Catholic, and had supported the Nationalists during the Spanish Civil War: he was to spend the war in Spain as a propagandist-cum-spy attached to the British Embassy, doing his bit to keep Spain neutral. In 1967 he succeeded Douglas Woodruff as the editor of the *Tablet*, steering it in a more liberal direction after the reforms of Vatican II, and appointing Graham to its board. In the meantime, he had moved from Sheed & Ward to Longmans, where he managed to persuade its 'somewhat bovine' board of directors to commission the Mexico book, paying an advance of £500.

In the limbo between losing his job on *Night and Day* and leaving for Mexico, Graham received a visit from one of his keenest admirers, Julian Maclaren-Ross. In later years Maclaren-Ross became a colourful chronicler of pub life in Soho and Fitzrovia, but when he visited Graham in Clapham he was still living in Bognor, selling vacuum cleaners to make a living and anxious to obtain Graham's consent to his adapting *A Gun for Sale* for radio. In his marvellous *Memoirs of the Forties*, published by Alan Ross many years after the event, he provided a vivid portrait of Graham in his mid-thirties, albeit one that needs to be taken with a pinch of salt. He tells us, for example, that he took with him a copy of *Brighton Rock* for Graham to sign, but the novel wasn't published until after Graham's return from Mexico; he claimed, wrongly, that Graham and Vivien were cousins, and that this explained the similarity of their handwriting, whereas nothing could be further removed from Graham's tiny, runic script than Vivien's florid, feminine hand.

Maclaren-Ross was invited to lunch, and at the appointed time he rang the bell of an elegant red-brick house on Clapham Common. Mistaking him – not unreasonably – for a travelling salesman, the housekeeper tried to bar him from entry, but then Graham appeared 'wearing a brown suit and large horn-rimmed spectacles, which he at once snatched off.' He suggested that they should take a large jug each and set off across the Common to buy beer for lunch from a pub. 'Greene took long lounging strides and his shoulders were well above mine as we walked across the grass,' his visitor recalled. 'Though very lean he had high broad straight shoulders from which his jacket was loosely draped as if still on its hanger.' Graham ordered a double whisky apiece while the jugs were being filled, and asked Maclaren-Ross what he did for a living. 'Good for you,' he said when told about the vacuum cleaners, no doubt recalling Herbert's own experience of the profession and, it may be, subconsciously storing it away for future use in *Our Man in Havana*. Back at the house, Maclaren-Ross was introduced to Vivien: 'handsome with black hair', she was 'placid and sedate like a young Spanish matron, and even the repeated crash of the dumb-waiter arriving at its destination failed to shake her poise.' 'It's an awful nuisance, but They are asking to see you, I'm afraid. I wonder if you'd mind,' Graham said after lunch was over. They went upstairs, and paused outside a room from which a 'strange twittering sound' emerged. Maclaren-Ross had a sudden vision of 'giant parrots or pet vultures brought from Africa, or even elderly female relatives not quite certifiable but confined nevertheless to their rooms', but when the door was opened 'two small, extremely pretty blonde children peered out at me unblinking from a cot'.

Back in the sitting room, Graham poured them each a large brandy. 'Who was it complained that not enough children get murdered in detective stories?' he wondered, and Maclaren-Ross deftly supplied the answer (Cyril Connolly). Before long they were joined by Vivien, who sat quietly doing her embroidery. Graham's eyes, his visitor noted, had 'an alert watchful quality, the eyeballs were slightly bloodshot, and one had a sense of tremendous energy and fun triumphing over inner fatigue.' 'His lean face was unlined then, but the skin was rough and a little worn: though his cheeks were carefully shaven there was still a suggestion of stubble,' Maclaren-Ross recalled. 'He smiled a lot and the set of his mouth was amiable rather than severe as in the photographs. His lightish brown hair was parted at the side and brushed in a slight curl over a broad bumpy forehead. He hunched forward in the low armchair with broad shoulders hunched up high and large knuckly hands hanging down with a cigarette fuming between the long fingers.' Graham was happy for Maclaren-Ross to adapt his novel for radio, but on his way back to the tube station Maclaren-Ross suddenly remembered that he had forgotten to ask Graham to sign his (non-existent) copy of *Brighton Rock*.

(Other accounts of visiting the Greenes on Clapham Common were provided by Tom Burns and Anthony Powell. The Greenes' house came as a 'complete surprise' to Burns, who remembered how 'his gentle and beautiful wife had it all arranged with such care. There was a serenity of order in every detail; so different from everything I had been able to observe of Graham himself.' Powell, never a great admirer of Graham or his writing, took a dimmer view. The Powells were invited to dinner, and were told that dress would be informal – only to have Graham ring back to say that 'I find we *are* changing.' Wearing a dinner jacket always made Powell feel like a conjurer or an 'orchestral player', and it took them an hour to get there by bus. 'We supposed at least the fellow-guests would be of a fairly high grade,' Powell recalled. 'Not a bit of it. They turned out to be a minor civil servant and wife of infinite dreariness, who lived in a house two doors up the same row as the Greenes. Vivien Greene, a woman of considerable pretentiousness and middlebrow views, was presumably responsible for insisting on evening dress.')

Once again, Graham was reluctant to set out on his adventures alone, and he hoped Hugh might fill the slot previously occupied by Barbara. 'This is all very sad about the *Telegraph*'s attitude to your coming to Mexico,' he wrote to his brother in Berlin after learning that Hugh couldn't take the time off. In February 1938 Graham and Vivien set out for New York on the *Normandie*: they would travel together as far as New

Orleans, at which point she would return to England, and he would head for Mexico and the semi-tropical southern states of Chiapas and Tabasco, where the anti-clerical purges initiated by President Calles had been particularly virulent and persistent. Felix spent two evenings with them in New York, and told his parents that Graham had 'improved enormously, a really friendly individual now, far more certain of himself, far less nervy', that Vivien was 'pleasant enough but vapid and ineffective', and that 'they both spoke in such warm terms about you two.'

The Lawless Roads, Graham's account of his travels in Mexico, is one of the great travel books of the twentieth century. Whereas Graham had felt ambivalent about the Spanish Civil War, he had no reservations about supporting the Catholic cause in Mexico, likening their persecution to that of their co-religionists in England during the reign of Queen Elizabeth. Churches were burned, priests harried and shot, and an aggressive secularism prevailed. He travelled by train, mule, ferry-boat and light aircraft; he came to feel an 'almost pathological hatred of Mexicans', priests and aviators always excepted; in the heat and dirt and dust he longed for England, and tried to assuage his homesickness with William Cobbett's Rural Rides and Anthony Trollope's Dr Thorne; and, of course, he gathered material and characters for The Power and the Glory, the novel which gave him 'more satisfaction than any other I had written' and, after a slow start, went on to become one of the most popular of all his works. 'This is an awful and depressing country for anyone like myself who doesn't care for nature,' he wrote to Elizabeth Bowen, whose novel The Hotel he had read while staying with the Norwegian widow of an American coffee-planter: he had been to his first 'bootleg mass', remarkable for their being 'no sanctus bell and the priest arriving in a natty motoring coat and tweed cap'. Back in Mexico City, the proofs of Brighton Rock were waiting to be read, along with a cable 'asking me to agree to apologise to that little bitch Shirley Temple', and a letter from Chatto to say that the Lord Chief Justice, Lord Hewart, who had presided over the libel case, had sent the file on to the DPP for a possible charge of criminal libel. During the course of the trial Hewart had described Graham's article as a 'gross outrage'; MGM had employed the best-known and most flamboyant barrister of the day, Sir Patrick Hastings, who told the court that Night and Day had published a 'disgusting libel'. Chatto was left with a bill of £3500, £500 of which was contributed by Graham. When Graham joined MI6 in 1940, 'they asked for traces of me from Scotland Yard and the Shirley Temple case was produced.' It was not considered sufficient reason for debarring him from the secret service, but when, nearly half a century later, Chatto asked if they could include the offending review in an anthology of *Night and Day*, Graham agreed on the strict understanding that Chatto and its lawyers would indemnify him against any risk of further action.

Graham sailed for home on a German boat carrying volunteers to fight for Franco in the Spanish Civil War. He returned to a London of gas masks and anti-aircraft guns and trenches dug in the parks. The Munich Agreement had, as it turned out, postponed the inevitable for another year – time in which one Greene in particular could do everything in his power to avert a war, at however high a cost.

Kristallnacht

As the world lurched from one international crisis to another during the course of the 1930s, Ben became ever more passionately convinced that war must be avoided at all costs, and that it was worth paying any price to avoid a repetition of the carnage of 1914–18. His pacifism went hand-in-hand with a conviction that Germany had been shabbily treated under the terms of the Treaty of Versailles, not least in the loss of territory to Poland and Czechoslovakia, and a belief – shared by Felix, and a good many other well-meaning people – that some aspects of Nazi social policy, such as their apparent abolition of unemployment by means of huge public works schemes, contrasted well with what was on offer in Britain, and that the brutality and intolerance of Hitler's regime would be mitigated if Germany's 'legitimate' grievances were met and she was welcomed into the community of nations. His being half-German no doubt swayed him to some extent, but however naïve or misguided they may seem in retrospect, his political views were infused with a genuine idealism, a desire to remedy injustices and to make the world a better place. Wherever he found himself on the political spectrum, he continued to think of himself as a socialist. He instinctively sided with the 'little man' against bureaucrats, party bosses and the sinister forces of inter-national capitalism. Nor was he alone in his views on Versailles: Lloyd George and Maynard Keynes both attacked the folly and unfairness of the terms imposed on Germany, and even Robert Vansittart, who after the outbreak of war declared that 'eighty per cent of the German race are the political and moral scum of the earth' and that Hitler was the end product of 'a breed which from the dawn of history has been predatory and bellicose', conceded that 'I have always thought that Germany got far too rough usage at Versailles and have always wished to see minimised the imprudences then committed.'

The ILP had always attracted those on the left of the party who found it hard to accept party discipline and the compromises involved in everyday politics. ILP members indulged in revolutionary rhetoric and guerrilla tactics, and frequently clashed with the Labour Party's leaders. After the crisis of 1931, when the former ILP member Ramsay MacDonald left the Labour Party to lead a coalition National Government, with Conservative and Liberal support, the running of the Labour Party was increasingly concentrated on the National Executive Committee or NEC, and power lay with the trade unions rather than with the demoralised and discredited rump of the parliamentary party. The ILP found itself more out on a limb than ever: later in the decade some of Ben's colleagues from the ILP would find themselves in dubious political company, but in the meantime Ben was cast in the traditional ILP role of harrying the powers-that-be on behalf of those Labour Party members whom he felt to be under-valued and under-represented. Despite having been defeated twice in parliamentary elections, he was active in local politics, both in the Hertfordshire County Council and the Berkhamsted Urban District Council, and he passionately believed that constituency parties and individual party members should be better represented in the Labour Party, not least at the annual Conference, where resolutions were put forward for debate and, in theory at least, policy was laid down.

In September 1932 Ben published an article entitled 'Local Labour Parties', in which he claimed that local parties lacked influence at national level because they were unorganised, and proposed a national organisation which could formulate policy and stand up against the all-powerful trade union bloc at Party Conferences. Two years later he launched an Association of Labour Parties, and was appointed its secretary: although he claimed at its inaugural meeting that there was 'no question of opposition to the leaders of the Party, and no sort of contest with the industrial elements', both the NEC and Transport House were vehemently opposed to the new organisation on the grounds that it could undermine the NEC's role in determining policy. It soon petered out, but Ben continued to work with activists at a local level, in the Home Counties in particular. Such areas had never been known to return a Labour MP, but Ben's campaign appealed to the middle classes, many of them university-educated and intellectually inclined, whose consciences had been pricked by mass unemployment at home and the rise of fascism in Europe, and who were regarded with deep suspicion by many working class and trade union members of the Party.

In June 1935 the Home Counties Labour Association or HCLA was established: Charles Garnsworth, a Reigate insurance agent and later a Labour peer, was its chairman and Ben its secretary, working from the

Kepston offices in Berkhamsted. Speaking at the Party Conference in Brighton that summer, Ben claimed that 'more and more local parties feel that representation at the annual conference has become an expensive futility.' He also attacked an NEC report calling for a boycott of German goods, but was unable to find a seconder: the Jews, he declared, were those most likely to suffer from such a boycott, and he suggested that the best way of dealing with the Nazis was to adopt the even-handed, uncensorious approach of the Quakers, whose Berlin office was already arranging for German Jews and their families to be settled in Britain and elsewhere. In November he stood again for Gravesend in the general election, and was again defeated. He continued to agitate for increased representation for constituency parties so that 'discussion can be done *inside the Party* on a wider basis than the present Party machinery allows for', and found himself increasingly unpopular with the Labour Party establishment. A plan to co-ordinate constituency party resolutions so as to present a united front at Conference was regarded as mutiny. He engaged in an increasingly heated correspondence with 'Jimmie' Middleton at Transport House, who told him, apropos the NEC's refusal to recognise the HCLA, that he took 'exception to activities which seem to usurp the functions and authority of the NEC'. 'I am bound to say that you have a most suspicious mind!' Middleton wrote in the summer of 1936, adding that 'You must get it out of your head that there is some kind of conspiracy afoot.' In his reply to 'My dear Jimmie', Ben said that he and his colleagues were 'not prepared to be treated by the National Executive as scallywags and hooligans, supported by arguments which are untrue and biased.'

Earlier that year, Ben had been involved in controversy over a proposed visit to Germany by members of the Labour Party, free of charge and under official auspices, which had been called off after adverse publicity in the *Daily Herald*. Ben had hoped to join the party, and from now on his work on behalf of constituency parties, and his reputation within the Party, was to be tarnished by his apparent sympathy for certain aspects of the Nazi regime. But it proved no bar to an uneasy collaboration between the HCLA and Stafford Cripps's Socialist League, a ginger group of left-wing public school and Oxbridge intellectuals which, like the HCLA, frequently clashed with the Party hierarchy, and was disliked and resented by the trade unions in particular. Following a revolt by the constituency parties at the 1936 Party Conference in Edinburgh, Hugh Dalton, the Party's Chairman-elect, and himself an Old Etonian, gave the HCLA a year in which to convince the NEC of its case, and gain the support of the TUC. A Provisional Committee of Constituency Labour Parties was set up, with Cripps (a Wykehamist) as chairman, Ben as secretary, and Aneurin Bevan among its members. Cripps's name lent weight to the proceedings, and his donation of £300 towards Ben's expenses was extremely welcome, but Ben was anxious not to alienate the Party hierarchy and the middle ground by seeming too close to the left-wing Socialist League, and to keep Cripps in particular at arm's length. When, the following year, the left-wing magazine *Tribune* was founded, Cripps suggested that the HCLA should be associated with it, and Ben was made a director: but he found himself out of sympathy with the Socialist League, and although, like the ILP, it continued to support his constituency parties campaign, he soon resigned from the post.

Altogether more important from the HCLA's point of view was the fact that Hugh Dalton had been won round to the cause of the constituency parties. He accepted most of their arguments and, in the face of trade union hostility, suggested that their representation on the NEC should be increased from five to seven. At the Party conference in Bournemouth in October 1937 Ben spoke for the constituency parties: after a good deal of horse-trading behind the scenes, Dalton's suggestion was accepted, and the news was greeted by a mighty cheer from the constituencies' delegates. Of the seven elected delegates, only one came from outside London, while two were Etonians, two were Wykehamists, and two were members of the working class. No doubt this confirmed TUC suspicions of middle-class intellectuals, but whereas the NEC had hitherto been powerful but mediocre, greater representation of the constituency parties injected new talent into the Party's governing body, giving it closer ties with the Parliamentary Labour Party, whose views it more accurately reflected. According to the historian Ben Pimlott, the effects of Ben's reforms were only really felt after 1945: they 'brought about a revolution in the Labour Party of far greater importance than anything achieved by noisier and more glamorous groups which captured the headlines and claimed, with no mandate whatever, to speak for the rank and file,' while 'Ben Greene's organisation succeeded in doing what no other group or faction has ever managed – mobilising the great army of fundamentally loyal constituency activists in a *united* campaign against the discipline imposed by the general staff at Transport House.'

Dalton's support had been invaluable, but Ben received no credit at the time. Transport House invented the myth that the NEC had 'generously and spontaneously' initiated the reforms, and Dalton went on to claim all the credit for himself, making no mention of Ben or his organisations in his memoirs or his published diaries. Despite representing 447,000 individual Party members as well as constituency parties, the HCLA was dismissed as a disruptive splinter group. In the spring of 1937 Ben had been the subject of an NEC enquiry after he had been accused of forcing the early retirement of his agent in Gravesend for suggesting that he had pro-Nazi sympathies: he was adopted as a Labour candidate for Hull South-West, but the NEC refused to endorse him on the grounds that he had attacked the Party leadership and the NEC at the Edinburgh Party Conference, as well as denouncing the NEC's call for a boycott of German goods.

Ben's attempts to expose a sugar beet scandal at a Party Conference confirmed his reputation as a trouble-maker – he later claimed that leaflets explaining a murky and complex financial scam intended to benefit the Party had mysteriously disappeared before they could be distributed to delegates – but his claims that socialists had much to learn from the Nazis, and that 'there is more socialism than nationalism in the Nazi movement', went down even worse with his colleagues. Ben complained to Dalton that, as Chairman of the Party, he had made speeches 'in which you either state or strongly imply that I am fascist or have fascist sympathies'; in his reply, Dalton said that Ben had 'made it clear on several occasions that your attitude towards the Nazi regime in Germany is not that generally adopted by the Labour Party', and reminded him of an article in which he had compared Nazi brutalities with those perpetrated earlier by German Social Democrats. In an article on 'Socialism and the German Boycott,' published in *The Labour Candidate*, Ben had written that 'the brutal treatment of prisoners and their murder is a stain as black in the history of German Social Democracy as it is in the history of Nazism in power,' and that 'Germany as a result of the war needed pulling up by the roots and planting again. Social Democracy could not do it. The Communist Party missed its opportunity, mainly through lack of courage. Now the Nazis have done it instead.' Years later Ben admitted that 'I did indeed feel that the vigour and drive with which the Nazis treated their unemployment problem and the support they gave to Schacht's policy was a lesson to us' – Hjalmar Schacht was Hitler's Economics Minister in the early years of the regime, closely associated with the policy of providing employment through ambitious public works schemes, including the building of the first autobahns – but he reacted furiously to Dalton's letter. 'I happen to have had a very close and intimate knowledge of German politics since the war and if I disagree with the Labour Party's attitude to Germany now, and if I consider this attitude deplorable and dangerous, then I have not only a right but a duty to express my opinions based on my own intimate experience,' he wrote in reply. As for the proposed visit to Germany by Labour Party officials, 'only by individual members of the Party seeing conditions for themselves can ignorance and prejudice be destroyed.' On foreign affairs at least, Ben and Dalton were poles apart: as the Labour Party's foreign affairs spokesman, Dalton was weaning the party away from its semi-pacifist past, rejecting Chamberlain's policy of appeasement and favouring rearmament.

Ben remained the secretary of the Constituency Parties Association until 1938, but he was asked to resign after making what was regarded as a speech in favour of Germany. After it was over, Charles Garnsworth joined him in a Lyons Corner House, and warned him that he would be thrown out of the Labour Party if he didn't change his views: Ben had no recollection of the meeting, and the two men never met again. Ben supported Chamberlain's role in the Munich Agreement, which he hoped would lead to a 'wider European settlement', and in October 1938 he resigned from the Labour Party with, he told Middleton, 'the very greatest regret'. He had joined the Party in 1920 'in the firm conviction that social and international justice without recourse to war or civil war would be the fundamental basis of our policy,' but it was now committed to 'a policy which means war of the most horrible and devastating kind in causes which have no historic justification. It appears that the Party is even committed to joining a War Cabinet, and even now conscription and compulsory military service is being advocated by Party members.' The Party had become increasingly undemocratic, so much so that 'even the appearance of consulting the Party in Conference . . . is completely dispensed with': its leaders had 'betrayed the historic mission of the Party by supporting and even advocating a policy of war', which in itself represented a threat to 'British democratic rights and liberties'.

Democratic rights and liberties were virtually non-existent in Nazi Germany, as Hugh was only too well aware. In May 1938 Wareing was transferred to the *Telegraph*'s Paris office, and Hugh found himself in charge in Berlin. Barbara visited him there at about this time, and remembered him dancing round the room chanting 'I'm a four-figure man, I'm a four-figure man' to celebrate the fact that he was now earning £1000 a year. Life for the Jews of Germany, on the other hand, was becoming ever more unbearable. That summer Hugh reported an increase in antisemitism, and although 'Berlin and certain other cities are more easy-going,' there was an outbreak of Jew-baiting in June. 'The final elimination of Jews from the economic and social life of Germany seems to be the object of the new anti-Jewish drive now being carried out,' Hugh told his readers. The Nazis hoped that Jews would be forced to emigrate, leaving their money behind, but 'Jews cannot emigrate from Germany without completely impoverishing themselves. Other countries then reject them because they have no means of subsistence. They must therefore remain and take what comes.' In the summer of 1938 he described boys between the ages of nine and thirteen daubing white-painted stars of David on Jewish shops, though onlookers seemed 'more sympathetic than hostile' to the Jewish victims. 'Hitler girls' were being told to report their parents if they bought from Jewish shops, and on the Unter den Linden he 'watched the usual squad of three painters led by a fourth man armed with a list of Jewish firms', followed by 'a small crowd, consisting mostly of young girls, who chanted "Jew, Jew, Jew" in a somewhat half-hearted fashion.' Jews without 'Jewish' names were ordered to add either 'Isaac' or 'Sarah' to their existing names, as a means of identification: Helga's cigarette case carried the initials 'HSG', and when asked what the 'S' stood for she made a point of claiming (untruthfully) the middle name of 'Sarah'.

Helga arranged for several Jewish families to be smuggled out of Germany, and after her death Christopher Serpell, a future BBC foreign news editor, remembered how, small as she was, she had earlier seen off some young Nazi thugs who were berating her for wearing lipstick. Life for foreign correspondents in Berlin was becoming increasingly difficult. 'Unlike German correspondents in London, Paris or elsewhere, they have no police passes – those issued in 1936 having been withdrawn – and are without the immunities and privileges granted by the police authorities to the Press in practically every other country in the world,' Hugh complained. The grimness of life under the Nazis was brought home by the suicide of young Graham's godfather, Paul Wallich, a prominent Jewish banker who was unable to take things any longer.

'The anti-Jewish campaign has gone so far that Germans of all classes are disgusted. "One is ashamed to be a German" said a working man to me this morning,' Hugh had written in June, but life became far worse for Germany's Jews after the assassination in Paris of Ernst vom Rath, a junior diplomat at the German Embassy, by a young Polish Jew called Herschel Grynspan: his family, like many others, had been expelled from Germany, and they had found themselves in limbo, camping out in no-man's-land, after the antisemitic Polish government had refused to take them in. On the night of 9 November vicious antisemitic riots broke out all over Germany, openly encouraged by Goebbels: more than a thousand synagogues were set on fire and destroyed, Jewish shops were smashed and looted, and over 30,000 Jews were sent into 'protective custody' (a euphemism for concentration camps) in revenge for what Goebbels described as 'the justified and comprehensible indignation of the German people at the cowardly assassination of a German diplomat'. Hugh was alerted to what was going on when his colleague Anthony Mann, noticing the smashed and looted glass showcases of a hotel in which he was spending the night, rang to say 'It's happened'. Picking his way through the broken glass on the Kurfurstendamm, Berlin's smartest shopping street, Hugh told a curious passer-by that he was 'observing German culture' ('Ich betrachte die deutsche Kultur'). 'An officially countenanced pogrom of unparalleled brutality and ferocity swept Germany today ... it puts the final seal on the outlawing of German Jewry,' he wrote in the *Telegraph*.

I have seen several anti-Jewish outbreaks in Germany during the past five years, but never anything as nauseating as this. Racial hatred and hysteria seemed to have taken hold of otherwise decent people. I saw fashionably dressed women slapping their hands and screaming with glee, while respectable middle-class mothers held up their babies to see the "fun". Women who remonstrated with children who were running away with toys from a wrecked Jewish shop were spat on and attacked by the mob. The attacks had started after midnight, when the beer halls closed, and the police shrugged their shoulders and refused to take any action.

Once again, children were encouraged to do their worst. 'I watched a gang of small boys, led by a member of the Hitler Youth in uniform, demolishing a corset shop in the Wielandstrasse. They then ran round the corner into the Kurfurstendamm, where they undressed the dummies in a women's dress shop and tore them limb from limb amid roars of laughter from the excited crowd,' Hugh noted, while 'conservative Germans in Berlin were particularly disgusted by the sight of German soldiers in uniform taking part in the looting of the fashionable Dobrin café. The soldiers speared cakes with their bayonets and waved them round their heads.'

Hugh continued to believe, or hope, that 'the great mass of decent-thinking Germans are astounded at the manner in which the wave of

antisemitic hooliganism has been carried through.' Three days after
Kristallnacht he reported that half-starved and panic-stricken Jews were
roaming the woods outside Berlin, and 'the holiday-makers shared their
picnic lunches with the Jews, and made no effort to hand them over to
the police' – quite why holiday-makers were picnicking in mid-November
remains a mystery – but the Jewish community had been understandably thrown into a state of 'hopeless panic'. *The Times* reported that
'desperate Jews continue to flock to the British Passport Control offices
in the hope of gaining admission to Great Britain, Palestine or one of
the Crown colonies.' Frank Foley, the Passport Control Officer in Berlin,
was later to be honoured by the state of Israel for the work he did in
saving Jewish lives and smuggling Jews out of Germany. Like most Passport Control Officers at the time, he doubled up as an MI6 agent, and,
as a close friend of Norman Ebbutt and Ian Colvin of the *News Chronicle*, he had been an occasional visitor to the Taverne. After Kristallnacht
he hid several Jews in his home, including the eminent Berlin rabbi Leo
Baeck: Foley invited Hugh and other journalists round to his house,
where Baeck briefed them about the repressive new anti-Jewish measures that had been introduced in the wake of vom Rath's assassination.

Back in London, Ben had been asked to investigate the anti-Jewish
riots on behalf of the Quaker Society of Friends and the Germany
Emergency Committee: he was well-known in Quaker circles, he spoke
fluent German, his experience in the Saar stood him in good stead, and
he had the support of the Jewish Centre in Woburn House. He travelled
out via Amsterdam, where he met the Dutch Prime Minister, who urged
him to report back on his return to Sir Samuel Hoare, the Home Secretary. In Berlin he went to see Ernst-Wilhelm Bohle, to whom he had
been given an introduction by John Scanlon. A Clydesider and a former
ILP colleague of James Maxton, Scanlon had become the labour correspondent of the *Daily Express* before going on to edit *Action* and *The
Blackshirt* for Oswald Mosley's British Union of Fascists. Bohle and his
brother Harry had been born in Bradford and brought up in South
Africa as British subjects: Ernst-Wilhelm was in charge of Goebbels's
Auslandsorganisation, which kept in touch with German citizens living
abroad, and he gave Ben introductions to colleagues in the Propaganda
Ministry, including his brother Harry. Ben remembered Harry Bohle as
a 'hale, hearty, well-made fellow', and 'a very pleasant man to be with',
but Hugh was not taken with Ernst-Wilhelm. 'Herr Bohle, leader of the
Nazi Foreign Organisation and Secretary of State in the Reich Foreign
Office, told me that in his view the methods by which Germany "regu-

lated" the position of the Jews in the Reich were her own affair and nobody else's,' he wrote in the *Telegraph*. 'For our part, we find the Jews disagreeable,' Ernst-Wilhelm told Hugh: he blamed them for losing the First World War, accused them of plundering Germany, and wondered 'Why cannot Britain, who rules over a third of the surface of the globe, find room for them somewhere if she is so fond of them?'

Ben crossed into Germany from Holland with a group of Dutch YMCA members, and 'along the frontier with Holland I saw groups of Jews encamping in bitter cold weather, unable to enter Holland till the Dutch government had made arrangements for their transit to other lands.' In Frankfurt he found children from a Jewish orphanage roaming the streets; he collected together some fifteen of them, took them to the railway station, bought them soup and rang the police, who took them to a Catholic children's home. In his hotel he met a weeping woman whose Jewish husband had been taken to a concentration camp. In the south of Germany he visited a community where every Jewish male between the ages of fifteen and sixty-five had been taken to a concen- tration camp. The police said they could do nothing about it, but referred Ben to the local Gauleiter; he expressed disbelief, and the men were released and allowed back home. People dared not speak out, and 'I was aware of a reign of terror not unlike that I had experienced in Russia.'

Shortly after his arrival in Berlin, Ben was arrested by the Gestapo on a currency irregularity and confined to his hotel for four days. Harry Bohle was, he told the police, the only person he knew by name in Berlin – Hugh seems not to have come into the reckoning – but Bohle 'said he did not know anything about me.' After his release Ben went round to the British Embassy, where the chargé d'affaires told him that 'he thought I was rather foolish, going round on the Jewish question in this way; he said I was causing more trouble to British officials . . .' Scanlon had already told Ben that he thought him an 'absolute fool' to get involved in Jewish relief, and when Ben finally made contact with Harry Bohle he was told that 'You are on this Jewish business. I can do nothing for you.' Bohle relented when Ben mentioned Scanlon's name, but despite vague promises he seems to have done nothing to help; no doubt he never had any intention of doing so, but they enjoyed an amicable and, on Bohle's part, jocular correspondence until the outbreak of war.

The Quakers were trusted by the Jews, and Harry Bohle had told Ben that they stood a better chance than most of being allowed to under- take relief work, but trying to find out what had happened and to organise relief for those affected was, Ben recalled, 'a most terrible bit of work to do . . . to go through wrecked shops and wrecked homes, often looked at with suspicion by the Jews themselves, to be continually under police supervision, never quite able to make your position quite honest and clear, never knowing what kind of treatment you were going to get from the local government authority.' It was important not to seem critical of the regime 'because you had to work with the Nazis', some of whom seemed ashamed of what had happened, and were even prepared to help. In a report for the Society of Friends, Ben wrote that 'above everything else the Jews want to get out of Germany. As a result of recent laws this desire has become almost hysterical, especially in the Frankfurt area.' Jews now had to deposit all their securities in the bank, and could not use them to pay fines or obtain relief, and it was rumoured that after 1 January 1939 Jews would not be allowed to earn money either: 'as the Chief Rabbi of Mainz told me, even slaves could work and could feed.' With Jewish village life wrecked, and their homes vandalised, uprooted Jews were flooding into urban areas, 'a vast mass of Jewish humanity living the lives of rats in and around the cities'. The Rabbi of Mainz told Ben that 'he knew of families that would die of starvation within the next month unless help came. He himself looked as if he hadn't eaten for a considerable time.' The suicide rate was so high that 'the Mainz town authorities have turned off the gas in every Jewish home,' and Ben was present when a Jewish woman tried to kill herself. Although, according to Ben's report, conditions varied from place to place – Berlin was better than most, Frankfurt was 'very desperate and could hardly be worse', Mainz was 'not much better except that the officials are less unkind' – many Jews saw themselves as facing a choice between death or 'the establishment of Jewish labour camps by the Authorities'.

The Jewish longing to leave Germany was compromised by the refusal of the German authorities to allow them to take any money with them – which, Ben believed, favoured either the very rich, who already had assets overseas, or the criminal classes, who could somehow fiddle the system – and by the reluctance of other countries, many of which were plagued by varying degrees of home-grown antisemitism, to accept huge numbers of penniless refugees. Ben himself claimed credit for persuading the British authorities to allow in a larger number of Jewish children than might otherwise have been permitted; and Wilfred Israel, the department store owner and the model for Bernhard Landauer in *Goodbye to Berlin*, many of whose shops had been wrecked, had urged him to put pressure on the British Government to let more children in. Ben had also been 'influential in getting a certain number of Jews out of concentration camps', but he soon became convinced that the answer lay in trying to relieve the situation in Germany itself rather than through emigration. 'All Jews begged me not to allow the question of relief to deter efforts to increase wholesale emigration,' he reported, but he had told them that it would take years before mass emigration could become effective, and Jews would welcome foreign relief 'provided that it was made with the full knowledge and consent of the central authorities in Berlin'. Roger Carter, who ran the Friends International Centre in Berlin, told his colleagues in London that although 'the relief of human need among the Jews would clearly be greeted with sympathy by thousands who have been looking with horror and shame on the recent pillaging and destruction,' German government hostility to relief schemes suggested that the Friends should concentrate their efforts on emigration schemes. But Ben always insisted that, as a Quaker, he was not interested in politics, giving aid irrespective of race or religion, and that 'I was in Germany in precisely the same way as I was in Russia in the early days.' The Friends in Berlin continued to help individual Jews and their families to leave the country, as well as promoting the *Kindertransport* scheme, whereby Jewish children were put on trains and sent to safety in Britain and elsewhere.

Back in London, Ben formed part of a delegation reporting on the situation to Samuel Hoare. He spoke to the Chief Rabbi, who told him that the Nazis were exploiting emigration schemes to clear the concentration camps of undesirable elements, and that those being allowed out included white slavers and drug smugglers. He also called on Victor Rothschild, who had initially supported Ben's plans for providing relief within Germany, but then turned against the idea on the grounds that such schemes would, in effect, involve paying money to the German Government. Ben later felt that he had made a dangerous enemy in 'that arrogant young man', but Jewish organisations in London shared Lord Rothschild's reservations. In December Ben returned to Germany to discuss the possible implementation of his plans, visiting Frankfurt and the Polish border. In Königsberg, a local rabbi asked him to get in touch with some of the 12,000 Jews who had been expelled from Germany and were camping out in no-man's-land. Ben found 150 men, women and children shivering under tarpaulins with nothing to eat: he got hold of sugar and blankets, which he pushed over the border in a handcart. He was arrested on his return, and put on a train to Berlin: he later claimed that he had been arrested for 'giving relief to a certain Polish refugee just on the border', and wondered whether he might have been mistaken for a member of the British army adrift in a prohibited area.

And with that Ben's well-intentioned if unrealistic relief plans came to an end. 'My ideas of relief are definitely not needed. The serious conditions are now past and all relief is available that is now needed,' he told Harry Bohle in March 1939, adding that he would not now be returning to Berlin, and that he had been offered a chance to do relief work among Arab orphans in Palestine, but had declined on the grounds that he couldn't speak Arabic. His optimism about the future of German Jews was sadly misplaced, and his passion for peace at any price meant that he would soon be consorting with people who not only admired Hitler, but shared his views on what they regarded as the 'Jewish problem'.

Peace at Any Price

'I was prepared to meet anybody who was prepared to work for peace,' Ben admitted in 1940, and 'this led me into extraordinarily strange company, a good deal of which I did not desire.' This may have been disingenuous – his long experience of political feuding within the Labour Party sits uneasily with the notion of him as a kind of political naïf, unaware of how wicked the world really was – and although Ben himself never displayed any signs of antisemitism, many of those with whom he associated after his resignation from the Labour Party were openly antisemitic, and espoused causes which were often implicitly – and sometimes explicitly – hostile to the Jews. (As it happened, Graham was the Greene accused of antisemitism for his portrayal of Jews in pre-war novels like *Stamboul Train*, *The Confidential Agent* and *Brighton Rock*. 'One regarded the word Jew as almost a synonym for capitalist,' he explained years later, with particular reference to Basil Zaharoff, the notorious arms dealer and a hate figure for pacifists and opponents of rearmament, whose origins in Anatolia were shaded in mystery. Graham's references to Jews seem mild by the standards of the day, but 'After the holocaust one couldn't use the word Jew in the loose way one used if before the war.')

In 1938 Lord Lymington and John Beckett founded the British Council Against European Commitments (BCAEC), which campaigned against Britain becoming involved in a war on behalf of Poland and Czechoslovakia, and supported German territorial claims in Central Europe. Lymington, later the 9th Earl of Portsmouth, was a pillar of the English Mistery, a back-to-the-land movement which celebrated organic farming and Morris dancing. Its members harked back to a pre-industrial England of guilds and archers and red-faced farmers, untainted by aliens (with the possible exception of those originating in the Germanic countries of northern Europe), and felt a strong kinship with German open-air movements, from the *Wandervogel* of the 1920s to the lustily-singing Hitler Youth, several members of which had been camping in Berkhamsted

and Little Wittenham. John Beckett was a tall, rubicund, jovial-seeming
character, a former stalwart of the ILP who had been first returned to
Parliament as a Labour MP in 1924, at the age of twenty-nine. His experiences during the First World War had turned him sharply to the left:
like Ben, he was outraged by the shabby way in which ex-servicemen
had been treated after the war, chairing the National Union of Ex-
Servicemen and founding the No More War movement. (Such resentment, however justifiable, was often combined with a dislike of war
profiteers, many of whom were assumed to be Jewish: a toxic mixture,
as the Germans soon discovered.) A rabble-rousing orator, he had
worked as Clement Attlee's agent in Limehouse, where Ben first met
him, and achieved a certain notoriety when, in 1929, he disrupted proceedings in the House of Commons by seizing the mace from the Speaker's
Table; he contemplated hurling it into the Thames as a mark of his
increasing contempt for parliamentary procedures, but then had second
thoughts. Despite having a Jewish mother, Beckett was stridently antisemitic. He claimed that Jews had profited from the First World War,
and, as a former manager of the Strand Theatre, was convinced that
Jews dominated the theatrical world. He joined the British Union of
Fascists soon after its foundation and edited *Action*, but left the party in
1937, along with William Joyce (the future 'Lord Haw-Haw', notorious
and much mocked for his wartime broadcasts from Berlin) and A. K.
Chesterton, to found the short-lived National Socialist League: according
to Robert Skidelsky, they 'disliked the BUF's half-hearted antisemitism,
and wanted to make it a central issue.'

The BCAEC's supporters included John Scanlon; General J. F. C. Fuller,
a well-known authority on tank warfare, supporter of far-right causes,
and erstwhile admirer of Aleister Crowley; Admiral Sir Barry Domvile,
a former Director of Naval Intelligence who had worked with Churchill
at the Admiralty during the First World War and, as an ardent admirer
of Hitler, had founded The Link, a far-right organisation devoted to
furthering friendship between Britain and Germany; and A. K. Chesterton,
a cousin of G. K. Chesterton, an Old Berkhamstedian, and a lifelong
fascist. The movement's magazine, *The New Pioneer*, featured articles on
organic husbandry, published an enthusiastic review of *Mein Kampf*, and
warned its readers in March 1939, the month in which Hitler swallowed
up what remained of Czechoslovakia, that 'the jackals of Jewish finance
are again in full cry for war'. Ben was among its occasional contributors, as were Arthur Bryant and Francis Yeats-Brown, the author of *Lives
of a Bengal Lancer*. According to John Beckett's son, Francis, 'the BCAEC

was a front organisation for every fascist, neo-fascist and antisemite in London, and a way in which they could link up with socialists, pacifists and anyone else who might be recruited to the anti-war cause in the wake of the Munich agreement.'

In June 1939 the BCAEC was subsumed into a new organisation called the British People's Party. Although Sir Barry Domvile once described Ben as 'the founder of the whole show – a genial giant', the BPP had been founded by the Marquis of Tavistock and incorporated his People's Campaign Against War and Usury. Tavistock was the president, Ben the treasurer, Beckett the secretary, and John Scanlon sat on the council. Ben got on well with Beckett, and provided him with an office in Berkhamsted. Beckett divided his time between Berkhamsted and the BPP's offices in Victoria: he remembered Ben as having 'a sort of constant melancholy lying under his surface panache. His size made him feel something of an outsider', while Beckett's third wife, Anne Cutmore, thought that Ben was 'always running away from himself'.

An evangelical Christian and a world authority on parrots and budgerigars, the Marquis succeeded his father as the Duke of Bedford in 1940. He strongly disapproved of drinking, smoking, cards and betting: according to his son, he was 'one of the loneliest men I ever knew, incapable of giving or receiving love, utterly self-centred and opinionated. Although he loved birds, animals, peace, monetary reform, the park and religion', his wife described him as 'the most cruel, mean and conceited person' she had met. Like Lymington, he was a keen believer in Major Douglas's theories of social credit, pressing for a radical reorganisation of the financial system and denouncing usury, in itself a covert and familiar form of antisemitism, since Jews had been synonymous with money-lending since the Middle Ages: while 'monetary reform' not only involved the abolition of interest, but a reduction in the power and influence of international capital and finance, with which Jews were invariably associated, not least by the Nazis. (The condemnation of usury was also an ingredient in the mediaeval nostalgia of romantic Catholics like Hilaire Belloc and G. K. Chesterton.) For rabid antisemites, Jews were undermining society from both the right and the left of the political spectrum: Hitler's demons of 'international Jewry' included the blubber-lipped, hook-nosed, cigar-puffing, top-hatted plutocrats depicted by the cartoonists in Julius Streicher's *Der Sturmer* as well as the bomb-toting Bolsheviks with whom, in August 1939, he would form a short-lived and lethal pact. In his memoirs, published after the war, Tavistock defiantly declared that 'the European fascist countries had some excellent features in their social service and economic plans,' and that, as far as Hitler was concerned, 'many of the measures he introduced for social services, for public works, and for the improvement of industry, though tinged with authoritarianism, appear to have been excellent' – views which Ben shared in 1939, though his innate insubordination and distrust of authority would not have endeared him to the regime had he lived in Nazi Germany. The Marquis also paid tribute to Ben's sister, Katharine, the youngest of the Hall Greenes, who 'rendered yeoman service' as his secretary, and later in his kitchen garden at Woburn Abbey.

The BPP's manifesto mixed elements from both extremes of the political spectrum. It included the abolition of a financial system based on usury, the abolition of all forms of land speculation, 'security for the small man against all forms of trustification', 'the security of labour in its industrial organisation and from the menace of all forms of international wage-cutting', the abolition of military alliances and political commitments which might involve Britain in wars which 'in no way affect the security and national independence of our peoples', 'the freeing of Parliament and all organs of public opinion from vested economic and sectional interests' (this was to become Ben's particular hobby-horse in later years), and – another item of covert antisemitism – 'safeguarding the employment and integrity of the British people against alien influence and infiltration'. At the Party's inaugural meeting in April 1939, Beckett explained that it had been 'decided by the committee that far more could be achieved in the campaign by refraining from direct attacks on the Jews, as it was felt by members of the committee that the campaign against "usury" would bring about the same results, and presented in this form would attract far more supporters to the ranks of the party.'

Ben later claimed that he was 'quite a minor person' in the BPP, 'except that I did cause a fair amount of difficulty over the antisemitic question', which, given his kindly nature and the work he had done for German Jews after Kristallnacht, was almost certainly the case. But his opposition to what he saw as the injustices perpetrated by the Treaty of Versailles was as strong as ever. A leaflet was distributed asking its readers to sign up 'if you agree that Poland is a bad cause', and quoting remarks made by Lloyd George in 1925 about the iniquity of parts of Germany, Russia, Lithuania and Ukraine having been ceded to Poland under the terms of Versailles. The following month Ben attended a meeting at which speakers asked 'why should British lives be sacrificed to prevent Danzig, a German city, going back to Germany by its own desire? There was only one answer to that and that was because there is a large amount of money invested in Polish concerns, money that was once British and is now being used by international financiers in the City of London to sweat the Polish worker and keep the British worker out of a job.'

As the Party's treasurer, Ben wrote to individuals and businesses to raise money for a body which, he claimed, aimed to 'avoid war and bring about a much-needed social regeneration'. He also produced a cyclostyled Peace and Progressive Information Service, sixteen issues of which were produced between March and September 1939. 'Ben has written to me about his information scheme . . . It is enormously encouraging to think of Ben as at last happy and full of fire and go,' Felix wrote from New York. 'Ben's pamphlets are very good. They are a very good antidote to the rising growl of hate and fear and distortion of fact,' he declared, after examining Ben's handiwork. 'Let him, however, keep to *facts* and eliminate his own feelings and views, and the bulletins will be yet more powerful.' 'I am making plans to start a Peace and Progressive Information Bureau to counteract the Communist activity now showing itself in the Labour Party due mainly to the Left Book Club,' Ben told Harry Bohle early in 1939. He would like to talk to Bohle 'with a view to my being supplied with as much information on Germany as possible. In return I would be only too glad to send you any information you may need.' In March he told Bohle that he was sending an early issue of his information sheet, much of which was devoted to Palestine, so 'by dealing with all these other things I cannot be accused of being a German propagandist!' This in itself struck a note of unease, and in a subsequent letter to Bohle Ben revealed that American Quakers would be taking over his relief work in Germany, but should Bohle come into contact with them 'please don't mention anything about my information service. They are not likely to understand my point of view, and it could lead to misunderstanding.' (Ben had been involved in discussions about the possibility of extending *Winterhilfe* to German Jews, and Bohle had asked him to submit a 'protocol'.) Of more immediate use than Harry Bohle was Dr Gottfried Rösel of the Anglo-German Information Bureau, who provided Ben with transcriptions of speeches by Hitler and other Nazi leaders. The London correspondent of the *Essener National Zeitung*, Rösel was also the Nazi Gauleiter for Central London. According to MI5, he was a member of the Gestapo, controlled Nazi propaganda in Britain, and reported back to Berlin on the movement of refugees from Germany and Austria. (Vansittart had encouraged a reluctant Vernon Kell to investigate the activities of the Auslandsorganisation: in 1935 MI5 sources within the German Embassy identified 288 Party members living in the United Kingdom.)

Rösel's expulsion from London in the spring of 1939 not only deprived Ben of a useful source of information, but led to the tit-for-tat expulsion from Germany of Hugh and five other Britons including a teacher, a businessman and the manager of a boot polish factory in Cologne. Hugh's expulsion made the headlines in the *Telegraph*, which had just started putting news on the front page in the place of classified ads. He was feeling increasingly embattled, still more so after Helga returned to England (the children had left the previous year). Iverach McDonald, who was sent to Germany in 1937 as deputy to *The Times*'s chief correspondent, James Holburn, wrote later that 'anyone who lived in Berlin during the last year or two before the war must recall the time with disgust and anguish', and that foreign journalists wildly socialised in dinners and dances that 'were deliberate withdrawals from the life outside.' (As Head of Chancery at the Embassy, Hugh's future colleague at the BBC, Ivone Kirkpatrick, considered most of the foreign correspondents in Berlin were 'a liability rather than an asset', in that 'they never obtain any news worth having, they waste the time of the staff, and often cause embarrassment by sending silly messages.') Hugh's letters home reflected his growing conviction that war was inevitable, and his days in Germany were numbered. His every movement was monitored: visiting Berlin in 1939, a future BBC colleague, Harman Grisewood, was alerted to the audible click as the Gestapo listened in to Hugh's phone calls; in a correspondence with his brother about who might inherit Harston after Sir Graham's death, Graham thanked Hugh for his 'opened letter', and suggested that his references to the 'Harston fight' and 'other candidates in the field' might be interpreted by the Gestapo as part of an 'elaborate code'.

Although it had been 'made clear to the British Embassy that Mr Greene's expulsion implied no criticism of his journalistic work, nor did it imply any dissatisfaction with the editorial policy of the *Daily Telegraph*,' Hugh's accounts of food shortages and anti-Jewish outrages had not endeared him to the authorities, nor did he have any illusions about Hitler's ambitions and his readiness to capitalise on the weakness of the French and the British in particular. 'Herr Hitler will be reassured by the nervousness over the dangers of war which is apparent in the outside world,' Hugh had written in the *Sunday Times* in January that year, adding that 'this nervousness he will be inclined to interpret as a sign of lack of confidence and confusion of purpose among potential opponents. In his opinion, this must make it easier for the Reich to pursue its own aims.' In March 1938 he had covered the *Anschluss* from Vienna following the expulsion of the *Telegraph*'s G. R. Gedye for denouncing antisemitic outrages: Hugh later wrote that 'from what I saw with my own eyes the Vienna mob behaved with a brutality to Jews which matched anything that happened in Germany.' A year later he covered the German takeover of Bohemia and Moravia, once again standing in for Gedye, who had been forced to take refuge in the British legation after the Germans marched in. Hugh had been forbidden to visit Prague, but infuriated the authorities by the simple expedient of booking a ticket to Vienna and changing trains en route. Many Czechs made it plain that they had lost faith in Britain: one official refused to touch Hugh's documentation when he learned that he was British, making instead a slitting motion across his throat.

Nor was Hugh a favourite of the Minister of Propaganda, Dr Goebbels. In May 1938 Hitler and Goebbels had left Berlin by train to visit Mussolini. Hugh arrived at the Potsdamer Bahnhof, and found himself following Goebbels up a steep flight of steps that led to the platform: the disparity between their heights provoked unseemly mirth among the Hitler Youth who were dutifully lining the staircase. On the platform Hugh found himself next to the Führer, who was talking excitedly to the Italian Consul-General and pounding his fist into the palm of his other hand. Sensing a coup, Hugh stiffened with excitement when he heard Hitler say 'Only in this way can we win!', but it turned out that they were discussing a motorcycle rally. Goebbels was still standing on the platform when the train drew out, so a 'large SS man leant out of a carriage window, caught Goebbels under the arse, and hauled him into the train with his short little legs kicking in the air.' 'Goebbels was not a man to forgive or forget anyone who made him look ridiculous,' Hugh recalled, 'and I have sometimes wondered whether this little incident may not have contributed to my expulsion from Germany almost a year later.'

The *Telegraph* was increasingly critical of Hitler, and sceptical about the policy of appeasement endorsed by Neville Chamberlain and supported by Geoffrey Dawson of *The Times* and J. L. Garvin of the *Observer*. The Foreign Office's leading opponents of appeasement, Robert Vansittart and Rex Leeper, had been sidelined when Chamberlain succeeded Baldwin as Prime Minister in 1937, but Vansittart continued to influence both Churchill, who became a frequent contributor to the *Telegraph*, and the *Telegraph*'s diplomatic correspondent, Victor Gordon-Lennox. But Chamberlain and his closest political advisor, Sir Joseph Ball, were ruthless exponents of 'spin', and did everything possible to stifle hostile views and keep up pro-appeasement pressure on journalists, editors and proprietors. Despite the dissenting views of some members of his staff, including Ivone Kirkpatrick, Nevile Henderson, who was appointed Ambassador in Berlin in April 1937, was sympathetic to the Anschluss and to German territorial claims in Poland and Czechoslovakia. According to Iverach McDonald, the Ambassador 'more than once warned me, with his eye on the latest issue of *The Times* on his desk, about the dangers of picking out German events which did not fit in with the picture of the amenable Reich which he saw and which he commended to London,' while the Foreign Secretary, Lord Halifax, on a visit to Berlin in November 1937, alluded to 'the need for the Press to create the right atmosphere if any advance were to be made towards a better understanding.' Such sentiments were shared by, among others, Robin Barrington-Ward of *The Times*: he was, according to McDonald, 'carried forward by a burning mission to save the world from another war', and sympathised with many of Germany's grievances and territorial claims. After the Munich Agreement of September 1938 the gulf widened between those papers which supported appeasement and those which opposed it. Iverach McDonald recalled how 'for those of us who worked on *The Times* the confusion and sense of unreality were the greater because the leading articles were descending, step by step with Neville Chamberlain, to the paper's nadir of appeasement.' At least Hugh had the consolation of knowing that his views were fully supported by both his editor and his proprietor.

Hugh was expelled in May 1939, soon after learning that, at the age of twenty-eight, he had made it into the pages of *Who's Who* ('Assuming that the next edition ever appears I should think Da will be able to claim a record with himself and three sons in it!' he declared). His secretary, Barbara Henman, who had unwisely fallen in love with an SS officer, was expelled at the same time. Hugh was seen off by a large party at the Friedrichstrasse Bahnhof, and by another when the train stopped at the Zoo Station, after which he was seen leaning out of his carriage window, waving his fencing foil and shouting 'Ich komme als Gauleiter zuruck!' ('I shall return as a Gauleiter!'). In Paris he learned that a warrant had been put out for his arrest should he set foot in Germany again; and from there he made his way back to England.

That July the BPP put up the celebrated Arabist Harry St John Philby as its candidate in the Hythe by-election. German propaganda supported the Arabs in Palestine and exploited British ambivalence in the Middle

East, and right-wing Arabists like Philby and Robert Gordon-Canning of the British Union of Fascists were invariably anti-Zionist and in favour of the Palestine Arabs. (Philby's son Kim had become a Soviet agent while still at Cambridge, but was now posing as a rabid right-winger: he had represented *The Times* during the Spanish Civil War, reporting from Franco's side of the barricades and being awarded the Red Cross of Military Merit by the Caudillo himself. He had also infiltrated the Anglo-German Fellowship, a milder version of Admiral Domvile's pro-Nazi The Link, attending a dinner in honour of the Kaiser's daughter at which Sir Barry Domvile and Herr Rösel were also present, and visiting Berlin for a meeting with Propaganda Ministry officials. His right-wing pose was persuasive, but Karl Robson, Hugh's former colleague from Berlin, who covered the Spanish Civil War for the *Daily Telegraph*, was made uneasy by Philby's persistent questioning about military details at press briefings.) The BPP produced an accompanying pamphlet entitled 'Alien Money Power in Great Britain', which attacked the Tory candidate on the grounds that the City firm he worked for was run by Jews. St John Philby denied that Hitler wanted war, and vehemently repudiated claims that the Führer was mad, since 'no madman had ever restored one of the greatest races in the world to the position of one of the greatest nations in the world.' According to the *Hythe and Sandgate Advertiser*, Ben spoke about 'the huge profits which were made in the armaments industry, and of the tremendous amount of money which was made out of the last war by a few people who, he said, "were the reason why peace was not sought by negotiation".' Philby scraped up only a handful of votes, but among those who spoke on his behalf were Lord Tavistock, Beckett, Ben, Admiral Domvile, Dr Meyrick Booth, an ardent admirer of Hitler, and Dr Maude Royden, a well-meaning innocent abroad and a leading light in the Peace Pledge Union.

Like a good many of his compatriots, Ben was also a member of the Peace Pledge Union, which helped to produce and distribute his Peace and Progressive Information Service leaflets. As Ben had explained at the PPU's AGM in April, it was essential to 'get in touch with every other body which opposes war and our present policy', still more so since 'we have been living under a dictatorship of vested interests which manipulates our democracy.' Founded by the Reverend Dick Sheppard in 1936, the Peace Pledge Union was the largest and best-known pacifist organisation in Britain, and included among its members Bertrand Russell, George Lansbury, Eileen Wilkinson, C. E. M. Joad, Siegfried Sassoon, Storm Jameson, Donald Soper and Vera Brittain. Gerald Heard and

Aldous Huxley represented the mystical end of the movement, advocating group meditation and a 'theology of pacifism' – the notion that pacifism could be employed to bring about a fundamental transformation in human nature. Their departure for America in April 1937 was greeted with relief by their more practical colleagues.

Writing from Berlin a month before the outbreak of war, Harry Bohle told Ben that he was unable to send a cheque to boost the BPP's coffers, but was contributing instead some copies of Professor A. P. Laurie's *The Case for Germany* to 'swell the party fighting fund' – Laurie being a particularly enthusiastic supporter of Hitler, and a contributor to the BPP's magazine, *The People's Post*. 'Forgive me for not talking about war as that subject is strange to us over here,' Bohle added in a PS. 'There *will be no war*! Sanity will rule the day!' 'Cheerio and many thanks again and once more power to your elbow in your political scrap,' Bohle wrote a few days later, signing off what may well have been his last communication with his friend in London.

Ben was not the only Hall Greene to have visited Germany in the thirties. With America and Britain importing coffee from 'new' producers like Colombia and Kenya, E. J. Johnston Ltd had taken advantage of a barter scheme worked out by Schacht whereby Germany would buy into Brazil's enormous coffee surpluses if Brazil would, in exchange, buy German goods to an equivalent value. Tooter had built up good relations with an official in the relevant ministry in Berlin – not a Nazi, he later insisted – who would tip him off when Germany was about to re-enter the market, so enabling him to nip in ahead of his rivals. Shortly before the outbreak of war, Tooter's agent in Germany asked him to fly over on urgent business. On arrival in Hamburg, Tooter was told by a Nazi official that E. J. Johnston had been put on a blacklist on the grounds that it was Jewish-owned, the founder's name being Juenstein. 'What utter nonsense!' Tooter declared: he later discovered that the rumour had been put into circulation by a rival firm.

Back in London, Tooter did his best to persuade Ben to desist from his political activities. Ben later claimed that he only made one speech after the outbreak of war, dealing with his old hobby horse of unemployment insurance relief, and that he severed all political connections thereafter, but this was far from the case. He continued to see his former associates, and to attend and even speak at public meetings. Nor did he contemplate a permanent withdrawal from politics. On the last day of October 1939 he told Beckett that 'the pressure and general conditions of my business make it imperative for me to withdraw from all political activity direct and indirect,' and asked him to accept his resignation as treasurer of the BPP and from its council, though 'I hope that as soon as conditions permit to be allowed to be associated again with the British People's Party.'

During the nine months of the Phoney War, between the outbreak of war in September 1939 and the German invasion of Norway, Denmark, the Low Countries and France in the early summer of 1940, many in Britain questioned the wisdom and desirability of war; nor were they restricted to the 'absolute' pacifists like the Peace Pledge Union or groups on the far right of the political spectrum. Lord Beaverbrook opposed the war until Churchill appointed him Minister of Aircraft Production in May 1940; Lloyd George continued to protest that Poland was not worth fighting for, most memorably in a long interview published in Beaverbrook's *Sunday Express*; duty-bound by the Nazi-Soviet Pact, the Communist Party of Great Britain opposed the war, as did ILP members like James Maxton and Jimmie McGovern. Sir Richard Stokes, a Catholic industrialist and an Arabist, founded a Parliamentary Peace Aims Group of like-minded Labour MPs, meeting Ben in late 1939 and Lloyd George in the spring of 1940 to encourage a negotiated peace, and visiting Ankara to meet the German Ambassador; as late as June 1940 the Foreign Office was making tentative overtures to its German equivalent through R. A. Butler and the Swedish Embassy in London. Oswald Mosley attacked 'Jewish capitalists' for starting a war in which Britain had no interest, while Sir Joseph Ball, the Chairman of the Conservative Party Research Department, announced in his magazine *Truth* that 'if we set aside the ideological passions of Mr Gollancz and his tribe in the tents of Bloomsbury, the truth is that no appreciable section of British opinion desires to reconquer Berlin for the Jews.' The editor of *Truth*, Henry Newnham, was an antisemite: the magazine praised BPP publications, attacked Leslie Hore-Belisha, the Jewish War Minister, and allowed General J. F. C. Fuller space to deny the existence of concentration camps in Germany.

Like an ever-changing amoeba, the BPP resurfaced in mid-September 1939 as the piously named British Council for a Christian Settlement in Europe (BCCSE). Ben, Beckett and Admiral Domvile met for lunch before going on to a meeting in Robert Gordon-Canning's flat, attended by members of The Link, the Nordic League and Captain Archibald Ramsay's violently antisemitic Right Club. Gordon-Canning was appointed treasurer and Beckett the secretary; Ben, formally adhering to his promise to eschew politics, was not on the committee, but he allowed Beckett to continue working from the Kepston offices. BCCSE supporters included veterans of the far right like Henry Williamson (of *Tarka the*

Otter fame), the writer Hugh Ross Williamson and St John Philby, as well as idealists and pacifists such as Donald Soper, the well-known Methodist preacher, Eric Gill, Laurence Housman and Richard Stokes, but neither Mosley's BUF nor Captain Ramsay's Right Club was associated with it. On 14 September the BCCSE held a meeting in the Conway Hall in Red Lion Square. Tavistock was unwell, so he asked Ben to take his place and, if the following day's newspapers are to be trusted, he did not restrict himself to unemployment insurance schemes. 'About 150 Britons met in London yesterday "to bring peace to the world". They praised Hitler. They reviled the British government. They ended by sending a resolution to Mr Chamberlain calling on him to start peace negotiations,' reported Beaverbrook's *Sunday Express*. 'From Mr Greene, who is 6´8˝ and very broad, you might have expected a rip-roaring, violent speech. But he doesn't even think we shall win the war. Nor does he think Hitler's invasion of Austria, Czechoslovakia and Poland were acts of aggression. He thinks Hitler was quite right. But he does think that our Government has taken the opportunity of war to kill the trade union movement.' According to the *Sunday Despatch*, Ben described the Government's foreign policy as so much 'bluff and treachery', while a woman in the audience 'referred to Christ having thrown the money-changers out of the Temple, and compared this with Hitler having thrown the Jews out of Germany.'

Ben later claimed that the *Sunday Express* had misrepresented him: he denied having said that Hitler was justified in invading Austria, Czechoslovakia and Poland, or ridiculing those who claimed that Hitler could not be trusted, or having referred to 'those of us who admire' the German leader: he denied claiming that Britain could not win the war, but he did admit to saying that the war could not be won by dropping leaflets over German conurbations, a policy much favoured at the time. According to the police's shorthand notes of the meeting, Ben urged his audience to 'look at the record of the men who can't trust Hitler. What have we had since the last war? Twenty years of misery, insecurity and unemployment. Twenty years of betrayal. Twenty years of bluff and hypocrisy.' Although he sat down to roars of applause, not all his listeners were convinced. A Mr Royden accused Ben of making 'certainly the most blatantly pro-Nazi speech I have ever heard'; a Mr Dickson thought it 'naked German propaganda', singling out for particular criticism a reference to the Führer's 'wise statesmanship', and Ben's claim that Hitler had invaded Czechoslovakia the previous March in order to save the Slovaks from Czech misgovernment. Maude Royden, her illusions finally shattered, wrote to the *Sunday Express* to say that she had been 'amazed to find that the other speakers, and the audience, seemed concerned much less with any such constructive policy than with denunciation of our own Government and praise of Hitler. I protested with extreme indignation ... My speech provoked an uproar of interruption and protests from the disgruntled audience.' Five days later the *Berkhamsted Gazette* reported a visit to the BCCSE's offices, 'just behind the town's war memorial': their reporter found Beckett and Katharine Greene hard at work, noted the presence of a large bronze eagle, which looked suspiciously Nazi but had, in fact, been brought back by Eppy after one of his American trips, and deplored 'the presence of this office and its works in our midst', still more so since BCCSE publications carried a Berkhamsted address. (In due course Felix inherited the eagle: he later donated it to Regent's Park, where it can still be seen in the Rose Garden.)

Despite the demands of his business, Ben found time to write all or part of an anonymous pamphlet entitled 'The Truth about the War', published in December by the BCCSE with a foreword by Beckett (who eventually claimed that his wife Anne was, in fact, its author). For some curious reason, it was distributed in Afghanistan by the Germans as anti-British propaganda. Ben's old boss, Clement Attlee, was shocked by its contents. In a letter to Leslie, written two days before Christmas, and enclosing a toy panda for his godson Paul, he said that he had 'glanced through Ben's book', and that

> frankly it strikes me as one of the nastiest pieces of pro-Hitler prop-
> aganda that I have met for a long time. It conforms closely to
> Hitler's description of propaganda which consists in giving one
> side only. I can understand the position of the genuine pacifist but
> I have no use for people who support Hitlerism. When you told
> me of the formation of your party I said that I thought its whole
> tendency was Fascist. This book confirms my view. I think it would
> be better, if these are the views that you and Ben now hold, that
> we should not meet.

Attlee signed off 'Yours affectionately', but he had made it clear that Ben's activities had put him beyond the pale with his former friends and colleagues in the Labour Party.

Much ridicule was heaped on the BCCSE when, in January 1940, Lord Tavistock, assisted by Lord Darnley, got in touch with the German Legation in Dublin and claimed to have elicited a set of peace proposals approved by the authorities in Berlin. Drawing on his experience as a prison visitor, Tavistock claimed that Hitler and Goering were a pair of rough diamonds who could be made to see reason if subjected to plain speaking from a peer of the realm. He reported back to Lord Halifax, the Foreign Secretary, who dismissed the German leaders as a 'set of gangsters', while Sir Alexander Cadogan, Vansittart's successor as the Permanent Under-Secretary at the Foreign Office, described Tavistock's peace proposals as 'absolute bilge and fraudulent propaganda', and the two peers as 'half-wits'. The *Daily Telegraph* was equally scornful, and Oswald Mosley dismissed Tavistock as 'woolly-headed', Beckett as a 'crook', and Ben as 'a good fellow, but not very intelligent'. Unabashed, Tavistock then asked Gerald Hamilton, of all people, to revive negotiations in Dublin, and reminded Halifax of how 'we should not forget that even in our boyhood the German Jew was a byword for all that was objectionable; and that there is good evidence of unfair treatment by Czechs of German minorities and ample evidence of unjust and even brutal treatment of Germans by Poles.'

Writing in the *Sunday Despatch* in February 1940, under the headline 'These Men Are Dangerous', the journalist Charles Graves listed St John Philby, Beckett, Ben, Gordon-Canning, Professor Laurie and Meyrick Booth, who lived with his German wife at Letchworth, not far from Berkhamsted. Ben, he declared, had 'particularly distinguished himself in producing certain propaganda sheets known as "the Peace and Progressive Information Service" constituting, in fact, National Socialist propaganda of a remarkably noxious kind.' Despite his disclaimers, Ben was reported as addressing a BCCSE meeting in Wellingborough the following month. He later claimed that no journalists were present, but according to the *Northamptonshire Evening Telegraph*, his speech tried to explain the purpose of the BPP: they stood, he said, 'for the regeneration of the land and a new pride in its work', and 'although we are not in the least antisemitic, only British folk are allowed to be party members.' Questioned after the meeting, he 'maintained that there was a definite menace from Jewish capitalists and when the war was over there would be a menace from American capitalists'. The following month Ben attended a gathering at the Criterion of all the 'patriotic' societies, addressed by Mosley, and joined Beckett in speaking at a meeting in Holborn Hall to discuss Tavistock's abortive peace proposals. At a BCCSE meeting in Kingsway Hall in May, chaired by Beckett, Hugh Ross Williamson attacked Churchill, who had recently succeeded Chamberlain as Prime Minister, while Jimmie McGovern praised what Hitler had done for the German working classes.

The police, in the meantime, were taking a closer interest in Ben and other members of his immediate family. A report in May 1940 claimed that despite being 'an admirer of the Nazis', Ben had been 'frightened into apparent inactivity'. Tooter was revealed, correctly, as living in Overstrand Mansions in the Prince of Wales Drive, in the same block of flats as his mother. His first wife had died in 1936 and, according to the police, he was now sharing a flat with his sister Katharine who, using the surname of 'Gray', worked for Tavistock, and their flat was used for occasional meetings of the BCCSE. That same month the Berkhamsted police quoted a 'reliable source' to the effect that Ben was 'pro-German, and has strong Nazi sympathies. There is no doubt that he is engaged in activities detrimental to the British cause, but nothing definite can be ascertained.' He was kept under regular surveillance, but spent most of his time in Kepston's, working late into the night before walking home in the dark. Once again, Eva Greene was not exempt from suspicion. 'Taking into consideration that she is of German birth and caused great trouble during the last war by her unconcealed German sympathies, it is probable that she also is assisting in anti-British activities,' the police reported, adding that she had 'caused considerable trouble to the Hertfordshire police by her public expressions of pro-German sympathy' and that she was thought to be writing a history of the Greene family in German: but according to MI5 reports, Sir John Maude – later Lord Redcliffe-Maude – 'carried out a search on [Sir Graham Greene's] house and interviewed Mrs Greene, who is a very proud aristocratic old German, but not a menace in any way.'

Beckett's blue van, with two loudspeakers on the roof, was often to be seen in the yard at Kepston's: the firm's finances were in a poor state, and the report suggested that as early as 1936 Ben had received £10,000 from the German authorities to subsidise propaganda, and that at some stage he had burned a large quantity of suspect 'German papers'. Kepston was the only split-wood pulley-maker left in the UK and, with German competition cut off by the war, it was overwhelmed by orders, many of them to do with the war effort. Ben and a retired colonel ran the business with the help of two girls, and worked flat-out all hours of the day.

Ben's name was not listed among the signatories to the BPP's 'For Peace and Prosperity: The British Peace Charter', ingredients of which included a currency based on labour rather than gold, hostility to speculators, the defence of small shopkeepers, the Co-op and agricultural labourers, hostility to party political machines, cheaper power and transport, devolution for Scotland and Wales, social services and equal opportunities for all. He denied contributing to Beckett's 'Headline Newsletter', but it was edited from the Kepston offices, and Ben admitted that he had provided information for it. In March 1940, for instance, Beckett told him about a letter he had received from a keen BPP supporter worried about a report in *The Times* claiming that Hitler planned to attack the Royal Navy bases in Gibraltar and Singapore: 'I have written telling him I know of no statement of Hitler's which warrants this concern, but that I am referring the letter to you as you speak German fluently and are able to hear the German Chancellor's speeches as they are made. Will you send him a reassuring letter, if possible, as soon as you can?' Earlier in the year Ben was taken ill with malaria, and had to spend time in hospital. 'I am delighted that you are going to start on the Party work when you get back,' Beckett told him. 'It will seem quite different when I have you with me once more.'

Chamberlain resigned as Prime Minister on 10 May 1940, following the German invasion of Norway, Denmark, the Low Countries and France, and was replaced by Churchill, who had resumed his role as First Lord of the Admiralty at the outbreak of war. At about the same time, MI5 received a report that the BCCSE was compiling a book about Churchill entitled 'An Appreciation of the First War Lord', the opening chapter of which was to have been written by Ben, and Beckett sent Tavistock a list of those who might be included in a 'Possible Coalition Government of National Security': Tavistock would have been Prime Minister, Mosley the Leader of the House, General Fuller the Minister of Defence, Beckett the Home Secretary, James Maxton the Foreign Secretary and Ben the Minister of Education, with junior ministerial posts going to Liddell Hart, Hugh Ross Williamson and Jenny Lee, the wife of Aneurin Bevan. Had he known of his elevation, Ben would almost certainly have been far too modest to make much of it, but time was running out for such fantasies. France's ignominious collapse had triggered off a panic, whipped up by the previously pro-Hitler Rothermere press, about treacherous fifth-columnists signalling to enemy aircraft, Mosley's possible role as a British Quisling, and the political and military reliability of the British fascists who had hurried to enlist. Enemy aliens, many of them Jewish refugees from Germany and Austria, had already been interned on the Isle of Man and elsewhere. Sir John Anderson, the Home Secretary, was keen to avoid extending internment to British citizens, but his liberal views were swept aside after the arrest on 22 May of Tyler Kent, a cipher clerk at the American Embassy, and Anna Volkoff of the Right Club for passing the Germans details of Churchill's correspondence with

President Roosevelt, who was sympathetic to Britain's predicament but hamstrung by isolationist tendencies at home.

Shortly before the outbreak of war the Government had rushed through an Emergency Powers Act empowering itself to make regulations by Orders in Council for the Defence of the Realm. Regulation 18B, tacked on a few days later, allowed the authorities to detain those suspected of 'acts prejudicial' to national security, and on 22 May a Clause (1a) was added to 18B, allowing for the internment without trial of members of organisations subject to foreign influence or control, or whose leaders had associations with leaders of enemy governments, or who sympathised with the system of government of enemy powers, and the Government no longer had to prove that the accused had contemplated or committed any subversive activity. As early as January 1940 Vernon Kell, the head of MI5, had urged the Home Secretary to intern members of the BPP: Churchill's instruction to 'collar the lot' was speedily implemented, and over 700 right-wingers were held and interned, including the Mosleys, Admiral Domvile, Ben, Captain Ramsay and Beckett, but neither Lord Lymington nor Lord Tavistock, who was by now the Duke of Bedford. Among those drafted onto the top-secret Home Defence Executive which recommended the detention of suspected subversives was Sir Joseph Ball, a former member of MI5.

Beckett was arrested on 23 May. When Katharine Greene heard the police banging on the front door of the BPP's office in Victoria she bounded up the stairs to the Becketts' flat on the top floor shouting 'John, the police are here!' She then climbed out of an attic window carrying BPP papers, some of which gave the names and addresses of party members, edged along the parapet, and came down via a neighbouring house. That evening Anne Cutmore took the incriminating papers up to Hampstead, and dumped them in a pond on the Heath. Beckett was to be interned in Brixton for longer than most, claiming that Herbert Morrison, by then the Home Secretary, bore a grudge against him for suggesting that he had fiddled some expenses back in the 1920s. Anne Cutmore was a particularly good-looking woman: 'I always assumed,' Ben's daughter Margaret said many years later, 'only Tooter can say if this was correct – that she was Tooter's mistress and that he kept her going . . .'

According to the minutes of a meeting held in the Home Secretary's office and attended by the Attorney-General, Sir Alexander Maxwell of the Foreign Office, and Norman Brook, a future colleague of Hugh's at the BBC, 'Sir John knew all about him [Ben], and had quite enough against him to make an Order.' Anderson signed the Detention Order on the 23rd, and Ben was arrested and taken to Brixton. His Kepston offices were searched: the police found 'ample evidence' that it had been the BPP's head office, and relevant papers were seized and taken away.

For the rest of his life Ben was outraged by the fact that he had been imprisoned without trial or charge under the terms of Regulation 18B. Professor Brian Simpson, the authority on wartime internment, has suggested that Ben was 'strong on sincerity' but 'to put it no more strongly, kept strange company and lacked discretion' in his passion to preserve the peace at any price. But his internment was far from the end of the story: it turned out that MI5 had employed the full gamut of dirty tricks to discredit and ensnare him, and Tooter was to play a major role in unmasking their agent provocateur.

The Greenes Go to War

None of the School House Greenes fought in the Second World War, but all were keen to do their bit, and all except Herbert made a useful contribution to the war effort, albeit in a civilian rather than a soldierly capacity. Graham joined the Officers Emergency Reserve shortly before the Munich Agreement, when war seemed imminent, trenches were being dug in the London parks, and children clutching gas masks were being prematurely evacuated to the countryside. The Emergency Reserve 'advertised for professional men, journalists, bankers, God knows what', and Graham was summoned before its draft board. He passed 'A' for health, amazed the major-general and two colonels who interviewed him by volunteering for the infantry rather than Intelligence, asked for and was granted more time in which to finish his novel *The Confidential Agent*, and was told to keep fit by walking to work rather than taking a bus. Hugh witnessed the German and then the Soviet invasion of Poland as a journalist and, on his return to England, was commissioned as a pilot officer in the Royal Air Force Voluntary Reserve. 'I can see, old boy, that you're a bloody fine linguist and shall report accordingly,' he was told at his interview after replying to questions posed in schoolboy French and German. Despite his Territorial Army commission, Raymond was too old for the regular Army, but he was to put his Everest experiences to good use on behalf of the Commandos, SOE agents dropped into enemy-occupied territory, and soldiers fighting in the Burma campaign. Herbert longed to prove his worth as a soldier, but his exploits as an amateur spy were held against him, and his war was to prove an inglorious, frustrated affair.

Graham told Walter Allen that he could have got rid of the Chamberlain Government by sending Mrs Chamberlain, Lady Simon and other Cabinet wives pornographic books carrying forged dedications by Sam Hoare, Leslie Hore-Belisha and other Cabinet Ministers, but he was too busy on his return from Mexico to concern himself with practical politics. He told Hugh, apropos *The Lawless Roads*, that 'consid-ering it was written in six months, I don't think it's too bad', and he had finished *The Confidential Agent* while simultaneously working on *The Power and the Glory*; as if this weren't enough, he reviewed film and books for the *Spectator*, and was commissioned by Stephen Potter to write a BBC radio play about the famous Master of Balliol, *The Great Jowett*. To keep awake, he dosed himself with benzedrine, and 'at five o'clock I would return home with a shaking hand, a depression which fell with the regu-larity of a tropical rain, ready to find offence in anything and to give offence for no cause.'

With war imminent, Graham sent Vivien and the children to stay with his parents in Crowborough. 'I miss you so much particularly in the evening which makes me rather moody and uncommunicative over my pint,' he told her. London was beginning to look 'very odd. Dim lighting, pillar boxes turned into white zebras in some parts. The Common a mass of tents, and nobody about on North Side.' The day after war broke out he reported the West End as being 'very lovely and impressive with all the sky signs gone and little blue phosphorescent milk bars and a hurdy-gurdy invisibly playing – rather like a Paris back street.' 'I'm very snug,' he assured her. 'Work in the morning, then go out and see people and have my three halves, and wander round.' His letters to Vivien were permeated with a nostalgia for the life they had led together. 'I wish one could twist a ring and be back before the war and before financial pres-sures got so bad. I'd choose the Campden period, with a nook for Francis and Lucy,' he told her, and 'Oh how I wish we had enough money to have a cottage in the country, and I'd come weekends.' 'Don't ever think I like this separation. It wouldn't have happened if we'd known how the war was going to turn out,' he wrote, emphasising 'how dearly I love you and how glad I am we got married,' and that 'there are good times coming, I feel sure.' Vivien, for her part, found life in Crowborough tedious. She read his proofs, Aunt Nono talked about making rock cakes for the WI, a good deal of time was given over to listening to the wire-less, and Da was reported as repeating, 'ponderously', 'One good thing the war *has* done is to draw the Empire together.'

A survey of Graham's writing by Arthur Calder-Marshall in Cyril Connolly's new magazine *Horizon* was good for the morale and the reputation, if an irritant in the long term – Calder-Marshall invented the notion of 'Greeneland', which Graham came to abhor – but with money in short supply and no further summons from the military, Graham needed a job. Writing to Vivien, he referred to the 'faint susurrus' of 'intellectuals dashing for ministry posts', and in April 1940, on the recommendation of Tom Burns, Graham succeeded his erstwhile literary agent, A. D. Peters, in charge of the writers' section of the Ministry of Information. A haven for writers, journalists and advertising men in particular, the Ministry had the dual role of putting out Government propaganda for use at home and abroad, and vetting and sometimes censoring what was published in England to make sure it did not give away information that might prove useful to the enemy. It was housed in part of London University's Senate House, later described by Graham as a 'high heartless building with complicated lifts and long passages like those of a liner and lavatories where the water never ran hot and the nailbrushes were chained like Bibles. Central heating gave it a stuffy smell of mid-Atlantic except in the passages where the windows were always open for fear of blast and the cold winds whistled in.' Malcolm Muggeridge, a colleague at the Ministry, described how Senate House retained 'intimations of its academic function: scientific formulae scrawled on blackboards, the whiff of chemicals and a dead dogfish in one of the laboratories, and even a tattered old gown hanging in one of the lavatories.' Graham, Muggeridge recalled, 'characteristically took a highly professional view of what was expected of us, coolly exploring the possibility of throwing stigmata and other miraculous occurrences into the battle for the mind in South America.' For domestic consumption, Graham commissioned the popular novelist Howard Spring to write a pamphlet on 'Life under the Nazis' and H. V. Morton's *I, James Blunt*, which also pondered the possibility of Britain coming under Nazi rule, and was reviewed by George Orwell. Along similar lines, he wrote a short story, 'The Lieutenant Dies Last', which described the German takeover of a sleepy village in the Chilterns, and was later made into Alberto Cavalcanti's marvellous wartime film, *Went the Day Well?* It has been suggested that Ben's internment may have made it awkward for Graham to stay on at the Ministry: be that as it may, he was eventually sacked by the Ministry's Director, Frank Pick, and after contemplating joining the Marines with Tom Burns, he succeeded Derek Verschoyle as the literary editor of the *Spectator*. Verschoyle worked for MI6 during and after the war, and the pre-war and early wartime *Spectator* was alive with spies and secret agents of a leftwards-leaning variety, including among its staff and contributors Anthony Blunt, Guy Burgess and Goronwy Rees.

Shortly before the war broke out, Graham had taken a studio flat in Mecklenburgh Square where he could write undisturbed by the demands of domesticity, and started an affair with his landlady's daughter, Dorothy Glover. Later described by Vivien – who always spoke kindly of her – as a 'stout short figure with blue glasses', Dorothy was hardly a typical *femme fatale*, but she was good company and never averse to a drink, as Hugh in turn discovered. A theatrical designer by training, she had literary ambitions, shared Graham's and Hugh's liking for Victorian crime novels, and would, in later years, collaborate with Graham on a series of children's books, for which she provided the illustrations. Although his letters to Vivien were as loving as ever, she sensed that his attentions were straying. 'Nice for the wife, to be treated as noble but not amusing, a sort of fortnightly pill "to be taken on retiring",' she noted in her diary. Wives sometimes fell in love with other people, but they remained faithful to their husbands: they 'want to *admire* the person they go to bed with: it is against their nature to have the "love" and "amusing" separated. But this is not difficult for men. We love each other and are friends and more than that – but O oneness and togetherness – it's not quite that any more . . . I thought we were the one pair, a unity, I mean, and no one had any right to it but us. But it is not for us now. I am so unhappy again.'

Wilson Harris, the editor of the *Spectator* and an upright Quaker, also lived in Mecklenburgh Square, and his wife was an air-raid warden. According to Walter Allen, Graham found Harris unbearably stuffy and pompous, and on the death of Frank Harris, the notorious debauchee and writer of pornographic memoirs, he sent an anonymous note to the *Evening Standard*'s 'Londoner's Diary' claiming that the two men were cousins. 'I would make a point of resigning at the weekend when he objected to the poetry I printed – for some reason he did not take to Kathleen Raine and Geoffrey Grigson,' Graham recalled years later. 'I also rather disapproved of the fact that he left the office during the Blitz before 5.30 when the alarm usually went off, leaving his wife in London driving an ambulance.' He was anxious that his editor should not spot him with Dorothy, so they took to meeting in her flat in Gower Mews.

Vivien was proud of Graham's new job at the *Spectator*, but 'I simply long for you to stay put in something: the changing about fills me with dread and depression. I think it would be harmful to have the reputation of instability ("Yes, but he never *stays* in anything").' She wished he could become a full-time publisher's editor or get a job in a Ministry with a view to becoming a civil servant after the war – 'I think it is necessary to make up our minds not to live precariously – i.e. not on possible film deals etc.' She and the children had moved from Crowborough to Oxford, where they were staying with the Master of Trinity and his wife:

she had begun her collection of dolls' houses, and included among her Oxford friends A. L. Rowse, Lord David Cecil, Maurice Bowra, Roy Harrod, Neville Coghill and A. J. P. Taylor and his wife Margaret. 'I do hope before this [wedding] anniversary comes round again we may be en famille again somewhere,' she wrote to Graham in October 1940. 'I do send all blessings and love and gratitude for everything you have done for me – you are so unfailingly unselfish and patient. I love you so much.'

The chances of their living *en famille* in London were reduced when their elegant Georgian house on Clapham Common, which Vivien had loved, was bombed in the early months of the Blitz. 'I've been leading a rather chequered and disreputable life,' Graham told Anthony Powell in December 1940. 'All my family are parked in Trinity: my house has been blasted into wreckage by a landmine, and I sleep on a sofa in Gower Street Mews.' 'I'm glad to say I saved practically all my books from the house, though poor Vivien lost most of her Victorian furniture and objects. It's sad because it was a pretty house, but oddly enough it leaves one very carefree,' Graham informed his American literary agent, Mary Pritchett: in fact, many of his books were destroyed, and others looted. Malcolm Muggeridge met him shortly after the house had been bombed, 'and he gave an impression of being well content with its disappearance', so confirming Muggeridge in his belief that his friend was 'one of nature's displaced persons'. The Blitz, Muggeridge recalled, 'was a kind of pro-tracted debauch, with the shape of orderly living shattered, all restraints removed, barriers non-existent. It gave one the same feeling a debauch did, of, as it were, floating loose; of having slipped one's moorings,' and Graham admitted that 'the whole war is good for someone like me who has always suffered from anxiety neurosis: I turn down work left and right just for the fun of not caring . . . [Vivien] has the thin end of things. I have a most interesting and agreeable time in London.'

'How completely those war years were his milieu,' Rose Macaulay later recalled. 'He loved walking the bombed streets, wrapped in a shabby mackintosh, admiring the craters, the fires and the tumbling buildings.' When not working at the *Spectator*, Graham spent his evenings as an air-raid warden at the height of the Blitz. He was based in Bloomsbury, near to Gower Street and the Senate House, and was at hand after one of the worst raids of the war, in April 1941. A bomb fell on the Victoria Club in Malet Street, killing – among others – over three hundred Canadian soldiers. 'It really was the worst thing yet,' Graham told his mother. 'On my beat which consisted of about three-quarters of a mile of streets we had one huge fire, one smaller fire, one HE and, worst of all, a landmine.

The casualties were very heavy, as the landmine which got the Canadian soldiers' home blasted houses right through Gower Street . . . Hardly three minutes would pass between two and four without a salvo being dropped.' He felt 'very stiff and bruised' after carrying a heavy young woman down from the top floor of the RADA building, and helping to carry 'a very fat, very vocal foreign Jew', whose foot had been crushed. 'One's first corpse . . . was not nearly as bad as one expected,' he declared, but 'what remains as nastiest were the crowds of people who were cut by glass, in rather squalid bloodstained pyjamas grey with debris.' While 'on fire guard', he replied to a desperate letter from Vivien, worrying that they were drifting apart. The suggestion that Vivien should join him in London 'makes me sick with worry', not least for the children's sake. 'You can't understand that the case is quite different from Hugh and Helga – not that I approve of them – not much family life there.' If Hugh and Helga were killed in the Blitz, 'their children would have plenty of money', whereas Lucy and Francis would have to rely on 'strangers for charity'.

The *Daily Telegraph* had sent Hugh to Warsaw in June 1939. 'I like this place and the people here enormously and it's an enormous mental relief to be working in a friendly country,' Hugh told his mother. 'It's very difficult to get news here but I'm getting the feel of the place now, so that I can work largely on intuition as I did in Germany.' Soon after his arrival he visited Danzig, where local Nazis were agitating to be incorporated into the Reich: Hugh described a 'sports rally' attended by 10,000 armed storm troopers as 'a dress rehearsal for an invasion of Danzig', and ridiculed Nazi claims that a Polish customs officer had tried to kidnap two storm troopers as 'a curious and rather foolhardy proceeding on an evening when the Free City was crammed with thousands of Brown Shirts from East Prussia.' The German Press denied that Himmler had visited Danzig, but Hugh proved that he had, and that weapons were being smuggled into the city. In a leader-page article headed 'Why a Free Danzig Is Essential to Polish Independence', he claimed that, once cut off from the Baltic, Poland would be reduced to the status of a German protectorate, and that local Nazis had already been equipped with laurel wreathes to celebrate their 'liberation'.

Hugh found Warsaw a thoroughly convivial city, well equipped with nightclubs and cabarets, and boasting a brisk, agreeably old-fashioned social life which involved the wearing of white ties and tails. But much as he enjoyed the café life and grand gatherings of the capital, Hugh sensed that war was imminent. 'Don't worry if you hear nothing from me,' he warned his parents, adding that 'I shall stay in this country as long as there is any possibility of getting the news out.' On 17 August he reported on the provocative activities of German minorities in Upper Silesia: a Polish policeman had been attacked by Nazi storm troopers on the frontier, but the German papers were raging against Polish atrocities. The Molotov-Ribbentrop Pact was announced on 24 August, and Hugh wrote home to say that 'My last will and testament is that you should keep the children out of the hands of the Guinnesses whatever happens!' The following day he crossed the frontier in Upper Silesia, and spent several hours in Germany. 'Everywhere I saw signs of the most intense military activity,' he reported: the German side of the border was littered with tank traps, barbed wire and machine-gun emplacements, but on the Polish side the locals seemed unconcerned, and denied Hitler's claims that the German minority was being persecuted. Back in Warsaw he was joined by the diminutive figure of Clare Hollingworth, who went on to become one of the best-known and most intrepid foreign correspondents of her generation. After working with refugees in the southern Polish city of Katowice and writing occasional pieces for the *News Chronicle* she had met Arthur Watson, the editor of the *Telegraph*, on a trip to England. He hired her on the spot, and told her to report to 'our man in Warsaw' as soon as possible. Pausing only to buy a new suitcase in Harrods, she took what turned out to be the last British passenger flight to fly over Germany before the outbreak of war. She reported for duty at the Europejski Hotel, where Hugh and other journalists were billeted in style. Hugh proved to be a 'tall, friendly character', and whereas 'few foreign staff correspondents would have so cheerfully welcomed an unknown female as an assistant, he could not have been more cordial.'

Sefton Delmer had earlier been in the Katowice area, 'playing my new game of checking up on Goebbels's stories of atrocities committed by cruel Slavs against innocent Germans.' Hugh suggested that one of them should report from the German-Polish frontier in the south of the country, and since she knew the area well, Clare Hollingworth set out for Katowice, where she found the Poles confident that they 'would give the hated Germans a good hiding'. She borrowed the British Consul's car and set off across the frontier with a Union Jack fluttering from the bonnet. On a hill near Gleiwitz she was overtaken by a swarm of dispatch riders and, looking to one side of the road, she noticed guns hidden behind hessian screens and hundreds of tanks, armoured cars and field artillery in the valley below, all part of von Rundstedt's 10th Army, poised to form the southern arm of a pincer attack on Poland. Back in Katowice, Clare Hollingworth phoned her findings through to Hugh, and filed a story, published in the *Telegraph* the following day, which carried the headline '1,000 Tanks Massed on Polish Frontier' and reported that 'The German military machine is now ready for instant action.' Two days later anti-Polish hysteria in Germany was whipped up when a team of SS men, disguised as Poles, stormed and captured the radio station at Gleiwitz, broadcast bogus Polish propaganda, and – as further evidence of Polish depravity – left behind the corpse of a local man supposedly killed in the attack. The following day, 1 September, Hollingworth was woken at dawn by the drone of planes flying overhead, the flash of explosions and gunfire that sounded like 'banging doors'. The Blitzkrieg had begun, and she immediately rang Hugh in Warsaw; as they were speaking the sirens began to wail in the capital. She also rang Robin Hankey at the British Embassy, and since he seemed to doubt her – 'Are you sure, old girl?' – she held the receiver out of her hotel window. Hugh rang the Polish Foreign Office who, despite the air-raid warnings, dismissed Hollingworth's report as 'absolute nonsense', and claimed to still be in negotiations with Germany.

On 2 September Hugh reported that fighting was concentrated on the Polish Corridor and the border with Slovakia, and that the outskirts of Warsaw were being bombed. He felt immense relief when he learned that Britain had declared war on Germany. The news was greeted with a 'tremendous outburst of joy in Warsaw', and shouts of 'Long Live King George' went up when Colonel Beck, the Polish Foreign Minister, appeared on the balcony of the British Embassy alongside the Ambassador, Sir Howard Kennard. 'Warsaw is now settling down to wartime conditions,' Hugh reported the following day. 'All windows are criss-crossed with strips of paper. At night there is complete darkness. Trams and buses, showing blue lights, rattle along at little more than a walking pace through black streets.' But despite the Poles' initial insouciance, their defences were rapidly overrun. As the Polish army withdrew, Clare Hollingworth helped consular staff in Katowice to burn official documents before leaving for Lublin, in the east of the country. From there she made her way to Warsaw. Hugh, she recalled, 'like most people in Warsaw at that time', had seemed 'singularly placid' when she first reported the bombing of Katowice, but when she called at the Europejski Hotel she found that 'although the maid seemed to think he would return,' he and all the other journalists had been ordered to leave Warsaw on 5 September, along with the British Embassy and the Polish Government itself; so, after helping herself to a bottle of Hugh's champagne, she set off back to Lublin.

Sefton Delmer, who had also been staying at the Europejski, described their 'nightmare retreat' from Warsaw 'across bridges crammed with small skinny horses, pulling low-wheeled carts piled to the top with bedding, clothes, bits of furniture and refugees', and how they were passed by gleaming limousines carrying diplomats and government officials to safety. After halting in a spa town, where they could hear the sound of alleged German spies and saboteurs being shot – 'the usual Fifth Column scare was on' – they pressed on towards the south. Hugh was travelling with a reporter from the *News Chronicle* and *The Times*'s correspondent, Patrick Maitland, a future Tory MP, who was clad in breeches, black jackboots and a black leather coat with a Union Jack brassard on one arm. Delmer later claimed that Hugh's car was a 'slow and decrepit affair', and that he 'could easily have passed them and got to the frontier with the news before them. But in times of war Fleet Street holds together' – a claim which Hugh treated with some scepticism when Delmer's memoirs were published.

'Safe Rumania future movements uncertain' Hugh cabled his parents on 10 September. Two days later he wrote from the Athenée Palace Hotel in Bucharest to say that 'between leaving Warsaw on Tuesday and crossing into Rumania on Friday night I didn't take off my clothes or sleep in a bed, and I was singularly filthy. I walked into this country through a delightful ornamental gate inscribed "Rumania", carrying a bottle of beer and a gas mask. Except for what I'd got on, I'd abandoned everything I own.' But he was not quite through with Poland. Eight days later he and Maitland took a taxi from Cernauti, in Rumania, to the Polish border. In Zaleszczyki, on the Polish side, they encountered Clare Hollingworth. She was accompanied by a Czechoslovakian Jew who had no visa for Rumania, and was reluctant to leave him behind. 'For Christ's sake come along now,' Hugh urged her. 'You can get him a visa in Cernauti.' They walked over a long wooden bridge that crossed the Dniester to where Hugh's taxi was waiting, and 'we must have looked an odd sight, Greene hugging a huge non-portable typewriter, and I my dirty pillowcase full of clothing.' Back in Cernauti, Clare Hollingworth learned that – as agreed in the Nazi-Soviet Pact – the Russians had begun their invasion and annexation of Poland, and although Hugh's initial reaction was 'Nonsense!' they hurried back to Zaleszczyki. Hugh slipped on the wooden bridge and 'plunged like a camel', but once safely on the other side they made their way to the village of Kuty, where the Polish government was briefly in residence. They found Sir Howard Kennard eating his lunch in the back room of a fly-blown grocery shop, and he told them how he had been driven in a motorbike sidecar to the Foreign Office, then installed in a farmhouse, before being told by Colonel Beck that the Russians had invaded. Later that day 'I saw a column of tanks which I thought to be an unusual Polish type,' Hugh told *Telegraph* readers, but 'when the conning tower of the leading tank was opened, an officer in a Soviet uniform looked out.' It seemed unwise to remain in Poland, so they headed back to the border, where a mass of lorries and buses and refugees were jostling to cross the bridge to Romania. A Polish officer in a cloak was trying to direct the traffic in a fruity alcoholic voice, a Rolls or Daimler swept by taking President Mościcki into exile, and Hugh reported that 'under the shock of the Russian invasion, the Polish armed forces are disintegrating completely.' Once across the river, Clare Hollingworth drove Hugh over the Carpathians to Bucharest: the car broke down en route, and Hugh 'made suggestions helpful and unhelpful'. From Bucharest Hugh reported on the assassination of the Prime Minister, Călinescu, by members of the fascist Iron Guard: he visited the scene minutes after, and 'found the chauffeur still collapsed on the running board of the car, and the bodies of the detectives still lying in pools of blood on the road.'

After a brief spell back in London, Hugh was sent in November to report on Germany from the temporary safety of Amsterdam, and he was there at the time of the humiliating Venlo Incident, in which a future member of the family was indirectly involved. Holland was officially neutral, and The Hague station of the SIS or MI6 had assumed a far greater importance than hitherto: it was heavily manned, and under strict instructions to keep a close eye on developments in Germany. Ever since the Russian Revolution of 1917, MI6 – like its domestic counterpart, MI5 – had concentrated its energies on combating the 'Bolshevik' threat, but by the end of the 1930s Nazi Germany had replaced the Soviet Union as the focus of its attentions. Stuart Menzies – who, as Head of Section II, had employed Elisabeth Greene as his secretary in 1938 – had just succeeded Admiral Sir Hugh ('Quex') Sinclair as 'C', in overall charge of the SIS. When London learned that the Passport Control Officer in the Hague had committed suicide – it was claimed that he had helped himself to money paid by German Jews for exit visas – Menzies sent Valentine Vivian to The Hague to investigate.

A former member of the Indian Police, Vivian was in charge of Section V, which looked after counter-intelligence and counter-espionage.

Vivian and his successor, Felix Cowgill, had built up Section V as a semi-independent service within SIS and, at Cowgill's suggestion, Vivian had appointed a Section V counter-intelligence officer to each overseas station. The Section V officer in The Hague was a young man called Rodney Dennys, who would in due course marry Elisabeth Greene. Bespectacled, six-foot three – two inches shorter than Raymond, and an inch taller than Graham – and, according to his future wife, 'extremely skinny', Dennys was the son of a Malayan civil servant. He had been educated at Canford and the LSE, and had spent six months in Germany in 1936. Back in England, he had joined the Foreign Office's Passport Control Department at a time when the SIS was under-funded, under-staffed and populated, for the most part, by retired soldiers, naval officers and members of the Indian police. He was posted to The Hague the following year: he was given a bedroom over the office, and noticed above the bed-head a hole in the plaster made by one of the bullets fired by his suicidal predecessor.

In May 1939 Dennys was made the first full time CE (counter-intelligence) officer in any overseas station. Dennys's friend and colleague Nicholas Elliott was also attached to the Legation, working for MI6. Richard Stevens, whom Dennys thought 'dangerously over-confident', was the Head of Station, and he worked closely with a senior SIS operative called Major Sigismund Payne Best, a member of Claude Dansey's 'Z' Organisation who wore spats and a monocle and claimed to run an import-export business. Dennys built up a network of informants in the Dutch capital, and one day in July 1939 he picked up the telephone to hear a mysterious foreign voice intoning 'Tell him [Stevens] next Monday in seven weeks.' Stuart Menzies was visiting Sir Nevile Bland, the Minister in The Hague, at the time: somehow he realised that the caller was referring to the German attack on Poland in early September, and alerted the powers-that-be in London. 'There cannot be many occasions in history when the British Government have had seven clear weeks warning of the outbreak of war,' Dennys wrote years later, adding that 'our report was only two or three days out.'

In the early stages of the war, British propaganda still distinguished between the German people and its leaders, and was ready to exploit any real or alleged disaffection in the German ranks, not least through the activities of the Joint Broadcasting Council. Established shortly after the Munich Agreement, the JBC was run, until her death in 1941, by Felix's old boss in the BBC's Talks Department, Hilda Matheson. It was partly funded by the SIS, and made use of Luxembourg-based *Freiheitsender* or bogus German radio stations, a form of 'black' propaganda that would be enthusiastically embraced by Sefton Delmer. Both the SIS and the JBC were keen to believe that dissidents in the Wehrmacht were poised to overthrow Hitler. Payne Best had been tipped off about a dissident plot, and was told that a senior Wehrmacht officer was ready to fly to London to discuss terms. A genuine attempt to assassinate Hitler in the Bürgerbräukeller in Munich on 8 November had been thwarted, and the following day, with the *Freiheitsender* or Freedom Station urging those involved in the bomb plot to rise up against the regime, Best and Stevens agreed to meet Walter Schellenberg of the Sicherheitsdienst, the intelligence-gathering arm of the SS, in the Café Bacchus, two hundred yards from the German border, near the Dutch town of Venlo. A Dutch Intelligence officer was shot and killed, while the two Britons were manhandled across the border by two SD men in plain clothes and taken to Düsseldorf, where they were interrogated separately. One of the two SD men, Alfred Nuajocks, had taken part in the Gleiwitz raid, and Schellenberg and the Sicherheitsdienst would, in due course, supplant Admiral Canaris's Abwehr, which was rightly regarded as being sympathetic to opponents of the regime. Rodney Dennys and his colleagues picked up a message, signed 'the German Gestapo', which read 'In the long run conversations with conceited and stupid people become boring. You will understand why we are cutting off communications. Your friends the German opposition send you hearty greetings'; and, as Dennys later admitted, they found it hard not to laugh.

Venlo was, from the German point of view, a brilliant and stylish operation, and a masterly exercise in deception. The Abwehr obtained the names of British agents in Europe, including members of the Z Organisation, the SIS's Hague station was virtually closed down, and had it not been for Rodney Dennys's protestations, all Intelligence activities in Holland would have been discontinued under orders from the Foreign Office. MI6's operations in the Hague had, it turned out, been compromised even before the outbreak of war – a young Dutchman working for the SIS had been 'turned' by the Abwehr, and had been submitting weekly reports on the activities of British agents in the Netherlands – but the episode proved so disastrous for British Intelligence that, after he became Prime Minister, Churchill forbade any future contacts with opposition groups in Germany, including those involved in the 20 July 1944 attempt on Hitler's life, on the grounds that they could well be double agents. Vansittart's belief that, with the Nazis in power, all Germans were by definition bad Germans prevailed, still more so after the Allies committed themselves to a policy of unconditional surrender.

Rodney Dennys was transferred to Brussels, but spent most of his time in The Hague. In the early days of May 1940 Dennys's informants reported a mass of Germans pouring into the city, posing as tourists or businessmen, and he later learned that arms and ammunition had been smuggled into the country in German diplomatic bags. In the early morning of 10 May he was woken by the blaze of searchlights, the sound of gunfire and the roar of planes overhead: the German invasion of Holland had begun. Dennys later learned that he was on a list of those to be shot on sight, and after feeding secret files, index cards and code books into a small stove in the Legation, he boarded the SS *Dotterel*, bound for Tilbury. The docks resounded to the boom of ack-ack guns, and his fellow-passengers included members of the Sadler's Wells Ballet, whose tour of the Low Countries had been rudely terminated. Back in England, he was posted to Section V's headquarters in St Alban's, monitoring Abwehr and SD activities in Holland. According to the journalist Leonard Mosley, 'Denzil Roberts' – the pseudonym he gave Rodney Dennys – was also involved in trying to track down an elusive German spy known as 'the Druid', said to be the only German spy in Britain not to have been detected and 'turned' by MI5's XX Committee, of which Dennys was a member. Although Mosley was a good friend, and had provided useful snippets of information in The Hague, the account he gave in his book *The Druid* was not thought (by Dennys at least) to be entirely reliable.

Hugh made his own way to Belgium, and was woken on the morning of 10 May by 'the scream of sirens and the crash of anti-aircraft guns'. Looking through the window of his Brussels hotel, he 'could see waves of German bombers like silver specks in the sunny spring sky'. The German Ambassador, he reported, had been summoned by the Foreign Minister, and 'it is believed that M. Spaak gave the Ambassador a severe talking-to.' The next day Hugh checked out of the Hotel Metropole in Brussels, leaving an IOU which was paid off by Marsland Gander of the *Daily Telegraph* in July 1945, after the Allies had liberated Belgium, and drove to Louvain with Geoffrey Cox of the *Daily Express*, a future colleague at the BBC: they watched the Luftwaffe bombing Louvain, and took shelter in a ditch as the German planes zoomed overhead. It was Cox's first experience of dive-bombing, but Hugh was a hardened veteran: '"Stukas," said Greene abruptly, drawing on his experiences of the Polish campaign.' At Tournai, Cox, Hugh, Edward Ward from the BBC and

Courtenay Young from Reuters squeezed into a five-seater Chevrolet with three overweight Belgian women. Ward drove, Hugh sat in front, with a Belgian lady on his lap, Young and Cox joined the other two ladies in the back, and together they slowly made their way to the *Daily Telegraph*'s office in Paris, where Eustace Wareing was still holding the fort. When they learned that the Germans were only fifteen miles from Paris, Cox and Hugh commandeered a lift in Wareing's car and set out in a south-westerly direction. 'Rain, grass, trees, a park, a lake./ Grass stretching to more trees under the gentle rain./ Bombers, owls, bats, a drone, a shriek./ Red Tunisian fezzes wet with rain,' Hugh wrote in a poem entitled 'From the Window of a Touraine Chateau', dated June 1940. The SS *Madura* was tied up at the quayside in Bordeaux, on its way from East Africa to Falmouth with 120 passengers on board, most of them colonial officials on leave. More than a thousand extra passengers clambered on board, among them diplomats, French government ministers and a bevy of journalists that included Hugh, Geoffrey Cox and Sefton Delmer, who had left the *Daily Express*'s Paris office on the day the Germans marched in. Although none of them possessed the obligatory dinner jacket for evening wear, they persuaded the captain to allow them to sleep on deck. Dodging German bombs, and escorted by two British destroyers, the *Madura* made its way to the open sea, and arrived in Falmouth the following morning.

Back in London, Hugh met Ian Fleming, who said there was nothing going in Naval Intelligence; but Victor Gordon-Lennox introduced him to an RAF officer over lunch in White's and, after dazzling his interviewers with his mastery of foreign languages, he was sent to Cockfosters to learn how to interrogate Luftwaffe pilots who had been shot down over England. As an RAF Intelligence officer, Hugh learned how to distinguish one German plane from another, practised his interrogation techniques on prisoners-of-war, and worked in Dorset, Plymouth and Tangmere before being sent to Kent during the Battle of Britain. His life was made easier by the fact that Luftwaffe crews often carried diaries and letters in their pockets, and he made use of his fluent German and his knowledge of their country; a dead Luftwaffe officer on Chesil Beach was found to be wearing pink silk women's underclothes and carrying lipstick and a powder puff. But he would soon be putting his knowledge of Germany and the Germans to better effect. He was asked if he would be interested in broadcasting to Germany for the BBC, and the matter was raised with Duff Cooper, the Minister of Information, and Sir Archibald Sinclair, the Secretary of State for Air. Arthur Watson of the *Daily Telegraph* provided a glowing reference, and MI5 could see no objections. For the rest of his life Hugh thought of himself as a journalist, but he was about to abandon newspapers for a world with which Felix was already very familiar; but whereas Felix had abandoned his career with the BBC after a brilliant and precocious start, Hugh would rise to the very top of the Corporation, and be remembered as one of its two outstanding Director-Generals.

★

Raymond had spent most of the thirties working as a GP in Oxford with Dr Counsell, with spells as a clinical assistant in the Radcliffe Infirmary and in the Westminster Hospital's department of endocrinology: he enjoyed obstetrics and, years later, took a retrospective pride in having delivered Antonia Fraser. Towards the end of the decade he took rooms in Wimpole Street, but when the war broke out he was working as a blood transfusion officer in Staines: he was bored and depressed, living away from home and with little to do except drink beer and play darts in a pub opposite the hospital. Life improved when he and Eleanor bought a Tudor house at Whitchurch, near Aylesbury, but although, as a medical officer in the Territorial Army, he longed to transfer from the Emergency Medical Services to become a full-time army doctor, he was considered too old for active service.

But his expertise was still in demand, and he would make a useful contribution to the military. Early in the war he was summoned to the War Office to meet Sir Roger Keyes, the Chief of Combined Operations, who wanted his advice – based on his experience as a mountaineer – about getting wounded Commandos away from the scene of battle. A long silence then ensued, only broken when Keyes was replaced by the rather more dynamic Lord Louis Mountbatten. Raymond bent his mind to the design of what would come to be known as the 'Greene Carrier', and in October 1941 he applied for a patent for 'an improved device to facilitate the carrying of loads'. Consisting of a light cane or metal frame with a seat or platform attached, it had 'for its primary object to devise simple and effective means whereby a wounded man may be easily carried upon the back of a soldier, while leaving free the arms and hands of the carrier.' It could also be used for carrying loads: a landing party, for example, could carry weapons and ammunition ashore in the stretcher, before using it to rescue wounded comrades. Nor was Raymond's involvement restricted to inventing the carrier. Himalayan friends and colleagues were keen to make use of his experience as a mountaineer to train soldiers in the School of Mountain Warfare. 'You sound as if you have a pretty full job of the "reserved" category,' Noel Odell wrote from the War Office in August 1941. 'Nevertheless I want to have you on my select list of mountaineers.' He mentioned the possibility of Raymond's being commissioned to run a course for Commando Medical Officers in 'casualty transport methods', and a fortnight later he wrote again to say that he had spoken to Combined Operations about the Greene Carrier.

Raymond ran courses in North Wales and the west coast of Scotland. They were well received by his pupils, one of whom was inspired to verse by the experience – 'Up the airy mountain/ Down the muddy glen/ The doctors go a-climbing/ To rescue wounded men' – but he found himself having to haggle over his expenses. In March 1942 Combined Ops wrote to say that it would be hard to get these through unless he could convince the Finance Department that he had no financial interest in his invention, and that 'you are willing to present your design to the country.' Later in the war Raymond was presented with a £300 'award to inventors' in recognition of the fact that the Carrier had been widely used during the Burma Campaign, and in due course his solicitor, L. A. 'Boy' Hart – eventually to become, with Graham, a director of The Bodley Head – negotiated some kind of royalty on his behalf.

Raymond's status was hard to define. As an official consultant, 'it might be a good idea if I were to receive an acting unpaid rank appropriate to the position,' he told Frank Smythe at Combined Ops. It would lend more weight to his views, 'but I do not insist on it and would be prepared to continue to help as a mere civilian.' He had, he went on, been pondering what Smythe had told him about the use of the Carrier during the disastrous Dieppe Raid earlier that year: there was no need for injured men to be carried in a horizontal position unless they were seriously wounded, in which case a conventional stretcher might be needed; it was perfectly feasible for a small man to carry a large colleague over rough ground using the Carrier, but he must be trained properly in its use. Smythe suggested that Raymond should be appointed Medical Officer to the School of Mountain Warfare; Raymond – who already held a position in the Emergency Medical Service equivalent to that of a lieutenant-colonel in the RAMC – finally decided against accepting a commission, but suggested that he should be made an honorary medical advisor to Combined Operations.

Raymond's work for Combined Ops had proved both rewarding and frustrating, and in a letter to Solly Zuckerman – a prominent scientific adviser to the government during the war and a zoologist, who would later be a colleague of Raymond's at London Zoo – he complained about the infuriating lack of co-operation between Combined Ops, the Medical Research Council and the War Office over the School of Mountain Warfare. In the meantime he was working in Aylesbury at Tindal House, a branch of the Middlesex Hospital, looking after the wards and teaching students. He was also involved with the top-secret activities of the Special Operations Executive, or SOE, which had a training school at Grendon Underwood, where they prepared men and women to be parachuted into Occupied Europe to work with the Resistance and sabotage enemy depots and lines of communication.

The Greene Carrier was a belated by-product of the 1933 Everest expedition, as was Raymond's interest in frostbite and associated disorders. Writing in the *Lancet* in December 1941, he reminded his readers that in wartime frostbite 'becomes an important military factor, either in its classical form or as the closely allied condition of trench foot', and evoked Napoleon's retreat from Moscow on the grounds that 'should the Germans in Russia be forced to dig in this winter, frostbite may be once more a potent weapon against Russia's enemies.' The symptoms of frostbite were very similar to those of trench foot, which had proved a particularly common ailment among those who spent long hours in cold, damp air-raid shelters or sat too still while on air-raid duty, and of immersion foot, which was associated with shipwrecked sailors. The important thing was not to try to revive chilled or frozen limbs by applying to them heat greater than that of the human body. 'I have more than once forcibly prevented Tibetans and Nepalis from roasting or boiling their chilled feet,' he recalled. Soldiers and civilians alike should avoid tight socks and boots, keep their feet dry, rub one another's feet with whale oil, keep their leg muscles active and their circulation going, make sure that trenches and duckboards were kept as dry as possible, take plenty of Vitamin C, eat fruit and vegetables, sleep with their feet up, avoid contact with cold metal in freezing conditions, and – this applied particularly to those spending nights in deck chairs in air-raid shelters – avoid sitting still in one place with the bar of a deckchair compressing the backs of the legs. He told potential sufferers from frostbite – those involved in the Arctic convoys, for example – not to be alarmed by the blackening of the skin that often resulted from severe frostbite: far too many blackened limbs had been unnecessarily amputated during the First World War, and – drawing again on his Everest experience – provided heat was not applied to the afflicted parts, the blackened crust would eventually drop off to expose the healthy skin below. Together with R. J. Simpson of the International Refrigerator Company, he had designed a freezing cabinet in which to test his theories, with holes for the insertion of hands and feet. In 1943 Raymond was elected the Hunterian Professor at the Royal College of Surgeons, not for the last time, and delivered his inaugural lecture on 'Frostbite and Kindred Conditions'. He was becoming an eminent figure in the medical world, and would achieve an even greater eminence in the years ahead.

Herbert's military career was also subject to frustration, but for very different reasons. In May 1939 he complained that he had tried to join the 'Searchlights' – presumably some kind of anti-aircraft battery – in Brighton, but was told that he could not join the Territorials because he had been in Spain during the Civil War. This seemed a poor excuse, but both MI5 and the War Office had taken a dim view of his activities as an amateur spy, and were determined not to allow him in or near any position of responsibility. 'We have considerable records to his detriment. He is entirely unsuitable for any position which may give him access to confidential documents, apparatus or information,' MI5 reported in September that year, and elsewhere he was described as 'a most undesirable type, given to drinking heavily and talking indiscriminately': both memos were initialled 'TAR', which suggests that 'Tar' Robertson of MI5's top-secret XX Committee had interested himself in Herbert's affairs. In October MI5 noted that a Mrs Joseph was about to break off her friendship with Herbert – whose 'relationship with her might be termed "would-be amorous"' – on the grounds that he was 'odd, not always likeable, and did strange things', while 'his philosophy seemed to imply that money was everything'. Quite what Herbert expected of Mrs Joseph remains a mystery, but shortly before the outbreak of war he had asked two ladies of his acquaintance to drop off letters to the German and Czech Embassies. Despite his earlier rebuffs by the military, he was now working in the orderly room of the Duke of York's barracks in Chelsea, where he had taken the liberty of signing a framed photograph of Winston Churchill and, on account of his height, had been unable to find a uniform that fitted him.

It was not an easy matter to find a suitable position for a man who claimed, against all the evidence, to have been commissioned in 1919 'after nearly three years service in the 3rd Suffolks', and the complexities of Herbert's wartime movements are sometimes hard to follow. In October 1939 he was reported as having enlisted in the Territorial Army's 1st Armoured (Middlesex Yeomanry) Divisional Signals after answering

an advertisement for a clerk at £3 a week: he had been posted to the
orderly room after claiming to have played cricket for his county and
worked on the docks, but he invariably drank 'a large quantity of beer'
while on duty, and was 'considered untrustworthy' as a result. Excessive
beer drinking and general unreliability soon took their toll. 'I should be
most grateful if you could take the necessary steps to get this man
removed from his present employ at the Duke of York's Headquarters,'
MI5 suggested to the War Office. 'It would be far better that he should
not be allowed to re-enlist in the Services ... Greene is a thoroughly
unreliable type of person, is addicted to drink, and should not be allowed
to hold a position in HM Forces.'

Despite MI5's insistence that he should not be employed in any position of trust, or allowed access to confidential documents, Herbert
clung on until the spring of 1941, when the Lieutenant-General
commanding the London District insisted that he should be transferred
at once 'in view of the confidential nature of the bulk of the work that
the Royal Corps of Signals handles'. In April Herbert was demoted to
the Pioneer Corps, responsible for digging ditches and latrines, and
exchanged St John's Wood for Huyton, near Liverpool. From there he
wrote a letter of complaint to the Prime Minister. 'As a nephew of Sir
Graham Greene, who was with you at the Admiralty and the Ministry
of Munitions as Permanent Secretary during the last war, I appeal to
you to get me out of this semi-penal battalion to which I have been
transferred,' he begged, before seizing the opportunity to keep the Prime
Minister abreast of iniquities being perpetrated in St John's Wood: the
Commanding Officer had forged his mileage claims, the rum intended
for despatch-riders carrying urgent messages to Chequers was being
drunk by warrant officers, and officers were not only siphoning off petrol
for their own use, but purloining their men's meat rations. In a letter to
the Secretary of State for War, repudiating claims of his unreliability, he
said that, according to Raymond, a dossier had been assembled which
would prevent him from regaining his commission. The War Office, he
claimed, had misread his *Secret Service* [sic] *in Spain*: 'Although most
reviewers took the book as fact it was fiction. Surely Military Intelligence
never really thought that I was acting as a secret agent in Spain?'

But it was all to no avail: Herbert was discharged from the Pioneer
Corps, and returned home to Plumpton. MI5 asked the local police to
keep an eye on him. He no longer spent so much time in the pub; in
March 1942 a detective-sergeant from the Sussex Constabulary called at
his cottage unannounced, and reported that Herbert seemed 'quite

pro-British', that he appeared to be badly off, and that he was earning a crust by breeding rabbits and by occasional journalism. A PC Chapman spotted him bicycling round the neighbourhood gathering food for his rabbits, and in December he failed to report for fire-watching duties. But his old spark had not entirely deserted him: as an old soldier who had once held a commission, he ticked off a correspondent who had addressed him as 'Mr' rather than 'Esq' on an envelope; he reported the local butcher for serving himself to more meat than he was entitled to, and heckled the speaker at a meeting of the Chailey Rural District Council.

MI5 continued to take a dim view of Herbert – he was, they declared in March 1943, 'a plausible liar', a 'born trouble-maker' and 'an unpleasant creature on whom no reliance can be put, and may easily get up to some sort of mischief in another connection' – but he was not entirely without friends. Tufton Beamish, then and for many years the Conservative MP for Lewes, told him that he seemed 'to have had a rough passage' and was 'worthy of much sympathy, and a completely honourable man', and that he planned to take his case to the highest authority. He wrote about Herbert to Duff Cooper, who referred the letter on to the SIS: Courtenay Young, now with MI5, reported that he had spoken about Herbert to Hugh, who said that 'his brother was not a reliable or pleasant character', but thought him no danger to security. In the spring of 1943 Herbert and Audrey moved to Reigate to work as wardens in a hostel for evacuated children, but by the end of the war Herbert was living in Bayswater and working for Toc H, the charity founded by 'Tubby' Clayton during the First World War. He applied for a job in India, but once again his past was held against him. 'How far he is a reformed character and even if he is how desirable it is for him to go to India is for you to judge,' MI5 informed the India Office. Their reservations must have struck home. 'What the hell do you mean cancelling my exit permit?' Herbert cabled the Director of Security at the India Office; and, thwarted once again, he and the long-suffering Audrey went back to their cottage in Plumpton.

Herbert's adventures as a spy had blighted his career, but other members of the family had happier experiences with the secret services. Elisabeth had been working for the SIS since 1938, and had enlisted Graham and Malcolm Muggeridge. They were formally recruited by a 'Wodehousian' character called Leslie Nicholson, who had earlier been the head of station in Riga. Graham had visited the city in 1934, and had struck up a friendship with Peter Leslie, MI6's agent in Estonia, after they discovered that they were both reading novels by Henry James on a flight from Riga to Tallinn. Muggeridge later recalled how he was told to 'present myself at an address in London with a view to being considered for special Intelligence duties. The summons was the consequence of a plot long before hatched with Graham Greene, whose sister, Liza, worked for someone important in the Secret Service. We hoped that she would recommend us both to her boss as suitable overseas representatives, and be able to pull the requisite strings to get us accepted.' The ploy worked, and Muggeridge was sent to be trained at Section V's headquarters in St Alban's, where Graham would find himself based later in the war. He learned about code-breaking, planting deceptive material and the use of invisible ink, and how to cipher and decipher and co-operate with other Allied counter-intelligence agencies. He was taken to meet Elisabeth's first employer, Sir Stuart Menzies – 'sandy-haired, liable to be kilted, with a soft handshake, and an air of indolence, belied by a glint of cunning in his brown eyes' – and noted that whereas pre-war MI6 types looked like conventional diplomats, soldiers or former colonial policemen, the wartime intake emulated Kim Philby by 'slouching about in sweaters and grey flannel trousers, drinking in bars and cafes and low dives rather than at diplomatic cocktail parties and receptions, boasting of their underworld acquaintances and liaisons.'

This was a world with which Graham would become very familiar, and he too was learning the ropes. He was sent for military and intelligence training in Oxford, and was lodged in Raymond's old college, Pembroke. A whole new aspect of his career was about to unfold.

'We Are All Guilty'

Far removed from the scene of war, and no longer working for the BBC, Felix took a lofty view of events on the other side of the Atlantic. In later years he attributed his anxiety not to be involved to a combination of genuine conscientious objection, his being German on his mother's side, and a dread at having to mix on terms of equality with the sort of people with whom, as a man of the left, he sided in principle, but avoided in practice. Jobless and momentarily adrift, he was unsure how and where he should direct his enormous energy and extreme efficiency, both organisational and practical. He was still involved with Peggy Bok and her husband in running Film Associates, and toured the Southern states to investigate the possibility of making a film about negro education, with the backing of the Rockefeller Foundation: but he soon lost interest, leaving Peggy and Henwar embittered at his 'rank desertion'. While in California in the autumn of 1940, ostensibly on Film Associates business, he met for the first time his distant cousin Christopher Isherwood, who had moved to the States shortly before the outbreak of war. Isherwood remembered meeting Eva Greene in Lisbon in 1937, presumably on one of her trips to or from Brazil, when she and his mother Kathleen had enlisted Sir Graham Greene to investigate the possibility of his German boyfriend Heinz being granted British citizenship or somehow shipped to safety in South America rather then face extradition to Germany to do his military service. Isherwood's odd and unstable brother, Richard, Sir Graham's godson, had been a contemporary of Felix at Berkhamsted prep school, and Felix had unhappy memories of walking down the High Street with the blubbering boy beside him, and longing to disown him.

Back East, Felix – like Ben before him – found himself working with the Quakers in the pacifist cause. Although America did not enter the war until December 1941, after the bombing of Pearl Harbor, Congress passed the Selective Training and Services Act in November 1940, as a result of which all men between the ages of twenty-one and thirty-five were ordered to register for the draft. Despite his British citizenship, Felix was not formally exempt, but in the meantime he helped to run a Quaker camp for conscientious objectors in Maryland. Inspired by his reading of Thoreau's *Walden*, he rented a cottage in the rolling Pennsylvania countryside, where he lived on prunes, lentils and home-made bread, got up at six every morning to read the Bible and Gerald Heard's *Code of Christ*, meditated several times a day, taught himself to knit, and set about making a scarf for Ben in prison. He sent home rhapsodic accounts of life in the camp, which involved hard physical labour and sitting round the campfire of an evening. 'The only thing that matters is to reach some kind of union with the Power we call God,' he told his mother; all his previous jobs had been 'important as experience', but none had proved 'quite the answer to my finding myself'. '"Busy-ness" is nothing but running away from thinking and feeling,' he declared, lest anyone should accuse him of evading the issue: 'it is when one is very quiet, very still, very alone that one dares to feel pain and really to face the implications of what is happening in the world today.'

With Tooter temporarily in the army, Felix contemplated coming home to run Kepston in Ben's absence. 'I am far less difficult and opinionated. I have lost a good deal of that aggressive self-confidence which made me arrogant and impossible to work with,' he told Eva, but he decided against it all the same. Roger Wilson, a friend from the BBC, suggested that he should transfer his activities to London, working with the Quakers on behalf of conscientious objectors: after some agonising, Felix declared that, with the war 'only a symptom of something infinitely more significant, a real mutation of man's spirit', he had opted for the 'high and terrible course' of staying put in the States. But he would not remain in Pennsylvania. Gerald Heard had selected him for the 'high honour' of helping to run a religious centre in California, so in June 1941 he said farewell to New Hope Cottage and headed out west. '*Think* what a wonderful opportunity it would be for me to widen my thinking,' Felix informed his mother. 'He is the *only* thinker who is meeting the world situation with courage and initiative', and 'at this point in the world's history, it has become essential for such a place to be founded.'

Gerald Heard had settled in North Carolina after leaving England in 1937, but had now moved to California with his partner Christopher Wood, the heir to a jam-making fortune. He was now busy elaborating a 'third morality' which would reconcile science and religion, and exploring his interest in Eastern religions and psychical research. Isherwood was a friend and admirer, as was Denham Fouts, who was once described by Isherwood as 'the most expensive male prostitute in the world' and had included among his lovers Prince Paul of Greece and Peter Watson, the margarine millionaire and backer of Cyril Connolly's *Horizon*. The three men had talked about establishing some kind of religious community, and asked Felix to set it up on their behalf. As a trial run, he was asked to organise a seminar at La Verne College, to be attended by thirty people. 'Felix Greene, my half-German cousin, was a very remarkable man, with a real genius for organisation. The blue eyes in his tanned hawk face blazed with rajasic power,' Isherwood recorded in his diary. 'Felix organised everything at La Verne – the sleeping accommodation, the work schedule, the menus, the activities of the hired cook – and he didn't merely give orders, he pitched in and fixed things himself: the plumbing, the electric light, the furniture. There was nothing he wouldn't tackle. He worked, as Gerald put it, with an energy "almost epileptic" . . . He was a born executive, but erratic, both in public and private life.' Isherwood added that 'again and again, according to Gerald, he had acted emotionally, hysterically, and left his partners in the lurch' – he cited in particular the case of Peggy Bok – and that 'Felix was desperate to win Gerald's favour, and Gerald, that old coquette, was cruel but slowly relenting. It was unofficially understood that this seminar was to be the probation period. If Felix made good, he would be admitted to Gerald's circle.'

Felix need not have worried: the La Verne seminar was so successful that Heard, Isherwood and Aldous Huxley decided to set up a permanent residential centre on the strength of a donation of $100,000 from a rich female enthusiast. Felix was asked to find and purchase a suitable plot of land, and to supervise the design and construction of the retreat, on the understanding that it must be in pleasant countryside, remote yet within easy reach of Los Angeles. He eventually settled on a farmhouse in Trabuco, in the foothills of the Saddleback Mountains. Set in the middle of a National Forest and game reserve, it enjoyed a view over wooded hills to the Pacific Ocean, yet was only fifteen miles from the house Gerald Heard shared with Christopher Wood on Laguna Beach. According to Isherwood, 'nothing noteworthy had happened in that area since the seventeenth century, when a Spanish soldier had lost an arquebus there, a "trabuco",' and he doubted whether 'Gerald would ever have bought any property at all – he was as undecided and full of excuses as Queen Elizabeth – if Felix Greene hadn't finally taken matters into his own hands, and bullied Gerald into the purchase of Trabuco.' A plot of land was purchased, the farmhouse was razed and, with the help of a

local architect, Felix set to work, camping out in a wooden hut when
not laying drains, designing the garden, and digging a storage tank and
a swimming pool. Isherwood was immensely impressed, noting in his
diary how Felix

> had worked all winter, with his superhuman energy, collecting mate-
> rial, bullying contractors, grabbing the last available supplies of
> wood and metal fixtures before the government froze them. Trabuco
> was three-quarters his creation, physically – ideologically also – for
> I soon began to realise that this place, this institution, was alto-
> gether in excess of anything Gerald's timid conservatism had ever
> planned or wished. The smug little anonymous retreat for four or
> five people, "Focus", had been swallowed up by "Trabuco College",
> which was capable of holding fifty. Already Felix was talking of a
> printing press to issue pamphlets, and was planning next year's semi-
> nars. For the present, Gerald went along with this, a little unwilling,
> but tremendously impressed and excited. It seemed to me that a
> new cult, Heardism, was being born, with Felix, a sunburnt and
> smiling Eminence, holding the real power behind the throne.

The result was a 'long, straggling building: a series of cloisters which
mounted, in flights of steps, the slope of a little hill', and 'the total effect
was beautiful.' As befitted southern California, the building was clad in
whitewashed adobe, with red tiles on the roof, an ecclesiastical dome,
and a central courtyard which contained a miniature orchard. There was
a dining room, a library, a store room, two patios, a large kitchen, and
an oratory set aside for non-denominational meditation; the bedrooms
faced onto the cloisters, with bathrooms in between. There was a pond
with goldfish, two green Chinese dragons stood guard, and oleanders,
pomegranates, oranges and scarlet zinnias made the garden a blaze of
colour. No radios or newspapers were allowed to pollute the atmosphere
with news of the world beyond: smoking was forbidden, vegetarianism
de rigueur, and whereas visitors were charged a modest fee, the full-time
inhabitants were not paid in any way. Not surprisingly, Isherwood 'could
never tire of being in it', though in due course he was to break Trabuco's
rule of chastity with Denny Fouts. The rules of the house were based
on those of the Benedictines: the inmates rose at 5.30 every morning and
meditated three times a day, and although Gregorian chants were sung
in the library before bedtime, they observed silence from before dinner
in the evening until after breakfast the following morning, and retired

to bed at nine. In a booklet designed to introduce Trabuco to the outside world, Heard, Isherwood and Felix announced that 'there are no "prophets" among us. We all start from the beginning, bringing nothing but our need for God and our trust in his grace.' Based on Huxley's notion of a 'perennial philosophy', Trabuco was dedicated to the search for God, and the discovery and exaltation of the elements common to all religions. Felix still felt homesick for England at times, but 'How few there are, how *very* few, who can still through God's grace remain aloof and thus prepare to be of greater use in the future,' he told Eva after a trip to New York, during the course of which he had paced the streets in an agony of indecision. In the end 'I came to the conclusion that to give way to my longing and homesickness would be an act of the utmost selfishness: my job is to stay here, with Gerald in California, and search human wisdom to see how these terrible things might be avoided in the future.' Far from being a retreat from the world, Trabuco was 'an advance post, a look-out'. Prayer, he told Eva, was 'the most difficult task that anybody can set their heart to accomplish: hard, painful, infinitely discouraging, and yet infinitely worthwhile. Beside it, every other activity seems like so much childish play-acting,' and 'to find that way, to find God, is the sole purpose of this human life.'

With the building completed, Felix helped to organise Trabuco's first seminar, attended by twenty-four 'learned' men, and 'Oh what a privilege it was to hear some of those present discuss and search aloud for the real meaning of life.' Aldous Huxley was among their number, and proved to be 'a wise, gentle, serene man – so touchingly considerate. He's always in the kitchen before meals to give me a hand – blindly (for his eyes are still very poor) he stumbles around and helps lay the table and peel the potatoes. What a change! No trace of the old arrogance or intellectual pride. Of all the people I know he is the source of my greatest encouragement.' While working in the kitchen one day, Huxley delivered a long lecture on gas and its influence on civilisation, at the end of which he turned to Felix and said, 'I suppose we'd better get on and do some cooking, but how do you light this thing?'

'I am not interested, really, in saving the world,' Felix told Sheila MacDonald. 'What I *am* trying to do, if needs be against the cynicism of the whole world, is to find a faith that can be pitted against the common despair: a belief – in God if you will – with which I can meet the stubborn unbelief of modern man.' In his diary he confessed that 'fortune combined with a streak of opportunism' had enabled him to lead a charmed life, but 'I have a haunting sense that one day I shall have

to answer for these wonderful years.' In August 1942, soon after the
Trabuco seminar, the war and the outside world intruded in the form
of a summons to appear before the Draft Board in New York. In a letter
to the Board, Felix assured them of his devotion and gratitude to the
United States, and that 'the least I can do is not in any way to hinder
her activities'. He decided against applying for conscientious objector
status, which would have involved his joining an 'alternative service'
camp, but to seek full exemption as a 'religious student'. Appearing before
the Board in New York in November, he was granted full exemption.
It made no sense, he was told, for him to register as a conscientious
objector – 'it's absurd for someone like you to have to go to camp to
sweep up leaves' – and he left 'in a kind of daze' after warm hand-
shakes all round. His case, he later discovered, had been referred to
Washington, as a result of which Trabuco itself was recognised as a bona
fide religious institution.

In January 1943, Felix crossed the Atlantic to find out how relief aid
provided by American Friends was being used by the Quakers in England.
He travelled in a Swedish cargo boat chartered to the US Navy: as the
slowest ship in the convoy, it occupied 'coffin corner' and was particularly vulnerable to U-boats, but nothing untoward occurred, and the time
was spent reading and playing chess. Safely on land, Felix appeared before
the Draft Board Appeals Court in Hampstead Town Hall, and was again
given an unconditional exemption from military service. He called on
Anthony Eden, the Foreign Secretary, and met the writer and pacifist
Vera Brittain, who was fiercely opposed to the saturation bombing of
German cities and had written a pamphlet on the subject entitled 'Seed
of Chaos'. She asked him to take it back to the States in the hope of
finding an American publisher, and he arranged for its eventual publication in Fellowship, a magazine edited by A. J. Muste, a Quaker pacifist
and civil liberties activist who, years later, became a leading opponent
of the Vietnam War. Vera Brittain noted in her diary that her article,
retitled 'Massacre by Bombing', had caused 'a real furore', so much so
that the New York Times had denounced her over three columns, and 'I
suspect this is actually the MS of 'Seed of Chaos' which Felix Greene
has now received and turned over as I suggested . . .'

Felix also paid a visit to Christopher Isherwood's mother, Kathleen, and
her half-mad son, Richard. 'The results were not satisfactory,' Isherwood
reported in his diary. 'He struck the wrong note. My mother was repelled,
in spite of herself, and therefore alarmed – wondering what kind of
bunch I had gotten myself mixed up with.' His duty done, Felix returned

to the States in style on board the *Queen Mary*, eating his meals in the officers' dining room and watching films in the evenings. After writing up his report for the Quakers, he made his way back to California.

During his absence in England, a new arrival had taken up residence in Trabuco. Elena Lindeman was a thirty-five year-old Mexican of German origin: she was extremely attractive, and before taking up teaching she had, with her two sisters, been a member of a singing trio called 'Las Cucherachas', performing in and around Los Angeles. Austere, gentle and serious-minded, she had left Palm Springs for Trabuco early in 1944, and was employed in the kitchen and the garden, as well as teaching the children who came to Trabuco for lessons. She was seeking self-fulfilment through the search for God, and was working her way through the reading matter recommended by Heard, who had gone to live in Trabuco full time in January 1943. It's not clear why Heard, who was shy with women and almost certainly regarded them as alien beings, had allowed her on the premises. He soon came to regret it, since Felix was all over the new arrival, and wouldn't take 'no' for an answer. Felix and Elena first met in the library, where she was reading: he bounded forward to introduce himself, and she was immediately struck by how English he looked in his smart shirt and high-cut trousers. He was 'absolutely fascinated, besotted, entranced' by her: he pursued her from room to room, and although she found him 'the most brazen man' she had ever met, and put up a fierce resistance, her defences soon began to crumble. 'He was very attractive to women,' she recalled. 'He had his way. He always has had.' In his letters to his mother, Felix waxed rhapsodic about his new conquest. She was a 'pure and lovely soul', radiating an 'inner calm' and an 'obvious purity' but 'too practical to have long slim hands'. Her pupils all loved her, and 'I always feel when I am with her that I am with someone who has the makings of a saint'. Nor were animals immune to her charms: 'Snakes will not attack or run away from her and often in the summer months she will quietly pick up a snake and let it wrap itself about her arm and she will gently stroke it, murmuring "You dear thing". I even saw her stroking a tarantula the other day,' he reported, adding that she had given him a wigging for killing some deadly black widow spiders.

Felix urged Elena to 'remember that God has given us this painful, wonderful love, in which there is no meanness, no littleness, no ugliness at all – only indescribable purity and loveliness – you and I, we are not of this world, quite – we belong to our own kingdom, which is somehow strangely apart.' Despite coming from a family 'in which non-conformity is the chief characteristic', his eldest sister, Ave, had married 'a man of limited outlook, of very restricted vision, who finds his chief security in life by believing what other people believe', but he and Elena were not in the business of living 'unlived lives'. 'Darling, we were not made for little lives, the half-efforts, the pretences, the mild respectabilities,' he insisted. 'Nothing but the noblest and the highest will ever satisfy your soul or mine.' Looking into the future, he worried in letters to Eva that 'she won't ever marry, for there is something in her that is quite solitary,' though 'of all the many women I have known, Elena will make the most beautiful and lovely of mothers . . . She is curiously like you in many little ways, which is why I love her.'

As it turned out, Elena and her future mother-in-law never got on, but of more immediate importance was the effect of their romance on the master of Trabuco. Heard, whose bedroom was bang next door to Felix's, was driven mad with jealousy and anger, clutching his head and striding wildly about the room when he learned that Elena – in all innocence, no doubt – had been spotted in Felix's room. He warned Felix that, as a Mexican, Elena would become extremely stout in middle age, told Elena that madness ran in the Greene family, and insisted that Felix should tell Elena about Peggy Bok and Betsy Barton – but all to no avail. 'That man will drive me insane,' he cried, before declaring that he would only stay on at Trabuco if the lovers departed forthwith. Despite his earlier infatuation with the man and the place, Felix was relieved to get away. Trabuco had been 'a much more morbid place than we can realise while we are there. Sick, a little unreal,' and 'a strange suffocation of the soul takes place there, unknown and almost undetectable.' As for Heard, 'he has no hold on me' and 'I am free of a strange and powerful domination that has lasted for years.' Heard eventually donated Trabuco to Swami Prabhavananda's Vedanta Society: in later years he became a pioneer of sixties counter-culture, taking a keen interest in flying saucers and the visionary power of LSD.

Quite what Felix should do next was undecided. He would like to write, since it would 'give me the independence and mobility, the freedom from meaningless routine and conformity to an office schedule and authority, and the range of interests that I really need'; on the other hand, he was thinking of training as a psychotherapist with a disciple of Jung named Fritz Kunkel, and he had become very taken with the thinking of the Indian sage Krishnamurti, who lived at Ojai, not far from Trabuco. A good-looking, charismatic figure with admiring disciples on both sides of the Atlantic, Krishnamurti had been acclaimed as a World Leader by

Annie Besant, the famous theosophist, as long ago as 1927: she had declared that the Divine Spirit had manifested itself in him and, egged on by Aldous Huxley, he had spent the war years writing his *Commentaries on Living*.

According to Felix, Huxley thought Krishnamurti 'the wisest and most enlightened man he had ever met' and, like many sages, he specialised in the long and meaningful silence. He had occasionally visited Trabuco, and even Heard had been impressed. Years later, Felix recalled how Krishnamurti had 'really shifted my thoughts and direction in life', and enabled him to 'see through mystical religion and all the hoo-ha about searching for God'. He was, he told Elena, learning so much from this 'lovable and strange Indian – how to *be*, how to escape from living on verbal levels and how to reach the deeper centres at which life becomes more vividly real . . . I have never met anyone who had a better balance of feeling and thought.' Felix and Elena decided to build themselves a house at Ojai to be near his new mentor. He designed the white adobe building with such success that it was featured in *Sunset* magazine, as a result of which Felix earned useful sums by designing similar houses for rich Americans; and, once again, he involved himself in every aspect of its construction while living in a tent alongside. He laid the drains, made bricks by hand, did the wiring and plumbing, and bought himself a second-hand concrete-mixer. Every now and then Krishnamurti would come to their tent, help them to cook, and sit in silence. 'He is aloof, gentle, quiet, authoritative; and when he slips quietly out of a group – even though he has said no word – everyone in that group feels that he has *lived* while Krishnamurti was among them,' Felix told Eva. He and Krishnamurti would sit for hours in companionable silence and if, at some point, Felix asked a question, the sage would ponder deeply and then 'his reply is always so simple, so true, so *apt*, that one feels that above and around the actual words there is a "field" of meaning.' Krishnamurti, he claimed, was not only teaching him 'how to *be*,' but also to 'become *aware*' and to 'take no authority but your own living experience, and to get back to that part of one that "is not educated or conditioned".' One evening the two men went to the cinema with Isherwood and Iris Tree, the daughter of Sir Herbert Beerbohm Tree, the Edwardian theatre manager; although the film in question was 'a devout attempt to portray a life of supreme holiness', Iris Tree walked out halfway through, while Isherwood ruined it all with his derisive remarks.

In February 1945 Elena finally agreed to marry Felix, and Aldous and Maria Huxley offered them their apartment in Los Angeles for their honeymoon. 'I didn't have a devoted husband. I had a man who had always been quite independent and wanted to be that way and stay that way,' Elena admitted years later, adding ruefully that 'I'd given up this, I'd given up that, for the wonderful occasion of marrying and giving my all, having my children and all of that. It didn't work out that way.' In the meantime, however, Felix told her that he intended to live 'a very simple and devout life of prayer and study, and raise our children. And one day, in some years time, I may be fit to deal helpfully with my fellow-men.' The time had come, he told Sheila MacDonald, for him to associate himself 'more closely again with people who are trying in outward ways to help the vast distress of the world', and Elena felt the same way: 'one of the most moving facts in the lives of even the great "contemplative" saints is the way they assiduously balanced their intense inner life of devotion with outer acts of love and charity for their fellows, and this is what I now intend to do.'

'I have an ever-deepening horror at what sheer naked violence is doing to the people of Europe, and an ever-growing sense of almost *personal* responsibility for it,' Felix informed Ben. 'I believe that anyone who points a finger at anyone else – Hitler, Chamberlain, the money magnates, Churchill – is really profoundly mistaken. They have missed the inner truth of this whole ghastly tragedy. We are *all* at fault, we are *all* guilty.' But for all the hand-wringing, he was unwilling to do more than pray. Eight years earlier, Gerald Heard had written to Dick Sheppard from North Carolina to say that he could do nothing for the Peace Pledge Union 'until I am far better myself', and that 'what is needed is not merely a political protest but another way of living,' and Felix was now taking a similar line. The Quakers in Philadelphia had asked him whether he would be prepared to do relief work on the Continent of Europe, very much as Ben had done after the First World War, but he found them 'lacking in humility and too buttoned-up'; and, he told Eva, 'I must go on working on my own sinful self before I can ever *dream* of working with the Quakers or the Germans or anyone else.' 'I need you to help me to grow,' he informed Elena: the misery and suffering reported from the countries recently occupied by the Germans were 'pitiful beyond words', but despite his organisational and practical competence, 'for the present we must face the fact that there is nothing we can give.' On a visit to Washington he met Tooter, who had spent the war working for the Ministry of Food, but although his brother talked of the possibility of mass starvation in Europe, and urged him to help out, 'I had to shake my head and tell him we were not yet ready to talk, because we were not yet living this truth.' Talking to Tooter 'brought home to me again the simply tremendous obligations we have on our shoulders, my darling. We *know*, we have been given the true message; the knowledge that God has given us through Gerald and through our life at Trabuco is what will bring life to thousands who are now suffering.'

Three months after his meeting with Tooter, Felix was still prevaricating. He was keen to help, but 'for the first few years it will be too mixed up with SHAEF and UNRRA and politics and strategy. So we can afford to wait a little. But sooner or later Elena and I will be over to do whatever we can to mitigate the appalling disaster we have inflicted upon the European people.' He never made it to Europe, but drew comfort from the fact that, as he told his mother, the Greenes were somehow both above the war and yet responsible for it. 'Our family in some wonderful and curious way – largely because of the way you brought us up, and the fact that we are of dual nationality – were able to transcend the violent national antagonisms of this war.' 'We *understood* Germany and Britain and the other nations, and to the extent that we understood them we did not judge them,' he told her. 'We saw that in the deepest sense we are *all* guilty.' With the war behind him, it was time to focus on other things.

Germany at War

'I have been through heaven and hell in my life, but I must say that I have never felt bored during the last years, and for that I thank God,' Barbara wrote to her sister Ave shortly after the war had ended. 'I used to pray as a girl that I might really *live* my life, experiencing every height and depth – and my prayers were certainly answered.' Whereas Felix had kept the war at arm's length, and made every excuse to avoid a devastated post-war Europe, his sister spent the war in Germany itself, and was so upset by the effect it had on children in particular, millions of whom had been bombed out of their homes, separated from their parents or become refugees, that she became a passionate supporter of many children's charities, both in Europe and in the wider world.

'Returning home after the trip, I resumed my cheerful life,' she wrote of her homecoming from Liberia. Although she liked to portray herself as a giddy London socialite, travelling through West Africa with Graham and writing a book about their adventures had made her more ambitious, more adventurous and, perhaps, a shade more serious-minded. Two years later, in the summer of 1937, she set off for Estonia in her Morris Minor with Tania Benckendorff, the daughter of Graham's friend Moura Budberg, to stay on the Benckendorff family estate. 'Barbara was always game for an adventure,' Tania Alexander, as she became, recalled in her memoirs. With Barbara at the wheel they made their way first to Berlin, where they stayed with Hugh. He had just been made the *Telegraph*'s chief correspondent in Berlin, 'and to celebrate his appointment we dined that night on a terrace, and every member of the party kept nervously looking over their shoulders, while talking in whispers and taking advantage of the fact that in the open air it was less dangerous to talk.' From Berlin they made their way east through Poland, Lithuania and Latvia, and Tania Alexander remembered 'the enormous relief of being able to talk freely with people after a week of the tense atmosphere we had experienced while travelling through Nazi Germany.' Estonia, Latvia and

Lithuania had all become independent states after the Russian Revolution, and Barbara recalled that the Benckendorffs' 'little house was crowded with Russian relatives and old governesses who had escaped from Petersburg and were living there penniless but still with great style, as if money did not matter. Conversation was carried on in five languages. There were books everywhere and vodka flowed like water. At night we wandered down to the lake, caught crayfish and sang Russian songs till the early morning.' In later years she looked back on her visit to Estonia as 'a kind of dream, perfect in itself and utterly remote from anything else that has happened in my life.'

Barbara was in Germany again that year, this time for the wedding in Hamburg of Fritz Schumacher, later to join the staff of David Astor's *Observer* and achieve fame as the author of *Small is Beautiful*. One of the other guests was Adam von Trott who, like Schumacher, had been a Rhodes Scholar at Oxford: he became a good friend of Barbara, and was eventually executed for his part in Claus von Stauffenberg's abortive attempt to assassinate Hitler on 20 July 1944. Most of those present were hostile to the regime, and Barbara noted how some, like Fritz Schumacher, had already decided to leave Germany and make new lives elsewhere, while others, including the Anglophile von Trott, with his influential connections in Britain and America, were prepared to stay on, in the vain hope that the regime might eventually be overthrown. A year later Barbara was in Berlin once more, staying with Hugh. Ben met her there after Kristallnacht, and 'she asked me not to see her again because my work for the Jewish refugees would cause her very considerable embarrassment', since 'if you are seen with Jews and things, it can be so terribly unpleasant', but there is no evidence of her having been remotely anti-semitic, then or at any other time.

While in Berlin, Barbara was introduced to Count Rudolf von Strachwitz. A member of an old Catholic family from Silesia, 'Rudi' was eleven years older than her; he had spent a term at an English public school before the First World War, and had been a diplomat since the early 1920s, serving in China, Japan and the United States. It was a lovely summer evening, and after dinner Barbara found herself walking with him in the Tiergarten. 'You two are going to get married one day,' a friend declared after seeing them together. Barbara was overcome with shyness and embarrassment, but her friend's intuition was spot-on: 'for the first time I had fallen completely and utterly in love.' Talk of marriage was soon in the air, although, as a civil servant, Rudi would need to obtain a marriage licence from his superiors in the Foreign Office – a regulation that pre-dated the Nazis and had been designed to obviate unsuitable alliances. Hugh, though well-disposed, took a sceptical view of it all. 'You're mad,' he told Barbara. 'Don't you know there might be a war at any time?' Despite Hugh's warning words, and an edict from Ribbentrop, the Foreign Minister, forbidding his civil servants from marrying foreigners, she longed to see more of her new admirer. Rudi was posted to Budapest, and although Hugh advised her against going, she joined him there for a weekend, and that winter she happily accepted an invitation to go skiing with Rudi and other members of his family

Back in London, 'I rather mooched around, getting on everybody's nerves.' Life was further complicated by the fact that she was semi-engaged to a brilliant young barrister called John Morris, who had taken silk in 1935, and would before long find himself as one of the judges who presided over the Appeals Committees set up to take evidence from those who, like Ben, had been interned under Regulation 18B. According to the *Dictionary of National Biography*, Morris was a 'tall, handsome man of great charm, a prodigious worker and a golden-voiced orator', noted for 'unfailing courtesy, instinctive kindness and an unsparing readiness to serve the public interest', but his virtues availed him nothing. Barbara felt overcome by gloom at the thought of having to marry him, quite apart from which 'I sometimes wondered how it was possible for such a very conventional man to fall in love with me.' He was, she had to admit, 'charming, kind, clever and obviously destined for a brilliant career – but he was not amusing, no *not* amusing, and I found it impossible to fall in love with him.' In August 1939 she set out for Germany again, and John Morris dutifully saw her on to the boat train. He never married, but years later, when he had become Baron Morris of Borth-y-Gest, and an Appeal judge, he would take her to tea in the House of Lords or dinner at the Athenaeum. 'What a nice man you are, but thank God I didn't marry you,' she would muse after the event. 'I would have died of boredom.'

She was met in Berlin by Rudi's sister: they drove to the Burgenland to stay with friends, and Rudi joined them from Budapest. War seemed unavoidable, but although Rudi had cold feet about Barbara's staying in Germany, she insisted on remaining where she was: 'I simply could not face the idea of waving good-bye again – probably for good, for war creates great barriers', and had she returned to England 'I would probably end by marrying poor old John, and feeling miserable for the rest of my life.' Her mother was staying with Sir Graham in Harston House, and Barbara rang to tell her that she would not be coming home. She had difficulty getting through, and the phone was eventually answered by a maid who told her that 'Mrs Greene is just changing for dinner. Please ring later' – the last spoken communication she had with any member of her family until the war was over. Barbara was staying with Louise Quadt, a friend of Marie Vassiltchikov, when war between Britain and Germany was declared on 3 September. They had been invited to dinner that evening, but Barbara said she would rather stay behind. Louise Quadt left her standing by a window of her ground-floor flat in Berlin, clutching the bars and staring ahead, and when she returned some four hours later, she was still standing by the window gazing out.

Determined, as always, to make the best of things, Barbara decided to find herself a job, and help was to hand in the improbable form of Hitler's interpreter. Five years earlier, in the aftermath of the Reichstag fire, the Nazis had tried to lend some kind of legitimacy or respectability to the trial of those accused of starting the fire by inviting some foreign lawyers to attend the proceedings. James Whitehead QC, a friend of Barbara's parents, had been among them, and on his return to England he declared that 'the only decent German he had met during his stay in Berlin' was Paul Schmidt, who had worked as an interpreter for the German Foreign Ministry since 1923 and would, as such, take part in Hitler's discussions in Munich with Neville Chamberlain, and remain in the job until 1945. The day after the outbreak of war, Guy Liddell of MI5 noted in his diary that Schmidt had been 'genuinely working for an eleventh-hour settlement behind the backs of his chiefs'. During the war he was to serve on the 'England Committee', other members of which included Roderich Dietze of the Reich Radio Service and a friend of William Joyce, and Erich Hezler, who had earlier liaised with Dr Rösel in London, and compiled a 'white list' of potential British collaborators. Schmidt was, in Marie Vassiltchikov's opinion, 'a nice and decent man': before the war he had been associated with the opposition to Hitler centred on Ernst von Weiszäcker, the head of the German Foreign Office, and he remained sympathetic to their aims. When James Whitehead's widow learned that Barbara had decided to remain in Germany, she made contact with Schmidt and asked him to look after her, and he was to prove a 'faithful and loyal friend'.

Schmidt found Barbara a job on *The Camp*, a newspaper which catered for British prisoners of war, who were thin on the ground in the early stages of the war but proliferated with the end of the Phoney War and the routing of the British Expeditionary Force, culminating in Dunkirk. The paper was supposed to show the regime in a sympathetic light, but Barbara and her colleague and close friend, Dusi Uxkull, a cousin of Claus von Stauffenberg, were left to their own devices. Their boss, a kindly character, soon fell for Dusi's 'youthful charms'; an official from the Ministry of Defence appeared once a week, and although he sometimes objected to what they had written and crossed it out, Dusi reinstated the offending material as soon as he had left the office. 'It was all very haphazard, and it became a kind of sport to see how far we could go,' Barbara later recalled. The Blitz began in September 1940, but although Barbara and Dusi were told to report German air raids over British cities, they did their best to avoid naming the towns and cities involved. 'German planes flew over England last week and some bombs were dropped at Random' passed without comment. Barbara interviewed P. G. Wodehouse, who was staying at the Adlon Hotel; she also found time to write two film scripts for her future brother-in-law, Arthur Strachwitz, neither of which was passed by the censors.

While America remained on the sidelines, Barbara could correspond freely with Felix, but after Pearl Harbor she was cut off completely from her family, though every now and then Adam von Trott would post letters for her from Switzerland. In October 1940 Felix told his mother that Barbara seemed well and happy, and that 'she does not seem to be blown about by circumstances as much as she seemed to be in the past.' 'I'm very impressed by the attitude of everyone towards me,' Barbara informed Felix. She had encountered no hostility towards the British, and 'everyone is trying to be as pleasant as possible'. Most of her friends spoke English, so she was making little progress with German – she had forgotten much of what she had learned as a child, and it remained erratic for the rest of her life – and although, as an enemy alien, she had to report to the police once a week, 'they could not have been more charming.'

All in all, she told Felix, 'I don't regret my decision to stay. I really had to be here. One day everything will turn out all right, and even if it doesn't I shall never regret this time. It's the point of my whole life. It's serious and deep and in these funny times it is the only thing that is quite real to me. The world is upside down, but I feel steadier in myself than I have ever done.' She had found herself, Felix reported, 'a very pleasant little flat, and even had a maid to help her look after it, and she was very busy with many poor English people who wanted special help or information.' Luise, the maid, was to stay with Barbara for the next thirty years: Barbara couldn't afford to pay her, but they shared Barbara's earnings, and when funds ran low they sold their cigarette coupons –

neither of them smoked – and Luise collected nettles in the Tiergarten to make into soup. 'I was never for one moment afraid,' Barbara later recalled, and 'being English made one quite sure that one was right under all circumstances, and – even in wartime – one was regarded by everyone as something special.' Hugh was by now running the German Service of the BBC, and although those caught listening to the BBC could face the death penalty, 'I loved hearing Hugh's voice even when he announced the Allied disasters before the tide turned.' Barbara 'never doubted that England would win the war. England always won wars. That is how we were brought up,' but German triumphalism in the early years was sometimes too much to be borne. Home on leave one weekend, Rudi took her with him to shoot on a family estate near Berlin. Recent German successes created a euphoric mood, to be celebrated with truffles and champagne brought back from France, which had recently been overrun. Barbara suddenly 'felt a complete stranger and utterly miserable'; after dinner she crept away to her room and wondered whether Schmidt could somehow arrange her return to England.

Rudi had been moved from Budapest to Barcelona. They were as keen as ever to get married – 'she thinks I may find him a trifle old-fashioned,' Felix informed his mother – and Barbara eased her loneliness and sense of isolation by joining the Catholic Church. She was received into the Church by Count Gustav von Preysing, the Bishop of Berlin, an opponent of the regime whom Goebbels once described as a 'clerical, un-German pig': one day, when she was in his palace to receive instruction from his chaplain, the Bishop took her to the window, pointed to a man lurking on the other side of the road, and told her that she was followed by a 'Spitzel' every time she came to see him. Nor was life on *The Camp* as easy-going as before. Germany was suffering its first reverses of the war on the eastern front, and the paper became a Nazi mouthpiece with no room for mild subversion. Schmidt advised her to resign, and found her a job working as a charwoman in a research institute in Berlin. She also gave English lessons to Dr Puhl, the vice-president of the Deutsche Bank: she worried at first that he might be spying on her, but learned later that he had been a friend of Hugh, and after the war was over she wrote testimonials for him and Paul Schmidt for use in denazification tribunals.

Years later, in an open letter to her son Rupert, Barbara said that although he had often asked her to write about her wartime experiences, she found it hard to do so. 'Part of the trouble is that there are so many people trying to justify themselves that one can hardly bear to hear those years mentioned. One longs to scream "But it wasn't like that at all!"'

she told him. 'I don't *think* we actually knew about the gas chambers, but we certainly knew about concentration camps, we knew of mass murders in Poland, and we had all heard of soldiers going mad because they had seen or had had to take part in the mass destruction of helpless old people, women, men and children in Russia. We saw the misery of the Jews and looked away as they shuffled miserably along with their yellow stars on their coats.' For all the kindness of individual Germans, she hated the regime, yet

the one time I had a chance to do something active, I didn't do it. In the cellar of the Victoria Luise Platz, to which we had to go during air raids, there was always a young man sitting alone reading a book. One night, to our surprise, he was wearing a yellow star on his coat, and it was whispered that he was a half-Jew. My heart, my conscience, told me to go and sit by him and talk to him. I didn't do it. I wasn't *afraid* to – that might have made it excusable – but partly my British upbringing of never making oneself conspicuous, partly a feeling that I might make things worse for him, and chiefly (I'm afraid) a kind of lethargy and indecision made me put off what I *knew* to be the right thing to do. Next time there was an air raid, he was no longer there. The chance had been missed forever and I knew then that I was no better than anyone else.

But occasional acts of defiance boosted the morale. She had to fill in a long form every time she reported to the police, and took to changing small details every time, so making it harder for the authorities to keep tabs on her. One day, in a friend's house, the porter arrived with a uniformed official, who shouted at Barbara, accusing her of making signals with a flashlight to RAF bombers. The friend interrupted his tirade to point out that this was no way to address a lady, to which he replied that there were no ladies in the Third Reich. 'How interesting,' replied the friend. 'I must tell Frau Goering next time I see her.' She had never met Frau Goering in her life, but the abuse came to a halt, and the officious porter and the man in uniform skulked uneasily away.

Rudi and Barbara were married at last in March 1943. Rudi had wangled a marriage licence by having himself temporarily seconded to another government department which did not forbid its officials from marrying foreigners, and they were wed with the minimum of fuss. The sister of their friend Axel von dem Bussche lent Barbara a wedding dress; Barbara wanted to put her profession as 'Putzfrau' or charwoman on the wedding certificate, but Rudi would have none of it. They took the train back to Berlin after the ceremony, arrived in the middle of a bombing raid, and spent their wedding night in the railway station. Rudi had never got on with Ribbentrop, who thought him politically unreliable, and very quickly found himself out of a job. They took rooms in Dahlem, a smart suburb of Berlin, where Rudi dug an air-raid shelter in the garden, and Barbara went back to work at the research institute. She became pregnant in due course, but had a miscarriage after her new boss, a deeply unpleasant man, had asked her to move all the books in the library from one wall to another, which involved carrying heavy weights, climbing up and down ladders, and stretching up to shelves that were almost out of reach. Rudi took her to hospital, but then had to leave for Silesia, and after taking six weeks' sick leave, Barbara decided not to return to work. In the late spring of 1944 she managed to send a message home via the Red Cross. 'How are you both and the children?' she asked Ave, then staying at Harston House. 'I have no baby yet, worse luck. Very sorry about it . . .'

One evening in Dahlem they received a message to the effect that they should leave all the lights off and the back door open, and in due course Bernd von Freytag-Loringhoven and another man turned up in the pouring rain. They were implicated in the 20 July plot to assassinate Hitler, led by Claus von Stauffenberg, and they told Rudi that his name had been taken off a list of people chosen for key positions in govern-ment after Hitler's assassination, since this would have exposed him to unnecessary danger, and that they would arrange for him to be drafted into the army to protect him, even though he was too old for military service. This, in effect, saved the lives of both Rudi and Barbara, since after his execution the amended list was found on the body of Carl Friedrich Goerdeler, a long-standing opponent of the regime who had been in regular contact with Vansittart before the war, enabling the Gestapo to round up almost all of those involved.

Although neither Rudi nor Barbara were directly involved in this or other plots to overthrow the regime, they knew many of those involved, and were broadly sympathetic to their aims. Rudi's cousin Hyazinth von Strachwitz had been marginally associated with various conspiracies, including an abortive plan, hatched by General Hubert Lanz, to kidnap the Führer on a visit to the Russian front. Rudi knew Rudolf von Scheliha, who had been so appalled by what he had seen when attached to the German Embassy in Warsaw that he had done his best to help Poles and Polish Jews. Scheliha was known to be one of the 'crew', and when the news came in that he had been arrested, tried and executed, Rudi 'went white with horror, and he never mentioned his name again, and nor did anyone else. Scheliha was simply wiped off the map' – a wise precaution, given the Gestapo's readiness to winkle out compromising connections, and act accordingly. (Years later, Scheliha's biographer discovered that, since 1941, Rudi had been on Ribbentrop's 'black list' of diplomats to be removed from the service.) Von Trott was a friend, as were the Uxkulls, the Schulenbergs, Marie Vassiltchikov and Axel von dem Bussche, a veteran of the fighting in France and Poland and, at the age of twenty-two, a holder of the Iron Cross. A lifelong friend of Barbara, von dem Bussche remembered meeting her for the first time, 'an incredibly beautiful girl in a black velvet thing, alone on a carpet, unattached.' He had joined the resistance after witnessing the massacre of 5000 Jews by the SS in Dubno, in eastern Poland, and in November 1943 he volunteered to become, in effect, a suicide bomber. As well as being a war hero, von dem Bussche was tall, blond and good-looking, the quintessential Aryan, and as such he was chosen to model a new army winter overcoat in Hitler's redoubt, the Wolf's Lair: he planned to carry a bomb in his pocket, seize the Führer in a tight embrace, and blow them both to smithereens. By a sad irony, the RAF bombed the truck that was carrying the new uniforms, and the fashion show had to be postponed. Von dem Bussche was posted to Russia, where he was seriously wounded, losing a leg. Others involved in the opposition to Hitler – and losing their lives as a result – included Raymond's former acquaintance, Albrecht Haushofer, and the genial Count Bernstorff, a friend and patron of Adam von Trott: Trott's biographer, Christopher Sykes, recalled how, as a Counsellor at the German Embassy in London until his recall in 1933, Bernstorff made no secret of his contempt for the Nazis, voicing his views to all and sundry in the Savoy Grill.

Many years later, Barbara wrote to Graham to thank him for sending her a copy of a speech he had given on 'The Virtue of Disloyalty'. 'It seemed to speak to me directly' she told him, 'as I have sometimes had to face the cold loneliness of the question concerning loyalty and disloyalty.' Only recently she had been discussing the war with two friends from wartime Berlin, 'one whose husband (who actually saved Rudi's life) was hanged after the 20th July attempt on Hitler's life, and one whose father was.' She had come to realise she only wanted to talk about those days 'with people who lived through them because no one else can possibly understand all the complications (which seem so strangely clear to other people *later*) and one only finds the picture becoming distorted. We talked and talked and our conversation turned to this question of loyalty and the difficulties of knowing the right road at the *time.*'

Rudi was enlisted in the Wehrmacht, and Barbara dutifully followed him as he was shunted from one posting to another. For the next few months she was to lead a peripatetic life, travelling the length and breadth of Germany. They were in Frankfurt an der Oder, by the former Polish border, when they learned of the abortive 20 July plot. At one stage Barbara found herself booking into what turned out to be a brothel, and had to jam a chest-of-drawers against the door of her room to keep customers at bay. She fell desperately ill, and underwent an agonising operation in Breslau at a time when medicine and painkillers were reserved for the armed forces. She remembered, years later, travelling in a cattle truck with Rudi: Russian guns were sounding in the distance, a woman had to leave her dead baby in the snow, and they were served a thin but warming goulash in the railway station where Rudi had to leave her. As Germany collapsed before the Allied advance, her life became increasingly chaotic. She spotted a group of Indian nationalists who had volunteered to fight against the British, looking cold and frightened and clutching umbrellas. She stayed in an inn, where there was a huge swastika painted on the ceiling of her room, and was told by the landlady next morning that she would have to leave at once as the Americans were advancing in their direction. She overheard a couple with an expensive-looking car say that they were making for Switzerland, and wondered whether she should ask them for a lift. Somehow she managed to ring Rudi for advice, and he told her to go with them, but only if they looked respectable – the last words she heard from him for the next two years. The man was a Belgian collaborator on the run, the woman his German girlfriend, and the boot of their car was crammed with black-market coffee, ham and sausages, which they used to barter for rooms in which to stay the night. They slept by day, all in the same room, and drove by night. Allied aircraft were bombing and machine-gunning traffic, so they drove without headlights, and dived into a ditch when a fighter buzzed low overhead. Barbara left her companions at Lindau. It was snowing and bitterly cold, and the little town was swarming with refugees. She took shelter in the porch of a church, and decided to ask the first person she met to give her a room for the night. A young woman appeared, but no sooner had she agreed to Barbara's request than the Belgian and his paramour resurfaced, and the three of them camped out on a sitting-room floor.

Rudi's youngest brother was married to the sister of the ruling Prince of Liechtenstein, Francis Joseph II. Wedged between Austria and Switzerland, the tiny principality had remained neutral throughout the war, and it had been agreed that should Rudi and Barbara be separated, they would make their way to Liechtenstein, in the hope of being reunited there. Somehow Barbara managed to squeeze onto an overcrowded train that was making its way to Feldkirch, just over the border from Austria. After asking her whether she was English, a young man in the train corridor told her that he knew the Liechtensteins, and volunteered to show her the way to where they lived, Schloss Amberg, and carry her suitcase up the hill. He gave a great shout as they arrived in the courtyard, and one of the Liechtenstein brothers opened a window, and hurried down to let them in. Barbara's adventures were over, but it turned out that she had had another narrow escape, since the young man who had carried her suitcase was a notorious flirt.

'One cannot believe that one is in the middle of a war-wracked Europe,' Barbara wrote to Ave from the Wald Hotel in Vaduz. Liechtenstein seemed like a land of plenty; she was learning to type and to cook, giving English lessons, and going for long walks in the hills. But she had no news of Rudi, and 'Perhaps Mama told you that I lost the baby I was expecting when we were fleeing. That was the second time it went wrong. So it is very unlikely, also because of my age, that I will have any children now. I was hopelessly upset at first, but there is nothing to be done. But because of that I have developed an enormous interest in my nephews and nieces.' She longed for news of Ave and her family, 'but I know what a bad letter writer you are.' Arthur Strachwitz told Felix that she was short of money, so he cabled her $250. 'Do not worry about me,' she told him. 'I am sitting on the top of a mountain getting brown in the sun.' But she often felt homesick, and 'sometimes I feel a bit old and my hair is beginning to go grey. I have lived through twenty novels.'

In October Barbara learned that Rudi was in a prisoner-of-war camp near Paris. She worried that he might be there for months or even years, but eventually he was released and made his way to Liechtenstein. Barbara had already started work on her second book, *Valley of Peace: The Story of Liechtenstein*, written in gratitude to the country that had given them refuge, and Rudi took the photographs. Their first child, Rupert, was born in Lucerne, over the border in Switzerland: life was returning to normal at last.

Stitch-Up

Little did she know it, but Barbara inadvertently contributed to Ben's woes after he had been detained under the provisions of Regulation 18B. The Home Secretary, Sir John Anderson, had been granted arbitrary powers to detain without trial those suspected of being over-sympathetic to the German cause or a danger to national security, without having to specify actual wrong-doing, and without those detained being given the details of any charges made against them. Ben was told that he had been held on the grounds of 'hostile associations', or having dealings with people who might in some way prove to be a security risk, and when in due course the authorities were persuaded to revise their 'Reasons for Order' and make them more specific, he learned that these included the fact that 'you were born of a German mother, and your sister has remained in Germany since the outbreak of the war, either being married or engaged to a German official, who either is or has been working for the Germans.'

Tooter was also regarded with suspicion, by MI5 at least, but unlike his mother or Barbara he was in a position to help. Leslie rang him as soon as she learned that her husband had been taken to Brixton, and he hurried round to find out what was going on. Ben was in a state of shock – asked to call at Scotland Yard on the night of 23 May, he had promptly been arrested – and had no idea why he was being held, or what the charges were against him. 'Conditions were appalling,' Tooter recalled. 'We were all ushered into one room. Ben sat at one side of the table; I on the other. There were hysterical women on the right and left of me; everyone shouting and screaming.' Since the 18B detainees were being held for custodial rather than punitive purposes – none of them had been charged with actual crimes – they were separated from other prisoners, and were, in theory, better treated: they were allowed to wear their own clothes, have food and drink sent in from outside, receive weekly visits and mix freely with their fellow-internees. But life inside was pretty grim, as were Ben's immediate prospects. After leaving the prison Tooter went to see Joynson-Hicks, the Greenes' family solicitors, but they claimed this was well outside their area of expertise, and declined to help. As it turned out, Tooter not only obtained help from a solicitor with the necessary bravado, persistence and ingenuity, but was himself to play a vital role in securing his brother's release; and between them they unravelled an extraordinary story which involved MI5 and agents provocateurs, and revealed the tensions that invariably exist between the demands of national security and those of individual liberty.

According to Jenifer Fischer-Williams, later to become an Oxford don and the wife of Herbert Hart, the Professor of Jurisprudence, Anderson had 'directed his mind to Greene's case personally'. Ben and John Beckett could have been interned as members of the BPP, but there was enough other evidence against both men to justify their detention. Fischer-Williams was to have a ringside view of Ben's travails: at the time of his detention she was working for Sir Alexander Maxwell, the Permanent Under-Secretary of State at the Home Office, who was closely involved with the fate of 18B internees, and in due course she moved from there to become the Secretary to the Advisory Committee headed by Sir Norman Birkett, which eventually recommended Ben's release. The Home Office files confirm her view that Anderson had been keeping an eye on Ben and his activities: 'Sir John knew all about him, and had quite enough against him to make an order without the allegation about contact with persons believed to be German agents.' But, according to Guy Liddell, who headed MI5's counter-espionage division, the Home Secretary 'seemed to have a great aversion to locking up a British citizen unless he had a very cast-iron case against him', and even expressed reservations about interning Mosley and members of the British Union of Fascists on the grounds that he did not believe they would actively help the German cause, while Alexander Maxwell 'believed fervently that the Home Office had a duty . . . not just to administer "Law and Order" but also to safeguard liberty'. The more liberal views of the Home Office – and, indeed, of those like Birkett and John Morris who served on the Advisory Committees set up to hear and investigate the cases of those interned – ran counter to the beliefs and the methods employed by the security services: for Liddell and his colleagues in MI5, 'the liberty of the subject and freedom of speech were all very well in peacetime but they were no good in fighting the Nazis.' As Ben would discover, the ends justified the means for the men and women of MI5.

'Intelligence organisations attract peculiar and unreliable people,' an expert on the subject once declared: and none was stranger than Ben's nemesis, Maxwell Knight of MI5, who had been recruited by the Director-General, Vernon Kell, in 1925, and worked under Guy Liddell in B division. A jazz drummer and clarinettist who had fought in World War I and smoked cigarettes through a long black holder, he was a crack shot, a busy socialite and a passionate animal-lover whose domestic menagerie included parrots, monkeys, snakes and, for a time, a bear which walked behind him on a lead. His three marriages were unhappy and, most probably, unconsummated; he disliked Jews and homosexuals, but was almost certainly homosexual himself; he wrote thrillers and, as a follower of the occult, admired Aleister Crowley and was a close friend of the novelist Dennis Wheatley. It was later claimed that Ian Fleming's 'M' was based in part on Maxwell Knight. His own political bias was to the right – in 1923 he had joined the British Fascisti, renamed the British Fascists Ltd the following year – but, as an expert in counter-intelligence and counter-espionage, his remit was to infiltrate extremist groups from both ends of the political spectrum. His agents and informers included Tom Driberg, whom he used to great effect to infiltrate the Communist Party of Great Britain, and John Beckett's former colleague William Joyce: it is generally assumed that Maxwell Knight alerted Joyce to his likely arrest only days before the outbreak of war, so enabling him to make his way to Berlin and resurface as 'Lord Haw-Haw'. In 1937 Kell authorised Knight to move his top-secret section B5(b) to Dolphin Square, where he had a flat, and from where he could keep an eye on Herr Rösel's Anglo-German Information Service. Geographical separation from his colleagues in MI5 encouraged operational independence, and still more so when, after the outbreak of war, Kell moved the main MI5 offices from Millbank to Wormwood Scrubs. Little money had been spent on MI5 between the wars, and although Kell's power was based on his archive, staff shortages made it hard, if not impossible, to check the vast mass of material that had been amassed, much of it by low-grade ex-army officers.

Maxwell Knight liked to employ women as agents, particularly if they were young and attractive, and able to charm or entice information from drunk or indiscreet sources by the calculated deployment of 'a little sympathy'. It was important, he once wrote, not to employ 'a woman agent who suffers from an overdose of Sex', since 'I am convinced that more information has been obtained by women agents by keeping out of the arms of the man than was ever obtained by sinking too willingly into them.' Some of his female agents were home-grown, like Joan Miller, who infiltrated Captain Ramsay's Right Club and helped to expose the activities of Anna Volkoff and Tyler Kent; others were foreign, like the Austrian-born Friedl Gärtner. Her sister, Lisel, had settled in London in the late thirties, posing in a pink diaphanous body-stocking at the London Casino before going on to marry Ian Menzies, the brother of Sir Stuart Menzies, the head of MI6. Friedl had been enlisted by the Abwehr before coming to England. She soon attracted the attention of Maxwell Knight, who used her to report on the activities of German nationals and right-wing groups, and also persuaded Dennis Wheatley to employ her as a research assistant, in which capacity she provided him with information about Nazi leaders for his Gregory Sallust novels. Working under the code name 'Gelatine', she became a successful double-agent, working for the top-secret 'XX Committee' run by J. C. Masterman and 'Tar' Robertson, and a colleague and lover of the Yugoslav 'Dusko' Popov, the most glamorous double-agent of the war.

In the meantime she found herself working with another German national, but since he was homosexual no romantic interest was involved. The grandson of a Yorkshire baronet, Harald Kurtz had come to England in 1937 while studying at Geneva University. His father, a publisher, supported the regime in Germany, as did his brothers, but according to Joan Miller young Harald had refused to join the Hitler Youth. After his arrival in England he worked as a bookseller and for Lord Noel-Buxton, a Labour politician and philanthropist who favoured a negotiated peace with Hitler, before meeting Maxwell Knight, who enlisted him as an agent provocateur. A large, fleshy figure with a scholarly bent, Kurtz liked his food and drink, smoked like a chimney and, being hopeless with money, was forever sponging off acquaintances. After the mass intern-ment of enemy aliens early in the war, Knight used him as a stool pigeon in various internment camps, posing as an unregenerate Nazi and winkling out useful information from the inmates. As Ben eventually discovered, both Kurtz and Friedl Gärtner played crucial roles in the events leading up to his arrest and internment.

Detention orders under Regulation 18B were made by the Home Office on the recommendation of MI5, and despite the more liberal views of Maxwell and his colleagues, who suspected the security services of exaggerating the dangers posed by members of the Nordic League or the White Knights of Britain, they had to rely on highly confidential information gathered by MI5. After their arrest, detainees were given a written 'Reasons for Order' indicating the 'grounds' or 'particulars' for their detention: and since neither the Home Office nor the Advisory

Committees were allowed free access to MI5 files or agents, MI5 effectively controlled how much – or how little – detainees were told. Ben had been detained on the basis of 'hostile associations', whereas Beckett faced the more serious charge of 'acts prejudicial' to national security: in due course Ben's lawyer would make good use of a bureaucratic blunder which resulted in his being erroneously accused of 'acts prejudicial'. For the time being, though, MI5 held all the cards, and since their activities were shielded from scrutiny they were not above using blackmail and false evidence against those whom they rightly or wrongly considered a threat to national security at a time when much of Continental Europe had been overrun by the Germans, and Britain stood alone.

Ben's membership of the BPP and the BCCSE had, of course, been noted by MI5, but so too had his involvement with and concern for German-speaking refugees, and Maxwell Knight exploited this to inveigle from him self-incriminating indiscretions which could then be used against him. One evening in the early months of the war Ben parked his car in Berkeley Square and walked towards Piccadilly to visit an all-night café. Just as he was about to go into the café he noticed a woman trying to attract his attention. She was still there when he came out, and spoke to him in German. She told him she had recognised him at once by his height, and that she had seen him in Amsterdam, where she had worked for a refugee organisation, and again in a refugee reception camp in Felixstowe which Ben had visited during his attempts to help German Jews after Kristallnacht. When Ben asked her what she was doing on the streets, she shrugged her shoulders and asked what else she could do: there was no way he could help her, and she had only spoken to him in order to warn him. 'I didn't know German well enough to know what she was warning me against,' Ben wrote in his account of their meeting: which seems odd in itself, since German had been his first language, and he must have made good use of it on his political and philanthropic missions to Germany before the war.

Ben forgot all about their encounter until he was rung in his office by a Mr Pope, who said that he worked in the aliens department of the Home Office, wanted to learn more about the report Ben had made to Sir Samuel Hoare after Kristallnacht, and wondered whether it would it be possible for them to meet at his home in Mill Hill later that evening. Ben told him that he would be in London that day, and since Mill Hill was on the way back to Berkhamsted, they agreed to meet outside Burnt Oak tube station at 11.30 p.m. Soon after Ben arrived, he was approached by a woman who introduced herself as Mrs Pope: she explained that her husband had been delayed, and had asked her to look after Ben in the meantime. 'The lady was charming – too charming, and very much made-up,' Ben recalled, adding that 'I find make-up on the whole repellent, and my suspicions were very much aroused.' Drinks and sandwiches were served by a maid, but there was still no sign of Mr Pope. Ben said he could wait no longer, at which Mrs Pope, ignoring Maxwell Knight's advice about employing sympathy rather than sex, 'suddenly turned all winsome, invited me to have some fun with her and even to get her into bed'. Ben 'managed to shake her off' and, after collecting his coat, prepared to drive home, only to find that two of his tyres had been let down. Heading back into the house, 'I could see the lady reflected in a mirror above the fireplace, and from her expressions I could see that she knew I would be back.' To her irritation, Ben insisted on ringing the AA, after which he sat down to wait, though he very sensibly 'kept [his] overcoat on'. The lady of the house disappeared in high dudgeon when Ben heard scuffling sounds outside the front door, which was opened to reveal two men and a police officer. Mr Pope's name was unknown to them, and looking out of the window Ben glimpsed his would-be seducer climbing into a car and being driven away.

Such crude attempts at blackmail were of no avail, but in March 1940 Ben received a letter from Harald Kurtz asking if they could meet. Kurtz introduced himself as a childhood friend of Ilse von Binzer, who had worked for Dr Rösel at the Anglo-German Information Service: MI5 had told him that they were keeping a watch on Ben, and suggested that Ilse might provide a useful introduction. This was, as it turned out, a shrewd move: she had been upset by Rösel's expulsion and had written to Ben about it; he felt bad about not having found the time to reply, and wanted to know what had happened to her. Kurtz added that he had attended a meeting in Central Hall, Westminster, in February 1939, during the course of which Ben had attacked the main speaker, Emil Ludwig, a popular biographer and an opponent of the Nazis ('I have never heard such terrible stuff,' Ben had told Harry Bohle afterwards). Rather reluctantly, Ben agreed to go round to Kurtz's digs in Ebury Street, which were more comfortable than he had expected, with ample supplies of wine and spirits. Kurtz told him that Ilse von Binzer had gone back to Stuttgart before the outbreak of war: what he didn't reveal was that – or so he claimed in a later statement prepared for MI5 – before she left she had urged him to get in touch with Ben as a 'great personal friend of Dr Rösel', and 'a man of definitely pro-Nazi views'. MI5 had instructed

Kurtz to express similar views when talking to Ben. Ben was puzzled by Kurtz, since he didn't conform to the pattern of the refugees he came across, almost all of whom loathed the regime in Germany. Kurtz told him that although he had never been a Party member, he was well-disposed to certain aspects of the regime, and was keen to do all he could to bring the war to an end. Ben found it hard to reconcile Kurtz's views with his claim that he had recently been released from an internment camp on the Isle of Man, and reclassified as a friendly alien. When Kurtz explained that he was keen to help the work of the BPP, Ben told him that he had broken off all contact with the party, but gave him their address.

Ben felt uneasy about Kurtz, and had no desire to see him again, but finally relented after his secretary had been deluged with imploring phone calls. Once again, they met in Kurtz's rooms in Ebury Street, and Ben later remembered how, early on in the proceedings, his host went into the next room and fiddled with something on the wall. Kurtz told him that a refugee friend of his was in real distress, and wondered whether Ben could help her. Ben explained that he was extremely busy at work and that since the outbreak of war he had devoted less of his time to refugees and their problems, and suggested that Kurtz should approach the Society of Friends instead. A third meeting took place, again in Ebury Street, at which Ben was introduced to Kurtz's distressed refugee, Friedl Gärtner. She explained that she was desperate to get a message through to her fiancé in Austria, and wondered whether Ben could help in any way, perhaps through Barbara, or a friend who worked for Reuters in Switzerland. Kind and well-disposed as ever, Ben pointed out that it would be extremely difficult to get past the censors in both Britain and Germany but, according to Kurtz, he suggested communicating with Germany through the Irish Free State, and recommended particular roads across the border from Northern Ireland. According to Kurtz, Ben went on to say that although he had no desire to see Britain under foreign rule, he had no doubt that Germany would win the war, and that there were people in Britain 'trained in and filled with the proper spirit of National Socialism – a British National Socialism' who were ready to take power, and would disassociate themselves from open political activity in order to build up an underground movement 'in readiness for the right moment', and that their supporters included members of the Royal Family. In a separate statement to MI5, Friedl Gärtner described Ben as being 'definitely defeatist' about the war and a 'strong believer in National Socialism', albeit one who could not support everything Hitler had done, especially with regard to the Jews. 'If this sudden desire of mine to set up a Nazi state in Great Britain is based upon a statement by Kurtz, then I must point out, in fairness to him, that I may have expressed admiration for certain aspects of the Nazi system in my endeavour to extract from him where he, a German refugee, just released from detention, stood,' Ben later declared. In the meantime, he felt more uneasy than ever about Kurtz and Gärtner, and decided that, as a JP, it was his duty to report his conversations to the authorities. He rang Scotland Yard, and was told to learn more and report back to them.

Ben's final meeting with Kurtz and Gärtner took place towards the end of April 1940. They attended a meeting in Holborn Hall, and had dinner afterwards. Ben invited them both to visit him in Berkhamsted, but later cancelled the invitation on the honourable grounds that he was 'not out to act as host to people I had reported to the police'. According to MI5, Ben told them that German soldiers would be marching through London within the year, and suggested – apropos contacting Germany – that they should speak to his sister Katharine, who was still working for John Beckett. Kurtz claimed that Katharine had visited him in Ebury Street, and spoke warmly about Lord Haw-Haw's broadcasts – no great sin in itself, since many patriotic Britons regularly tuned in, half-fascinated and half-amused by his strangulated upper-class accent and nasal delivery. Ben mentioned that he had recently spotted a member of the SA at large in London – he remembered him from his time in the Saar – and spoke of his friend Meyrick Booth, whose benign demeanour concealed a keen admiration of Hitler and his works.

A month later, on 23 May, Ben was in Leicestershire on business when he heard on the news that Mosley, Captain Ramsay and other right-wing activists had been arrested. He rang home, and Leslie told him that Beckett had also been arrested, and that Scotland Yard was anxious to talk to him. Assuming that the police wanted to follow up his earlier report about Kurtz and Friedl Gärtner, Ben rang Scotland Yard, and asked if he could call in there the following day. They insisted that he should come at once, so he hurried back to London and reported to the Yard at 11.45 p.m. Far from finding himself a welcome visitor, with useful news to impart, Ben was told that a detention order had been issued against him, and he was bundled off to Brixton. Scotland Yard later denied having any record of Ben's phone call about the suspicious activities of Kurtz and Gärtner, but Maxwell Knight may well have persuaded them to forget all about it.

'At least it's better than St John's,' Ben once remarked of his accommodation in Brixton – 'St John's' being Uncle Charlie's old house at Berkhamsted – but prison life was hardly luxurious. His cell was extremely draughty, aggravating his sciatica and lumbago, and his narrow bunk was so much too short that it had to be extended with a pile of bricks, which was prone to collapse in an air raid. His daughter Anne remembers making an unannounced visit: he was unshaven and clad in a blue fisherman's jersey, and he told her how he had unintentionally kicked the prison doctor across the room after suddenly straightening his leg to cope with an agonising twinge of sciatica. After his daughters' last visit they found the conditions 'so foul' that, according to Margaret, 'we were both in tears and I vowed at the time that I would *never* go there again.' Food could be brought in from outside, but warders had to be bribed: Tooter, who came for half an hour every week, bearing dried fruit or chocolate, reckoned that every visit cost him £2 in bribes. Ben was starting work on his book about the British Constitution, designed to show how factionalism and party politics had corrupted the spirit of the Magna Carta and eroded the liberties of the average man, and he presented Tooter with a reading list of books he needed: he became very agitated if these weren't provided, leading Tooter to brand him a 'difficult patient'. But for all that Ben was popular with staff and inmates alike. He may have been irritated by the 'general rowdiness' of the younger detainees, but his friend T. C. P. Catchpool, who had been interned as a pacifist in the First World War, and had run the Quakers' office in Berlin for much of the previous decade, remembered visiting Ben in 'a small bright room overlooking a garden', and being told by a warder that 'Greene is a good lad, and not troublesome like some of them are.' Among his fellow-detainees, Ben disliked Oswald Mosley, but got on well with Admiral Domvile, George Pitt-Rivers and Captain Ramsay: they often met to discuss the state of the world, and Ben claimed to be the only left-winger among them. Captain Ramsay, whose mind was still aflame with lurid fantasies about Judaeo-Bolshevik conspiracies, was an Old Etonian, and urged Ben to put his son Paul down for the school as soon as possible. Uncle Graham's influence was enlisted, and after consulting the Master of Magdalene, Cambridge, he suggested to Leslie Greene that she should write to various Eton housemasters, but to 'be careful not to mention the fact of Ben's detention. That would be fatal.' When not being kept waiting in freezing conditions to see the hospital doctor, Ben worried about Kepston, which was being run in his absence by two girls and a retired colonel.

Soon after his arrival in Brixton, Ben was told by the Governor that

he could appeal to an Advisory Committee, and that he had to hand in
his appeal within the next three days. This was no easy matter: he had
no copy of the detention order, and he was unaware of the exact reasons
for his detention. He was not allowed legal representation at this stage,
though lawyers could help detainees to prepare their cases, and were
sometimes allowed to appear before the Committee themselves. MI5
agents, on whose testimony the charges so often relied, seldom appeared
before the Committee, though they occasionally gave evidence from
behind a screen. After interrogating a detainee, the Advisory Committee
would prepare a report and submit its recommendations to the Home
Office for its decision, but hearings and verdicts were often subject to
frustrating delays. Ben was given a sheet of foolscap paper, but there
were only two pens and two inkpots for sixty prisoners. Eventually an
'officer took me down into the cell used by prisoners for shaving and I
had to address my appeal there and then under impatient threats from
the officer that he could not wait', and, of course, 'I had to address my
appeal to the Advisory Committee in ignorance of what I was appealing
about.'

Once Ben had handed in his appeal, he was given a copy of the 'Reasons
for Order', from which he learned that he had been detained on the
following grounds: as a member of the BPP and the BCCSE, he had
claimed that the war was being waged solely on behalf of financial interests, urged a negotiated peace, described British policy as one of 'bluff
and treachery', and justified Hitler's invasion of Poland; he had been
privy to John Beckett's pro-German propaganda in his 'Headline News
Letter'; before the war he had been in touch with figures close to the
German Government; since the outbreak of war he had been complicit
in sending messages to Germany through illicit channels, as well as asso-
ciating with German agents and helping them to avoid detention, and
he had expressed himself as being 'desirous of the establishment of a
National Socialist regime in Great Britain, with the assistance if necessary of German armed forces.' The supporting 'Statement of the Case'
listed Ben's pre-war contacts with Felix's friend Herr Bennemann and an
official called Hoffmann in Goebbels's Propaganda Ministry; Ben's dealings with Harry Bohle on behalf of his Peace and Progress Information
Bureau; his newsletters, including one in which he had referred to the
mistreatment by British police of Arabs in Palestine, and his recommendation of Beckett's wife Anne as a typist for Bohle. Reference was
made to speeches made by Ben since the outbreak of war, and to the
evidence gleaned by Kurtz and Friedl Gärtner: the Committee was keen

to interview them both, but MI5 refused, and written statements were provided instead.

Ben eventually appeared before the Advisory Committee in Burlington Gardens on 24 July 1940. He claimed that he was given no advance notice of this, and that he was summoned before the Committee unshaven and without having had any breakfast, was seated in the middle of a darkened room facing the members of the Committee, and given a lunch of dry bread and corned beef. The first day was given over to Ben's prewar activities, and the second to the charges of treachery. The detailed questions about his political activities made Ben wonder whether he had not, in fact, been under surveillance for years. The Committee was unimpressed by his failure to remember what he had or had not said in speeches made since the outbreak of war; they accepted MI5 statements as being 'substantially accurate', and seemed convinced that although Ben would not have helped German forces in the event of an invasion, he expected them to win the war and 'intended and planned to take advantage of the situation which would then arise. Greene hoped and believed that he might then find his opportunity to secure a position of influence for himself and so further his own peculiar political and religious views.' 'I felt very dissatisfied with the whole procedure and my weak position,' Ben wrote after the event. 'The total absence of legal assistance, the total absence of evidence, documents or anything in the nature of proof. I felt that the confiscation of my notes was most unfair.' The Committee was not prepared to accept his assurances about his behaviour were he to be released, and recommended his continued detention, for 'it was quite clear that the Committee had not accepted my explanations and they had made it clear that they did not believe in my truthfulness', and 'I thought it best to work on my theory that Kurtz to save his own skin had denounced me to the police . . .'

But Ben would not be friendless for much longer, and his suspicions about Kurtz would soon be vindicated. Tooter had proved a pillar of strength for Ben's family and business, helping to run Kepston in his spare time and sometimes commuting to his office in London from Berkhamsted. Active as ever on his brother's behalf, he had got in touch with Oswald Hickson, a solicitor who already represented the Mosleys and Captain Ramsay, and was regarded as an infernal nuisance by the authorities. 'He reminded me of a character out of Dickens: big fellow, huge fellow, hair standing all on end,' Ben recalled. Tooter told this reincarnation of Mr Jaggers that Ben had made 'some rather foolish statements'. 'All right, I'll see what I can do,' Hickson replied before roaring into action. He wrote at once to the Home Office, demanding to know on what grounds Ben had been detained, and as soon as he received an answer he summoned Tooter to his office in Covent Garden. Tooter was 'horror-struck' and wanted to know why Ben hadn't been charged under criminal law and put on trial at the Old Bailey. 'Exactly; that is my opinion too,' Oswald answered. 'Now if you agree and Ben agrees, I will write to the Public Prosecutor and demand an immediate trial.' Nothing happened. 'All right, something smells,' Oswald announced. 'We will get down to this.' He wrote again to the DPP to say that Ben wanted to stand trial for trying to make contact with Germans associated with the Nazi regime, for trying to send illicit messages, for wanting to establish a National Socialist regime, and for trying to help Germans avoid detention: would they kindly prosecute his client?

Still nothing happened, so Oswald tried a different tack and applied to the Divisional Court for a grant of Habeas Corpus, a move which reflected Ben's own obsession with the gradual infringement of English liberties. Ben's appearance in court – he dispensed with counsel, and argued his own case – proved acutely embarrassing to the Home Office. To begin with, he pointed out that the 'Reasons for Order' had wrongly accused him of 'acts prejudicial' rather than 'hostile associations', a legal point which Hickson exploited to the full. MI5 put pressure on the Home Office not to disclose the names of their agents in open court, and the Home Office itself was reluctant to be associated with the use of agents provocateurs.

Ben's case was also causing concern in Parliament itself. Tooter had spoken to Richard Stokes, who saw Russia rather than Germany as the real enemy, had favoured the redistribution of the Polish and Czech borders in Germany's favour, and recommended a negotiated peace whereby Germany would be left to dominate Continental Europe; Irving Albery, a Conservative MP who had earlier been Ben's opponent in a by-election, had promised to raise his case in the Commons ('Dear old Ben, he's got his head in the clouds but by no stretch of the imagination could he be a traitor to this country. Impossible!' he told Tooter); Lloyd George wrote to Hickson to say of Ben that 'although I did not share his political opinions, I have always held a high opinion of his character, and heard him well spoken of for his integrity and straightforwardness . . . I feel certain that he is not the kind of person who would be guilty of any act of disloyalty or treason to the country.' Although the Divisional Court accepted the Home Office's affidavits, and refused Ben's application, it recommended that he should be given a new hearing in front of a different Advisory Committee. Ben and another internee then took their appeals to the Court of Appeal: although the Law Lords declared that it was not up to the courts to intervene with the Home Office – now headed by Ben's old enemy Herbert Morrison – in matters concerning national security, Ben's persistence was casting doubts on the procedures employed for dealing with internees. The new 'Reasons for Order' correctly gave 'hostile associations' as the cause of Ben's detention, and were expanded to include the fact that he had a German mother, and a sister living in Germany who was married to a German official. Hickson immediately replied demanding further particulars, and mentioning in particular Kurtz, Gärtner, Barbara, Ilse von Binzer and Dr Rösel.

Oswald Hickson had made all the difference to Ben's prospects – and then MI5 overstepped the mark, with fatal results for its case. Ben was not the only member of his family to fall under suspicion: Barbara had been described as the 'mistress' of a high-ranking German official, Ben's mother was still assumed to be pro-German, Kurtz believed Leslie to be an 'ardent admirer of Hitler', and Tooter's innocence could not be assumed, since – or so it was claimed – a political meeting chaired by the Duke of Bedford had been held in his flat in Prince of Wales Drive. Soon after Ben's detention two men turned up at Overstrand Mansions and insisted on searching Tooter's flat. He was about to leave for the office, so he told the housekeeper to show them around. The following day they appeared in his office to interrogate him about a broadsheet they had found, but were interrupted by the imposing figure of Arthur Whitworth, the Chairman of E. J. Johnston Ltd and a Director of the Bank of England, who tore them off a strip ('How dare you . . .') and sent them on their way. But Maxwell Knight was not to be put off so easily. Kurtz himself was sent round to call on Tooter, claiming that they had met at a meeting addressed by the Duke of Bedford. He explained that, following his release from an internment camp on the Isle of Man, he was planning to make a new life for himself in Brazil, and he had just been issued with a Brazilian visa: and he wondered whether Tooter, with his knowledge of the country, could provide him with letters of introduction to expatriate Germans in Brazil. Tooter didn't take to his visitor: he found him 'very smooth', and 'it seemed to me at the time that Kurtz was nothing more or less than an agent provocateur of the type one knows exists extensively on the Continent but does not expect to encounter in this country, even at a time of war.' When he asked his visitor about conditions on the Isle of Man, Kurtz replied that they were 'pretty awful, but the worst feature was that I had to mix with Jews' – after which he tried to provoke Tooter into making antisemitic remarks. 'Now I could see with half an eye that he was a Jew himself,' Tooter remarked (wrongly). 'An alarm bell rang: there's something fishy; so I just asked him to leave.' After his visitor had left, Tooter rang the Brazilian consulate, who confirmed that no visa had been issued to a Mr Kurtz. He also rang Oswald Hickson. 'My God, if you had given him those letters you would have been in gaol within five minutes. Obviously a trick,' Hickson told him. The Home Office had informed him that the charges against Ben were made in a report drawn up by Kurtz, and Hickson told Tooter to do all he could to track Kurtz down.

This seemed a hopeless task until, in October 1941, Tooter encountered Kurtz by chance outside the Café Royal and asked him to lunch later that month. Towards the end of their lunch in Simpson's in the Strand, Kurtz asked about Ben, and Tooter told him that there seemed to have been some misunderstanding at the Home Office about Ben's work for the Quakers on behalf of the Jews. Tooter said he thought Kurtz might be able to help them, and – as agreed beforehand with Hickson – he suggested that they should go together to his solicitor's office, five minutes' walk away in Covent Garden. Tooter briefly left the table under the pretence of making a phone call to Hickson, and on his return Kurtz agreed to go with him. Hickson introduced himself to Kurtz, told him that he was going to read out the charges that had been made against Ben, and suggested that they had been made on the basis of a report made by Kurtz. 'This is a trap. I refuse to say anything more,' replied Kurtz, who had begun to sweat with fright. He said he wanted to get in touch with his own solicitor, and gave the name of a well-known practitioner. Hickson picked up the phone and said he would ring Kurtz's lawyer right away, to which Kurtz replied 'No, leave it. I'll deny everything' – in effect withdrawing all the evidence he had fabricated against Ben. Hickson then dictated and had typed a memo describing exactly what had happened, signed it, gave one copy to Kurtz and had another sent to the Home Office.

Kurtz reported back to MI5, who complained to the Home Office that Hickson had used dirty tricks against their agent. 'Kurtz had been lured into making a rather foolish statement to Hickson about Ben Greene,' Guy Liddell noted in his diary. 'The whole matter has obviously been a trick by Hickson, aided and abetted by Edward Greene.' To prevent Kurtz's name becoming common knowledge, he suggested to Sir William Maxwell that it should not be mentioned in a parliamentary question in the House of Commons. Hickson, in the meantime, continued to gather ammunition for use in Ben's defence, writing to Sheila MacDonald in Canada and to the current headmaster of Berkhamsted, who denied that Ben had been involved with Herr Bennemann's Anglo-German Youth Camp. A curious twist to the tale was provided by Lord Rothschild, who was himself involved with the secret service. He invited Tooter to Tring to talk about Ben's predicament: he spent most of their time together quizzing Tooter about his pre-war trips to Germany on coffee business, but as his guest was leaving he gave him a jar of home-made jam to pass on to Ben.

Ben's second Advisory Committee was more liberal-minded and well disposed than its predecessor. Its unpaid Chairman, Sir Norman Birkett, was one of the best-known, best-paid and highly regarded barristers of the day: he had been appointed by Sir John Anderson in September 1939 and, abjuring the enormous fees he was accustomed to earning at the Bar, he heard more than 1500 cases over the next two years. 'The work is important, of course, for on our decision the freedom or imprisonment of the individual depends,' he declared, and 'the paramount consideration at all times has been national safety and national security', as well as the need to 'keep some small element of justice alive in a world in which we are fighting for it.' He found chairing the Committee a 'rather thankless task', not least because MI5 'want everybody interned, while I cannot bring myself to send some simple German girl for years of detention when I am quite satisfied that she has been in the country in some household for years and is not the slightest danger to anybody.' 'The work I do now, though very important, is beset with frustration, and I am very far from happy in it,' he confessed in December 1940. 'The delays are grievous and many people are in prison this Christmas who have been there since last May without any trial or reasons given for their detention. I suffer in spirit daily.' The Secretary to the Committee, Jenifer Fischer-Williams, had initially supported internment, but had 'more and more come to feel that it had not been necessary, even considering the desperate situation of Britain in the summer of 1940, to take action against many of the detainees.' Birkett, she claimed, 'felt that no one should be detained unless there were clear grounds for regarding this as absolutely necessary. This attitude rapidly brought him into conflict with MI5, whom he considered illiberal, disorganised and incompetent.'

It had been agreed that Oswald Hickson could appear before the Committee on Ben's behalf, and he opened the proceedings with a fine rhetorical flourish. His client, he declared, is a man who is vouched for by respectable people everywhere as a thoroughly straight and honourable man. He may be a bit of a crank, but Oliver Cromwell was considered a crank when he started his political career. He may be perhaps rather difficult: at any rate he has had difficulties with members of the Labour Party who are now members of the Government, and therefore you have the peculiar position that a Minister of the Crown, Mr Herbert Morrison, who is the Home Secretary now, has had political disagreements with a man who is now detained and whom he persists in detaining.

He ridiculed the notion that having a German mother made Ben a security risk – would the same apply if he owned a dachshund, or professed a liking of German beer or sausages? – and subpoenaed both Kurtz and Friedl Gärtner to appear before the Committee. Maxwell Knight and Sir William Maxwell had both been to Burlington Gardens to try to persuade Birkett and Miss Fischer-Williams that it would be fatal if either name was leaked to the world at large, and the Treasury Solicitor had asked that Gärtner should be referred to by her initials only, but although Birkett agreed that national security had to take precedence, Kurtz appeared before the Committee, which also interviewed Tooter and Maxwell Knight. The Committee was impressed by Ben's performance: he denied having made his Wellingborough speech, and said that if released he would do nothing to impede the war effort – he no longer believed in a negotiated peace, and was 'quite clear that the war must be fought out' – and would no longer associate with John Beckett or the Duke of Bedford. But he would continue to campaign against what Birkett referred to as 'the injustices of 18B', describing them as 'fundamental wrongs which strike at the very roots of our constitution'. Tooter found the Committee hostile, with the exception of Birkett: when Birkett eventually dismissed him he told him not to leave by a particular door since Kurtz was waiting behind it, 'and I don't think it would be advisable for you two to meet!'

By now the focus of attention had switched from the well-trodden ground of Ben's German connections and political activities to the hapless agent provocateur. Kurtz was 'severely cross-examined' by Birkett: Maxwell Knight felt that Kurtz had been a victim of the 'combined deceit of the brothers Greene and Hickson', while Guy Liddell ruefully referred in his diary to 'what can only be described as an onslaught on the unfortunate Kurtz', designed to 'tear his evidence to pieces'. After it was all over, MI5 operatives rallied behind their man. Toby Pilcher was convinced that the Committee had set out to discredit an MI5 informant, claiming that 'even if Kurtz's evidence is not accurate in every particular he was certainly present at a treasonable conversation with Greene', and that Birkett had ignored the fact that Scotland Yard had denied ever receiving a phone call from Ben about the activities of Kurtz and Gärtner. A Mr Noakes said that although Kurtz had been attacked for telling lies, lying was 'an almost indispensable necessity if the agent is to have any success in his duties', and that 'the Committee seem to have no realisation whatever of the circumstances in which the security services work' – a view echoed by Sir David Petrie, who had been appointed the Director-General of MI5 after Vernon Kell had been sacked by Churchill in 1940. An agent's work, he told Sir William Maxwell, 'may necessarily involve him in deliberate lying', was 'often uncongenial and sometimes dangerous', and 'it does not seem to have occurred to the Advisory Committee that such officers employed on security duties often have to live a life which is a complete "lie", but do so from the highest motives and often at the risk of their lives.' And although Frank Newsam, the deputy Under-Secretary of State responsible for security matters at the Home Office, disapproved of using agents provocateurs, he felt that 'the whole business of Greene shows only too clearly how hopeless it is to establish any reasonable degree of security under this quasi-legal system by which the prosecution and its witnesses are subjected to severe cross-examination whereas the word of the accused is accepted without question.'

The Committee recommended that Ben should be acquitted of the charges made against him. On 7 January 1942 an official from the Home Office wrote to say that the Home Secretary had reviewed his case and had decided to 'suspend the operation of the order for your detention', and a week later Sir William Maxwell confirmed that the charges of treason had been dropped. Ben was in poor health, and Tooter took him straight to St Mary's Hospital Paddington after collecting him from prison. But clearing Ben's name was a grudging and provisional business. Kurtz's allegations may have been withdrawn, but when, two days before Ben's release, Herbert Morrison was asked whether action would now be taken against those on whose evidence he had been detained, he replied that Ben had not been detained on the evidence of one man only, and that 'there was undisputed information derived from various sources that he had hostile associations; and these associations were of such a character that it was necessary to exercise some control over him. Even at this date his release from detention has been made subject to conditions imposed for this purpose.' Ben's release was conditional on good behaviour, and he was expected to report to the police on a regular basis.

Hickson remained as active as ever on Ben's behalf. To his great distress,

Ben had been struck off as a JP after his internment, and Hickson wrote to the Lord Chancellor, Lord Simon, to demand his reinstatement, but with no success. He complained to the Advisory Committee that since Ben had been detained on the basis of false accusations, it was an insult to release him on conditions. He wrote to Sir William Maxwell about the charges still listed in the revised 'Reasons for Order', he dismissed allegations about Ben's pre-war visits to Germany and his meetings with German officials as footling, and – somewhat disingenuously – claimed that there was no evidence that his client had made controversial speeches after the outbreak of war, or that Ben had helped John Beckett during that time. And he sprang into action when Ben decided to sue the Home Secretary for libel and false imprisonment. Tooter employed Searle's Detective Agency to track down and issue subpoenas to Kurtz and Friedl Gärtner; others subpoenaed by Hickson included the Lord Chancellor, Lloyd George and Birkett.

Ben's action was heard by Mr Justice Lawrence and a special jury in September 1943, and lasted for less than two days. The court, Mr Lawrence declared, was not concerned with the truth or falsity of the charges, but had to decide whether Sir John Anderson had a 'reasonable cause' for detaining the plaintiff. Ben's case was not helped by Herbert Morrison claiming that the relevant official documents were privileged material; nor did he prove to be an impressive witness. He sought to present himself as a blameless pacifist, but the Attorney-General had no difficulty in showing that his pre-war political activities and speeches could be interpreted as suggesting a degree of support or sympathy for Nazi Germany. Kurtz took his revenge on Hickson and Tooter by withdrawing his denial, and said that he was prepared to repeat his original account of Ben's conversations with him. Since he had been called as one of Ben's witnesses, his evidence would have to be accepted by Ben's counsel. After an adjournment, Ben's counsel withdrew the case, and costs of £1243 were awarded against his client. Tooter's boss, Arthur Whitworth, contributed £1000 towards Ben's costs, and various well-disposed MPs, the Quakers and a political organisation called the Liberty Restoration League also chipped in.

Maxwell Knight had attended the case, and in a memo written afterwards he vented his spleen and frustration on the Greene family in general. Ben, he claimed, had been embarrassed by his wife's presence in the courtroom, since 'he knows her to be thoroughly pro-German', and worried that she might intervene to his detriment. He noted that a cousin of Ben, 'a thoroughly unscrupulous individual', was in the public gallery – this must have been Herbert, about whom MI5 were all too well

informed – while Tooter was included in a group of 'right-wing extrem-
ists', along with John Scanlon. 'I have no hesitation in saying that this
man is an unscrupulous rascal and hypocrite,' Knight fulminated.

> I think Greene's German blood came well to the top: he had that
> touch of arrogance so symptomatic of the Teuton; he was ready to
> crumple up on any occasion when he was sternly tackled by the
> Attorney General . . . He has that touch of egotism which is noted
> in many persons of abnormal size, and he is ready, at almost a moment's
> notice, to assume the role of Democratic Martyr, Religious Reformer,
> or even the man who is the Victim of other people's malice.

Ben was already suffering from the sense of persecution that was to
blight him for the rest of his days. He was convinced that Maxwell Knight
in particular was warning people against him, and that he was viewed
askance by the inhabitants of Berkhamsted. Leaving others to run
Kepston's, he moved his family to Braefoot in Kinross-shire, where he
set up another business involving the manufacture of furnaces used for
brazing metals. They were visited there in the spring of 1943 by Felix,
who was over in Britain on behalf of the Quakers. 'He was coming over
to Europe to write a report on how we were taking the bombing and
things like that,' Ben's daughter Margaret recalled. 'How dare he! Quite
a head of hostility had built up towards him before he arrived.' But 'he
was so sweet, and so charming, and so natural, and so loving, and so
completely helpful in every way, in everything he did for everybody; it
was all so absolutely right that he got us eating out of his hand in no
time at all.' The two brothers went for long walks over the hills, and
Felix reported 'such an intensity of frustration bottled up in the unhappy
man, that once released it pours forth as from a volcano,' and urged Ben
to remain on good terms with Tooter, whose 'never-ending patience,
constant kindliness and firmness' had enabled them to survive it all. Felix
was convinced that 'Ben's whole unrest and misery could have been
avoided if only he would look *inwards* to himself and a little less often
outwards for the source of all these aggravations,' and that he should pay
more attention to prayer 'as the first basis of reform'. He should work
on the land instead of 'all this fooling around with Kepston', so that 'the
genius within him may develop and become of some account.' 'It is
increasingly clear that what God is doing to that poor brother of mine
is forcing him, step by step, into a complete breakdown,' Felix told their
mother. 'It is wilfulness that lies at the root of Ben's ailment – "The gods

will not abide an implacable man", and there is grown in Ben an element of the implacable. His self-pity, his wilfulness, his egotism, his sense of personal grievance, have driven him into a prison from which total madness may be the only escape.'

★

Harald Kurtz joined the BBC later in the war: he was not, as some Hall Greenes suggested, employed by Hugh in the German Service, but worked for the Monitoring Service in Evesham, listening in to and reporting on German-language broadcasts alongside such future eminences as George Weidenfeld and E. H. Gombrich. He served as a translator during the Nuremberg trials; in later life he settled in Oxford, where he wrote well-received biographies of Marshal Ney and the Empress Eugenie. Both were published by Hamish Hamilton, who were asked to pay part of the advances in the form of cigarettes. He was a convivial and hospitable figure, though Hugh Trevor-Roper claimed that he stole books from libraries in Oxford to pay for the drink. He became a regular at the King's Arms, next to Wadham College; Ben's son Paul, then an undergraduate at Oxford, was another frequent visitor, but they never met. After Kurtz's death in 1972, Christopher Sykes wrote in *The Times* that 'his ready humour and wide learning made him a delightful companion,' while Lord Longford spoke of his 'buoyant temperament' and his 'lovable combination of wit, irony and enthusiasm.' Maxwell Knight's standing in MI5 never recovered from the Greene fiasco, with the result that his prescient warnings about Communist infiltration of the security services were ignored by his superiors. After his retirement from MI5 he reinvented himself, appearing on BBC nature programmes as the benign, animal-loving 'Uncle Max', and writing books for children about hedgehogs, garden birds, newts, spiders and other livestock.

Tooter, the hero of the hour, had been granted a deferment of his military service in order to help run Kepston's, but was called up after Ben's release despite a message from the Ministry of Food to the effect that they could obtain his exemption. His life as a soldier was cut short when he fell out of the back of a lorry at Sandhurst, hitting his head on the kerb and remaining unconscious for several days, and he spent the rest of the war with the Ministry of Food. In later life he confirmed that Ben never recovered from his experiences. 'He always saw plots against him,' he told a gathering of Greenes after Ben's death. 'If anything went wrong, it was because they had heard about his 18B and were plotting against him; it was pathetic.' Jane Wootton, who had worked as Ben's secretary, claimed that he was 'a bad judge of character, and this in itself had led him into dangerous company.' Despite his spell in Brixton, and the promises he had made to the Advisory Committee, Ben continued to consort with former friends and colleagues from the far right of the political spectrum. He was a 'vice-governor' of the English National Association, which was, according to a 1943 MI5 memo, 'ostensibly devoted to restoring English Liberties' as set out in Magna Carta, but in fact was 'designed to give effect to the dictator principle'. Even at this late hour it favoured a negotiated peace with Germany, under the terms of which Hitler would be left in control of the mainland of Europe. The ENA was eventually merged with the National Front After Victory, the driving spirit of which was A. K. Chesterton: a planned merger with the BPP was thwarted after both bodies had been infiltrated by the British Board of Jewish Deputies, and denounced in the House of Lords by Robert (now Lord) Vansittart. Ben busied himself co-ordinating the activities of organisations devoted to monetary reform and the reduction of officialdom, including the Union to Curb Bureaucracy, the Honest Money Association and the Farmers' Action Council. In June 1944, according to MI5, he hosted a lunch to celebrate Magna Carta, 'a measure which his study of constitutional law had led him to believe to be, primarily, an antisemitic document.' Ben was by then dividing his time between Braefoot and Hertfordshire: Captain Ramsay was a frequent visitor to Berkhamsted after his release from Brixton in 1944, and the local police reported that he had come to share his visitor's views ('Greene holds extremely anti-Jewish sentiments, and has been heard to refer to Jews as the curse of the country').

Shortly after the war had ended, Ben received an unexpected visit from a former MI5 operative. 'I hope you do not recognise me,' were his opening words, and he went on to explain that although he had worked on Ben's case, and had even met him in Brixton, he had come to apologise. He told Ben that MI5 had forged an incriminating letter which was used against him – some of his notepaper had been stolen when his office was searched after his arrest, as well as a rubber stamp of his signature – and, according to Ben, 'some of his colleagues had become very uneasy at the part they were required to play in the case of some of the detentions and he was particularly uneasy about the part he had played in mine.' All in all, it had been a wretched story: Ben may have been, as the headmaster of Dartington told Leslie Greene, 'one of the honestest and nicest people I have known', and MI5 could plead national security in justification of their dirty tricks, but neither emerged with their reputation unscathed.

German Service

The Second World War was fought on the airwaves as well as on the battlefield, and as the head of the BBC's German Service from January 1941 Hugh was to prove a cool, clear-minded combatant who knew exactly what he wanted to achieve and employed his forces to maximum effect. He was, by temperament and training, a newspaperman, but the German invasion of Norway and the unavailability of esparto grass from North Africa had deprived newspapers, magazines and book publishers of their major suppliers of paper, and they were subjected to the indignities of rationing and quotas. Television, then in its infancy, had been put on hold for the duration: with most of Continental Europe out of bounds for even the most intrepid foreign correspondents, radio came into its own, on the foreign as well as the domestic front.

The outbreak of war led to an immediate expansion of foreign-language broadcasting, and by 1943 the BBC would be transmitting news and feature programmes in forty-five different languages. Broadcasting to occupied countries like France had the great advantage of a largely sympathetic and well-disposed audience, but running the German Service was a far trickier proposition: not only were BBC broadcasts jammed by the authorities in Germany, but those caught listening were severely punished, not to mention that, in the early years of the war in particular, most of the BBC's target audience enthusiastically supported Hitler and his policies. As the *Daily Telegraph*'s Berlin correspondent, Hugh had been fearless in describing developments in Nazi Germany, and as head of the German Service he was to be a great champion of the BBC's policy of telling the truth in its all-important news items, however unwelcome or inconvenient that truth might be. With the Government taking a greater interest than usual in the content of BBC broadcasts, leading to a baffling proliferation of boards and committees, he became a sure-footed denizen of the corridors of power, simultaneously toeing the line and going his own way, and combining the need to present an official

'line' with a degree of editorial independence. By so doing he acclimatised himself to the bureaucratic world of acronyms, initials, office
memos, meetings and sonorous job descriptions in which he would spend
the rest of his working life.

The BBC had begun broadcasting in German, French and Italian after
the Munich Crisis, and early in 1939 transmissions to Germany were
extended to half an hour a day. Straightforward news items were
combined with *Sonderberichte* or talks based on the news, and it was noted
how 'the calm voice of the BBC announcer evoked special admiration
from abroad, in contrast to the excited accents of the American
announcers and the extreme anti-Czechoslovakian propaganda from
Germany.' The BBC prided itself on its independence from government,
and – unlike its German equivalent – was loath to be seen as an instru-
ment of propaganda, but after the outbreak of war all broadcasting to
enemy countries, including that of the BBC, came under the formal
control of Sir Stuart Campbell's Department for Enemy Propaganda,
based initially in Electra House, a large office block on the Embankment,
and later in various out-houses in the grounds of Woburn Abbey, the
home of Ben's old colleague the Duke of Bedford. 'EH' was responsible
to the Ministry of Information, and although it provided political
'guidance' or advice to the BBC's German and other foreign language
services, it concentrated its energies on straightforward news until the
arrival at Woburn in 1941 of Hugh's rival from the Berlin Press corps,
Sefton Delmer, who was to specialise in mendacious, misleading and
often extremely entertaining 'black' broadcasting, of a kind far removed
from that provided by the BBC's German Service.

Woburn was always referred to as 'the Country': according to Leonard
Miall, who joined the embryo German Service before the war and
composed several *Sonderberichte*, great secrecy prevailed and 'one wasn't
allowed to know where "the Country" was.' Life was complicated further
by a ruling, later abandoned, whereby the BBC was often prevented from
using news items until they had appeared in the Press, which gave an
impression of slow-footedness, still more so if German radio picked
them up first. With – or so it was claimed – thirty per cent of the adult
population regularly tuning in to Lord Haw-Haw's broadcasts and
German propaganda in triumphalist mood, British broadcasters got off
to an uneasy start, despite an Electra House memo of January 1940
insisting that 'the BBC's German broadcasting must aim at stimulating
doubt among the confident and encouraging defeatism and irritation
with the regime in the apathetic.' In May 1940, following the German

invasion of France and the Low Countries, the BBC's Overseas Services were reorganised and reinvigorated. Noel Newsome was brought in from the *Daily Telegraph* as European News Editor. Hugh would have little time for Newsome, professionally at least, but in the meantime he provided much-needed energy and enthusiasm.

That same month Ben's old sparring partner from the Labour Party, Hugh Dalton, was appointed the Minister of Economic Warfare and charged by Churchill with setting up the Special Operations Executive. SOE was divided into two parts: SO2, which concerned itself with the more glamorous business of infiltrating agents into Occupied Europe and perpetrating acts of sabotage, and SO1, which interested itself in psychological warfare and in propaganda. SO1 was merged with EH and, after Sir Stuart Campbell's return to Canada, placed under Vansittart's former colleague Rex Leeper, the Director of Enemy Propaganda, who – as if this weren't confusing enough – also headed the Foreign Office's Political Intelligence Department or PID, which was responsible for spelling out the ministry's policy as it changed from day to day.

EH, the PID and the Ministry of Information were not the only intermediaries between the Government and the BBC. In January 1941, the month in which Hugh joined the German Service, Ivone Kirkpatrick was seconded from the Foreign Office to the BBC to act as a 'Foreign Adviser', representing and explaining Government policy and acting as a bridge between Whitehall and those responsible for foreign-language broadcasting. Last encountered as the Head of Chancery and First Secretary at the British Embassy in Berlin, Kirkpatrick was, according to his deputy, Harman Grisewood, 'quick-witted and sure-footed, like a mountain animal, with a good head for heights and used to rough weather. Despite his manicured "Mayfair" appearance there was little of the diplomat in him: he won his points by attack rather than persuasion.' Robert Bruce Lockhart, who had worked with him at PID, admired him for his 'quick, decisive' approach, and claimed that he was 'always at his best in a crisis'. Once installed at the BBC, Kirkpatrick proved to be a poacher turned gamekeeper, defending its interests from over-zealous Government intervention and proving, from Hugh's point of view, an invaluable ally.

A few more acronyms and bureaucratic bodies need to be introduced before we can move on to the BBC's foreign services in general, and the German Service in particular. In July 1941 Churchill's crony Brendan Bracken succeeded Duff Cooper as Minister of Information. Churchill was indifferent to propaganda warfare, which he derided as 'killing Hitler with your mouth', and deeply suspicious of the BBC, which he once referred to an 'an enemy within the gates, doing more harm than good', but Bracken, like Kirkpatrick, was to prove an ally rather than an irritant. Confrontation gave way to co-operation, and he regularly defended the BBC against prime ministerial assaults. In September 1941 what became known as the Political Warfare Executive or PWE assumed embryonic form in the shape of regular ministerial meetings between Anthony Eden, representing the Foreign Office, Bracken and Dalton. The following month Kirkpatrick was promoted within the BBC to Controller (European Services): as such he was to pursue an increasingly independent line vis-á-vis both the PWE and the Foreign Office, and encouraged foreign service editors like Hugh and Darsie Gillie of the French Service to follow his example.

In 1942 the PWE was formally established after Dalton had departed for the Board of Trade. Eden and Bracken were now the only Ministers formally involved, with Eden deciding policy and Bracken looking after its administration. Robert Bruce Lockhart – who had been condemned to death as a British spy during the Russian Revolution, and edited the *Evening Standard*'s 'Londoner's Diary' for much of the thirties – was appointed PWE's Director, responsible for conveying Government views and policy to programme-makers and propagandists alike.

The BBC's two criteria when broadcasting overseas were truth and consistency. Goebbels's Propaganda Ministry had persistently employed exaggeration, bombast and lies in order to advance the German cause, and before his retirement as Director-General in 1938 Reith had insisted that his broadcasters should 'help in stifling rumour and sensation by the presentation of fully authoritative and carefully presented news.' 'No permanent propaganda policy can in the modern world be based upon untruthfulness,' the *BBC Handbook* declared in 1941, while Harold Nicolson, himself a frequent broadcaster, insisted that 'totalitarian methods of propaganda are not only foolish as such but totally inapplicable to a civilised society.' The truth must be told, however inconvenient, and Allied defeats and reverses had to be reported with the same impartiality and objectivity as any other items of news. In the early years of the war, with the Wehrmacht sweeping all before them, there was little good news to report. Disasters like Dunkirk and Tobruk and the Dieppe Raid were neither denied nor covered up, partly for idealistic reasons, and partly for reasons of realpolitik: by telling the truth the BBC came to be trusted by enemies and friends alike, and it was felt that a reputation for honest, trustworthy reporting would pay dividends when the tide of the war began to turn: as Hugh put it years later, 'one knew perfectly well that if we lost the war, if there was a German invasion, we'd all be shot anyway. So why not tell the truth? Whereas if we held out and the tide turned, the fact that we told the truth would mean the Germans would believe us, as indeed they did.' When Hugh's colleague Lindley Fraser broadcast details of the fall of Singapore in February 1942, a German listener said of the British that 'if they can admit a catastrophe so openly they must be terribly strong.' The French politician Leon Blum declared that 'in a world of poison, the BBC became the great antiseptic.'

Consistency was as important as truth. Each foreign language service had its own flavour, and feature programmes were designed for particular national audiences, but the facts given in the all-important news bulletins had to be the same in every language, even if the emphasis altered from country to country. It was important to allow for what became known as 'cross-listening', 'eavesdropping' or 'twiddling dials', for Poles or Czechs listening into the German Service to be given the same news as they would have received on their own services broadcast from London. Once again, the BBC took a radically different approach from that adopted by German broadcasters, who placed no value on consistency and truth, assumed its listeners had short memories, exaggerated German triumphs and had little to fall back on when the Allies began to prevail, and had no compunction about attacking Churchill in particular on personal as well as political grounds – whereas the BBC refrained from personal attacks on Hitler and Goering on the grounds that, given their popularity, this could well be counter-productive, and merely suggested that the policies pursued by the German Government could prove to be unwise.

Policy lines were laid down at weekly meetings between the PWE's regional directors – in Hugh's case the future Labour politician Richard Crossman – and the heads of regional services, and because such meetings were on a weekly basis this left editors like Hugh room to manoeuvre, with Kirkpatrick's support. The news itself was less amenable to PWE interference, coming in as it did in a ceaseless flow. As European News Editor, Noel Newsome was responsible for collecting the news and disseminating it to the various foreign language services: Broadcasting House and the national newspapers could provide him and his editors with domestic news, but news from Occupied Europe was gleaned from the BBC's Monitoring Service in Evesham and from agency tapes. The News Desk in Bush House was on duty around the clock, with news being constantly sifted and updated. Newsome held two news conferences a day, at eleven in the morning and again at five in the afternoon, and daily directives were prepared. Every now and then the Foreign Office, the Ministry of Information or PWE objected to the inclusion of a particular item of news, but by then it was almost always too late.

Newsome was also in charge of the Central Talks staff, members of which included the future historian Alan Bullock, and he edited an English-language overseas service called *London Calling Europe*. According to Harman Grisewood, Newsome had little knowledge or understanding of Europe, which he believed to be 'variously enslaved to the Pope and other corrupt and despicable authorities', while Hugh thought him 'completely ignorant of the basic tenets of propaganda'. Newsome paid little attention to PWE directives, but Hugh was more likely to agree with Crossman than with Newsome, and Kirkpatrick was able to prevent Newsome from imposing his ideas on the German Service. The other major foreign-language broadcast was the French Service run by Darsie Gillie, whom Hugh had got to know as *The Times* correspondent covering the Anschluss, and who felt exactly the same way about Newsome. 'I couldn't stand Noel Newsome, and Noel Newsome couldn't stand me,' Hugh recalled. 'Newsome used to issue a daily directive and they were really quite fantastically silly. He was very energetic, and as far as Darsie Gillie and I were concerned, we regarded it as one of our contributions to the war effort to see that no traces of Newsome directives were ever seen.'

Hugh found Crossman, by contrast, both sympathetic and congenial, and very much a kindred spirit. A forceful and fast-talking former Oxford philosophy don, with swept-back hair and Arthur Askey spectacles, Crossman had made his mark as the author of *Plato Today*, a brilliant analysis of the totalitarian mentality, and would in due course become one of Harold Wilson's best-known Cabinet Ministers, and the editor of the *New Statesman*. Early on in the war he had delivered several *Sonderberichte*, aimed at German workers. After being recruited into Military Intelligence (Research) he had worked in Electra House before being moved to Woburn in the spring of 1940. He and Dalton had been allies in the Labour Party, trying to combat pacifism within the party, and Dalton decided that Crossman should run the German Section within what was to become PWE, with responsibility for overseeing both 'black' propaganda of the kind produced by Sefton Delmer, and 'white' propaganda as provided by Hugh and the German Service. His house in Apsley Guise, near Woburn, became the headquarters of what was to become the first clandestine radio station broadcasting to Germany from British soil, *Sender der Europeanischen Revolution*, a 'grey' left-wing station

set up with F. A. Voigt, formerly the *Manchester Guardian*'s Berlin correspondent. Energetic, disrespectful and hard to control, Crossman spent
two days a week in London, representing the views of the Government
to the broadcasters in Bush House, delivering talks on the German
Service, and taking part in a weekly brains trust, *Was Wollen Sie Wissen?*
along with Hugh, Lindley Fraser and the actor Marius Goring: it was
claimed that questions came in from all over Europe, but most of them
were concocted by Crossman and Leonard Miall, the programme's
producer and the European News Talks Editor, and an early member of
the German Service.

Crossman was, and would remain, a controversial figure. Bruce Lockhart, his superior in PWE, claimed he was extremely unpopular and
widely known as 'Double Crossman'; Rex Leeper of the PID found him
a difficult character but 'much superior to Greene and Miall at the BBC,'
both of whom 'eat out of his hand'. According to Harman Grisewood,
Kirkpatrick 'spoke of Crossman in general as under-developed and undergraduate, and a person who enjoyed "spoofs"', while Dalton confided
to his diary that he regarded 'this able and energetic man with some
detachment. He is loyal to his own career, but only incidentally to anything
or anyone else.' Malcolm Muggeridge, who saw a good deal of Crossman
at this time, admired him as 'one of the most versatile, engaging, and
irresponsible of contemporary minds', and remembered how 'whatever
position Crossman took up was defended with vigour and panache, though
he was quite likely, on another occasion, to demolish it with equal vigour
and panache.' He conducted proceedings like a philosophy seminar or a
Socratic dialogue, and by saying less Hugh usually managed to win him
round or get his own way. (Years later, Hugh's son Graham defied
precedent, and outraged the Establishment, by publishing Crossman's
ministerial diaries shortly after their author's death – and at his request.)
Because Crossman was Hugh's superior, there may have been an element
of friendly rivalry between them: in a diary entry for April 1942, Patrick
Gordon Walker noted that Hugh was gaining ground in the hierarchy
at Crossman's expense, and that 'there is clearly going to be very little
support from higher up against [Hugh] even though they don't like him.'

Crossman also worked very closely with Sefton Delmer. According to
a colleague at PWE the two men were 'incompatible', but whereas
Crossman supported Delmer's activities, Hugh thoroughly disapproved,
even if he had to admit that some of the material broadcast to German
troops on Delmer's *Soldatensender Calais* programme was 'so funny that
I have sometimes wondered whether they did not raise rather than depress

morale.' 'I spent nearly two years as overall director of political warfare against the enemy, trying to control and co-ordinate the black propaganda of PWE with the white propaganda of the BBC German Service', Crossman wrote in a review of Delmer's wartime memoirs. 'Delmer and Hugh Carleton Greene, the BBC chief, detested each other and waged a departmental war in which no holds were barred.' Their dislike was professional as well as personal, reflecting opposing and incompatible views on the philosophy, function and morality of broadcasting to Germany, with Hugh adhering to the BBC philosophy that truth must prevail at all times, while Delmer believed that every trick of the trade was justified in the cause of discomforting and bamboozling the enemy.

Early in the war Delmer had been asked by the then Minister of Information, Duff Cooper, to 'improve' the BBC's German broadcasts by giving occasional *Sonderberichte*, while continuing to work on the *Daily Express*. During the course of one of these talks he famously rejected a 'final peace appeal' from Hitler, made during a speech to the Reichstag in July 1940. 'Herr Hitler, you have on occasions in the past consulted me as to the mood of the British public,' Delmer replied, after gaining approval from Crossman, Leonard Miall and Noel Newsome, but without consulting any member of the Government. 'So permit me to render your Excellency this little service once again tonight. Let me tell you what we here in Britain think of this appeal of yours to what you are pleased to call our reason and common sense . . . We hurl it right back at you, right in your evil-smelling teeth.' According to William Shirer, Delmer's retaliation amazed and outraged its German listeners: it was violently attacked in the House of Commons by Richard Stokes, but stoutly defended by Duff Cooper, speaking on behalf of the Cabinet.

Not long afterwards Leonard Ingrams, who worked on psychological warfare for the Ministry of Economic Warfare, suggested to Delmer that he should leave the *Daily Express* and set up a 'Freedom Station' – euphemistically referred to as a 'research unit' – to broadcast to Germany. Delmer thought it a waste of time trying to appeal to the all-conquering Germans by reason: trickery and deceit would prove more effective, and he suggested to Ingrams a new approach that 'undermines Hitler, not by opposing him but by pretending to be all for him and his war'. (His approach to broadcasting had much in common with Claud Cockburn's passion for 'preventive journalism', whereby facts were reordered, distorted or invented to promote a particular course of action.) Ingrams told him to 'stop gassing' and get on with it, Crossman was all in favour, and in the spring of 1941, after spending three months in Lisbon interviewing refugees from Nazi Germany, Delmer moved to Woburn full time to concentrate his enormous energies on 'black' propaganda. 'A "black" news bulletin mixing truth and calculated fiction had for long been my dream,' he recalled. 'I longed to show the BBC the difference between the stodgy news presentation of the old-fashioned journalism to which the BBC bowed down, and the sharp and vivid style of my side of Fleet Street which I hoped to adapt to radio. I wanted to demonstrate the mass appeal of the significant "human story", until now absent from the air, the technique of "personalising" the news.'

Ostensibly broadcast from inside Occupied Europe, stations like *Atlantiksender* and *Soldatensender Calais* were aimed at German troops in particular – *Calais* even purported to be broadcast by German troops – and specialised in disinformation, confusing and demoralising their listeners and misleading them about Allied activities. As such, they were seen as an adjunct of the military, and were supported by Ian Fleming and Donald McLachlan of Naval Intelligence in particular: according to Crossman, Naval Intelligence provided Delmer with a flow of military secrets 'on the basis of which the black broadcasts were able to tell bigger lies and provide more accurate information about the course of the war and about life in Germany than any other radio station or newspaper in Europe.' Churchill found Delmer's buccaneering approach very much to his taste. Delmer's team – which included Hugh's former colleague from Berlin, Karl Robson – worked partly on hunch and pure invention, partly from information gleaned from Axis newspapers flown in from neutral Portugal, and partly from interviews with neutral diplomats and prisoners-of-war. In an attempt to undermine enemy morale, they made much of corruption within the Nazi Party, exploited real or imaginary differences between the Wehrmacht and Nazi leaders, contrasted the lives of luxury-loving Party officials with the misery endured by troops on the Russian front, and interlaced the ravings of a garrulous Party official known as 'Der Chef' with jazz and dance music of a kind *verboten* in Nazi Germany. And whereas Germans caught listening to the German Service could face severe penalties, soldiers tuning in to *Soldatensender Calais* could plead ignorance, and get away with it. The trappings of 'The Rookery' – Delmer's house-cum-office in Apsley Guise – were suitably piratical, as was its name (the German for 'rookery' is *Krahenhorst*, a German underworld term for a 'den of thieves'). Otto John joined the 'Delmer circus' late in 1944, after he had been flown to Britain from Lisbon, and worked for *Soldatensender Calais*. He was driven from London to Apsley Guise, and eventually 'the car stopped before an iron grille behind which was a door leading into a guard room. Through the half-open door I could see men in uniform and sub-machine guns with their barrels glistening against the wall.' Delmer himself proved to be a 'corpulent gentleman in mufti', whose flawless German 'belied his somewhat bohemian appearance'.

The efficacy as well as the morality of Delmer's efforts were the subject of fierce debate. 'Jack [John Wheeler-Bennett] is not a great believer in "black", thinks that Delmer had a very amusing war, but is very doubtful whether his efforts were anything like as successful as Tom claims. Here, too, I agree, and so does Kirkpatrick,' Bruce Lockhart noted in his diary towards the end of the war. George Martelli, a former head of PWE's Italian Section, thought Woburn 'a gigantic waste of human effort and public money', while conceding that 'there is a place in war for a foreign information service, as was shown by the BBC, which by eschewing propaganda and sticking strictly to the truth, however unpleasant, acquired an enormous influence on the course of the war.' Crossman had mixed views on the matter. 'Subversive operations and black propaganda were the only aspects of war at which we achieved real pre-eminence,' he declared, in the cause of which 'we trained a small army of gifted amateurs for all the dirtiest tricks from lying, bugging, forging and embezzlement to sheer murder – all, of course, in the name of preserving the democratic way of life.' Years later, even Hugh had to concede that '"black" propaganda seems to have an irresistible attraction for those in authority and the mere mention of the word "black" will sometimes open up sources of valuable intelligence which might otherwise be withheld. It seems so much more fascinating and romantic than the slowly grinding mills of orthodox propaganda. It appeals to the small boy's heart which still beats under the black jacket and the beribboned tunic.'

'Judged in terms of the numbers of its listeners and readers, our black propaganda by the end of the war in Europe had become a serious rival to the Nazi radio and press, and may well have outstripped the German Service of the BBC,' Crossman declared after the war, adding that Delmer's staff 'had to be prepared to carry out any form of subversion, however odious, on the orders of a chief who not only ate, drank and looked like Henry VIII but equalled that monarch in the genial absolutism with which he ran his kingdom.' Black propaganda, Crossman concluded, was 'nihilistic in purpose and solely destructive in effect', and 'I am more doubtful than ever whether this decision to plunge far below the Nazis' own level of lying, half-lying and news perversion was justified even by its undoubted results.' Delmer himself remained defiant. White, grey and black propaganda all had their parts to play,

> nor am I in any way disparaging Carleton Greene and his men when I say that the spinsterish insistence of the BBC on its freedom from government control made it inevitable that the Services would look around for an alternative medium without these virginal complexes. The whole of our "white" radio output suffered under the system of divided responsibility by which the BBC, an independent corporation, controlled what was broadcast to Germany in the name of Britain, while the government's planners and policy-makers, sitting in my department, were merely consulted by the BBC as advisers. This meant it was never possible to gear BBC output to operational requirements as perfectly as could be done with a unit where policy-making, planning, intelligence and production were all under one hat.

His own department's attention to detail and relevance to military planning had, he claimed, spurred the BBC into emulative action, and 'had they not done so I fear the BBC might well have continued to plod along in the dreariness and the pious unrealism which had so irritated Duff Cooper in 1940.'

Hugh, for his part, saw no reason to admire Delmer's 'genial and Rabelaisian nature', let alone his Falstaffian girth – he himself was, Leonard Miall recalled, 'a very tall, thin, bespectacled shambling man' – and he thoroughly disapproved of the whole business of black propaganda on the grounds that it compromised Britain's reputation for objectivity and truthfulness. But he continued to attend weekly meetings at the riding school in Woburn, and in summer these were enlivened and made more bearable by cricket matches. Hugh founded and captained a team known as the 'Bushmen' – its original members all worked at Bush House – and matches were played against EH or the PWE. Hugh was the wicketkeeper, and regular players included Patrick Gordon Walker, Leonard Miall, Maurice Latey, Lindley Fraser, Noel Newsome (recalled in Latey's history of the Bushmen as a 'burly buccaneering' figure) and even some scholarly German émigrés; Crossman and Delmer (by now sporting a piratical black beard) watched from the wings. On one occasion a messenger rushed onto the field in the middle of a match to announce that Rommel had taken Tobruk, but Hugh ordered play to continue. A good deal of beer was drunk during and after matches, and occasional dinners were addressed by eminent speakers, including Jan Masaryk and Harold Nicolson. The Bushmen continued to flourish after the war: matches were played against a variety of teams, including one representing *Private Eye*, and the team's guest players included Edmund Blunden, Graham's friend Michael Meyer, a leading authority on Scandinavian literature, and the great West Indian player Learie Constantine.

Hugh was proving himself a leader of men off as well as on the cricket field. Julius Gellner, a member of the German Service staff, was a Jewish refugee from Czechoslovakia who had been a theatre director in Prague, and had been introduced to Helga by Hugh so that she could help him with his English. He remembered that whereas Crossman bubbled over with ideas and never stopped talking, Hugh said very little at meetings: but, unlike Crossman, he was a 'real leader', in that 'the power was there, but none was displayed. He had a certain amount of humour and his was the most analytical mind. He could reduce complex arguments to a few words.' Martin Esslin, who joined the German Service from the Monitoring Service in Evesham, remembered how Hugh exploited his height and a misleading air of vagueness to give the impression of being somehow aloof and above it all. But some colleagues had their reservations. Gellner admired Hugh's work (as well as having a long affair with his wife), but thought him lacking in imagination, while for Marius Goring 'there was something philistine about Hugh's approach.' Hugh once described himself as 'a beast, but a just beast': he could be ruthless when necessary – he once sacked a member of staff on the spot for making an antisemitic joke – and he had no qualms about standing up to authority. On one occasion Churchill was reported as saying, after a heavy lunch, that the Allies were fighting that Austria might be free. Allied policy towards post-war Austria was as yet undecided – was she to be regarded as an integral part of Germany, or a vassal state? – and the Foreign Office rang to suppress the story. 'I'm sorry, old boy, it's about to go out in a few minutes, so Austria will have to be free, won't it?' Hugh replied. He was highly regarded by his superiors, and this was reflected in his salary, which rose from £1100 to £1200 in 1944 alone 'on the ground of the increased importance of the German Service, the outstanding value of Greene's control of it, his rarity value, and the fact that he could earn £2000 p.a. if he went back to the *Daily Telegraph*.'

The German Service's staff list for 1941 lists Hugh as the German Editor, Leonard Miall as his Deputy and Talks Editor, and Maurice Latey as the Deputy News Editor: others included Lindley Fraser, Marius Goring, Patrick Gordon Walker, Tangye Lean, the jazz buff Spike Hughes, the actor Herbert Lom and the all-round entertainer Hubert Gregg. Patrick Gordon Walker was another Oxford don and future Labour Cabinet Minister, whose daughter Judy later married Hugh's son Graham. In the early days of the German Service he gave some early-morning *Sonderberichte* aimed at German working men about to leave home for the factory floor, and in 1942 he delivered a talk on the newly-published Beveridge Report, on the assumption that German workers, and the few Social Democrats who had managed to survive, would like to know what was being planned outside *Festung Europa*. Before joining the German Service, Lindley Fraser had been a Fellow of the Queen's College, Oxford, and a Professor of Political Economy at Aberdeen University. A heavy drinker, he spoke good German with a strong Scots accent, and became one of the German Service's most regular contributors, with a keen following in Germany.

One of the most obvious differences between the German Service and Darsie Gillie's French Service was that whereas Gillie put Frenchmen on the air, Hugh's programmes were almost exclusively 'fronted' by Britons: there was no equivalent of the popular *Les Français Parlent aux Français*. Sefton Delmer, an occasional contributor, recalled that 'the talks were terrible. They sounded like émigrés talking to émigrés or, as I used to say at the time, like Maida Vale calling Hampstead, not like London calling Berlin. They were addressed not to the mass of Germans who supported Hitler and his war of aggression, but to the infinitesimal few who wanted to lose it. To the ordinary German they were bound to sound like arid enemy propaganda and would be dismissed as such.' He was, almost certainly, misremembering. Thomas Mann gave talks for the German Service – they were recorded at his home in Hollywood, flown to New York, and sent by radio to London – as did the theologian Karl Barth, but for the most part German voices were excluded from the airwaves: it was felt that émigrés could well be regarded in Germany as traitors, whose views could be safely disregarded. Jewish accents could be counter-productive (Hugh himself complained about 'a most unpleasant Jewish voice with a guttural accent' that had briefly surfaced on a programme being beamed into Austria, adding that 'this is just the kind of voice that would render most Austrians more suspicious than even the most pronounced German accent'); and it was important that the German Service should represent the British point of view, with voices and accents to match. German émigrés were employed behind the scenes, writing scripts, converting news reports and talks into fluent and colloquial German (one of Hugh's pet obsessions), providing editorial and factual advice, and keeping up-to-date with German slang and jargon. During lunch breaks or after work the émigrés tended to gather in the canteen, while Hugh and his cronies drank beer in a nearby Finch's pub. (Hugh's lifelong passion for beer manifested itself in cryptic diary entries to the effect that Ansell's still brewed a 'good clear-tasting beer of considerable strength', though Young's proved 'thin and with little taste'.)

The foreign services had started out in Broadcasting House, but after it was bombed in December 1940 they endured a short, uncomfortable spell in a disused ice rink in Maida Vale before moving into Bush House in the Aldwych, which was to remain its base for the rest of the war, and still houses the World Service. Lockhart and other members of the PWE moved into the floor above the European Service, leaving Woburn to Sefton Delmer and his co-conspirators. 'Conditions in which staff – especially editorial – work are terrible. Forty to fifty feet below ground. No air conditioning, too little space, and very indifferent ventilation,' Lockhart noted in his diary. Members of staff often slept in the office overnight: Kirkpatrick was known to sleep on top of a desk, while Newsome strode about in a sarong. Hugh and Helga lived in the same places throughout the war, and every now and then she invited some of Hugh's colleagues to the parties she gave in Bayswater, and later in South Eaton Place: regular guests included Marius Goring, George Weidenfeld, Herbert Lom, Julius Gellner and Richard Crossman, with whom Helga would later have what her son James described as a 'dalliance'.

A 'Layout of BBC Broadcasts in German' circulated in 1940 declared that the Service's four main objectives were to convince its listeners that the Allies would eventually win, to make them want the Allies to win, to undermine their morale, and to encourage passive resistance: 'on the whole news is the primary means of convincing the Germans, first that they may lose, and later that they will lose.' 'BBC broadcasts to Germany rightly confine themselves to straight news, and to comment thereon,' Delmer wrote in July 1943. 'They refrain from revolutionary agitation against the regime as such agitation, coming from the mouth of the openly enemy BBC, would be ineffective.' Such provocation should be left to black propaganda, he declared, adding that 'Black says "we", where the BBC says "you".' Lindley Fraser defended the sobriety of German Service broadcasts despite 'accusations of dullness', claiming that 'nobody would have listened to this part of British radio propaganda with a view to being excited or amused . . . in really serious matters sobriety of presentation carries conviction where brightness merely annoys and in the end bores,' while a German listener later recalled how 'the sincere voices, the calmness of the operation, made an enormous contrast with the heroic shouting and neurotic heroism of the German broadcasts.'

Certain hours of the broadcasting day were set aside for particular audiences, with eight in the evening to midnight the peak listening time. German workers were expected to tune in at the crack of dawn, the educated elite came last of all on the grounds that 'listeners at this time of night can be expected to be more sympathetic to the Allied cause', and in between were programmes designed for women, soldiers, sailors, airmen and Austrian listeners. (The Austrian Service got off to a bad start on the grounds that it was 'so vulgar as to be incomprehensible to all except Viennese cab-drivers', while a programme for peasants was swiftly axed.) According to Fraser, 'one invaluable bait for the listeners after the early stages was the regular practice of reading out the names of German prisoners-of-war in Allied hands', sometimes adding details of their state of health and the treatment they were receiving; German airmen were demoralised by the listing of Luftwaffe crews who had been shot down. Martin Esslin came up with the idea of recording particularly boastful or bombastic speeches by Hitler and other Nazi leaders, and then playing them back, with lethal effect, after their claims had proved false; a German prisoner-of-war was quoted as saying that the most effective programmes were those which quoted from Hitler's speeches and from *Mein Kampf*, only to make them seem absurd. 'This is where we do the dirty work: where our colleagues try and raise their listeners' morale, we try to lower it,' Leonard Miall told the Queen when the Royals paid a visit to Bush House.

Feature programmes amounted to less than ten per cent of the output, but the best of them made a strong and favourable impact on their listeners, as well as enabling some émigrés to take to the air. *Die Gefreite Hernschal*, featuring a Berlin corporal, was Konrad Adenauer's favourite programme; *Kurt und Willi*, a dialogue over the air suggested by the poet Norman Cameron, was reluctantly admired by Goebbels, who conceded that Willi was an all-too-accurate representation of one of his Ministry of Propaganda officials (Goebbels was, according to Kirkpatrick, 'a professed admirer of the BBC German Service'); 'Frau Wenicke', played by Annemarie Haase, a former Berlin cabaret singer, proved immensely popular with Berliners in particular. In 1942 Goebbels allowed a new light entertainment programme featuring dance music to be broadcast over German radio, so the German Service retaliated with *Aus der Freien Welt*, in which Delmer and Spike Hughes played jazz and swing records, and songs were performed live by Marius Goring's wife, Lucie Mannheim. Refugees working for the Monitoring Service, among them George Weidenfeld, regularly came up with news and ideas, enabling the Service to react quickly to events and overall trends.

The Gestapo estimated that whereas a million Germans or German-speakers had listened to the German Service in 1941, this figure reached 15 million by the end of 1944 despite the severe penalties for tuning in to 'enemy poison' and the jamming to which BBC broadcasts were subjected – having encouraged all Germans to buy a radio before the war, and even distributed them free of charge, the Nazis had been hoist on their own petard. Neither the BBC nor the Government favoured jamming broadcasts from Germany, and British listeners were free to listen to Lord Haw-Haw or Mrs Eckersley, the wife of a former Chief Engineer of the BBC, who had moved from the ILP to the far right of the British political spectrum, settled in Germany before the war, and offered her services to the New British Broadcasting Company, a German 'black' station. 'Jamming is really an admission of a bad cause. The jammer has a bad conscience,' the BBC announced in May 1940. 'We have no such fears and to jam broadcasts in English by the enemy might even be bad propaganda.'

In 1942 Hugh was flown to Stockholm in a Mosquito to test the effect of jamming on BBC broadcasts from as near as he could get to the German mainland. He reported that jamming could be circumvented provided broadcasters spoke slowly and clearly: young and deep voices were more likely to get through than reedy or high-pitched ones, and the news should be read by two announcers, since alternating voices counteracted the weariness induced by jamming. Matters were further improved when, in January 1943, the European Services were allowed to use 'Aspidistra', the giant 500-kilowatt medium-wave transmitter known as the 'dreadnought of the ether'. Based in Crowborough, it had been bought from the States at Churchill's insistence, was shared with the RAF and PWE, and drowned out German medium-wave broadcasts.

One of the many problems facing Hugh and his colleagues was the extent to which they could, or should, encourage resistance to the regime in Germany. In the early days of the war, before the Venlo Incident, broadcasters were encouraged to emphasise and exploit any differences between the German people and their leaders. 'Peace with the German people, certainly; peace with the Nazis, never,' was a popular slogan, and in September 1939 Lord Macmillan, the Minister of Information, emphasised that British 'hostility is not to a people but to its rulers and their policy.' But although Robert Vansittart had been sidelined in terms of immediate access to Government ministers since his 'promotion' to Chief Diplomatic Adviser, 'Vansittartism' increasingly prevailed in the corridors of power. He believed that although 'good' Germans existed, the opposition was ineffectual and of no value or importance, and that even if Hitler was somehow removed, Prussian militarism and Ruhr industrialists would still prevail. His views were shared by Churchill and by Eden, and by influential journalists like F. A. Voigt, who dismissed 'workers' broadcasts' of the kind prepared by Patrick Gordon Walker as a waste of time. Vansittart had been employed as an adviser by Hugh Dalton, the Minister of Economic Warfare: as such he had quarrelled violently with Richard Crossman, who accepted that Hitler was supported by the vast majority of the German people, but was keen to exploit any signs of opposition. Hugh was uneasy about the Vansittart doctrine: he accepted the guilt of the German people as a whole, but thought it important to encourage opposition and disunity. A row broke out within the German Service in December 1941, when a faction led by Tangye Lean objected to Hugh's decision – supported by Crossman – to try to exploit potential disagreements between the Wehrmacht and the Party after the dismissal of General von Brauchitsch. Hugh instinctively agreed with a European Service *Monthly Intelligence Report* of earlier that year which declared that 'until Britain is ready to issue peace aims and unless these offer the Germans some satisfactory inducement to throw Hitler overboard, British propaganda to Germany is at a fatal disadvantage.'

The Allied policy of unconditional surrender, agreed with the Americans at the Casablanca Conference in January 1943, made life even harder for Hugh and those who thought like him. When news came through of the 20 July 1944 bomb plot, Hugh famously declared over the air that 'in Germany civil war has broken out': he had not, by then, learned that the plot had failed, and that Claus von Stauffenberg and his fellow-plotters had been rounded up, and he hoped that his words might encourage other potential rebels to join in. He had not been briefed in advance by Kirkpatrick or Bruce Lockhart, and it was, he later admitted, the only time during the war when he knowingly exaggerated in a broadcast. He was in liberated Paris in August 1944 when he was told, in confidence, that Rommel had been involved with the opposition to Hitler, and he decided to broadcast this over the German Service after learning of Rommel's suicide in October. Newsome, in the meantime, was furious when the German Service continued to broadcast *Kurt und*

Willi during the trial of the 20 July conspirators. To do so, he told Hugh, was 'quite out of tune with the electric atmosphere that must prevail in the Reich, and is completely false psychology'. The German Service, he continued, needed to be rethought and restructured: it no longer reflected a rapidly changing military situation or the fact that 'the clock really has struck twelve and is now ticking away Germany's future', and Hugh had to convince his listeners 'that there is not a moment to lose if unspeakable disaster is to be averted.'

With the Allies advancing through Europe, broadcasting to the enemy was in a state of flux. In 1943 Crossman had left PWE to work in Algiers before moving on to work for Eisenhower at the Supreme Headquarters of the Allied Expeditionary Force, or SHAEF. He later wrote that the feuding between Hugh and Delmer had driven him to 'take refuge in Eisenhower's headquarters', though Hugh strenuously denied this. British and American propaganda and broadcasting were becoming more closely co-ordinated, and as a member of the new Psychological Warfare Division (PWD) based in London, Crossman made sure that the policy directives received from PWE and the American Office of War Information tied in with strategic demands. Many of those working at the BBC, Hugh among them, were unhappy about the activities of SHAEF's 'creative planners': Hugh always claimed that dons and journalists made the best 'white' broad-casters, and he despised the advertising men who were being employed by PWD to churn out meaningless slogans. In the summer of 1944 US troops entered Luxembourg, and PWE took over Radio Luxembourg, broadcasting 'black' propaganda designed to alarm the civilian population and create confusion as the Allies advanced into Germany itself. Newsome was seconded to it, as were Gordon Walker and Leonard Miall.

Despite the activities of SHAEF and PWD, the audience for Hugh's programmes continued to expand as Allied troops pushed into Germany. According to a Luftwaffe officer, 'it was in the second half of 1945 that my friends and I began listening regularly to the German news bulletins emanating from London. We relied on this source for accurate and trust-worthy information regarding the change in military situations.' The old rivalry between Hugh and Delmer persisted to the end. Delmer had been posted to Bush House as Director of Special Operations, and as Germany descended into chaos, he and his 'black' colleagues issued bogus instruc-tions to civilians, while the German Service still insisted on telling the truth.

Hugh revisited Dachau in April 1945, just as it was being liberated by the Americans. The ground was littered with emaciated corpses and the stench was overpowering; among the survivors was a French journalist whom Hugh had known in Berlin. With the war drawing to a close, Hugh and his colleagues were deluged by letters from appreciative German listeners, and as the Russians finally took Berlin the last *Kurt und Willi* programme was broadcast from London. It ended with Willi saying 'I must go out now and see if there is any news', followed by an announcement that Hitler's death had just been declared on Hamburg Radio.

★

'Dear Lindley Fraser/ Dear Carleton Greene/ We've often you heard/ But never you seen' ran the anglicised version of a rhyme circulated among some German listeners of the German Service, and in September 1945 some of Hugh's grateful admirers had a chance to meet their hero when he returned to Berlin for the first time since his expulsion six years earlier. He expected to find a 'dead city', in which 'the peculiar atmosphere of Berlin (the feeling that one always had that something interesting was happening round the corner) had gone for ever', but although he found himself walking through 'acre after acre of complete and absolute ruin', it soon became apparent that 'people have not lost their faith in the future and are not willing to just lie down and die', and that the incessant tapping of hammers as people boarded up windows was at least a sign of life. The block of flats in Viktoriastrasse where he and Helga had lived before the war no longer existed; he visited the site of the Taverne, but although 'I thought I identified the site amidst the rubble, the only sign that there had ever been a Nachtlokal was one empty bottle of Rheinwein standing on the pavement.' He worried about 'an unhealthy tendency to speak always of "'fascism'" rather than "National Socialism". Fascism is a remote term which is apt to give people the comfortable feeling that the events of the past twelve years really had nothing to do with them.' His involvement with Germany was far from over: back home, he turned down a job with the *News of the World*, and found himself writing love letters to Helga, with whom he had spent little time during the war, and pining in vain for letters from her. His private life was unresolved, but at least he had had a good war.

Secret Agents

'Only after recruitment did I realise the meaning of all those parties, given by a mysterious Mr Smith, to which I had been invited in London where, in spite of the Blitz and the rationing, there seemed no lack of liquor and where everybody seemed to know each other. I was being vetted,' Graham wrote years later of his initiation into the Secret Intelligence Service, otherwise known as MI6. He was to retain his connections with the secret service for the rest of his working life, but his career with MI6's Section V began in what may well have seemed a remote and unimportant posting.

By the end of the Phoney War in the early summer of 1940, MI6 no longer had stations in France and the Low Countries. Denmark and Norway, and the capitals of neutral Europe – Stockholm, Berne, Madrid and, above all, Lisbon – became increasingly important for gathering intelligence and planting disinformation. Graham would, in due course, work for the Iberian Section of Section V in St Albans, but in the meantime he ventured further afield. Felix Cowgill, the head of Section V, was determined to place Section V representatives in all of MI6's important overseas stations: Malcolm Muggeridge was sent to Laurenço Marques in Mozambique, Nicholas Elliott to Istanbul, a nest of spies and secret agents, while Trevor Wilson, whom Graham would get to know a good deal better in South-East Asia in the 1950s, was in due course dispatched to Algiers. In August 1941 Graham told his mother that he was being sent out to Sierra Leone to work for the Colonial Office, and that 'the pay is very good, and the job interesting.' Counter-espionage in Freetown, together with parts of North Africa, was controlled by the Iberian Section, headed by Kim Philby. Graham was attached to him 'for a brief period of training', and so met for the first time a man with whom he was to have a long and controversial friendship, remaining loyal to him through his defection to the USSR in 1964, the revelations of his involvement with Burgess and Maclean and his betrayal of British agents during the early years of the Cold War, and his long years of exile in Moscow. 'After very few sessions, I came to like and respect him as someone quite out of the ordinary run of SIS trainees,' Philby recalled. 'The mechanics of the work presented no problem to a man of his intelligence. But he showed, in flashes, profound doubts about the relevance of whatever he might do in Freetown to the war against Hitler.' Philby 'shared his doubts', but did his best to persuade Graham that the ports of West Africa were swarming with enemy agents, and that Freetown would prove to be an invaluable 'observation post'. Graham 'listened with invariable courtesy, but I am quite sure he remained unconvinced.'

Graham travelled out to Freetown on an Elder-Dempster cargo ship, leaving Liverpool in a convoy in December 1941 and spending long hours anchored in Belfast Lough before finally heading out into the Atlantic. His fellow passengers included a gentle American Byzantologist, who seemed quietly pleased when news came through that Germany had declared war on the United States. In between drinking with the chief steward and taking his turn on watch – looking out for submarines on one watch, enemy aircraft on the next – Graham wrote *British Dramatists*, a volume in the elegant 'Britain in Pictures' series published by Collins. Rightly suspecting that his new posting would leave plenty of time for reading, he brought with him a sizeable library, including a dozen novels by Trollope; on the voyage out he read a crime novel by Michael Innes, which partly inspired him to write *The Ministry of Fear*, and Eric Ambler's *The Mask of Dimitrios*.

After three months' training in coding and decoding in Lagos – he stayed with a colleague in a 'disused police bungalow in a mosquito-haunted creek', devoting their evenings to cockroach-hunting – he took up his post in Freetown, where he moved into a 'dingy little Creole villa' near a swamp on the edge of the town, much favoured by flies and other insects, and by rats which swung off the bedroom curtains. It was not the most salubrious spot: the locals used the swamp as an outdoor lavatory and, he told his mother, 'I never quite get used to seeing a vulture sitting complacently on my roof as I come home,' but despite the discomfort and the tedium of his fellow Britons, Graham came to love the country he had visited six years before with his cousin Barbara: as he wrote in *Ways of Escape*, 'my love of Africa deepened there, in particular for what is called, the whole world over, the Coast, this world of tin roofs, of vultures clanging down, of laterite paths turning rose in the evening light.' Cuts turned septic in the humid, malarial heat, and every drop of water had to be boiled before use. He employed a cook to prepare his meals and converted the tiny dining room into an office: after writing five hundred words of *The Ministry of Fear*, a thriller set in wartime London, he devoted the mornings to decoding and replying to telegrams, snoozed in the afternoon, and in the evening walked along an abandoned railway line to look at the boats anchored in Freetown Bay.

Rather to his regret, these ships had a professional interest for him. With the Mediterranean dominated by the Axis powers, convoys to Egypt and North Africa had to take the long route out via the Cape, and Freetown was the main port of call between England and South Africa. One of Graham's jobs was to search Portuguese ships for illicit or revealing correspondence and for industrial diamonds from Angola which might otherwise make their way to Nazi Germany. On one occasion he had to interrogate a young Scandinavian seaman from Buenos Aires who was suspected of being a German agent; on another, after searching the cabin of a Swiss passenger, he confiscated a notebook in which he found the name and address of his French agent and translator, Denyse Clairouin, who had been arrested as a member of the Resistance and later died in a concentration camp. Graham's cover was that of a Special Branch officer, and he hated the work, which he felt was better suited to a policeman or an MI5 operative. In *The Heart of the Matter*, the novel he based on his experiences in Freetown, he described in agonising detail the miserable business of tricking and cajoling a Portuguese sea captain into handing over a compromising correspondence, and 'one such interrogation that I had to make of a prisoner so disgusted me that I never made another.'

Sierra Leone was hemmed in on three sides by Vichy-controlled French West Africa, and Graham was expected to keep an eye on developments there. His suggestion that he should open a brothel on a Portuguese island off Dakar was rejected; since 'nothing pleased the services at home more than the addition of a card to their intelligence files', he was tempted at times to send home bogus information gleaned from imaginary sources, a notion he put to use, years later, in *Our Man in Havana*. He communicated his findings in cipher to Section V's headquarters in St Alban's, where they were collated and put to use, exchanged coded telegrams with Malcolm Muggeridge in East Africa, and achieved a certain notoriety within the Service by realising his ambition to include the word 'eunuch' in a professional communication: invited to spend Christmas with colleagues in Bathurst, he replied 'Like the eunuch I cannot come'. 'The results of his work there were frankly meagre, and he was kind enough not to overload the bag,' Philby recalled, adding that 'too many overseas stations did so, creating a lot of useless work.' 'I didn't at that time know that he was my boss in London' Graham declared years later, but before long he would be working on a day-to-day basis with Kim Philby.

'This isn't an ideal spot,' he told Raymond, but 'I have a house of a kind to myself and can close the door when I want to be as morose as I like.' 'I suppose one never enjoys what one is doing at the moment – even writing books, and I rather envy you the sense of a useful job' he continued. He wondered whether he mightn't be better employed in a munitions factory back home, 'and certainly one would prefer any factory town to this colonial slum.' Hugh wrote to say that 'a very nice piece and a good drinking companion' was coming out to work for the government in Freetown, adding that he was seeing something of Dorothy Glover, and that they were planning a book on 'the sights of London'. Though 'grateful for your tasteful and reliable pimping', Graham wouldn't rise to the bait. 'I'll look out for the girl, but I don't really feel inclined for a playmate,' he replied, before going on to explain that 'a drinking companion would be a boon if there was anywhere to drink and anything to drink. But there's only one hotel, and nothing to get but bad bottled export beer of uncertain kinds, Scotch if you are lucky, gin which is a depressant, and South African wines which make you feel like hell next morning.' As for Dorothy Glover, with whom Hugh was having an occasional fling of his own, 'I wish you'd told me how she was looking, whether she seemed well, could down her pint and Irish as readily, etc.' 'This place will be most amusing to look back on, I daresay, but it's extraordinary how dull and boring the bizarre can be at the time,' he concluded. 'I'm getting grey, more and more bad-tempered, and rather a bully.' 'His current preoccupation seemed to be the shortage of contraceptives in Sierra Leone,' remembered Nicholas Elliott, who was making his way, circuitously, from London to Cairo, and encountered Graham in Freetown: fellow passengers from the boat which had brought him to West Africa agreed to make up the shortfall.

Graham's regrets at not being in England were exacerbated when, in November 1942, he received a telegram to say that his father had died, followed shortly after by another reporting him as being seriously ill. 'I feel it was rather a selfish act taking on a job abroad at this time, and I ought to have been home,' he wrote to his mother. 'I can't write about how sorry and sad I feel: he was a very good person in a way we don't seem able to produce in our generation . . . I'm glad it all happened so quietly and suddenly, so that he had no time to miss Elisabeth being away at the end. And I'm glad too that I belong to a faith that believes we can still do something for him.' In a PS he added 'This may seem Popish superstition to you, or it may please you, that prayers are being said every day for Da in a West African church, and that rice is being distributed here in his name among people who live on rice and find it very hard to get.' He told Raymond that he felt bad about not having visited his father more often, but 'when one did go down his rather noble old Liberalism was always inclined to make one bring out one's cynicism stronger than need have been.'

Graham worried that 'quinine and the dreary colonials and the even drearier services turn one into a complete nitwit': the consumption of food and drink over the Christmas period had been 'quite enough to fill a cargo boat', and 'one will be glad to get back to decent austerity again and at least the possibility of air raids.' 'The Africans at least contribute grace,' he told Raymond, 'but how tired one is of little plump men in shorts with hairless legs, and drab women, and the atmosphere of Balham going gay. People say the African is not yet ready for self-government. God knows whether he is or not: the Englishman here certainly isn't.' He would not have to put up with the knee-length shorts and frumpish wives for much longer. He had never got on with his superior in Lagos, and after a 'violent quarrel' he handed in his resignation. 'This is a quite useless spot,' he reported home, and 'you'll probably hear of me yet cleaning latrines on Salisbury Plain.' He lingered on for another six months, but after the North African landings, SIS interest in West Africa waned, and by March 1943 he was back in England.

On his return Graham was sent to work for the Iberian Section of Section V, based in 'a large, ugly house on the outskirts of St Albans', where six officers worked in 'what had been a spacious drawing room'. Spain and Portugal were swarming with spies and secret agents, and the work of the Iberian Section was of particular importance in the two years between the fall of France in May 1940 and the first Allied landings in North Africa in November 1942. It was feared that Spain might enter the war on Hitler's side, that Gibraltar might be taken by the Germans, and that even if Spain stayed out of the war its ports might be used by German warships, and by U-boats in particular. Every effort was made to counter the activities of the Abwehr in Spain, but although the Ambassador in Madrid, Sir Samuel Hoare, was anxious not to jeopardise Franco's neutrality and kept a tight control over MI6 activities, he simultaneously encouraged Graham's friend Tom Burns to pursue his own course as a propagandist-cum-spy. Otto John, who was involved with German resistance movements, including the 20 July 1944 conspiracy, took advantage of his status as a Lufthansa employee to make frequent visits to Lisbon and Madrid in vain attempts to win Allied support for the opposition to Hitler, as was Dusko Popov, whom Graham liked, and his girlfriend, Friedl Gärtner, who had earlier been involved in MI5's entrapment of Ben. Ralph Jarvis, who ran Section V, claimed to have identified and 'turned' almost all the Abwehr agents working in the country. Lisbon was an all-important outpost of MI6, and this reflected well on the status of the head of the Iberian Section in St Albans, Kim Philby.

Philby had joined MI6 in July 1940, on the recommendation of Guy Burgess, and began by teaching a course in 'underground propaganda' at an SOE training school, during the course of which he sought advice from both Sefton Delmer and Richard Crossman. Tomas Harris, a half-Spanish art dealer and MI5 operative, tipped him off about a possible position with Section V's Iberian Section, and Dick White, the future head of MI5, recommended him to Cowgill. The knowledge of Spain he had acquired while reporting on the Civil War for *The Times* provided an additional qualification for the job. Cowgill's great rival, Colonel Valentine Vivian, had worked in India with St John Philby, Kim's father, who had been shipped home from India in 1940 after making speeches in favour of Hitler, whom he had likened to Christ. He appeared before an Advisory Committee chaired by Norman Birkett, and – according to his son – 'bored them into submission', so prompting his release. Vivian invited father and son to lunch at his club, and when Kim briefly absented himself he asked St John about the rumours that his son had been a Communist at Cambridge. 'Oh, that was all schoolboy nonsense,' the old maverick explained. 'He's a reformed character now.'

According to Hugh Trevor-Roper, who worked for Section V at St Albans, Cowgill was 'a conscientious but worried official who sorely needed an efficient deputy in the private empire which he jealously, not to say frantically, guarded against every supposed rival or critic.' He looked to Philby to bring order to the running of the Iberian Section, and whereas 'Colonel Vivian doted on him, Major Cowgill clung to him.' A genial-seeming, hard-drinking character, Philby was efficient but curiously remote. John Cairncross, who joined the German Section of Section V from Bletchley Park, and was later discovered to have been the 'Fifth Man' of the Cambridge spies, remembered how 'Philby was widely regarded as an up-and-coming man and certainly had a very clear mind, writing memoranda which were always crisp and "going somewhere"', and that 'he was always smiling, in good humour, and seemingly indefatigable.' For Trevor-Roper, Philby stood out among the 'part-time stockbrokers and retired Indian policemen, the agreeable epicureans from the bars of White's and Boodle's, the jolly, conventional ex-naval officers and the robust adventurers from the bucket shop': he was generally thought to be an intellectual, 'yet he never allowed himself to discuss any intellectual subject', and although he seemed so much more sophisticated than his colleagues – Trevor-Roper greatly enjoyed his 'casual, convivial conversation' – he 'never allowed himself to be engaged' and if he criticised MI6 in any way 'it was always unspoken, implicit only in his benign, distant, Aesopian irony.'

Malcolm Muggeridge recalled how Philby came to dominate Section V, despite a stutter which 'was liable to become truly agonising, his lips moving convulsively and his hands clawing the air as he tried to get words out. It was more like a kind of fit than just a speech impediment.' He 'gave an impression of great energy and determination, which in some mysterious way his stutter only seemed to enhance', yet 'the prevailing impression I had was of a kind of boyishness, even naïvete.' He emanated a sense of suppressed violence, which manifested itself in 'the often infantile plots and stratagems his Section V work involved', and he had a soft spot for heavy drinkers, womanisers and disreputable figures like Guy Burgess. Nicholas Elliott remembered him as a 'formidable drinker', but 'it never affected his concentration, nor did it lead him into indiscretion.' He did not seem particularly interested in politics, literature or artistic matters: he took a keen interest in cricket, and his favourite author was Rex Stout.

Philby inspired loyalty and affection in most of his staff, but 'beneath his veneer of charm lay an emotional but ruthless personality,' Elliott recalled. 'You were either completely taken in by him or you disliked him,' a secretary from the typing pool remembered years later. She liked him, 'but I didn't like his single-mindedness, what I saw as his calculating ambition, and his cold-hearted way of handling his staff. If you made a blunder in the typing, old Cowgill would snort and bellow, but you knew he didn't mean it and it didn't hurt. Philby would call you into his office, point to the error, and say coldly, "Would you correct that, please."' Nor were his colleagues and drinking companions immune, even if, as in Graham's case, they were eight years older than Philby: 'I can remember walking into Graham Greene's office and he was gripping the chair and his eyes were glinting with anger. I asked him what was the matter and he said, "I've just had a caning from the headmaster."'

Philby, for his part, remembered how Graham 'worked quietly, coolly and competently, writing terse, sometimes devastating marginalia on incoming correspondence, occasionally breaking silence with some explosive comment on official idiocy.' Much to his regret, they were seldom alone together: colleagues 'put a distance between us', but 'I also felt in him a more personal factor: a deeply held sense of privacy on matters which seriously engaged him, contrasting with his easy attitude to the superficial aspects of work and play.' As a result, 'our relationship remained friendly to the point (I hope and think) of warmth,' but neither of them 'wanted to get more seriously involved'. Philby noticed how Graham combined 'a capacity for fierce contempt' – usually reserved for 'the powerful and pretentious', and 'self-important senior officers' – with a 'profound charity'. 'He seemed irresistibly drawn to the lowly and apparently dull', 'his voice grating in rising excitement, eyes blazing in kindly wonderment' as he pondered the characters and activities of clerks and salesmen. And 'in a man of obvious maturity and wisdom, there survived an almost adolescent itch to shock.'

John Cairncross first encountered Graham at St Pancras Station, while waiting for a train to St Albans. He was joined by a 'tall, lanky figure whom I recognised as a colleague of Kim Philby'. Graham asked him what he was reading, Cairncross told him *England Made Me,* Graham said it wasn't a bad book, Cairncross thought *The Power and the Glory* was better, and Graham agreed before owning up and introducing himself. Years later, after Cairncross had been denounced as the Fifth Man, Graham stood up for his old colleague, whom he always referred to as 'Claymore' in deference to his Scottish origins. Cairncross, for his part, thought that Graham 'was far closer to sainthood, with all his erratic traits, than the austere but cardboard figures which are still served up to us as the genuine article.' He greatly admired Graham's work for Section V, which 'seemed to me free from the anguish and tensions which he accepted when religion inspired or weighed upon him. There was no sign of a constant rebellion against conventional standards. On the contrary, he showed a dispassionate and impressive sense of realism.' 'His passionate dislike of injustice and his sympathy for the underdog never distorted his judgement in threading his way through the treacherous maze of espionage and counter-intelligence', nor was his understanding of intelligence operations 'blurred by the romanticism visible in the work of many other writers.' He showed no interest in power or office politics: he had no desire to succeed Tim Milne, the son of A. A. Milne, when Philby moved on to higher things, but happily stood aside for his friend Desmond Packenham. Cairncross remembered that Graham and Philby 'formed an excellent team inside and outside the office, and I remember seeing them, after Section V had moved back to London, going merrily off to a sex show in Soho.'

The work done in the Iberian Section was often of critical importance to the war effort – in November 1942, for instance, German plans to monitor Allied shipping passing through the Straits of Gibraltar by means of infra-red cameras and radar were intercepted and frustrated – but Graham remembered life in St Albans as 'a question of files, files, endless files', and despite the occasional caning from the headmaster, 'no melo-drama or violence disturbed us: only a certain boredom and lassitude induced by the closed-in life, since the nature of our occupation forced our small sub-section of five men to live too closely together.' No doubt it came as a relief when, in July 1943, Section V was transferred from St Albans to Ryder Street in St James's. The building also housed several officers from the OSS – the American equivalent of MI6 – including the mysterious James Jesus Angleton, later to play a part in the saga of the Cambridge spies. According to Muggeridge, Philby was 'more than ever the dominant personage', not just within the Iberian Section, but within Section V as a whole. Graham was given particular responsibility for the Azores, which Churchill was keen to capture since U-boats attacked convoys round the islands, but although he produced a 'Who's Who' of German agents in the area, circulated to twelve people *in toto*, his days in Section V were drawing to a close. Philby's duties, as far as his Russian controllers were concerned, were to keep them informed about any Anglo-American plans to make a separate peace with Germany or any divergence from the Allied policy of unconditional surrender, and to provide them with as much intelligence as possible without betraying his own position. As such, he fought hard but in vain to prevent Otto John from being flown from Lisbon to London in 1944, fearing that his involvement with the resistance movement in Germany might lend strength to those in Britain who opposed unconditional surrender, and worked to undermine the activities of Tom Burns in Madrid on the grounds that he was too well-disposed to Franco's regime and unsympathetic to those who yearned for a left-wing revolution in Spain.

Section V was privy to the top-secret Ultra decrypts, and responsible for the security of signals intelligence, and with the British increasingly well informed about Germany's order of battle on the Eastern Front in particular, fierce debates broke out within Section V about how much information could be passed on to the Russians without making it apparent that the dons and cryptographers in Bletchley had cracked the Germans' Enigma code. Cowgill favoured telling the Russians as little as possible, and protecting Bletchley material; Cairncross, on the other hand, had earlier leaked information which had played a critical role in helping the Russians on the Eastern Front.

Worries about compromising Ultra coincided with the realisation in some quarters that, once Germany had been defeated, Russia might well prove to be the new enemy of the Western democracies, and as the war swung in favour of the Allies, MI6 began to revert to its pre-war role as an anti-Communist organisation. Early in 1944 Stuart Menzies decided to recreate Section IX to combat Communist infiltration of the secret services. Cowgill was the obvious man to head such a body, but the KGB told Philby to put himself up for the job, since – from their point of view – no one could be better suited for it. Philby exploited the animosity between Cowgill and Vivian to his own advantage; Sir David Petrie, the Head of MI5, recommended Philby to Menzies; Cowgill resigned, and Philby came into his own. 'Philby at one stroke had got rid of a staunch anti-Communist and ensured that the whole post-war effort to counter Communist espionage would become known to the Kremlin. The history of espionage records few, if any, comparable masterstrokes,' Robert Cecil declared after the event. Graham was shocked by what he considered a piece of 'office jobbery' on Philby's part. In later years he took a more lenient line. 'I attributed it then to a personal drive for power, the only characteristic in Philby which I thought to be disagreeable,' Graham wrote in his foreword to Philby's *My Silent War.* 'I am glad now that I was wrong. He was serving a cause, and not himself, and so my old liking for him comes back.' According to Philby, he recommended Graham as the 'obvious man' to replace him as head of the Iberian Section, but he declined the job and resigned from the service on the grounds that 'he had not minded chivvying Portuguese from above but had no intention of taking personal responsibility for doing so' – quite apart from which 'the war was virtually won, nothing that he could do would hasten the end, and I had given him a pretext for cutting loose from a dreary and distasteful routine.' 'We were very sorry to lose him,' Philby concluded. 'His good company, trenchant talk and outbursts of amused exasperation had been for many months a reliable tonic for us all – the equivalent of a lot of stiff whiskies. And his work remained competent to the end.'

In the early spring of 1946 Malcolm Muggeridge recorded that he had 'got rather tight' at a party given by Graham's sister Elisabeth, attended by 'all the old MI6 chaps'. No doubt Graham was among them, for although he had resigned from the secret service in July 1944, he still kept a foot in that world. He worked briefly for the PWE in Bush House: his friend Antonia White worked for the French Section, and Graham edited *Choix: Les Ecrits du Mois à travers le Monde*, a magazine distributed in France. It has been suggested that he may have encouraged Hugh to make his contentious 'civil war' broadcast on the day after the 20 July plot, having learned about Stauffenberg's activities from Otto John, and that Philby, under orders from Moscow to oppose any co-operation with resistance movements in Germany, had done everything he could to discredit his source. Graham also prepared a film treatment for Alberto Cavalcanti, loosely based on the activities of the Ostro Ring, a network of agents based in Lisbon. The film was never made, but Graham's central character was a salesman of Singer sewing machines who set up a ring of imaginary agents, and resurfaced years later in *Our Man in Havana*.

*

When the war broke out, Elisabeth was working as a 'G girl' under Captain Cuthbert Bowlby, a dashing, good-looking sailor who had joined the Navy in 1912 at the age of seventeen and fought in the First World War before joining the SIS. The 'G' Section of MI6 was responsible for the administration and control of overseas stations, and in August 1939 her department was moved from Broadway, near St James's Park, to Bletchley Park, an 'incredible Victorian monstrosity', soon to be populated by code-breakers and cryptographers. A year later she was told that she was being sent out to Cairo, once again working for Captain Bowlby. In September 1941 she boarded a Dutch boat bound for West Africa, and Graham saw her off at the dockside. Freetown, she told her mother, was 'a dilapidated dump of corrugated iron-roofed houses and a few shops filled with cheap-looking stuff from Manchester and Birmingham'. She had drinks with the Governor, and wondered what Graham would make of it all. From Sierra Leone she made her way to Lagos, and on by air across the middle of Africa, to Sudan and on to Egypt, flying down the Nile and catching sight of the Pyramids as they came in to land. Her first letter home was written from the Anglo-American Hospital: somewhere in Africa she had been afflicted with boils and, to make matters worse, they were infested with maggots.

Despite the presence of Rommel's Afrika Korps in neighbouring Libya, Cairo was a haven by wartime standards, an exotic, cosmopolitan city crammed with spies, refugees and Allied soldiers of every kind. Officers on leave could join brass hats, politicians and visiting socialites in playing golf or polo at the Gezira Sporting Club or dining at Shepheard's Hotel: familiar figures on the Cairo scene included the playboy King Farouk, Brigadier Enoch Powell, the writers Lawrence Durrell and Olivia Manning, and SOE officers like Patrick Leigh Fermor and David Smiley, enjoying bibulous evenings at Tara, Sophie Tarnowska's house on Gezira Island, before being sent back to guerrilla warfare in Crete or Albania. The pantherine Barbara Skelton, who had travelled out by exactly the same route as Elisabeth and was working, at Donald Maclean's sugges-tion, as a 'cipherine' attached to the British Embassy when not in bed with King Farouk or the actor Anthony Steele, remembered Cairo as 'oppressive, dusty and colourless. Trams ran in all directions hooting, limp little donkeys loaded with fruit trailed along the gutters surrounded by horseflies. The pavements were crowded, women with frizzy black hair hurried along on taloned cork sandals, and tarbooshed men shuffled with limp arms or stood picking their noses and spitting into the dust.' Elisabeth was overwhelmed by the noise and the smells, by 'hundreds of beggars and people selling fly-whisks, balloons, dark glasses, nuts, fruits – rather like an outsize fun fair.' She rented a flat on Gezira Island, on the banks of the Nile. It backed onto the Gezira Club, the only green space for miles around, and from her balcony she could see the Pyramids gleaming in the distance. Before long she had employed two *safragis*, or domestic servants, including a cook. Cairo was 'impossibly expensive', but despite the dust and the noise and the drunken soldiers being sick in the gutters over Christmas ('perfectly foul') it seemed like luxury after London. She played tennis, went to the races, danced with officers on leave, took tea and cakes at Groppi's, and went duck shooting in the desert. 'I feel quite ashamed at the amount of food we eat here,' she told her parents and, recalling the austerity of wartime England, she admitted to being 'slightly repelled by the amount of money which is spent on food and drink in overcrowded restaurants'. Rozanne Colchester, who was to become a lifelong friend, remembers spotting a 'tall, slim, obviously English girl making her way on foot to the MI6 office'. She took to 'Liza' at once, noting how her soft voice and apparent vague-ness disguised the fact that she was, in fact, 'intensely observant'.

Elisabeth enjoyed her work as well as her social life, even though her first office was a tiny tiled room which had once been a lavatory. 'Cuth' Bowlby had been asked by Stuart Menzies to run the MI6 station in Cairo, operating under the cover name of the Inter-Services Liaison

Department (ISLD) and sharing a building with Security Intelligence Middle East (SIME). SIME was run by Brigadier Raymond Maunsell, who ran his own elaborate network of informants and double-agents, including drug-runners, brothel madames, gun-runners and deserters, as well as employing Maurice Oldfield, later to become a friend of both Graham and Rodney Dennys and, in due course, the director of MI6. In November 1941 Felix Cowgill appointed Rodney Dennys to be the station's Section V officer. He was commissioned into the Intelligence Corps – 'he's only a bogus soldier, of course,' Elisabeth once wrote apropos his then rank of captain – and after travelling out to Lagos in a 'leisurely convoy' he made his way across Africa to Cairo 'to set up a sort of miniature Section V' in ISLD, known as 'B' Section, at GHQ Middle East. More often than not, civilian and military intelligence agencies regarded one another with deep suspicion, but, Dennys recalled, 'we were fortunate in a complete absence of internal rivalries and generally close and amicable relations with SIME,' despite the fact that, as part of SIS, ISLD reported to the Foreign Office, was not under military command, and was not paid by the Army. Cuthbert and Maunsell were on 'close and friendly terms', and Dennys found the SIME officers with whom he had dealings 'civilised, intelligent and amusing'. ISLD's territory ranged 'from Italy to Persia and from the Balkans to East Africa', and 'B' Section worked closely with indigenous intelligence and security operations in these countries as well as in neutral Turkey. ISLD had its own separate ciphers and communication with London, and more than once Archibald Wavell, the Commander-in-Chief made use of this when he wanted to communicate with Churchill in London. There was, Dennys remembered, 'a certain buccaneering eccentricity about the officers and secretaries of SIS, including Section V, which allowed us to cut corners and arrange things outside the rules.' Rozanne Colchester thought that Rodney Dennys was more like an Oxford don than a conventional military man. He was, she recalled, 'a dear man, tall, gangly, slim, slow, humorous, but *not* on the ball.' Her husband, Halsey Colchester, who worked as Dennys's deputy, combined devotion to his superior with occasional frustration at his apparent inability to make up his mind.

'I made my reputation in the field of strategic deception,' the everdiscreet Rodney Dennys admitted forty years after he arrived in Cairo, and as such he found himself working with a man who, according to Field Marshal Alexander, did as much as any other individual to win the war for the Allies. A dapper professional soldier, Colonel – later Brigadier – Dudley Clarke was a humorous, inventive individual: according to Edgar

Williams, Montgomery's Intellligence chief, he had 'a face like a sort of merry-eyed potato,' while Dennis Wheatley, who was an inventive and convivial member of the London Controlling Section as well as providing Friedl Gärtner with 'cover' as his research assistant, remembered him as an 'excellent raconteur and great company in a party' – though he outraged some of his colleagues in the Intelligence community when he was arrested in Spain for appearing in public dressed as a middle-aged woman. Clarke's brother, T. E. B. Clarke, made his name after the war writing scripts for Ealing comedies: Dudley Clarke deployed a similar wit and ingenuity to deceiving the Italians and then the Germans about the strength and intentions of British troops. According to his entry in the *Oxford Dictionary of National Biography*, 'The misleading clues he scattered round the Mediterranean theatre led the enemy to overestimate allied strength there by nearly a quarter of a million men and tied down troops which otherwise might have been used to resist the allied invasion of Normandy. He thus blazed a trail successfully followed by the sister organisations of Colonel John Bevan in London and Lieutenant-Colonel R. Peter Fleming in the Far East.' It has been claimed elsewhere that Clarke and Sefton Delmer were the war's two great masters of deception, but whereas Delmer's 'black' propaganda was directed at German 'other ranks', Clarke aimed to deceive the enemy's top brass. Like scriptwriters, those who worked behind the scenes never became household names, and Clarke and his colleagues, including Rodney Dennys, never had – or expected – the public recognition they deserved.

Wavell, as Commander in-Chief in the Middle East, appointed Clarke to be his 'Personal Intelligence Officer', and Clarke's 'A' Force – which was initially housed above a brothel – was set up to mastermind deception in December 1940, when Allied fortunes were at a low ebb, with 40,000 British troops vastly outnumbered by Marshal Graziani's army in Libya and the Mediterranean in danger of becoming an Axis-controlled inland lake. Dummy tanks, gliders, railway sidings and bombers were built out of plywood and painted by *camoufleurs* to deceive enemy aircraft; Jaspar Maskelyne, the most famous conjurer and illusionist of the day (Elisabeth saw him on stage in Cairo) lent his expertise, and imaginary units of paratroopers were conjured up to mislead and overawe the enemy. By the time Rodney Dennys arrived in Cairo in early 1942, Wavell had been sacked by Churchill and Auchinleck put in his place: Rommel had replaced Graziani as the main threat to British power in the Middle East, but the techniques used against him remained the same. Rodney Dennys became 'the key member' of the 'remarkably successful

"Deception Committee" run by Dudley Clarke in 1942–43' according to J. M. Bruce Lockhart, a veteran of those days: Dennys's 'ability to put your mind inside the mind of a turned German agent – who sometimes didn't even *exist*, except in your mind – was quite remarkable.'

MI5's XX Committee was responsible for 'turning' enemy agents, and in Cairo Rodney Dennys managed a 'Special Section' to run double agents. Set up by the heads of 'A' Force, SIME and MI6, and housed in a requisitioned villa, it was 'effectively controlled by Colonel Dudley Clarke, the commander of the ghostly "A" Force', and Dennys suggested that it should be called the 'XXX Committee' on the grounds that 'we might go one better than London.' Captured spies who could be 'turned' were used to supply misleading information: 'Torch', the codename for the Allied landings in North Africa, was preceded by intimations of landings in Greece, while a 'turned' Abwehr agent in Istanbul was equipped with a radio transmitter and codes and went on to spread disinformation about 'Overlord', the invasion of Normandy. Dennys was involved in 'turning' Renato Levi, codenamed 'Cheese', an Italian Jew living in Cairo who proved to be an 'important and amazingly durable double agent'. Masterminded by Maunsell's deputy at SIME, W. J. Kenyon-Jones, 'Cheese' supplied the Abwehr and SIM, Italian military Intelligence, with plausible disinformation which was then passed on to Rommel's headquarters.

Dennys also played a crucial role in the capture and turning of a German spy operating in Cairo. With Rommel expected to attack Egypt at any moment – Elisabeth enrolled in the Auxiliary Territorial Service (ATS) so that she could claim prisoner-of-war status if she was captured – the Abwehr decided to smuggle a spy and a radio operator into Cairo to report on British military strength and movements. Johann Eppler was half-German, half-Egyptian; he had been born and brought up in Egypt, and spoke English well enough to be mistaken for a British officer. 'Operation Condor' involved flying Eppler and his companion, 'Sandy', to Rommel's headquarters, from where they were taken across some of the most remote and barren stretches of the Sahara by a dashing Hungarian called Count Ladislaus de Almaszy, who had made his name before the war as an explorer in the desert. Almaszy took them as far as the Egyptian border, where they changed into civilian clothes, carrying with them a briefcase containing £50,000 in British bank notes: as it turned out, the £5 notes were German forgeries, while the pound notes were genuine, but had been collected from banks in neutral countries such as Spain and Portugal.

Once in Cairo, Eppler and 'Sandy' hired a houseboat, set up their radio transmitter, and spied out the land. Eppler was a likeable, convivial figure who passed muster when disguised as an officer in the Rifle Brigade, and was happy to spend long hours propping up the bar with, as he hoped, drunk and indiscreet British officers. Eppler's pleasure-loving ways were viewed askance by the puritanical Anwar Sadat, the future President of Egypt, who sided with the Germans in his determination to end British control of his country, and was one of Eppler's Egyptian contacts. Doubtless to Sadat's disapproval, one of Eppler's most useful contacts was a beautiful belly dancer and German agent called Hekmath Fakmy, who performed at the Kit Kat Cabaret, lived in the houseboat next door and had an electric effect on susceptible and homesick British officers – none more so than hapless 'Major Smith', who was unwise enough to bring his briefcase with him on a visit to the houseboat. It contained vital information about forthcoming British military operations, and while he lay in a drugged post-coital slumber, Eppler removed the contents of his briefcase. As it happened, his radio operator was unable to get through to the Abwehr office in Athens, but – for the time being at least – luck was on Eppler's side.

But not for much longer. While all this was going on, two German radio operators had been captured on a raid into Libya. They had with them a copy, in English, of Daphne du Maurier's novel *Rebecca*. The price on the endpapers was given in escudos, and through Section V in London it was learned that several copies of the novel had been bought by the wife of the German military attaché in Lisbon. There was no reason to connect this to the harmless-seeming Eppler, were it not for the fact that he had unwisely allowed himself to become involved with another beautiful woman – only this time the *femme fatale* was working for the Jewish Agency. She felt uneasy about him, and reported her suspicions to Major A. E. W. Sansom, a stocky, 'rather unattractive Levantine Englishman' who had spent most of his life in the Middle East, spoke fluent Arabic, Greek and Armenian and, as the head of Field Security, was ready to impersonate a drunken Greek businessman in order to elicit compromising information from Eppler. Eppler's £5 notes were revealed to be forgeries, and Rodney Dennys – 'Robby' in the version of events provided by Leonard Mosley, who was working as a journalist in Egypt at the time – suggested that Eppler's houseboat should be raided at once. A copy of *Rebecca* was found: Dennys realised that it was being used as a code book, and spent a long night breaking the code. Eppler's transmitter was also retrieved from the bottom of the Nile – he had hurled it overboard during the course of the raid – and, using the *Rebecca* code, it was used to transmit misleading information to Rommel's headquarters. Eppler was tried and condemned to death in what was, in fact, a sham trial, designed to mislead the enemy: the Abwehr were led to believe that their agent had been shot, but in fact he was sent to a prisoner-of-war camp, and returned to Germany after the war.

Nor was that the end of the Eppler affair. The wretched 'Major Smith', facing court martial for his amorous indiscretions, ended his days as a precursor of 'The Man Who Never Was', the corpse disguised as a British officer which was dropped by submarine off the coast of Spain in April 1943 carrying bogus top-secret papers suggesting that the Allies would land in Greece and Sardinia rather than Sicily – a celebrated and highly influential deception ploy codenamed 'Operation Mincemeat', in which Dudley Clarke was inevitably involved. In August 1942, Rommel mounted what proved to be his last offensive against Montgomery's Eighth Army at the Battle of Alam Halfa. Shortly before the battle began, troops of the German 90th Light Division came across a blown-up British scout car. The dead body at the wheel, allegedly that of 'Major Smith', had in its pockets documents giving details of non-existent British minefields and misleading information about the state of the terrain and the deployment and strength of British forces. The Panzer division changed direction as a result, only to find itself bogged down in acres of soft sand, and Montgomery went on to win a decisive victory which paved the way for El Alamein, the turning point in the war in North Africa.

Leonard Mosley's *The Cat and the Mice* reads like fiction, and the story of Eppler's arrest and detection inspired two films and a novel: many years later, Elisabeth provided a full-time novelist, Michael Ondaatje, with background material for *The English Patient*, which is set in North Africa during the war. Mosley described 'Robby' as 'a long, lean, pale man', while the unnamed Elisabeth was 'as long in her body as her husband, but much better looking'. Rodney Dennys had met Elisabeth when she was working with Bowlby on evacuation plans for Cairo at a time when Rommel's forces were sweeping all before them in North Africa: she faced prosecution for wandering out of bounds near the Suez Canal, Rodney helped to get her off, and one thing led to another. When she had to move house, she moved into the flat Dennys shared with two colleagues, albeit on a temporary basis. 'Everyone always likes him,' she told her mother. 'He's got all the qualities I like most', including 'heaps of sense of humour'. They visited Luxor and Karnak together, and before long they had announced their engagement. 'Vices: smokes cigars and can out-drink most men. In temperament she is very like myself and

also has the kindest heart and the sweetest character,' Rodney Dennys
wrote to his mother in Richmond-on-Thames, adding that they both
'laughed at the same things'. 'Elisabeth's engagement was pleasing,'
Graham told Hugh in August 1942. 'The man is very nice and intelligent.
[Quite when Graham had met Rodney Dennys remains unclear.] I was
afraid she was emotionally tied up with the middle-aged married sailor
[Cuthbert Bowlby]. God knows what size the children will be, as the
man is a good bit taller than me.' The only obvious snag about getting
married was a ruling – unenforced, as it turned out – that husbands and
wives could not work in the same office. 'I could quite easily get another
job here,' Elisabeth told her parents, 'but I'd hate to leave our comic
organisation and stop working for Cuth.'

Two months later Elisabeth had broken off the engagement, and
Graham provided moral support. 'I'm sorry things have not gone too
well,' he wrote from Freetown. 'Things can be hell, I know. The peculiar
form it's taken with me has been in loving two people as equally as makes
no difference, the awful struggle to have one's cake and eat it, the inability
to throw over one for the sake of the other . . . Yours is different and I
imagine just as hellish. I always used to laugh at emotional situations and
feel they couldn't any of them beat toothache. One lives and learns.' As
he knew from his own experiences in Sierra Leone, the heat provoked
a fatal combination of 'feverish mental sexuality with much impaired
vitalities': he suggested that Elisabeth should wait and see if they felt the
same way once they were back in a 'reasonable climate'. A brisk social
life provided an antidote for both parties. Elisabeth took a holiday in
Palestine, and was surprised to hear German spoken all about her in Tel
Aviv – the city was populated by German Jews – and sauerkraut and
sausages the staple fare in restaurants despite the midsummer heat; at a
party in Cairo she spotted Clare Hollingworth, who spent the war years
reporting from the Middle East; she got to know 'Graham's friend'
Malcolm Muggeridge, 'liked him enormously' and found him 'a most
amusing person'. (Years later, Rodney Dennys described Muggeridge as
'that mosquito of the Western world, whom I refused to have nearer Cairo
than Lourenço Marques as he was such an incompetent CE officer', but
by then both he and Elisabeth had fallen out with their old acquaintance,
as had Graham himself.) The conviviality of Cairo life was interrupted
by news of her father's death. 'I hope he hadn't been very sad and depressed
about the war,' Elisabeth told her mother. 'He was so essentially a kind
and gentle person, and such a loving one too. You know, don't you, what
a very dear and perfect "pair" you have been as parents for me.'

All Elisabeth's letters home had to be passed by the censor, and were stamped accordingly, so it is hard to get a clear idea of exactly what her work involved. What we do know is that she was awarded a certificate for outstanding service by the Commander-in-Chief, Middle East. Rodney Dennys – who was awarded the OBE in 1943 – was involved in an abortive plan to capture the dashing Count Almaszy: had this succeeded, Almaszy would have found several pre-war friends in Cairo working for irregular units like the Long Range Desert Group. As the tide of war turned in favour of the Allies, 'A' Force's activities expanded from the Middle East into North Africa, the Balkans and Greece. Rodney Dennys busied himself preparing 'black' and 'white' lists for Greece, Yugoslavia and Albania, a chore which involved the compilation of some 25,000 index cards, and he made frequent visits to Istanbul, where he had appointed his friend Nicholas Elliott the MI6 agent. Dennys was there at the time of the celebrated 'Cicero' affair, in which the Albanian valet to the British Ambassador, Sir Hughe Knatchbull-Hugessen, photographed top-secret documents for his German masters. By now Cuthbert Bowlby was spending much of his time on his travels, and Elisabeth found herself at a loose end: she stood in for Rodney Dennys's secretary, and in July 1943 she flew with him to Algiers; she was the only woman on the eight-hour flight, and tin drums behind a canvas screen served as lavatories when they stopped to refuel ('Luckily I am very continent,' she told her mother).

Almaszy had proved too elusive, but Rodney Dennys had no intention of allowing Elisabeth to make her escape. After Elisabeth had broken off the engagement, he considered hurling her engagement ring into the Nile, but decided against and exchanged it for a 'dis-engagement ring' with a large sapphire embedded in platinum; and when she accepted it, he knew he was still in with a chance. 'Malcolm [Muggeridge] always said I would marry Rodney in the end,' Elisabeth admitted after the event, and their wedding finally took place in January 1944. Cuthbert Bowlby was out of the country, so Elisabeth was given away by John Teague, who had been in temporary command of ISLD before Bowlby's arrival. The reception was given by Angela and Denis Greenhill, who became lifelong friends: at Rodney Dennys's memorial service in 1993 Sir Denis Greenhill, who had spent his working life in the Foreign Office and ended his career as head of the Diplomatic Service, revealed how, in their time together in Cairo, Dennys had invented such a plausible German agent, to whom he supplied seemingly useful but misleading information, that his imaginary character was awarded the Iron Cross.

The newly-weds spent their day-long honeymoon lost in the Nile Delta, and the following morning Rodney Dennys left for Istanbul. They were to enjoy only occasional encounters for the rest of that year. After the Allied landings in North Africa, Bowlby was posted to Algiers to open an SIS station. Elisabeth followed him there, flying from Cairo in 'one of the uncomfortable planes where one sits on a tin shelf with nothing to lean against except rivets and the side of the plane is curved in the most uncomfortable way.' No longer working for ISLD, Rodney Dennys visited Washington and New York on behalf of MI6: he noted how many Americans regarded England as a 'decadent aristocracy with communistic leanings', while in liberated Paris he found Trevor Wilson 'as vague and feckless as ever'. Elisabeth, increasingly restless in Algiers, longed to be with him after his eventual return to London. 'Please see that I do not get an administrative job of *any* description in Head Office if you possibly can,' she begged him. 'I have *had* it. I'd rather have a lowlier job in the more active sections than a higher grade one with the big old boys ... Without reducing my war effort I'd like more time with you – you are sure to be working overtime, so let's have one of us with time to cook the dinner. I'm not really an *ambitious* secretary any more.'

In January 1947 Rodney Dennys was appointed by Ernest Bevin, the Foreign Secretary, 'to serve in an unestablished capacity as a Temporary Principal in the Foreign Office', and after a brief spell back in England his footloose life resumed once more. He travelled to Palestine, reporting to the Foreign Office's Security Department on the activities of Jewish terrorist groups, before flying on to India, Ceylon and Singapore. That same year, Kim Philby was appointed MI6's station head in Istanbul, under cover of being the First Secretary at the British Consulate. Rodney Dennys had shared an office with him for six months, but 'while we continued to remain friends, our relationship was at arm's length' – which suggests that he must have felt some unease about Philby's activities. Two years earlier Philby had a narrow escape when an NKVD agent named Constantine Volkov approached the British consulate in Istanbul, promising to reveal the names of three Soviet agents working for the Foreign Office in London; Philby realised that he must be one of the three, and arranged for Volkov to be bundled back to Moscow in the nick of time. Turkey was on the front line of what had become the Cold War, and Istanbul was, once again, abuzz with spies and secret agents, as well as being MI6's base for its operations in the Balkans, Central Europe and the southern reaches of the USSR, where it encouraged the activities of the 'Promethean League', exiled anti-Soviet minorities from Georgia, Belarus and the Ukraine. Philby worked closely with these right-wing exiles, infiltrating them into the Soviet Union before tipping off the KGB.

Albania formed part of Philby's remit, and Istanbul was a haven for Albanians who had fled from, or were opposed to, Enver Hoxha's Communist regime, which had been in power since the country was liberated from German occupation in November 1944. Philby knew a good deal about British- and American-backed schemes to infiltrate agents into Albania. Rodney Dennys was working back in Cairo when the plans were being hatched by an indiscreet and amateurish combination of Albanian royalists and old SOE hands like Colonel David Smiley, who had fought in Albania during the war, and had come to loathe Hoxha and all he stood for: as Rodney Dennys recalled, Albanian operations represented 'the dying twitches of the SOE', in the course of which, 'years after it had been disbanded, SOE came back into its own, with agents in the field, and in the Balkans, SOE's favourite area.' In August 1949 Kim Philby left for Washington, where he had been appointed the Liaison Officer with US Intelligence, and his place in Istanbul was taken by Rodney Dennys. The Dennyses and their three young children lived in Turkey until 1953, and on their return to England Elisabeth gave several talks on the BBC's Home Service about their life and travels in the Middle East. On his way to Washington, Philby stopped off in London, where he was briefed about the impending Albanian operations: he tipped off the KGB, and the agents were rounded up and shot as soon as they set foot on Albanian soil. It is very likely that the Albanian landings would have failed without Philby's intervention, but Rodney Dennys, who knew, or knew of, many of those whom his old colleague had betrayed, was less forgiving and less well-disposed than his brother-in-law, who always retained a soft spot for his former colleague from the Iberian Section. The Dennyses had always thought of Philby as a close friend – their daughter Amanda went to school with one of the Philbys' children, and remembered him as 'very charming and charismatic' – and Rodney Dennys never forgave 'the worst traitor to have defiled this country'.

Scenes from Office Life

'Have you heard that I'm now contracted to be a full-blown publisher immediately the war's over: after 18 months training I am to have full charge of Eyre & Spottiswoode, which should be fun – but is anything fun when one gets down to it?' Graham asked Elisabeth in August 1943. 'I'm sorry Graham is so fed up,' Elisabeth had written from Cairo a month earlier. No doubt he had felt in limbo after his return from Sierra Leone, and if a job in publishing seemed rather removed from the war effort, at least it gave him an arena in which to expend his energies. Eyre & Spottiswoode was a long-established firm which was allowed to describe itself as the 'King's Printer', and shared with the Oxford and Cambridge University Presses the exclusive right to publish the Authorised Version of the Bible; despite an aura of extreme respectability, it had also been the British publisher of that notorious antisemitic forgery *The Protocols of the Elders of Zion*. Both the proprietor, Oliver Crosthwaite-Eyre, and the chairman, Douglas Jerrold, were Roman Catholics, and Graham had been recommended to them by Tom Burns. According to Malcolm Muggeridge, Graham thought life would be hard for writers like himself in the post-war world, and wanted a 'secure economic base', and Graham told James Hadley Chase, the author of *No Orchids for Miss Blandish*, that he was thinking of concentrating his energies on publishing and film-making rather than writing novels.

Wartime publishing was a curious and paradoxical trade. Paternoster Row, where many of the leading publishers had their offices, had been bombed to smithereens in December 1940, and many warehouses and printing works were destroyed in subsequent raids; metal printing plates were compulsorily purchased and turned into armaments, making it hard or impossible to reprint existing titles. Publishing was not a reserved profession, and publishers, printers and binders lost qualified staff to the forces, and had to rely increasingly on women and old retainers, most of them overworked and underpaid. They had to make do with poor-quality materials, and the dispiriting demands of the Book Production War Economy Agreement; most vexingly of all, paper supplies were severely restricted by a quota system, and publishers had to compete for what little there was with government departments like the Ministry of Information. And yet publishers flourished as never before. Civilians and servicemen alike read to escape from the world about them, to fill in the long hours of the blackout or fire-watching duties or waiting to go into action, and to prepare themselves for life and work after the war was over. There was a seemingly insatiable market for Trollope and Jane Austen, for thrillers like *No Orchids for Miss Blandish*, for Penguin paperbacks that fitted neatly into a battledress pocket, and for leftwards-leaning tracts about the future of post-war Britain. As Kenneth Sisam of the Oxford University Press put it, publishing was 'the luckiest of all trades and professions in wartime, having somehow got on towards doubling their sales at a time of price control and drastic rationing of labour and materials.'

Graham found himself sharing an office with Douglas Jerrold and, according to Muggeridge, 'a telephone call by either produced a sort of anguished silence in which a third person found himself listening intently to every word spoken into the receiver, however softly.' Both men were Catholic converts, but whereas Graham was, according to Muggeridge, 'a fervent advocate of Catholic-Marxist dialogue', Jerrold was a right-wing Catholic, and a keen admirer of Mussolini and the corporate state. A founder of the Friends of Nationalist Spain, he had helped to charter the plane which flew Franco from the Canary Islands to Morocco in July 1936 to launch his revolt against the Republican government, and he had toured Franco's front line in the company of Francis Yeats-Brown and General J. F. C. Fuller. A 'tall, saturnine figure' with a tiny head and thin hair, and a left arm that had been badly damaged on the Western Front, Jerrold came to work in a black jacket, striped trousers, a stiff collar and highly polished black shoes from Lobb's. Tom Burns described him as 'a Counter-Reformation Catholic, a High and hard-headed Tory, a one-time Treasury official with a computer mind in that small head of his.' Anthony Powell remembered him as 'large, sombrely dressed, immensely gloomy (sounding on the telephone as if already in purgatory)', and claimed that 'Jerrold's whole life was a perpetual round of making paper mountains out of political molehills and breaking literary butterflies on the wheels of publishing.' Jerrold had founded the Right Book Club before the war in a vain attempt to emulate the success of the Left Book Club, the brainchild of his former colleague Victor Gollancz. He was also the founder and editor of the *English Review*, a literary and political magazine of conservative disposition, and when not 'breathing out dire threats to withdraw his support from Winston Churchill', he could often be found working on its behalf in the Authors' Club in Whitehall Court or The Lamb & Flag off Garrick Street, usually in the company of its literary editor, Hugh Kingsmill, and the right-wing historian Charles Petrie.

Graham, by contrast, retained 'the look of a perennial undergraduate engaged in working out some ingenious joke or impersonation', but despite their temperamental and political differences the two men worked well together: as Graham recalled, 'Jerrold and I had exactly the opposite political ideas, but we had no quarrels and remained friends to the end.' In an article for *Picture Post*, Jerrold compared his protégé to a brilliant child who liked to trick and confuse the grown-ups: Graham invented an imaginary author called Mrs Montgomery, played by Dorothy Glover, who rang up every now and then in a filthy mood to complain about a missing manuscript; according to Jerrold, 'in her righteous anger she summoned all and sundry to urgent meetings at impossible times in inconvenient places.' Jerrold shared Marion Greene's doubts about Graham's youthful dalliance with Russian roulette, the details of which were first published in *The Saturday Book*, an annual anthology of new writing edited by John Hadfield, and included in *The Lost Childhood and Other Essays*, published by Eyre & Spottiswoode in 1951. (According to Raymond's wife, Eleanor, the revolver had been brought back from the war by Ian Lake, a cousin of the Greenes, and never contained any bullets; others have suggested that it was, in fact, a starting pistol.)

When not engaging in practical jokes, Graham 'would settle down to the serious business of the day, telephoning with rapid succession to his bank, to his stockbroker, to his insurance agent, to his literary agent, to a film company or two, and, if it was a really busy morning, to two or three editors. During these conversations, the tortured conscience so frequently, and so movingly, on exhibition in his novels was notably absent.' Jerrold's belief that 'he is, and does not wish you to know it, an absolutely first-class man of business' was confirmed by Anthony Powell. Although Powell told Malcolm Muggeridge that Graham 'always seemed to him like a scholarship boy who was putting up a really wonderful performance', he also thought him 'a man of very considerable practical ability (unlike many writers)', whose 'nervous energy, organising faculty, taste for conflict, sudden bursts of rage, would have made him successful in most professions: indeed, I can think of few in which he would not

mming the veteran engine of Eyre
come increasingly hard-headed and
lishers and literary agents, and his
rse, The Bodley Head – benefited
publisher.

ottiswoode, Graham had arranged
Chatto & Windus had turned down
uggested that he should send it to
had made substantial revisions and
ercilessly frank – I was very disap-
wanted to wring your neck because
ling a first-class book by laziness,' he
that 'I'm hitting hard because I feel
it's the only way. Any ... h his salt would have welcomed such
frank and fearless editorial adv... and most would have welcomed his
suggestion that 'if you want to call me out, call me out – but I suggest
we have our duel over whisky glasses in a bar.' He persuaded R. K.
Narayan to join the list and promised to reissue some of his earlier novels;
he started a thriller list, publishing Edgar Lustgarten's first novel and
James Hadley Chase's *More Deadly than the Male*, and commissioned
Dorothy Glover to design the jackets; he took on *The Ides of Summer* by
Marc Brandel, the son of his old hero J. D. Beresford, a novel that was
much admired by John Betjeman, Peter Quennell and Anthony Powell.
On a trip to Paris he signed up the Catholic novelist François Mauriac;
he took the art historian John Rothenstein to lunch at Rules and told
him that he should 'let Eyre & Spottiswoode sign you up for life'; he
started a reprint list, the Century Library, devoted to reissuing neglected
masterpieces like J. D. Beresford's *The Hampdenshire Wonder*, and asked
Walter de la Mare, V. S. Pritchett and George Orwell to suggest titles
and write introductions. And he took on one of the finest memoirs of
the Second World War, Robert Kee's *A Crowd is not Company*, an account
of the author's experiences as a prisoner-of-war in Germany. The boom
in wartime memoirs had not yet taken off, and Kee thought his book
might do better as a novel. Graham asked him how he would like to
have it published, and 'it was a measure of his talent for encouragement
that he let me have my way.' As Peter Quennell pointed out to Kee at
the time, it was a mistake on the part of both author and editor: the
combination of an unmemorable title and its being published as a novel
proved fatal, and although the book was reissued as a memoir by Jonathan
Cape in 1982, it has never had the credit it deserves.

Nor were Graham's activities as a publisher restricted to editorial matters. He visited Amsterdam to buy paper 'which we badly needed to print our bestsellers – the Bible and the novels of a certain American lady called Mrs Parkinson Keyes whose books I found quite unreadable', so circumventing the paper quotas which remained in force until 1951; he paid his hotel bills in cigarettes, drank a great deal of Bols, and 'learnt that the comradely thing to do was to slap my hostess's backside as she sat down'. He chivvied literary editors like John Betjeman at the *Daily Telegraph* to review a new novel by Frances Parkinson Keyes, and put his publishing knowledge to good effect in his dealings with his own publishers, Heinemann. 'As a publisher I dislike and disapprove of authors who complain of lack of advertising,' he told David Higham before asking him to find out what plans were being made to advertise his *Nineteen Stories*. When it came to sending advance copies of the same book to his fellow writers, 'speaking as a publisher I have always found that personal copies to these people have produced good results.' After speaking to Alan Pryce-Jones, the editor of the *TLS*, about *The Heart of the Matter*, he made sure that Heinemann followed this up with an early copy of the book; and, like many other authors, he worried about libel and misprints, and what was to go on the jacket. Heinemann embarked on a uniform edition of his works, and Frere warned B. S. Oliver at the Windmill Press that Graham was now a director of Eyre & Spottiswoode, 'and from that position of eminence he has some ideas about production.' Graham insisted on being shown specimen pages and typefaces, and was soon in touch with Oliver about binding materials. 'My own preference is for the Mono Goudy,' he told Frere, who was keen to get his approval for the typeface for a new book. 'I don't feel very strongly between it and the Granjon, but I think it is a little bit clearer and blacker to the eye. It has the advantage, too, that it makes a slightly longer book.' Graham was devoted to Frere, as were most of his authors, though Muggeridge, who had a part-time editorial job at Heinemann in the late Forties, thought him 'an odd, unhappy little fellow' and a 'ludicrous character'. 'Like all people of his type, his uneasiness and aggressiveness are developed by alcohol,' he noted in his diary after meeting Frere for a drink at the Garrick, adding that 'he said he hated authors, and particularly women novelists', and that he 'spoke in an emotional way about Graham Greene who, he complained, didn't like him.'

'I think you should be careful about any information from Malcolm Muggeridge,' Graham told his biographer many years later. 'I got him his job as a reader for Heinemann after the war and his curious character means that anyone who has done him a favour has sooner or later a knife in the back. Frere certainly did him a favour and you might well find a few knives in the corpse.' Graham saw a good deal of Muggeridge during his four years with Eyre & Spottiswoode, and Muggeridge's diaries provide useful insights into his personality, and his career as a novelist and publisher. Graham was, he thought, 'a Jekyll and Hyde character, who has not succeeded in fusing the two sides of himself into any kind of harmony. There is a conflict within him, and therefore he is likely to pursue conflict without. I remember him saying to me once that he had to have a row with someone or other because rows were almost a physical necessity to him.' But despite the rows, 'Greene is a very lovable character', and 'the great quest of his life has not been virtue but sin, and this quest has been completely fruitless. He is a sinner manqué. In the Blitz we used to spend a good many evenings together, and I remember the longing he had for a bomb to fall on him, but of course it didn't, and I told him it wouldn't.'

Muggeridge reported that Heinemann was pleased by Anthony Powell's anonymous review of *The Heart of the Matter* in the *TLS*, but Graham, 'as I had foreseen, detected that it was much more critical than appearances might suggest', while George Orwell – a close friend of both Powell and Muggeridge – expressed grave reservations about the novel in his review for *Tribune*. Powell was inadvertently responsible for Graham's departure from Eyre & Spottiswoode. They had been at Balliol together, but had barely spoken to one another. Despite finding *Venusberg* 'a mildly amusing, rather tiresome book in the Evelyn Waugh manner', Graham had commissioned Powell to write the Eton chapter in *The Old School*, and persuaded him to contribute to *Night and Day*. Oxford University Press had offered Powell a derisory advance for *John Aubrey and His Friends*, and Muggeridge suggested he should take it instead to Graham at Eyre & Spottiswoode: although Powell's 'Dance to the Music of Time' sequence of novels would be published by Heinemann, he was not committed to them, and no doubt Graham hoped that Eyre & Spottiswoode would be able to publish his fiction as well as this study of a seventeenth-century gossip and man of letters. The contract was signed in May 1946 on the understanding that the book would be published some nine months later, but publication was endlessly postponed. Graham found it a 'bloody boring book', and although Powell later claimed to find this 'hilarious', he was understandably irritated at the time. In September 1948 Muggeridge enjoyed a 'curious lunch' with Graham and Powell, during the course of which a blazing row broke

ut Aubrey being postponed yet again. 'Graham looked pretty
ed, unshaved, bad colour. Said he'd now got a yacht. Had the
that he was melancholy, and rather unhappy, doing what he
rstood rich men did,' Muggeridge noted in his diary, adding that
ham has an insane love of conflict. This, as I said to Tony, is an
vitable consequence of there being no sort of relation between what
purports to believe and what he does. Very typical figure of this time
which is why his novels are so successful' Powell, for his part, recalled
a 'colossal row', adding that Graham 'would go white on such occasions,
admitting that he had to have rows from time to time for his health,'
and that 'we neither of us liked the other's books.'

A month later, Muggeridge 'gathered from Douglas Jerrold that he
was about to have another of his rows with Graham, this time about
Graham's agreement to release Tony from his novel contract with Eyre
& Spottiswoode.' Jerrold was annoyed by his deputy managing director's
cavalier behaviour, telling Powell that 'Graham has no more power to
release you from your contract with the firm than I have to sell the
company's furniture,' and *John Aubrey and His Friends* was duly published
by Eyre & Spottiswoode. 'Your case really brought matters to a head,'
Graham told Powell, adding – and here the author prevailed over the
professional publisher – that he 'was not prepared to remain on the board
of a company that kept any author to the letter of a contract.' 'Now
that we are again in the position simply of friends and not of author
and publisher, do look in for a drink!' the letter ended. But the friendship never blossomed. Powell later admitted that 'from the word go I
had found [Graham's] books unreadable' and 'absurdly over-rated', and
although he 'always got on pretty well with him, chiefly just before the
war', he came to see him as 'an odd, unhappy, restless man, never
somehow seeming to achieve the "image" he himself wants' and
'completely cynical, really only liking sex and money and his own
particular form of publicity'. Although Oliver Crosthwaite-Eyre tried
to lure Graham back to the firm after Douglas Jerrold's retirement,
Graham's career as a publisher was in temporary abeyance; and after his
departure, his former agent David Higham recalled, 'most of his plans,
intelligent and practical plans, were dropped, and the list once more sank
into obscurity.'

Hamburg, and a femme fatale

Eighteen months after the war had ended, Hugh found himself working once again in Germany, this time as a broadcaster rather than a newspaperman, and based in Hamburg rather than Berlin. 'Hamburg is a depressing and sobering sight,' Rodney Dennys had told Elisabeth in October 1945. 'Vast areas of the town are a desert of rubble and tangled masonry, piled high in endless chaotic dunes, with broken and twisted walls like surrealist trees standing amidst the desolation. It's infinitely worse than anything to be seen in London.' The city had fallen to British troops on 3 May 1945: three officers and a handful of men took control of Radio Hamburg, and within twenty-four hours the station was on the air again. It was the only radio station in what was to become the British Zone that was still in working order: both the studio and a powerful transmitter nearby were fully operational, and a team of German engineers was on site to ensure a smooth transition from Nazi propaganda to something acceptable to the Allied armies of occupation. In due course studios were rebuilt in Cologne and the British sector of Berlin – a German engineer remembered that valuable broadcasting equipment had been stored in a salt mine in the Harz Mountains, and it was put to good effect – but, for the time being, Hamburg was the centre of broadcasting activity, and because radio was less vulnerable than newspapers, magazines or books to a shortage of raw materials, it assumed great importance in efforts to recreate a liberal, democratic society in Germany, and to eradicate all traces of Nazi thought and behaviour.

Major-General Alex Bishop was a professional soldier and a former member of the PWE, and as the officer in charge of press, film and broadcasting in the British Zone, he converted Radio Hamburg into the *Nordwestdeutscher Rundfunk* or NWDR. But although experienced broadcasters and technicians, both British and German, were employed by the station, the Broadcasting Controller for the British Zone, Rex

Palmer, was generally regarded as a disastrous appointment. He had done good work as 'Uncle Rex' in *Children's Hour* before the war, but knew nothing about Germany or the nuts and bolts of broadcasting, and was no administrator. After Palmer's dismissal, Bishop asked William Haley, the BBC's Director-General since 1944, if he could recommend a replacement: he saw Haley's new Home Service as a model for the programme itself, and hoped that, in due course, NWDR would become a public corporation along the lines of the BBC. Hugh was recommended for the job, and since he felt he had reached a dead end in the European Service, he happily accepted the challenge.

He arrived in Hamburg in October 1946, and in his opening address to the staff he declared that 'I am here to make myself superfluous.' He shared Bishop's views about the future status of NWDR, and was determined to establish it as a public corporation modelled on the BBC, run by a Director-General responsible to a Board of Governors, and independent of political parties. Under the Nazis, broadcasting had become an arm of government, but even before 1933 German broadcasting had lacked both vitality and independence, with the Post Office owning the transmitters, and the state and political parties interfering with management and output to an extent that would never have been tolerated in Reith's BBC. By the time Hugh arrived, NWDR had its full complement of staff and equipment: his mission, as he saw it, was to provide programmes that were informative, entertaining and not too obviously bent on reforming the German character; to continue the BBC's wartime philosophy of truthfulness and objectivity; and to work out a constitution for the station that would enable it to remain independent of local and national politicians once the British were no longer involved. Remote but benign, Hugh's management of NWDR anticipated the approach he would take, in due course, as the Director-General of the BBC: once he had established the rules and the framework, he interfered as little as possible with his broadcasters, was happy to delegate, and encouraged discussion and debate on and off the air. A Reithian distinction was made between news and comment, broadcasters were told to avoid the portentous language employed by their Nazi precursors, to adopt a more demotic and less reverential approach, and to identify themselves by name, so enabling them to build up a popular following among their listeners. Outright attacks on the Occupying Powers were not allowed, but mockery, criticism and discussion programmes based on the BBC's *Brains' Trust* were encouraged. As Hugh recalled, 'we tried to demonstrate in practice that democratic freedom involved the right to show up and laugh at the inevitable failures, and the occasional corrupt practices, of a new democratic system.' By a curious irony, given German notions of England as 'the land without music', the NWDR was also admired for its musical output. The Hamburg Radio Orchestra had survived the war, and was revived under the baton of Hans Schmidt-Isserstedt: Stravinsky's 'Rites of Spring' was performed for the first time in Germany, as were works by British composers including Britten and Tippett, and a series of children's concerts were modelled on those arranged in London by Sir Robert Mayer. 'Nobody cared – it was like working in an empty room,' lamented Friedrich Schnapp, the orchestra's director, after Hugh had returned to England and handed over control to his German colleagues.

'Life in general is a curious mixture of luxury and discomfort,' Hugh wrote to his mother after reflecting how curious it felt to be lord and master of all he surveyed. 'I have an office which would have made Goering green with envy; a car about the size of a railway engine which used to belong to an SS general; and a very big pleasant room in the mess looking out over the Alster with my own bathroom. But there is only hot water once a week, so far no heating.' The car in question was a huge black Maibach tourer with red upholstery, which had previously belonged to Karl Wolff, a general in the SS and Himmler's chief-of-staff; the absence of heating made itself felt in the freezing winter of 1946– 47 – a particular irritation was finding his shaving cream frozen hard every morning – and the cold weather brought him into conflict with local politicians, already uneasy about Hugh's determination to keep them at arm's length from NWDR. Huge quantities of peat had been stockpiled: the local authorities insisted that it was not of high enough quality to be used for domestic use, but a radio journalist was sent to interview the nightwatchman guarding the stockpile, found him burning peat on his brazier to good effect, and reported the peat as being more than adequate to warm the Hamburgers' bombed-out houses. Nor did NWDR's practice of broadcasting the movements and the whereabouts of trains carrying coal endear Hugh to the authorities. Despite the shortage of fuel and power, he decided against cutting broadcasting time to save on power: newspapers were, as yet, available only twice a week, and radio was a vital source of information and entertainment. 'I enjoyed my rows with the representatives of the parties: after all, I had the whip hand,' Hugh remembered, 'but it left a residue of anxiety for the future.'

Germany was, in effect, ruled by the Control Commission, a body

established by the four occupying powers and, as an official of the
Commission's Information Control, Hugh was one of those charged with
re-educating the Germans and, wherever possible, removing all traces of
the country's recent past. NWDR employees were subjected to the rites
of denazification, which involved filling in a detailed questionnaire or
Fragebogen and being interviewed in Hugh's office. According to Hugh,
this sometimes resulted in 'some painful surgery', with the writer George
Clare and another member of the Control Commission as his 'scalpel-
wielding assistants'. Clare recalled how Hugh sat 'comfortably curled up
on a settee at the back of the room', and 'listened without ever interfering or saying a word either during or after an interrogation . . . his
motive was to look after his staff and also to ensure that no one we interviewed could later claim he had been roughly handled.' Twelve former
Nazis were dismissed from NWDR as a result: the toughest case of all,
according to Clare, was one Hans Zielinski, who looked disconcertingly
like Reinhard Heydrich but persistently and persuasively claimed to have
been hostile to the Nazi Party, and produced letters from Jewish émigrés
in Britain and America to support his argument. He was interviewed five
times before finally signing a confession of guilt. 'Hugh was sitting
upright, shaking his head in disbelief,' Clare remembered. 'Nothing was
said. We watched Zielinski writing and when he had finished Hugh came
over and witnessed his signature.'

After Zielinski had finally admitted to a long-standing membership of
the Nazi Party, Hugh and Clare drove to Berlin in the red-upholstered
Maibach tourer. Both men loved German cabaret, and that evening they
went along to see the Ulenspiegel Cabaret, accompanied by a bull-necked
Russian from the Soviet Military Administration. The star of the show
was a popular singer and actress called Tatjana Sais. In 1932 she had made
her name in a Berlin cabaret called 'The Catacombs', and since Hugh
had a passion for political cabaret, he may well have seen and even met
her in his early days in Berlin, when it was still just possible to criticise
and ridicule the regime in public; she had also appeared in a number of
pre-war German films, including an allegedly antisemitic musical comedy
called *Robert und Bertram*, in which she played a Jewish girl, Isidora
Ipplmeyer. She was married to a songwriter and composer called Günter
Neumann, sometimes described as the German Noël Coward, with whom
she had appeared in 'The Catacombs'. The bull-necked Russian rocked
with laughter throughout the show, slapping his thighs with glee, but
Hugh had eyes only for the star of the show. One of Hugh's English
colleagues at NWDR remembered him as 'very lovable' and a 'lonely,

unhappy man who wasn't quite sure whether he could achieve happiness': but he had fallen for Tatjana Sais, and they started what was to prove a long-lasting if interrupted love affair. Because she was married, and her husband was well-known, it was, to begin with, a covert affair; when Anthony Mann, Hugh's former colleague from the *Daily Telegraph*'s Berlin bureau, bumped into them by chance at a frontier post NAAFI canteen, Hugh made it plain that he did not want to be recognised.

Helga, in the meantime, was making a life of her own in England, still more so after their sons were despatched to boarding school in 1942. 'There's nothing I'd like so much as another Vienna honeymoon with you. I miss you and love you always,' Hugh had written from Vienna, but this and other passionate letters remained unanswered. Hugh's mother, and other members of the family, criticised Helga for not returning to him, but Hugh, fair as ever, would have none of it. 'I think it's time somebody expressed sympathy with Helga instead of me!' he told his mother. 'I don't need it. I can truthfully say that I've never been so happy in my life.' They were divorced in 1948, and Helga began to make her own way, at first in the theatre as Julius Gellner's assistant, and then in the literary world. She was briefly involved in *Contact*, the quarterly magazine run by George Weidenfeld, and worked at Collins on the New Naturalist list before setting up on her own as a literary agent with a list of clients that included Heinrich Böll, Lancelot Hogben, Marie Stopes, Erich Kästner, Roald Dahl, Constantine FitzGibbon, Thea Holme, Michael Meyer, Frank Norman, Andre Simon, Michael Wharton, Richard Crossman and, most famously of all, Raymond Chandler, who became one of her closest friends as well as her lover, and bequeathed her his literary estate.

By the time Hugh left Hamburg, NWDR had a staff of 2,000, and stations in Berlin, Cologne and Hanover. With an estimated twenty million listeners, it was the third largest broadcaster in Europe after the BBC and *Radiodiffusion Française*. Hugh spent his last months travelling round the British Zone, talking to politicians, trade unionists, academics and clergymen about the station and its future. In November 1947, with the handing over of its Charter, NWDR became the first post-war German radio station to acquire a legal status. 'My period of complete personal dictatorship came peacefully to an end last Saturday when the Board of Governors of NWDR came together for the first time,' Hugh told his mother the following March. 'It's a very good lot of people on the whole . . . Now I've got to find a D-G and then I shall have turned myself out of a job.' Hugh stayed on as

Director-General for the next seven months, reporting to a Board of Governors headed by Adolf Grimme before handing over to Grimme in November 1948. In his farewell speech he emphasised once again how important it was that broadcasting should remain independent of politicians and political parties. 'You will fail, Mr Greene, you will fail,' growled the Burgermeister of Hamburg, who was sitting beside him. As predicted, NWDR failed to live up to Hugh's expectations, but he looked back on his time in Hamburg as a time of 'gaiety and irreverence', and running a broadcasting station had provided him with invaluable experience.

Back in London, in the meantime, changes had occurred at the BBC which would also greatly influence Hugh's future, the most important of which was the appointment of Major-General Sir Ian Jacob as the Director of Overseas Services. A neat, brisk, orderly figure, educated at Wellington, Woolwich and Cambridge, Jacob was a professional soldier, and had spent the war working closely with Churchill as Military Assistant Secretary to the War Cabinet. After the war ended, the foreign language services of the BBC suddenly found themselves depleted as dons made their way back to their universities, journalists resumed their careers on newspapers, and émigrés returned to their countries of origin. Ivone Kirkpatrick, that great champion of the German Service, had joined the Control Commission in Berlin, and William Haley, the new Director-General, was determined to replace him with someone who could stand up to, and understand, the ways of Whitehall, and resists any cuts to the grants-in-aid which funded foreign language broadcasting. Ian Jacob fitted the bill better than most, and in 1946 he joined the BBC from the Cabinet Office, initially as Controller of European Services, and then as Director of the Overseas Services. Six years later, when Haley moved on to become the editor of *The Times*, Jacob succeeded him as Director-General. Though overshadowed in his lifetime by the memory of Lord Reith and by Hugh's more flamboyant innovations, Jacob was to prove a resilient and enterprising Director-General: whereas Haley had little interest in television, Jacob not only saw its potential – most obviously manifested at the time of the Queen's Coronation in 1953 – but dealt with the advent of commercial television three years later.

Jacob was keen to promote British values overseas, and, like David Astor at the *Observer*, or Allen Lane at Penguin Books, he wanted these to reflect a 'socially progressive Britain' in which a planned economy was combined with individual freedom. Hugh himself subscribed to such views – which were prevalent in post-war Britain, and helped to explain Labour's electoral victory in 1945 – and, as a rather unexpected kindred spirit, Jacob was to prove one of Hugh's greatest supporters in the years ahead. The East European Service had been set up in 1946, in the early stages of the Cold War. Hugh joined in January 1949, when relations with Russia were at a particularly low point: Berlin was still blockaded, and the Russians began to jam BBC broadcasts in April. There had been no Russian Service during the war, but Hugh was now in charge of broadcasting to ten Eastern European countries, including Russia, with a brief to make programmes sharper and more aggressive. Although Hugh agreed to give Albanian exiles extra airtime in the hope of destabilising Enver Hoxha's regime, the Eastern European Service was designed to maintain its listeners' links with Western culture and values rather than encouraging sabotage or revolt, or dreams of liberation. As Hugh once put it, his job was to 'get our audience to accept our view of events' and 'to shake faith in Stalin'.

Once again, Hugh found himself having to keep politicians and pressure groups at bay. In May 1950, for example, he was summoned to a meeting with John Profumo, Selwyn Lloyd, Lord Simon and the Conservative MP Sir Tufton Beamish (who had earlier rallied to Herbert's defence), who were worried about the employment of Communists in the Russian Service. Hugh vigorously rose to the defence of his staff, and suggested that the BBC's foreign languages services should come under the direct control of the Foreign Office through an equivalent of the wartime PWE, and that if broadcasts to France were reduced, more time could be devoted to Eastern Europe. He had to remind them that General Jacob 'took the view that in present circumstances the combating of Communism in Western Europe was just as important if not more important than broadcasting to the countries under Soviet domination.' Anti-Communist material was provided by the Information Research Department, which had been founded by Christopher Mayhew, included Robert Conquest on its staff, and worked closely with MI6.

Hugh's experience in the German Service, at NWDR and now in the East European Service had made him expert in both psychological warfare and political manoeuvring; and when, in the summer of 1950, Ian Jacob summoned him to his office and asked him 'Hugh, how would you like to go to Malaya?' he hurried to accept. Tatjana Sais, who had been living with him in London, had returned to Germany to resume a theatrical career which, because of her poor English, she had not been able to maintain in England: Hugh had nothing to lose, and could apply his expertise in a very different arena.

★

Graham's marriage, like Hugh's, had fallen apart, but whereas Hugh's separation from Helga had been a relatively painless affair from her point of view, Graham's rejection of Vivien was an agonising business, involving utter misery and a lifelong sense of rejection on her part, and feelings of terrible guilt and remorse on his. Perhaps because guilt so easily turns into resentment, into a need to lash out at the person who provoked it, however undeserving, Graham treated her, at times, in the cool, brusque, disconcertingly hard-headed way that he treated publishers, agents and film producers, far removed from his kind, gentle and generous alter ego, and from the shy young man she had met in Oxford twenty years before.

Vivien had settled in Oxford during the war, and was to spend the rest of her life there, and although Graham had led an increasingly separate existence, in West Africa and then in London, his wartime letters to her were as fond and affectionate as ever. 'I love you and only you,' he told her on one occasion. 'I have so much admiration, affection and tender-ness for you, and you are the best companion I have ever known.' Vivien was delighted to be involved in his life and work whenever possible. She gave a party in Oxford when the play of Brighton Rock started its run at the New Theatre in 1943: the guests included Maurice Bowra, David Cecil and A. L. Rowse, and after the show was over 'A. J. P. Taylor and Raymond went behind the stage to find Hermione Baddeley and Richard Attenborough who were also guests.' Nor did his affair with Dorothy Glover, or the fact that, while working at Eyre & Spottiswoode, he spent the weekdays at her flat in Gordon Square and the weekends in Oxford, alter his feelings towards Vivien: the fire may have gone out of their marriage and, like Hugh, he was not by nature a domesticated or family-minded man, but his fondness for her was never in doubt. But then, like many middle-aged men before and since, Graham fell violently in love, and his wife and children were left to bear the consequences.

One day in 1946 Vivien received a letter from a woman called Catherine Walston, who explained that she was converting to Catholicism, and wondered whether Graham, whom she had already met through John Rothenstein, would be her godfather. Quite why Mrs Walston couldn't or didn't write to Graham directly remains unclear, but Graham was a famous name, and she was keen on collecting famous names; and, as Vivien came to realise, she was the sort of woman who liked to get on good terms with the wife before prising the husband out of her grasp. Vivien, all unsuspecting, was pleased to welcome another convert, and set the wheels in motion. Mrs Walston was received into the Church; she sent the Greenes a Christmas turkey from her farm in Cambridgeshire

– a welcome offering at a time when rationing was in full force – and the two women discussed the possibility of their going on a retreat together (Mrs Walston liked to go on retreats, but on this occasion Vivien didn't think Graham was up to coping with the anthracite boiler on his own, let alone getting the children's breakfast). She invited the Greenes to stay in their converted farmhouse in Thriplow, near Cambridge, and rather than have them make their way back to Oxford by train, she hired a light aircraft and flew with them to Kidlington. Before flying back to Cambridge, she kissed Graham when Vivien's back was turned, and nothing was the same thereafter.

Tall, slim and stylish, Catherine Walston was in her early thirties when she met Graham: she was, Malcolm Muggeridge recalled, 'so *belle*, but *sans merci*', with, according to Antonia Fraser, 'a perfect milky complexion and huge blue eyes' and 'wildly curling hair'. Half-English and half-American, she had been brought up in the States, and had dropped out of Barnard College. Her sister Binny had married a member of the Straight family, and in 1935 the eighteen-year-old Catherine also married into money. Harry Walston was, by all accounts, a kindly, generous man: his grandfather had made the family fortune; his father was a don at Cambridge, and had changed the family name from Waldstein. After Eton and Cambridge and a spell as a research fellow in bacteriology at Harvard, Harry had settled in Cambridgeshire, where he farmed, was appointed a JP, and sat on local and national committees. Despite his great wealth, his political sympathies were on the left: he stood four times as a Labour candidate in parliamentary elections (without success), and in due course he was made a Labour peer. The Walstons were famed for their house parties, at which a great deal was drunk, and Labour politicians of the grander kind were usually in attendance. Regular visitors included Richard Crossman, Hugh Dalton and Hugh Gaitskell, as well as Ben's champion, Richard Stokes, who had spent the war denouncing the bombing of German cities and the policy of unconditional surrender, and, as a fierce anti-Communist, had supported the activities of far-right groups like the Promethean League. He had a soft spot for his hostess, and left her money in his will.

Frances Donaldson, a frequent visitor to Thriplow and then to Newton Hall – the enormous Edwardian Queen Anne house, requisitioned during the war, to which the Walstons returned in 1950 – remembered her hosts as 'a rather odd couple': Harry had a 'natural friendliness', but although Catherine was 'exceptionally beautiful', she seemed 'slightly dotty', 'less kind' than her husband, and liable to disconcert her guests by appearing in jeans when they were in their finery, and vice versa. 'I went to such an extraordinary house on Wednesday,' Evelyn Waugh told Nancy Mitford after visiting Thriplow. It represented

a side of life I never saw before – very rich, Cambridge, socialist, high brow, scientific, farming. There were Picassos on sliding panels & when you pushed them back plate glass [in fact the Walstons never owned a Picasso] & a stable with a stallion looking at one. No servants. Lovely Caroline silver unpolished. Gourmet wine and cigars. The hostess at six saying "I say shall we have dinner tonight as Evelyn's here. Usually we only have Shredded Wheat. I'll see what there is." Goes to tiny kitchenette and comes back. "Well there's grouse, partridges, ham, a leg of mutton and half a cold goose" (literally) "What does anyone want?" Nanny eats with them, dressed with tremendous starched frills & celluloid collars, etc and everyone talking to her about lesbianism and masturbation.

'At the age of twenty I was completely mesmerised by this strange, utterly beautiful, unconventional being, wearing jeans at dinner when the rest of England hardly knew what they were, a see-through summer dress at Mass in the drawing room, and so forth – and all done with the greatest style in which defiance mixed with humour,' Antonia Fraser recalled many years later, while Waugh reported how his hostess had bare feet and liked to squat on the floor. But although Waugh's first impression was of someone 'unaffected to the verge of insanity', exuding 'simple friendliness and generosity and childish curiosity', she often comes across as pretentious, affected and ruthless in pursuit of what she wanted. On one occasion, or so he claimed, Evelyn Waugh visited a bootmaker in Cambridge, and Catherine burst into the shop, barefooted, while his feet were being measured. 'She ramped round the shop looking in boxes and produced a circular shoe, like the shoes horses used to wear to cut the grass. "I have never seen anything so chic." Mr Thrussel, "That, madam, is my own shoe. I regret to say I have a misshapen foot." Mrs Walston, "You must make me a pair exactly like them",' Waugh informed Ann Fleming, who shared his passion for overcharged gossip in which ludicrous exaggeration was combined with lethal powers of observation. Some years later, Ann and Ian Fleming had lunch on Capri with Gracie Fields, and were joined afterwards by Graham and Catherine. 'She behaved much as you described her in the shop of a lame shoemaker,' Ann Fleming told her old friend. 'She seized my battered straw hat and declared it a most enviable possession, she tried it on at various angles and prinked and preened, then she displayed the same idiotic enthusiasm for Ian's old walking stick and pranced about with the uninteresting object expressing a violent desire for it. I suggested a swop for her frock at which she started violently undoing the bodice – she's a very maddening woman.'

Maddening or not, she was devastatingly attractive, and her combination of good looks, wealth and sophistication must have been hard to resist. Wives with small children are always at a disadvantage in such a situation: Vivien was no exception, and Beaumont Street in Oxford had a hard time competing with the worldly company, hard drinking and high living on offer in Thriplow. John Rothenstein, the art critic and future head of the Tate Gallery, got to know both Greenes at about this time, and observed that Graham was 'manifestly unsuited' to the 'small-scale and slightly self-conscious elegance' of Beaumont Street. He was, and would remain, a neglectful father, showing sudden bursts of interest and then drifting away, and Oxford dons and Oxford politics bored him rigid. Despite the turkey and the talk of retreats, Vivien became increasingly uneasy about her husband's new attachment. She was, Graham told 'Mrs Ralston' (as Ann Fleming affected to call her), 'thoroughly fed up' with the idea of his spending a long weekend in Cambridgeshire, and 'in return for those four days I have clamped the handcuffs on my wrists and said that in future I would be spending *all* my weekends in Oxford . . . Am I happy? The answer is definitely negative.' Water turned to ice when, under the pretence of going to Holland on publishing business, Graham went with Catherine to her cottage on Achill Island, in the west of Ireland. He looked back on their time together as an idyll, but Vivien was understandably upset when she and the children returned from a weekend in Bath to find her husband and Catherine sitting on the Beaumont Street doorstep, fresh off the Irish Mail, with Catherine expecting a bed for the night. The two women went to Mass in Blackfriars the following morning, but Vivien was uneasily aware that her fellow communicant was hell-bent on stealing her husband's affections away. He was hopelessly 'in love with a Bacall profile', and Vivien felt powerless to resist.

Matters deteriorated still further when Vivien confronted him with a letter he had written to Catherine in New York, which had been marked 'return to sender' and had made its way back to Oxford. Passionate declarations were combined with a reference to 'comforting Vivien for vague unhappiness' and a longing to escape from a 'rather dreary Oxford'. Vivien's unhappiness was far from vague, and reached its nadir at a party given in Beaumont Street for François Mauriac, whom Graham published at Eyre & Spottiswoode. Graham had been campaigning for Mauriac to be given an honorary degree, and Vivien's friends from the academic world, David Cecil and Maurice Bowra among them, were invited, along with the Rothensteins, Rex Warner, Rosamond Lehmann, the Walstons and Catherine's friend and neighbour Barbara Rothschild. Vivien looked back on this party as the 'cruellest' moment of her betrayal. 'He sat on the little stone patio behind the glass doors, with Catherine Walston, and I was left to cope alone,' she recalled over thirty years later. 'I came after an hour to ask him to open some bottles, please, and he looked at me so scornfully and so spitefully. "I'm not the butler," he said, and that was all.' Not long afterwards, Graham invited Vivien to dinner in a London hotel. He told her that he was leaving her for Catherine, and that he wouldn't be coming home, 'and I was on the floor by his knee, crying, and he said (could he have been meaning to console?) "I shall always like you to see my work and tell me what you think."'

There was no doubting Graham's passion for his new mistress, or hers for him, but although their affair dragged on for years, their plans to live together never advanced beyond the odd holiday in Italy. Harry, who was not a model of fidelity, was prepared to tolerate his wife's affairs provided she didn't leave him, and although their children may at times have found Graham an awkward and unwelcome presence, he was a regular guest at Thriplow and later at Newton Hall. He was there when Evelyn Waugh paid his first visit, and Waugh noted how, at a dinner of lobster bisque, partridge and cheese, preceded by two bottles of champagne in silver goblets and washed down with claret, port and brandy – and this at the height of rationing – 'we talked all the time of religion. She and Graham had been reading a treatise on prayer together that afternoon. Then she left the room at about one and presently telephoned she was in bed. We joined her. Her bedside littered with books of devotion.' Waugh and Graham had become close friends, and were to remain so for the rest of Waugh's life: they enjoyed each other's company, and admired each other's books, with some reservations on Waugh's part. Both liked to drink, but whereas Graham had led a comparatively austere life, Waugh was more at home in the opulent, cigar-puffing, country house life for which Graham was acquiring a taste. Waugh disapproved of adultery – 'I do not know what the connexion is between them,' he told Nancy Mitford. 'I would not swear carnal, though GG plainly likes it to be thought so. Mrs W is good at heart I think but she has lived in a terrible underworld of Jews and socialists and Cambridge dons and is not really house-trained' – but before long he was inviting them to stay

in Somerset. Graham had warned him that he and Catherine were 'both
drinkers rather than eaters,' but 'G. Greene behaved well & dressed for
dinner every night,' Waugh informed Nancy Mitford. 'Mrs Walston had
never seen him in a dinner jacket before and was enchanted and will
make him wear one always.' A couple of years later, Ann Fleming met
Graham and Catherine in Jamaica. 'Mrs Walston was dressed as a French
porter but it did little to disguise her charms,' she reported to Evelyn
Waugh. 'Mr Greene was very over-anxious about the making of dry
martinis, and offering peanuts, and quite impossible to engage in seductive conversation . . . He remained remote from all, totally polite and
holding the cocktail shaker as a kind of defensive weapon.' To complicate life still further, Graham's flat in St James's Street was next door to
the Walston's London house: he and Harry shared a secretary for a time,
and Harry had an affair with Graham's French literary agent, Marie Biche.

'You know I am fond of you,' Graham told 'Dear Vivien' in the summer
of 1948, before trying to explain his actions, and signing off 'with affection'.

But, mainly through my fault, we have lived for years too far from
reality, & the fact that has to be faced, dear, is that by my nature,
my selfishness, even in some degree by my profession, I should
always, & with anyone, have been a bad husband. I think, you see,
my restlessness, moods, melancholia, even my outside relationships,
are symptoms of a disease & not the disease itself, & the disease,
which has been going on ever since my childhood & was only
temporarily alleviated by psycho-analysis, lies in a character
profoundly antagonistic to domestic life. Unfortunately the disease
is also one's material. Cure the disease & I doubt whether a writer
would remain. I daresay that would be all to the good.

'Graham, you were once my husband and I was your wife and I
completely belonged to each other,' Vivien told him. 'You have learned
brutality in these last eighteen months; you were always so kind to me
when you lived with Dorothy.' He had 'changed so dreadfully': his words
seemed to be those of 'a hysterical malevolent woman – not you, my
friend for twenty years', and she felt that he was *being made to hate*
someone who has only sadness and affection for you and you hit out to
take away the last remaining feeling of security I have.' In a fragment
entitled 'Life', written in the early 1950s, Vivien wrote of how she
had felt 'unwanted and undesired' since 1938; she looked back on the

'desolate Crowborough bleakness' in the first months of the war, and
the difficulties of bringing up their children in other people's houses,
and lamented her 'utter lack of confidence' and the 'lack of FUN' in her
life. Graham was, by nature, 'wary, not spontaneous', and the 'coldness
of heart and critical detachment are freezingly discouraging'. He had no
time for 'the unsuccessful, the gauche, the naïve, the "enthusiastic"', but
went instead for 'the "smart", expensively scented, poised, the hidden
riches: hair loose, heavy white coat and a diamond and topaz chip on it
– this is the country simplicity he appreciates.' He had, she confided to
her diary, abandoned his home and his children for 'a loose American
blonde, married, licentious and spreading ruin and desolation in at least
two families.'

Not surprisingly, friends and family rallied round, and none more so
than Graham's mother, whose letters to Vivien flatly contradict the
widespread notion of Marion Greene as a chilly, remote figure interested
only in her family, and Graham in particular. 'What can I say? I have
heard it all from Graham. You seem to have been a saint under terrible
provocation,' she wrote. 'It absolutely makes my heard bleed,' she
continued a few days later. Vivien's letter had reduced her to tears: 'I
could never have believed it of Graham,' and 'I am ashamed of my son.'
As for Catherine, 'I could kill her. Nasty minx.' 'Your letter has distressed
me beyond words,' she told Vivien after learning more of what was going
on. 'You poor, dear thing. I think it is too sad for words. That horrid
woman. Of course Graham is too soft-hearted.' He should make a fresh
start with Vivien, 'and let that horrid woman commit suicide – I don't
suppose she would.' Remembering the shy, gentle boy he had been, 'I
simply *cannot* understand how such a tender-hearted person as he is being
so cruel to you. I am glad Da has not lived to know all this.' Aunt Maud
wrote from Berkhamsted to say that she could not understand it 'as
Graham was so devoted to you and he is such a dear kind person. I feel
it must be an illness and will pass away.' Elizabeth Rothenstein urged
Vivien not to put herself in the wrong as lawyers began to arrange a
judicial separation. Catherine, she warned her, 'is the most experienced
woman it is possible to conceive of in the arts of winning a man', and
although she 'always manages to sound so frank, so honest, so fair, so
sporting,' her real aim was 'that you should know as much as possible
to turn you against Graham.'

Such advice was sorely needed, but Marion Greene's hopes of a
reconciliation were doomed. Not only was Graham infatuated with
Catherine, but he was finding it increasingly hard to reconcile himself

with the demands of domesticity and fatherhood, and from now on he would lead a peripatetic, lonely life, moving restlessly from country to country in search of material and to keep boredom and depression at bay. Even without Catherine hovering in the wings, home life in Oxford might have seemed anti-climactic after lunching with Rex Harrison in Hollywood or cruising round the Mediterranean on Alexander Korda's yacht with Laurence Olivier, Vivien Leigh and Margot Fonteyn, 'a companion spirit' with whom he shared a liking for retsina. 'How far away Torcello seems,' he wrote to Catherine from a family holiday at Burnham-on-Crouch, after confessing that he found it hard to drum up much interest in 'Lucy prattling on about the small details of life at Oxford'. (In fact, Graham was interested in children and fond of his own: both his children looked forward to his Oxford visits, and enjoyed the competitive games he devised when he walked with them through the side streets of the city, and stories such as 'The Basement Room' and 'The End of the Party' reveal his sympathy and understanding of a small boy's mind.)

Amorous and marital tribulations were taking their toll. 'Things have been battering me about like no one's business,' Graham told Waugh, who reported bumping into a 'shambling' and 'unshaven' Graham outside the Catholic church in Farm Street, and whisking him off for a restorative cocktail at the Ritz. James Lees-Milne met him for a drink with John Lehmann, and thought he looked 'like a raddled Noel Coward with a bad colour'. John Rothenstein remembered how 'even then the blue eyes in his small round youthful face seemed, in startling contrast, the rheumy eyes of an oldish man.' Graham's penchant for high society coincided with his earning huge sums from the publication of his books on both sides of the Atlantic and in foreign-language editions, and from the sale of film rights in his work, driving hard bargains with agents, publishers and film producers, scrutinising every sub-clause with an expert eye and extracting every penny owing from Norwegian serial rights or a Spanish-language paperback deal. 'GG thinks of *nothing* but money, in very small sums. It is odd. He must be the richest man we know,' Waugh remarked to Nancy Mitford. But life for Graham had become a much more expensive business. He was, by nature, a generous man, and in the years to come he would not only help less well-off members of his family with school fees and the like, but would do good by stealth to impoverished or novice writers whose work he admired. He had moved into the flat in St James's Street, was still involved with Dorothy Glover (and was too soft-hearted and too fond of her to give her the push), and holidaying with Catherine in Italy was an expensive business, despite the currency restrictions. In 1948 he bought a house in Anacapri, the Villa Rosaio, which he lent to friends and family (including Herbert), and which provided him thereafter with a retreat in which to write and escape from the world, and strike up a friendship with that old reprobate Norman Douglas and his friend Kenneth Macpherson, who lived on the island.

He was punctilious about meeting his obligations to Vivien and his children. His letters to her from then on make melancholy reading: every now and then they would squabble over school fees or her allowance, and he would write – or ask his secretary, Josephine Reid, to write – the cold, even brutal letters he reserved for refractory publishers, but more often than not he was full of remorse, and anxious to explain his behaviour. 'I never cease to be sorry about what I've done, and never cease to think of you with love – so discount any stories to the contrary,' he told her, and five years after his fateful meeting with Catherine, he wrote to say that 'I'd so like to say you wouldn't be alone any more and that I'd be back, but I'm still in love with another woman, and she with me. It brings us very little happiness, but I'd be a poor husband as long as that love lasted. I love you even though I've done you such a lot of wrong.' 'You mustn't feel that you are not loved. It's true that I've been unable to love exclusively one person . . . perhaps it is a frequent penalty of having a writer's temperament,' he wrote in 1962, by which time he had settled in France for tax reasons, and was only an occasional visitor to England. 'Just as you hate solitude, I seek it. I don't particularly like being alone, but I have to if I'm to work, and that's not a good thing for marriage . . . I'm sorry that writing has been born on this particular type of soil, a compost of restlessness, fear of boredom, the necessity to escape from things and people I love. I know I have made you and three other people unhappy, and it's not a nice thought in the twilight.'

Vivien's feelings wavered between sorrow and resentment, and a desire to protect her children. 'Graham of course is kind,' she wrote to a friend: 'a kind man, often generous, but he won't give himself: he won't be bored or tired or involve himself – a cheque represents the time he can't stand. He wants to disconnect so much that he can't imagine feelings . . . when I see Graham, twice a year perhaps, he looks so lost and liable to be pitied.' Years later, she re-read a letter Graham had sent her during the war in which he told her how, through all his forays to Mexico or Sierra Leone, 'like in that Prior poem "You are my home", and back I come and ask you to like me and go on liking me', and another, written while he was still deeply involved with Catherine, in which he told her not to think of herself as a failure – 'I was the failure – and never write off the happiness you gave me' – and how 'there is a store of love and gratitude to you that can't be used up.' 'How to read or copy out these without floods of tears,' Vivien commented. 'All changed – it is a part of Graham totally gone. He would not recognise himself if he read them now. When I meet him (approximately yearly) I see no trace of the person that he was: either or both are or were "real", but this person died a long time ago.'

Graham's relationship with Catherine is best remembered for having inspired, however loosely, one of his best-known and most popular novels, *The End of the Affair*. After criticising its 'supernatural' ending as 'hideously unreal', Vivien noted that 'the Catholic scruples are not (of course!) those of Catherine Walston, to whom the book is dedicated, but of Dorothy Glover', and whereas she felt an understandable loathing for Catherine, she always felt sympathy for the dumpy, hard-drinking Dorothy. 'I want you to know something that I have often wished to convey to you, and that is that I have never at any time had any feeling about you except that of the greatest sympathy,' she told Dorothy in a letter which may or may not have been sent. 'You must have suffered very much, and so have I. We have both cared for the same person and I want you to know that if ever I can do anything for you, or be of any help, I would gladly do it.'

'No one dares to ask Walston what he feels about the novel, which is all the more embarrassing because Mrs Walston talks all the time about Graham Greene,' Richard Crossman noted in his diary in May 1953, two years after publication of *The End of the Affair*. He was staying at Newton Hall, and remarked on how, during the afternoon, while the other guests played croquet, Catherine 'rather ostentatiously immersed herself in reading a translation of St Thomas Aquinas . . . Looking up, she said to me, "Strange how 'the heart of the matter' has become a cliché since Graham's novel." I said it was a cliché long before – and then I knew she didn't like me.'

Graham, for his part, adored Catherine as much as ever – 'My dear, I never knew love was like this, a pain that only stops when I'm with people, drinking' – but as it became increasingly apparent that she would never leave Harry, he found solace and distraction in travel and affairs with other women. He sought Raymond's advice, since he had 'the hygienic strictly honest view of a doctor', and Raymond told him that Catherine had told him that she loved having Graham to stay but that he spread 'nerves and gloom', and that she would have a more

peaceful life without him (after their affair had finally petered out, Harry
Walston told Frances Donaldson that 'they had at last forbidden Graham
the house because he would criticise the food'). '*Please* don't be angry
with Raymond,' Graham begged her, but 'I persuaded him against his
will because he could see I was worried.' None of this affected his friendship with Gustavo Duran, the Spanish-born husband of Catherine's
sister Bonte. A composer turned diplomat, Duran had fought for the
International Brigade in the Spanish Civil War, becoming close friends
with Ernest Hemingway, before settling in the States, where he worked
for the UN and was eventually denounced by Senator McCarthy.

   Graham made a point of keeping in touch with – and, ideally, on good
terms with – the women in his life. He remained friends with Dorothy
Glover, promoting her work as an illustrator and collaborating with
her on children's books. According to Vivien, Dorothy Glover felt
increasingly guilty about her involvement with Graham and threatened
suicide on more than one occasion, as a result of which he had bars
erected on the landing outside her flat. She converted to Catholicism,
occasionally visiting Catherine at Newton Hall, and became an alcoholic.
Her death in 1971 came as a 'nasty shock': after the funeral Graham and
Hugh visited her flat, which was 'like an Algerian slum' and 'for days I
couldn't get it out of my mind.'

   Altogether less fraught was a brief affair with Jocelyn Rickards, a lively,
good-natured and easy-going Australian set-designer who made no
emotional demands, and whose other lovers included A. J. Ayer and John
Osborne. They met at a party at the National Book League in Albemarle
Street in the early summer of 1951: Graham suggested that she should
come on to dinner with Freddie Ayer and Rose Macaulay, 'and by
midnight', Jocelyn told her friend Barbara Skelton, 'I was hoping that
Freddie would be overcome with desire for Rose and would leave me
curled up forever in Graham's lap.' Barbara too had recently met Graham,
through John Sutro. 'We drove down to Brighton and lunched with him
and did a pub crawl,' she told Jocelyn. 'He and Sutro are great buddies,
sharing numerous private jokes and giggling like schoolgirls while I sat
by confounded.' Nine months later Jocelyn confessed that although she
was 'hopelessly and romantically IN LOVE with Graham,' their relationship 'must be called an *amitie amoureuse*': they met several times a
week, going to a film, a play or an art gallery, having dinner together in
Wilton's in Jermyn Street, or 'eating smoked salmon sandwiches or
drinking in his St James's Street flat'. Graham felt guilty about Catherine,
and Jocelyn about Freddie Ayer, 'although God knows why, when he's

laying every woman in London the evenings I spend with Graham.' Graham, she informed Barbara, 'has made me swear that I will never turn to the Catholic church as all the other women involved with him have – a promise I was only too happy to give.' As for Catherine, 'She's one of those American women with square shoulders and good bones and looks her best in a man's shirt.' Jeans and bare feet alternated with a black Balenciaga dress and a sable fur, Jocelyn reported, adding that 'I don't like her (nor she me), but oddly I'm not jealous of her.' Later in the 1950s Graham became more seriously involved with the Swedish actress Anita Bjork. He met her through his friend Michael Meyer, and in due course she succeeded Ingmar Bergman as the Director of the National theatre in Stockholm.

Always a heavy drinker, Catherine also became an alcoholic, but Graham continued to see her until, and even after, he met Yvonne Cloetta, a trim, level-headed Frenchwoman whose husband was working in Africa, and who provided Graham with the companionship and love he craved, and lived near him on the Côte d'Azur for the rest of his life, dividing her time between Graham and her husband. 'You are the greatest love I can ever have – & it continues,' Graham wrote to Catherine from Israel in September 1967. '*My love for you wiped out all small loves*,' he added, 'but Y cannot wipe out my love of you (nor would she want to) nor can you wipe out my love of Y (& wouldn't want to either).' Catherine died in 1976. She had been the great passion of Graham's life. No doubt she loved him too, but terrible damage had been done along the way.

Eastern Promise

'Hugh is off to Malaya, and last night I dreamed he was dead and awoke in tears,' Graham wrote to Catherine from Alexander Korda's yacht in August 1950. Hugh, for his part, had been suffering from a fearful hangover when Ian Jacob suggested sending him to Malaya – 'I came into his office feeling like death' – but he had agreed to go, and it was too late to turn back.

A British colony since 1824, Malaya's economy was largely dependent on its rubber plantations, and the British had imported large numbers of Chinese and Indian workers to act as clerks, servants, shopkeepers and the owners of small businesses. The fall of Singapore to the Japanese in 1942 had been a major military disaster, and a humiliating blow to British prestige. Operating as guerrillas from camps deep in the jungle, the Communists had been particularly effective in organising opposition to the Japanese occupying forces, and after the war had ended they determined to continue their struggle, this time against the British, and establish a 'People's Republic'. A conference of the World Federation of Democratic Youth and the International Union of Students – both Communist front organisations – was held in Calcutta in 1948, and it was agreed that a more militant approach should be taken towards colonial powers in South-East Asia, involving guerrilla warfare and 'liberation armies'. That same year a state of emergency was declared in Malaya, following the murder of three European rubber planters, and the Communist guerrillas, most of whom were Chinese, withdrew into the jungle to organise a campaign of terror.

Hugh's old colleague from the German Service, Patrick Gordon Walker, was now the Secretary of State for Commonwealth Relations in a Labour government that was nearing the end of its days: he told James Griffiths, the Secretary of State for the Colonies, that a psychological warfare expert was needed to advise the authorities in Malaya, and recommended Hugh for the job. Hugh's experience at the German

Service, in Hamburg, and at the East European Service had made him an authority on the subject, and the year he spent in Malaya gave him an opportunity to put theory into practice. Years later, he defined psychological warfare as 'the attempt to impose your own way of thinking, your own view of the situation, on the enemy's fighting force and civil population and then, this having been achieved, lead them to behave in the way you desire'. In a memo written at the time, he suggested that 'wars are not won by bullets alone,' and that 'ideological propaganda' must be 'auxiliary to the ideas which are supposed to guide our actions and which, if they are to be effective, must themselves be expressed in action.' Louis Heren, who covered the Emergency in Malaya for *The Times*, remarked that the British campaign against the Communist 'bandits' was essentially a police operation, reliant on the use of informers, intelligence and individual arrests, and far removed from that employed by the Americans in Vietnam ten years later, with its use of area bombing and military might; and Hugh was sent out to add his professional expertise.

He arrived in Kuala Lumpur in September 1950, and was appointed a Staff Officer (Emergency Information) to the Director of Operations, Sir Harold Briggs. Briggs's superior was the High Commissioner, Sir Harold Gurney, a liberal-minded colonial administrator who was keen to gain the confidence of the Chinese and promote good relations between them and the indigenous Malay population; and, once the Emergency was over, he planned to set the country on the path to self-government. Hugh thought him 'one of the greatest men I've ever met', but he was assassinated in 1951, and his reputation was overshadowed by those of his successor, Sir Gerald Templer, whom Hugh despised, and the Commissioner-General for South-East Asia, Malcolm MacDonald, the brother of Felix's old friend Sheila MacDonald, and an acquaintance of Graham's from Oxford. The 'bandits' consisted of the MRLA, a uniformed and disciplined army of some 5,000 men, which lurked in the deep, almost impenetrable jungle, emerging from time to time to murder rubber planters and their families and terrorise the civilian population: those who defied or betrayed them could be buried alive, cut into strips, beaten to a pulp or crucified. This austere and elusive fighting body was supported by the Min Yuen or Communist underground, which provided them with supplies, recruits and intelligence. Hugh recalled that 'the underground was all about you in Malaya,' and that the friendly-seeming shopkeeper or laundryman or domestic servant might well belong to it. The MRLA was outnumbered by 100,000 members of the British-officered Malay Police, and some 40,000 British, Gurkha and Malay troops: but, like all professional guerrillas, they travelled light, had the advantage of the terrain, emerging from the grey, humid jungle and then vanishing back again, and enjoyed the support – voluntary or coerced – of much of the population.

Hugh began by touring the country with an armed escort, and after familiarising himself with the situation he decided that two jobs needed to be done: improving civilian morale and confidence in the Government, and thereby increasing the flow of intelligence to the authorities; and undermining Communist morale by driving a wedge between the MRLA's leaders and their followers, and encouraging the rank-and-file to surrender. Detailed intelligence should replace general exhortations; too much emphasis had been placed on the dropping of leaflets, and too little on broadcasting and film. In November 1950 Hugh was put in charge of all broadcasting to do with the Emergency. He reinstated his predecessor, Alex Josey, who had been sacked for suggesting that socialism might be the way ahead for Malaya, appointing him Controller of Emergency Broadcasting, and appointed from the BBC Eliot Watrous, who had worked on SOE's Albanian operations during the war, and wrote and broadcast a radio series entitled 'This is Communism'. Hugh encouraged 'community listening', with programmes aimed specifically at Chinese, Malays and Tamils. Features and talks about the Emergency were included in regular Radio Malaya schedules, and Chinese storytellers were encouraged to include anti-Communist jokes and asides.

Nor did Hugh restrict his activities to the airwaves. Co-operation between the Emergency Information Services and the police, army and civil authorities had been poor before he arrived: he insisted that the EIS should be involved early on in planning military and police operations, and established a weekly meeting with the Director of Intelligence. By the time he left 'there was seldom a major military operation which was not preceded and accompanied by a propaganda barrage.' Leaflets were dropped from the air: some, following the example of Sefton Delmer's 'black' broadcasts to German troops, spelled out unsavoury details of Communist leaders' private lives, while others contrasted pictures of happy, smiling civilians with mangled bodies of dead terrorists above a slogan reading 'Which Would You Rather Be?' Safe conducts were offered – according to Hugh, 'the task of propaganda is to persuade a man that he can safely do what he already secretly wants to do because of disillusionment, grievances, or hatred of life in the jungle, and to play on those feelings' – as were offers of hospital treatment to potential defectors suffering from jungle diseases, and rewards to those prepared to hand over weapons or information. 'In many parts of the country the only human emotion which can be expected to be stronger than fear among a terrorised population is greed,' Hugh declared, and the scale of rewards was increased, ranging from $60,000 for the Secretary-General of the Malayan Communist Party down to $2000 for the rank-and-file. Disillusioned Communists who had surrendered were sent out on lecture tours of towns and villages, on the grounds that 'there is no better anti-Communist than one whose own god has failed.' Mobile film units and public address systems were deployed, and, at the most practical level, Hugh suggested that grass verges should be trimmed, so depriving guerrillas of temporary cover.

Shortly after his arrival, Hugh told his mother that he had 'fallen completely under the spell of the country', and in November 1950 he wrote to say that 'it is an awful job to find staff to plan for the future and at the same time to do single-handed a job which by last war's standards one would have employed a dozen or more people. But I continue to find it all great fun.' In due course his suggestions began to take effect. 'It's over a year now since I met my first bandit, a very ordinary and harmless-looking little Chinese in a white shirt and brown drill trousers. He sat there, desperately tired and desperately unhappy,' Hugh recalled in a radio talk entitled 'On Being a Bandit'. Operations tended to be small-scale, but invaluable none the less. 'The best coup to date came two weeks ago when four bandits surrendered in a body – all propaganda surrenders. Nothing like that has happened since the very early days of the emergency,' he told Graham, and in his broadcasting memoirs he recalled 'one cheerful ruffian who walked in from the jungle with a reward leaflet, carrying his commanding officer's Sten gun – and his commanding officer's head'.

Graham, in the meantime, was planning to visit his brother in Malaya. Even – or especially – when his emotional and domestic life was at its most turbulent, he had, as a determined and hard-working professional writer, travelled abroad when occasion demanded. He had visited Vienna in 1948 to write the script for *The Third Man* – Korda had asked him to write another film following the success of *The Fallen Idol*, working once again with Carol Reed – and 'the fifties were for me a period of great unrest' in which travel provided an escape from boredom, 'my own manic-depressive temperament', and an unhappy love affair. 'I had no employer from whom to escape – only myself, and the only trust I could betray was the trust of those who loved me,' he wrote in *Ways of Escape*, and he found himself following exotic substitutes for 'the long road back to Berkhamsted Common, where as a boy I had played at Russian roulette to escape an unhappy love.' Sometimes he contemplated suicide, but his courage failed him. Restless and rootless, 'it became a habit with me to visit troubled places, not to seek material for novels but to regain the sense of insecurity which I had enjoyed in the three blitzes on London.' As often as not these travels prompted a novel, but publishers' advances were supplemented by handsome commissions from newspapers and magazines. The *Sunday Times* and *Figaro* enabled him to visit Indo-China four times between 1951 and 1955 to cover France's war against the Viet Minh, and the *Sunday Times* also sent him to Kenya in 1953 to report on the Mau Mau's campaign against the British. More immediately, *Life* magazine had commissioned him to cover the Emergency in Malaya, and had offered him a fee of $2500 for anything he wrote.

Before he left England he asked Hugh whether he should bring a dinner jacket, and whether he would be expected to wear shorts, which he hated: he would far sooner not stay with people – 'I always find the burden of hospitality appallingly tiring' – and since *Life* was paying him so well, he could easily afford to stay in hotels. He arrived in Singapore in late November 1950, and was 'overjoyed' to find Hugh there to meet him. But he became bored and lonely when Hugh was at work – 'I haven't even got him to drink with' – and was missing Catherine dreadfully. 'I love you more than my children, more than my God, more than all my family lumped together,' he told her. 'I feel a wretched useless failure away from you.' As for his Malayan *raison d'être*, 'the war was like a mist: it pervaded everything, it sapped the spirits, it wouldn't clear.' Relief of a kind was provided by an invitation to go out on patrol with the Gurkha Rifles, and he asked Catherine to think of him in his 'jungle-green uniform and anti-leech boots'. They had to hack their way through dense jungle, which was waterlogged, dark and stank of decaying vegetation; Graham's rubber-soled boots slipped on the mud, he had to sleep in his sodden clothes, and although he was carrying a revolver rather than a rifle, he was exhausted. 'I felt utterly uninterested in bandits – the only effort was to keep up and not delay the patrol,' he told Catherine. No bandits were encountered, but some time later Graham wrote to say that he had seen his first dead body. 'It was a nasty sight and I'm a bit off meat. It was a young Malay special constable. He'd been stripped naked, beaten about the face and then stabbed through the heart with a bayonet,' and 'I had to nerve myself to take a close-up photo of him.'

Thanks in part to Somerset Maugham's short stories, Malayan rubber planters had a poor reputation, reputedly spending their days drinking stenghas in their clubs, tyrannising their workers, and having affairs with each other's wives. Few of them were prepared to tolerate trade unions, and more often than not they blackballed or cold-shouldered non-Europeans who applied to join their clubs. One of their number turned out to be an unwelcome figure from Graham's past. A 'tall, foxy-faced rather heavy man' introduced himself as Wheeler, the boy who, with Carter, had made his life such misery at school. 'Here he was back again, after thirty-five years, in a shop in Kuala Lumpur, rather flash, an ardent polo-player,' Graham told Catherine. 'And instead of saying "What hell you made my life thirty years ago" we arranged to meet for drinks!'

Like many Englishmen abroad with no great gift for languages, Graham preferred former French or Spanish colonies to their British equivalents, peopled as they were by Wheeler and his ilk – he found Kenya 'the dreariest of dreary holes,' on a visit in 1953 to cover the Mau-Mau revolt – and with Hugh hard at work most of the day, he had no desire to linger in Malaya. He wrote his article for *Life* – Hugh showed a first draft to the local CID, and 'I was rather wistfully asked whether you would be willing to soften your remarks about the "laziness and stupidity of the Malay Police"!' – and moved briskly on to Vietnam. 'This is a fascinating place, so different from dreary Malaya,' he wrote to Catherine; on his return home he informed Evelyn Waugh that 'my trip to Malaya was rather dreary and wet, but I loved Indo-China and finding a new Eastern religion in which Victor Hugo is venerated as a saint.' 'The spell was first cast, I think, by the tall elegant girls in white silk trousers, by the pewter evening light on flat paddy fields, where the water-buffaloes trudged fetlock-deep with a slow primeval gait, by the French perfumeries in the rue Catina, the Chinese gambling houses in Cholon, above all by that feeling of exhilaration which a measure of danger brings to the visitor with a return ticket,' he recalled in *Ways of Escape*. He relished the food and the wine, the French restaurants, the beautiful women and, in due course, the opium dens, and he was relieved to learn that there was 'no nonsense of black ties' when dining with General Jean de Lattre de Tassigny. According to Louis Heren, de Lattre was 'a great soldier in the romantic Gallic tradition', responsible for delaying France's inevitable and humiliating defeat and withdrawal from Indo-China. De Lattre took against Graham after his son had been ambushed and killed near Phat Diem – he got it into his head that Graham was somehow responsible, since he had made an unauthorised trip to the area – and accused him of being a British spy. He also expelled Trevor Wilson, Graham's former colleague from Section V. Graham's friendship with Wilson hampered his activities as a foreign correspondent – 'very politely all doors are closed' – and, fond as he was of his 'very lecherous companion', he told Catherine that he was 'bored and irritated to the point of screaming with Trevor. He is so vague and woolly and behaves half like my adjutant and half like my pimp.'

'What a damned silly life this is that I'm leading, traipsing all the way round the world so as to give you the six months you need to get me out of your system', he wrote to Catherine in November 1951. It took a good deal longer than six months for her to get him out of her system, if she ever did, while Graham's fascination with Indo-China brought him back to Vietnam again and again over the next four years, prompting him to visit Dien Bien Phu, the scene of France's defeat at the hands of the Viet Minh in the spring of 1954, to take tea with Ho Chi Minh in Hanoi, and, after the Americans had replaced the French in an attempt to stem the spread of Communism, to write *The Quiet American*, a novel inspired by a CIA agent's exposition of the need for a 'third way' between communism and capitalism. 'I will go to almost any length to put my feeble twig in the spokes of American foreign policy,' Graham once declared after admitting that he felt oppressed by 'the terrifying weight of this consumer society', and Alden Pyle, the lethal innocent abroad, embodied all that he most disliked about American intervention in what would later be referred to as 'third-world' countries. Graham always denied that Pyle was based on General Edward Lansdale, the CIA's counter-insurgency 'expert': no doubt he was gratified when, during the course of a congressional hearing, William Colby, the Director of the CIA, admitted to having read *The Quiet American*, but he was appalled by Joseph Mankiewicz's film of his novel, which made the Americans the heroes of the story, and he dismissed it as a 'complete travesty'.

On his first trip to Saigon, Graham had a brief affair with a lively, good-looking American girl called Elaine Shaplen, whose husband was a war correspondent covering South-East Asia. Shortly afterwards, Hugh met her in Singapore: she was alone, he was on leave, and they spent ten days together. It was, Hugh told his brother, 'a strangely happy episode, the only trouble being that we both got far too deeply engaged. But there's no future in it, so if you meet her again in Saigon or else-where, remember that I haven't even mentioned her to you.' Despite Hugh's provisos, they had fallen in love, with all that that involved. Elaine's husband, Bob, had sensed that something might happen if she were left alone with Hugh – 'he seemed like the kind of guy you like,' he warned her – and Elaine told Hugh that, as a result, life had been 'sheer hell –

with Bob being unutterably charming, understanding, sad, and me just being rather sick . . . I keep telling myself that I have been hoist by my own petard, and richly deserved it. I was so damned superiorly sure that I wasn't going to fall in love with *you*. Somebody upset the schedule.' Elaine was, Graham reported home, 'a very generous, open character, with the right amount of "toughness" . . . she is obviously very much in love with Hugh. She's not exactly pretty, but definitely attractive. I'm sure you'll like her.'

With Bob bowing out, Elaine returned to the States to obtain a 'Nevada divorce', and Hugh asked Dorothy Glover to look after her in London. 'This is just for you and Dorothy at the moment. I am quite extraordinarily happy about it. I feel unusually confident that it is a Good Idea,' Hugh told Graham from Kuala Lumpur, adding that 'I know about the Saigon incident, so don't let that cause any embarrassment.' Nor did it: Hugh's marriage to Elaine was to become an unhappy, embattled affair, but Graham remained very fond of her through it all. 'I liked her very much when I ran into her in Saigon, and there certainly won't be any kind of embarrassment on my side,' he replied, adding 'now that you are breaking with Tatjana perhaps I can applaud that too without offending you! I like Elaine a great deal more.' Tatjana was far from a spent force, as it turned out, but with Elaine preparing for married life in London after Hugh's return, Graham set about advancing the career of his future sister-in-law. Elaine had worked for Alfred Knopf in New York before going out East, and – like Helga – she was keen to set up as a literary agent. She would become a distinguished, effective and much-liked practitioner, working under her own name, and including P. D. James, Michael Frayn, William Sansom, Bill Bryson, William Shawcross and Conor Cruise O'Brien among her clients. In the meantime, MCA, the New York talent agents, had asked her to start a book department in London and, generous as ever, Graham asked A. S. Frere to give her help and advice, and introduce her to the London literary scene.

Sense and Sensibility

Far away in the Californian desert, Felix was still deep in contemplation when the war ended in 1945. 'What the world needs above all – certainly above new financial schemes, new Leagues of Nations, new laws and new inventions – is a new gospel,' he told his mother in the autumn of that year, so relegating the United Nations Charter and the Bretton Woods Agreement to their rightful place in the grand scheme of things. 'I feel inside me that the cause of our human ills lies very deep,' he declared. 'There is nothing in the long run that will be altered in saving a few thousand lives in Europe now if we miss the opportunity to get at the deeper root of the trouble.' Tooter, who was involved in providing food for the displaced peoples of Europe, was unimpressed by his brother's abstention, but Felix redeemed himself by sending food parcels and clothing to his relatives in Germany. He was outraged when he learned that Tante Nina's house in Heidelberg had been requisitioned by the US Army. She didn't seem too concerned, but he wrote to General Eisenhower to protest at her 'atrocious treatment', nor did he forget to remind Winston Churchill of Sir Graham Greene's forthcoming birthday. That done, he told Elena that they should concentrate on leading 'a very simple and devout life of prayer and study', as a result of which, 'in some years time, I may be fit to deal helpfully with my fellow men.'

Felix and Elena were now living in the adobe-covered house he had built, almost single-handed, in Happy Valley, near the village of Ojai. Elena spent the weekdays teaching at Trabuco, while Felix helped the residents of Ojai with their plumbing and other chores in exchange for fruit and vegetables (300 of its 500 inhabitants were vegetarians, so they were never in short supply). Ojai, he sensed, was 'more in touch' than Trabuco, as a result of which it '*may* bring something good into the world'. They founded a Happy Valley school, the trustees of which included Aldous Huxley and Krishnamurti. Like Felix and Elena, Huxley spent three hours a day in meditation, and sometimes helped out in the kitchen. In him, Felix declared, 'one of the greatest minds and one of the humblest spirits combine in a devout conviction of God's reality', but 'having said this,' Felix warned his mother, '*don't* read *Time Must Have a Stop*.' Krishnamurti, in the meantime, gave open-air speeches under the oak trees, which were extremely well attended.

'Until a man is free from either the need to be rich or the need to be poor, he is caught in the "I" process,' Felix declared. He had discovered Buddhism and, as a pacifist, was still contributing to A.J. Muste's magazine *Fellowship*, but whereas at Trabuco he had been actively seeking God, he now sought liberation from all earthly attachments, objects and even ideas. This involved a massive bonfire of possessions, including papers, letters and Greene family records. 'Papa's illness and death; your Little Wittenham days and troubles; anxieties over Barbara, Ben and Kate; the Munich crisis; the beginning of the war; Ben's imprisonment and release; Kepston worries and crises; Harston, Ave . . . all went into the flames,' he informed Eva after the event. More clothes were parcelled up and sent to Germany, and much of his library was sold. Too late to halt the conflagration, Eva came to stay for three months, sleeping in Felix's study while Elena camped out in one of the tents. Felix fussed about her, bringing her breakfast in bed, and she went for walks in the desert in hat and gloves. She was, at first, kind if condescending to Elena, but became increasingly hostile as the weeks wore on: she talked a great deal about Peggy Bok, and failed to hide her disappointment that Felix had married Elena instead. Elena became convinced that her mother-in-law had come to reclaim her son, and consulted Dr Kunkel, who described Felix as a 'Faust'.

Felix's relations with Elena were almost as unsatisfactory as his affairs with Peggy Bok and Betsy Barton. 'From Elena I have learned a supremely important lesson – that most of us who are called clever or intellectual are skimming the surface,' he informed his mother before she made her unfortunate visit. 'We live in the *verbal* level of life, and know all about it without really knowing or experiencing it . . . Elena has this extraordinary *simplicity* and a kind of direct contact with real life.' This was all very well, but – as he himself admitted – no sooner were they alone together than he buried himself in a book or a copy of *Time* magazine. He was to spend an increasing amount of time away from home, travelling, giving lectures and, in due course, researching his books; he was passionate about Elena from a distance, declaring his love in ecstatic tones and vowing to make a fresh start on his return home, but found it impossible, emotionally and sexually, to convert theory into practice once he was with her again, and longed to be on his way once more. She dreamed of having children and a devoted husband, but admitted, years later, that not only had their sex life been non-existent, but that they had never even shared the same bed.

'The important thing is not to get too tied to any particular career and thus lose one's freedom,' Felix believed, but although he was, and would remain, gullible and emotionally immature, he was far too energetic, practical and well-organised to devote the rest of his days to prayer and contemplation. In 1949 he took Elena to Europe for the first time: they visited France, Italy, Austria and his Tante Nina in Germany. In London Felix met his old mentor, Sir John Reith, who had never found his feet again after leaving the BBC in 1938, and introduced Ben to Sir James Cragg, the official who had signed the order for his arrest in 1940. Elena did not enjoy the trip, and after she had gone back to the States Felix stayed on in London. He had decided to import English antiques and furniture into California, which would involve him spending a good deal of time in England, so he took a house in Egerton Crescent, opposite the Brompton Oratory. Elena claimed later that the business was her idea, but, efficient as ever, Felix set about organising it alone, which he incidentally regarded as a 'work of self-knowledge'. Before shipping his purchases to San Francisco, he cleaned and catalogued them, marking their prices in invisible ink: items for sale included flintlocks, antique commodes, a crossbow and Rowlandson prints. He ran a lucrative business single-handed until 1957, diversifying into pottery, textiles, cashmere jerseys and tweeds, and, for a brief period, importing German cars into California, and he spent part of each year travelling round England, attending country-house sales, visiting antique shops, and grumbling about the weather, the food and the stuffiness and dullness of English life. He may or may not have had a fling with Tooter's second wife, Olwen, a former dental receptionist, and briefly contemplated opening a restaurant with her. As always, he bombarded Elena with letters, some accusatory, the majority passionate. He told her that he couldn't be himself when he was with her, that he feared her disapproval, that she made him wretchedly aware of his own inferiority, that she stifled his spontaneity, and that 'I couldn't have a full sex life with you because you had become to me the symbol of restraint'; on another occasion he reported a moment of ecstasy while walking to catch a bus in the Brompton Road, as a result of which 'I am in love with you all over again, but with no agonies and no fears' and 'I love you but do not wish to bind you.' Elena had two phantom pregnancies, and on one of their trips to London they adopted their daughter, Anne.

In 1951 Felix and Elena moved into a house in Palo Alto: 'Elena is being enthusiastically hospitable – an obviously neurotic person but she and Felix seem devoted to each other, and Anne is sweet,' Raymond reported on a visit to California some years later. Importing antiques was a useful source of income, but Felix still felt unfulfilled. 'There isn't a single thing in this world I can do well,' he told Elena in a moment of self-doubt. 'Nothing. Amateur stuff. Half-baked, everything I do.' He was too hard on himself. His private life was a muddle, and his yearning for all-explaining, all-consuming systems of belief made him more credulous than most, but although he was competent and efficient at everything he turned his hand to, he was too self-absorbed for his own good, and lacking in direction. He did some work for a local radio station, a 'miniature BBC' which depended on subscribers rather than advertising: his fellow broadcasters included Alan Watts and the poet Kenneth Rexroth. 'Sometimes, in the welter of controversy here about McCarthyism, we forget how much freedom there still is here compared to anywhere else in the world,' he told his mother. 'Where else would a radio station permit me to say *anything*?' A lively and entertaining public speaker, he became a fixture on the flourishing lecture circuit, travelling the country and spending even less time at home. He wrote some short stories, but had no luck in placing them with magazines. He sent Graham a copy of 'An Enquiry into the Nature of Belief ', which reflected his own hostility to the Catholic Church: he claimed that this had blighted their friendship, but Graham later wrote that he didn't 'remember being offended by Felix's article', and that 'I don't believe it caused any rift in a relationship which didn't really exist.'

'I am forty-two, getting a little bald, just a bit fat around the middle, and a little frightened of the advancing years and already conscious of powers that are waning and a mind that is getting somewhat dull and imprecise,' Felix recorded in the spring of 1953. 'I have not yet lived. I have *done* things; I have moved about; but I haven't been alive. I have reacted to events, been led by compulsions, lived vicariously through others; but never have I operated from my own centre. Perhaps I have no centre.' To other people he seemed 'competent, businesslike, in control – clear of mind, and a source of strength', but he knew himself to be

competent in only quite a limited and superficial sense within quite narrow boundaries; unable to follow a steady line of work; knowing nothing really well; unable to make friends; incapable of deep feeling; too vacillating to engage myself in any commitment; somewhat feminine; too insecure to meet my contemporaries in an adult or equal feeling; hiding my insufficiencies, my shynesses and my inability to relate to my fellow men behind a "cleverness" which is purely verbal, unsupported by any grounding of pure knowledge or a really developed character.

He felt himself to be over-earnest, lacking in humour and spontaneity, and 'unable to play or "act silly"'. 'Am I following Papa's stern unhumorous attitudes?' he worried. 'Nonsense was no part of our home. Why am I so fearful of being laughed at?' – and to what extent was his 'administrative aptitude based on quickness and imagining all the things that could go wrong and guarding against them?' Other manifestations of his 'neurotic disorders' included an inability to make close friends, a desire to keep people at bay, a reluctance to become involved, a sense of worthlessness, and a tendency to take charge.

Needless to say, his problems could be traced back to what he had come to see as an embattled childhood, in which (according to Felix) his mother compensated for an unhappy and loveless marriage by doting on Felix in particular. This, he believed, explained his own feelings of guilt about sex, and his inability to form satisfactory relationships with other women. The hapless Elena 'has represented my mother, to whom I most defer, whom (as a baby) I loved and hated: and therefore to Elena also I have brought an attitude of love and hate, of appeasement, of a constant fear of a loss of her good opinion; and therefore of resentment if attention is not given to me.' Elena was all too well aware of the problem, and of the fact that, as Felix put it, 'I feel more when away from wife/mother.' 'From the moment I married you I was challenged; I was never made to feel secure,' Elena told him years later. He was kind and thoughtful, but she was 'never made to feel that you really cared for me. In brief, I was never a real wife to you': he was 'never giving of your real self, always holding back', and although they worked extremely well together when building houses or making films, 'our relationship has in fact been one of subtle and hidden resistance to each other.' In the meantime, he told her, 'all my life has been a flight, and now there is nowhere to go. And always – this is the real horror – there is a falsity which lies a little deeper, and there is no bottom to it.'

'I am not surprised that Ben sees nothing in what I am doing or trying to do,' Felix told Eva in the early days at Ojai, but Ben's continuing problems enabled his youngest brother to bring all his organisational skills to bear, and to good effect. Ben was dividing his time between Berkhamsted and Braefoot, combining the running of Kepston with his new business, based in Scotland, of making hydrogen furnaces. Ben's house in Berkhamsted was, Felix reported, 'the one place in England where there never seems to be shortage of good food', including duck, pheasant and jugged hare. After a visit to Braefoot early in 1952, Felix was, as always, impressed by Ben's 'immense knowledge and the originality of his thinking', but although he found him 'immensely warm and lovable', Ben's business was dogged by financial crises and 'haunted by creditors'. Whereas Kepston continued to manufacture split-wood pulleys, Ben had, while in Berkhamsted, begun to make metal V-pulleys for use inside power-generating machinery. This involved the brazing or knitting together of different metals, and despite his lack of scientific training, Ben had single-handedly discovered how to make large, water-cooled hydrogen atmosphere furnaces, an invention involving a particular kind of brick which made it possible to achieve enormous temperatures inside the furnace. Ben often claimed that if he had read physics rather than history at Oxford he would never have dared to go ahead with what could have proved a dangerous procedure. As it was, he had become an authority on the heat treatment of metals, and – since his furnaces were both cheaper and quicker than their predecessors – he was soon fulfilling orders from huge American corporations from a small and primitive factory in the Scottish countryside. But for all his inventive genius, 'Ben, being Ben, was not able to run it in a businesslike way,' and was for ever teetering on the verge of bankruptcy.

Ben's business affairs deteriorated still further in the summer of 1954, when a firm called Howden's acquired a majority shareholding and threatened to take over altogether. Ben's position was so precarious that he could have lost Kepston as well as his house and business in Scotland. Felix galloped to his brother's rescue. He arrived in Glasgow with a lawyer and an accountant in tow, discovered irregularities in the minutes of the most recent board meeting, summoned a meeting of independent shareholders, and eventually got Howden's thrown off the board. Two years later Ben's affairs were again in a critical condition. 'We have so often – Tooter and I, and Papa before us – merely given in and helped him out, which has undoubtedly done him harm and mucked up any chance of having a realistic relationship with him,' Felix lamented, but once again he was there to help out. Felix and Tooter went to see Ben in Berkhamsted to talk about business 'in a rather strict way'. The three brothers went for a long walk, which was devoted exclusively to Ben and his woes. 'I do not see how he can carry the strain and anxiety for much longer without cracking up. His face is the face of a sick man. Self-enclosed, generating one problem after another which could have been avoided,' Felix told Elena. Ben was 'helplessly drifting under the control of compulsions too deep for him to understand', and 'I have never felt more certain than today that Ben's affairs are doomed to disaster – and in a strange way willed to come to disaster.' By now Felix was acting, to some extent, as Ben's part-time agent, visiting engineers, braziers and potential customers in Britain, the States and Canada on the firm's behalf. When, the following year, Ben got into a muddle over American patents, Felix visited both General Electric and Westinghouse on his behalf.

Nor did Felix restrict his views to business matters. Ben had sent his daughters to Dartington Hall at his suggestion, but he was appalled when they both became Roman Catholics, on the grounds that they had 'got caught in a deadly – in my view a profoundly evil – organisation which prevents them from using their own intelligence and clarity of thought and holds their minds within a prison of superstition and fear.' Both daughters were to prove fearless and outspoken figures in later life. Margaret, the eldest, became a friend of both Tom Driberg and Randolph Churchill: as a member of the League of Empire Loyalists, she made the headlines when she stormed the stage just as Sir Anthony Eden had mounted a podium in Bradford, snatched the microphone from his hand, and denounced the Government for abandoning the Empire. Not surprisingly, she thought Felix too 'soft' on Chairman Mao and Communist China. Anne, the younger daughter, became a doctor: she outraged the Catholic hierarchy by opening a birth-control clinic in Liverpool, and was forever grateful for her father's support.

Ben was not the only member of the family in need of Felix's support and advice. Katharine's marriage had not proved altogether satisfactory since, like the Lammles in *Our Mutual Friend*, both parties had assumed the other to be richer and grander than proved to be the case. The Collacotts lived in a village near Aldeburgh, and when, in January 1954, Jimmy Collacott suddenly died of a stroke, various members of the family rallied round to support his widow and help her to sort out her affairs. 'Kate is copying almost exactly Mama's procedure with us – without the one thing that Mama gave to us – a clean and orderly home with things of beauty around us,' Felix reported, adding that Katharine's children were spoilt and out of control. Barbara came over to lend a hand, and was all for letting Katharine sort herself out as she saw best.

'The children are *very* undisciplined, but they are healthy and seem to have good characters,' she told Eva after she had returned to Rome. 'I found it perfectly ghastly there, and I couldn't live like that for a day – but I doubt whether Kate could live my life ... I am sure we must stop talking about the "Kate problem". We can't change her, and we must let children bring up their children as they want.' According to Felix, Ave proved a pillar of strength, 'simple, direct and quite undisturbed by anything', and 'companionable, cheerful, matter-of-fact and helpful.' Ben, on the other hand, could talk only of himself: he saw conspiracies on every side, threatened legal action, spoke of his business going into receivership, and worried how, if he were bankrupt, he would be able to pay Paul's fees at Eton. 'What a family we are! I see myself in every one of them' Felix continued. 'I see the family set-up clearly, and I *hate* it.' Only Ave seemed to have escaped, and Felix now decided that she was his favourite sibling.

★

With the war over, Raymond was appointed a physician at the Metropolitan and, later, the Royal Northern Hospital (which later became the Royal Free Hospital), while continuing to see patients at his rooms in Harley Street: but he was to become best-known for his work at the New End Hospital as a pioneer endocrinologist, studying and operating on goitres and thyroid diseases. During the 1920s endocrinology had come to be associated with quacks and charlatans – W. B. Yeats was among those treated with the 'rejuvenating' power of monkey glands – and Raymond himself wrote that it had 'suffered not only from the dubious products of a few commercial houses, but from the ignorance of the basic facts of the science displayed by a large proportion of practising physicians.' With help from the King's Fund, Raymond and his colleagues not only established endocrinology as an important medical discipline, but made New End into a world-famous unit, to which patients were referred from all over Europe and beyond. The endocrine unit also included Jack Piercey and Sir Geoffrey Keynes, the brother of Maynard Keynes, a brilliant surgeon who was equally well-known as a bibliographer, a world authority on William Blake, and the biographer of, among others, his Cambridge contemporary, Rupert Brooke. Between them they put into clinical practice advances which had been made in the laboratory as a result of the introduction of chromatography and radioactive isotopes of iodine. Raymond was elected President of the Thyroid Club, a convivial gathering of specialists who combined expert knowledge with a taste for expensive food and drink and waggish after-dinner speeches, and Chairman of the Fourth International Goitre Conference.

His medical expertise was not restricted to goitres and thyroids or helping to train the victorious Oxford crew in the 1946 Boat Race. He took a lifelong interest in the symptoms and treatment of migraine, and was a founder of the Migraine Trust; in 1953 he and Dr Dalton produced an influential paper in which they argued that the pre-menstrual syndrome was a hormonal rather than a hysterical condition, and could lead to violent or erratic behaviour: this was to have a profound effect on the outcome of court cases in which women were accused of murdering their husbands, as well as earning Raymond the gratitude of many women in general, and the feminist movement in particular. He retained his literary interests, producing well-turned occasional verse as well as a slim and urbane volume of memoirs. *Moments of Being* was published in 1974 by Heinemann: Raymond had acted as an adviser to Heinemann Medical Books since 1950, joining its board in 1973, acting as Chairman for ten years, and pushing the firm in the direction of scholarly monographs. When General de Gaulle visited Britain in 1960, Raymond was appointed his honorary physician, for which he was made a Chevalier of the Legion of Honour; he had to arrange ambulances along the processional route, and be ready to treat the President at a moment's notice. He served on the Council of London Zoo under his old colleague Solly Zuckerman, and as the Zoo's honorary endocrinologist he treated Guy the Gorilla's thyroid problems. When it became clear, in the weekend before the Coronation in 1953, that Everest would almost certainly be climbed, the BBC came down to Whitchurch to record him announcing the news, and his words were broadcast to the crowds waiting in the Mall and Whitehall for the procession to pass by. Tall, fit and lean, he remained a keen walker after his mountaineering days were done. He was still extremely strong: an awestruck colleague once saw him lift one end of a badly-parked car, and manhandle it into place.

As a colleague Raymond was, according to the *British Medical Journal*, 'painstaking, shrewd and sympathetic, and a wonderful ally in need': he was also regarded as a first-rate teacher, and a witty public speaker. After his death in 1982, his obituarist in *The Times* suggested that although he shared with Graham and Hugh a 'detached outlook on life, caustic sense of humour, and somewhat supercilious manner which could be quite off-putting on superficial acquaintance', to his patients he was 'understanding and sympathetic, a tower of support in times of trial', with 'a sparkle in his eyes which cheered many a patient through a difficult period of stress and strain'; and if he didn't get all the credit he deserved – something he minded – 'this was probably the result of his caustic, if witty, tongue, and an unfortunate air of superiority. He was not an easy man to get to know, and within his profession his mannerisms tended to alienate those who never really got to know him. 'I can just remember an elderly Raymond Greene, in an elegant white suit, looking like a character from one of his brother Graham's novels,' a colleague recalled apropos a meeting of the Royal Society of Medicine's Section of Endocrinology in the 1960s. In later life he took to wearing a monocle, which was tucked into a waist-coat pocket when not in use: it was a professional accessory, in that he would examine patients through his good left eye, and use his monocled right eye when writing up his notes.

Though somewhat remote as a parent, at least as far as small children were concerned, and seen by some as a rather grand figure, prone to pontificate, Raymond was increasingly regarded as the head of the family, dispensing advice, recording the family history, and providing Graham with the medical details he needed for his novels. He had, in earlier years, acted as an intermediary between Graham and their father, with whom Graham was never on easy terms, and he also provided a bridge between the Hall and the School House Greenes, in that he was respected and generally liked by members of both families. Graham and Tooter had been friends since boyhood, and Graham retained a soft spot for Ave; Barbara, who considered herself an honorary School House Greene, was far friendlier with Graham and Hugh than with her siblings, some of whom regarded her as a bit of a snob; there was not much contact or even much liking between the two families, but Raymond was familiar to both sides. But he was not, it has to be remembered, the oldest of the School House children. Molly had long ago vanished into domesticity, but Herbert was still living in Sussex, ready for mischief, and about to erupt for one last time. Graham and Hugh found it hard to forgive him, but Raymond was on hand to pick up the pieces.

Civil War in Greene Land

Hugh was much in demand on his return from Malaya in September 1951. Malcolm Muggeridge, the deputy-editor of the *Daily Telegraph*, floated the possibility of his rejoining the paper as its resident expert on Communist affairs, but he decided against it; he was offered a job with MI6, but the pay wasn't good enough; Ian Jacob, the Controller of Overseas Services, suggested that he should follow in Felix's footsteps and become the BBC's man in New York, but he had had enough of foreign parts, and wanted to settle down in London with Elaine. Ian Jacob, his mentor, saw him as a rising star, and felt that he should gain experience of every aspect of the BBC, including finance, administration and management: he was initially seconded to an Efficiency Committee, before becoming Assistant Controller, and then Controller, of the Overseas Services.

During his time with the German Service, Hugh had seen little of his colleagues at Broadcasting House, catering as they were for the domestic market. He tended to dismiss them as dull, stuffy and out-of-touch; and in the post-war years a battle was fought within the BBC between the old guard and the revolutionaries, with whom Hugh instinctively sided. The old guard was embodied in the admirable and often rather maligned figure of William Haley, the Director-General. Like Hugh, he was by background and training a journalist but, unlike him, he was a self-taught man who had left school in his teens and never been to university. He had started life as a copy-taker on *The Times* and as a reporter on the *Manchester Evening News* before becoming, in due course, Editor-in-Chief of the *Manchester Guardian*, from where he had moved to the BBC. Like his most famous predecessor, Sir John Reith, he was a firm believer in the cultural and educational role of the BBC, even if this involved an element of *de haut en bas*; like Allen Lane at Penguin Books, another self-taught man, he was eager to make the best available to the many, so long as no dilution of standards was involved.

After the war Haley had divided the BBC's radio output between the Third Programme, the Home Service and the Light Programme, representing as they did highbrow, middlebrow and lowbrow tastes. He liked to compare his arrangement to a pyramid, with the Third at its apex, catering for a tiny minority, and the Light at its base, broadcasting material that appealed to the masses while at the same time reflecting the BBC's commitment to producing the best of its kind, at whatever level. He believed in a benign trickling down – or raising up – from one level to another, in that a Home Service listener who inadvertently tuned in to a talk or a concert on the Third might be so intrigued or overwhelmed that he or she would make further forays into the highbrow world; and that this would, with luck, lead to an overall raising of 'brow' levels. Such an approach would come to be seen as elitist and condescending, but its guiding principles were noble and idealistic, and Haley's belief in excellence and self-improvement was shared by bodies like the WEA, Penguin Books and, in its early years at least, the Arts Council. 'While satisfying the legitimate demand for recreation and entertainment, the BBC must never lose sight of its cultural mission,' Haley once declared: far from being an end in themselves, 'the wireless set and the TV receiver are only signposts on the way to a full life', in which listeners and viewers would be equipped and encouraged to read books and attend plays or concerts that might otherwise have seemed daunting and out-of-reach.

'Television will be of no importance in your lifetime or mine,' Bertrand Russell informed Grace Wyndham Goldie, one of the BBC's brightest talents and a keen proponent of change, and Haley shared the sage's suspicion of a medium which had been in a state of suspended animation during the war, but was resuscitated with the return of peace. During Haley's time as Director-General the BBC acquired the Lime Grove studios from Rank Films and bought the site in White City on which Television Centre would open in 1960, when Shepherd's Bush replaced Alexandra Palace as the hub of television film-making; but Haley starved television of funds, and regarded it as an altogether inferior form. At his last meeting with his staff before he left to become the editor of *The Times*, he urged them to 'fight against lowering of standards' and any suggestion that television should be allowed on air more than five hours a day, and never on Sundays: it must not 'become a film industry', but should remain 'civilised and adult'. But not everyone agreed. In 1950 one of the BBC's rising young producers, Norman Collins, handed in his resignation. A former director of Victor Gollancz and the author of the bestselling novel *London Belongs to Me*, Collins was regarded with grave suspicion by some of the BBC Governors, who worried that whereas the Director of Television, George Barnes, who had previously run the Third Programme, could be relied upon to keep television 'within the system', Collins, if given his head, would make it too popular for its own good.

Two years later a Conservative White Paper, backed by young MPs like Enoch Powell, Iain Macleod and Edward Boyle, proposed the establishment of a second television channel, funded by advertising and in direct competition with the BBC. Supported by most Labour MPs and quite a few Conservatives, the BBC mobilised opposition. Lady Violet Bonham Carter headed the National Television Council, the organiser of which, Christopher Mayhew, described commercial television as a 'barbarous idea'; its rival, the Popular Television Association, was supported by, among others, Malcolm Muggeridge, A. J. P. Taylor, Rex Harrison, Somerset Maugham and the cricketer Alec Bedser. A second White Paper suggested the setting up of an Independent Television Authority, which would supervise the operation of commercial television, owning the transmitters and renting facilities to the new companies, each of which would cover a particular region and be free to sell their programmes to one another. In 1954 the BBC's monopoly, on television at least, was broken by the Television Act, and commercial broadcasting began in September 1955. The Act had coincided with the end of food rationing, and the early years of commercial television were to benefit hugely from a boom in the advertising of consumer goods. Among those who were instrumental in setting up commercial television was the still-youthful Norman Collins.

Sir Ian Jacob, who succeeded Haley as Director-General in December 1952, would almost certainly have been on Collins's side in one respect. Unlike Haley, he believed in television: he saw it as the future of broadcasting and was prepared to fund it properly, and as a result the balance of power and prestige within the BBC gradually shifted from radio to television. He was, as befitted a military man, a firm believer in planning: after a year in the job he announced a ten-year plan for the Corporation, the ingredients of which included the setting up of a second television channel, and colour television. He realised that, with the arrival of ITV, the BBC had to appeal to a mass audience if it were not to atrophy and become a rarefied minority cult, but, in good Reithian fashion, he was determined at the same time to uphold standards. He wanted to extend the range of programmes, to offer the listening and the viewing public a choice and a service, and (within reason) to reduce the element of paternalism and cultural mission which so affronted the Young Turks, most of whom claimed that the Old Guard were only really interested in radio, and the better class of programmes at that. He extended the hours of television broadcasting from five to seven (Sundays included), developed outside broadcasts, pressed for a higher licence fee, and improved salaries to enable the BBC to employ the best scriptwriters and commentators and prevent them from being poached by ITV, which was already awash in cash. He was lucky, too, in his timing: the Queen's Coronation occurred the year after he took over, and not only was Richard Dimbleby on hand to describe the proceedings in reverential tones, but the Queen herself insisted that the cameras should be allowed inside the Abbey. Millions watched, with the result that the number of television licences rose from 7000 in 1946 to 350,000 by 1954, putting the BBC in a better position to confront the challenge of ITV.

One inescapable by-product of what Hugh always referred to as 'commercial' television – he refused it the epithet 'independent' – was that, for the first time, the BBC had to think in terms of ratings and audience figures. 'To seek success in popularity alone is a trivial use of a great invention. Mass without mind always comes a cropper,' warned George Barnes, but his successor as Director of Television, Gerald Beadle, declared that 'the one big strategic weapon of television competition' was 'the lowering of the proportion of intelligent programmes in main viewing hours below the level of one's competitor': the BBC should try to reflect 'the advancing tastes and aspirations or the perplexities of an educated democracy in the making', and to do otherwise would create 'a vast wasteland which would have been impossible to recover afterwards'. Hugh shared Beadle's belief that, while maintaining standards, the BBC should aim to reflect people's lives and interests, and be topical, controversial, irreverent and humorous: but whereas, by the late 1950s, Ian Jacob felt that for BBC TV to have a 35 per cent audience share justified its claim to be a national broadcaster, and that to have a 50 per cent share would have been a cause for concern 'because in doing so we would have made our output indistinguishable from that of ITV', Hugh would happily have gone for a half share at the expense of the detested opposition.

But in every other way Hugh and Jacob saw eye-to-eye. Jacob was keen to employ and promote young, aggressive and, if needs be, iconoclastic directors and producers, Hugh among them; and, as a veteran of Whitehall and the corridors of power, he was anxious to protect the

BBC from overbearing politicians, setting Hugh an example that he would follow when he succeeded his mentor as Director-General in January 1960. The Suez Crisis of 1956 provided Ian Jacob with his finest moment. Anthony Eden fully expected the BBC to rally behind the Government, and tried to justify the British, French and Israeli attack on Egypt over the airwaves. He was outraged when the Chairman of the Governors, Sir Alexander Cadogan, gave the Leader of the Opposition, Hugh Gaitskell, an immediate right of reply on television, on the Home Service and, most heinously of all, on the Arabic Service, and threatened to cut off Bush House's grant-in-aid as a result. Jacob stood firm, and the embattled Prime Minister backed away.

Hugh had got used to running his own show in Hamburg and in Malaya, and to begin with he found life as an Assistant Controller a frustrating business. His immediate boss was 'a nice old boy but no good at all', but Ian Jacob was more than willing to expand his protégé's horizons. Despite some doubts about the morality of the BBC dabbling in trade, or accepting commercial sponsorship in any way, it was agreed that they should at least explore the possibility of making programmes for, or selling programmes to, overseas markets, and the United States in particular. Nowadays this is a vital and hugely profitable aspect of the BBC, but Jacob, once again, was opening new frontiers. In the spring of 1952 Hugh was sent to New York to talk to American broadcasting corporations, and despite his own reservations about commercial television at home, he proved a tough and hard-headed negotiator. There was, he reported, a huge appetite for BBC programmes, particularly if they were devoted to major figures like Churchill or (as she had recently become) the Queen Mother. His great coup, engineered in conjunction with the William Morris Agency, was to sell three half-hour programmes on the forthcoming Coronation: in the event, film of the Coronation was flown in a Canberra bomber to Labrador, and on to New York in an RCAF and then a USAF fighter.

Hugh was in New York and Toronto the following year, again on Overseas Services business. In 1955 he visited Salisbury, Rhodesia, to advise on the future of broadcasting in the colony ('Nobody has called me Bwana, but I have been called Baas – and as that is what Allan Quatermain was called, it's much more exciting' he told Elaine); and over the next fifteen years he was to spend a good deal of time sitting on commissions and attending broadcasting conferences around the world, from Stockholm to New Zealand. He was becoming, perforce, an all-round practitioner, combining his instinctive libertarianism and mischief-making cast of mind with authority and a familiarity with bureaucratic ways. His under-standing of the nuts and bolts of broadcasting was reinforced when, in the summer of 1956, Jacob moved him from his post as Controller of Overseas Services to Director of Administration, in charge of personnel, administration, finance, copyright and industrial relations. To his surprise, and that of his colleagues, he enjoyed the job a great deal: but two years later he was moved again, this time to a post which could not be more immediately involved with broadcasting itself, and was to bring him into conflict with his brother Herbert.

Despite, or because of, ITV's success in the ratings, the powers-that-be in the BBC had tended to look down on their rivals: Lew Grade and Sidney Bernstein were all very well, but they were essentially showbiz folk rather than serious broadcasters, and this was reflected in the programmes they produced. But ITV soon began to provide real com-petition, and not just in the realm of soap operas and panel games. Stirred on by keen and impatient young producers and directors on its own staff, the BBC began to take a livelier interest in the whole area of news and current affairs. Two figures in particular were responsible for this: Grace Wyndham Goldie and Cecil McGivern, who has been described as the 'true architect of BBC TV'. Recalled by Alasdair Milne as a 'small, birdlike woman with a striking finely chiselled face', Grace Wyndham Goldie had been employed by Hugh's old German Service colleague Leonard Miall as an Assistant Head of Talks. In 1948 she had been made a producer in the TV Talks Department at Alexandra Palace, where she set up an almost autonomous current affairs unit, employing Woodrow Wyatt, Christopher Mayhew and Aidan Crawley as presenters, persuading politicians to perform before the cameras, and asking academics like David Butler and Robert Mackenzie to analyse election results and political trends. In due course she moved to Lime Grove, where she recruited young producers like Michael Peacock, Geoffrey Johnson Smith and Donald Baverstock: according to Ian Trethowan – like Alisdair Milne, a future Director-General – 'her sharp tongue and angry, snapping eyes were feared and respected by newer and more junior members of staff, but the older hands held her in deep respect, even awe.'

Cecil McGivern, as Controller of Programmes for BBC TV, shared many of the beliefs and attitudes that Hugh came to embody in the 1960s: in the late 1950s he gave his backing to Richard Dimbleby's *Panorama* and John Freeman's *Face to Face* as well as to *Z Cars*, *6.5 Special* and *Hancock's Half Hour* – all of them innovative and controversial at the time – and to the immensely popular early evening programme, *Tonight*, a combination of interviews, topical sketches and travel pieces dreamed up by Grace Wyndham Goldie. The programme's editor, Donald Baverstock, was a powerful, bombastic Welshman, brimming over with ideas and much given to thumping the table. According to Derek Hart, Baverstock had 'all the graces of an untamed labrador', and his irreverent, journalistic approach to interviewing politicians in particular was hugely influential. Milne, the programme's director, remembers Hugh coming to a showing of *Tonight* and how, after the show was over, he 'disputed with us vigorously over much gin until late in the night'.

By then Hugh was already installed in his new post as Director, News and Current Affairs. John Green, who recommended him for the job, once said of Hugh that 'he's totally insensitive. If he's sensitive it's because it suits his own interests. I think he's got the stuff of which Cromwells are made; his absence of sensitivity doesn't worry him.' If so, that was all to the good, since Hugh's first priority would be to get rid of a man whom he detested in person, and saw as the embodiment of all that was wrong with the BBC's handling of news and current affairs. According to Gerald Priestland, then a very junior dogsbody, Tahu Hole, who ran the News Division, was 'a massive bloodhound-like New Zealander, a figure out of some black-and-white Hitchcock movie' who 'inspired nothing but terror' among his staff, while Leonard Miall remembered him as a 'tall, massive man with jowls like a bloodhound, who usually wore a black Homburg hat and a long overcoat.' BBC news had established a worldwide reputation for truthfulness and reliability during the war, and, according to Miall, 'Hole thought he could maintain that reputation by following a line of extreme caution. Insecure, and uncertain in his news judgement, he ran the News Division on a policy of safety first. There must never be a mistake, no matter how slow and pedestrian the bulletins were, and all items must be supported by at least two sources.' Alasdair Milne, who joined the BBC in 1955, thought 'the news was a joke' and 'pathetic' under Tahu Hole, while Donald Baverstock dismissed it as 'laughably bad'. Not only did royal stories have to take precedence over all others, but Hole distrusted scoops of any kind, bullied his staff, refused to co-operate with other departments of the BBC, spent too much time searching for mistakes in the previous day's news and punishing those responsible, and regarded television news with grave suspicion at a time when Independent Television News or ITN was coming into its own, with Robin Day, Christopher Chataway and Ludovic Kennedy making their reputations as presenters and Nigel Ryan providing the editorial flair. 'Remember, Priestland, there is no harm in being dull', a future foreign correspondent was told: 'the idea was to produce a service like the gas, water or electricity: useful, but unremarkable.'

Hugh shared the views of his younger colleagues. Not only did he regard the News Division as the 'Kremlin of the BBC,' but he detested its leader so much that he once confessed, apropos Hitler, Himmler and Goebbels, that 'I have never had such a sense of evil from any of them as I had from Tahu Hole.' Ian Jacob may not have felt quite so strongly about Hole, but he gave Hugh his full support. He was determined to reorganise and revitalise, combining news and current affairs, radio and television in one department, and Hugh took command in August 1958. According to Leonard Miall, Hugh always claimed that giving Tahu Hole early retirement at the age of fifty-one was his finest achievement at the BBC. On a more positive note, he commissioned a report into the state of television news from Baverstock, Michael Peacock and Ian Atkins (Tahu Hole disagreed with all its recommendations), brought in Donald Edwards and Stuart Hood from Bush House, and set about implementing his own vision of news and current affairs.

Public service broadcasting and television, Hugh declared, 'only exists to serve the public', and as such it 'can dare to be experimental and adventurous. It can resist pressure groups and ill-informed criticism. It is not tied to a rigid pattern.' He brought a more journalistic approach to the news, favouring news value over 'balance', removing royal stories from the head of the queue, or dropping them altogether, suggesting ideas for programmes, chairing weekly meetings with his editors and producers, and taking a tougher, less reverential line with politicians and public figures. At meetings he would listen carefully to both sides, without saying much, before making up his mind ('Right, we do this'): those who queried or defied his decision were treated to 'an icy stare and a way of looking at you almost as if you weren't there'. 'Hugh was tough enough to cope, so that when things went wrong one was aware of a purposeful, powerful, decisive fellow,' a colleague recalled. 'He always exuded a sense of power as well as authority. He would sit in his chair, and one had this sense of his personal as well as his corporate authority.' According to Leonard Miall, Hugh had 'great charm, combined with a strong streak of mischief. He was often aloof, and he could be ruthless.' His ruthlessness was to be tested in 1959, when he decided to move the time-honoured nine o'clock evening news on the Home Service forward by an hour. Many listeners were outraged

by such a break with tradition, and none more so than his brother
Herbert.

★

After the war, Herbert had returned to Oak Cottage, from where he made
sporadic attempts to find employment. One scheme, floated in 1946,
involved investing in a garage in Lewes, and he approached both Raymond
and Graham about the possibility of his being advanced some of the
money that would come his way after Marion Greene's death. Graham,
who continued to subsidise Herbert and provided him with cast-off vests,
socks and underpants in exchange for duck eggs, vegetables and the occasional rabbit, took a dim view of the matter. Herbert would be getting
the 'largest proportion of Da's estate' in due course, but neither he nor
Raymond was prepared to risk releasing the money. 'You are in fact asking
two married men whose first responsibility is towards their wives and
children to advance you £1200 without interest or much in the way of
security for an indeterminate period,' Graham informed his eldest brother.
'It can't be done.' He told Marion Greene that Herbert had come to see
him at Eyre & Spottiswoode, and had told him that the garage-owner in
Lewes would pay him £2 a week, but would put this up to £5 a week if
the family would invest £250 in the business. Graham remained adamant.
'I'll send Audrey my usual Christmas box,' he informed his mother. 'I
told Herbert when he came to see me that while I still felt some responsibility as a brother, it counted as nothing compared with my responsibility to my children and I saw no reason why he should have anything
which should go to them . . . If only one could definitely compound for
so much a week, one would feel inclined to do it, but it would never stop
at that.' He suggested that they should pay Herbert thirty shillings a week:
he would pay half of this, and 'any extra things, like spectacles, you would
then refer to me and not pay yourself.'

Nor was that the end of Graham's activities on Herbert's behalf. He
got his accountant to check Herbert's accounts and income tax forms,
sent him and Audrey tickets to see his plays on their pre-London runs
at the Theatre Royal in Brighton, and advised him about job opportunities. Herbert showed him a booklet he had produced for Sabena Airlines,
seemingly on spec, but no more was heard on that front, and he tried,
in vain, to persuade Graham to invest in Vacuum Brakes. Graham was
not interested in going into the antiques business, advised against taking
a job at the Hampstead Cricket and Tennis Club, and wrote to say how

'Mumma has told me of the success you had at Seaford in spite of the weather and I was interested in the cuttings.' Quite what Herbert was up to in Seaford remains a mystery – he liked to drink at the windswept Buckle Inn, but that was unlikely to win him plaudits or press cuttings – but when he suggested that Graham might like to invest in a new but equally mysterious publishing company he received short shrift. 'Even if I had available capital I would not put it into a small publishing firm – it is the quickest way to lose one's money,' Graham told him, drawing on his long experience of the book trade.

It could be that the 'small publishing firm' in question was responsible for *Wanted a Lead, and Other Trifles*, a slim volume which carries neither a date of publication nor a publisher's imprint, and contained a selection of Herbert's verse plus various prose oddments, including unpublished letters to the Press. 'Wanted a Lead', the first poem in the book, refers to Herbert's hero, Winston Churchill:

> We ask for men to lead us,
> Not 'conchies' with a plan;
> Not separate Party interests
> But leaders of one clan;
> Pack up, you puerile planners,
> This country needs a man!

Combining elements of Chesterton, Belloc, Kipling and Robert Service, Herbert's poems reflect a nostalgia for a vanishing, largely rural England, a love of old pubs, and a Ben-like hatred of party politicians, form-filling bureaucrats and the activities of the post-war Labour Government ('Attlee, for God's sake, Go!' one poem ends):

> I'll work my way to Canada,
> Brazil or Palestine,
> Where 'Vermin' like ourselves can drink
> Without a form to sign;
> Where no Controllers hang about
> To count up all your gins,
> Nor State officials stand behind
> The bars of country Inns.

Saddest of all is a poem which reflects his frustration at not having fought in either war:

> I sit in my armchair wondering
> If those times were really true
> When I landed 'somewhere' in the night
> With my black-faced silent crew,
> Ears straining for those sudden rattles
> From a Sten gun out of sight . . .
> I'm spending my time with memories,
> Till the Post arrives at three,
> To say where my country will need me
> For I'm sure there's work for me.

A would-be short story includes club-men sitting around a fire on a stormy night, among them a 'famous surgeon', while another features 'a famous Harley Street specialist': the unpublished letters fulminate against war profiteers, pen-pushers, Herbert Morrison and identity cards.

But dealing with Herbert was never easy or harmonious. He threatened to sue Graham and Hugh for including the reference to him in *The Spy's Bedside Book*, and he embarrassed Hugh by bombarding the BBC with long and incoherent telegrams in which he complained about the increasing 'Americanisation' of its service. 'As a great believer in Sir John Reith is it not possible to bring him back to our Broadcasting House because I am quite certain he would not have sold us to America,' he cabled Sir Ian Jacob. 'Can you not persuade my young brother that a lot of us have American wives that some of us have still got married and kept them and they are English but right or wrong I think that it will be a good thing to take Lord Reith away from his present job and take him back to where I did not like him but in getting older his place in England is head of the BBC.' Graham leaped to Hugh's defence. 'I have just heard from Hugh that you're continuing to send these long absurd telegrams to the BBC, now directed towards the Director-General,' he wrote in furious vein. 'If any further telegrams of this kind are sent I shall assume that you no longer are in financial need of my allowance and will stop it herewith, nor can you expect any presents, financial or otherwise.'

A few days later Graham returned to the attack. 'No one is objecting to your having views about American influence on television,' he told Herbert.

What I object to is your writing to me one week and asking for money and almost the next week sending a long telegram which must have cost pounds to the BBC . . . the telegram was not

merely an attack on their so-called American policy but an attack
on your brother to his employer for no better reason than that
he had married an American wife. This I think would be regarded
by most people as caddish if the whole tone of the telegram had
not shown that you were not quite responsible for your actions.

Hugh, for his part, had never had many dealings with his oldest
brother – 'He's a sad character,' he told his biographer. 'He'd have been
a sounder character if he hadn't been so fundamentally nasty' – but
he had to consult his solicitors when Herbert threatened to sue him
over an uncomplimentary remark he had made about him in the *Sunday
Express*. 'I am glad that this thoroughly unpleasant business has now
been disposed of,' Raymond wrote to their distant cousin Ian Lake, a
partner in Payne, Hicks, Beach and Co of Lincoln's Inn, who had advised
Hugh that his remarks were not defamatory, and that since legal aid
was not available in defamation cases, Herbert could find himself facing
sizeable lawyers' bills. 'I am glad the Third World War is now over'.
Herbert told Hugh, adding that 'it would never have happened if the
unwarranted way in which I was treated by the War Office in the last
war had not made me very touchy.'

Graham was on the warpath again a year later, when he learned that
Herbert was – or claimed to be – in discussions with the publishing firm
of Robert Hale about a possible autobiography. 'I do strongly object to
an autobiography of yours flying under the false colours of a biography
of your brothers,' he told the would-be family historian. He and Raymond
and Hugh should be shown what Herbert had written – 'nobody cares
a damn what you write about yourself, you are your own property, but
equally so are we our own property.' 'I owe you too much gratitude not
to fall in with your wishes if you will let me know what they are,' a
penitent Herbert replied: the book was, he explained, 'almost entirely
autobiography', and contained 'nothing you can possibly object to except
the title which reads "The Four Greene Brothers"!! which I am doubtful
of myself.' The idea had come to him 'during a visit from a Sunday
newspaper reporter after the uncalled-for and spiteful remarks made by
Hugh to the *Sunday Express* about me.' He claimed to have written 50,000
words, and that Hale, who had published *Secret Agent in Spain*, were very
interested indeed, and a Sunday paper had asked for a copy of what he
had written. Sad to say, Robert Hale have no record of any correspondence with Herbert, and *The Four Greene Brothers* was probably a figment
of his imagination.

Hugh's decision to switch the nine o'clock news to ten, and to expand the programme to half an hour by following the news with comment and debate, prompted William Haley to express concern in *The Times* about new 'magazine' programmes, and whether they were compatible with the much-prized separation of news and comment. Hugh wrote a letter to the paper, assuring its readers that there would be no blurring of boundaries, and that the BBC would continue to be strictly impartial. The ending of the nine o'clock news also roused Herbert to a final frenzy of indignation, which came to a head in October 1960, ten months after Hugh had replaced Sir Ian Jacob as Director-General of the BBC. The nine o'clock news had only been a fixture since September 1938, but Herbert was horrified by what he regarded as yet another assault on Old England. He organised a nationwide protest, and promised that unless Hugh's decision was reversed thousands of protesters would march on Broadcasting House and/or the Houses of Parliament, headed by Herbert and General Sir Frederick Morgan, a veteran of D-Day. Equally outrageous was a report in the *Radio Times* which claimed that not only would the 'bongs' of Big Ben be recorded rather than live, as hitherto, but only the first 'bong' of ten would be heard before the newsreader took to the air. Herbert placed small ads in *The Times* soliciting support for the chimes, and The Big Ben Silent Minute movement lent vociferous assistance: Hugh thought it all a 'silly rumpus', but after receiving over 3,000 angry letters, he agreed to a more gradual phasing out of the 'bongs'.

Olga Franklin of the *Daily Mail* hurried down to Sussex to find out what Herbert was up to, and wrote up her findings in a full-page article entitled 'Civil War in Greene land', with photographs of the four Greene brothers running along the top of the page. She arrived to find Herbert correcting the proofs of his latest collection, *Big Ben and Other Verses*, which was published soon afterwards by the right-wing journalist John Connell and dedicated to 'my wife and the millions who want the return of Big Ben and the nine o'clock news'. Herbert told Olga Franklin about his unhappy schooldays at Marlborough and how he had tipped the future Archbishop of Canterbury into a gorse bush, before moving onto the vexed issue of the nine o'clock news. He saw little of Hugh, he said, but 'I am very fond of Graham, he is always very kind. But he phoned the other day and was very annoyed about the BBC business.' He was also very fond of Raymond, who 'kept a dignified silence, but it was whispered that he had strong opinions too.' But, Olga Franklin soon discovered, Herbert really wanted to talk about his book of poems, the first of which was given over to the subject of his protest:

From the shores of far New Zealand,
   From all men of worthy stock,
Sounds the call across the Oceans,
   'Bring us back the nine o'clock!
Bring us back the Chimes that cheered us
   In the darkest days we knew,
Bring us back the voice of Big Ben,
   Coupled with the famous 'Few'.

Graham had earlier given Herbert a wigging on Hugh's behalf – 'I see from the *Express* that you've been at it again with a lot of public nonsense to do with Hugh. I warned you before over those telegrams that if they continued I should stop your allowance. This is my last warning. Any further publicity of this kind and your allowance will stop automatically. If you prefer to make a fool of yourself to having that money you are at liberty to do so' – but that had proved no bar to his lending the Sussex Greenes his villa in Anacapri, so prompting a letter from his cousin Barbara, now living in Rome. 'I had a letter from Herbert of all people this morning,' she told Graham. 'I have not seen him for about forty years. He says he is passing through Rome one of these days and will have an hour at the station between trains and would I meet him for a drink. But I won't be in Rome that day, so that problem is solved.' 'Herbert to my surprise has gone and borrowed my villa for two weeks,' Graham explained. 'He won some money on the Derby winner, and God knows what he'll be up to down there!'

Barbara had settled in Rome by a circuitous route. After the war, she and Rudi had made their way from Liechtenstein to Argentina, and although he spoke little or no Spanish, he had found a job teaching political economy at the university in a remote provincial town called Mendoza. They lived in a small house with their two children, and in due course they were joined by their Berlin maid, Luise, who had come out from Germany. In his South American travel book *The Condor and the Crows*, Christopher Isherwood acknowledged 'my cousin Barbara and her husband Rudolph von Strachwitz', and wrote that meeting them in Buenos Aires 'was, for me, the happiest accident of the entire journey'. But such excitements were few and far between: Barbara was often extremely bored, and to pass the time she compiled an anthology of prayers, which she described as 'my escape into a private world of my own'. Ten years later she sent it to Victor Gollancz, a forceful character who described himself as a Judaeo-Christian and had (or so he claimed) been contemplating just such an anthology himself. He was very excited by Barbara's collection, appointed himself co-editor, added a good many suggestions of his own, bombarded her with telegrams, and offered her an advance of £250. *God of a Hundred Names* was published in the autumn of 1962 under the slogan 'Give God for Xmas'. John Betjeman described it as 'a book to cling to when the world seems falling to bits', Edith Sitwell declared it to be a 'great and noble book', and Christopher Isherwood found it 'a work of true love and art': it went into a third edition and sold some 40,000 copies. 'VG is rubbing his hands with joy!' Barbara told her mother. 'Well, so am I! It seems to be THE bestseller for Christmas.'

All this lay in the future: in the meantime, Rudi received a letter from the West German Foreign Ministry inviting him to rejoin the diplomatic service, and in 1951 the family left Mendoza for Rome, where he had been appointed Counsellor to the German Embassy. Rudi's health was poor, and he increasingly preferred birdwatching and a more solitary country life to the busy social life of a diplomat, but he knew where his duty lay, and made sure that Barbara played her part to perfection. 'Rudi always gives me a little lecture at lunchtime so that I don't make too much of a fool of myself by not knowing enough of what is going on below the surface,' Barbara noted. In 1957 Rudi was appointed Ambassador to the Vatican, and Barbara found herself making polite conversation with, among others, Charles de Gaulle, the Queen Mother, the Pope and Konrad Adenauer: at a less formal level, she recorded a dinner with Alan Moorehead, Lettice Cooper and Lionel Fielden at which 'we talked a lot of Felix, and his ears must have burned.' She found diplomatic life interesting, 'though when one gets tired one does long for a more natural life.' 'Remember that for years, patiently and smilingly, I have been arranging diplomatic dinners which have often been so boring that I feel I could burst. And so pointless too – all that money given out for so little return,' she told Graham, her closest confidant. When, in 1961, Rudi finally retired, and they went to live in a house they had bought in Berchtesgaden in Bavaria, she told him that although she was 'leaving quite a chunk of my heart' in Rome, 'it is quite a cheering thought that all those diplomatic lunches have come to an end.' (Barbara almost certainly enjoyed diplomatic life more than she let on: in this particular case she probably wanted to assuage Rudi's anxiety that she would be bored by life in Berchtesgaden – which she was – but she also worried that her family might feel that her addiction to the grandeur of Roman life was a betrayal of their left-wing tendencies.)

The year before they left, Barbara decided, on an impulse, to arrange a bazaar in a tiny church in the Vatican, to which Graham contributed £5. 'Now suddenly all the blood of our Harston aunts has risen in me,' she told him. Harston and its future had provided a recurrent motif in letters between Graham, Hugh and Raymond in particular. 'I had cherished the hope that you and Helga would follow Mary and me at Harston and that you would share our life and I think that you wished your two boys would share all our interests,' a melancholic Sir Graham had written to Hugh after learning of his nephew's divorce in 1948. Sir Graham died in 1950 and Aunt Polly a year later: Hugh once again contemplated the possibility of taking it over, and Graham too wondered whether, given its proximity to Newton Hall, it might not make sense for him to stay in Harston rather than be an uneasy guest of the Walstons, but nothing came of either plan.

Hugh and Elaine now had two sons, Christopher and Timothy. His two elder boys, Graham and James, had been sent to Eton. Hugh had been a neglectful parent, and James, the younger boy, had suffered from his father's remoteness, and from being sent to boarding school. In a poem entitled 'Letter from Eton' – he described it as 'an unsent letter to my parents', and presented Hugh with a copy on his seventy-fifth birthday – James wrote that

> I know you're very busy making names for yourselves
> And, one of you, gunning for that knighthood . . .
>
> Running the BBC is a full-time, fatherly occupation,
> As we know, but don't forget you have a son here too
> And that turning *two* blind eyes is one too many
> Even for the BBC . . .

'Please come soon. I do feel abandoned,' the poem ends. Years later, James showed Graham a copy. 'Whatever induced Hugh to send you to Eton?' Graham wondered. 'I realise what a civilised school Berkhamsted was by comparison, and Hugh was happy at Berkhamsted.' Despite his earlier diatribes against his in-laws, Hugh had been too preoccupied with his own affairs to pay much attention to his sons' education. Sam Guinness was prepared to pay the difference between sending the boys to St Paul's – Hugh's first choice – and Eton, and Raymond had a word with his Everest climbing partner, Tom Brocklebank, who agreed to take them both into his house.

Hugh's private life was once again in a turbulent state, but his career was going from strength to strength. In July 1959 a handwritten letter from Sir Arthur fforde, a former Headmaster of Rugby and now the Chairman of Governors of the BBC, was pushed through the door of his house in Addison Road inviting him and Elaine to lunch. Over lunch fforde told Hugh that the Governors were keen that he should succeed Sir Ian Jacob as Director-General, but there was only one possible hitch: was he by any chance a Roman Catholic, since the Northern Irish governor wouldn't approve him if he were? Hugh's successor in the post, Charles Curran *was* a Catholic, but by then – thanks in part to Hugh – the BBC was a rather more liberal institution. In the meantime, Hugh assured his host that he was, in fact, a 'respectful agnostic'. 'Well, that's all right,' fforde told him. 'Have a drink. You will be the D-G.'

That same year Marion Greene died. On a visit to Rome, Graham told Barbara that 'she lost all interest in life long ago, could not reconcile herself to old age, and was really dying of boredom. So one can only be glad that it was a peaceful ending.' 'Perhaps as a Catholic I am more "cold-blooded" because I believe there is a future & that she is probably happier at this moment than any of us,' he informed Aunt Nono, who, many years earlier, had gone to live in Crowborough with Charles and Marion Greene. 'I want to be of any help I can & I want you to feel that anything I was able to do for Mumma at the end, I would like to transfer to you. Please between us of the School House days, between the favourite aunt & the most difficult nephew, don't let's have any shyness.' Cold-blooded or not, Graham's love for his mother was never in doubt, and was fully reciprocated. Herbert had been a permanent source of anxiety, but Elisabeth and Rodney Dennys were planning to move to Crowborough; the prospect of their company, and the success of three of her sons, must have been a source of justified pride and pleasure.

China Hand

'I *love* the Chinese. Why didn't I ever realise how beautiful and gentle and kind they are? Why have we such an utterly erroneous idea of them?' Felix wrote to Elena in the autumn of 1957. He was in Hong Kong, stocking up with toothpaste and ballpoint pens before crossing into mainland China for the first time. Felix is best remembered for his two books on China, *The Wall Has Two Sides* and *A Curtain of Ignorance*, the publication of which led him to be seen by some as a lyrical and generous-minded admirer of a country which was trying to recover from a long and bloody civil war, to create a new and fairer form of society, and by others as a gullible propagandist for Mao Tse-tung's brutal and incompetent regime, a reincarnation of Lenin's 'useful idiots', who had visited Soviet Russia in the 1930s and returned home with rhapsodic accounts of smiling peasants gathering in the grain and firm-jawed workers singing lustily on the way to work. Within days of his arrival in Hong Kong, Felix felt himself to be 'a much nicer person': he never learned to speak or read Chinese, and although his political sympathies were genuine enough, his enthusiasm for Communist China may have had more to do with his own psychological and emotional problems, with his restless search for his 'true' self and for an all-explaining system of belief than with what he encountered there.

Quite what prompted Felix's interest in China remains unclear – Elena later claimed that she planted the seeds some ten years earlier – but he was well-disposed to the Communist regime from the outset. Getting to China was no easy business for someone who, like Felix, lived most of his life in the United States. America had refused to recognise the People's Republic of China after the Communists finally defeated Chiang Kai-shek and the Kuomintang in 1949, treating mainland China as a pariah state and regarding the Nationalist government in Taiwan as its legitimate rulers. Edgar Snow, the author of the pre-war bestseller *Red Star over China*, was persistently refused permission to visit China, and threatened with the confiscation of his passport, but Felix had the advantage of being both an American and a British citizen. While he was pondering on how and when to go to China, Lord Reith's daughter Marista came to stay with the Greenes in Palo Alto. Reith was extremely grateful, and gave Felix lunch at the Dorchester on his next visit to London in search of antiques. He asked Felix if he could help in any way, and when Felix said he wanted to visit China, he put him in touch with an official at the Foreign Office's Far Eastern Section, who in turn promised to cable Peking about the possibility of Felix interviewing some of the Chinese leaders.

Before leaving London Felix had a drink with James Cameron, a hard-boiled but sentimental journalist who had recently visited China and published an account of his experiences. Cameron proved rather the worse for wear, but he came up with some useful tips and advice. 'He sees the whole picture, and the tragedy of America's misconception of what Mao and those around him are trying to do,' Felix told Elena. Cameron, he went on, had 'caught the gentleness of the Chinese, the "Middle Path" philosophy, the quiet timing of their lives', and he had showed Felix 'photographs of the leaders he had taken – such quiet, wise faces.' A year later these quiet, wise faces would launch the Great Leap Forward, a combination of enforced industrialisation and collectivisation of the land which led to a lethal drop in grain production, as a result of which – it has been claimed – between twenty and thirty million of their countrymen died of starvation. In the meantime, Felix informed readers of *The Wall Has Two Sides*, 'I expected to find a country of vast impoverishment and dreadful squalor and disease. I prepared myself to see a people embittered by the rigid coercions of a police state. I expected to see fear as I had seen it in Russia in the early thirties and later in Germany and Italy,' but 'no one can be in China for more than a few hours without sensing an almost tangible vitality and an enormous optimism.' Crossing the frontier from Hong Kong, he felt that he had entered 'a country totally different from what we had been led to believe existed', the inhabitants of which were 'a smiling, relaxed, poor – yes – very happy people, energised in a way I had never known before.'

Reporting home from Peking nine days after leaving Hong Kong, Felix was ecstatic about everything he saw. 'They really are so kind – humorous, quick-witted and gentle. Never have I seen one moment's hostility or resentment, only a smiling curiosity,' he told Elena. 'I have never seen, in the midst of great poverty, so natural a grace and mutual kindliness.' He was bowled over by 'a thousand darling, utterly human incidents: a soldier stepping out of line to comfort a small boy who is crying; a policeman chasing a youngster and both laughing, as if it were a game; the look in the eye of a very old man as he walks hand-in-hand with a wee child.' More importantly, perhaps, 'my whole "world feeling" is being stretched and enriched. I know I shall never be quite the same person again.' The editor of a Chinese newspaper in Hong Kong told him that he had really 'got under the skin' of the Chinese, and begged him to return; back in America, he embarked on a lecture tour, during the course of which he told his listeners that the Chinese had 'released a collective energy which is reforming the face of their land. I saw not one single undernourished child; not once did anyone beg . . . They are gentle with each other and (what the Russians can never do) they can laugh at their government.' The *Saturday Evening Post* rejected an article he had written as being too favourable to the regime, but despite a momentary loss of faith – 'the doubt creeps into me – was my view of China naïve?' – his enthusiasm soon revived.

Fifteen years after his first visit to China – years in which Mao had unleashed his savage and disastrous Cultural Revolution – Felix wrote of how he had

come to the conclusion that knowing a great deal about China, accumulating many facts about China, has very little meaning in itself unless we can in some way relate it to ourselves, to our own society, to ourselves as individuals . . . What China has done and is doing – especially since the Cultural Revolution – has acted like a powerful searchlight illuminating our own society, the relationships that we take for granted here and, again speaking personally, my own behaviour and my own consciousness and my own relationship to other people.

Whereas Americans valued competitiveness and the gratification of the individual's material needs, the Chinese emphasised co-operation and mutual support. Westerners were imprisoned by notions of the self, and self-fulfilment, whereas the Chinese had a far stronger (and altogether preferable) sense of community, and 'democracy, to my way of thinking, has much more to do with the way we feel and act towards each other than the mere machinery of voting.' Maoism was about changing human nature as well as society at large, as a result of which 'the Chinese message is universal, it is not just for China. It is in the very air around us if we listen to it; for it is expressing what we all have in our hearts: the need for a world in which we can be really human.'

Felix was not alone in thinking that human nature had been changed for the better in Communist China. The number of foreigners allowed to live in or visit the country had been tightly controlled since 1949. Visitors were treated as honoured guests: they were put up in luxury hotels, showered with gifts, treated with grave courtesy, taken on carefully planned itineraries, kept at a distance from the man in the street, and only allowed to meet specially selected Chinese who had been told how to behave with foreigners. Chinese who had been taught how to deal with foreigners in Chou En-lai's *waishi* schools presented themselves as being, like their master, frank, accessible and considerate: whereas Mao was seen as a remote, god-like figure who devoted his life to serving his people, Chou, whom Felix interviewed twice on later visits, came across as a friendly, urbane, rather diffident figure with whom one could see eye-to-eye. The fact that so few Western visitors could speak or understand the language or knew anything about Chinese history or culture made it all the easier for them to be bamboozled, and to idealise both the Chinese themselves and the Communist Party's achievements. Simone de Beauvoir noted 'a certain freshness in the soul', whereas 'we have gone stale somehow,' while the actress Shirley MacLaine waxed rhapsodic about the 'glorification of selflessness'; and their views were shared by, among others, the left-wing writer Basil Davidson, the Swedish economist Jan Myrdal and Professor Fairbank of Harvard University. Felix, for his part, claimed that China 'allows one to be *oneself*, in a way no other society can.' He felt himself to be 'a "better" person here, kinder, more outgoing even to total strangers, a less "me-enclosed" person', where he could 'cry without feeling ashamed'.

The pronouncements of such well-meaning visitors excited a mixture of envy and derision among the few journalists who lived full time in China, spoke the language and had some idea of what was going on. According to Jacques Marcuse, the only resident correspondent who could remember pre-war and pre-Communist China, journalists like himself had to rely on official handouts from the Chinese News Agency and read between the lines of what appeared in the Communist Party's *People's Daily*; travel was severely restricted, there were no press conferences or interviews with officials, and the foreign Press corps were united by 'bonds of common frustration'. By contrast, well-disposed visitors like the American sinophiles Edgar Snow and Anne Louise Strong, who had done relief work for the Quakers in Southern Russia the year before Ben, were not only given the full treatment, but were kept away from their more jaded professional colleagues. Marcuse was scathing about the 'fellow-travelling salesmen' who made their brief appearances in Peking, and ridiculed them as 'the regime's blue-eyed Foreign Devils, who turn up again and again to be pampered, cajoled, bamboozled and put to their appointed use.' 'Special correspondents' like Snow and Felix were 'crammed like poultry, in the hope, often gratified, that the proof will be found in the reading.' 'Their sources of information are strictly Chinese and their audience largely Anglo-Saxon,' Marcuse declared. 'They are shown a greater area of the surface than others, it being understood that they will not ripple it or indulge in unseemly soundings.' They were, he suggested, given the 'VIPP (Very Important Potential Propagandist)' treatment: the honoured guest was made to feel that nothing was being withheld from him, and although he felt sure that he was being shown a typical Chinese market place, 'he does not always realise that it is a *special* market and a sham market' – and 'what his eye does not see, his conscience will not grieve over.' Snow and Felix did not tell 'deliberate untruths', but were carried away by 'blind faith'. Another French-speaking veteran of the Chinese scene, Simon Leys, mocked those idealistic visitors who claimed that nothing got stolen in China, that the waiters didn't expect to be tipped, and that beggars were unknown.

Marcuse thought that whereas Edgar Snow's *Red Star Over China* was useful and informative, Felix was 'a comparative newcomer, who writes with much greater ignorance of China's past and with greater advertising zeal.' He read *The Wall Has Two Sides* in 1962, the year of its publication, and 'thought Greene's scholarly and literary background slim' after noting that the bibliography contained nothing published before 1944. The following year he met Felix at a Danish Embassy reception in Peking. They dined together afterwards, and 'I did not ingratiate myself by asking whether he had ever seen a one-sided wall.' He dismissed as 'balderdash' Felix's enthusiastic account of Peking's new railway station, and told him that 'his good faith had been taken advantage of'. Felix had written of how the station restaurant was open day and night, of how there were televisions in all the waiting rooms and nurseries for young children, and how tickets could be ordered by phone. After Marcuse had pointed out, inter alia, that the crèche was 'permanently locked and padlocked', Felix admitted that he had not visited the station by himself but had come on a pre-arranged visit. 'I reminded him that the Chinese were masters of stage management, but that was something he did not particularly want to hear,' Marcuse recalled, adding that 'after that session I saw no more of him except from a distance when he was filming Wang Fu Ching, which had been cleared of traffic and down which a sprinkler was operating, a thing never witnessed before in broad daylight.'

Unfazed by such mean-minded scepticism, Felix was riding high as a China expert. Han Suyin, the Chinese writer, remembered meeting him in Hong Kong, his 'eyes shining' with excitement as he told her that visiting China had been 'the most significant thing that has ever happened to me'. Felix had asked her for help when planning his second visit in 1960, and she had spoken about him to Chou En-lai, describing Felix as a 'very good man' who was 'truly concerned about the future of the world' – which was accurate enough – and emphasising his 'usefulness and enthusiasm'. 'Would we be able, Edgar Snow, Felix Greene and myself, to establish better understanding between China and the Western world, so that China was no longer to be considered a threatening, hostile planet on its own?' she wondered. 'When would China be seen as she really was, neither Heaven nor Hell, but simply a very large country with an enormous number of hard-working, poor people, frighteningly poor, but indomitable in their determination to achieve prosperity and social justice and get swiftly into the twentieth century?'

After his first visit, Felix met Adlai Stevenson and talked to him about China; he was disappointed not to receive any reactions from Stevenson, Eleanor Roosevelt or ex-President Truman to a paper he had written on the subject, but he was consumed by 'a growing sense of my own responsibility' to shed light in dark places, compared with which the 'buying of antiques seems a ludicrously irrelevant occupation!' His morale was boosted by a visit to Cambridge, where he called on Joseph Needham, the eminent left-wing scientist and authority on Chinese life and culture, who told him that 'this new development in China will go down as one of the great events in human evolution.' Like many others at the time, Felix compared China favourably with India, which seemed hopelessly poverty-stricken, over-populated and caste-ridden. Felix visited India in 1959, and told Elena, apropos the poor of India, that 'there's no flow of sympathy that runs between these people like there runs between the poor of China.' Krishna Menon, the Foreign Minister, arranged for him to meet Nehru, but it was not a success: 'I think he got nothing from me at all,' Felix reported home. 'I left Nehru feeling that I had failed – that I had wasted the time of a very great and very busy man.' While in Delhi he visited Krishnamurti, whom he found sitting up in bed reading a detective story, and met Han Suyin for the first time at a dinner party given by Malcolm MacDonald.

Far removed from the squalor and chaos of India, Felix discerned in Peking 'grandeur here and a sweep of history, and a new wind blowing; it is a human change on a cosmic scale – and the meanest of these grey houses is part of the grandeur, and the laughter of the children under my window is part of the new wind.' The Chinese, he told Elena in the summer of 1960, had no sense of guilt or 'individual consciousness', and he wondered 'why do we never see children fighting here? Why is the personal gain, personal achievement motive so apparently lacking in adults?' Felix may have admired their apparent lack of competitiveness, citing it as evidence of a change in the very nature of humanity, but he found it hard to follow his hosts' example: he stiffened when he learned that Edgar Snow was returning to China for the first time since 1942, and was planning to write a book about modern-day China, and reacted with alarm when, in later years, he heard of rival film-makers invading his patch. He visited steel works, cotton mills, a prison and model farms, and attended a dinner hosted by Chou En-lai for Field Marshal Montgomery. 'It is a people's government, not a government imposed upon the people,' he declared after the dinner. 'Where else could you see, as I have seen, working men in working clothes sitting in the same banquet hall, aglitter with light and wine, as the heads of the govern-ment, and feeling quite at home?' Some months later he returned to China for a second interview with Chou. The Chinese Prime Minister seemed nervous, and their conversation was less relaxed than Felix had hoped: as for his interlocutor, 'if only people knew how much this *outward* experience of mine hides the shyness and fears of a very young boy.'

Felix returned to China in the autumn of 1963, armed with a film camera. As a cameraman-cum-film director, Felix was entirely self-taught: when he first went to China he could not load, let alone use, a cine-camera, but he learned the job as he went along and brought to it the same extraordinary competence he had displayed at the BBC, as a house-builder in California, as a dealer in antiques, as a public speaker and, most recently, as an author. Like Leni Riefenstahl, he excelled at crowd scenes and shots of men at work, as often as not against a dramatic backdrop; and over the next twenty years he was to make a series of remarkable documentaries in China, Tibet, Cuba and East Africa which, however politically naïve or credulous they may be, were masterly in cinematic terms. He was equally persistent and enterprising about show-ing his films back in the States: unable to find a distributor for his first film about China, he hired Carnegie Hall for three weeks at the cost of $20,000. Huge queues snaked around the block, his technique as a film-maker was rightly admired, and to the State Department's dismay, he established a huge following among students, radicals and anti-war protesters. He was equally successful as a lecturer, spending weeks on end travelling across the States on lucrative lecture tours. 'He is an exceptionally able speaker, fluent, never fumbling for a word, and above all relaxed and at ease,' his mother reported after listening to him in London's Conway Hall.

In later years Felix would be helped by Elena and their daughter Anne, neither of whom had any formal training as film-makers, but on this particular trip he was working alone. The film, he told Elena, 'must not even remotely smell of propaganda; it must be authentic and real' and, in search of authenticity, he visited schools, hospitals, houses, a market and an art college. 'Just picture me, in my khaki short-sleeved shirt, directing lights, cameramen, crowds, children, trying to record and film at the same time,' he instructed, adding that 'no foreigner has been given such freedom of movement as I am being given this time.' Not only was he getting to know the Chinese, but – it went without saying – all this was having a profound effect on Felix himself. 'This is the first time in my life that I have experienced working with a bunch of chaps as equals, and it's doing something very important to me,' he told Elena. 'Somewhere along the line, way back in my childhood, I missed the experience. I was always the lone worker. I never had a gang. I never had friends. It took coming to China to give me the experience of having a gang and having companions. This is a deeper therapy than I could find in any other way. I am learning to trust utterly the essential goodness of the people around me.' Not only did he feel 'enormously relaxed and at peace with the world and my fellow men', but – as always happened when he was far from home – 'this may be just what I needed before our relation could really find its foundation. I am sure that something very important is happening to me.' Back in the public arena, he assured his London publisher, Wren Howard of Jonathan Cape, that American reports of famine in China were regarded as a 'standing joke' by those in the know: 'China is now *full* of food, the people relaxed more than they have been for years, the department stores jammed with buyers, the sidewalks piled high with vegetables that are virtually given away before the next load comes in.' He had lunch with a group of Western journalists, including Hugh's old *Daily Telegraph* colleague Clare Hollingworth, but 'Oh Lord what a huge gap between their thinking and the Chinese.' He ticked off Hollingworth – who had been appointed the *Telegraph*'s China correspondent in 1973 after covering the Vietnam War, eventually settled in Hong Kong, and wrote a book about Mao Tse-tung's China – for persistently referring to the Chinese as 'they', as in 'Why do they keep us cooped up in Peking?'

Bernard Levin was to ridicule Felix in *The Times* as one of those 'useful idiots' who 'consciously devil away at their task of putting out propaganda on behalf of Chinese communism', and Barbara felt much the same way. 'Felix's enthusiasm for anything Chinese got a bit on one's nerves, and he wrapped himself in a blanket of silence after a while,' she told their mother after he had visited her in Rome, fresh from his first trip to China. 'Felix of course feels he KNOWS everything about China now, having been there for four weeks. He swept aside any arguments against Communist China, talking like an expert to poor fools who know nothing. He reminds me of Pat Sloane and others who used to come back from Russia in the 1920s, starry-eyed about what was happening there.' 'How CAN anyone know anything about the Far East, except most superficially, who has been there such a short time and speaks none of the languages?' she wanted to know on another occasion. 'I have seen in Germany how easily some people were transported to heights of enthusiasm by a little gentle flattery, by special interviews with Hitler, and what untold harm they did,' she told Eva. 'Do write and tell me his views. I don't feel at all happy about it all.' Barbara's reservations echoed discussions between Felix and Rudi, who had lived in China for several years between the wars, but she rallied round when she heard that he had written a book about China, albeit with some reservations ('I hope he does not spoil it by wild over-enthusiasm'), and ordered a copy since 'I felt I must support home industries.'

Whatever the views of more cynical critics and commentators, *The Wall Has Two Sides* was well received by non-specialist readers. William Plomer, one of Jonathan Cape's readers, wrote an enthusiastic report when the typescript came in, and in due course Wren Howard posted a copy to Field Marshal Montgomery. 'The book is in all respects a first-class portrait of the new China and I have enjoyed it immensely and agree with everything Greene says,' 'Monty' wrote from the SS *Stirling Castle*, en route to South Africa. 'Especially do I agree with him that the American attitude to the People's Republic is unworthy of the leading nation of the Western world.' As a British citizen, Felix had found it easier to visit China than his American counterparts, but new legislation made it harder for foreigners living in the States to go there without a 'public interest' permission from the State Department. Felix could find himself unable to re-enter the States, and he had asked Wren Howard to write on his behalf to the State Department, so facilitating his later visits. His second book on China, *A Curtain of Ignorance*, was published in 1965. James Cameron thought well of it, but the Labour MP Desmond

Donnelly declared Felix to be the 'soapiest seller of doctrine since Dr Frank Buchman', while the *Observer* described his book as 'unbalanced, simplistic and naïve'.

Felix's next book, *Let There Be a World*, was an impassioned plea for an end to the nuclear arms race. Enterprising as ever, Felix decided to publish it himself, and he set up the Fulton Publishing Company in his garage in Palo Alto. The book sold 85,000 copies in 1963, with peace groups in the States placing bulk orders, and it was reissued in Britain in 1982 by Gollancz, who sold a further 25,000. Combining text and photographs, Felix's next book, *Vietnam! Vietnam!*, was also self-published, and reflected his belief that 'what is happening in Vietnam is cruel and terrible'. Felix and Elena visited North Vietnam in 1966, and were horrified by the way in which America was 'bullying and terrorising a small land' with massive bombing raids. The Fulton Publishing Company sold over 100,000 copies of *Vietnam!, Vietnam!* in the American market, and it was published in Britain by Felix's regular publisher, Jonathan Cape. Hugh's son, Graham C. Greene, had succeeded Wren Howard as the firm's managing director, and he sent a proof to his uncle Graham, who would shortly resign from the American Academy of Arts and Letters in protest against the war, a move from which Isaiah Berlin sought to dissuade him, but which was supported by Bertrand Russell, C. Day Lewis and Herbert Read. 'I am afraid I can't say anything very favourable,' Graham told his nephew. 'Naturally I sympathise entirely with his motives in publishing as I am entirely against the war, but this book seems to be a compilation of familiar facts (with a few errors), familiar photographs and familiar propaganda. It's not the kind of book that will do any good to anyone, I think.' Claud Cockburn mentioned to Graham that he had bumped into Felix for the first time in years, and that he seemed to be doing a 'tremendous job'. 'I have never liked Felix and I found his books on China very boring as well as rosy-eyed,' Graham replied, but despite his views on *Vietnam! Vietnam!* he conceded that 'he has been doing a good job in North Vietnam.' (Years later he told Felix's biographers that he remembered nothing about it, and that 'I can't for the life of me remember Felix asking me for a blurb.') Undeterred by Graham's lack of enthusiasm, Tom Maschler, Cape's stylish and charismatic chairman, decided to publish jointly with Penguin Books. 'This is really great and I hope it will really have an effect', Tony Godwin of Penguin told him. Cape and Penguin eventually published in 1967, after some nightmare dealings with Felix's printers in California.

That same year Felix visited North Vietnam for the *San Francisco*

Chronicle (the *New York Times* had decided against commissioning a series of articles on the grounds that Felix would almost certainly prove too well-disposed to the Vietcong). The Prime Minister, he was told, had read and approved *Vietnam! Vietnam!*, and he was treated as an honoured guest. He felt 'utterly at ease' with the Vietnamese – 'much more so than I did this time with the Chinese': he had recently visited China, and although 'everyone is discussing like mad!' – the Cultural Revolution was under way – he was aware, for the first time, of 'tension and stress in the air'. He filmed smiling Vietnamese working in paddy fields – they included a song and dance group, and a girl who beat a drum to warn of an impending American air raid – and 'there was a simplicity, a kind of *purity* about it, that appealed to me immensely.' Listening to 'darling' peasants singing their 'heroic' songs, he was – once again – 'struck by their extreme purity – in their singing, in their quick readiness to help me, their laughter when mistakes were made.' Arriving in Hanoi from China, he marvelled at the ubiquitous 'laughter and giggling', and by the way in which 'the pretty girls give one (even me!) a flirtatious glance and smile', while 'little children, barefoot and in rubber sandals, looked up as I passed and screamed something childish and cheeky which made the others burst into shrieks of mirth.' They were poor, cold and shabby, 'bless their hearts', but 'these people are among the kindest in the world'. 'I warm to these people. I really love them,' he told Elena, and by comparison the Chinese now seemed 'correct' and lacking in spontaneity. While in North Vietnam he encountered a group of Quakers ('well-meaning but pretty hopeless') as well as members of Bertrand Russell's War Crimes Tribunal, who were gathering evidence of American atrocities. He worried that Russell's sidekick, Ralph Schoenman, would pip him to the post with a film for CBS. Felix considered his own film, *Inside Vietnam*, 'the best and most moving film I have made': it included an interview with Ho Chi Minh, and 'Fulbright told me that it had done more to arouse public opinion against the Vietnam War than all the marches and pamphlets and speeches that had been made.' The BBC refused to screen it, but CBS paid him $2500 for a brief extract, and the *Washington Post* published extensive excerpts after the whole interview had been broadcast over Radio Hanoi. The film was shown in thirty-five countries, and, as with his films about China, it was widely and enthusiastically received in American universities.

Once again, Felix found it hard to exclude his own yearnings from his reflections on the war and the people of North Vietnam. 'This is the kind of place we must have, and will have, once we get outside the *money* world, which means the fear world,' he told Elena after visiting an area which to him looked like a tropical paradise, replete with bamboo huts and beaming peasants. 'The wish to get away from the money-fear world is getting very strong in me.' With Elena half a world away, Felix continued to agonise over their relationship, posting off mingled protestations of love and remorse. 'It obviously cannot go on as it is, half right, half pretence, too self-conscious to be spontaneous, too full of mutual resentments from the earlier times,' he told her, but yet again they were presented with 'a real opportunity to see whether we can make a true and open relationship . . . the pretending must stop. A fake relationship with you is just one aspect of a whole life that is hitting rock bottom.' He and Elena spent much of 1969 in Paris, where he worked on *The Enemy: Notes on Imperialism and Revolution*, which was published the following year by Jonathan Cape. In July he flew to Hanoi for Ho Chi Minh's funeral: General Giap thanked him for all he had done on behalf of North Vietnam, but the heat and the rain were unbearable. He failed to take a photograph of the great leader's body lying in state, the *Observer* rejected a piece he had cabled through, and, alone in his hotel, he was overwhelmed by 'the sense of incapacity and all-round failure with everything I have done in my life.'

The North Vietnamese may have ousted the Chinese in his affections, but Communist China still exercised its magic. 'I have never been in a revolution before. This one is a revolution conducted by words and writing, not by fighting,' Felix reported from Peking in the early stages of the Cultural Revolution. The streets were filled with crowds waving banners and posters. 'It is Mao and the young people, plus many of the workers, against the bureaucrats. I have never witnessed anything more exciting and more misunderstood,' he told Elena. 'If it works, China will emerge as an extraordinary country – a really new people, basing their lives on utterly different value systems.' It was 'like nothing that has ever happened before in human history,' and amounted to 'a discussion of the very nature of man'. Five years later he was back in China at the time of President Nixon's groundbreaking visit. He was invited to a banquet given by the President in Peking, but refused to drink the champagne that had been flown in from California and, ignoring Nixon's toasts, Felix and his translator 'quietly drank toasts to the future of the people everywhere and to Mao Tse-tung'. He scorned Nixon's speech after the meal, and ridiculed his very obvious make-up. 'I felt far more at home among the Chinese than among the Americans,' he informed Elena. He found the American visitors alien and arrogant, 'and even when I couldn't communicate in words, I found myself, whenever I was with the Chinese, feeling at *home* again.'

By the late seventies Felix was becoming increasingly disillusioned with Communist China. He had come to realise that the Chinese government specialised in making credulous foreigners feel uniquely important, with 'everyone, like I have in the past, swallowing it whole. The Chinese are past masters at this, and once one has seen it in operation one is staggered by the smooth way it operates.' Felix was no longer deceived, and the Chinese were now 'looking at me with (or am I fooling myself again?) a new respect.' The news that Coca-Cola would soon be on sale in mainland China came as a further blow. 'Dear God, the very symbol of American expansionism – and bad for the teeth and health as well,' he expostulated. 'I think I had better put them straight on a number of things.' But old loyalties persisted, still more so after the Chinese Ambassador in London had visited him at home to extend an invitation to visit China once again. 'They can't afford to have me become doubtful about their present course – too many people have seen me as a staunch ally, and if I, of all people, begin to waver, lots more people, especially in the US, will waver too,' Felix brooded in his journal, adding that 'the problem is in me: how can I guard against being influenced?' Gullible as he often was, Felix always kept one foot on the ground: he invariably reported back to the Foreign Office and the State Department after his trips to China, and he recalled how, after he had told Chou En-lai that he was planning to have a heart operation under acupuncture on his next trip to China, the worldly Prime Minister had advised him to go instead to the London Clinic.

Visiting Peking with Elena and Anne en route to film in Tibet, Felix was still 'filled with certainty that the future of the human race belongs here'. They spent six weeks in Tibet, and were greatly impressed by all that the Chinese had done to modernise the country, building roads and schools and hospitals, breaking up feudal estates and cutting the lamas down to size. Thirty years earlier, Raymond had encountered a lama clad in a brocaded waistcoat and a white cloak embroidered with silver and gold, accompanied by a retinue of retainers, and displaying 'the coldest, harshest face I have ever seen', and Felix felt the same way about Tibet's *ancien régime*. 'You must cast from your mind all images of this being the holy land, with lamas in deep prayer seeking enlightenment in sacred monasteries,' he told his mother: far from being benign and other-worldly, the lamas were rich, corrupt and debauched, and their monasteries were equipped with torture chambers and dungeons where serfs had their eyes gouged out or their hands cut off, the stumps being sealed with burning yak butter. Freed from such horrors, the Tibetans proved to be 'wonderfully jolly and open', running across the fields to wave and smile as the Greenes passed by. Although Felix complained that his Chinese assistants only wanted him to film 'the happy-happy stuff', the Tibetan Society in London was outraged by his film, and tried to persuade the BBC not to show *Tibet!*, on the grounds that it was essentially Chinese propaganda. The reviews were unkind, with Derek Malcolm in the *Guardian* suggesting that Felix was 'so anxious to find goodness and light that we are trapped inside his own wishful optimism and soon screaming to be let out'. It seemed an apt summing-up of a man who had always combined generous instincts and a laudable desire to support the underdog with naïvety, self-loathing and a longing to move on to whatever new system would, however briefly, assuage his own doubts, anxieties and feelings of inadequacy.

Man of Letters

In the early spring of 1959 Graham arrived in the Belgian Congo to research a novel set in a leper colony, and eventually published as *A Burnt-Out Case*. 'Osbert and I are horrified to learn of your proposed sojourn among the lepers,' Edith Sitwell wrote from the Sitwell family house in Italy. 'But we feel you ought to have a little preliminary experience – think of us as *moral* lepers, and come here on your way.' Graham declined his old friend's invitation, and made his way without diversions to the country's capital, Leopoldville. No sooner had he booked into his hotel than his afternoon siesta was interrupted by a schoolmaster who banged on his door and asked him if he would read a novel he had just completed. 'I think if I found myself washed up on a desert island with one inhabitant he would have a novel he wanted published,' Graham complained to his mother.

The Sitwells' invitation and the persistent schoolmaster were indicative of Graham's standing as a writer who had not only appeared on the cover of *Time* magazine, but had the rare and enviable distinction of being admired by his literary peers while at the same time writing novels that sold in their hundreds of thousands around the world. He was as restless and as footloose as ever, drawn like a moth to the squalid, steamy and dangerous places of the earth, and in the years to come he would set *Our Man in Havana* in Batista's Cuba, *The Comedians* in Haiti (prompting 'Papa Doc' Duvalier to publish *Graham Greene Finally Exposed*, in which Graham was revealed as, in Papa Doc's words, 'a sadistic negrophobe, a drug addict and a torturer'), *Travels with My Aunt* in Paraguay and *The Honorary Consul* in Argentina. He was generous and helpful as ever to fellow writers whose work he admired, beating the drum on behalf of Brian Moore, Paul Theroux and Beryl Bainbridge before they became famous names, helping Antonia White with a libel case, putting Mervyn Peake's wife in touch with Raymond when he learned that his old author was suffering from Parkinson's disease and, in the case of Muriel Spark, combining very welcome cheques with 'a few bottles of red wine to take the edge off cold charity'.

As men of letters go, Graham was modest, workmanlike and unpretentious. 'I am not a genius,' he told Yvonne Cloetta, whom he had first met on his way home from the Congo. 'I am a craftsman who writes books at the cost of long and painful labour,' and whereas Dickens was a great novelist, 'I write novels, some of which are a little better than others.' Nor did he have any illusions about the likely lifespan of his own work, or that of his contemporaries. 'But what twentieth-century books will survive thirty or forty years more?' he asked Gavin Young, who was interviewing him about *The Human Factor* for the *Observer*. 'How long will *anyone* be read?' (During the course of a long and convivial lunch at the Travellers' Club, the two men worked their way through a brace of pink gins apiece, an undisclosed quantity of wine and some Calvados before returning to the Ritz Hotel, where they made inroads on a quart bottle of Teacher's whisky in Graham's room.) He saw himself working in the tradition of Robert Louis Stevenson, who had 'made the storyteller respectable in literature', and he told a correspondent who was compiling a bibliography of Arthur Conan Doyle that 'I can re-read him as I find myself unable to re-read Virginia Woolf and Forster, but then I am not a literary man' (a rather disingenuous claim, since he was exceptionally well read.) Writing was, he told Yvonne Cloetta, 'a very painful process, but I feel infinitely more upset and depressed when I'm not writing': as a young man he had tried to write a book a year, 'a reaction against the Bloomsbury people, most of whom seemed content to do a few things, build a reputation, and rest on it', but as he grew older he began to slow down. He disliked literary gatherings, hated being bracketed with Iris Murdoch and Kingsley Amis ('two of the worst novelists of the period'), and doubtless felt exhausted when, as they often did, the Australian writer Shirley Hazzard and her American husband, Francis Steegmuller, an authority on French literature and culture, knocked on the door of his house on Annacapri or arranged a meal in a nearby restaurant. They had met in the early sixties, in that very same restaurant: Greene had recited out loud a stanza of Browning, a poet he particularly admired, but forgot the last line, and Shirley Hazzard thoughtfully refreshed his memory. The Steegmullers' conversation was relentlessly literary, with quotation succeeding quotation and aphorisms abounding, and it took its toll. Graham and the Steegmullers continued to see one another, though he found that Shirley Hazzard 'intruded herself too much' and tended 'to talk a great deal,' as a result of which 'as time went on he sometimes ended up discreetly trying to escape.' His brief friendship with another over-eager literary admirer, Anthony Burgess, ended with him accusing his neighbour on the Riviera of being 'either a liar' or 'unbalanced'. After Burgess had interviewed him for the *Observer*, Graham claimed that 'he put words into my mouth which I had to look up in the dictionary', and he told Richard Ingrams that he was 'delighted' by *Private Eye*'s *Oxford Book of Pseuds*, partly for its 'exposure of poor Burgess', and partly because it confirmed his belief 'that the true home of the Pseuds is in the so-called "quality" press.'

'During my life I have spent more time living with fictional characters than with real people,' Graham once declared, and he warned Yvonne Cloetta that 'Fifty years of living with fictional characters, of dreaming their dreams, picking up their jealousies, meannesses, dishonest tricks and thoughts and betrayals doesn't make one easy to live with.' A hard-lived life was beginning to take its toll when the Steegmullers met him. 'In physiognomy and bearing he was clearly an Englishman of his era, but his looks belonged to no convention and fluctuated with mood,' Shirley Hazzard wrote in her elegant and evocative memoir, *Greene on Capri*. He looked pale and drawn, with red-rimmed eyes, and 'in his sixties, the short upper lip of sensitive youth was lengthening and toughening, the mouth pursing, the lower face growing jowly, the cheeks and nose pinkly veined from a past of serious drinking.' She noted his beautiful prehensile fingers held out on the table before him, the elegant hands twisted by Dupuytren's contraction (an affliction which, like backwards-bending thumbs, ran in the family), his alarming bright blue eyes, and his sudden flashes of rage.

Ever on the lookout as a publisher, Graham commissioned Francis Steegmuller to write *Flaubert in Egypt* for The Bodley Head, one of the many books he was to recommend to the firm over the years. Its owner and managing director, Max Reinhardt, was a suave, genial and benign figure who had settled in England and exchanged the family import-export business for publishing. One of that brilliant generation of Jewish immigrant publishers who had revitalised London publishing after the war – other members included George Weidenfeld, André Deutsch, Walter Neurath of Thames & Hudson, Paul Hamlyn, Ernest Hecht and, the rogue elephant, Robert Maxwell – Reinhardt had bought The Bodley Head from Sir Stanley Unwin in 1957. The board members included Graham's old adversary J. B. Priestley; Sir Francis Meynell, whose elegant Nonesuch Press editions were sold and distributed by The Bodley Head; and, reflecting Reinhardt's lifelong involvement in the theatre, the actors

Anthony Quayle and Ralph Richardson, an old squash-playing friend of Reinhardt whose performance in Graham's play *Carving a Statue* had driven its author wild with irritation ('Ralph is *impossible*,' Graham declared. 'Last night I lost my temper with him completely at two in the morning').

Graham and Reinhardt had been introduced to one another by Raymond's erstwhile solicitor, L. A. 'Boy' Hart, a director of The Bodley Head and of Ansbacher's, the merchant bank which had financed the takeover of the firm from Stanley Unwin, and a friend of Ralph Richardson. (Earlier in the decade, Graham, drawing on his experience as both writer and publisher, had engaged in a public row with Sir Stanley on the vexed issue of authors' royalties. The most parsimonious of publishers, Unwin had suggested that with book prices rising as fast as they were, it might make sense for authors to accept reduced royalty rates, since a lower royalty on a higher price would bring them the same income as before. 'The cost of living for the author has risen as well as for the publisher and the bookseller' Graham told readers of *The Times*. 'He has his raw materials, too, of food, lodging, paper, typing. Why is it always the middleman who seeks protection against rising costs? The author has in the past been able to live without publishers, but the publishers cannot live without authors. May I suggest a more equitable way of keeping down the price of books would be for publishers to make a substantial cut in their own salaries and directors' fees?' Graham and Reinhardt took to each other at once, and Graham was invited to join the board. Over the next thirty years – initially as a director, and later as The Bodley Head's prize author – Graham would provide the firm with a ceaseless flow of advice, tips, gossip, laudatory quotes and suggestions about where to send proofs or early copies of new books, and Reinhardt and his wife Joan would invite him to a supper of roast sausages from Paxton & Whitfield, washed down with plenty of red wine.

Graham's most celebrated coup was to persuade Charlie Chaplin to publish his autobiography with The Bodley Head. The firm was still living on past glories but, as Reinhardt recalled, Chaplin's memoirs 'launched us onto the international market as a major publishing firm'. Graham had met Chaplin earlier in the decade, and had defended him in print when he fell victim to Senator Joseph McCarthy's campaign to expose the activities of alleged Communists in American political and cultural life. Graham, Reinhardt and Reinhardt's wife Joan visited the Chaplins in Switzerland, and after the ladies had retired to bed Chaplin read the two men what he had written. 'This could be a wonderful book,' Graham told Reinhardt afterwards, and over breakfast next morning he told their host that 'I don't believe in many things, but I do believe in good writing, and what you read to us last night was first-rate.' Although they had not, as yet, a contract for the book, Graham set about cutting and editing what had been written so far: in due course Max Reinhardt bought the world rights for $500,000, and almost immediately sold the serial rights to the *Sunday Times*, the American rights and a raft of foreign rights. Graham, for his part, relished the cut and thrust of publishing, and the chance to advance the careers of writers he admired. He told Gillian Sutro that he had finished editing a new novel by his old protégé R. K. Narayan, whom he persuaded to join The Bodley Head, 'and now have to start on Charlie Chaplin. No work of my own.'

Things did not always turn out as he might have wished. A year before he joined The Bodley Head, Graham had chosen Vladimir Nabokov's *Lolita* as one of his three Books of the Year in the *Sunday Times*. Heinemann, who had published Nabokov's *Pnin*, had turned it down on grounds of possible obscenity: the previous year the firm had been prosecuted for publishing Walter Baxter's *The Image and the Search*: Frere had been compelled to spend days on end in the dock at the Old Bailey, and could not face repeating the ordeal. With publishers on both sides of the Atlantic shying away, *Lolita* had eventually been published in Paris by Maurice Girodias's Olympia Press. Graham's advocacy of *Lolita* had been attacked by John Gordon, James Douglas's successor in the *Sunday Express*, a Presbyterian pugilist who liked nothing better than writing journalistic hellfire sermons, and had earlier weighed in against *The Image and the Search*. Graham's immediate reaction was to set up the John Gordon Society with his old friend John Sutro. A few years earlier, Graham and Sutro, inflamed by several glasses of black velvet drunk on board the London to Edinburgh express, had invented the Anglo-Texan Society, highlights of which had included an inaugural meeting at Sam Guinness's house in Cheyne Walk, a dinner at the House of Lords to which the Duke of Edinburgh was invited, and a giant barbecue in the Denham film studios to which the American Ambassador and 1500 Texans from US Air Force bases turned up to eat hamburgers and listen to hill-billy bands. The John Gordon Society was in the family tradition of elab-orate practical jokes, which included Graham, Hugh and Elisabeth writing pseudonymous parodies of Graham's work for competitions in the *New Statesman* and the *Spectator*: a recent manifestation had involved Graham ringing Cyril Connolly in the guise of a chimney sweep; Connolly was giving a party to which Graham had not been invited, and was told to

SHADES OF GREENE

cover all his furniture with sheets to protect it from the soot. The Society, Graham and Sutro told the *Spectator*, had been set up in John Gordon's honour, 'in recognition of the struggle he has maintained for many years against the insidious menace of pornography, in defence of our hearths and homes and the purity of public life'. Those attending the initial meeting of the Society included Frere, Ian Gilmour (the Society's Vice-President), Moura Budberg, André Deutsch, Gerald Hamilton, A. J. Ayer, Christopher Isherwood, Peter Brook, Dorothy Glover and Angus Wilson. Facetious suggestions were advanced and discussed, and John Gordon was invited to attend a debate at the Horseshoe, a vast and cavernous bar at the bottom of Tottenham Court Road. Gordon rose to the occasion, defending himself with great aplomb, and the proceedings were enlivened by a drunken Randolph Churchill shouting his views from the wings.

'Mr G. Greene is making an ass of himself – first advertising an indecent book called *Lolita* and then trying to organise a rag of the editor,' Evelyn Waugh complained to Lady Diana Cooper. Graham assured Leonard Russell of the *Sunday Times* that he was perfectly serious in his admiration of *Lolita*, which 'seems to me one of the most amusing and interesting novels of the last ten years'. So serious was he that he pressed hard to have the novel published at The Bodley Head, at his own risk and expense if needs be. Nabokov was keen that he should go ahead, but Priestley wouldn't hear of it. He 'wasn't going to remain a director of a firm which published muck like that,' he muttered to his colleagues. 'It'll only encourage dirty old men.' While Bodley dithered, George Weidenfeld took the risk and went ahead. On the advice of his lawyer, he printed and distributed a modest number of copies, one of which was sent to the Director of Public Prosecutions, and when no writs were forthcoming he printed and sold 200,000 copies in hardback, establishing his firm as a major commercial publisher as a result.

No doubt Priestley was greatly relieved, but relations between the two directors remained uneasy. Not long after *Lolita* had been lost to the firm, Graham attended a grand dinner in Paris arranged by George Ansley, a director of Ansbacher's and The Bodley Head. Nancy Mitford reported that 'Priestley was furious because Graham Greene was at the grand table with Gladwyn [Jebb, the British ambassador] and neither of the Priestleys were.' Some years later the two men clashed again, this time over Terry Southern's novel *Candy*. It was now Graham's turn to threaten to leave, this time as an author rather than director, on the grounds that he objected to the board dictating the firm's editorial policy. Once again Bodley dithered, and a rival firm snapped it up. Shortly afterwards Priestley was persuaded to resign as a director, on the grounds that he seldom attended meetings any more, but he and Graham would occasionally encounter each other in the entrance hall of the Albany, where they both had rooms for many years.

A feud of a more serious kind had earlier broken out between Graham and his – and Priestley's – long-standing publishers. Heinemann had been an extraordinarily successful firm in terms of both commerce and quality, but by the late 1950s it seemed to have lost its way. Like its great rival, Collins, it owned its own printing works – sited, together with the warehouse, a social club and a cricket ground, at Kingswood in the North Downs – and its overheads were far higher than those of its competitors. Unlike Collins, it had made no effort to set up or invest in a paperback imprint to rival Allen Lane's Penguins or middlebrow lists like Pan Books; profits were worryingly low, and the cash flow was so sparse at times that suppliers could not be paid on time. Buying elegant but unprofitable literary publishers like Secker & Warburg and Rupert Hart-Davis had added lustre to the proceedings, but had done little for the profit-and-loss account, and although Frere was adored by his authors, and by Graham in particular, he was by nature an editor rather than an organisation man or a businessman. Alan Hill remembered how Frere combined 'genuine warmth of personality, with a charm which could be quite irresistible. He was helped in all his dealings by an instinctive sensitivity to other people, which enabled him to perceive your thoughts before you could express them in words', and the literary agent Laurence Pollinger once described him to Frieda Lawrence as 'the cleverest man in London', but he was far too secretive and detached from the everyday running of the firm to be a successful manager. Although Hill worked with him for seventeen years, 'I never once knew him to leave the first-floor office to visit the staff on the upper floors.'

Doubleday, the New York publishers, had a sizeable stake in Heinemann when Graham was first published by the firm, but by the late 1950s it was largely owned by Thomas Tilling, an industrial conglomerate famous for its fleets of buses. In 1960 Frere, now in his mid-sixties, persuaded Lionel Fraser, the boss of Tillings, that he should sell Heinemann to the American firm of McGraw Hill. British publishing was going through a paranoid phase at the time, with predatory American publishers as the villains of the piece, and when the news leaked out Fred Warburg and Rupert Hart-Davis, neither of whom had been consulted, made a great fuss, and persuaded McGraw Hill to withdraw their offer. (A year or two later, having extracted his firm from the group, Rupert Hart-Davis promptly sold it to another American publisher, Harcourt Brace.) Despite being offered the honorific post of President, Frere stumped off in high dudgeon, spending far more time in his house on the Riviera than in the Heinemann headquarters in Mayfair, and Tillings bought up the remaining shares in the group.

The following year Lionel Fraser came up with a plan of his own to restore the fortunes of the ailing publisher. Ansbacher's owned 51 per cent of The Bodley Head, and Fraser and George Ansley proposed merging Heinemann and The Bodley Head, with Max Reinhardt as one of the two managing directors, Frere as president, and Graham sitting on the holding company board as literary adviser. Reinhardt was never enamoured of the idea, but Graham seemed smitten, and was happy to take credit for thinking it up. 'It looks as though Tillings are agreeing to my great merger of Bodley Head and Heinemann – Max joint managing director, myself on the board of the Heinemann companies, and Frere back in control with me. Deadly, deadly secret!' he confided in Catherine Walston; a few days later he assured her that 'Heinemann won't really mean extra work – I'll only attend board meetings . . . I'm really becoming a tycoon!' But excitement soon turned to disillusionment, with Graham finding 'this publishing imbroglio . . . very tiring and disappointing'. Frere had assured Lionel Fraser that the entire board of Heinemann supported the idea, but once again he had not told any of them about it, let alone obtained their agreement. Warburg, Hart-Davis and Dwye Evans, the son of Graham's old publisher, Charles Evans, were strongly opposed, and no more was said about a possible merger. Frere, more isolated than ever, resigned from the board the following year, and Graham took the whole thing as a personal insult, telling Max Reinhardt that 'he refused to be associated any longer with a bus company'. He warned Lionel Fraser that Heinemann could no longer assume that they would be publishing his next book – 'I must in self-protection hold myself free to consider any offers from other firms' – and in a letter to the *Observer* he noted how quickly the character of a publishing firm could change, and how 'the sense of trust between author and publisher may vanish in a season. Perhaps this change happens more frequently now, when the City has begun to move in. Authors are not factory hands, nor are books to be compared as commodities with tobacco, beer, motor-cars and automatic machines.'

With Frere no longer involved, and about to retire altogether, Graham had no desire to stay with Heinemann. He told Max Reinhardt that, come what may, The Bodley Head could publish his next work, a short travel book entitled *In Search of a Character: Two African Journals*. Laurence Pollinger told Graham's New York publisher, Tom Guinzburg of Viking, that this would be announced in the *Bookseller*, and that although Frere knew all about it, 'I have been told to say nothing to Heinemann for he [Graham] wants them "to have an unpleasant surprise . . .".' (Graham had also changed literary agents: David Higham and Laurence Pollinger had gone their separate ways, and although Higham was, with A. D. Peters, the most distinguished agent of the day, Graham had taken against him for very personal reasons – he was irritated by his Old Testament whiskers, and by his singing in the Bach Choir – and had opted for Pollinger instead.) Frere, who would soon be appointed to the board of The Bodley Head, was more than happy to conspire against his former colleagues. He summoned some of his authors to his rooms in the Albany to see if they would be interested in defecting to The Bodley Head. Priestley decided to stay put – 'They made me. I must stand by them now' – but in due course Eric Ambler, Georgette Heyer and the SOE veteran George Millar would follow Graham into the rival camp. Nor were authors the only target. The poet and translator James Michie, then considered to be the most brilliant publishing editor in London, was invited round to see Graham in the Albany. Graham had urged Reinhardt to 'steal James Michie from Heinemann', and Michie remembered Graham 'saying fairly early on "Let's get this straight. I've got you here to seduce you."' Michie moved to The Bodley Head, but his heart was no longer in publishing, and although he edited some of Graham's early books for Bodley, the two men eventually fell out, and Graham was edited thereafter by Jill Black.

Graham finally left Heinemann in 1962, after completing *The Comedians*. 'You have been my publisher for more than ten years and my greatest friend for close on twenty years, and I owe you an explanation,' he told Frere in a long apologetic letter. The 'personal rebuff' implicit in Heinemann's rejection of the proposed merger 'could have been laughed easily off if I had not become more and more aware of the fact that I no longer had any personal contact with anyone in the firm and that – to speak frankly – I could no longer depend on you to look after my work.' 'I understand very well all your reasons, for we have often discussed them,' Frere replied; and, with that out of the way, Graham suggested that they should 'have lunch together and discuss tactics against Heinemann'. These tactics ranged from the petty to the genuinely disruptive. When David Machin, an editor at Heinemann, asked whether Graham would be prepared to provide a laudatory quote for a novel he had praised in a letter, he received a frosty reply from Graham's long-serving secretary, 'the wonderfully discreet if stern' Josephine Reid, to the effect that Graham 'saw no reason at all to assist the publishing firm of Heinemann from whom he has withdrawn his books, and considers it rather an impertinence that they should have asked him.' At a more damaging level, Graham waged a long but futile battle to force Heinemann to relinquish the rights in all his titles published by them, and transfer them to The Bodley Head. Provided Heinemann kept the books in print, they were under no contractual obligation to agree to his demands, and because Graham's backlist was a valuable and much-needed source of revenue, the demands of commerce were bound to prevail, however many angry and insistent letters he wrote. As a former publisher, Graham must have known that he was on extremely shaky ground, but, aided and abetted by Pollinger and Frere, he persisted in his epistolary trench warfare. And he persuaded Eric Ambler and the best-selling Georgette Heyer to follow his example, gleefully informing Frere that 'This will get the cold war down to zero.'

'From my publishing experience I would have judged it to be a sound measure to maintain all my titles at a stock figure of not less than 2000. That you should so flatly disagree only exacerbates a situation which can scarcely stand any further deterioration. The financial owners of your firm already know my views on your policy of holding authors on a list against their will, but I wonder if they know enough about publishing to realise how unnecessarily offensive is your attitude to my request,' he told Dwye Evans, now addressed as 'Evans' rather than 'Dwye'. His insistence on Heinemann keeping 2000 copies of each title in print in hardback had no contractual basis, nor would a failure to do so have prompted a reversion of rights to the author, but Graham would try anything to bully Heinemann into submission, including telling the Daily Telegraph that his former publisher 'clings to my old books like some divorced woman who fights over every chattel not for its intrinsic value but because she considers herself to be a wronged woman'. Graham disliked Dwye Evans, but in due course he found himself dealing with Heinemann's managing director, Charles Pick, a hard-headed publisher who had started life as one of Victor Gollancz's reps in the 1930s, knew the business backwards, and wasn't to be brow-beaten by Graham or anyone else. Pick was polite, friendly and firm. He wrote Graham a three-page letter refuting his claims that his books were out of stock; 'Dear Pick' became 'Dear Charles', and invitations to lunch were gladly accepted. Pick paid no attention when Pollinger, at Graham's suggestion, proposed that Heinemann should forgo their standard 40 per cent share of the very handsome paperback advances Pick had negotiated with Tony Godwin of Penguin. (Like many other authors, Anthony Powell among them, Graham detested the jackets Tony Godwin willed upon him: Allen Lane flew out to Antibes to assure him that Godwin's days were numbered, and that more tasteful designs were in the pipeline.) Max Reinhardt offered £50,000 for the rights in Graham's backlist, and suggested that The Bodley Head should buy up Heinemann's existing stock, a mind-boggling operation which would have involved stripping off the bindings and tipping in new title pages before rebinding and rejacketing the lot. Pick pointed out that with over 100,000 copies of Graham Greene titles in print this was hardly feasible, but – to the satisfaction of all parties – it was agreed that the two firms should jointly publish a handsome Collected Edition, with jackets designed by The Bodley Head's John Ryder, with lettering by Michael Harvey. (Graham had agreed that the Penguin editions should carry small, stylish drawings by Paul Hogarth, but insisted on plain lettering jackets for his hardbacks: he thought very highly of both Ryder and Harvey, who created an elegant and instantly recognisable 'look' for his books.)

Although he continued to turn to Frere for editorial advice – 'I couldn't trust Max's judgement but I do trust Frere,' he told Hugh – he found The Bodley Head the most congenial of publishers, and Reinhardt a loyal, urbane and supportive friend who gave him useful advice about financial matters and shared his liking for the South of France. He persuaded Muriel Spark to move to The Bodley Head, masterminded the republication of Ford Madox Ford's major novels, and remained on the board until 1968, when he was advised to resign for tax reasons. Every now and then he disagreed with the firm's decisions – he was particularly annoyed with James Michie for rejecting Paul Theroux's novel *The Black House*, which resulted in The Bodley Head losing its best young writer to Gillon Aitken at Hamish Hamilton: 'They said his new manuscript wasn't his best. But one can't always be at one's best,' he sagely observed – but he was to remain with The Bodley Head until, at the very end of his career, he found history repeating itself, with himself once again at the centre of events.

*

Graham's letters to publishers and agents tended to be cool, tough and terse, but his dealings with, and letters to, young people in particular often reveal a very different and more engaging side of his character. After Tom Guinzberg of Viking had been given the sack for querying the title of *Travels with My Aunt* – 'Easier to change publisher than title' Graham famously cabled back – he was published, for a time, by Michael Korda, the young whiz-kid then in charge of editorial matters at Simon & Schuster in New York. Korda was the nephew of Graham's old friend Alexander Korda, and he first met Graham on board his uncle's yacht. Their fellow sailors included Randolph Churchill, Carol Reed and Vivien Leigh, and the fifteen-year-old Mike felt over-awed and out of place. Early on in the proceedings he was handed a dry martini by 'a tall, lean Englishman with thinning sandy hair and penetrating bright blue protuberant eyes – rather like intelligent gooseberries, I thought.' 'Drink up. You look as if you need it,' this kindly apparition told him. 'It can do you no possible harm.' Korda took to Graham at once, comparing him to a 'mischievous, darting schoolboy', and relishing his 'intuitive sympathy' with the young and his 'sly, subversive determination to help them break the rules.' Graham had, he observed, 'a curious way of speaking, very English, clipped to the point of being old-fashioned and high-pitched, with a slight trace of a voice impediment and a tendency to turn every sentence into a question.' The owner of this curiously 'donnish voice' then declared that 'the main thing is to have a *lot* of women, then you'll discover that looks aren't even the half of it' – Korda had confessed his admiration for Randolph Churchill's wife, the famously beautiful but badly behaved Pamela Harriman – and urged him to smoke, drink and drive his uncle's sports car without a licence.

Claud Cockburn, who resurfaced in the sixties to ask Graham if he could lend him £200 to meet a debt incurred through 'the malevolence of a Cork lawyer', once said of his old friend that he was a 'classic case of arrested development', and his wife Patricia remembered how 'Claud always said that one of the nicest things about Graham was that all his life he had retained the enthusiasm and energy of an eighteen-year-old. In fact he said that he never really grew up', and how he wished that he had seen more of him in later life. Like many writers, Graham had an endearingly juvenile streak, and the relish with which he cocked a snook at pomposity, self-importance, pretension and the Establishment in general made him, like Cockburn, a natural ally of the young and disrespectful. He outraged readers of the *Daily Telegraph* by wondering whether he was 'one of a minority in feeling admiration for the skill and courage behind the Great Train Robbers', comparing their thirty-year sentences with 'a life sentence (twelve years at most in practice) for the rape and murder of a child'. A keen reader of *Private Eye*, he regularly supplied candidates for 'Pseuds' Corner', and Richard Ingrams likes to recall a *Spectator* lunch at which Graham interrupted a long and extremely boring monologue by the Italian writer Luigi Barzini with a cry of 'Hands up who doesn't find the Cloggies funny!', 'The Cloggies' being a comic strip in *Private Eye*, drawn by Bill Tidy and featuring the Blagdon Amateur Rapist, an elderly gentleman who caused havoc among the ladies, clad only in a tie and a pair of black socks. Auberon Waugh once told Graham that 'you are the only person I know who is universally revered by all my friends, even such hard-bitten cynics as Ingrams,' and it comes as a relief to turn from Graham's business letters to those he wrote to young men like Auberon Waugh, Richard Ingrams, Patrick Marnham and Christopher Hawtree.

Hawtree, who went on to edit *Yours Etc*, a collection of Graham's letters to the papers, and a handsome anthology of *Night and Day* articles and reviews, wrote to Graham out of the blue about John Hampson's long-forgotten novel *Saturday Night at the Greyhound*: Graham shared his enthusiasm, and a genial correspondence ensued. The *Night and Day* selection had included a marvellous piece by a forgotten writer called P. Y. Betts, and after Hawtree had persuaded Ernest Hecht at the Souvenir Press to publish the octogenarian's memoirs, *People Who Say Goodbye*, Graham volunteered, with typical generosity, to provide them with a well-deserved quote. Hawtree also persuaded Chatto to reissue a little book about the famous Dreadnought Hoax, which had involved Virginia Woolf, Adrian Stephen and other pranksters dressing up as the Emperor of Abyssinia and his entourage and being given a guided tour of one of the Navy's most up-to-date warships. Uncle Graham, then at the Admiralty, had smoothed down ruffled feathers after the hoax had come to light. 'Having been a bit of a practical joker myself perhaps I appreciated it the more,' Graham told Hawtree. 'I'm glad my uncle took the Dreadnought Hoax so calmly. He was not a man to get over-excited – even when my brother Herbert confessed to him that he had been doing some work for the Japanese.'

As a young journalist working for *Life* magazine, Stanley Price was sent to Cuba to cover the filming of *Our Man in Havana*, and found himself standing next to his hero while a scene was being shot. Graham proved 'most affable': he suggested that they should go for a drink, and Price found that he had 'an amazing capacity for putting one at one's ease'. Duncan Fallowell, on the other hand, encountered Graham in one of his capricious moods. Graham had only agreed to an interview when told that it would appear in *Penthouse* magazine, and no sooner had Fallowell arrived in the South of France – he was travelling with his parents – than he began to prevaricate. 'Give it twenty-four hours, darling, and ring him again,' Fallowell's mother advised, to good effect: Graham could not have been more charming when Fallowell rang again, apologised for having seemed irritable the day before, and agreed to be interviewed. 'He looks far younger than he is – so much so that there is something artificial about his appearance,' Fallowell noted, but although 'his manner was genial and open', he did not strike him as a 'man of large culture' and there was 'something parsimonious in his make-up' (this may have reflected the fact that Graham offered him no refreshment of any kind). Graham went on to reveal that he regularly wrote 200 to 300 words every morning after tea and toast and before he shaved; that he read the *Spectator* and *Private Eye*; that writing up his dreams was an invaluable antidote to writer's block; and that when he went to see the psychiatrist Eric Strauss about the possibility of his having electric shock treatment to counteract his depression – which Graham described as 'complete boredom, complete disenchantment' – Strauss very wisely advised him to embark on his memoirs instead.

Graham's sense of mischief and his desire to shock or annoy the powers-that-be was combined with a reluctance to toe the line or join organisations of any kind. Evelyn Waugh and Richard Stokes once put him up for membership of White's, the famously High Tory club in St James's Street, a haunt of red-faced country squires and patrician figures in chalk-striped suits which had an almost hypnotic appeal for middle-class writers like Waugh and Cyril Connolly. 'I hope you have ordered high white collars, a hard hat, an umbrella, a tie-pin, black brogues and all the other requisites,' Waugh wrote to his old friend after learning that he had been accepted, but, much to his sponsors' disappointment, Graham never came to the club. Nor did Waugh fare any better when he tried to persuade Graham to reconsider his refusal to accept a Companionship of Literature from the Royal Society of Literature, an award extended to only ten writers at any one time. 'If you refuse, you snub not only the Council but all the quite respectable people who have accepted. A sin against courtesy is a sin against charity,' Waugh wrote, but although Graham gave way in the end, it was not without a struggle. 'Really you old school prefect come off it,' he replied. The Fellows of the Society had not been consulted, and 'it seems to me pretentious nonsense that "a body of well-intentioned people" should assume the right to separate ten authors from the multitude for special honour.' Years later, Brigid Brophy and Maureen Duffy wrote to him on behalf of the Writers' Action Group, which was campaigning for a Public Lending Right royalty to be paid to authors. 'I am not keen on the idea of unionisation,' Graham told them. 'A union seems to me only of value when it has sanctions at its disposal – the sanctions of a strike or a go-slow. I can't see a union of writers stopping to write or anybody caring if it did. I am not myself against "ivory tower loneliness". It's only in an ivory tower to which I can retire that I find it possible to write at all.'

As a denizen of an ivory tower who was, by nature, shy and retiring, Graham guarded his privacy more fiercely than most. A no-nonsense man of letters, he cunningly combined reticence and a reclusive reputation that bordered at times on misanthropy with a strong sense of his own worth and an almost intuitive sense of how best to publicise his work. Anthony Powell, who combined a dislike of Graham's books with shrewd insights into his character, once said that 'Graham is a master of publicity. Refusing interviews and acquiring the reputation of a hermit was all part of his publicity equipment.' 'I hate biographical notes and always refuse to give them,' Graham told Frere when the Heinemann sales department asked for more information about him; he was furious when they gave his phone number to a journalist, and insisted that 'I never under any circumstances want to be approached by newspapers'. He told Pollinger that he would prefer it if Penguin replaced their usual jacket photograph with one of him wearing dark glasses and clutching a glass, since 'the great point nowadays is to be unrecognisable.' (Graham's author photographs were always a matter of dispute, and Christopher Isherwood provided a possible explanation. 'Graham looked quite sleek and handsome – much younger than in his photographs,' he noted in his diary after meeting Graham, John Lehmann and Henry Green for a drink. 'He said that this is because he is always photographed when he has a hangover.')

Graham loathed being the centre of attention – he was 'speechless' with rage when he went to a restaurant in Vienna with the Reinhardts and Allen Lane, only to have their table picked out by a spotlight while the zither-player Anton Karas played his theme music from *The Third Man* – yet no one was more adept at backing into the limelight. Every new novel was greeted not just by reviews, but by profiles and extensive interviews, with V. S. Naipaul, Gavin Young and Martin Amis among those who wrote up their encounters. As Fallowell discovered, publishing such pieces could be a nerve-wracking business. Michael Mewshaw was a young American novelist whom Graham thought well of and recommended to The Bodley Head. Mewshaw visited Graham in Antibes, where he was struck by the way Graham answered the phone with a barked 'Who is this?' rather than a conventional 'Hello', and noted how 'he stooped at the shoulders, more as if to incline an ear and listen closer', and how 'his eyes alone betrayed his age' and seemed 'always on the verge of brimming over'. He wrote up his encounter in the *Nation* and Alan Ross's *London Magazine*. Graham expressed 'real horror' at the result. 'I don't think that any journalist has done worse for me than you who are such a promising novelist,' he told the hapless Mewshaw. 'It gave me a great deal of pain for its inaccuracies and its absurdities.' An embattled correspondence ensued, with Mewshaw citing chapter and verse in his defence. And then, quite suddenly, Graham suggested that they should 'forget all about it'. When, years later, Mewshaw wrote to say that he would like to include the piece in a forthcoming collection of essays, and asked Graham for a list of corrections, he was told that Graham couldn't remember there being any inaccuracies.

But that was not the end of the affair. Two years after the profile had appeared, in 1979, Penelope Gilliatt published a long profile of Graham in the *New Yorker*, and this time Graham and Michael Mewshaw were up in arms together. The *New Yorker* was famed for its fact-checkers and for the scrupulous editing and re-editing of its pieces, but Graham told its editor, William Shawn, that he had spotted 'more than fifty misstatements, misquotations and inaccuracies in Mrs Gilliatt's profile'. 'I was never invited to an internment camp in Argentina, if any exist, there are no vultures in Antibes, I never saw Miss Tutin act in Russia, no Communist from the Czech Federal Ministry of Foreign Affairs has ever called me a "liar"', he declared. Penelope Gilliatt – who was by now a heavy drinker – had a 'very odd imagination' and a 'very imperfect memory', and 'I advise her in future to use a tape recorder and make sure there is no vulture under her bed.' It then turned out that whole chunks of her piece had been lifted from Michael Mewshaw's contentious profile, and that the sanctimonious Shawn had known this all along, but liked to think of it as a case of 'unconscious plagiarism'. Neither Mewshaw nor Alan Ross was in a position to sue the *New Yorker* for breach of copyright, but Shawn eventually offered Mewshaw $2000 by way of compensation. Graham, who admired and occasionally contributed to the *London Magazine*, kept abreast of the proceedings, and told Mewshaw how glad he was 'that horrible woman got her comeuppance.'

★

Graham was, by now, an extremely rich man, yet he had worried about money since those far-off days when he and Vivien lived in Chipping

Campden, and the habit was hard to shake off. He liked to stay in expensive hotels like the Ritz, and although he was not above wangling a free flight to Barbados in exchange for an extract from his forthcoming novel in the in-flight magazine, his travelling expenses must have mounted up. As visitors invariably remarked, his flat in Antibes was small and austere (Barbara Skelton remembered it as being 'in a large modern block where you announced yourself by shouting into a grille') and his day-to-day needs were restricted to meals in Chez Felix, a nearby restaurant. His generosity was not restricted to his fellow writers. He may not have been the easiest or most involved of parents or husbands, but he never stinted on his obligations to Vivien and their children.

A passionate collector of antiques, Vivien lived in an elegant, comfortable house in Oxford, and was assured of a large and comfortable income which, in the early days at least, Graham was sometimes hard-pressed to meet. He also funded her famous collection of dolls' houses, which was housed in a building known as the Rotunda: on one occasion in the 1950s Graham spotted a 'tiny carpenter's bench' and a 'miniature billiards table' in a toyshop in Lisbon, and buying them and having them delivered to Oxford involved the combined efforts of Miss Reid, two literary agents, a Portuguese publisher, a Portuguese diplomat and Graham himself. Since they never divorced, Vivien continued to describe herself as 'Mrs Graham Greene'. Not long before Graham's death, Euan Cameron, The Bodley Head's publicity director, visited her in Oxford to discuss a possible book about her collection, and after tea she offered to show him round the house. 'This is Graham's room,' she said as they entered one of the bedrooms. The bed was turned back, and a pair of men's pyjamas was laid out on the pillow. 'It's ready for when Graham comes home', she told him, misleadingly perhaps.

Nor was Vivien the only member of the family to benefit from Graham's generosity. In the mid-sixties, Raymond told him that although he was in no need of financial assistance, Elisabeth and Rodney Dennys were 'rather worried about educational expenses' for their three children, and Graham immediately insisted on paying their school fees. (Elisabeth in due course replaced the admirably discreet Miss Reid as his secretary, typing up pre-signed letters which had been dictated onto a tape and posted to her from France. 'Her foresight, her good sense, her wise advice were irreplaceable,' according to a close friend of Graham's later years, while Euan Cameron recalled how his life was 'transformed': 'Instead of the blanket "no" which Josephine [Reid] felt impelled to give, my requests for information or even the pleas for an interview with a favoured journalist, were treated with kindliness, humour and under-standing.')

On one particular occasion, Graham's anxiety about money proved counter-productive, prompting his decision to move from London to Paris in 1965. T. W. C. Roe CBE was a solicitor based in Geneva who specialised in the financial affairs of rich and glamorous clients who wanted to pay as little tax as possible, and escape paying surtax altogether. His clients included Graham, Noël Coward, Charlie Chaplin, the saturnine actor George Sanders, James Hadley Chase and the film cameraman Jack Cardiff. Graham's finances are baffling at the best of times, but when – for example – Tony Godwin at Penguin paid Heinemann £33,750, an enormous sum in the mid-sixties for the paper-back rights in ten of his novels to Penguin, Graham's 60 per cent share of the advances was passed to Roe's company, Roturman SA, which in turn paid Graham an annuity before transferring the rights to Graham's holding company, Verdant SA, also based in Switzerland. Graham put his trust in 'Tom' Roe, but in August 1965 the *Sunday Express* reported that Roe had been arrested near Lausanne for cashing sixty forged $100 notes. His car had been searched, and forged notes to the value of $365,000 had been found. 'Everyone is terribly sorry about what has happened to poor Tom,' Noël Coward was reported as saying, but it turned out that 'poor Tom' had not only swindled his clients, Graham included, but may well have been laundering money for the Mafia.

Graham had a soft spot for rogues and 'pirates' – Roe had offered to advise Francis Greene, newly graduated from Christ Church, Oxford, about possible jobs, and after meeting Robert Maxwell at 'Boy' Hart's, Graham suggested him as 'another pirate who would be interested if you got in touch with him' – but he worried about scandal as well as monetary losses, and, faced with a possible battle with the Inland Revenue, he decided to move to France for tax reasons, visiting England for no more than ninety days a year. 'Today I have been clearing drawers, destroying letters, preparing for the new life,' he told Yvonne Cloetta as he prepared to leave the Albany. He would be having a farewell dinner with the Reinhardts, the Sutros and Miss Reid, and 'the next day I take the train at 10 a.m. and arrive at the Gard du Nord at 6.15 – a free man!' Not long afterwards Evelyn Waugh gave Nancy Mitford Graham's Paris address, warning her that 'he is more social than his books would give one to think.'

★

Some years later, Diana Athill, then an editor at André Deutsch, found herself sitting next to Graham at a dinner given by Norah Smallwood, who had worked as a secretary on *Night and Day* and was now the formidable managing director of Chatto & Windus. For the first ten minutes or so he glared angrily at her, and made no attempt at conversation – like Hugh, he had no time for small talk – but then she said something which made him laugh and engaged his interest, and from then on he was the best of company, and more than happy to talk to her to the exclusion of all others. Far from being a cold fish, he was, she decided, a kind but shy man who hated being – as he invariably was – a famous name and the centre of attention, and she wouldn't hear a word against him thereafter.

28

Director-General

Graham was visiting Barbara in Rome when they read about Hugh's appointment as Director-General of the BBC in an airmail edition of *The Times*. 'Graham's first reaction was how pleased his mother would be, which I thought was rather nice,' Barbara recalled; his second was to fire off a congratulatory telegram ('currency forbids full expression enthusiasm excitement love graham'). 'It's all very strange, isn't it? I never thought I should climb as high as I had already done. But to be D-G! Inconceivable!' Hugh told Tatjana Sais, his old flame from post-war Hamburg, with whom, two years later, he would resume a long-interrupted affair.

Reactions outside the family were equally positive. Writing in the *Sunday Pictorial*, Malcolm Muggeridge hailed Hugh as a 'capital choice' and 'a man of unusual intelligence and perception, tall, whimsical, adventurous and kindly', and hoped he would purge the BBC of the 'old mandarins' who had ruled the roost for far too long. Peter Black, the most influential television critic of the day, wrote approvingly of a 'Greene light at the BBC', the *Observer* welcomed Hugh's arrival, while describing him as a 'cold fish' and a 'lonely tower of a man', and the *Star*, one of London's three evening papers, described him in glutinous terms as 'the best kind of uncle – the kind who isn't stuffy, prefers chuckles to a frown; wants his nephews and nieces to treat serious things seriously, but doesn't wish to spoil anybody's fun.' Lord Reith, on the other hand, was all for spoiling the fun: he was 'horrified' when told of Hugh's elevation, and felt sure that 'the appointment of a divorced man, remarried and an un-believer, would be an immense delight and encouragement to those set on the paganisation of the country.' Curiously enough, the man who had done most to advance Hugh's cause had some misgivings of his own: Sir Ian Jacob worried that Hugh could be too tough for his own and others' good, was impervious to criticism, and had 'no values' or firm convictions, and 'his marital career didn't inspire one with great confidence.'

Whatever Sir Ian's views on the matter, Hugh had strong enough convictions about the duties and responsibilities of broadcasters in general, and the Director-General in particular. Radio and television, he told a gathering in Frankfurt, should hold 'a mirror up to society, and I don't care whether what is reflected in the mirror is bigotry, injustice and intolerance or accomplishment and inspiring achievement. I only want the mirror to be honest, without any curves and held with as steady a hand as may be.' The broadcaster had 'a duty to take account of the changes in society, to be ahead of public opinion, rather than always wait upon it'; the BBC should concern itself 'with the whole of life in Britain', and if viewers and listeners were presented with 'only the familiar, the comfortable, the reassuring, then surely we have failed them, for the world is not like that.' He rejected the paternalism of Reith and Haley, the notion that the BBC should provide the public with what would do them good, both morally and culturally. 'Democracy rests in the last resort on faith in the common man,' he declared, but although he insisted that 'people must turn to the BBC to find what they want, whatever it is,' he had enough in common with his predecessors to take a dim view of 'the cynicism that provides a flow of trivial entertainment for the masses while despising it and them', which was 'very close to the political cynicism which regards them as dupes to be manipulated'.

Ian Jacob's suggestion that Hugh lacked 'values' reflected his successor's belief that 'a core of scepticism and curiosity is just as important as a core of belief'– views which echoed, almost word for word, those held by Graham vis-à-vis the Roman Catholic Church. Hugh was by temperament a libertarian, for whom few subjects, if any, should be out of bounds or beyond discussion – Stuart Hood once described him as 'the most effective, most liberating figure in the history of the BBC', to work with whom 'was to know that possibilities existed which had not been thinkable before' – but the BBC should not be 'neutral, unbiased or impartial' when 'the basic moral values – truthfulness, justice, freedom, compassion, tolerance' came under attack. Recalling his experience of Nazi Germany, Hugh insisted that 'racialism' or 'extreme forms of political belief' were beyond the pale, since 'being too good "democrats" in these matters could open the way to the destruction of democracy itself.' Even so, many viewers and listeners were to be outraged by the programmes Hugh tolerated or encouraged during his ten years as Director-General, and for Mary Whitehouse and her followers he seemed the incarnation of everything that was most distressing and offensive about the Permissive Society. 'I realise I am probably too tolerant,' Hugh told Tatjana six years after he took on the job. 'All the same I take some pride in the fact that we have achieved a freedom of speech unmatched anywhere in the world. Sometimes inevitably one goes too far.'

Although Hugh is best remembered for the controversy provoked by *That Was the Week That Was*, the Wednesday Play and Kenneth Tynan saying 'fuck' on television, he once claimed that he was only responsible for suggesting two programmes during his time as Director-General: *Perry Mason*, recommended to him over drinks by Ian Fleming, and *Songs of Praise*, which must have been approved of by Mary Whitehouse and her friends in the Moral Rearmament movement. Hugh instinctively aligned himself with social and cultural change and what his successor, Charles Curran, described as an 'open-hearted libertarianism', but as Director-General he was, above all, an 'enabler': he believed in encouraging bright young talent, creating the environment in which such people could flourish, allowing them to experiment and make mistakes, trusting in an informal sense of how far they could go rather than in written directives. Editors, he once declared, 'should have an instinctive feeling for the limits of their freedom', and work within 'a framework of general guidance which arises from the continuing discussion of programmes'. He shared with Graham what his colleague Robert Lusty described as 'an engaging element of mischief': Lusty evoked 'that slow, cool, calculated voice which is so authoritative an ingredient of his manner', but warned those in danger of being seduced by it that 'not every pronouncement made by Hugh Greene is to be taken at its face value, nor is his every remark a considered one.' But although Hugh inspired great devotion, especially among his younger colleagues, he remained, as he had been in his German Service days, a remote and distant figure. 'Hugh lacked a certain viability with other human beings,' a Governor of the BBC recalled. 'Hugh is in some ways a detached cold fish, in other ways very warm. He hadn't quite the human touch somehow. In conversation he was lucid, but he made no small talk, and had very few of the minor human graces.' 'He tends to create a loneliness around him and that is why he likes a coterie of friends' with whom he could drink in the pub, another colleague remembered, adding that 'he tends to envelop himself in a cocoon of isolation and loneliness.'

Hugh took over as Director-General on 1 January 1960. He told Tatjana that he found it hard to recognise himself in the innumerable newspaper profiles published at the time, and that the social side of the job could be tiresome at times – he never had lunch alone, and was expected to don a white tie and tails at least twice a week – but it was a relief to know that 'in the end one is the person who decides.' True to his journalistic training and instincts, he merged his previous job as Director of News and Current Affairs with that of the D-G, appointing himself the Corporation's Editor-in-Chief; and, with that settled to his own satisfaction, he turned his mind to doing battle with commercial television. Although the BBC hierarchy, Hugh included, looked down on ITV, it was run by shrewd operators like Sidney Bernstein, Lew Grade and Norman Collins, all of whom had a showman's sense of the popular market, and by 1958 the BBC's share of the television audience had slumped to 28 per cent.

Seven months after Hugh took office, the Government set up the Pilkington Committee to examine every aspect of broadcasting, from the BBC's licence fee and the renewal of its charter to a proposed third television channel, the future of colour television, and the workings of local radio. Hugh not only loathed 'commercial' television – he once declared that 'it would be a sad thing for mankind if the music of the spheres turned out to be no more than the jangling of cash registers' – but he despised Sir Robert Fraser, the ITA's managing director. He set out to make the strongest possible case for the BBC, and to demolish the opposition, using the techniques and insights he had acquired as a psychological warrior at the German Service and in Malaya. Although he hated public speaking, Hugh made speeches on behalf of the BBC up and down the country. He lobbied MPs of every party, after making a careful study of their particular interests and enthusiasms, he wined and dined newspaper editors and opinion-makers, and he compiled a 'black book' which contained details of the methods, finances and personalities of those involved in independent television, the existence of which earned him a reproach from his old boss Ivone Kirkpatrick, now at ITA. And when Hugh learned that the detested Tahu Hole had leaked information about the BBC to Norman Collins, he summoned his old enemy to Broadcasting House and banished him for ever ('Tahu, get out, and never show your face in this building again').

The ITA made little effort to match Hugh's missionary zeal, and when, in June 1962, the Pilkington Report was published, the BBC achieved all it desired, including a renewal of its charter, a £5 licence fee, the use of the third television channel and colour TV. 'What a splendid vindication for the BBC. My warmest congratulations,' William Haley wrote from his office at *The Times*. 'In the final outcome the BBC was to emerge from Pilkington so much whiter than white that it proved positively embarrassing,' Robert Lusty recalled. Critics of Pilkington claimed that members of the Committee shared Hugh's prejudice against commercial television, and condemned ITV for being too popular and too good at making money – the Committee's most influential member was Richard Hoggart, the author of *The Uses of Literacy*, and one of Allen Lane's closest advisers at Penguin Books. Be that as it may, Hugh had carried the day. 'What a lot of Russians you are – clapping yourselves,' he told a gathering of BBC staff who had given him a standing ovation after the Report was made public.

The office of the Director-General was separated by a small typing pool from that of the Chairman of the BBC. Hugh found Sir Arthur fforde extremely sympathetic, but in 1964 fforde was replaced by Lord Normanbrook, a former Cabinet Secretary and Head of the Home Civil Service. Unflappable and, according to Donald McLachlan, a 'model of *gravitas* and courtesy', Normanbrook had, in Lusty's words, 'taken quiet command', and presided over 'a singularly united and informed Board of Governors'. Hugh liked and respected him, and Normanbrook was to stand by him in the turbulent times that lay ahead, defending the BBC and its Director-General against accusations of immorality and iconoclasm. But there was one man whom Hugh longed to win over: the formidable Lord Reith, who had been restlessly seeking a role in life ever since he resigned as Director-General in 1938, and, at just over six-foot six, was a quarter of an inch taller than Hugh. 'Although I did not have the honour of serving under you myself, I have always during my time at the BBC been impressed by the feeling of loyalty which you still inspire among those who did. It would be a great satisfaction to all of them if we could have you among us from time to time,' Hugh told the old titan in December 1959, and he enlisted his support vis-à-vis the Pilkington Committee, which, Lusty warned him, it was 'never wise to assume', since Reith was 'predictably unpredictable and capable of hurling a thunderbolt against the citadel of his own making'. The historian Asa Briggs acted as an intermediary between the two men, and a charm offensive was launched. Reith was invited round to Hugh's house in Addison Avenue to meet old colleagues, and if he never warmed to his host, he was very taken with Elaine. On another occasion, Hugh waited on the pavement outside Broadcasting House to give Reith a tour of the building, summoning up old colleagues like Harman Grisewood and John Snagge, pointing to the bust of Reith in the lobby, and showing him his old office ('much deteriorated'), after which he was driven round to Lime Grove to be interviewed by the steely John Freeman on *Face to Face*.

Richard Crossman, Hugh Greene, Marius Goring, Lindley Fraser and Leonard Miall (in cubicle) broadcasting *Was Wollen Sie Wissen*?

Foreign correspondents: Claud Cockburn (right) and Sefton Delmer (below)

Felix's mentors: Gerald Heard and Aldous Huxley at Trabuco (Courtesy Vickie Zahn)

Peace at any price: Ben Greene
during his Labour Party days

The Marquis of Tavistock
(later the Duke of Bedford)

John Beckett

Maxwell Knight

Elaine Shaplen

(*Above right*) Tatjana Sais

Felix with Chinese Premier
Chou En-lai

Graham with Kim and
Rufina Philby in Moscow

Ave, Graham and Barbara
at Raymond's seventieth
birthday celebrations

Graham with Felix and Tooter
at the same party

But disillusionment soon set in. Reith was disgusted by the BBC's coverage of the Profumo affair in the summer of 1963, raging in his diary about 'vulgarity and cheapness' and how 'the BBC has lost all I put into it', and admitting that 'if I were not committed (as it were) to friendliness with the Director-General I am pretty sure I would make a serious attack on the BBC in the Lords.' 'The BBC, particularly on television, has utterly discarded everything I did,' became a leitmotif of his private and public musings. 'I don't think I am going to have anything more to do with Carleton Greene or Lady Greene, as she has become today' he declared after publication of the 1964 New Year's honours list. A day or two later Elaine rang to ask why he hadn't rung to congratulate Hugh on his knighthood, and 'I said I was pretty disgusted by what was happening at the BBC.' Over lunch, he told Elaine that he and Hugh were fundamentally incompatible, in that 'I lead; he follows the crowd in all the disgusting manifestations of the age . . . Without any reservations he gives the public what it wants: I would not, did not, and said I wouldn't. I am very annoyed that I ever got on terms with him.' He told Sir Arthur fforde that 'the BBC has lost dignity and repute; in the upper reaches of intellectual and ethical and social leadership it has abdicated its responsibility and its privileges; it is no longer "on the Lord's side". I am sorry I ever had anything to do with it,' and in his diary he mourned the 'eclipse, or rather complete overthrow and destruction, of all my work at the BBC. It was my being prepared to lead, and to withstand modern laxities and vulgarities and immorality and irreligion and all . . .' He referred to Hugh as 'that fellow Greene', and called for his resignation in a letter to *The Times*: not only would he take the job of Director-General if it were offered him, but he could do it 'more or less in my sleep'. His last encounter with Hugh was provoked by a comedian appearing on the cover of the *Radio Times*. 'Don't you think, Hugh, that dignity is the most important quality?' Reith asked. 'I'm afraid, John, I do not' was the succinct reply.

Hugh was to infuriate a great many people during his time as D-G. The deferential were outraged by the disrespectful songs and sketches aired on *That Was the Week That Was*; politicians, and Harold Wilson in particular, found Hugh less amenable than they wished; moralists like Lord Reith and Mary Whitehouse were disgusted by the views and the language expressed in television dramas, as damaging to the fibre of the nation as Penguin's publication of the unabridged *Lady Chatterley's Lover*, the songs of the Beatles and the Rolling Stones, and beads, bangles and the smoking of pot.

Like Graham, Hugh was a great encourager of the young, many of whom shared his subversive tendencies, but generosity of spirit was combined with ruthlessness. Leonard Miall, his old friend and ally from the German Service, was removed from a job he particularly enjoyed, making way for Grace Wyndham Goldie as Assistant Controller of Talks and Current Affairs, and 'after days of being threatened with Hugh's particular form of Siberia – Scotland' he was put in charge of staffing the new BBC2. Donald Baverstock felt that he had been shabbily treated when, after Stuart Hood's defection to Rediffusion in 1964, he was passed over as Controller of Programmes in favour of the less truculent Huw Wheldon – Hugh told him that he had provoked too much hostility over the years – and left the BBC the following year, taking with him Alasdair Milne and Anthony Jay, the future writer of *Yes, Minister*. Kenneth Adam, once Hugh's closest colleague at the BBC, left in 1968, by which time the two men were barely on speaking terms.

All this lay in the future: in the meantime, *That Was the Week That Was* (familiarly known as *TW3*) embodied all that people loved or loathed about Hugh as D-G, and was produced by many of the Young Turks with whom he was associated. Hugh claimed to have been inspired by his memories of Berlin nightclubs and cabarets, while Kenneth Adam recalled Herbert Farjeon and the Gate Theatre's pre-war reviews, in which songs and satirical sketches were interlaced. Alasdair Milne and Ned Sherrin drafted ideas under Baverstock's guidance, and Milne was given editorial responsibility for the show, which Sherrin produced. David Frost and Gerald Kaufman were involved from an early stage, and Sherrin sought out the young talent who would appear before the camera, including Willie Rushton, Roy Kinnear, Bernard Levin and Millicent Martin. 'I had been directing and producing live TV for eight years when we started *TW3*, but there was nothing quite like the intoxicating effect of that show in its early days,' Milne recalled in his memoirs, adding that 'it was the combination of good writing and good performance that made *TW3*, at its best, such an electrifying experience.' The show was topical and relentlessly up-to-date, and no one, from the Prime Minister down, was spared. Willie Rushton provided masterful lethal impersonations of Harold Macmillan, and after the first episode Reginald Bevins was asked whether, as the Postmaster-General, he would take action against the show. 'I hope you will not, repeat not, take any action about *That Was the Week That Was*,' Macmillan told him. He had not seen the show himself, but 'It is good to be laughed over. It is better than to be ignored.'

Not everyone was as tolerant, or as complimentary. Hugh had decided, very shrewdly, that *TW3* should be produced by Current Affairs rather than Light Entertainment, which was just as well, since Tom Sloan, the Head of Light Entertainment, declared that he had never been so ashamed of the BBC in his twenty-five years with the Corporation. Kenneth Adam disapproved of an episode entitled 'A Consumer's Guide to Religion', and although Hugh told those involved that 'I take my hat off to them', some of the BBC's Governors were unhappy about it. There was much worried talk about the high levels of 'smut' in the show; Sir Arthur fforde thought it would be 'a pity to spoil the ship for a ha'porth of tar', while Grace Wyndham Goldie, under whose aegis many of the Young Turks had flourished, found *TW3* 'amateurish in its endeavours to seem casual, and politically both tendentious and dangerous.' By the time the programme entered its second series, Hugh was coming under pressure from the public in particular. In October 1963 Milne rang Hugh at home to get his approval for a sketch by Christopher Booker which claimed that the electorate was faced with a choice of 'Dull Alec versus Smart Alec' (Sir Alec Douglas-Home or Harold Wilson). Hugh gave him the go-ahead, but the BBC received over 600 angry phone calls, and over 300 equally outraged letters. The General Advisory Committee was hastily summoned, and the programme was declared both offensive and unamusing.

The following month the BBC announced that *TW3* would be taken off the air at the end of the year. Hugh told the *Guardian* that he was, by nature, a 'subversive anarchist', and as such he had agreed to broadcast *TW3*, but 'it was as a pillar of the Establishment that I yielded to the fascist hyena-like howls to take it off.' 'Who will rid me of this turbulent show?' he quipped, but in fact he had decided, while at home with flu, that *TW3* threatened the unanimity of the Board of Governors, and that with Tory Cabinet ministers and their Labour shadows venting their unease, it might be wiser to pre-empt Government action. 'I knew that 1964 was bound to be an election year, and the BBC has to be especially impartial during an election,' he told the BBC's Michael Cockerell. 'It is very difficult to be fair with laughter. When I took the programme off the air, the political parties hastened to issue statements saying, quite rightly, they had brought no pressure to have the programme removed. They knew it would be politically damaging to be in any way associated with my decision.' Looking back, he thought that *TW3* had assumed an 'exaggerated importance' in the minds of both the public and the BBC: it had become 'a gigantic red herring, diverting attention from the real achievements of the BBC and prejudicing judgements of broadcasts on important and difficult social themes.'

'Nobody in Britain seriously regards the BBC these days as a servant of government,' Hugh declared in 1961, and he meant to keep things that way. Anxious to hold importunate politicians at arm's length, he relied on his Chief Assistant – initially Harman Grisewood, and later Oliver Whitley – to liaise with party leaders and pressure groups. Macmillan insisted on the right of ministers to address the nation at critical moments, and Hugh came up with a formula whereby the BBC would, from time to time, invite the Prime Minister or one of his Cabinet colleagues to take to the airwaves: the Opposition would only be granted the right of reply if the ministerial broadcast seemed like a party political broadcast in disguise. When, for example, Macmillan was invited to speak about the Common Market in September 1963, Hugh Gaitskell demanded, and was granted, a right of reply. Harold Wilson proved a far trickier proposition than Macmillan. He was determined to master television, speaking straight to the camera and paying attention to the small but telling details of how he looked and performed, and, like many Prime Ministers since, he was convinced that the BBC was prejudiced against both him and his party. He assumed that because the Press was largely Tory, it was particularly important for Labour to exploit and enjoy a good relationship with the BBC: he claimed that during the 'thirteen wasted years' of Tory rule, Labour had been persistently under-represented, and complained that, in the run-up to the 1964 election, he had been treated far more harshly by Robert Mackenzie than the Prime Minister, Alec Douglas-Home.

Hugh's own leanings were to Labour – 'I long for a Labour victory. I have never felt so intensely about an election,' he told Tatjana – but he soon discovered how nimble Wilson could be at exploiting the media. The BBC had scheduled a showing of the hugely popular television comedy *Steptoe and Son* for eight o'clock on the evening of election night, an hour before the polls closed, hoping thereby to capture a large share of the audience and retain it while the results came in. Wilson, obsessed by notions of a 'BBC plot', and uneasily aware that Labour voters were more likely than most to abstain from voting rather than miss a favourite show on television, urged Hugh to postpone *Steptoe* until nine, facetiously suggesting that he should plug the gap with *Oedipus Rex*. Later that evening he rang to say 'Thank you very much, Hugh. That will be worth a dozen or more seats to me.' Labour squeaked home with a tiny majority, and, Hugh recalled, 'I've often wondered in view of the eventual outcome whether I should have a bad conscience.'

'Harold Wilson thought he had money in the bank with the BBC, but when he came to cash his cheque it bounced,' Hugh told Michael Cockerell apropos the 1966 general election. Wilson, who wanted to be seen as a soothing, sensible family doctor, resented Hugh's preference for lively debate over pipe-wagging platitudes, and his growing hostility to the BBC was combined with warmer feelings towards ITV which, despite its commercial culture, was thought to appeal more to Labour voters. Unlike the BBC, the ITA, which represented commercial companies like Granada and Rediffusion, did not produce programmes, never argued back, and was regulated by an Act of Parliament rather than a Royal Charter. Hugh wanted to cover election campaigns like a newspaper, combining sharp reporting with live debate. Wilson found him far less accomodating than before, and bitterly resented Hugh's refusal to postpone *The Man from UNCLE* until after the polls had closed. 'I fear that a small man who, I thought, had some elements of greatness, is going to show himself smaller and smaller as his power increases,' Hugh told Tatjana, 'but I have not lost my taste for a fight.' After giving his final election broadcast in the old Lime Grove studios, Wilson launched into a fierce attack on Paul Fox, who had replaced Grace Wyndham Goldie as television's Head of Current Affairs. The BBC had arranged to film him travelling by train back from his Liverpool constituency to London, but Wilson locked its representatives out of his carriage and, in a deliberate snub to the BBC, offered John Whale of ITN his first post-election interview.

Relations between the two men steadily deteriorated after Labour had been returned to power with a greatly increased majority. (That same year Hugh took part in a very different kind of election, voting for the winning candidate when his old tutor, Edmund Blunden, was elected the Oxford Professor of Poetry.) Wilson, Hugh recalled, became 'even more suspicious of the BBC. He developed an almost paranoid belief in plots – in which some of his colleagues and the BBC were involved to do him down or even replace him.' The election was followed by endless emergencies – a sterling crisis, a seamen's strike, a wage and price freeze, cuts in public expenditure – and the embattled Prime Minister became convinced that Robin Day, Paul Fox, Ian Trethowen and Robert Mackenzie were all aligned against him. Wilson wanted the right to appear on television on a regular basis, and was furious when Hugh, who suspected him of trying to blur the distinction between BBC broadcasts and party political broadcasts, refused to allow him to explain his economic policies to viewers, and when Hugh and Normanbrook granted

Ian Macleod the right of reply to a broadcast by George Brown about Labour's National Plan.

Hugh and Normanbrook were summoned to Number 10 – they entered by a side door in case they were spotted by the Press – and subjected to a deluge of complaints. The BBC's finances were in a poor way, and Wilson threatened not to increase the licence fee. He was livid when Hugh and Normanbrook threatened in turn to expose his attempted blackmail, and he backed a plan by the Postmaster-General, Tony Benn, to reform the BBC by partly funding it with commercials, and hiving off some of its radio output to commercial operators. 'We had treated him too casually,' Hugh later declared. 'We didn't treat him with quite the respect due to a Prime Minister; we forgot that he was no longer "dear old Harold".'

A year later Wilson was still complaining to his Cabinet colleagues about the BBC, comparing its 'prejudice and bias' unfavourably with the alleged impartiality of ITV, and instructing the Chief Whip, Sam Silkin, to write a formal letter of complaint. Although Edward Short, who succeeded Benn as Postmaster-General, warmed to Hugh on account of 'this marvellous charm of manner, this smile of his, which charmed all sorts of people throughout his life', Wilson was not alone in his dislike of the Director-General. The pound was devalued in 1967, and Edward Heath, as Leader of the Opposition, demanded an immediate right of reply to Wilson's Prime Ministerial broadcast. Hugh offered him the following evening, but that was not good enough. Heath rang Hugh in a towering rage, and 'was kind enough to call me a liar among other things' before telling Hugh that 'one of his aims would be to break the tyranny of the BBC – as if that were the most important thing in the world.' 'That frightful man Hugh Greene was responsible for *That Was the Week That Was* and for the fashion to knock things down and doubt a man's integrity,' Ted Heath recalled, adding that 'the BBC is extraordinarily arrogant – and that comes from Reith.' 'I saw what an awkward cuss Hugh is,' Richard Crossman recalled after noting how Hugh had succeeded in uniting all three party leaders against him. 'Hugh is a wonderful Director-General, but he's certainly no negotiator.' Despite Hugh's enthusiasm for one of his pet projects, the Open University, Wilson's vindictive fury persisted to the end of Hugh's time as Director-General – in 1969 he complained about David Dimbleby's coverage of a visit by Richard Nixon, as a result of which Hugh and Normanbrook had to apologise to the American Ambassador – and in due course he would take his revenge.

Politicians were not alone in objecting to Hugh's innovations. In 1961 Sydney Newman joined the BBC from ABC as Head of Television Drama, and Hugh encouraged him to commission new writers and expand the repertoire in terms of both style and subject matter. Newman's *The Wednesday Play* attracted up to twelve million viewers a week, and included 'gritty', allegedly working-class dramas like Nell Dunn's *Up the Junction*, Jeremy Sandford's *Cathy Come Home* and early plays by Dennis Potter and David Mercer. They were loved and loathed in equal measure, as were popular series like *Dr Who*, *Steptoe and Son*, and *Till Death Us Do Part*, in which Warren Mitchell played the foul-mouthed bigot Alf Garnett. Hugh was delighted to support young, subversive dramatists, though neither he nor Normanbrook objected when the Governors of the BBC banned the showing of Peter Watkins's *The War Game*, a play about the effects of a nuclear explosion over London, which was thought to be too strong meat for the viewing public, and was not shown until 1985.

The Wednesday Play and *Till Death Us Do Part* were both regarded as abominations by Hugh's most vocal and unforgiving critic, Mary Whitehouse. A teacher from the West Midlands with white permed hair and bat's-wing glasses, Mrs Whitehouse regarded 1963 as an *annus horribilis*, blighted as it was by kitchen-sink plays, *That Was the Week That Was*, the Profumo affair, the rise of the Beatles, Bishop John Robinson's *Honest to God* and, most outrageous of all, a programme called *This Nation Tomorrow*, in which the poet and self-proclaimed sex expert Alex Comfort not only talked about 'prostitution', 'sexual intercourse' and 'homosexuality', and defined a 'chivalrous' boy as one who took a packet of contraceptives with him when meeting his girlfriend, but did so at an hour when children and young people could still be tuning in. She wrote at once to Hugh to protest about the BBC's enthusiasm for the 'New Morality', and asked for a meeting. Hugh – who never agreed to meet his arch-enemy on the grounds that she was unelected and entirely self-appointed – was abroad at the time, so she met Harman Grisewood instead. He seemed sympathetic to her views, but resigned shortly afterwards: he was, she declared later, 'too sincere and too gentle a Christian to be at ease among the demolition men who frequented the BBC at that time'. Mrs Whitehouse and a vicar's wife then went on to found the 'Clean Up TV Campaign', later renamed the National Viewers' and Listeners' Association, designed to give voice to those who objected to the 'propaganda of disbelief, doubt and dirt' broadcast by the BBC, which pandered to 'the lowest in human nature' and presented 'promiscuity, infidelity and drinking as normal and inevitable' activities.

Hugh was amused by Mrs Whitehouse, and liked to look down on her as an absurd and reactionary embodiment of the lower middle classes at their primmest and most narrow-minded, but her persistent campaign against him must have had some effect, like water on a stone, as well as providing ammunition for those who had their own reservations about the tone he had set at the BBC. 'She has chosen to pick on me as a sort of Antichrist engaged in a conspiracy to undermine the morals of the nation,' he told Tatjana. 'There are some pretty nasty people round her . . . real Nazi types and the lunatic fringe.' Mrs Whitehouse claimed, with some justice, to represent the millions who resented and felt patronised by university-educated, liberal-minded London intellectuals: 2000 people attended the first meeting of the 'Clean Up TV Campaign' in Birmingham Town Hall, and Kenneth Tynan's bold expletive triggered massive protests and five hostile motions in the House of Commons. 'If you were to ask me who, above all, was responsible for the moral collapse which characterised the sixties and seventies, I would unhesitatingly name Sir Hugh Carleton Greene,' Mary Whitehouse declared: in open letters to the Press she repeatedly called on him to resign – 'You're not the man for the job, Sir Hugh' – though Brian Walden, the Labour MP-turned-television interviewer, warned her that calling on Hugh to resign was a 'hopeless task', since 'Sir Hugh Greene is the Establishment.' In later years, Mrs Whitehouse liked to claim credit for Hugh's resignation: no doubt she made a contribution, but, in Normanbrook's words, 'the forces aligning themselves against the Director-General were becoming more formidable, and derived from sources of much greater consequence than Mrs Mary Whitehouse.' Not surprisingly, the opposition was led by none other than the Prime Minister, Harold Wilson.

When Hugh's ally Lord Normanbrook died in the summer of 1967, Wilson decided to replace him with Charles Hill, the Chairman of ITA. (Edward Short, Wilson's Postmaster-General, claimed in his memoirs that he decided to appoint Hill: if so, he was acting as his master's voice.) A bluff, owl-like figure whose large round spectacles gave him a look of Billy Bunter, Hill had trained as a doctor, and his mellifluous, reassuring tones as the BBC's 'radio doctor' during the war had made him a national figure, best remembered for his enthusiasm for prunes (those 'black-coated workers', as he called them). As secretary of the British Medical Association he had done battle with the Labour Minister of Health, Aneurin Bevan, and had served as a minister under Macmillan, who made him a life peer in 1963 and appointed him Chairman of ITA in the wake of the Pilkington Report. He heard the news of his impending elevation from a journalist on the *Sun*, whose call woke him as he and his wife were dozing in front of the television; he then rang Edward Short, who told him to get in touch with Harold Wilson. Hill was summoned to Downing Street the next day, where he found Wilson smoking a large cigar. Wilson told him that he wanted him to become the new Chairman of the BBC. 'There will be an almighty row if I do that,' Hill replied, all too well aware of the enmity between the BBC and ITA, and Hugh's detestation of 'commercial' television and of him. 'You and I are used to almighty rows,' Wilson insisted, and later that evening, at an *Economist* party, he told Robert Mackenzie that the news, when it broke, would 'leave the BBC on its beam ends'. Edward Short claimed that Wilson had no desire to force Hugh's resignation, and that far from being an 'anti-Greene' measure, Hill had been appointed as 'a disciplinarian who would put the BBC in its place', but others were not convinced. 'So Harold has coolly switched Hill to the BBC to bring it to book and above all to deal with Hugh Greene,' Crossman noted in his diary.

Like Hill, Hugh learned the news indirectly, through Robert Lusty, who had been appointed a Governor of the BBC by Macmillan in 1960. 'If I have an utterly reliable friend (and with all my love of Graham I could hardly say that of him!) it's Bob Lusty,' Hugh told Tatjana. A contemporary of Felix at Sidcot, Lusty was a professional publisher, and a year or two earlier, as managing director of Hutchinson, he had threatened to resign after his colleagues had torpedoed his plan to reissue *Mein Kampf*: 'Wait until you are sacked,' Hugh had urged him from the sidelines, and in due course Lusty got his way. Shortly afterwards Hugh himself was outvoted by the Governors after he had revealed plans to have the Hitler Youth leader Baldur von Schirach interviewed on his release from prison: Hugh also considered resigning, and wished Lusty had been there to lend him support ('It's your own silly fault, you should never have raised the issue,' Normanbrook told him).

As Vice-Chairman of the BBC, Lusty was summoned to St Martin's le Grand, the headquarters of the Post Office, for a meeting with Edward Short. Hugh had no idea what was involved, but thoughtfully lent Lusty his car and his chauffeur. Short apologised for summoning Lusty at such short notice, but the Government's plans for the BBC had leaked out, and since the Queen would be holding a meeting of the Privy Council in the Royal Box at Goodwood racecourse that very afternoon, it was imperative to let the BBC know in advance that its new Chairman would be 'Charles Smith'. 'Charles Hill, sir, not Charles Smith,' a civil servant whispered in his ear. 'I hope he will realise that we are a horse of a very different colour,' Lusty told him, bravely attempting a racing analogy, but Short was unimpressed. 'Lord Hill is a very wise man. He will be getting in touch with you,' he told a stunned Lusty, who hurried back to Broadcasting House to break the news to Hugh.

'Hugh, I am sorry, but I bring you the worst possible news,' Lusty blurted out, and 'I might just as well have shot the D-G. He is a large man, and he bounced – almost out of his chair.' Oliver Whitley joined them: he had heard rumours, and a BBC reporter had bumped into Harold Wilson, who seemed very pleased with himself and said he had done something the BBC wouldn't like. 'But how can I work with such a man?' Hugh groaned, his head in his hands. Kenneth Adam, the Director of Television, remembered how Hugh 'sat behind his desk with a dark baffled face', and how, at a dinner party that evening, a huge amount was drunk, 'so that a kind of frenzied gaiety prevailed.' According to Hugh, Hill was a 'despicable man', and his appointment a 'calculated insult' on Harold Wilson's part. He 'had never felt the BBC so united from top to bottom as in its rude shock at this, I can only use the term, disgraceful appointment. He did not have the intellect or the character that one had become used to in a Chairman of the BBC.' The day after the news broke, the Board of Governors met at Broadcasting House. It was, according to Lusty, 'a shocked and numbed assembly', and 'something akin to despair prevailed'. Hardiman Scott, the BBC's Political Correspondent, had persuaded Hugh not to resign, but it had been a close-run thing. Hill's appointment was, Hugh told Tatjana, 'an appalling blow. My first reaction was to resign immediately; my second to stay and fight it out. But it means the end of all pleasure in my work.'

Lusty dutifully invited Hill to lunch – his guest complained that he had received no letters of congratulation from the Governors, and wrote later of 'the pettiness and childishness of some people at the top of the BBC before and after my arrival', and of how a patronising Lusty had suggested that he should attend his first Board meeting as an 'observer' – but Hugh was sulking in his tent: the tent being, in this case, Earls Hall, the house in Suffolk which he shared with Elaine and their sons. He told Tatjana that although he was officially on holiday, 'Behind the scenes I've guided the *Observer* and the *Sunday Times*, two papers with which I've got very good and confidential relations. You will have seen by now what they wrote, which I found very helpful. You see, I'm rather a ruffian.' Hill, in the meantime, contacted the Director of Engineering at the BBC to see if he could arrange a meeting with his Director-General, and the Director rang Hugh at Earls Hall. 'I am on holiday, and Charles

Hill is not part of it,' Hugh told him, but in the end he relented, and agreed to break off his holiday and meet Hill for tea at the Reform Club. (Neither the place nor the occasion were well chosen: Hugh was never a clubman – he is said to be the only man ever to have spurned honorary membership of the Athenaeum – and tea was not a meal he enjoyed.) Hugh introduced Hill to his chauffeur ('who, I thought, was in urgent need of a haircut'); Hill went on to affront some sensitive souls at the BBC by bringing his own secretary with him, and by revealing that he already had a car provided by a chemical company of which he was a director, and a television set courtesy of the ITA.

Hill took up his post in August 1967, and although David Attenborough compared Hill's arrival at the BBC with Rommel being put in charge of the Eighth Army – he told him that the staff 'need convincing that you are fighting for the same things as the last one' – he was to prove as sturdy a defender of the BBC's independence and public service role as his predecessors and, as Lusty conceded, 'stood four-square against political and commercial pressures'. 'Harold appointed Hill to bring the BBC into line. He thought the BBC needed someone from the world of politics to tell them what the real world was about – to bring in some discipline, some curbs,' Harold Wilson's press secretary, Joe Haines, told Michael Cockerell. 'But it did not work. Hill went native. He ceased to be a politician; he became a television chairman. He became just as bad as everyone else at the BBC.'

Native or not, Lusty was convinced that Hill and Hugh would never get on together: Hill was understandably suspicious of Hugh, and displayed 'an almost total inability to understand him'; Hugh was 'intellectually contemptuous of Hill and found him devious in his ways', and persistently underrated him. (One bone of contention had to do with cigarette advertising in the *Radio Times*. Hugh worried about the loss of revenue if it was banned: Hill appeared to support him, but turned up at the next meeting of the Board of Governors with the BBC's doctor in tow, and voted in favour of a ban. Hugh was so furious that he cadged and lit up the first cigarette he had smoked in years.) Hill later wrote that although Hugh seemed at first to be 'aloof, cautious, telling me very little', they eventually reached a civilised modus vivendi: but he never got to know him well, finding him 'approachable' enough, but with a 'central area in him which no one sees', and 'a man of obstinately rigid judgements, seldom failing a friend or forgiving an enemy.' Hugh later admitted that he got on better with Hill than expected, though 'a great deal of the pleasure and exhilaration seems to have gone out of my work.' Unlike Hugh, Hill was prepared to meet Mary Whitehouse, and he treated her courteously, 'recognising that the central theme of her campaign could not be contemptuously dismissed, even though I was rarely able to agree with her.' She wrote to him to complain about the inclusion of the line 'You've been a naughty girl, you let your knickers down' in the Beatles film *Magical Mystery Tour*, due to be broadcast on Boxing Day 1967: she claimed that Hugh refused to remove the offending line when asked to do so by his Chairman, and thereby 'sealed his fate'. 'Could it be,' she wondered, 'that our letter had played a key part in triggering off the palace revolution that was to follow?'

Probably not, but in the summer of 1968 Hugh told Lusty that he was going to resign as Director-General, and that Hill had got Harold Wilson's agreement to his being made a Governor. 'It's one up on Reith, isn't it?' Hugh told Lusty – Reith had been upset not to be made a Governor after his resignation as D-G – 'and the glint of Greene mischief was in his eye.' Hill had suggested that he should leave the following April, but Hugh was worried about his resignation being linked to what was about to become his second divorce. Seven years earlier Hugh had spent a weekend with Tatjana in Geneva, and had fallen in love with her all over again, provoking a stream of passionate love letters. 'You matter in my life far more than my work, my family, my friends, my country,' he told her in words reminiscent of those used by Graham towards Catherine Walston: he read her letters to him in the lavatory at work, the only place where he could peruse them in peace. 'And then poor Hugh!' Graham told Yvonne Cloetta. 'I drank with him last night at the BBC, and saw his beloved. Apparently I knew her in 1948–9, but I'd forgotten. An old artificial anxious nervy Jewess who looks her near sixty years, but Hugh regards her with eyes swimming with love.' (Tatjana was not, in fact, Jewish, though Elaine was.)

There were other distractions to hand. Hugh had joined the board of Greene King, the family brewers, in 1964, eventually becoming its chairman. Earls Hall was only a few miles from Bury St Edmunds, and Hugh told Tatjana how he enjoyed 'the beer side of my life, the brewery and the sort of people I was with tonight, so much more, in many ways, than the more intellectual company in which I have to spend more of my time.' 'I went down to Hugh's house near Bury at the weekend,' Graham told Yvonne Cloetta. 'O my the cold and the damp. I wore a sweater over my pyjamas and a dressing gown over the sweater, and I had a hot-water bottle and an electric fire on all night, and I couldn't sleep properly for cold.' Weekends in Suffolk became bleaker still as relations with Elaine deteriorated. 'Last night was terrible; tears but no words; no communication,' he told Tatjana. 'There is nothing I can do but grit my teeth.' He escaped to a deckchair in the garden, clutching a large glass of Cutty Sark and brooding on his distant love, but to no avail. 'What I am finding increasingly difficult is not so much the occasional crying fit as the atmosphere of ferocious bad temper in which one spends one's days: not a word spoken to one except in the ugliest and rudest terms,' he wrote. Elaine saw a certain amount of Graham in Paris, and he provided much-needed moral support. 'It will be interesting to see what line Graham has taken,' Hugh told Tatjana; Graham reported that he had just had lunch with Elaine: 'Not too gloomy now, but I think when I come back during the summer I ought to play the uncle (not a favourite role) and take the boys to a matinee.' Hugh talked to Raymond about his problems, and 'What really emerged was that in his heart of hearts, I am quite sure, he envies me . . . How extraordinarily different we three brothers are, to say nothing of the fourth. Perhaps the result of the marriage of cousins?' Hugh told Lusty that Elaine had asked for a divorce on the day Lusty told him about Charles Hill's appointment. She was granted a decree nisi on account of Hugh's adultery with (or so *The Times* had it) 'a woman named Elsa Neumann', and Hugh moved out of Addison Avenue into a flat in Cornwall Gardens. Much to her credit, Elaine spoke generously about Tatjana to their sons.

Lord Reith was delighted to learn that the 'wretched Director-General' was to retire at the end of March 1969, and no doubt Mary Whitehouse, Tahu Hole and Tangye Lean felt much the same way. More generous sentiments were in evidence elsewhere. 'I should like to say how much I have come to enjoy our personal association in recent months,' Hugh told Lord Hill, adding – apropos his successor as Director-General, Charles Curran – 'I think, if I may say so, that the future of the BBC is in good hands.' A series of leaving parties were held, 'and for the first time in this long process of farewell I was really moved, and had to fight back tears. Very odd. One was surrounded by love. I had never really expected anything like that.' At midnight on 31 March he ceased to be the Director-General, and 'for the first time since March 1st 1934 I am on nobody's payroll.'

Hugh's spell as a Governor of the BBC was short-lived and uneventful. His fellow Governors took a dim view of the matter when, despite his professed contempt for 'commercial' television, he became a consultant for Thames Television on a series based on *The Rivals of Sherlock Holmes*, the first of the anthologies of late-Victorian and Edwardian detective stories he edited for The Bodley Head. Hugh unveiled a painting of himself by Ruskin Spear, which was hung in the Council Chamber at Broadcasting House; but his attendance record as a Governor was poor, and in August 1971 he finally severed his connection with the BBC on the grounds that he did not want to embarrass Charles Curran.

Hugh's period as Director-General was, according to Robert Lusty, 'one of the most beneficial, progressive and liberating eras in public service broadcasting that any society has experienced. Above all there was compassionate understanding and a probing into human problems not previously thought appropriate. Its assumptions were that democracy was adult and that those who lived under it were percipient, questioning and reasonable', while for John Freeman he was, quite simply, 'the other great D-G'. The last word should go to the erstwhile 'radio doctor', whom Hugh had so maligned before they worked together. 'A born leader, he can exhibit both a considerable maturity and a juvenile capacity for mischief,' Charles Hill wrote of Hugh in his memoirs. 'He loves to be thought outrageous. Unpompous and unstuffy, an apostle of joy and pleasure, he passionately believes in total freedom within the law, wherever it leads. An ace, if lowbrow, professional, with reactions as apparently slow as his bulk is great, he has the discernment of a top-grade politician.' One couldn't say fairer than that.

The Old Firm

Graham's old friend Alexander Korda had grown up in Hungary, and when, in 1956, the Hungarians rose up against the Soviet Union, his nephew Michael was determined to visit Budapest. Before he left, he met Graham for a drink at the Ritz, where he was introduced to an MI6 man wearing a Brigade of Guards tie, with a rolled umbrella and a bowler hat at the ready. He urged Korda to photograph the markings on Soviet tanks and the shoulder flashes worn by Russian troops, after which he should 'place the film cartridges in a French letter and shove it up your rectum', adding as an afterthought 'Vaseline helps.' 'You'll see,' Graham told his young friend as the MI6 man strode off down Piccadilly, 'they always look after their own.'

Years later, when Korda was Graham's American editor at Simon & Schuster, Graham asked him if he would try to get hold of his FBI file, since he longed to know what it contained. Early in the 1950s, when Senator McCarthy's baleful campaign was at its most effective, Graham half-jokingly told an American consular official that he had, very briefly, been a Communist Party member while at Oxford, and ever since he had enjoyed an uneasy relationship with the United States authorities, not least in terms of visiting a country for which he had little liking or sympathy. He enjoyed thwarting American immigration authorities whenever possible, and was vocal in his support for anti-American movements in Central America. Korda managed to get hold of the file, but far from bulging at the seams it turned out to be a very modest affair, consisting of press cuttings, a long account of the 1948 International Congress of Intellectuals in Warsaw, and sixteen blacked-out pages, with no mention of Graham's meetings with Castro or Kim Philby, or his travels in North Vietnam.

According to Yvonne Cloetta, Graham 'often said that he would have made an excellent priest or a bad spy, because he forgot what he was told the moment he heard it.' Because he found the world of espionage so fascinating, and liked to shroud his doings in an air of mystery, it is generally assumed that Graham combined his foreign travel with some work for MI6, and continued to associate with colleagues from the 'old firm'. For the time being at least, we can only rely on tantalising hints. Alexander Korda, his host on a Mediterranean cruise in the early 1950s, told him that MI6 had given him a generous currency allowance to photograph the Yugoslavian coastline. When, again in the early 1950s, Graham interviewed Ho Chi Minh for an article he was writing about Indo-China, he contacted MI6 on his return to Britain and gave them a full report of their meeting. It has been claimed that MI6 encouraged Graham to join a trip to China in 1957, organised by Margaret Lane, in order to find out what had happened to a Chinese dissident (Graham drank a great deal of sake, and was intensely irritated by a Labour peer who was also in the party). An MI6 official claimed that Graham 'went to Poland at our instigation during the Cold War', ostensibly to investigate the publication of books from the West by Pax, a government-backed Catholic body. In 1957 Graham lunched with the head of MI6, Maurice Oldfield, and 'we were by ourselves and it was most interesting.' With the MI6 files still closed, one has little to go on beyond hunch and hearsay, but in a letter to Auberon Waugh pointing out howlers in an article Waugh had written for the *Sunday Telegraph* Graham revealed that 'I was never an MI6 *agent*. You should know the difference between an officer who lives in perfect safety and an agent who leads a dangerous career. I was always in perfect safety.' He had never owned a pistol 'loaded or unloaded,' nor had he ever 'indulged in fantasies of a shoot-out with Guy [Burgess]. My fantasies include the possibility of his friends getting rid of him, but I have never had that ambition.'

Graham may not have felt too kindly about Guy Burgess, but his old friend Kim Philby was a different matter. 'I never believed in the prime importance of loyalty to one's country. Loyalty to individuals seems to me to be far more important,' he told Marie-Françoise Allain, and Philby was to be a beneficiary of Graham's loyalty. Burgess and Maclean fled to Moscow in 1951, and the following year Philby was interrogated by Helenus Milmo QC at MI5's headquarters in Leconfield House. Philby later told Phillip Knightley that he broke off his friendship with Graham after the interrogation so as not to cause him any trouble. In 1955 Philby was named as the 'third man' in a New York newspaper; Harold Macmillan cleared his name in the House of Commons, but in the meantime Philby and his second wife, Aileen, took refuge from the Press in his mother-in-law's house in Crowborough. In due course he moved to

Beirut as a stringer for the *Observer* and the *Economist* before defecting to the Soviet Union in January 1963 on board a cargo ship travelling from Beirut to Odessa. The first journalist to write about his disappearance was Hugh's former colleague, Clare Hollingworth, who was then covering the Middle East for the *Manchester Guardian*: she had got to know Philby in London in the late 1930s, and had seen a fair amount of him in Beirut. To her intense frustration, the editor, Alastair Hetherington, sat on the story for fear of libel, but four months after Philby had vanished she persuaded his deputy to run it in his absence. In her belated article she thought it unlikely that Philby had gone to Moscow, but other papers took up the story, and soon afterwards his defection was made public.

Quite how much Graham knew, or suspected, of Philby's activities is a matter of conjecture. When, in February 1948, he went to Vienna to research *The Third Man*, he saw a good deal of *The Times*'s correspondent in the city, Peter Smollett, né Hans Peter Smolka, who, like Graham, had worked for the Ministry of Information during the war, and is best remembered for having tipped off Graham about Harry Lime's lethal racket of selling diluted penicillin, and for having advised Jonathan Cape not to publish George Orwell's *Animal Farm*. Smollett himself may have been a Soviet agent; he had got to know Philby in 1934, when civil war had broken out in Vienna between the socialists and Engelbert Dollfuss's paramilitary Heimwehr, and Philby had helped members of the Schutzbund to escape through the sewers of the city. Smolka had briefly employed Philby at the London Continental News Agency, set up in London in 1934 to collect and distribute news from Central and Eastern Europe, and it may be that he and Graham found themselves discussing their mutual friend in the freezing Vienna winter.

Five years after his defection, Philby's *My Silent War* was published in London, carrying an introduction by Graham in which he famously compared his old friend with Catholic priests suffering for their faith during the reign of Queen Elizabeth. 'I was flabbergasted when I read it,' Philby later declared. 'He understood what I had done and why I had done it.' 'I always thought that you were one of the few people in England who would really understand,' he told Graham.

> Even so, I was overwhelmed by the warmth of your tribute (I can call it no less). You will not of course expect the humbling thought to have escaped me that you may have over-written my virtues and most charitably have ignored my many failings. Nevertheless I must accept what you say as a corrective to much of the nonsense that

has been written about me, notably the many libels on my father, whom I always regarded, with abundant justification, as a great, if rather remote, friend.

Nicholas Elliott thought Graham's preface 'shameful'. Years later, over lunch with Graham in the South of France, he spoke 'pretty sharply' to him about it, and claimed that Graham 'certainly seemed rather shame-faced' about what Elliott conceded to have been an 'act of political naïvety'. But Graham was unrepentant: he genuinely liked Philby, as did Malcolm Muggeridge, and a tendency to side with the underdog was combined with a writerly readiness to see both sides of an argument, and a good many others in between. In his contribution to three short talks on the role of the writer given on the 'Third Programme' in October 1948 – the other speakers were Elizabeth Bowen and V. S. Pritchett – Graham claimed that 'disloyalty is our privilege', and that 'the one privilege [the writer] can claim, in common perhaps with his fellow human beings, but possibly with greater safety, is that of disloy-alty'; and in a speech entitled 'The Virtue of Disloyalty', delivered in Hamburg in 1969, he suggested that it was the writer's duty to 'act as the devil's advocate' and to be 'a piece of grit in the state machinery'.

Even so, Shirley Hazzard recalled that whenever Philby's name was mentioned by Graham in conversation, it was 'never without bravado'. Graham himself told Catherine Walston that writing an introduction meant that 'I shall be in trouble with the Patriots', and that John Sutro for one 'behaved very queerly when Kim Philby's name cropped up. Apparently he gets worked up like an old Anglo-Indian colonel whenever he's mentioned.' Philby wrote again to congratulate Graham on a letter to *The Times* protesting against the sentences passed on the dissident writers Daniel and Sinyavski – Graham had said that he would no longer allow his books to be published in the Soviet Union if the authorities refused to pay his royalties to the writers' families – and added a hope that conditions would change 'not only because what you did is just and honourable, but because it might result for us in some unexpected gratification, some meal together, for instance, when we could talk about old times.' A fitful correspondence ensued, covering such diverse topics as the Russian war in Afghanistan (of which Philby disapproved), the Ayatollah Khomeini, and whether or not Graham and Malcolm Muggeridge had been seen riding bicycles in 1951: Graham denied the charge ('I hate to be confused with Muggeridge. Yes, we were friends even before the war, but I have learned too well that his underpants conceal a stiletto'), and Philby explained his confusion on the grounds that 'you were the two literary characters among the rest of us Section V philistines.' Graham later told the *Sunday Telegraph* that their correspondence was, for the most part, personal and nostalgic, but 'if there was anything political in it, I knew that Kim would know that I would pass it on to Maurice Oldfield.' The *New York Herald Tribune* suggested that Philby's letters contained 'disinformation', but in their author's modest opinion, 'they contained no information at all, dis- or otherwise.' Graham was not best pleased when Anthony Burgess suggested in an article that he had been 'in almost daily correspondence' with Philby. 'I received ten letters from him in the course of nearly 20 years,' he told Burgess, adding that 'you must be very naïf if you believe our letters were clandestine on either side' (all Graham's correspondence with Philby was passed on to MI6 through Rodney Dennys).

Graham found himself once again rising to Philby's defence shortly before the publication in 1979 of Andrew Boyle's *The Climate of Treason*, an account of the Cambridge spies which prompted the exposure of Anthony Blunt as the 'fourth man' later that year. Boyle told Graham that he had quoted him as saying of Philby, 'I might have guessed there was something fishy about his rise. If he'd blurted out the truth at the time, I suppose I'd have given him twenty-four hours to clear out. Then I'd have denounced him.' 'The "rise" refers, of course, to his intrigue to supplant Felix Cowgill', Boyle explained in his covering letter. 'I think he tried to inveigle you by offering you promotion. If this quote is true, please let me know.' Graham was having none of it. 'I don't at all like you having me say that "I might have guessed there was something fishy about his rise",' he replied. 'I saw nothing fishy about Kim Philby's rise – he was a very able man. What I think I have written somewhere is that I was glad to discover years later that his supplanting of Cowgill was not simply the desire for personal power. I would never use the phrase "blurted out the truth".' He went on to say that during all the years he had known Philby he 'never once saw him the worse for drink', and was unimpressed to learn that Boyle had spoken to Malcolm Muggeridge – 'Don't trust a word that Malcolm Muggeridge says to you without checking with me,' Graham told his biographer some years later. 'He is a complete liar. As some of his information will deal with the secret service it's as well to be accurate'. He concluded by saying that 'I would much rather you left me out of your book.'

A year earlier Graham had sent Philby a copy of his novel *The Human Factor*, in which an idealistic Soviet agent finally defects to Russia and ends his days alone in a gloomy Moscow flat. Graham had written before about the shady world of spies and double agents – famously in *The Third Man*, set in Vienna after the war, farcically in *Our Man in Havana*, most realistically, perhaps, in his posthumously published novella *No Man's Land* – and he had long wanted to write 'a novel free from the conventional violence which has not, in spite of James Bond, been a feature of the British Secret Service.' Maurice Castle – the 'Maurice' was borrowed from Maurice Oldfield, who had been appointed head of MI6 in 1973 – lives in Berkhamsted and commutes to London every day to a job at MI6. 'I was very uneasy about it and would have liked to put it in a drawer for publication after my death, but Frere proved unexpectedly and irrationally enthusiastic,' Graham told Catherine Walston. He sent a copy to Maurice Oldfield, who wrote a letter of thanks after reading the blurb. '"Maurice" – yes; "Castle" – no, but does mean something in that he was one of the cleverest fellows I introduced (we didn't keep him); "dull" – yes; "brilliant with files" – who knows – at least not formidable. And now I'll leave the dust jacket and begin reading,' Oldfield replied, adding that he was now retired, so 'I can meet at civilised times.' Like many other novelists, Graham resented any suggestions that his novels could be read as covert autobiography, and he insisted that Castle bore no resemblance to Philby, and that *The Human Factor* should not be read as a *roman-à-clef*. Be that as it may, Philby told him that he had made Castle's new life in Moscow bleaker than it should have been, while Graham admitted that he had based the furnishings of Castle's Moscow flat on details provided in *The Spy I Loved* by Philby's third wife, Eleanor, who had returned to America in 1965, unable to bear life in Moscow a moment longer. Before long he would have a chance to see for himself.

In his letter to *The Times* about Daniel and Sinyavski, Graham famously declared that 'If I had to choose between life in the Soviet Union and life in the United States, I would certainly choose the Soviet Union.' The historian Sir Dennis Brogan wrote in to say that if Graham went to live in Russia he would find it hard to worship as he liked given the scarcity of Roman Catholic churches, to which Graham replied that 'Christianity is surely more important than Catholicism,' and that Orthodox churches would fit the bill perfectly well. 'I am an admirer of the Soviet Union, and an admirer of the Communist system,' he told a meeting of PEN. 'But in any government there grows up an Establishment of stupid men.' 'If I live in a capitalist country, I feel Communist; if I am in a Communist country, I feel a capitalist,' he told the writer Gaia Servadio: he became increasingly interested in politics as he grew older, but just as, in religious matters, he came to describe himself as a 'Catholic agnostic' on the grounds that 'I've always believed that *doubt* was a more important thing for human beings. It's *human* to *doubt*,' he brought to politics the same scepticism, the same urge to react against the prevailing orthodoxy, and the same instinctive desire to support the weak against the strong. He had endorsed Charter 77 after the Soviet invasion of Czechoslovakia in 1968, and now, in old age, he backed those movements in Central America which sought to distance themselves from the United States, and was entertained to be included in the Panamanian delegation which attended the signing of the Panama Canal Treaty in Washington in 1977. In the same spirit, he attended meetings of the Writers' Union in Moscow, and used his fame to agitate on behalf of dissident writers. On one such visit he and Yvonne Cloetta paid a visit to Kim Philby and his Russian wife, Rufina, in their flat in Moscow.

'Rufa said, without any prompting from me, that the three days we spent on and off together were among the happiest in her life,' Philby told his old friend. 'As for myself, I find myself suffering from an acute attack of the *esprit de l'escalier*: so many things I wanted to ask, but didn't, so many things I wanted to say, but didn't. Well, you can't bridge a gap of thirty-four years in a few hours.' He was, he said, 'more than surprised that you had expressed some doubt about our willingness to meet you. So as to clear up any misunderstanding, please regard this as a standing invitation (or rather a peremptory insistence) that you should see us when you are next in our neighbourhood.' Rufa had dreaded meeting Graham: she had been led to believe that he was a 'man of sarcastic character', but in the event he turned out to be 'a very charming man who laughs a lot and whose eyes are filled with childish naïvety', and she 'liked him a lot'. The pleasure was far from one-sided. 'We loved our visit to you and the strong feeling of how our friendship has survived all these years untouched,' Graham replied, and two further visits followed. 'They were the most rewarding meetings in our long friendship,' Philby told Phillip Knightley of the *Sunday Times*. 'For the first time we were able to speak frankly with each other. We were able to discuss doubt, a matter of great importance to us – the nagging doubt we both feel, him as a Roman Catholic, and me as a Communist.'

In 1987 Phillip Knightley spent some twenty-five hours talking to Philby about his life. Philby was keen to repudiate rumours that he wanted to return to Britain; the KGB had wanted him to talk to Graham, but 'I told them that Greene is a friend and former colleague. I wanted to talk to someone who would be objective.' Philby died in Moscow in 1988,

the year in which Knightley's book about him was published, and Graham
wrote to Rufa about his 'good and loyal friend'. Some time later, Knightley
met a Moscow journalist called Genrikh Borovik who told him that,
shortly after Philby's death, he had, at Graham's suggestion, obtained
access to Philby's KGB file. 'Prepare yourself to have your views about
Philby and the KGB shattered. Thank God Philby himself never saw his
KGB file,' Borovik told him. Philby had remained loyal to the KGB, but
they, it seems, had long ago lost interest in him, and some in the KGB
had always suspected the Cambridge spies of being treble agents. In 1997
Markus Wolf, the East German spymaster, published his memoirs, in
which he claimed that Philby was disillusioned rather than unhappy in
Moscow. 'He would complain to me bitterly about the miserable economy
and the gap between the rulers and its people,' he wrote, and 'Philby
did not have much opportunity in Moscow for conversation with cultured
people.' According to Wolf, the KGB worried about the damage that
would be done to Soviet prestige should Philby ever find his way back
to Britain, and 'Philby told me that the British secret service in Moscow
found ways of making him several offers to return.' It occurred to
Knightley that Graham might have been involved as an intermediary,
acting on behalf of M16, and he put the possibility to Markus Wolf.
Knightley wrote of how Wolf's 'eyes behind his rimless glasses gleamed
with professional appreciation of the cunning of the British plot,' and
then said 'I never thought of Graham Greene, but it makes sense.' It is
a tantalising notion, and no doubt more will be revealed when the MI6
files are made public.

Graham was loyal to another old friend from MI6, John Cairncross,
who, like Philby, Maclean and Burgess, had been recruited while at
Cambridge by Arnold Deutsch, the Comintern's ace recruiter. Cairncross
denied ever having been a member of the Communist Party, but readily
admitted that, as a young man in the 1930s, he had been appalled by the
British Government's failure to stand up to Nazi Germany and had
advocated a united front with the Soviet Union; and that, while working
at Bletchley Park during the war, he had passed to the Soviet Union
Ultra decrypts about Luftwaffe formations which had materially affected
the outcome of the Battle of Kursk, a turning-point in the war on the
Eastern Front. Anthony Blunt had tipped off MI5 about Cairncross's
wartime activities, but – like Blunt – he had been granted immunity from
prosecution in 1964. Graham had remained in touch with 'Claymore',
who had gone to live in France and become an authority on, and translator of, Molière and Racine. In the autumn of 1990, Cairncross wrote

to Graham to ask him if he would provide him with a reference for a French residential permit, since 'the hounds of Granada TV are after me as the only survivor of what they so inaccurately call the Cambridge Group – although (unlike theirs) my only motive was to strengthen the Allied cause against the Nazis, and nothing else.'

Cairncross felt still more embattled when he learned that *The Times* was planning to serialise *KGB: The Inside Story* by Christopher Andrew and Oleg Gordievsky, which had named him as the 'fifth man'. Although Graham was, by now, in very poor health, he immediately rallied to his old friend's defence. He introduced Cairncross to Ronnie Challoner, a long-standing member of SIS, and a 'great friend apart from being Consul-General in Nice and obviously still attached however distantly with intelligence'. Challoner 'agreed that the security people had broken their promise to you' by leaking information to writers and journalists – Peter Wright's *Spycatcher* had included several references to Cairncross – but 'Claymore' worried that Challoner's advice to say nothing 'has a suspicious convergence with the command of the authorities to be quiet'. He felt he was being both 'let down' and 'set up', and that there was 'a definite campaign of misinformation – or tolerance of misinformation – by the boys up top', and he asked Graham how he should react. Graham urged him to lie low until his right of residence had been confirmed and, in due course, to state his case in a book. He introduced Cairncross to his niece, Amanda Saunders, who helped Cairncross to plan his memoirs, and remembered him as 'a very charming and sweet man'. Graham was amused by 'the angry exchanges between the various authors of books about the secret service who had no experience of the service themselves', as he told his old friend. 'I hope my advice is not a dangerous one but it's the best I can think of . . . I wonder when the hacks will begin to look for a sixth man!' Cairncross took Graham's advice: Ronnie Challoner helped his widow to complete his autobiography, *The Enigma Spy*, in which Cairncross remembered how 'though terminally ill and subject to constant blood transfusions, [Graham] remained untiring in his support for me', and how he had proved to be 'one of the kindliest, most unaffected and most human persons I have ever met'.

★

Graham's loyalty tended to be directed towards individuals rather than institutions, and near the end of his working life he found himself once again leaving a long-established publishing house in order to show his support for a particular person whom he considered, rightly or wrongly, to have been badly treated, and to whom he owed his principal allegiance. In the early 1960s he had left Heinemann after A. S. Frere's demotion; a quarter of a century later, he left The Bodley Head when Max Reinhardt decided to set up on his own. An already complicated situation was made more difficult by the fact that another member of the Greene family was involved: Hugh's oldest son, Graham, ran the holding company which now owned The Bodley Head, and found himself on the other side of the barricades from his eminent and subversive uncle.

The post-war years had been a golden age for the independent and independent-minded publisher. Some of the great names in the trade were long-established family firms, like Collins, Longmans and Murray; some, like Hamish Hamilton, Michael Joseph or Rupert Hart-Davis, had set up in business before or shortly after the war; and some, like Weidenfeld & Nicolson, André Deutsch and Thames & Hudson, had been created after the war by Jewish immigrants from Austria and Germany. Many still occupied elegant if ramshackle Georgian houses in Bloomsbury or Covent Garden, and all were run by benign despots on a very personal and often idiosyncratic basis. In the late fifties London publishers had worried about being taken over by their predatory New York equivalents. Ten years later the City, for some inexplicable reason, began to show an interest in publishing, and over the next thirty years most of the famous names in British publishing, including such long-established family firms as Murray and Collins, would be swallowed up by huge multinational conglomerates, and exchange their decaying Georgian houses for single floors in modern concrete blocks in Hammersmith, Pimlico or the Euston Road.

Unlike educational, legal, medical or even academic publishing, 'trade' or 'general' publishing has always been a tricky, marginal business in which the occasional bestseller and a backlist of steady-selling books about gardening or chess subsidise first novels, biographies, poetry and memoirs, and 'literary' publishing is the trickiest area of all. In 1969 two of the most distinguished literary publishers in London, Jonathan Cape and Chatto & Windus, decided to join forces from the waist downwards: each firm retained its identity and its offices, and each had its own editors, publicists and rights managers, but sales, distribution and administrative chores like the collection and payment of royalties were shared by the two firms, and run by a separate but jointly owned service company. The idea was to keep predators at bay, to be in a position to compete with larger firms, and to share some of the ever-rising over-heads that form so large a proportion of the published price of a book. Graham C. Greene, the managing director of Jonathan Cape, was co-chairman of the Group, and in 1973 he and Ian Parsons of Chatto were joined by Max Reinhardt, who was worried about the The Bodley Head being taken over, and was persuaded to take cover with Cape and Chatto.

Reinhardt had owned almost all the shares in The Bodley Head, and since his firm contributed 35 per cent of the turnover of the enlarged Group, he became its largest single shareholder. He later claimed that he had never felt happy about joining Chatto and Cape, but in the early years at least all was sweetness and light. Life began to turn sour in the 1980s, reflecting changes in the publishing world at large. Not only was the era of the independent gentleman publisher drawing to a close, but publishers were abandoning their long-held position as the ringmaster of the literary circus. Max Reinhardt, like his equivalents in Cape and Chatto, had grown up in a world in which the advances paid to authors represented a modest proportion of the royalties that a book would expect to earn in hardback, but literary agents were flexing their muscles, extracting advances that bore no relation to likely sales and threatening to move bestselling authors elsewhere if their demands were not met. The new book chains were demanding far higher discounts than their modest, down-at-heel precursors, and insisting that stock was provided on sale-or-return basis, with the result that publishers all too often reprinted books only to have copies from the first printing returned to the warehouse, so converting a modest profit into a thumping loss as well. The fragile ecology of trade publishing was being undermined, with disastrous effects on both cash flow and profit-and-loss accounts.

As all publishers were only too well aware, overheads and production costs were soaring, but the Group's particular problems were exacerbated by the cost of building a new warehouse and installing a computerised management system; and whereas, in happier times, a large proportion of the Group's books had been sub-licensed to Penguin, with author and publisher sharing the proceeds, the Group was now at a disadvantage in that unlike many of its larger rivals it did not have its own paperback imprint. Nor were matters helped by the loose structure of the Group: the managing directors of its component parts concentrated their ener-gies on the welfare of their particular firms, and were happy to leave the running of the Group and the service companies to Graham C. Greene, who was not only involved in managing Chatto, Bodley Head and Cape and its various subsidiaries but was, at various times, the President of the Publishers' Association, a director of Guinness Mahon, the merchant bank, and Greene King the brewers, and was on the board of the British Museum and the *New Statesman*'s holding company.

Publishing is a capital-intensive business at the best of times, with money – often borrowed from the bank at high rates of interest – tied up in advances to authors, work-in-progress and slow-selling stock, and steadily eroded by inflation; and, unlike their larger rivals, the Group did not have educational, academic or reference book lists to rely upon. Bestsellers were, by definition, few and far between. Working capital was in increasingly short supply, and funds were reduced still further in 1984, when the Group bought back Granada's 20 per cent share. Uneasy about one man owning so large a slice of the business, Tom Maschler of Cape and Graham C. Greene bought half Reinhardt's shares in the business. Reinhardt felt increasingly marginalised: he worried that the three firms were, in effect, competing for the same restricted market – not just in the bookshops but in terms of the funds available to pay the inflated advances needed to compete with their rivals – and he felt that the Group was being run in the interests of Cape, its largest and most profitable constituent part.

In 1985 the Group's losses amounted to £508,000, and the overdraft had to be increased to £2.8 million. After the National Westminster Bank refused to raise the overdraft limit to £3.8 million, Tom Maschler and Graham C. Greene raised £923,000, personally guaranteeing the money to the bank – a commitment which gave Maschler, who had no private means, more sleepless nights than he cared to remember. Fearful that his beloved Bodley Head would be dragged down, and that the Group as a whole was heading for bankruptcy, Max Reinhardt refused to take part in a rights issue the following year, or to invest any more money in the Group. Tom Maschler and Graham C. Greene increased their joint stake in the company to 76 per cent, while Max Reinhardt's was reduced to 11 per cent. Two years earlier, Reinhardt had suffered a heart attack, and thereafter spent more time working from home. After The Bodley Head moved from Bow Street to Bedford Square in 1986, sandwiched between Cape and Chatto, he became convinced that his old firm was about to be subsumed into Jonathan Cape – there were twenty-six redundancies, and copy-editing, production, publicity and rights were shared between the two firms – and he came into the office no longer. After seventeen years with the firm, Euan Cameron – then in his mid-forties, and with three small children – was made redundant: his modest compensation was suddenly doubled, and 'I learned later that this was done at the behest of Hugh, urged on by Graham and Elisabeth.'

Graham had allowed his niece, Louise Dennys, who was running her own publishing firm in Toronto, to edit and be the primary publisher of his second volume of memoirs, *Ways of Escape* – 'I do think you are a wonderful publisher – apart from Frere much the best that I have known,' he once told her – but The Bodley Head had, as usual, published it in Britain and the rest of the Commonwealth. Graham was extremely fond of Max Reinhardt, albeit with some professional reservations: he once said that authors like to keep 'good company' on a publisher's list, and although The Bodley Head was greatly admired as a children's publisher, its adult list was too dependent on Graham himself and, to a lesser extent, William Trevor. But he thought his old friend was being hard done by, and rallied to his defence. 'If I felt that under the new organisation I would not have the same attention under your personal care that I have had in the past, I would have to consider transferring to another publisher my new book when ready, and any of my old books which The Bodley Head have so far published,' he told Reinhardt in the summer of 1986. 'I rely on you to keep an eye on my personal interests as you have done in the past, whatever your final status in the company is to be.' 'Graham, with whom I had dinner last night, has been aware of the situation for some time and told me that he would not entrust his new novel, which is nearly ready, to The Bodley Head if he felt that its financial problems had not been solved,' Reinhardt informed Graham C. Greene early the following year, and Graham Senior was fully behind him. 'I have been thinking about our conversation in London and urge you again to try and buy back The Bodley Head and see that it is run as it used to be,' he told his publisher. 'If my suggestion is not practicable then I propose to offer to your private company my next novel, which should be ready within a few months. If you accept to publish it, I would also like a promise from you that you will do your utmost to secure the transfer of all my other books published by The Bodley Head.' Reinhardt had retained the Reinhardt Books imprint for his own use and, despite his poor health, the idea of making a fresh start under his own name was extremely attractive – still more so since Peter Mayer, the flamboyant American boss of Penguin, Graham's long-standing paperback publisher, had assured his author that he was 'completely available to you and The Bodley Head, or even to you and Max privately, to achieve either the current purpose or any that may develop.' Reinhardt sent a copy of Graham's letter to Graham C. Greene, who told him that 'to pursue the course you are proposing would seem to me an act of very considerable aggression.'

Things were turning nasty, and they became nastier still after Graham wrote a letter to *The Times*, complaining about the tendency of large firms to swallow up their smaller rivals, threatening to take his books away from the Group, and accusing his nephew of running the Group into the ground. Graham C. Greene had earlier been quoted in *The Times* diary to the effect that rumours of changes within the Group – including a justified claim that the feminist publisher Virago, which had joined the Group in 1984, was planning to buy itself out – were 'pure fantasy'. This, his uncle suggested, seemed to suggest that 'he himself is living in a fantasy world. Publishers depend on authors, and I am sure that I am not the only author who will consider leaving the Group should there be none of the necessary changes in the administration.' Graham's letter had a profound effect: as Michael Davie wrote in the *Observer*, 'one brief letter destabilised the Group', intensifying rumours in the incestuous, gossip-ridden world of publishing – so much so that his nephew, who wished that his uncle had done his homework before rushing into print, subsequently told Michael Davie that 'Uncle Graham should be held responsible' for the impending sale of the Group to an American publisher. Two days later, Max Reinhardt resigned as joint Chairman of the Group. He favoured selling the Group, or The Bodley Head alone, to Penguin, but in an interview with the *Independent* he said that he would like to buy back his old firm so that it was no longer run by a committee, and confirmed that Virago was negotiating to buy itself out of the Group.

In the meantime Tom Maschler had been rung by Bob Gottlieb, the former editorial supremo at Alfred Knopf, who told him that Si Newhouse was interested in buying the Group. One of the richest men in America, Newhouse owned the Random House publishing group in New York, of which Knopf formed a part, as well as a string of magazines, including the *New Yorker*, now edited by Gottlieb. Maschler and Graham C. Greene entered into negotiations with Newhouse and Robert Bernstein of Random House, and although Greene had great reservations, they eventually sold the Group in its entirety to Random House, which also paid off debts of £3 million. 'I knew, and Graham knew, that we had been offered more than double the value of the company,' Tom Maschler recalled in his memoirs. 'We knew that Max Reinhardt would be furious as this was a deal he had not engineered. However we were not obliged to consult him.' Reinhardt, who received an 11 per cent share of the £17 million paid for the Group, later claimed that the deal was done 'without my knowledge or consent': according to Maschler, 'We were scared that he would muck things up in any negotiations. We had just been sold down the river with the Graham Greene letter.' 'The recent flurry of publicity has been very distressing and I feel it would be a good idea if we had a talk,' Graham C. Greene wrote to his uncle shortly after the sale had been announced, but by now it was too late. In a letter to the *Independent* reminiscent of those he had written a quarter of a century earlier about Heinemann's attempts to persuade him to stay, Graham claimed that 'if the new American owners allow the administration of the group to remain in the same hands as in the past, I think that many authors besides myself will prefer to take their books elsewhere. An author is not a chattel. My loyalties are to a publisher, Max Reinhardt, and not to a group.' 'Before writing to you, Graham Greene clearly needed briefing by his publisher, Max Reinhardt,' 'young' Graham replied the following day in a letter to the *Independent*.

As it turned out, Random House soon appointed new managers to run their acquisition, but Graham had already decided that his future books should be published by Reinhardt Books. Reinhardt resigned as Chairman of The Bodley Head in October 1987, and Penguin agreed to handle the sales and distribution of the list. Graham's new novel, *The Captain and the Enemy*, was published the following year, but it was not a particularly distinguished piece of work. Reinhardt Books went on to publish *Yours Etc*, a collection of Graham's letters to the Press, a collection of essays edited by Judith Adamson, and *A World of My Own*, a posthumously published anthology of his own dreams, which Graham had thought of calling *The Night Life of a Sexagenarian*: it included a dream in which Graham found himself sitting next to the Queen, and found himself trying not to laugh when Prince Philip appeared in a scout-master's uniform, prompting the Queen to confide to Graham that 'I can't bear the way he smiles.' Graham's backlist remained with The Bodley Head, and Reinhardt Books itself was a short-lived affair which petered out after Reinhardt's death in 2002. After it was all over, Graham visited his nephew, who was no longer involved with Random House despite the promise of a ten-year contract, and expressed a degree of remorse. It had been an unhappy story, in which Graham had displayed three of his enduring qualities: loyalty to old friends, support for the underdog, and a strong sense of mischief.

30

Closing Time

Graham was only in his late fifties when he told Hugh that he had been pondering the possibility of being buried in Harston churchyard. He had talked to Raymond on the subject, and Raymond too had expressed interest in reserving a plot for himself and Eleanor: how did Hugh feel about it? Graham felt he should give the vicar 'a vague idea of the number of corpses or rather corpse space required', so any thoughts on the subject would be gratefully received. Molly, their oldest sibling, had died in 1963, and Graham had heard the news in Mexico, on his way to Havana. 'It's a good thing – finally it must have come very quickly and without pain,' he told Yvonne, adding that 'Now there are only five of us.'

None of the brothers was buried in Harston, but as they grew older the School House Greenes became increasingly intrigued by their family history. Raymond wrote his history of the Greene family, which was circulated in typescript to interested members; Graham's lifelong fascination with Robert Louis Stevenson showed no signs of abating, and Hugh spent his weekends in the village of Cockfield, twenty minutes drive from the family brewery in Bury St Edmunds. Nor were the Hall Greenes immune from a fascination with the past. Ben still brooded on his internment, and a new book about the Labour Party in the 1930s revived his sense of persecution; Felix, racked by a sense of inadequacy and failure, laid the blame on his hapless parents, and his mother in particular, much to Barbara's indignation.

Graham had always regarded Robert Louis Stevenson as a kindred spirit, and in 1949 he had been commissioned by Heinemann to write a biography of his distant cousin. He set about it with great aplomb: Janet Adam Smith, later the literary editor of the *Listener* and a writer of biographies, helped him collect Stevenson's letters; Roger Lancelyn Green sent him transcripts of material he had collected while attempting his own aborted life of Stevenson; he spent long hours in the National Library of Scotland, and got in touch with Stevenson's stepdaughter,

Isobel Osborne, by then in her eighties and living in California. He abandoned the idea when he discovered that J. C. Furnas was working on a rival biography, *Voyage to Windward*, published two years later by Faber, but not before learning that changes and corrections made by Stevenson to his novel *The Wrong Box* had never been incorporated into the published version. Scribner's, Stevenson's New York publishers, had sent the proofs to Hawaii, but they had not been returned on time, and had been languishing in a vault at Yale University ever since. Eager to take up his kinsman's cause, Graham raised the matter in a letter to the *Times Literary Supplement*, and, in later years, hoped to reissue the corrected version at The Bodley Head. (It was eventually published by Francis Meynell's Nonesuch Press, which was owned by Max Reinhardt.)

Nor was that the end of the Greene brothers' interest in Stevenson. Graham asked his bookselling friend David Low to keep an eye out for books by or about the author and his family, who were well-known for having built many of Britain's most famous lighthouses, and supported a campaign to have him commemorated in the Lothian Road in Edinburgh rather than in Princes Street. Raymond wrote to say that 'looking through my untidy files' had made him realise what a good book could be written about the Balfours and the Stevensons, 'if only I had the time and the ability, and I have neither'; and Hugh found himself devoting his spare time in Suffolk to chasing up Stevenson connections. Earls Hall was in the village of Cockfield, and Nicholas Rankin, who was writing a book about Stevenson, had discovered that in 1873 Stevenson had come south to visit his cousin Maude Wilson, who had married the Reverend Churchill Babington and was living in Cockfield Rectory. Stevenson's mother, Maggie Balfour, and Maude's mother, Marion Balfour, were sisters; Maude's sister, Jane, had married the melancholic vicar, the Reverend Carleton Greene – Stevenson had attended their wedding in Bury St Edmunds – and their daughter, another Marion, had married Charles Greene, the future headmaster of Berkhamsted. Hot in pursuit of the Stevensons and their kin, Rankin arranged to visit Hugh at Earls Hall. Peering through a window, 'I could see a tall bespectacled man with a sunburned bald head reading *The Times*. He was wearing a cardigan, grey flannels and old Dunlop tennis shoes, and when he opened the front door I could see just how big Sir Hugh Carleton Greene was.' They drove over to Cockfield rectory, where the young Robert Louis Stevenson had first met Sir Sidney Colvin, the Slade Professor of Fine Art at Cambridge, who had introduced him to London literary life; and over a pint in The Three Horseshoes in Cockfield Hugh told Rankin how Graham always thought of Stevenson as 'one of the family'.

This was more than could be said for Herbert, at least as far as Hugh and Graham were concerned. Despite Graham's threat to withdraw his subsidy, Herbert had continued to fire off the occasional missile in the direction of Broadcasting House. A telegram to Hugh, sent during Hugh's early days as Director-General, struck a Blimpish note. 'As your brother I think it is a damned disgrace that your news uses the word the Englishmen fled repeat fled from Assam,' it read. Hugh forwarded it to Graham after scribbling across the top 'Gad, Sir, there's still one right-minded Englishman,' to which Graham added 'Perhaps you should have used the word crept.' Nor was Herbert best pleased when he learned that Hugh's son Graham had married Judy Gordon Walker, the daughter of a Labour Cabinet Minister. He told the returning officer in Smethwick, Gordon Walker's constituency, that he planned to stand against young Graham's father-in-law in the 1959 general election, but nothing came of it. Hugh's least favourite cousin, on the other hand, felt more kindly disposed to the 'black sheep' of the family. 'I have always had a warm spot in my heart for him just because all the other members of the family have done him down and disowned him,' Felix told his mother after visiting Herbert in Plumpton. 'I found him astonishingly well, very genial, and a little mad. Very like Ben – even to look at.' As a child who knew nothing of his uncle's misdemeanours, Nick Dennys was taken by his parents to meet Herbert. 'I liked Herbert a lot,' he recalls. 'He was a huge, warm and friendly figure', less alarming and less preoccupied than his brothers, while Audrey seemed 'beautiful and calm'.

But all was not well with Herbert. He and Audrey were still living at Oak Cottage, Plumpton, the walls of which were decorated with framed official photographs of famous men, including Churchill and de Gaulle, which Herbert – an autograph-hound as a boy – had solicited from their subjects, and proudly displayed. A year after Felix's visit, Raymond reported that his brother was 'now almost incapacitated by Parkinsonism', and that Audrey, now in her mid-seventies, was 'unable to cope with his immense weight'. Raymond had provided his elder brother with the psychological support he needed, just as Graham continued to help on the monetary side. They would have to give up their cottage, and 'the question of what to do with Herbert seems almost insoluble', since their income of £800 a year was not enough to pay for a nursing home. 'One of the few good traits in his character is his devotion to Audrey, and he will certainly refuse to be separated from her,' Raymond told Hugh. 'One of the troubles, of course, is that he has done his best to alienate both you and Graham, and I shall tell him that I do not think he can expect very much help from either of you under the circumstances.' Herbert and Audrey struggled on somehow, and he died in hospital in October 1968. 'I am sure he had wished for death for some time,' their doctor informed Raymond, adding that he could not 'remember a case of Parkinsonism deteriorating to quite such an appalling state before.' 'It was, of course, a release for him and Audrey from that ghastly Parkinson's disease, but one feels sad for him all the same', Graham told his daughter Caroline (as Lucy preferred to be known). 'He didn't have much luck in his life – except Audrey.' 'The whole family owes an enormous debt of gratitude to Audrey for her unselfish devotion to Herbert,' Raymond told Hugh. 'She has relieved us all of a terrible responsibility.' She had been left with an income of £500 a year and, at the suggestion of Raymond and Graham, it was agreed that she should continue to receive the income from a trust set up for Herbert under the terms of their father's will.

Like Herbert, Ben had proved an embarrassment to some members of the family, but whereas few had a good word to say about his feck-less cousin, Ben was loved by all who knew him, and invariably described as the kindest of men, and a 'gentle giant'. After retiring from business he inherited a house in Whittlesford in Cambridgeshire, not far from Harston, left to him in the will of Aunt Helen's long-time companion, Marie Hall. Ben and Leslie spent much of their time in Aldeburgh, where they had a large ground-floor flat in the same house as his mother, Eva. Ben loved solitude, and spent days on end alone at Whittlesford, surrounded by his books and writing an ambitious but uncompleted study of the English Constitution, in which he inveighed about the perni-cious influence of party and the ways in which the pure democratic waters derived from Magna Carta had been polluted over the past 150 years; and another uncompleted work, entitled 'The Great Betrayal', which interlaced his ideas about the corruption of politics with self-justi-fying accounts of his pre-war activities and his internment in Brixton. He worried that were his works ever published, his disillusionment with current politics and the workings of Westminster might strike a chord with far-right groups, including the National Front and former supporters of Oswald Mosley. 'I cannot risk the slightest association with them,' he told Felix, because 'they are interested in promoting schools of thought with which I have no sympathy whatsoever.' Since, as he readily admitted, he was unable to write in a popular and accessible manner, there was little chance of his finding a publisher for either book, but his past was about to resurface, albeit in an unintended form.

In 1977 a young historian, Ben Pimlott, published *Labour and the Left*

in the 1930s: it was his first book, and Ben first became aware of it through
a favourable review by John Grigg in the *Sunday Telegraph*. Pimlott felt,
very strongly, that Ben had never been given due credit by Labour politicians or Labour historians for democratising the Party in the 1930s by
giving individual members and constituency parties a greater say in
formulating policy: he had no idea that Ben was still alive, and greatly
regretted not having interviewed him during his researches. Ben was a
hero of *Labour and the Left* and yet, by a sad irony, he was so affronted
by a reference to his 'pro-Nazi sympathies' that all else was forgotten as
he sought, once again, to clear his name. After reading in John Grigg's
review that he 'had been conveniently dropped from Labour's Roll of
Honour because he was a Nazi sympathizer, later sent to Brixton under
Regulation 18B', Ben swung into action. Indignant letters were fired off
to the Cambridge University Press and the *Sunday Telegraph* by Greene
& Greene, a firm of solicitors in Bury St Edmunds which had been
founded by William Greene's brother John, the father of Carleton Greene;
Anthony Scrivener was engaged as counsel and, since Ben was short of
funds, his son Paul agreed to pay the preliminary costs. By another strange
irony, Cambridge University Press was represented by Oswald Hickson
& Collier, the firm which had defended Ben so ably all those years before,
but Mr Sheerin of Greene & Greene was unawed by the opposition. He
told Pimlott's publishers that, following publication of the *Sunday Telegraph* review, his client had 'received abusive messages which have
distressed him considerably'. He demanded a retraction and an apology,
plus damages and costs, and threatened them with a writ for libel should
these not be forthcoming. Ben, for his part, said that although his assets
amounted to only £1000 in cash, plus the value of his house in Whittlesford, he was quite ready to sell this and move full-time into the flat
in Aldeburgh rather than withdraw.

Privately, however, both solicitors and counsel advised Ben not to take
things any further. Mr Sheerin and Anthony Scrivener urged him not to
go to court or 'go too far along the line in litigation': should Ben take
Cambridge University Press to court, he would have to disclose his documentary evidence, and, Mr Sheerin warned him, 'once these documents
have been seen by them . . . their hand would be very considerably
strengthened in any pleading of justification.' Such evidence as Ben
possessed, and planned to cite in his defence – press cuttings, material
produced by the British People's Party and his pre-war information
service, the proceedings of the Appeals Committees, reports of the court
cases that had followed his release from Brixton – would have to be

shown to solicitors and counsel acting for the defence, and, in the opinion of both Greene & Greene and Anthony Scrivener, they would have an adverse rather than a positive effect, lending support to claims that what Pimlott had written had been 'justified' (true, in other words). Mr Sheerin told Paul Greene that he could not advise Ben to take the case to trial, since 'if we issue a writ your father will become caught up in proceedings which sometimes become difficult to stop,' but that did not prevent him from making a good deal on Ben's behalf at a meeting with Cambridge University Press. They could not have been more co-operative, which suggests that although Ben's lawyers worried that his case would not stand up in court, the defendants thought he had right on his side. They agreed to change the wording he objected to in existing stock, either by printing an erratum strip or dismantling the books and reprinting the section in which it occurred, to freeze all stock until a revised wording had been agreed, to ask major bookselling accounts to return any unsold stock, to indemnify Ben Greene's costs, and to pay compensatory damages of £250. It was also agreed that Ben Pimlott would write to the editor of the *Times Literary Supplement* and to the literary editors of all the main papers. Ben was, Pimlott wrote, 'a huge, open-hearted man of restless energy, high principle and dogged determination, with a tendency to hold unfashionable opinions and to refuse to keep quiet about them which did not endear him to colleagues' – but by then it was too late.

Ben died in March 1978. Kind and concerned as ever, Felix had hurried to Suffolk when he learned that his brother was dying. It was agreed that Felix would drive Eva to the service at the Quaker burial ground, and that Elena would go on ahead with the other mourners. In an absent-minded moment, Elena went off with the car keys, and since there was no taxi service in Aldeburgh, Felix and Eva – then in her mid-nineties – had to hitch a lift with a corset salesman. Despite this inauspicious start, Eva was so impressed by the Quaker service that she asked to be buried alongside Ben in the same burial ground. 'I do miss him more and more,' she told Felix two months after his death. 'What wonderful friendship he gave me. We shared so much, interesting letters, articles in the papers, ideas, plans and talks, as well as talks about history, religion, politics etc . . . There was so much to talk about and discuss, until Ben would laugh and say, "I must go down, or poor Leslie will feel neglected."'

Tooter, like Ben, had retired from business: he enjoyed a modest success as a part-time painter, and ran an antique shop in Castle Hedingham in Essex with his third wife, Inka. Felix was as restless as

ever. He decided to leave Palo Alto, and in the late sixties he and Elena
spent a year in Paris, where he had been lent a flat by the playwright
Arthur Miller. Miller was annoyed when Felix then lent the flat to Alvarez
del Vayo, whom he had got to know during the Spanish Civil War,
when del Vayo was the Foreign Minister in the Republican government,
and much involved with wining and dining visiting journalists. Felix and
Elena lived in Henley for a time, before buying a large and comfortable
flat off the Marylebone Road, but for the rest of his life he was based
in Mexico, where Elena's family originated, and where he built a house
in 1976. Barbara still sounded faintly disapproving. 'It is a pity that he
gave up the BBC all those years ago,' she told Eva. 'That was the tide
in his affairs that would have swept him on to a fortune. But he is the
kind that may get a second wind and do something great still. I hope
so, for he has it in him, though I do not think that buying a house in
Mexico and "writing" there is just the thing. But one never knows. He
is so practical and clever that the future is safe in his own hands.'

Felix was, in fact, as busy as ever, though film was now the medium
in which he excelled, with the willing co-operation of both wife and
daughter. 'Elena and Anne have been magnificent. I don't know of any
other two women who would have worked so hard, often in the broiling
sun, often in the thick dust,' he reported from Cuba. 'Elena does the
sound recording, and looks after the tapes and the microphones. Anne
does the clapperboard, and the records of the scenes; she also connects
all the wiring, the batteries, the cameras, the recording apparatus. I do
the camera work.' But practicality and efficiency were, as ever, combined
with brooding and self-doubt. In 'Thoughts on Becoming Seventy' he
agonised over his failings as a husband – he had, he confessed, caused
Elena 'unbelievable suffering', and 'of course the sexual relationship has
never been full-blooded' – and expatiated, in familiar vein, about the
need to 'simplify! simplify! simplify!' and to 'order my life so that *meaning*
(discovery of it) is more important than *doing*, inner rather than outer
experiencing'. Before long he would be given an excuse for further
introspection and breast-beating, much to Barbara's annoyance.

Barbara was not always popular with the Hall Greenes, who thought
her snobbish, stuck-up and, as befitted the wife of a former ambassador
to the Vatican, dauntingly formal and keen on protocol: her two children met many of their Greene relations for the first time at Graham's
memorial service, nine months before Barbara's death in September 1991.
Barbara's alleged hauteur was misleading. She may have been bored by
many aspects of diplomatic life, but had learned to put up a good front,

and after Rudi's retirement she was often restless and lonely. Rudi suffered from depression, and spent his days at Berchtesgaden gardening, shooting game birds, communing with nature and worrying about their finances. Barbara tried to write, but although an American firm published *The Chance of a Lifetime: An Anthology for the Ageless*, compiled with Eva with a foreword by Gerald Heard, and Graham was always happy to put in a good word with Max Reinhardt, nothing satisfactory emerged. She did work for the Sue Ryder and Leonard Cheshire homes, and became involved in the SOS Children's Homes, set up after the war by Hermann Gmeiner to look after homeless and displaced children. She disliked the opulence and materialism associated with the post-war German economic revival ('I'm afraid my Quaker upbringing does not allow me to accept that as the object of the greatest importance,' she once wrote). Although she lived in Germany, and had a German family, Barbara remained something of an outsider, and showed little interest in her mother's German relations. But she became increasingly close to Eva, and still more so after Ben's death. 'I know only too well that nothing (except my love) can make up to you all you have done for us,' she told her mother. 'The older I get, the more I realise it. It is *you* who has given us an appreciation for all things lovely, it is *you* who has taught us to keep our eyes and hearts open to all things "of good report", and it is *you* who has taught us that the joys of friendship are one of the greatest joys the world can give.' Eva had given them a strong sense of right and wrong, and had 'succeeded in making us a tightly-knit family who hold together'.

A year later, in 1969, Rudi had a stroke while on a shooting holiday. The funeral was an extremely grand affair. The Abbot of a Benedictine monastery in Salzburg conducted the service; a military guard of honour reflected Rudi's service in the First World War; members of the Order of Malta stood alongside the coffin, which was draped with their flag; there were long speeches, after which the coffin was lowered into the ground to the rolling of drums. The Last Post was played, and afterwards there was a huge reception. 'I think they found it very British that I did not shed a tear,' Barbara told her mother. In due course she sold the house in Berchtesgaden, and from now on she spent part of each year in a house she had bought on the island of Gozo. While in Italy she had resumed her old friendship with Graham – 'It was good to be with people to whom I could say "we, we, we",' he recalled after dining in Rome with Barbara and Rudi – and an epistolary friendship flourished. 'You would like him very much now,' she assured her mother, who may have had lingering reservations. 'He has mellowed so much, and is one of the very few people who has learned to get old very well.'

Barbara's literary ambitions may have been frustrated, but her first and finest book was about to enjoy a new lease of life. A small publisher decided to reissue *Land Benighted* in hardback, albeit under the more anodyne title of *Too Late to Turn Back*. 'Your book is really much better than you think it,' Graham told her, though he wished, as a former publisher, that she'd shown him the contract before signing it: she had gone to Raymond for advice, but 'I don't think Raymond is much of a judge of these things.' 'I really rather left it all to Raymond as he seems to know what's what', Barbara explained, but Graham was unimpressed. Raymond's suggested title, 'A Walk with Graham', was vetoed, and Graham was pleased to learn that Paul Theroux, a keen admirer of Barbara's book, had sided with her against Raymond on the subject of her foreword, since 'Raymond is a very good endocrinologist but I don't know that I would approve of him as a literary critic.' 'Please don't have any misgivings at all about the reissue of your wonderful book – it will get superb reviews,' Graham reassured her, as publication loomed.

'I was glad to see a good review by Theroux saying that your book was nearly as good as mine. Perhaps he should have said a better book than mine,' Graham wrote shortly after the book had been reissued. All this was well and good, but both Hugh and Graham continued to wax indignant about the contract Barbara had signed with her 'little gangster', not least because it didn't include a reversion clause enabling her to claim back the rights when it went out of print. 'Poor Raymond', Hugh sighed. 'Graham and I are both unable to understand how he allowed you to sign that contract.' According to Hugh, Paul Theroux planned to ask his agent, Gillon Aitken, to write to the publisher 'threatening them with all sorts of horrors because of the crooked contract.' Quite what happened to the contract, or the publisher, remains unclear, but Theroux went on to provide an enthusiastic foreword to the Penguin edition of Barbara's book, which was published in their Travel Classics series. Barbara also found herself the subject of a play by Brian Pearce, *The Widow of Gozo*, which drew on her wartime experiences.

Raymond may have given Barbara dud advice about her contract, but, Graham told him, 'You are the real heart of the Greene family and we have always depended on you more than you know.' He remained an impressive figure – tall, elegant and good-looking, as often as not in a three-piece suit, with a watch-chain across the waistcoat. His daughter Annabel recalled how, not long before his death, they walked down Bond

Street together, and 'I was very aware that the eyes of everybody we passed were drawn to him', while his nephew, Nick Dennys, remembers going into a pub with Raymond and overhearing a woman say 'What a handsome man! I have never seen such a handsome man!' His mountaineering days were over, but he still enjoyed strenuous cross-country walks. Alan Hill, a colleague from Heinemann, once joined him in the Lake District. Raymond was then in his mid-seventies: there was ice on the high ground, but Raymond was only wearing a string vest under his anorak, and was often up to his knees in freezing mud. By the time they got back to their cottage, he was blue with cold, but next morning he was as bright as ever, and warning his companion about the perils of trench foot. But his physical fitness was misleading. In October 1972 Graham reported that Eleanor was 'very worried': Raymond was 'in bad shape' after falling down stairs, but he still insisted on seeing his patients, 'who are very demanding.' Three years later he was suffering from cancer of the throat. Graham told Catherine Walston that he had 'diagnosed it himself very early and they put in gold spots and made them radioactive, and they said he was cured but he suffered terribly afterwards.' The following year Hugh learned that the Royal College of Physicians had wanted to put Raymond up for a knighthood, but he had been turned down as he was no longer connected with the National Health Service. Graham was understandably incensed. 'How very stupid about Raymond,' he wrote. 'One feels inclined to tell the Department of Health that they ought to consult Mrs [Barbara] Castle, whose life he practically saved – she wouldn't be troubling us now if it hadn't been for Raymond.'

Graham continued to take a gloomy view of matters. 'I'm afraid Raymond is on the way out,' he told Hugh in May 1981, eighteen months before Raymond's death, 'but I had a very cheerful dinner alone with him – the first in years – and all his anxiety was for Eleanor.' Not long before he died Raymond had lunch with Roland Gant, a novelist, Heinemann editor, SOE veteran and fellow-mountaineer. 'He was as alert and amusing as ever,' Gant recalled, 'but, he said, "My legs won't go any more and every walker knows how frustrating that can be."' Raymond rang his son Oliver, and asked him to join him for lunch in The Prince Regent, a pub near Harley Street. He told Oliver that his heart was no longer working properly, that he was unlikely to last more than a year at most, that he would not survive a bypass operation, and that he would not want to be brought round in the event of a heart attack. In November 1982 he suffered a heart attack, and was taken to the Middlesex Hospital. Oliver visited him there, and found him sitting up in bed. 'That was a narrow escape,' his father said, but shortly afterwards he lapsed into a coma, and died of kidney failure. Hugh's son, James, was among the many Greenes who attended Raymond's funeral, and when Graham walked into the church he 'was struck and moved to tears by his resemblance to my dead grandmother, his mother', and noted how Graham 'looked intensely grave and preoccupied, as if deeply experiencing his brother's death. His manner touched me in a way my father's didn't.' Graham and Hugh sat next to each other during the service, and afterwards (as James recalled in an unpublished poem) they went off together to the nearest pub 'to toast an endocrinologist' with 'the liquids of consoling, carnal resurrection'.

'I've got a lot to learn about life as an ordinary citizen,' Hugh told Tatjana after trading in the Director-General's chauffeur-driven car for travelling on the Tube, but his prospects were far from ordinary. David Astor invited him to join the *Observer*'s Board of Trustees; Roy Thomson nearly offered him the editorship of *The Times*, but changed his mind at the last minute; the Royal Court Theatre announced that he was to be its next chairman, but he decided not to go ahead; he was offered, but declined, the editorship of *Punch*; the *Sunday Telegraph* asked him to write occasional reports from overseas as a special correspondent ('It would be rather fun to see whether I can return with success to my beginning,' he told Graham, to whom he went for advice about terms). On the day he resigned as D-G, he had lunch with Max Reinhardt, who asked him to join the board of The Bodley Head, and become its Chairman ('Max, in case you change your mind before lunch is over, I will say yes now,' Hugh replied). Hugh was surprisingly nervous about attending his first board meeting – Max Reinhardt told him afterwards that it was the first time that books rather than money had been discussed at such a meeting – and other members of the firm thought him a remote, rather chilly figure. Reinhardt, on the other hand, found him very easy to deal with, recalling how they 'used to have lunch together before the meetings so that I could explain our problems and prime him to ask questions that would come better from him than from me.' Hugh published the memoirs of several BBC colleagues at The Bodley Head and edited his anthologies of Victorian and Edwardian crime stories: *The Rivals of Sherlock Holmes* was followed by *More Rivals of Sherlock Holmes*, *The Crooked Counties* and, at Graham's suggestion, *American Rivals of Sherlock Holmes*. On his deathbed he told his son Graham how glad he was that he – Graham – had published Jeffrey Archer's first novel. Graham later discovered that Hugh had been overruled by his colleagues when he suggested that The

Bodley Head should publish *Not a Penny More, Not a Penny Less*, on the grounds that it would make its publisher a great deal of money: it had eventually been taken on by Jonathan Cape.

Hugh also busied himself suggesting titles for the Bow Street Library, a hardback series given over to resurrecting neglected Edwardian classics. It provided Hugh and Graham with a golden opportunity to re-read and promote the adventure stories they had loved and read together as boys, and Graham's letters to Hugh are crammed with suggestions. Graham once said that if he hadn't been a writer he would like to have been a second-hand bookseller, and his trips to England were given over to scouring second-hand bookshops with Hugh when not eating lunch together in Rule's. Both men hugely enjoyed these hunting expeditions. Hugh told Tatjana after one such trip that 'the old relationship' between them had been 're-established'; he was not 'someone of many friendships', and 'the friendship of Graham has meant a great deal to me and has been somewhat interrupted.' They planned elaborate itineraries, often including a visit to Scarborough to see Charles Laughton's brother Tom, a fellow-bibliophile with an extensive cellar (Hugh in particular had a discriminating and well-informed knowledge of wine). The Bow Street Library's first offerings included novels by Stanley Weyman, Anthony Hope, A. E. W Mason and W. W. Jacobs, dimly remembered by them both as a denizen of Berkhamsted, and plans were made to reissue all the novels of the Anglo-Irish novelist George Birmingham. Two of Hugh's interests, Germany and Edwardian writers, were curiously combined when a play he had written in Germany after the war, based on Roy Horniman's novel *Bellamy the Magnificent* and translated into German by Tatjana, was performed at a theatre in Lübeck in 1977; and his passion for second-hand books, for Nelson sevenpennies and long-forgotten reprint series, took tangible form when, in 1983, he became a director of his nephew Nick Dennys's Gloucester Road Bookshop, where he could sometimes be seen with a leather pouch strapped round his waist in which to carry change.

Thirteen years earlier, Hugh announced that he had 'a new cause' to support. After meeting the Greek journalist Helen Vlachos in London, he joined the campaign to overthrow the repressive right-wing regime of the Colonels in Greece, and became an energetic and effective Chairman of the European Atlantic Action Committee for Greece, other members of which included Denis Healey and Senator Edward Kennedy. He interviewed Colonel Papadopoulos at length in the *Sunday Telegraph*, describing the Greek Prime Minister as a 'small man with receding black hair, a muddy complexion and a military moustache' and 'expressionless eyes which do not change when he smiles'. Hugh was not optimistic about the imminent restoration of democracy in Greece, but he had the satisfaction of learning that Papadopoulos was infuriated by the piece, which was headed 'The Greek Dictator Drops his Mask'. In 1971 he flew to Washington to drum up support, meeting Arthur Schlesinger, Edward Kennedy and Hubert Humphrey, and giving evidence before a House of Representatives Foreign Affairs Committee hearing on Greece. Three years later, after the Colonels had been ousted, he was given a standing ovation in the Greek Parliament, during the course of which, he told Graham, 'Someone called me the only unifying factor in Greek politics!' The new Prime Minister, Constantine Karamanlis, asked him to draw up a plan for the modernisation and democratisation of Greek broadcasting, but although his suggestions were much admired, they were never implemented. But Greece continued to play a part in his life: Paris Tacopoulos, whom he met while campaigning against the Colonels, became his closest friend, and was his best man when, in December 1984, he married for the fourth and final time. Hugh's activities in Greece, combined with a congenital interest in spies and spying, may or may not have put him in touch with MI6: he seldom spoke of such matters, but his last wife, Sarah, knew that he had been meeting secret service connections whenever, after a trip abroad, he came back from a lunch in a Spanish restaurant off Regent Street to which she had not been invited.

But for all his activities, Hugh at the time seemed a lonely figure, not least because Tatjana was still pursuing her career out of a sense of duty to her colleagues. Although he joined her at her home in Switzerland, and they travelled together, she spent more time in Germany than in England. 'To Cockfield alone' is a recurrent motif in his telegraphic diaries, which are otherwise given over to the weather, and the state of the garden and the greenhouse in Suffolk: the only long entries are devoted to detailing the runs scored when the Bushmen came to play at Cockfield, and the amount of food and drink consumed ('14 lb ham – nearly all gone, 2 lbs stilton – nearly all gone, 2 cucumbers, very fat ones, 16 pints from pub and 20 bottles of Abbot'), though we do learn that when 'the two Grahams' and Elisabeth and Rodney came to dinner they worked through three bottles of Chateau Margaux 1959, a bottle of 1792 Madeira and four pounds of sausages ('a few left'), and that the following day was given over to visiting Greene King pubs in the neighbourhood, inspecting the pub signs and sampling the beer within. Like Graham, he did not drive, and although Elaine had been a notoriously bad cook, his own efforts in the kitchen were restricted to boiling potatoes, roasting sausages, putting a chicken in the oven and making compotes from the fruit in the greenhouse. Raymond had put Hugh on a diet after his return from Malaya, but like Graham he retained his passion for sausages, and he once suggested that he and Graham should collaborate on a book on the subject.

Ever the publisher, Graham was all for Hugh writing his memoirs. 'Why don't you give him a good lunch and try to get him to write about his life: it is an interesting one,' he suggested to Max Reinhardt. He thought Hugh should write a personal rather than a political book, and that he should 'build the whole thing around' what Hugh described as 'the agonies of shyness which I used to suffer, and about my whole career (you don't think of journalists as being shy men) being an attempt to overcome that, ending with a realisation when I was D-G at the BBC that suddenly it was all behind me.' It was sound advice, and Hugh acted upon it, but although the completed chapters are extremely good, with a tone of voice very similar to Graham's own *A Sort of Life*, 'A Variety of Lives' was never completed, and peters out after Hugh's arrival in Germany in 1934. In 1969 The Bodley Head published Hugh's *The Third Floor Front: A View of Broadcasting in the Sixties*, a collection of pieces which, despite the title, touched also on his work in Germany after the war and in Malaya: it is a tantalisingly short book, small in format and few in pages, and one can only regret that he never followed Graham's advice through to the end. In the meantime, he had to make do with an interim biography by Michael Tracey, carrying the same title as his aborted memoir and published by The Bodley Head. In 1984 he visited Berlin to see about its translation into German: 'I expect it will be better in German than in English!' he told Barbara.

Biographers can blight the lives of writers and public figures, and are best kept at bay till after death. Hugh's biography appeared in his lifetime and, in James Greene's opinion, The Bodley Head had 'cut off the balls and removed the heart of the book'; but he was not the only Greene to suffer a biographer's attentions. Graham was, inevitably, a prime target, while Felix found himself having to deal not just with a single practitioner, but with a brace of biographers. Graham read Christopher Sykes's biography of Evelyn Waugh shortly after its publication in 1975, thought very little of it, and was determined not to suffer the fate of his old friend. Michael Meyer, the biographer of Ibsen and a good friend with whom he had played Scrabble on a voyage through the South Seas, was keen to play the biographer's role, but Graham tactfully dissuaded him.

And then, in 1977, Graham relented, and agreed to appoint an English academic, Norman Sherry, as his official biographer. 'I felt certain that someone would do a book, but I hope it won't appear till I'm safely dead, and I didn't want it to be a kind of Christopher Sykes, who mixed up personal memories with biography,' Graham told Catherine Walston; and he informed his son, Francis, that having read the Sykes biography, he was 'determined that nobody who knew me should have my support and it had to be a non-Catholic.' He had admired Sherry's two books about Joseph Conrad, but this wasn't enough to convince his old friend Mario Soldati of Sherry's suitability. Sherry was, Soldati warned him, 'not intelligent enough to make up for a deep strain of vulgarity which is in him . . . Certainly Sherry devotes himself earnestly to the study of Conrad, but Conrad remains a giant whose feet are the only thing Sherry likes to look at. That is the way he proceeds in his literary investigations; attending only to small things, small facts, small ideas, small feelings, everything small.'

Although Frere shared Soldati's reservations, it was agreed that Sherry should go ahead. He was not, Graham assured Francis, a 'scandal-monger', and 'from my point of view there is one great thing in his favour – that he doesn't bother me. He only bothers my friends and relations!' 'I don't in the least want to influence you to see him or not to see him,' Graham told Catherine Walston. 'Elisabeth and Hugh and Raymond have all seen him and like him, but I keep very carefully in the background.' Inspired, perhaps, by a sense of mischief, Graham suggested that the hapless Sherry should make a point of visiting all the places he had visited in his restless travels about the world. 'That poor Sherry, who has been trying to follow in my footsteps in Mexico, Haiti and Paraguay, has returned to England very unwell. I hope I'm not going to be the death of him,' Graham reported only a year after Sherry had embarked on what was to prove an enormous and adulatory three-volume life that would be published over fifteen years and include among its many illustrations a photograph of the biographer astride a mule, somewhere in Mexico. Quite why Sherry felt it necessary to visit Haiti or Paraguay so early in the proceedings remains unclear, but he was equally active on the home front. 'Norman Sherry kept the Sutros up till half-past five in the morning,' Graham warned Hugh. 'God knows what he got out of them.' He told Jocelyn Rickards that she could say what she liked about their brief affair, since Sherry was 'a nice man and I don't think he is going to bother much about the private life.' This proved a misjudgement on Graham's part, and in due course he not only ordered his biographer to 'lay off'

Muriel Spark, but wrote to say that Anita Bjork was 'distressed by your letters as, quite naturally, she likes to keep her life private. I don't see why people should be punished because of the affection they have had from me. I have advised her to put any letters from you straight in the wastepaper basket.'

Biographical life was further complicated when, noticing that not a word of Sherry's Life had been published ten years after he started work on it, Random House in New York decided to commission a rival, unauthorised biography from an English writer called Anthony Mockler. Sherry, who could never be accused of a lack of diligence, and had spent much of the last ten years battling through rainforests and tropical swamps, was understandably alarmed. 'Yes, Norman is really paranoid. I don't see that after ten years he can really hold out against any competition. For myself, I would much rather nothing was published before I died, but I gave way to Norman,' Graham told his nephew Graham, who would be publishing the authorised biography at Jonathan Cape. 'I won't be giving Mockler any personal help, nor will Vivien or Elisabeth or Francis. He will only have written sources to play with.' He assured Sherry that he was doing his best to 'keep Mockler at bay', while warning him that it was 'vital that you should precede' him, and urged his friends to have no truck with the opposition. 'He has been plaguing my wife and even making menaces towards her,' he told Julia Stonor. 'He has no right to be interfering in our affairs.' And he urged Vivien not to talk to Mockler, reassuring her that 'You *must* know that none of this information about you and your mother comes from me.' In the meantime, he assured Sherry that he trusted him enough not to insist on reading it in typescript, but was 'quite ready to read it first in proof', so enabling him to pick up the occasional howler ('Really! The Madeleine is a very famous church and not a brothel!').

The first volume of Sherry's biography was eventually published in the summer of 1989. 'I am sorry to think of you ploughing through all that immense book of Sherry's. It's not badly written but it really goes on for far too long,' Graham wrote to Barbara. Sherry, he continued, 'is someone who unlike me obviously enjoys publicity. I found his book long and tedious reading although the second half was a bit better as it was so often written by you and me. I can't imagine who is going to buy and read it, and I am rather surprised at the favourable notices.' 'I think you were right to keep your distance,' Paul Theroux told his old mentor. 'In the end I thought it was okay – too much about your courtship, though; I imagine it must have set your teeth on edge.' 'Understanding

your fears, I will try to keep away from the personal, where this is irrelevant . . . If I seem to be moving into the private sphere I'll consult with
you hurriedly,' Sherry had assured Graham back in 1975, but Graham's
courtship of Vivien was covered at inordinate length. Nor was Graham
best pleased to receive a furious letter from Alastine Lehmann, the
daughter of his old Oxford tutor, Kenneth Bell. Sherry had claimed that
Bell had been sacked from Balliol after leaving his wife for a student, and
had eventually committed suicide: none of this was true, but Sherry had
told her that Graham had approved the contents of the first volume.
'Professor Sherry is quite wrong in saying that I approved all that he had
written in his biography,' Graham assured her. 'I only saw later proofs
when it would have been impossible to change anything substantial. I
very much loved your father and I still remember my sadness at his death
but I have completely forgotten the circumstances of it.' 'I am glad that
I have been promised galley-proofs in the case of your second volume,
but of course I think it highly unlikely that I shall be alive to read them,'
he told his biographer. Details of Graham's love life would once again
be interlaced with extensive summaries of his novels, and one shudders
to think what he would have made of the ludicrously self-indulgent and
self-obsessed Volume Three.

Felix was not as obvious or well-known a subject, but he had led a
more interesting life than most, and was understandably flattered when
an Australian couple called the Flanagans approached him about writing
his life. Based in Spain, they had given up their jobs in order to write
Felix's biography, and were worryingly short of funds. Graham C. Greene
at Cape eventually paid them the first part of an advance, but, they
assured Felix, their motives were entirely altruistic: 'The book is our gift
to you,' they insisted. 'It is only my sense of my own worthlessness that
allowed your ego-boost to so greatly influence me,' he told them. They
must not flinch away from the truth, he declared, as they embarked on
'the biography of a man who knows that at bottom he is "second-rate".'
He was, he warned them, one of life's 'flitters', 'human humming birds,
tasting as many aspects of life as they can cram into their lives. They
are too busy experimenting with life ever to be confined to a single
occupation. They can never decide who they really are,' and 'they often
– very mistakenly – *appear* to be free souls.'

The Flanagans spent long hours interviewing Felix, pondering his
replies, and writing up the results, all of which gave Felix a justifiable
excuse to re-examine every aspect of his life. But although the book gave
him 'a tiny niggling sense that I haven't really been such an utterly useless

worm as I have felt for the whole of my life,' it proved an unhappy experience, and was eventually aborted. Part of the problem was that Felix and the Flanagans got on each other's nerves. Felix was a desultory correspondent; he worried that their exhaustive approach might be 'appropriate for a biography of some world figure, but certainly not for a non-entity', shared Barbara's views about their prose style and their use of 'pseudo-scientific language', and addressed them as 'you dear people' while running them down to family and friends. The Flanagans alternated between unctuous servility and outright abuse, complaining bitterly about his negative attitude and lack of co-operation, and reminding him that they had devoted an enormous amount of time to the book, and that they only wanted to make him a gift of his life. 'You seem to find it difficult to recognise freely given friendship, let alone value it in non-monetary terms,' Julie Flanagan told him. It was all very well for Felix to tell them that he had no friends, but 'you are intensely lovable, and admirable in many ways. I think you just don't value freely given friendship.' Three months later, the Flanagans wondered whether there was any point in carrying on, given Felix's ambivalent attitude. They had come to dread his letters, since they never knew 'whether it will be an affectionate one, or whether you have yet one more complaint.'

Nor were other members of the family entirely happy about the planned biography. Anne worried about what the Flanagans might have to say about Felix's marriage and about his affairs with other women; Tooter was put on the spot when Felix suggested that he might get in touch on his behalf with Peggy Bok, despite the fact that she had begged Felix again and again not to try to see her, and not to keep in touch ('I do not want to fade away unreconciled,' he claimed); and Barbara was frankly appalled. Pat Flanagan wrote to her about Felix's long-standing claim that their parents' marriage had been unhappy, and that he had enjoyed a 'quasi-erotic' relationship with Eva. 'It is complete nonsense to suggest that the love relation between my father and mother was not satisfactory,' Barbara replied. 'It is also nonsense to think that it is significant that my mother did not remarry after her husband died. Why should she? I didn't . . . To put it baldly, I think you had better leave the family out of your book altogether, and just stick to Felix's adventures through life.' Pat Flanagan assured Felix that 'Truth is always dangerous and threatening to those with defensive fears and repressed anxieties,' and that they were as committed as ever to telling the 'uncensored truth', but with Barbara on the war-path Felix felt called upon to read the riot act. 'You must, must, *must* be careful in the way you approach people about me,' he told his biographers. 'I thought I had told you enough about Barbara's general character – a "real snob", I think I called her – to caution you about approaching her about the intimacies of the family.' Barbara, he warned them, 'has very decided and very inflexible opinions, and views everything written or said about our side of the family only as it may affect her more exalted "aristocratic" relations in Germany', and he worried that she could prejudice Graham and Hugh against the book, and persuade them not to talk to his biographers.

Felix had never felt at ease with the School House Greenes, and with Graham and Hugh in particular. Hugh had never liked him, and Felix felt towards Graham 'a sense of inferiority, slight fear, envy at his extra-ordinary writing ability'. Years earlier, in 1965, he had attended the first night of Graham's play *Carving a Statue*. It was generally regarded as, in Felix's words, 'an appallingly bad play', and it enjoyed none of the commercial or critical success of its predecessors, *The Living Room*, *The Potting Shed* and *The Complaisant Lover*. 'Very flashy affair – everyone of importance there,' Felix reported back to Elena. 'All in evening dress but me. Graham and Raymond and Hugh and Elisabeth and young Graham and his wife Judy. Graham hid himself in the dress circle and disappeared afterwards – as well he might.' Raymond was 'elegant', Elisabeth 'tall and gentle and very nice', but Hugh, 'the great Sir, ignored me'. Felix went on to dinner afterwards with Graham C. Greene, Judy and Helga Greene. 'Even this part of the family had lost its hold, and I was much nicer than I usually am with them,' Felix admitted. 'I suppose Graham's failure helped – it made my own non-emergence into the Greene lime-light less noticeable. Whatever the reason, I was at ease with them all and enjoyed myself enormously.' Nearly twenty years later, Felix felt emboldened to write to Graham about *Ways of Escape*, a collection of autobiographical essays. 'I had an affectionate note from the older Graham,' he informed the Flanagans. 'I had written to him to tell him I thought he had chickened out of his latest biography by not going into the personal relationships – his love relationships – which had meant as much to him as mine have meant to me. He said he didn't think he had chickened out, but was old-fashioned enough to avoid mentioning the people he had slept with.' The Flanagans, in the meantime, had been in touch with Graham, who seemed better disposed than Felix might have feared. 'I am perhaps nearer to him than he thinks,' he told them apropos their political differences, adding that 'I think it very likely that I did say jokingly to somebody "That's my Communist cousin."'

'Elena, Anne and I have reached a kind of plateau of serenity where

I think we could all live quite happily in the tiniest and simplest of cottages, for I think in the end there is *no* security except that which comes from our relationship with others', Felix told Tooter in the summer of 1984, but their happiness was not to last. 'I received a letter from Felix which moved me a good deal,' Graham told Barbara three months later. Graham himself had been operated on for intestinal cancer in 1979, and now Felix was 'facing a nasty situation very courageously. The Greene family seem addicted to cancers. On your side there is Felix and my uncle Eppy, and on our side Molly, who died from it, Raymond, who recovered from it, and myself who touch wood has recovered also after an operation.' Felix sent him a poem he had written, and Graham wrote back to thank him, and commiserate. 'Our two families seem, more than the average, addicted to it,' he wrote of Felix's illness, before striking a more personal and conciliatory note. 'My last happy memory of you was in the fifties when you showed me your warehouse of antiques. I may have disagreed with you about Mao, but I think we should agree now over Nicaragua and El Salvador, and I liked the poem you sent me very much. Stick to life as long as you can, and write more of them.' Three months later, Felix told Tooter that he would not be coming to England from Mexico, since he could no longer stand or walk or even sit up in bed. 'We were looking forward so much to talking over so many things but that is clearly out of the question now,' he told his brother. 'But you know with what deep affection I have always thought of you.' Two months later he was dead. 'I was very sorry to hear of Felix's death,' Graham told Barbara. 'At the end of his life he seemed to have become a much more likeable character, and I had a poem from him about dying which was really rather good. It might be worth finding out what other poems he had written.' Felix's poem may well have been a 'one-off': he was, perhaps, the most naturally gifted of his generation of Greenes, but his career had been blighted by the ease with which he could turn his hand to whatever needed to be done, and by his longing to find some system of belief that would explain not just the workings of the world at large, but his own sense of inadequacy and worthlessness.

Tatjana died alone in Berlin in 1981 at the age of seventy-one, and was buried next to Günter Neumann. Before she died she wrote Hugh a letter hoping that he would remarry and find happiness again. Years earlier, in 1968, while on a Commonwealth Broadcasting Union visit to New Zealand, Hugh had met Sarah Grahame, an Australian working in television. He invited her to join him for a drink after work, and they had kept in touch ever since. They were married by Special Licence –

thereby avoiding reporters – in Chelsea Register Office in December 1984. Despite the difference in their ages, they were devoted to one another. Far from finding him a cold and remote figure, 'he was more fun and better company' than anyone she had ever met, before or since. They divided the two years they spent together between Earls Hall and Hugh's splendid 1930s flat in Palace Gate, designed by the modernist architect Wells Coates.

But Hugh's health was not good. He had fallen foul of the family disease, suffering from prostate and bone cancer as well as severe anaemia. On what proved to be the last Sunday of his life he wanted to watch *The Antiques Roadshow*, one of his and Sarah's favourite television programmes, 'to see if my brain is still working because my body will not do what I want it to.' He was admitted to the Edward VII Hospital in February 1987, taking with him as reading matter Trollope's *The Way We Live Now* and the latest Dick Francis thriller. Despite being in great pain, he made light of it when ringing people from the hospital, or never mentioned his being there. The two people he particularly wanted to see were Graham and Paris Tacopoulos; he said he slept better when Sarah was with him, so she slept curled up in a blanket on a chair, but could not hold his hand because the pressure on his bones was agonising. Graham returned back from a trip to Moscow, and stood at the bedside of his favourite brother, repeating 'Poor boy, poor boy' over and over again. Ashen-faced and breathing heavily, Hugh lay in a coma for two days, but then, quite suddenly, he sat bolt upright, his eyes wide open. Sarah rushed from the room to fetch a doctor, but he was dead by the time they returned. Three of Hugh's sons, who had spent the day with their father, had gone to the pub for a drink; the television was still on, since Sarah had been waiting for the seven o'clock news to see who had been appointed the new Director-General of the BBC. Graham had left the hospital only hours earlier, on his way home to Antibes. 'I don't need to tell you how shattered I was by Hugh's death,' he told his nephew James. 'It was terrible sitting beside him the day I returned, in his coma, and when you rang me up at Bentley's it was a sort of relief, knowing he wouldn't have to struggle any more with his breath.' 'The death was a bad shock,' he wrote in a later letter to James. 'We had shared a great many experiences including the war in Malaya. I had also interested him in pirates and read aloud to him when he was six years old. I found the sight of him very painful, and the breathing was so heavy and strained. I find it difficult to get it out of my mind.'

Graham was not at Hugh's funeral: 'Moscow and Hugh's death have knocked me out. I still find it difficult to do anything – the last sight of his face comes between the lines when I read . . . Please forgive me for not being there. I couldn't bear the thought of all the strangers.' 'I found Sarah wonderful,' he said of his sister-in-law's demeanour in the hospital; he had suggested to James that, at the funeral, he should read a poem he had written about his father, and told him that, according to Elisabeth, he had done so very well. (The poem was set in the garden at Earls Hall, and after evoking Hugh's 'brewer's bulk in the enlightening dusk', it told of how 'He rises, Canute-like, to cut the grass with blunt and favourite shears, / Then vanishes behind a bush to pee . . .') Although they seldom met, James Greene and his uncle had struck up an epistolary friendship some years earlier. James had written to Graham in the hope that he might shed light on 'the intricacies and the strangeness of the family and the family history', but Graham said he was far too busy to 'help you "exorcise and transcend" your personal life'. Years later, James took to sending him his own poems and his translations of Mandelstam; Graham gave his frank opinions for good and for bad, and was delighted to learn that The Bodley Head would be publishing *Dead-Man's-Fall*, a book of James's poems ('It will be the first Greene verse since *Babbling April*, but I have every expectation that it will be a good deal better!'). In 1984 Graham, Hugh, James and other family members travelled down to Crowborough by train for the wedding of Louise, Rodney and Elisabeth's eldest daughter, and 'so far as I can remember, Graham and Hugh talked exclusively about food and drink.' James found Graham a 'generous, considerate, sympathetic and, from time to time, irritatingly opinionated and quirky correspondent'.

As a father, Hugh had been far more involved with Christopher and Timothy than he ever had been with Graham and James. 'I don't suppose you always had a very happy youth, but somehow it is good to have a father to be proud of,' Barbara wrote to 'young' Graham after learning of Hugh's death, while James wondered whether his father 'never really forgave Helga for leaving him and that consequently his relationship with his children by her was always tainted. I must admit his death has been something of a relief to me: for me, he was always so tantalisingly unavailable.' 'As I said to the congregation, Hugh is probably enjoying himself in hell – if there is one, which I doubt,' James wrote to Graham shortly after the funeral. 'Certainly the world seems less lively without him.' 'I imagine you may have had – still have – an almost parental feeling for him. I do know of his (sometimes almost jealous-making) loyalty to and admiration of you,' James wrote a week later. 'Of course he was not a bad man (although there was something of a dictator in him he was unaware of, projected outwards and consciously opposed in Hitler, the Greek Colonels etc rather than ever in himself) but he was always more a boy than a "father". Naturally I'm ambivalent about this. I liked his spirit of adventure.' 'Poor Hugh. Don't you think you ought to forgive him?' Graham wondered, but for all his feelings of resentment and neglect, James insisted that he had forgiven his father. 'You are wrong to infer that I don't forgive Hugh. I don't think that forgiving someone requires blinding oneself to their shortcomings,' James replied. 'He was a cold fish, but a not uninteresting one', and 'he lacked hypocrisy at least.' Remembering how Graham used to read young Hugh stories about pirates, James once suggested that his father 'was something of a pirate himself – although sailing under a flag of seeming legality'. Hugh had led an extraordinary life, and although James told Graham that he didn't 'expect we'll ever agree about him', he continued to 'find him a fascinating character'.

Hugh's memorial service was held at All Souls, Langham Place, immediately opposite the entrance to Broadcasting House. 'The service was lovely as the choir at All Souls sing beautifully and so thank heavens the Greenes did not have to drone through the hymns as they did at the funeral,' Elisabeth informed Graham. Graham's friend Leopoldo Duran assisted at the service, Graham C. read a speech by his father entitled 'The Conscience of the Programme Director', and two of Hugh's old colleagues from the BBC, Maurice Latey and Joanna Spicer, gave the addresses (Sarah Greene had wanted to include a reading of Lord Rochester's 'Song of a Young Lady to her Ancient Lover' – Hugh had recited that particular poem to Sarah on the way home from the White Tower, his favourite Greek restaurant in London – but was overruled by Sir Marmaduke Hussey, and opted instead for Philip Larkin's 'The Whitsun Weddings'). Afterwards they all filed into Broadcasting House to watch a showing of 'Greene's Germany', a programme made for German television and devoted to his time in the country. Hugh, who had once described himself as a 'respectful agnostic', is buried in Cockfield, and his tombstone is engraved with words that had come to him in a dream: 'Because I believe in nothing, I am unwilling to disbelieve in anything.'

Rodney Dennys had retired from MI6 in 1958 after an unsatisfactory attachment to the Embassy in Paris: he felt that his generation was being pushed aside, and that the Foreign Office had not purged itself sufficiently after the defections of Burgess and Maclean. He had taken up a new career in the arcane and colourful world of heraldry, joining the College of Arms, initially as First Rouge Pursuivant and then as Somerset Herald, before retiring as Arundel Herald Extraordinary. He wrote two books on the subject, and helped to organise Winston Churchill's funeral and the Investiture of the Prince of Wales in Caernarvon Castle. Elisabeth had continued to act as Graham's secretary but, two years after Hugh's death, she had a stroke, and was confined to a wheelchair. Graham provided generous financial support so that she could be looked after at home, and her eldest daughter, Amanda, took over as Graham's secretary-cum-personal assistant. 'I am so sorry about your parents,' Barbara wrote to Amanda. 'I have always felt that your mother was the pearl of the family and it seems so unfair that she should now suffer.' Both branches of the family seemed suddenly exposed. Kate, the youngest of the Hall Greene girls, died of cancer in 1985 and in October 1990 Ave Barham wrote to Graham to say that Tooter, Graham's 'first companion,' had been ill for some time with cancer. Not long afterwards he was taken into hospital with a fractured leg, and died in his sleep. 'Poor Tooter,' Barbara told Graham. 'His earliest days with you and his Cambridge time were probably his happiest time. He had a dull life, and his wives were all dull too.' 'My generation of the family are all gradually dying off or getting incapacitated – poor Ave, who till recently kept me up to date, is now very blind and it is only rarely that I get a few scribbled lines from her', Barbara declared. 'We were such a huge family long, long ago. I seem to be the only one that is going on and on and on.'

Ave, whom both Graham and Herbert had so admired in their youth, would in fact outlive Barbara, who died in 1991. She had seen little of Graham over the years, and was far removed from the literary world, but in November 1990 she wrote to him to say that she had just heard one of his stories being read on the radio. 'What a wonderful story!' she exclaimed. 'Do please let me know if there is a book of your short stories – it would make a wonderful Christmas present to take with me when I go to spend Christmas with Snooks [her daughter] in America!' 'The Greenes are going through a rather bad period what with Elisabeth in her wheelchair, and I am suffering from anaemia and have to have blood transfusions every two weeks which means five or six hours in a hospital. It's a very tiring business getting old,' Graham replied. In 1979 he had been operated on for cancer of the stomach, but even in his eighties, Shirley Hazzard recalled, 'there was something valiant in his refusal to mellow. He remained fired, as in youth, with engagement

and indignation, and by the rightful written word', and behind the rheumy
blue eyes and the mottled features 'one would still perceive the gangling,
narrow-shouldered, self-communing youth.' He remained devoted to
Yvonne, and dedicated much time and emotional energy to a courageous
defence of her daughter, Martine, in her battle with her estranged
husband, Daniel Guy, a member of the Nice underworld and a Mafia
drug baron who had the support of the corrupt Mayor of Nice. Yvonne,
her husband Jacques and Martine were all beaten up, and Graham's own
life was threatened. Graham devoted a short, angry pamphlet to the
subject, entitled *J'Accuse*: Jill Black, his editor at The Bodley Head, took
the proofs to Antibes, and despite what Graham had told Auberon Waugh
about never owning a gun, she remembers how, as they left the flat to
go out to dinner, Graham tucked a revolver into the back pocket of his
trousers. Not long after its publication, Anthony Powell found himself
sitting next to the historian Richard Cobb at a dinner in Balliol. Cobb
told him that the *Sunday Times* had refused to print his review of
J'Accuse for fear of libel, but The Bodley Head had sent Graham a copy.
'In answer to this he received two furious letters from Graham Greene
in one day, complaining about the review. I gather Cobb had complained
that there was insufficient information in the book to derive any idea of
what had really happened,' Powell noted in his journal. 'Cobb said he
thought Graham wanted to end his life by being murdered at the hands
of a Nice Mafioso. I certainly think Graham has always felt, from his
earliest days, that somehow his life is not glamorous enough, although
he is always doing things to make it sound exciting.'

Excitement of a less alarming kind was provided by trips to Spain
with Father Leopoldo Duran, a Spanish priest and the model for the
endearing hero of *Monsignor Quixote*. Much wine was drunk, and they
particularly enjoyed visiting the Cistercian monastery at Osera. Duran,
who had permission from his bishop to use the Latin rite, said Mass in
Graham's flat in Antibes, or in a hotel room when they were travelling
together. Graham told John Cornwell, who interviewed him at length
for the *Tablet*, that he regularly confessed to Father Duran 'although I've
nothing much to confess at the age of eighty-five', and that he took the
host 'because that pleases him'. Graham had always hated being described
as a Catholic novelist – it was, he wrote, 'the last title to which I had
ever aspired' – and his attitude to religion, and to the Catholic Church,
was fond but sceptical. 'His Catholicism is with lots of *grani salis*', Arthur
Koestler remarked when they met at dinner with Rose Macaulay during
the war, but Graham told Father Duran that although he found it hard

to believe, 'I don't believe my unbelief.' He disapproved of the Pope's views on contraception, and was unable to believe in hell, yet he still thought of himself as 'to a certain extent an agnostic Catholic'. All in all, he told Father Duran, 'I have faith, but less and less belief in the existence of God. I have a continuing faith that I am wrong not to believe and that my lack of belief stems from my own faults and failure in love.'

Graham was never quite the same after Elisabeth's stroke in 1989, Yvonne later recalled. By the summer of 1990 he was enduring a blood transfusion every fortnight, vitamin injections three times a week, and a heavy dosage of pills. He was told to lay off the alcohol, 'but I have interpreted that to allow me a small vodka at lunchtime and a glass of beer at lunch and dinner!' Barbara was keen that he should visit her in Gozo, but 'I am afraid my travelling days are over.' He was in Vevey in Switzerland, near to where his daughter Caroline lived, when, in March 1991, the doctors confirmed that his body was rejecting the transfusions, which were no longer having any effect. Graham decided that there was no point in burdening his body any more, and prepared himself for death. Yvonne was in Antibes at the time, and hurried to be with him. He looked quite different, she remembered, 'his eyes shining, his mind lucid and clear, his voice firmer', and he seemed unalarmed by the imminence of death. '"There's nothing more to be done," he said. "It may be an interesting experience. I will at least have the answers to my questions. Will I see a flash of light like Freddie Ayer?"' (Ayer, an unbeliever, had famously undergone an 'after-death experience'.) Yvonne told Gillian Sutro that Graham 'did not seem to care any more, he was taking death in his stride with his usual writer's curiosity'; he told her that he was not frightened of death, but dreaded being separated from her. Norman Sherry, in the meantime, continued to badger him with questions about his wartime activities in West Africa: he wanted Graham's permission to quote from letters and unpublished material, and the day before he died Graham signed a document giving his 'authorized biographer' permission to quote, carefully adding a comma which denied Sherry the exclusivity he sought.

Father Duran claimed that Graham wanted him to be there when he died, and on Easter Sunday the priest was summoned to Graham's bedside in the Hôpital de la Providence in Vevey and gave him the last rites. Next morning, over breakfast, Father Duran was told that Graham was dying; he gave him absolution and sat with him when he died. Caroline and Yvonne were also present, and remembered him murmuring 'Why does it take so long?', the last words he spoke. Both Vivien and Yvonne were at the graveside, and in due course the Greenes gathered in Westminster Cathedral for his memorial service. Of Graham's generation, only Ave, Elisabeth and Barbara were still alive, but a new generation was making its mark.

Acknowledgements

As readers of the Preamble may have gathered, this book owes its existence to Graham C. Greene, and without him it would never have come
into being, at least in its current incarnation. I first encountered Graham
in the 1980s, when I was an editor at Chatto & Windus and he was the
managing director of the group of publishers of which Chatto formed
a part. He was invariably referred to as 'Graham C.' or 'young Graham'
to differentiate him from his famous uncle, and he remained, as far as I
was concerned, a benign but remote presence, encountered as a beaming
presence at staff outings or office parties, with whom I exchanged a
hundred words at most over the course of ten years. Eight years after I
left Chatto he wrote to me out of the blue to say how much he'd enjoyed
my biography of Cyril Connolly and to point out that Eton has a
'Head Master' and not a 'Headmaster', a correction dutifully made in
the paperback. A few years later, he gave me some invaluable help with
my biography of Allen Lane; and then, at a party in the Wallace Collection, he suggested that I should write about the Greenes. I cannot thank
him enough for the suggestion: not only have the Greenes proved to be
far more fascinating than I ever imagined, but Graham himself has proved
to be a marvellous mixture of impresario, editor and friend, and getting
to know him better has been one of the many happy by-products of
writing and researching this book.

Graham introduced me to a bewildering array of Greenes. Itemising
their various contributions – including enormous lunches and a great
deal of hospitality – would be a long and invidious business, but I am
immensely grateful to the following for allowing me access to family
letters and papers, for reading the book through to pick up howlers and
omissions, and, where relevant, for permission to quote from their
parents' writings, published or unpublished: John Barham, Nick Dennys,
Annabel Gooch, Anne Greene, Francis Greene, James Greene, Paul
Greene, Oliver Greene, Sarah Greene, Tim Greene and Rupert von

Strachwitz. I also enjoyed long and useful conversations with Ann Biezanek about her father, Ben. Richard Greene, who edited Graham Greene's letters, is not related to the family, but knows more about them than most: he has proved an invaluable friend and ally, calming me down when I teetered on the edge of panic or despair, and answering emailed queries within minutes of their arrival on the shores of Lake Ontario.

I am very grateful to the following for their help and advice: Judith Adamson, Rupert Allason, Frank Archer, Deborah Asher, Diana Athill, Roderick Bailey, Phil Baker, Michael Beloff, Jill Black, Michael Bloch, the late Richard Boston, Mark Bostridge, Clive Bradley, Montagu Bream, Piers Brendon, Hugo and Mary Rose Brunner, Michael Burleigh, David Burnett, Tim Butcher, Peter Calvocoressi, Euan Cameron, Adam Clapham, Francis and Charlotte Clarke, Rozanne Colchester, Gerard Conway, Jane Conway, Michael Estorick, Duncan Fallowell, Harry Frere, Jonathan Fryer, Reg Gadney, Patrick Garrett, Sarah Gibb, John Hale, Jon Halliday, Selina Hastings, Christopher Hawtree, Frank Hermann, Bruce Hunter, Richard Ingrams, Richard Johnson, Alan Judd, Roger Kirkpatrick, Phillip Knightley, Alexander Kulpok, David Kynaston, Peter Janson-Smith, Christine Jennings, the Hon. John Jolliffe, Mark Lambert, Lucy Lethbridge, Deirdre Levi, Roger Lewis, Giles MacDonogh, David Machin, Partrick Marnham, Douglas Matthews (a masterly indexer and eagle-eyed sleuth), Emily Mayhew, the late James Michie, Anthony Mockler, Malcolm Moore, Charlotte Mosley, Andrew Nash, Graham Page, Stanley Price, Alexandra Pringle, Joan Reinhardt, Barbara Ruffell, Pam St John, Jean Seaton, Professor A. W. B. Simpson, Christopher Sinclair-Stephenson, the Hon. Julia Stonor, Paris Tacopolous, Judy Taylor, Ian Thomson, Abbie Todd, Harriet Tuckey, Nigel Viney, Alexander Waugh, Sara Wheeler and Ilsa Yardley.

Burrowing in archives and spending long hours in libraries are among the perks of the biographers's life, and I'd like to thank the following for their help: Yvonne Sibbald at the Alpine Club; Jeff Walden and Jacquie Kavanagh at the BBC Archives, Caversham; Dennis Archer at Bedales School; Judith Priestman, Helen Langley, Paul Cartledge and Colin Harris at the Bodleian Library; Robert O'Neill, David Horn and Robert Bruns at Boston College; Claire Knight at the Churchill Archives Centre, Churchill College, Cambridge; Nicholas Scheetz at Georgetown University; the late Ken Sherwood, David Pearce, Sally Bartlett, Richard Lewis, Dermot Gilvary and Colin Garrett at the Graham Greene Birthplace Trust in Berkhamsted; Pat Fox at the Harry Ransom Humanities Research Center, University of Texas, Austin; Amanda Corp and Helen O'Neill at the London Library; Brenda Brown at the McFarlin Library, University of Tulsa; Dr T. E. Rogers at Marlborough College; Jean Rose at the Random House archives in Rushden, Northants; Michael Bott, Verity Andrews and Brian Ryder at Reading University Library; Lucy McCann at Rhodes House library; Fiona Colbert at St John's College, Cambridge; Christine Gladwin at Sidcot School; Tabitha Driver at the Society of Friends Library in the Euston Road; and Cliff Davies and Cornelia Carson at Wadham College, Oxford. I am very grateful to the Society of Authors for a grant which enabled me to visit libraries in America in search of Greene material. Thanks are due to David Higham Ltd for permission to quote from the *Journals of Anthony Powell*, and to PFD Ltd to quote from *The Letters of Evelyn Waugh*.

My agent, Gillon Aitken, has been, as always, a model of good humour, reassurance and sage advice. I had forgotten what a pleasure it is to be published by Dan Franklin at Jonathan Cape, and how his cool, laconic manner makes his praise all the more potent; it's good to know that we will be working together on my next book, a biography of David Astor. Tom Avery of Cape is all that I should have been when I was his age, and starting life as a publisher's editor – calm, efficient, always in the office when needed, and miraculously polite and patient when I bombarded him with last-minute changes and corrections, some of them provided by members of the Greene family who had suddenly unearthed folders of letters and box-files of papers long after I thought I had finished the book.

My daughters, Jemima and Hattie, have expressed polite interest in the proceedings, as have their husbands, Henry and Tom; my wife, Petra, has not only endured unusually high levels of absent-mindedness and distraction, but has kept me going with mugs of hot chocolate, and hosed me down in moments of despair.

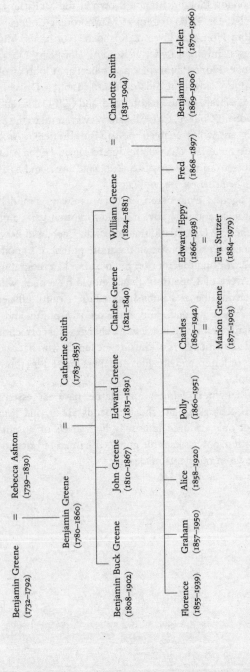

THE GREENE FAMILY TREE

Benjamin Greene (1732–1792) = Rebecca Ashton (1739–1830)

Benjamin Greene (1780–1860) = Catherine Smith (1783–1855)

Benjamin Buck Greene (1808–1902)

John Greene (1810–1867)

Edward Greene (1815–1891)

Charles Greene (1821–1840)

William Greene (1824–1881) = Charlotte Smith (1831–1904)

Florence (1855–1939)

Graham (1857–1950)

Alice (1858–1920)

Polly (1860–1951)

Charles (1865–1942) = Marion Greene (1871–1903)

Edward 'Eppy' (1866–1938) = Eva Stutzer (1884–1979)

Fred (1868–1897)

Benjamin (1869–1906)

Helen (1870–1960)

THE SCHOOL HOUSE GREENES

Marion Greene = Charles Greene
(1871–1959)   (1865–1942)

Molly   Herbert   Raymond   Graham
(1896–1963)   (1898–1968)   (1901–1982)   (1904–1991)
=   =   =   =
Lionel Walker Audrey Nutting (1) Charlotte Mackenzie   Vivien Dayrell-F
(1874–1951)   (2) Eleanor Gamble   (1904–2003)

(4) Se...

THE HALL GREENES

Edward 'Eppy' Greene = Eva Stutzer
(1866–1938)   (1884–1979)

Benjamin (Ben) Eva 'Ave'   Edward 'Tooter'   Barbara   Felix   Katharine
(1901–1978)   (1903–2001) (1904–1990)   (1907–1991)   (1909–1985)   (1914–1985)
=   =   =   =   =   =
Leslie Campbell Jack Barham (1) Lola Bell   Count Rudolf Strachwitz Elena Lindeman James Collacott
(1898–1989)   (1904–1988) (1911–1936)   (1896–1969)   (1909–1997)   (1898–1954)
                             (2) Olwen Armstrong-Maddocks
                             (3) Immingard Fischges
                             (1917–1998)

Abbreviations

ABC: American Broadcasting Company
ATS: Auxiliary Territorial Service
BCAEC: British Council Against European Commitments
BCCSE: British Council for a Christian Settlement in Europe
BPP: British People's Party
BUF: British Union of Fascists
BW: Brazilian Warrant Company
CBS: Columbia Broadcasting System
CE: Counter-Intelligence Officer
CIA: Central Intelligence Agency
CID: Criminal Investigation Department
DPP: Department of Public Prosecutions
EH: Electra House (Department for Enemy Propaganda)
EIS: Emergency Information Services
ENA: English National Association
FBI: Federal Bureau of Investigation
FO: Foreign Office
HCLA: Home Counties Labour Association
ILP: Independent Labour Party
ISLD: Inter-Services Liaison Department
ITA: Independent Television Authority
ITV: Independent Television Authority
JBC: Joint Broadcasting Council
JCR: Junior Common Room
MCA: Music Corporation of America
MGM: Metro-Goldwyn-Mayer
MRLA: Malayan Races Liberation Army
NAAFI: Navy, Army and Air Force Institutes
NAR: North American Radio
NBC: National Broadcasting Company

NEC: National Executive Committee

NJCSR: National Joint Committee for Spanish Relief

NKVD: People's Commissariat for Internal Affairs

NWDR: Nordwestdeutscher Rundfunk (North-West Germany Radio Station)

OSS: Office of Strategic Services

PEN: Poets, Essayists and Novelists (worldwide association of writers)

PID: Political Intelligence Department

PPU: Peace Pledge Union

PWD: Psychological Warfare Division

PWE: Political Warfare Executive

RAMC: Royal Army Medical Corps

RCA: Radio Corporation of America

RGS: Royal Geographical Society

SD: Sicherheitsdienst (Nazi party intelligence service)

SHAEF: Supreme Headquarters of the Allied Expeditionary Force

SIM: Servizio Informazioni Militari (Italian military intelligence)

SIME: Security Intelligence Middle East

SIS: Secret Intelligence Service (also known as MI6)

SOE: Special Operations Executive

SS: Schutzstaffel (Nazi military unit)

Toc H: (Charity)

TUC: Trade Union Council

TVA: Tennessee Valley Authority

TW3: *That Was the Week That Was*

UNRRA: United Nations Relief and Rehabilitation Administration

WEA: Workers' Educational Association

Bibliography

Adamson, Judith *Max Reinhardt: A Life in Publishing* (Palgrave Macmillan, 2009)

Adamson, Judith (ed.) *Graham Greene: Reflections* (Reinhardt Books, 1990)

Allain, Marie-Francoise, translated by Guido Waldman *The Other Man: Conversations with Graham Greene* (The Bodley Head, 1983)

Allen, Walter *As I Walked Down New Grub Street* (Heinemann, 1981)

Amory, Mark (ed.) *The Letters of Evelyn Waugh* (Weidenfeld & Nicolson, 1980)

Amory, Mark (ed.) *The Letters of Ann Fleming* (Harvill, 1985)

Alexander, Tania *A Little of All These: An Estonian Childhood* (Jonathan Cape, 1987)

Amory, Mark (ed.) *The Letters of Evelyn Waugh* (Weidenfeld & Nicolson, 1980)

Anderson, J.R.L. *High Mountains and Cold Seas: A Biography of H.W. Tilman* (Gollancz, 1980)

Andrew, Christopher *The Defence of the Realm: The Authorised History of MI5* (Allen Lane, 2009)

Bacha, Edmar and Greenhill, Robert *150 Years of Coffee: Marcellino Martins and E. Johnston* (privately published, 1992)

Balfour, Michael *Propaganda in War, 1939–1945: Organisations, Policies and Publics in Britain and Germany* (Routledge, 1979)

Barber, Michael *Anthony Powell: A Life* (Duckworth, 2004)

Barham, John E. (ed.) *Alice Greene: Teacher and Campaigner: South African Correspondence 1887–1902* (Matador, 2007)

Bartlett, Vernon *Report from Malaya* (Derek Verschoyle, 1954)

Beckett, Francis *The Rebel Who Lost His Cause: The Tragedy of John Beckett MP* (London House, 1999)

Bethell, Nicholas *Spies and Other Secrets* (Viking, 1994)

Biezaneck, Anne *All Things New: The Declaration of Faith* (Peter Smith, 1964)

Blond, Anthony *Jew Made in England* (Timewell, 2004)

Boustead, Hugh *The Wind of Morning* (Chatto & Windus, 1971)

Boyle, Andrew *'Poor, Dear Brendan': The Quest for Brendan Bracken* (Hutchinson, 1974)

Brady, Anne Marie *Making the Foreign Serve China: Managing Foreigners in the People's Republic* (Oxford: Rowman & Littlefield, 2003)

Briggs, Asa *The BBC: The First Fifty Years* (Oxford University Press, 1985)

Briggs, Asa *The Golden Age of Wireless: The History of Broadcasting in the United Kingdom, Volume II* (Oxford University Press, 1965)

Briggs, Asa *The War of Words: The History of Broadcasting in the United Kingdom, Volume III* (Oxford University Press, 1995)

Briggs, Asa *Competition: The History of Broadcasting in the United Kingdom, Volume V* (Oxford University Press, 1995)

Bright-Holmes, John (ed.) *Like It Was: The Diaries of Malcolm Muggeridge* (Collins, 1981).

Brittain, Vera *Wartime Chronicle: Diary 1939–1945* (Gollancz, 1989)

Burns, Jimmy *Papa Spy: Love, Faith and Betrayal in Wartime Spain* (Bloomsbury, 2009)

Cain, John 'Dealing with Deprivation: The Origins of Social Action Broadcasting in Britain between 1923 and 1973', Open University PhD thesis, 1996.

Cairncross, John *The Enigma Spy: An Autobiography* (Century, 1997)

Cameron, Euan 'A Guiding Light' (Paper delivered to the Berkhamsted Graham Greene Festival, October 2005)

Camoys, Julia *Sherman's Wife* (Desert Hearts, 2006)

Cardiff, David and Scannell, Roddy *A Social History of British Broadcasting. Volume I 1922–1939: Serving the Nation* (Blackwell, 1991)

Cash, William *The Third Woman* (Little, Brown, 2000)

Clare, George *Berlin Days 1946–47* (Macmillan, 1989)

Clarke, Nick *Alistair Cooke: The Biography* (Weidenfeld & Nicolson, 1999)

Cloetta, Yvonne, as told to Marie-Francoise Allain, translated by Euan Cameron *In Search of a Beginning: My Life with Graham Greene* (Bloomsbury, 2004)

Cockerell, Michael *Live from No 10* (Faber, 1988)

Cooper, Artemis (ed.) *Mr Wu & Mrs Stitch: The Letters of Evelyn Waugh and Artemis Cooper* (Hodder & Stoughton, 1991)

Cockburn, Claud *Cockburn Sums Up: An Autobiography* (Quartet, 1987)

Cockburn, Patricia *Figures of Eight* (Chatto & Windus, 1985)

Cockett, Richard *Twilight of Truth: Chamberlain, Appeasement and the Manipulation of Truth* (Weidenfeld & Nicolson, 1989)

Cooper, Artemis *Cairo in the War 1935–1945* (Hamish Hamilton, 1989)

Cox, Geoffrey *See It Happen* (The Bodley Head, 1983)

Cox, Geoffrey *Countdown to War: A Personal Memoir of Europe 1938–40* (William Kimber, 1988)

Curran, Charles *A Seamless Robe: Broadcasting – Philosophy and Practice* (Collins, 1979)

Davie, Michael (ed.) *The Diaries of Evelyn Waugh* (Weidenfeld & Nicolson, 1976)

Davies, Robertson *The Merry Heart* (Penguin, 1998)

Davison, Peter (ed.) *Orwell: A Life in Letters* (Harvill Secker, 2010)

Deacon, Richard *'C': A Biography of Sir Maurice Oldfield* (Macdonald, 1985)

De Bellaigue, Eric *British Book Publishing as a Business since the 1960s* (British Library, 2004)

Delmer, Sefton *Trail Sinister: An Autobiography. Volume I* (Secker & Warburg, 1961)

Delmer, Sefton *Black Boomerang: An Autobiography. Volume II* (Secker & Warburg, 1962)

Donaldson, Frances *A Twentieth-Century Life* (Weidenfeld & Nicolson, 1992)

Dorril, Stephen *MI6: Fifty Years of Special Operations* (Fourth Estate, 2000)

Dorril, Stephen *Sir Oswald Mosley and British Fascism* (Viking, 2006)

Drazin, Charles *In Search of the Third Man* (Methuen, 1999)

Drazin, Charles *Korda: Britain's Only Movie Mogul* (Sidgwick & Jackson, 2002)

Duran, Leopoldo, translated by Euan Cameron *Graham Greene: Friend and Brother* (HarperCollins, 1994)

E. Johnston & Co. Ltd. *One Hundred Years of Coffee* (privately published, 1942)

Elliott, Nicholas *Never Judge a Man by His Umbrella* (Michael Russell, 1991)

Elliott, Nicholas *With My Little Eye* (Michael Russell, 1993)

Fallowell, Duncan *20th Century Characters* (Vintage, 1994)

Farndale, Nigel *Haw-Haw: The Tragedy of William and Margaret Joyce* (Macmillan, 2005)

Fielden, Lionel *The Natural Bent* (André Deutsch, 1960)

Fraser, Lindley *Propaganda* (Oxford University Press, 1957)

Fry, A. Ruth *The Quaker Adventure: The Story of Nine Years Relief and Reconstruction* (Nisbet, 1927)

Gannon, Franklin Reid *The British Press and Germany 1936–1939* (Oxford University Press, 1971)

Garnon Williams, R. H. *A History of Berkhamsted School 1541–1972* (privately published, 1980)

Gibbs, Victoria 'Dr Raymond Greene on Everest' (BSc thesis, Imperial College, London, 2009)

Gilbert, Martin *Kristallnacht: Prelude to Destruction* (HarperCollins, 2006)

Goldie, Grace Wyndham *Facing the Nation: Television and Politics 1936–1976* (The Bodley Head, 1977)

Goodman, Martin *Suffer and Survive: The Extreme Life of Dr J. S. Haldane* (Simon & Schuster, 2007)

Greene, Barbara *Land Benighted* (Geoffrey Bles, 1938) Reissued as *Too Late to Turn Back* (Settle Bendall, 1981)

Greene, Barbara *Valley of Peace* (Liechstenstein, 1947)

Greene, Barbara and Greene, Eva, (eds) *The Chance of a Lifetime: An Anthology for the Ageless* (Bond Wheelwright, 1968)

Greene, Barbara and Gollancz, Victor (eds.) *God of a Hundred Names: Prayers of Many Peoples and Creeds* (Gollancz, 1962)

Greene, Eva 'A Short History of the Greene and Stutzer Families: For her Grandchildren and Great-grandchildren' (Privately circulated TS, n.d.)

Greene, Eva 'The William Greenes at Bedford' (Privately circulated TS, n.d.)

Greene, Felix (ed.) *Time to Spare: What Unemployment Means, by Eleven Unemployed* (Allen & Unwin, 1935)

Greene, Felix *The Wall Has Two Sides* (Jonathan Cape, 1962)

Greene, Felix *Let There Be a World* (Victor Gollancz, 1963)

Greene, Felix *A Curtain of Ignorance* (Jonathan Cape, 1965)

Greene, Felix *Vietnam! Vietnam!* (Jonathan Cape, 1967)

Greene, Felix *The Enemy: Notes on Imperialism and Revolution* (Jonathan Cape, 1970)

Greene, Felix *Peking* (Jonathan Cape, 1978)

Greene, Graham *Journey without Maps* (Heinemann, 1936)

Greene, Graham *The Lawless Roads: A Mexican Journey* (Longmans, 1939)

Greene, Graham *The Lost Childhood and Other Essays* (Eyre & Spottiswoode, 1951)

Greene, Graham *Collected Essays* (The Bodley Head, 1969)

Greene, Graham *A Sort of Life* (The Bodley Head, 1971)

Greene, Graham *Ways of Escape* (The Bodley Head, 1980)

Greene, Graham (ed.) *The Old School: Essays by Diverse Hands* (Jonathan Cape, 1934)

Greene, Graham *Yours etc.: Letters to the Press 1945–1989* Christopher Hawtree (ed.) (Reinhardt Books, 1989)

Greene, Graham *Getting to Know the General: The Story of an Involvement* (The Bodley Head, 1984)

Greene, Graham *A World of My Own: A Dream Diary* (Reinhardt Books, 1992)

Greene, Graham and Greene, Hugh Carleton (eds) *The Spy's Bedside Book* (Rupert Hart-Davis, 1957)

Greene, Graham C. 'A Glance Back at Fifty Years in the British Book Trade' in Wm. Roger Louis (ed.) *Penultimate Adventures with Britannia: Personalities, Politics and Culture in Britain* (I.B. Tauris, 2007)

Greene, Hugh Carleton *The Third Floor Front: A View of Broadcasting in the Sixties* (The Bodley Head, 1969)

Greene, Hugh Carleton 'A Variety of Lives' (unpublished memoir, n.d.)

Greene, Raymond (ed.) *The Practice of Endocrinology* (Eyre & Spottiswoode, 1948)

Greene, Raymond *Moments of Being* (Heinemann, 1974)

Greene, Raymond (ed.) *Sick Doctors* (Heinemann Medical Books, 1971)

Greene, Raymond 'The Family of Greene' (Privately circulated history, n.d.)

Greene, Raymond Unpublished 1933 Everest Diary, (private collection)

Greene, Richard 'Owning Graham Greene: The Norman Sherry Project', (*University of Toronto Quarterly*, Fall 2006)

Greene, Richard (ed.) *Graham Greene: A Life in Letters* (Little, Brown 2007)

Griffiths, Richard *Fellow-Travellers of the Right: British Enthusiasts for Nazi Germany 1933–39* (Constable, 1980)

Griffiths, Richard *Patriotism Perverted: Captain Ramsay, The Right Club and British Anti-Semitism 1939–40* (Constable, 1998)

Grisewood, Harman *One Thing at a Time* (Hutchinson, 1968)

Hare, Steve (ed.) *Allen Lane and the Penguin Editors* (Penguin, 1997)

Harris, Percy Wyn Unpublished memoirs, (Alpine Club, n.d.)

Hart, Jenifer *Ask Me No More: An Autobiography* (Peter Halban, 1998)

Hart-Davis, Duff *The House the Berrys Built* (Hodder & Stoughton, 1990)

Hart-Davis, Rupert (ed.) *Two Men of Letters: Correspondence Between R.C. Hutchinson and Martyn Skinner 1957–1974* (Michael Joseph, 1979)

Hastings, Duke of Bedford *The Years of Transition* (Andrew Dakars, 1949)

Hawtree, Christopher (ed.) *Night and Day* (Chatto & Windus, 1985)

Hazzard, Shirley *Greene on Capri: A Memoir* (Virago, 2000)

Higham, David *Literary Gent* (Jonathan Cape, 1978)

Hill, Alan *The Pursuit of Publishing* (John Murray, 1988)

Hill, Charles *Behind the Screen: The Broadcasting Memories of Lord Hill of Luton* (Sidgwick & Jackson, 1974)

Hollander, Paul *Political Pilgrims: Travels of Western Intellectuals to the Soviet Union, China and Cuba 1928–1978* (Oxford University Press, 1981)

Hollingworth, Clare *The Three Weeks War in Poland* (Duckworth, 1940)

Hollingworth, Clare *Front Line* (Jonathan Cape, 1990)

Holman, Valerie *Print for Victory: Book Publishing in England 1939–1945* (British Library, 1945)

Holt, Thaddeus *The Deceivers: Allied Military Deception in the Second World War* (Weidenfeld & Nicolson, 2004)

Holzel, Tim and Salkeld, Andrew *The Mysteries of Mallory and Irvine* (Jonathan Cape, 1986)

Howard, Anthony *Crossman: The Pursuit of Power* (Jonathan Cape, 1990)

Howe, Ellic *The Black Game: British Subversive Operations against the Germans during the Second World War* (Michael Joseph, 1982)

Ingrams, Richard *Muggeridge: The Biography* (HarperCollins, 1995)

Isherwood, Christopher *Goodbye to Berlin* (Vintage, 1989)

Isherwood, Christopher *Kathleen and Frank* (Methuen, 1971)

Isherwood, Christopher *Christopher and His Kind 1929–1939* (Eyre Methuen, 1977)

Isherwood, Christopher *Diaries Volume One: 1939–1960* Katherine Bucknell ed. (Methuen, 1996)

Jennings, Christine *Widnall: A Capital Contriver* (Folly Press, 2003)

John, Otto, translated by Richard Barry, *Twice through the Lines* (Macmillan, 1972)

Kirkpatrick, Ivone *The Inner Circle: Memoirs* (Macmillan, 1959)

Knightley, Phillip *Philby: The Life and Views of the KGB Masterspy* (André Deutsch, 1988)

Knightley, Phillip *A Hack's Progress* (Jonathan Cape, 1997)

Korda, Michael *Another Life: A Memoir of Other People* (Random House, 1999)

Kotani, Ken *Japanese Intelligence in World War II* (Osprey, 2009)

Lambert, J.W. and Ratcliffe, Michael *The Bodley Head 1887–1987* (The Bodley Head, 1987)

Latey, Maurice *The Quest for the Bushmen* (privately published, n.d.)

Lewis, Roger *Anthony Burgess* (Faber, 2002)

Leys, Simon, translated by Steve Cox *Broken Images: Essays on Chinese Culture and Politics* (Allison & Busby, 1979)

Low, David *Dear David, Dear Graham: A Bibliographic Correspondence* (Alembic Press, 1989)

Lusty, Robert *Bound to be Read* (Jonathan Cape, 1975)

McDonald, Iverach *A Man of the Times: Talks and Travels in a Disrupted World* (Hamish Hamilton, 1976)

Maclaren-Ross, Julian *Memoirs of the Forties* (Alan Ross, 1965)

Mansell, Gerard *Let Truth Be Told: Fifty Years of BBC External Broadcasting* (Weidenfeld & Nicolson, 1982)

MacDonogh, Giles *1938: Hitler's Gamble* (Constable, 2009)

Marcuse, Jacques *Leaves from the Notebook of a China Correspondent* (Arthur Barker, 1967)

Maschler, Tom *Publisher* (Picador, 2005)

Masters, Anthony *The Man Who Was M: The Life of Maxwell Knight* (Blackwell, 1984)

Meehan, Patricia *A Strange Enemy People: Germans under the British* (Peter Owen, 2001)

Mewshaw, Michael *Do I Owe You Something? A Memoir of the Literary Life* (Louisiana University Press, 2003)

Meyer, Michael *Not Prince Hamlet: Literary and Theatrical Memoirs* (Secker & Warburg, 1989)

Miall, Leonard *Inside the BBC: British Broadcasting Characters* (Weidenfeld & Nicolson, 1994)

Miller, Joan *One Girl's War: Personal Exploits in MI5's Most Secret Station* (Brandon, 1986)

Milne, Alasdair *DG: The Memoirs of a British Broadcaster* (Hodder & Stoughton, 1988)

Mockler, Anthony *Graham Greene: Three Lives* (Hunter Mackay, 1994)

Montgomery Hyde, H *Norman Birkett: The Life of Lord Birkett of Ulverston* (Hamish Hamilton, 1964)

Moore, Charles and Hawtree, Christopher (eds) *1936 as Recorded by the Spectator* (Michael Joseph, 1986)

Morgan, Janet (ed.) *The Backbench Diaries of Richard Crossman* (Hamish Hamilton and Jonathan Cape, 1981)

Mosley, Charlotte (ed.) *The Letters of Nancy Mitford and Evelyn Waugh* (Hodder & Stoughton, 1996)

Mosley, Charlotte (ed.) *The Letters of Nancy Mitford* (Hodder & Stoughton, 1992)

Mosley, Leonard *The Cat and the Mice* (Arthur Barker, 1958)

Mosley, Leonard *The Druid* (Eyre Methuen, 1982)

Mosley, Nicholas *Beyond the Pale: Sir Oswald Mosley and Family 1933–80* (Secker & Warburg,1983)

Mosley, Oswald *My Life* (Nelson, 1968)

Muggeridge, Malcolm *The Infernal Grove: Chronicles of Wasted Time, Volume Two* (Collins, 1973)

Muggeridge, Malcolm Unpublished Diaries 1948–50 (private collection)

Mure, David *Practice to Deceive* (William Kimber, 1977)

Nashel, Jonathan *Edward Lansdale's Cold War* (University of Massachusetts Press, 2006)

Ondaatje, Michael *The English Patient* (Bloomsbury, 1992)

Overy, Richard *The Morbid Age: Britain Between the Wars* (Allen Lane, 2009)

Parker, Peter *Isherwood: A Life* (Picador, 2004)

Pearce, Brian Louis *The Widow of Gozo: A Play in Two Acts* (Magwood, 2002)

Pearce, Robert (ed.) *Patrick Gordon Walker: Political Diaries 1932–71* (Historians Press, 1991)

Pettifer, James (ed.) *Cockburn in Spain: Despatches from the Civil War* (Lawrence & Wishart, 1986)

Pimlott, Ben *Labour and the Left in the 1930s* (Cambridge University Press, 1977)

Philby, Kim *My Silent War* (MacGibbon & Kee, 1968)

Powell, Anthony *To Keep the Ball Rolling, Volume III: Faces in My Time* (Heinemann, 1980)

Powell, Anthony *Journals 1982–1986* (Heinemann, 1995)

Preston, Paul *We Saw Spain Die: Foreign Correspondents in the Spanish Civil War* (Constable, 2008)

Priestland, Gerald *Something Understood: An Autobiography* (André Deutsch, 1986)

Pugh, Martin *'Hurrah for the Blackshirts': Fascism and Fascists in Britain between the Wars* (Jonathan Cape, 2005)

Quennell, Peter, *The Marble Foot* (Collins, 1976)

Rankin, Nicholas *Dead Man's Chest: Travels after Robert Louis Stevenson* (Faber, 1987)

Rankin, Nicholas *Churchill's Wizards: The British Genius for Deception 1914–1945* (Faber, 2009)

Raverat, Gwen *Period Piece* (Faber, 1952)

Reinhardt, Max *Memoirs* (privately published, n.d.)

Rickards, Jocelyn *The Painted Banquet: My Life and Loves* (Weidenfeld & Nicolson, 1987)

Rose, Norman *Vansittart: Study of a Diplomat* (Heinemann, 1978)

Rothenstein, John *Time's Thievish Progress: Autobiography Volume III* (Cassell, 1970)

Rowse, A. L. *A Cornishman at Oxford* (Jonathan Cape, 1965)

Ruttledge, Hugh *Everest 1933* (Hodder & Stoughton, 1934)

Scannell, Paddy 'Broadcasting and the Politics of Unemployment', Polytechnic of Central London, 1980)

Seale, Patrick and McConville, Maureen *Philby: The Long Road to Moscow* (Hamish Hamilton, 1973)

Sebba, Anne *Enid Bagnold: The Authorized Biography* (Weidenfeld & Nicolson, 1986)

Shelden, Michael *Graham Greene: The Man Within* (Heinemann, 1994)

Sherry, Norman *The Life of Graham Greene. Volume I: 1904–1939* (Jonathan Cape, 1989)

Sherry, Norman *The Life of Graham Greene. Volume II: 1939–1955* (Jonathan Cape, 1994)

Sherry, Norman *The Life of Graham Greene. Volume III: 1955–1991* (Jonathan Cape 2004)

Shipton, Eric *Upon that Mountain* (Hodder & Stoughton, 1943)

Shirer, William *Berlin Diary* (Knopf, 1941)

Shirer, William *Twentieth-Century Journey: A Memoir of the Life and Times. Volume II: The Nightmare Years 1930–1940* (Little, Brown, 1984)

Short, Edward *Whip to Wilson* Macdonald, 1989

Simpson, A.W. Brian *In the Highest Degree Odious: Detention without Trial in Wartime Britain* (Oxford University Press, 1992)

Skidelsky, Robert *Oswald Mosley* (Macmillan, 1975)

Smith, Michael *Foley: The Spy Who Saved 10,000 Jews* (Hodder & Stoughton, 1999)

Smythe, F. S. *Kamet Conquered* (Gollancz, 1932)

Smythe, F. S. *Camp Six* (A&C Black, 1937)

Smythe, F. S. *The Adventures of a Mountaineer* (Dent, 1940)

Smythe, F. S. *The Spirit of the Hills* (Hodder & Stoughton, 1946)

Sorley Walker, Kathrine *Remembering Helga* (privately published, 1987)

Steele, Peter *Eric Shipton: Everest and Beyond* (Constable, 1998)

Stephen, Adrian *The 'Dreadnought' Hoax* (reissue) (Chatto & Windus, 1983)

St John, John *William Heinemann: A Century of Publishing 1890–1990* (Heinemann, 1990)

Stuart, Charles (ed.) *The Reith Diaries* (Collins, 1975)

Suyin, Han *The House Has Two Doors* (Jonathan Cape, 1980)

Symonds, John and Grant, Kenneth (eds.) *The Confessions of Aleister Crowley: An Autohagiography* (Jonathan Cape, 1969)

Taylor, John Russell *The Pleasure-Dome: The Collected Film Criticism 1935–40 of Graham Greene* (Secker & Warburg, 1972)

Thomson, Ian (ed.) *Articles of Faith: The Collected Tablet Journalism of Graham Greene* (Signal Books, 2007)

Thurlow, Richard *Fascism in Britain: A History 1918–1985* (Blackwell, 1987)

Tracey, Michael *A Variety of Lives: A Biography of Sir Hugh Greene* (The Bodley Head, 1983)

Trevor-Roper, Hugh *The Philby Affair* (William Kimber, 1968)

Unsworth, Walt *Everest* (Oxford Illustrated Press, 1989)

Vassiltchikov, Marie *The Berlin Diaries 1940–1945* (Chatto & Windus, 1985)

Walker, Martin *The National Front* (Fontana, 1977)

Waugh, Evelyn *A Little Learning* (Chapman & Hall, 1964)

Webb, Barry *Edmund Blunden: A Biography* (Yale University Press, 1990)

West, Nigel *MI6: British Secret Intelligence Service Operations 1909–45* (Weidenfeld & Nicolson, 1983)

West, Nigel *Counterfeit Spies: Real or Bogus?* (St Ermine's Press, 1998)

West, Nigel (ed.) *The Guy Liddell Diaries Volume I: 1939–1942* (Routledge, 2005)

West, W. J. *Truth Betrayed* (Duckworth, 1987)

West, W. J. *The Quest for Graham Greene* (Weidenfeld & Nicolson, 1997)

Wheeler-Bennett, John *Knaves, Fools and Heroes* (Macmillan, 1974)

Whitehouse, Mary *A Most Dangerous Woman?* (Lion Publishing, 1982)

Wilson, R. G. *Greene King: A Business and Family History* (The Bodley Head and Jonathan Cape, 1983)

Winterbottom, D. O. *Doctor Fry: A Study of Thomas Charles Fry* (Clobury Cottrell Press, 1977)

Wolf, Markus *Man Without a Face: The Autobiography of Communism's Greatest Spymaster* (Jonathan Cape, 1997)

Woodehouse, C.M. *The Rise and Fall of the Greek Colonels* (Granada, 1985)

Young, Kenneth (ed.) *The Diaries of Sir Robert Bruce Lockhart, Volume II: 1939–1965* (Macmillan, 1980)

Ziegler, Philip *Rupert Hart-Davis: Man of Letters* (Chatto & Windus, 2004)

Reference Notes

Where it is obvious who is writing to whom, I have given the date only (or 'n.d.' where unknown) of letters, followed by the source from which it is quoted or the collection in which it is to be found. I have used the following abbreviations:

Barbara: Barbara Greene
BG: Ben Greene
FG: Felix Greene
GG: Graham Greene
HCG: Hugh Greene
HG: Herbert Greene

Barham: *Alice Greene: Teacher and Campaigner*
Flanagans: material gathered for unpublished biography of Felix Greene by Pat and Julie Flanagan
ODNB: Oxford Dictionary of National Biography
TS of *Variety of Lives*: uncut and unedited version of Michael Tracey's biography of Hugh Greene
BL: British Library
Bodleian: Bodleian Library, Oxford
Boston: Boston College
Caversham: BBC Archives, Caversham
Georgetown: Georgetown University Library
HRHRC: Harry Ransom Humanities Research Center, Austin, Texas
Morgan: The Morgan Library and Museum, New York.
NA: National Archives
p.c.: private collection
Reading: Reading University Library
Rushden: Random House archives, Rushden, Northants.
Tulsa: McFarlin Library, University of Tulsa

Chapter 1: Ancestral Voices

p.1 'fills me with distaste . . .': 5 Dec. 1974, Boston.

p.1 'I must admit . . .': 16 Dec. 1974, Boston.

p.1 'one of the family': q. in Rankin, *Dead Man's Chest*, p.68.

p.3 'He is king . . .': 25 Nov. 1892, Barham, p.195.

p.4 'the scene of continuous hospitality . . .': Isherwood, *Kathleen and Frank*, p.3.

p.6 'hair like spun gold . . .': Eva Greene, 'The William Greenes at Bedford'.

p.6 'frustrated romantic nature': *A Sort of Life*, p.94.

p.6 'nervous, highly-strung man . . .': Eva Greene, *ibid*.

p.7 'I left him . . .': q. in *A Sort of Life*, p.94.

p.7 'Like Mama . . .': q. in *A Sort of Life*, p.95.

p.8 'as if there had been a leaf . . .': 1 Jan. 1883, q. Eva Greene, *ibid*.

p.8 'There's nothing like . . .': 6 March 1881, q, Eva Greene, *ibid*.

p.8 'Macaulay made . . .': 24 Jan. 1882, q. Eva Greene, *ibid*.

p.8 'It seems his intention . . .': to Alice 10 May 1901, Barham p.559.

p.8 'felt he must . . .': to GG, 16 Sept. 1971, Boston.

p.9 'the octopus of Whitehall': q. in Raymond Greene. 'The Family of Greene'.

p.9 'Very remote my uncle . . .': *A Sort of Life*, p.30.

p.9 'one of those half-dead men': q. in *ODNB*.

p.9 'The place looked very cold . . .': to Alice Greene, 25 Feb. 1890, p.c.

p.10 'Nothing doing': October 1927, Churchill Archives Centre, Churchill College, Cambridge.

p.10 'It was most interesting . . .': q. in Raymond Greene, 'The Family of Greene'.

p.10 'a conscientious, zealous . . .': *The Times*, 11 Sept. 1950.

p.11 'the centre of my youthful . . .': *Period Piece*, p.63.

p.11 'dear muddle-headed Polly . . .': *A Sort of Life*, p.32.

p.11 'afflicted with insanity': Edward Greene to Alice Greene, 8 July 1891, q. in Barham, p. 162.

p.11 'a merciful end . . .': 1 Dec. 1897, Barham, p.399.

p.11 'It would have been better . . .': 17 Sept. 1891, Barham, p.163.

p.11 'It is sad, but . . .': 30 Jan. 1890, Barham, p.125.

Chapter 2: Two Brothers

p.12 'Of course you have heard . . .': 2 May 1889, Barham, p.89.

p.13 'I am looking forward . . .': 28 Sept. 1887, Barham, p.25.

p.13 'coal-heavers . . .': 8 July 1889, Barham, p.104.

p.13 'The only thing . . .': *ibid*.

p.13 'after lurching around a bit . . .': 10 Dec. 1890, *ibid*, p.145.

p.13 'Dear old Eppy . . .': 25 Feb. 1891, *ibid*, p.150.

p.13 'I can't tell you . . .': 26 April 1891, *ibid*, p.152.

p.13 'I am glad to say . . .': 8 July 1891, *ibid*, p.162.

p.13 'Rio itself . . .': *ibid* p.161.

p.15 'they are dealing . . .': q. in Bacha and Greenhill, *150 Years of Coffee*, p.177.

p.15 'Miss Sewell . . .': 21 Oct. 1892, p.c.

p.16 'is much older . . .': 19 Aug. 1901, Barham, p.574.

p.16 'did not go much beyond . . .': Eva Greene, 'A Brazilian Boarding School in 1896', n.d., p.c.

p.16 'Poor Eva came in . . .': 21 March 1901, Barham, p.552.

p.17 'even mother, . . .': 19 Aug. 1901, Barham, p. 574.

p.17 'a gracious William and Mary building . . .': Eva Greene, 'A Short History . . .'

p.17 'ordinary daily life . . .': *ibid*.

p.17 'very serious . . .': *ibid*.

p.17 'giving her an almost nun-like appearance . . .': *ibid*.

p.19 'The condescending way . . .': 25 Sept. 1909, p.c.

p.19 'He could not live . . .': 3 Jan. 1910, p.c.

p.19 'I do wish . . .': 16 Sept. 1971, Boston.

p.20 'middle-aged, small . . .': Eva Greene, *op. cit.*

p.20 'forgetting all his English . . .': 29 Sept. 1909, p.c.

p.20 'A beautiful little boy . . .': Eva Greene diary, 10 July 1910.

p.20 'He takes all the little . . .': to Alice, 29 Sept 1909, p.c.

p.20 'wailing in piteous tones . . .': to Alice, 11 Oct. 1909, p.c.

p.20 'rather slow . . .': to Alice 11 Oct. 1909, p.c.

p.20 'In spite of being . . .': Eva Greene diary, 10 July 1910.

p.21 'I do miss you . . .': 18 Aug. 1909, p.c.

p.21 'I found him . . .': 17 Aug. 1909, p.c.

p.21 'as soon as we dropped anchor . . .': 25 Aug. 1909, p.c.

p.21 'He eats so little . . .': 28 Aug. 1909, p.c.

p.21 'half angels . . .': 8 Sept. 1909, p.c.

p.22 'so happy here . . .': 31 Sept. 1909, private collection.

p.22 'a charming little fellow . . .': to Alice, 25 Oct. 1909, p.c.

p.22 'Ben must go to school . . .': to Alice, 20 Feb. 1910, p.c.

p.22 'as gentle as an old cow': to Alice, 31 Sept. 1909 p.c.

p.22 'in a wonderland . . .': to Alice, 5 Nov. 1909, p.c.

p.22 'He is a queer little fellow . . .': n.d. 1909, p.c.

p.22 'Eppy begins . . .': to Alice, 11 Jan. 1910, p.c.

p.22 'A few white-clad Englishmen . . .': 17 Nov. 1909, p.c.

p.23 'The ball is flying high . . .': Eva Greene diary, 10 July 1910.

p.23 'Alas, I have given up . . .': Christmas 1887, Barham, p.38.

p.23 'Helen is to go': 12 Jan. 1894, ibid, p.233.

p.23 'It is rather amusing . . .': to Alice, 22 Feb. 1894, ibid, p.236.

p.24 'Charlie spoke to me . . .': 10 Oct. 1995, ibid, p.311.

p.24 'I have been very far from happy . . .': 3 Nov. 1895, ibid, p.312.

p.24 'I have no doubt . . .': 23 Nov. 1895, ibid, p.317.

p.24 'Marion is a good . . .': to Graham Greene, 3 Nov. 1896, ibid, p.312.

p.24 'I do hope Marion . . .': to Alice, 10 Oct. 1895, ibid, p.311.

p.24 'a fine example . . .': to Alice, 23 Nov. 1895, ibid, p.317.

p.24 'To Helen . . .': ibid.

p.25 'went off capitally . . .': to Alice, 22 Jan. 1896, ibid, p.343.

p.25 'Charlie is purchasing . . .': 31 Oct. 1896, ibid, p.374.

Chapter 3: Hall and School House Greenes

p.26 'drab, prosaic town': *The Marble Foot*, p.57.

p.26 'I walked down . . .': *The Lawless Roads*, p.17.

p.26 'ugly alms-houses . . .': *Twenty-One Stories*, p.47.

p.27 'the Grand Junction canal . . .': *A Sort of Life*, p.11.

p.27 'The long secret trek . . .': ibid, p.66.

p.27 'began to develop a love . . .': *The Lawless Roads*, p.17.

p.27 'across the canal bridge . . .': *The Human Factor*, p.17.

p.27 'Part rosy Tudor . . .': *A Sort of Life*, p.12.

p.28 'humdrum institution': *The Marble Foot*, p.64.

p.28 'a repulsive redbrick chapel . . .': ibid.

p.28 'sinister sadistic predecessor . . .': *A Sort of Life*, p.66.

p.29 'considered opinion . . .': Walter Versfeld to GG, 9 April 1972, Boston.

p.29 'a great pest . . .': to Walter Versfeld, 24 April 1972, Boston.

p.29 'I remember your tall, beautiful mother . . .': A.G. Pearson to GG, 28 June 1974, Boston.

p.29 'the young dandyish man . . .': *A Sort of Life*, p.24.

p.29 'very beautiful, very dignified . . .': q. in Tracey, *A Variety of Lives*, p.5.

p.29 'I never thought of it . . .': to GG, 16 Sept. 1971, Boston.

p.29 'I associate my mother . . .': *A Sort of Life*, p.17.

p.30 'even more distant . . .': ibid, p.26.

p.30 'I think my only real moments . . .': ibid, p.23.

p.30 'sitting in a pram . . .': ibid, p.14.

p.30 'struck out for the shore': ibid, p.21.

p.30 'my mother's remoteness . . .': ibid, p.27.

p.31 'was far more used . . .': Barbara

Greene, autobiographical sketch, p.c.

p.31 'my life's first tragedy . . .': *ibid.*

p.31 'There were few rules . . .': *ibid.*

p.31 'we heard the dreaded words . . .': *ibid.*

p.32 'We lived in an atmosphere . . .': FG to the Flanagans, p.c.

p.32 'our cousins at the School House . . .': *ibid.*

p.32 'an intimidatingly exotic air': *A Sort of Life*, p.18.

p.32 'were inserted between us . . .': *ibid*, p.19.

p.32 'I used to be embarrassed . . .': *ibid.*

p.33 'no stone of it now remains . . .': *ibid*, p.35.

p.33 'terrified by a witch . . .': *ibid*, p.29.

p.33 'occasionally disturbed . . .': HCG, 'A Variety of Lives', Bodleian.

p.33 'Two countries just here . . .': *The Lawless Roads*, p.13.

p.34 'In the land of the skyscrapers . . .': *ibid*, p.14.

p.34 'she paid occasional state visits . . .': *A Sort of Life*, p.17.

p.34 'I am alone, unobserved . . .': HCG, 'A Variety of Lives', Bodleian.

p.35 'my trailing skirts . . .': *ibid.*

p.35 'My father and mother were remote . . .': *ibid.*

p.35 'Those hours of listening . . .': HCG, 'Childhood with Graham': unpublished memoir, Bodleian.

p.36 'I hated every minute . . .': *Daily Mail*, 17 Oct. 1960.

p.36 'a good deal of undeserved contempt': *A Sort of Life*, p.59.

p.36 'minor cuts and bruises':Raymond Greene, *Moments of Being*, p.3.

p.37 'except that I once teased . . .': *A Sort of Life*, p.63.

p.37 'The clouds of unknowing . . .': *ibid*, p.70.

Chapter 4: A Country under Occupation

p.38 'we often sighted . . .': *The Marble Foot*, p.65.

p.38 'efforts were made . . .': *Cockburn Sums Up*, p.18.

p.39 'In my youth . . .': *op. cit.*

p.39 'I liked your portrait . . .': 21 Oct. 1971, Boston.

p.39 'was never during school hours . . .': *A Sort of Life*, p.112.

p.39 'the tone of the school . . .': q. in *A Variety of Lives*, p.11.

p.39 'a dear old man . . .': q. in Hart-Davis (ed.), *Two Men of Letters*, p.42.

p.39 'I had a great respect . . .': Walter Versfeld to GG, 9 April 1972, Boston.

p.40 'Although he had to give me . . .': Charles Seltman to Marion Greene, 17 Nov. 1942, p.c.

p.40 'Through his learning, . . .': q. in Williams, *A History of Berkhamsted School*, p.252.

p.40 'were not so much history . . .': *op. cit.*, p.19.

p.40 'that sleepy little town . . .': *The Spirit of the Hills*, p.12.

p.40 'Well, the little squit . . .': *High Mountains and Cold Seas*, p.32.

p.40 'because he had been seen . . .': *A Sort of Life*, p.64.

p.40 'in case the "enemy" . . .': *op. cit.*, p.13.

p.40 'A German master . . .': *A Sort of Life*, p.64.

p.40 'I actually met . . .': Lady Harrigan to GG, 20 June 1972, Boston.

p.41 'Next day . . .': *The Marble Foot*, p.73.

p.41 'manifest indications . . .': Cockburn, *op. cit.*, p.20.

p.41 'his slightly bulbous . . .': *op. cit.*, p.19.

p.42 'not at all fashionable . . .': *op. cit.*,p.64.

p.42 'we were constantly hungry . . .': *Evening Standard*, 16 Oct. 1965.

p.42 'the system of education . . .': *op. cit.*, p.13.

p.42 'There was a schoolroom . . .': *A Sort of Life*, p.72.

p.43 'pale red hair . . .': W.A. Saunders to GG 29 Nov. 1971, Boston.

p.43 'I cannot imagine . . .': *Hertfordshire Countryside*, April 1979.

p.43 '"Well, there must have been . . ."': Cloetta, *In Search of a Beginning*, p.41.

p.43 'I had not realised . . .': 16 Sept. 1971, Boston.

p.43 'What a lot began . . .': *The Lawless Roads*, p.

p.44 'Graham was a very sensitive child . . .': Marion Greene to Vivien Greene, 29 June 1948, Tulsa.

p.44 'I suppose I complained . . .': *A Sort of Life*, p.90.

p.44 'felt great pride . . .': *ibid*, p.91.

p.44 'to express himself in writing . . .': *op. cit.*

p.45 'the six months I spent . . .': 27 Aug. 1971, *A Life in Letters*, p.313.

p.45 'but then he said no . . .': q. in Shelden, *Graham Greene*, p.126.

p.45 'a quiet, withdrawn boy': letter from Hilary Root to GG, 24 Sept. 1971, Boston.

p.45 'His talk had had an exuberantly . . .': *The Marble Foot*, p.98.

p.46 'he would leave the bacon . . .': *Cockburn Sums Up*, p.21.

p.46 'the heaviest forward . . .': St John's House Record Book, 1918.

p.46 'an engineer . . .': 'Eppy's children: 1914', misc. notes, Nov. 1914, p.c.

p.46 'a coffee merchant . . .': *ibid*.

p.47 'the Government are justified . . .': *The Berkhamstedian*, Dec. 1917.

p.47 'one nation would . . .': *ibid*, April 1919.

p.47 'he exhorted . . .': *ibid*, Oct. 1919.

p.47 'loved mountains . . .': *Moments of Being*, p.1.

p.47 'the great pioneer . . .': *ibid*, p.2.

p.47 'We want contributions . . .': *The Berkhamstedian*, Dec. 1919.

p.48 'Believe us, reader . . .': *ibid*, July 1920.

p.48 'spoke at some length . . .': *ibid*, March 1922.

p.48 'a quantity of fossils . . .': *ibid*, July 1922.

p.48 'was like a great wave . . .': HCG, 'A Variety of Lives', Bodleian.

p.48 'when the time came . . .': *ibid*.

p.49 'completely docile . . .': q. in Tracey, *A Variety of Lives*, p.16.

p.49 'a tall, remote intellectual': A.G. Pearson to GG, 28 June 1974, Boston.

p.49 'I learned for the first time . . .': HCG, 'A Variety of Lives', Bodleian.

Chapter 5: Oxford Adventures

p.51 'doctrinaire socialism': Ben Greene, unpublished writings, p.c.

p.51 'my spiritual home . . .': *ibid*.

p.53 'C.R. Greene is . . .': *The Berkhamstedian*, Dec. 1922.

p.53 'the hatred of institutional life . . .': unpublished MS, p.c.

p.53 'I didn't know . . .': unpublished MS, p.c.

p.53 'I have looked upon literature . . .': unpublished MS, p.c.

p.55 'possessed every qualification . . .': Crowley, *Confessions*, p.904.

p.55 'very attractive . . .': *Moments of Being*, p. 20.

p.56 'Naturally one's first impulse . . .': 1 March 1923, p.c.

p.57 'a bunch of very queer . . .': 30 Sept. 1968, Reading.

p.57 'He was a big man . . .': *Moments of Being*, p.25.

p.57 'the architect . . .': *Moments of Being*, p.3.

p.57 'the most terrifying weekend . . .': *ibid*.

p.58 'I didn't think . . .': *ibid*.

p.58 'when I knew . . .': *ibid*.

p.59 'rumours had reached . . .': *ibid* p.17.

p.59 'Cockburn and G. Greene . . .': *The Berkhamstedian*, Dec. 1922.

p.59 'I guessed you . . .': to Marion Greene, n.d., BL.

p.59 'tall, spectacled . . .': *A Little Learning*, p.200.

p.59 'schoolboyish zest . . .': *Oxford Dictionary of National Biography*.

p.59 'rather tedious . . .': *The Marble Foot*, p.113.

p.60 'the impression that . . .': *op. cit.*

p.60 'I was not suffering . . .': 10 Sept. 1964, BL.

p.60 'For nearly one term . . .': *A Sort of Life*, p.135.

p.60 'Why Graham . . .': *The Marble Foot*, p.113.

p.60 'There was also . . .': 10 Sept. 1964, BL.

p.60 'overwhelmed . . .': 15 Nov. 1923, BL.

p.61 'I hope it will not be . . .': n.d., Bodleian.

p.61 'extraordinarily nice . . .': to Marion Greene, 15 June 1923, BL.

p.61 'your comprehension . . .': 15 June 1923, BL.

p.61 'I enjoyed . . .': 23 Jan 1925, Georgetown.

p.62 'extraordinarily youthful . . .': *A Cornishman at Oxford*, p.207.

p.63 'nearly a giant . . .': q. in Sebba, *Enid Bagnold*, p.112.

p.63 'he was such a complete . . .': to Julia Stonor, 30 March 1987, Bodleian.

p.63 'I thought in those days . . .': q. in Sebba, *op. cit.*

p.63 'I can remember still . . .': *A Sort of Life*, p.139.

p.63 'everybody glowered . . .': to Marion Greene, 17 April 1924, Bodleian.

p.64 'one insignificant . . .': *A Sort of Life*, p.143.

p.65 'like a recurring flu': *ibid*, p.146.

p.65 'How miserable . . .': to Marion Greene, n.d., BL.

p.65 'I can't help now . . .': q. in Tracey, *A Variety of Lives*, p.16.

p.65 'totally rational . . .': n.d., Bodleian.

p.66 'a miserable affair . . .': to Eva Greene, 17 Feb. 1923, p.c..

p.66 'Houses stand . . .': *ibid*.

p.67 'as big as Tooter's bedroom . . .': to Eva Greene. 1 March 1923, p.c.

p.67 'a priceless sort of place . . .': *ibid*.

p.67 'Lucy Sampson . . .': *ibid*.

p.67 'Ben almost fills . . .': March 1923, p.c.

p.67 'they will be very useful . . .': to Edward Greene, 6 March 1923, p.c.

p.68 'the Bolsheviks . . .': to Edward Greene, 26 May 1923, p.c.

p.68 'Bolsheviks were not half . . .': to Felix Greene, 19 April 1923, p.c.

p.68 'A 100 per cent . . .': *ibid*.

p.68 'one goes to . . .': 6 April 1923, p.c.

p.68 'has lifted Russia . . .': *ibid*.

p.68 'as only a German . . .': to Felix Greene, *op. cit.*

p.68 'I am getting keener . . .': *ibid*.

p.69 'proud flag . . .': to Edward Greene,19 July 1923, p.c.

Chapter 6: Climbing Ahead

p.71 'this damned desire . . .': GG to Catherine Walston, 25 Dec. 1950, Georgetown.

p.71 'I learned more . . .': *Moments of Being*, p.45.

p.72 'we made snide remarks . . .': *ibid*, p.87.

p.72 'I've been let into . . .': 13 June 1925, BL.

p.72 'My precious baby . . .': 4 Oct. 1925, HRHRC.

p.73 'I was interested that . . .': *A Sort of Life*, p.161.

p.73 'I was feeling . . .': March 1925, HRHRC.

p.73 'I've never really . . .': 26 May 1925, HRHRC.

p.73 'an excess . . .': 27 Feb. 1991, q. in *A Life in Letters*, p.420.

p.73 'I am so glad . . .': n.d., HRHRC.

p.73 'Darling pusskin . . .': n.d., HRHRC.

p.73 'I always feel . . .': n.d., HRHRC.

p.74 'the months passed . . .': *Ways of Escape*, p.13.

p.74 'Uncle E . . .': 14 April 1925, BL.

p.74 'so it would put . . .': to Marion Greene, 16 Aug. 1925, BL.

p.74 'I'm awfully sorry . . .': 4 June 1925, BL.

p.75 'an awfully nice man . . .': 22 May 1925, BL.

p.75 'When I read Dickens . . .': *A Sort of Life*, p.157.

p.75 'Everyone hates him . . .': 17 Dec. 1925, BL.

p.76 'the illegitimate child . . .' Bodley Head files, September 1971, Reading.

p.76 'It was only fair . . .': *A Sort of Life*, p.161.

p.76 'a very tall . . .': *ibid*, p.162.

p.76 'It was on the ground . . .': *ibid*, p.164.

p.77 'I can think of no better . . .': *ibid*, p.171.

p.77 'I've been through . . .': 23 Feb. 1928, BL.

p.77 'I'm afraid Herbert's . . .': 31 May 1928, May.

p.78 'a memory of which . . .': diary entry, 11 Aug. 1933, HRHRC.

p.78 'Are people who write . . .': 13 Oct. 1926, HRHRC.

p.78 'There is a splinter . . .': *A Sort of Life*, p.185.

p.79 'I've never met . . .': 17 Aug. 1925, HRHRC.

p.79 'Ooo darling . . .': 1 April 1927, HRHRC.

p.79 'I'm going to marry . . .': 28 Sept. 1927, HRHRC.

p.79 'My mother-in-law . . .': q. in Shelden, *Graham Greene*, p.136.

p.79 'I haven't had . . .': 29 March 1928, BL.

p.80 'I could never . . .': 2 July 1928, Bodleian.

p.80 'wildly happy . . .': Oct. 1930, Bodleian.

p.80 'I'm simply parched . . .': n.d., Bodleian.

p.80 'Nothing in . . .': *A Sort of Life*, p.191.

p.80 'It could only . . .': *ibid*, p.193.

p.80 'With his bald head . . .': *ibid*.

p.80 'trembling with . . .': *The Pursuit of Publishing*, p.36.

p.80 'he had the air . . .': *Literary Gent*, p.170.

p.81 'The bearer . . .': *ibid*.

p.81 'We went to . . .': 26 June 1929, Georgetown.

p.81 'great fun . . .': 13 Jan. 1929, *A Life in Letters*, p.32.

p.81 'foresaw a time . . .': *A Sort of Life*, p.195.

p.82 'I thought I was . . .': *ibid*.

p.82 'it was a thoroughly . . .': q. in St John, *William Heinemann*, p.294.

p.82 'I think it was Stevenson's . . .': to Sir James Marjoribanks, 12 Nov. 1985, Georgetown.

p.82 'I'm glad that you . . .': n.d., Georgetown.

p.82 '*The Man Within* is . . .': 20 Oct. 1929, BL.

p.82 'Herbert is again . . .': 21 May 1931, p.c.

p.83 'the eternal Herbert . . .': 9 May 1931, p.c.

p.83 'Uncle Charlie was . . .':to Sir James Marjoribanks, 12 Nov. 1985, Georgetown.

p.83 'Raymond and Charlotte . . .': 10 June 1930, p.c.

p.83 'caged feelings': to Eleanor Gamble, 12 April 1933, p.c.

p.83 'I know that . . .': to Marion Greene, 11 Oct. 1930, BL.

p.83 'Raymond ménage . . .': 21 Oct, 1930, p.c.

p.83 'What a pity . . .': 11 Oct. 1930, BL.

p.84 'It is strange how . . .': 21 Dec. 1930, p.c.

p.84 'a rather frail . . .': *Moments of Being*, p.94.

p.85 'tried always . . .': *ibid*, p.95.

p.85 'a period of calm . . .': *ibid*, p.96.

p.85 'Your friend in . . .': *Kamet Conquered*, p.32.

p.85 'the man who is . . .': 'A Doctor on the Mountain', n.d.

p.86 'thoroughly understood . . .': *Kamet Conquered*, p.34.

p.86 'I was never . . .': *Moments of Being*, p.94.

p.86 'must be something . . .': 'A Doctor on the Mountain', n.d.

p.87 'ragged and odorous . . .': *Kamet Conquered*, p.44.

p.87 'analgesics . . .': 'A Doctor on the Mountain', n.d.

p.87 'look on the boiling . . .': *ibid*.

p.87 'stentorian bellows . . .': *Kamet Conquered*, p.78.

p.88 'exuded strong odours . . .': *ibid*, p.105.

p.88 'lumbered along . . .': *ibid*, p.140.

p.88 'even Greene's . . .': *ibid*. p.119.

p.88 'we saw Kamet . . .': *Adventures of a Mountaineer*, p.162.

p.88 'after my own heavings . . .': *Kamet Conquered*, p.155.

p.88 'tapping out . . .': *Alpine Journal*, Nov. 1949.

p.89 'at a rhythmical pace . . .': *Kamet Conquered*, p.217.

p.90 'we could not help . . .': *ibid*, p.235.

p.90 '"Certainly", replied . . .': *ibid*, p.244.

p.90 'it was amusing . . .': *ibid*.

p.90 'a scene of utter . . .': *Moments of Being*, p.109.

p.91 'partly because . . .': to 16 Oct. 1931, Reading.

Chapter 7: No Love Lost

p.92 'a restrictive . . .': 'Analytical Therapy': unpublished TS, n.d., p.c.

p.93 'real dramatic . . .': FG's school report, 1926. p.c.

p.94 'I am getting to know . . .': 1 Jan. 1928, p.c.

p.94 'Thank goodness . . .': 7 Jan. 1928, p.c.

p.95 'only talk to one . . .': *ibid*.

p.95 'I looked over . . .': 22 March 1928, p.c.

p.95 'and extraordinarily . . .': to Flanagans, 3 Aug. 1983, p.c.

p.95 'She is the most . . .': n.d. 1928, p.c.

p.96 'There are eight . . .': 18 Sept. 1929, p.c.

p.96 'disowned me . . .': interview with Flanagans, 28 June 1982, p.c.

p.96 'I have completely . . .': to Flanagans, 7 March 1983, p.c.

p.96 'Well, never . . .': FG to Flanagans, n.d., p.c.

p.96 'I want to leave . . .': to parents, 24 May 1929, p.c.

p.96 'There is no feeling . . .': 30 April 1930, p.c.

p.97 'It seems like . . .': 22 March 1930, p.c.

p.97 'When I get . . .': 6 April 1930, p.c.

p.97 'Up to now . . .': 30 Sept. 1930, p.c.

p.98 'deprived me . . .': 16 Sept. 1930, p.c.

p.98 'If only Papa . . .': 6 April 1930, p.c.

p.98 'They always make . . .': 27 May 1930, p.c.

p.98 'you will not be . . .': 4 July 1930, p.c.

p.99 'terribly ashamed . . .': q. in Flanagans, draft chapter, n.d.

p.99 'when he plunges . . .': 5 Aug. 1930, p.c.

p.99 'Ramsay . . .': ibid.

p.99 'Ben has never . . .': 30 Sept. 1930, p.c.

p.99 'failed at Kepston's . . .': 16 Sept. 1930, p.c.

p.99 'Dear, magnificent . . .': Eva Greene to FG, 28 June 1930, p.c.

p.99 'that old hopeless . . .': 24 May 1929, p.c.

p.99 'There are strange . . .': 14 June 1931, p.c.

p. 99 'Heard the full . . .': diary, 23 Nov. 1932, HRHRC.

p.100 'I first knew . . .': to Flanagans, n.d., p.c.

p.100 'I had fled . . .': unpublished MS, n.d., p.c.

p.101 'I knew full well . . .': to Flanagans, n.d., p.c.

p.101 'You are my very life . . .': n.d., p.c.

p.101 'I can see myself . . .': HCG, 'A Variety of Lives', Bodleian.

p.102 'noted for . . .': ibid.

p.102 'Mr Greene, sir . . .': ibid.

p.102 'he looked the . . .': ibid.

p.102 'If I was able . . .': ibid.

p.102 'a sport fit only . . .': ibid.

p.102 'Beware of . . .': 25 May 1930, Georgetown.

p.103 'Mrs Roberts . . .': q. in Tracey, A Variety of Lives, p.27.

p.103 'obnoxious cocktails . . .': n.d., Bodleian.

p.103 'three of the main . . .': q. in Tracey, op. cit., p.25.

p.103 'mildly disappointed . . .': HCG, 'A Variety of Lives', Bodleian.

p.104 'stressing her . . .': ibid.

p.104 'very reluctantly . . .': 12 Oct. 1933, Reading.

Chapter 8: Aspects of England

p.105 'what I suffered . . .': diary, 14 July 1932, HRHRC.

p.105 'My faintings . . .': diary, 19 July 1932, HRHRC.

p.106 'My nerves . . .': diary, 10 July 1932, HRHRC.

p.106 'the noise of mice . . .': 25 Oct. 1932, HRHRC.

p.106 'the courage and understanding . . .': Ways of Escape, p.31.

p.106 'we are on the verge . . .': 20 July 1932, Georgetown.

p.106 'I felt great . . .': diary, 7 June 1932, HRHRC.

p.106 'since then . . .': Ways of Escape, p.26.

p.106 'Graham is very unattractive . . .': q. in Ziegler, Rupert Hart-Davis, p.78.

p.107 'I want to approach you . . .': ibid.

p.107 'my three guaranteed years . . .': A Sort of Life, p.207.

p.107 'There is no spark . . .': ibid, p.202.

p.107 'An unfavourable . . .': Ways of Escape, p.19.

p.108 'deliberately set out . . .': ibid, p.26.

p.108 'The best I could do . . .': ibid.

p.108 'trembling hands': diary, 9 Aug. 1932, HRHRC.

p.108 'the pages are too laden . . .': A Sort of Life, p.208.

p.108 'any losses . . .': diary, 1 Sept. 1932, HRHRC.

p.108 'under the influence of sun . . .': Ziegler, op. cit.

p.109 'offered little hope': diary, 1 Sept. 1932, HRHRC.

p.109 'a piece of sheer . . .': diary, 1 Nov. 1932, HRHRC.

p.109 'His family had all . . .': 29 Nov. 1932, BL.

p.110 'never been more uncertain . . .': 4 April 1933, Georgetown.

p.110 'was arrested . . .': diary, 4 Jan. 1933, HRHRC.

p.110 'Wrote to Raymond . . .': diary, 30 Sept. 1932, HRHRC.

p.110 'I can't bear . . .': diary, 18 April 1933, HRHRC.

p.110 'terribly broken . . .': diary, 21 May 1933, HRHRC.

p.110 'Aunt Eva was . . .': diary, 2 July 1933, HRHRC.

p.110 'I don't care . . .': diary, 29 Dec. 1933, HRHRC.

p.111 'went up and down . . .': diary, 1 Sept. 1932, HRHRC.

p.111 'a trying position': diary, 19 Oct. 1932, HRHRC.

p.111 'One sees his blood . . .': diary, 12 Jan. 1933, HRHRC.

p.111 'I'm terribly sorry . . .': 12 May 1931, BL.

p.112 'Marion was the driving . . .': q. in Shelden, Graham Greene, p.137.

p.112 'I seem to have gate-crashed . . .': diary, 28 Feb. 1934.

p.113 'How extraordinarily . . .': 15 March 1932, BL.

p.113 'of course the ubiquitous . . .': to HCG 11 March 1934, Georgetown.

p.114 'I stand firmly . . .': q. in Flanagans, n.d.

p.114 '"Felix kept on . . ."': Barbara to Flanagans, 5 Feb. 1982, p.c.

p.114 'a futile body': FG to Eva and Edward Greene, 18 Feb. 1933, p.c.

p.114 'It astonishes me . . .': 18 Aug. 1932, p.c.

p.115 'He was reported . . .': P.N. Furbank, E.M. Forster: A Life Vol. 2, p. 136.

p.117 'I remember the shock . . .': Nash's Magazine, June 1935.

p.118 '"Time to Spare" is shattering . . .': Daily Herald, 5 June 1934.

p.119 'there are neighbours . . .': Radio Times, 25 May 1934.

p.119 'a piece of impertinence . . .': q. in Cardiff and Scannell, A Social History of British Broadcasting, p.390.

p.119 'the idleness . . .': 15 July 1934, p.c.

p.119 'and then had to go . . .': interview with Flanagans 31 Jan. 1983, p.c.

p.119 'his looks . . .': ibid.

p.120 'it will make you shake . . .': Listener, 6 March 1935.

p.120 'there exists . . .': BBC memo, Nov. 1934, BBC Archives, Caversham.

p.120 'There is no getting away . . .': BBC memo, 23 Jan. 1935, BBC Archives, Caversham.

p.121 'deplorably lacking in grip': 9 March 1935, p.c.

Chapter 9: Everest Unbeaten

p.123 'Smythe, Birnie and Shipton . . .': 30 Sept, 1932, p.c.

p.123 'a bad mountaineer . . .': q. in Unsworth, Everest, p.160.

p.123 'He tends to worry . . .' Everest diary, p.c.

p.123 'he was equally good . . .': obituary of Frank Smythe, Alpine Journal, 1949.

p.123 'morally and physically fit . . .': 'Some Medical Aspects', in Ruttledge, Everest 1933, p.248.

p.124 'the most delightful of men . . .': Everest diary, 11 April 1933, p.c.

p.124 'a small, powerful . . .': Everest diary, 17 April 1933, p.c.

p.125 'the rations were . . .': unpublished memoir, n.d., Alpine Club.

p.125 'it was not Dr Zilva's fault . . .': 'Some Medical Aspects', in Ruttledge, op. cit.

p.125 'looked on as off-side': The Wind of Morning, p.101.

p.126 'the highest points . . .': C.G. Bruce, q. in Goodman, Suffer and Survive, p.337

p.126 'MacLean and I, . . .': q. in Unsworth, op. cit., p.166.

p.126 'peacefully occupied . . .': q. in Steele, Eric Shipton, p.38.

p.126 'both keen and delighted': Boustead, The Wind of Morning, p.98.

p.126 'and all the memories . . .': Everest diary, 12 March 1933, p.c.

p.127 'felt again that delightful . . .': ibid, 23 Feb. 1933, p.c.

p.127 'it was curious . . .': ibid.

p.127 'a quiet and exceptionally pleasant . . .': ibid, 12 March 1933, p.c.

p.127 'cheap seaside hotel': ibid.

p.128 'My most vivid memories . . .': Boustead, op. cit., p.100.

p.128 'neither in moderation . . .': 'Some Medical Aspects', in Ruttledge, *op. cit.*, p.255.

p.128 'for though collectively . . .': *ibid*, p.249.

p.128 'we spent much time . . .': *Everest 1933*, p.62.

p.128 'fine, free movers . . .': *ibid*, p.50.

p.128 'These hordes of animals . . .': *Camp Six*, p.18

p.128 'I am only tonight . . .': Everest diary, 23 March 1933, p.c.

p.128 'a wind blew continuously . . .': *ibid*.

p.129 'it is impossible to deny . . .': 'Some Medical Aspects', in Ruttledge, *op. cit.* p.256.

p.129 'the most beautiful . . .': *Moments of Being*, p.144.

p.129 'I have cast off England . . .': Everest diary, 22 April 1933, p.c.

p.130 'fat and jovial . . .': *Moments of Being*, p.145.

p.130 'Greene, himself . . .': *Everest 1933*, p.91.

p.130 'Every expedition . . .': Everest diary, 5 May 1933, p.c.

p.130 'ridiculously self-conscious . . .': *Upon that Mountain*, p.107.

p.131 'rolling Gibbonian . . .' q. in Steele, *op. cit.*, p.46.

p.131 'In Greene we discovered . . .': *Everest 1933*, p.68.

p.131 'a great raconteur': *The Wind of Morning*, p.100.

p.131 'I seem to have been pushed . . .': Everest diary, 2 April 1933, p.c.

p.132 'giant pine trees . . .: *Geographical Magazine*, May 1936.

p.132 'showing signs . . .': Everest diary 27 March 1933, p.c.

p.132 'At lower altitudes . . .': *ibid*, 29 April 1933, p.c.

p.132 'he seems to me . . .': *ibid*, 3 May 1933, p.c.

p.132 'None of us had been . . .': *Camp Six*, p.209.

p.132 'Bill has begun to behave . . .': Everest diary, 8 May 1933, p.c.

p.132 'once again entertained . . .': *Camp Six*, p.209.

p.133 'Life on Mount Everest . . .': 'Some Medical Aspects' in Ruttledge, *Everest 1933*, p.263.

p.133 'Unlike our forebears . . .': *ibid*.

p.133 'It seemed that . . .': 'Anoxia', in *British Medical Journal*, 4 May 1957.

p.133 'the most disgraceful day . . .': Everest diary, 20 May 1933, p.c.

p.133 'attempt to overcome . . .': *ibid*, 21 May 1933, p.c.

p.134 'and when I felt for . . .': *Moments of Being*, p.159.

p.134 'Completely exhausted, . . .': Everest diary, 23 May 1933, p.c.

p.134 'very done in': *Camp Six*, p.130.

p.134 'By establishing Camp V . . .': Everest diary, 27 May 1933, p.c.

p.134 'each time I put my foot . . .': *The Wind of Morning*, p.103

p.135 'looked a rather pathetic . . .': Everest diary, 30 May 1933, p.c.

p.135 'I use my dilated heart . . .': *ibid*, 3 June 1933, p.c.

p.135 'in the arctic tent . . .': *ibid*, 30 May 1933, p.c.

p.135 'frightfully pleased . . .': *ibid*, 5 June 1933, p.c.

p.136 'Anxiously waiting . . .': telegram dated 14 June 1933, p.c.

p.136 'Anyone leaving Camp VI . . .': *Adventures of a Mountaineer*, p.202.

p.136 'he just gazed..': q. in Steele, *Eric Shipton*, p.30.

p.136 'at the brown Rongbuk Valley . . .': *Adventures of a Mountaineer*, p.207.

p.136 'With the exception of Hugo . . ..': Everest diary, 4 June 1933, p.c.

p.137 'the laziest bloody doctor . . .': *ibid*, 6 June 1933, p.c.

p.137 'a smile of infantile . . .': *ibid*, 26 June 1933, p.c.

p.137 'longing for home, . . .': *ibid*, 27 June 1933, p.c.

p.137 'Greene, Crawford and I . . .': *Everest 1933*, p.186.

p.138 'got so much clinical material . . .': Everest diary, 24 June 1933, p.c.

p.138 'I have been hideously overworked . . .': to Hinks at RGS, 10 Feb. 1934, Royal Geographical Society, RGS Library.

p.138 'Would that you could be . . .': to Hinks at RGS, 18 May 1934, Royal Geographical Society, RGS Library.

Chapter 10: Foreign Correspondent

p.139 'if one book . . .': HCG, 'A Variety of Lives', Bodleian.

p.139 'A venerable figure . . .': *ibid.*

p.140 'No need to feign . . .': 16 Dec. 1934, Georgetown.

p.140 'more than I should have . . .': to Charles and Marion Greene, 23 Dec. 1933, Bodleian.

p.140 'a tiny little man . . .': *ibid*, 11 Jan. 1934, Bodleian.

p.140 'above all I caught . . .': HCG, 'A Variety of Lives', Bodleian.

p.140 'All I can remember . . .': *ibid.*

p.141 'the guards were quite . . .': n.d., Bodleian.

p.141 'Please make no comment . . .': n.d., Bodleian.

p.141 'I don't think the Catholic Church . . .': to Marion Greene, 15 Jan. 1934, Bodleian.

p.141 'inevitably destroyed . . .': *ibid*, 16 Jan. 1934, Bodleian.

p.141 'large, grey-moustached . . .': HCG, 'A Variety of Lives', Bodleian.

p.142 'a wonderful Nazi . . .': Shirer, *Berlin Diary*, p.28.

p.142 'the News Editor . . .': q. in Hart-Davis, *The House the Berrys Built*, p.75.

p.143 'never since I left school . . .': *ibid.*

p.143 'A likeable figure . . .': q. in Tracey, *A Variety of Lives*, p.45.

p.143 'I fear Putzi's words . . .': *Berlin Diary*, p. 17.

p.144 'a big bluff German . . .': *The Nightmare Years*, p.255.

p.144 'the foreign correspondents dine . . .': *Goodbye to Berlin*, p.20.

p.144 'a momentary haven . . .': *The Nightmare Years*, p.259.

p.144 'was able, on occasion, . . .': *Knaves, Fools and Heroes*, p.40.

p.145 'sat in a corner . . .': *The Nightmare Years*, p.255.

p.145 'I do my utmost . . .': q. in *ibid*, p.206.

p.145 'Over the next few years . . .': *ibid.* p.138.

p.146 'duck into stores . . .': *Berlin Diary*, p.15.

p.146 'while the rest of his colleagues . . .': 'Drawing the Line', n.d., Bodleian.

p.146 'a rather pedantic . . .': Robson, n.d., Hugh Greene papers, Bodleian.

p.146 'though he's not . . .': to Marion Greene, 14 March 1934, Bodleian.

p.146 'much too lackadaisical . . .': Robson, *op. cit.*

p.147 'a pretty cold fish . . .': q. in Tracey, *A Variety of Lives*, p.41.

p.147 'Though I do like talking . . .': 5 March 1934, Bodleian.

p.147 'My own dearest . . .': 14 March 1934, Bodleian.

p.147 'people who act as informants . . .': n.d., Bodleian.

p.147 'I only feel sorry . . .': n.d., p.c.

p.148 'following my brother . . .': to Marion Greene, 10 March 1934, Bodleian.

p.148 'a Continental seventeen . . .': 14 March 1934, Bodleian.

p.148 'not dark, but . . .': 24 March 1934, Bodleian.

p.148 'I am really painfully ignorant . . .': n.d., Bodleian.

p.148 'fairly pleasant people': 4 April 1934, Bodleian.

p.148 'for someone exceptionally silly . . .': 13 April 1934, Bodleian.

p.148 'a terribly uninteresting man . . .': 11 May 1934, Bodleian.

p.148 'The church on Monday . . .': q. in Tracey, TS of *A Variety of Lives*.

p.149 'a brothel in Talinn . . .': GG to HCG, 16 April 1934, Georgetown.

p.149 'both physically and mentally': n.d., Bodleian.

p.149 'it's my own responsibility . . .': n.d., Bodleian.

p.150 'Wareing was looking . . .': q. in TS of Tracey, *A Variety of Lives*.

p.150 'gay and expansive . . .': *Trail Sinister*, p.236.

p.151 'We knew something . . .': TS, n.d., Bodleian.

p.151 'grim satisfaction . . .': *Trail Sinister*, p.235.

p.151 'an entrée . . .': *op. cit.*, p.41.

p.151 'I remember that . . .': *Listener*, 24 April 1969.

p.152 'There is a feeling of horror . . .': *Daily Telegraph*, 4 July 1934.

p.152 'has got into my blood . . .': n.d., Bodleian.

p.152 'rang the Propaganda Ministry . . .': *Daily Telegraph*, 16 July 1934.

p.153 'that was the end . . .': *op. cit.*, p.236.

p.153 'I wonder if I shall . . .': 1 Aug. 1934, Bodleian.

p.153 'to make my dirty tweed . . .': to Helga, 10 Aug. 1934, Bodleian.

p.153 'one of the most extraordinary . . .': *Daily Telegraph*, 8 Aug. 1934.

p.153 'from a hotel . . .': HCG notes on Hindenburg's funeral, n.d., Bodleian.

p.154 'breathed forth . . .': q. in Tracey, *A Variety of Lives*, p.47.

p.154 'The answers foreign . . .': *Daily Telegraph*, 17 Aug. 1934.

p.154 'Tell Da . . .': 27 Nov. 1934, Bodleian.

p.154 'I know no people . . .': 15 Jan. 1935, Bodleian.

p.154 'One sensed that . . .': n.d., Hugh Greene papers, Bodleian.

p.155 'one couldn't live the life . . .': q. in Helga Greene, notes, n.d., Bodleian.

p.155 'He neither considered . . .': Helga Greene, notes, n.d., in HCG papers, Bodleian.

p.155 'I actually went . . .': to Marion Greene, 1 Jan. 1937, Bodleian.

p.155 'opted out of fatherhood . . .': Helga Greene, notes, n.d., in HCG papers, Bodleian.

p.155 'I thought you were . . .': 28 Jan. 1935, Georgetown.

p.155 'blessedly independent . . .': HCG to Marion Greene, 8 Feb. 1935, Bodleian.

p.155 'felt smaller than ever': *ibid*.

p.155 'the most dangerously . . .': Delmer, *op. cit.*, p.244.

p.156 'The Saar was . . .': 9 Feb 1935, p.c.

p.156 'approved as . . .': Society of Friends minute, 14 Feb. 1936.

p.156 'and were quite satisfied . . .': *passim*: unpublished writings by BG, p.c.

p.157 'knife in his belt . . .': FG to Eva Greene, 9 July 1935, p.c.

p.157 'It was a shock to me . . .': 15 July 1935, p.c.

p.157 'I cannot help feeling . . .': *ibid*.

p.158 'as I went round . . .': FG to Flanagans, 13 Aug. 1983, p.c.

p.158 'Laughingly I said . . .': *ibid*.

p.158 'highly influential . . .': FG to Eva and Edward Greene, 15 July 1935, p.c.

p.158 'For far too long . . .': *ibid*.

p.158 'Berlin must know of this . . .': FG to Flanagans, 13 Aug. 1983, p.c.

p.159 'Some of them looked . . .': 23 July 1935, p.c.

p.159 'He has this marvellous . . .': interview with Flanagans, 31 Aug. 1983, p.c.

p.159 'It was rather a nice change . . .': 18 Oct. 1935, Bodleian.

p.159 'most journalistic . . .': 'Dear Mumma' in Moore and Hawtree, *1936: As Recorded in the Spectator*, p.124.

p.159 'eye on General Werner . . .': *ibid*, p.125.

p.159 'as white as a sheet . . .': *The Nightmare Years*, p.243.

p.160 'neither Wareing nor I . . .': Moore and Hawtree, *op. cit.*, p.125.

p.160 'depressing times . . .': 1 May 1936, Bodleian.

p.160 'already there is no beef . . .': to Marion Greene, 16 Sept. 1936, Bodleian.

p.160 'After Benito . . .': 15 Oct. 1937, Bodleian.

Chapter 11: Real and Imaginary Adventures

p.161 'luckily for me . . .': *Ways of Escape*, p.46.

p.161 '"Papa," I said timidly . . .': introduction to *Too Late to Turn Back*, p.xiii.

p.162 'we never had a great deal . . .': *Land Benighted*, p.6.

p.162 'a period when "young authors" . . .': *Ways of Escape*, p.45.

p.162 'You will, I am sure, . . .': 18 Dec. 1934, Rhodes House, Oxford.

p.163 'Do you know anyone . . .': 26 Nov. 1934, Georgetown.

p.163 'I wept a little . . .': *Land Benighted*, p.3.

p.163 'somehow managed . . .': *ibid*, p.2.

p.163 'his method of conversation . . .': *ibid*. p.68.

p.163 'it seemed rather unreal . . .': *ibid*, p.16.

p.164 'should the reader . . .': *ibid*, p.43.

p.164 'I was far too stolid . . .': *ibid*, p.124.

p.164 'here it seemed dead . . .': *ibid*, p.122.

p.164 '"I wish he would . . ."': *ibid*, p.126.

p.164 'I expect you have . . .': to Eva and Edward Greene, n.d., p.c.

p.164 'I had never got used . . .': *Journey without Maps*, p.96.

p.164 'enormous bowls of rice . . .': *Land Benighted*, p.60.

p.165 'continually astonished . . .': *ibid*, p.6.

p.165 'His brain frightened me . . .': *ibid*.

p.165 'a long journey backwards . . .': *Journey without Maps*, p.97.

p.165 'It is strange . . .': *Land Benighted*, p.48.

p.166 'I began to see the beauty . . .': *ibid*, p.38.

p.166 'whose stern eyes . . .': *ibid*, p.22.

p.166 'looking as if he had just left . . .': *ibid*, p.34.

p.166 'followed the sentry . . .': *Journey without Maps*, p.198.

p.166 'after the fish . . .': *Land Benighted*, p.162.

p.166 'It all sounded horrible . . .': *ibid*, p.147.

p.167 'a kind of hope . . .': *Journey without Maps*, p.192.

p.167 'the moments of extraordinary . . .': *ibid*, p.158.

p.167 'looked ghastly . . .': *Land Benighted*, p.170.

p.167 'I felt quite calm . . .': *ibid*, p.174.

p.167 'I went into his room . . .': *ibid*, p.176.

p.167 'had discovered in myself . . .': *Journey without Maps*, p.213.

p.168 'suddenly she nearly made me . . .': *Land Benighted*, p.191.

p.168 'wanted to laugh . . .': *Journey without Maps*, p.223.

p.168 'were capable of quarrelling . . .': *ibid*, p.216.

p.168 'because its people . . .': *ibid*, p.224.

p.168 'after a trek . . .': *ibid*, p.244.

p.168 'the sense of taste . . .': *ibid*, p.225.

p.168 'a stupid and unnecessary . . .': q. in West, *The Quest for Graham Greene*, p.97.

p.168 'if this was an adventure . . .': *Ways of Escape*, p.48.

p.169 'only in one thing . . .': *ibid*, p.47.

p.169 'surprisingly good . . .': 27 Nov. 1938, Bodleian.

p.169 'Da is worried . . .': to Marion Greene, 18 Oct. 1935, Bodleian.

p.169 'disgraceful behaviour': 6 March 1934, NA.

p.169 'The club, as usual . . .': Greene, *Secret Agent in Spain*, p.271.

p.170 'a nephew of Sir Greene . . .': 1 Feb. 1934, NA.

p.170 'worth nothing . . .': *Secret Agent in Spain*, p.272.

p.170 'open and produce . . .': Feb. 1934, NA.

p.171 'I saw Greene yesterday . . .': 29 Sept. 1934, NA.

p.171 'pointed out to Greene . . .': 26 March 1934, NA.

p.172 'like the meeting covered': memo from 'B', 12 Nov. 1934, NA.

p.172 'I am warning you . . .': *Secret Agent in Spain*, p.18.

p.172 'I understand that . . .': 20 Jan. 1935, NA.

p.173 'All the scoundrels . . .': *Journey without Maps*, p.16.

p.173 'signed chits . . .': q. in Sherry, *The Life of Graham Greene*, Vol.1, p.496.

p.173 'financially utterly . . .': to Eva Greene, n.d., p.c.

p.173 '"failure, Empire Tobacco" . . .': *Journey without Maps*, p.20.

p.173 'I wish he wouldn't choose me . . .' *passim*: q. in Sherry, *op. cit.*, pp.496-9.

p.175 'somewhat reluctantly . . .': George Orwell to Tosco Fyvel, 15 April 1949, in *Orwell: A Life in Letters*, p.460.

p.175 'a thousand congratulations . . .': n.d., Morgan Library, New York.

p.175 'I do not wish you to come . . .': *Secret Agent in Spain*, p.18.

p.176 'conscience is a . . .': *ibid*, p.72.

p.176 'patiently waiting . . .': *ibid*, p.90.

p.177 'Don't shoot him . . .': q. in Sherry, *op. cit.*, p.615.

p.177 'lending this lorry . . .': *Secret Agent in Spain*, p.131.

p.177 'there is a document . . .': *ibid*, p.141.

p.178 'on the top of my wardrobe . . .': *ibid*, p.247.

p.178 'dabble no further . . .': *ibid*, p.266.

p.178 'my reward was experience . . .': *ibid*, p.13.

p.178 'in a state of considerable . . .': MI5 memo, 2 Nov. 1937, NA.

p.178 'Mr W. Herbert Greene . . .': 30 Oct. 1937, NA.

p.178 'I hear Herbert's been contributing . . .': to Marion Greene, 20 Jan. 1938, Bodleian.

p.178 'this story must . . .': to HCG, 16 Jan. 1938, Georgetown.

p.178 'let the Empire . . .': 22 Dec. 1937, *Daily Worker*.

p.179 'lot of further stuff . . .': 29 Dec. 1937, NA.

p.179 'a man, who appeared . . .': MI5 report, 3 March 1938, NA.

p.179 'I think it advisable . . .': *The Spy's Bedside Book*, p.29.

p.180 'the only civil mention . . .': John R. Allwork, 31 July 1938, p.c.

p.180 'I went to Spain . . .': 13 Nov. 1937, NA.

p.180 'Mrs Guest may have . . .': *Secret Agent in Spain*, p.286.

p.180 'I could be of use . . .': 9 Oct. 1935, NA.

Chapter 12: Westward Look

p.181 'most attractive boys . . .': FG to Eve and Edward Greene, 25 July 1935, p.c.

p.181 'I know Felix Greene well . . .': 4 Sept. 1935, Caversham.

p.182 'with books stacked on . . .': to Charles Graves, 29 Dec. 1935, Caversham.

p.182 'The authority of broadcasting . . .': report to BBC, 11 Dec. 1935, Caversham.

p.182 'immense potentialities . . .': 27 Dec. 1935, Caversham.

p.182 'Propaganda is becoming . . .': 11 Dec. 1935, Caversham.

p.183 'obsessed increasingly . . .': 29 Feb. 1936, p.c.

p.183 'the availability . . .': 16 Jan. 1936, Caversham.

p.183 'prodigious amount . . .': FG to Flanagans, 7 Feb. 1984, p.c.

p.183 'take a subject . . .': q. in Clarke, *Alistair Cooke*, p. 135.

p.183 'Don't you think . . .': *ibid*.

p.184 'Why cannot we have . . .': 'American Tour No.1', 25 March 1936, Caversham.

p.184 'I love them . . .': 27 May 1936, p.c.

p.184 'they showed us where . . .': FG to Flanagans, n.d., p.c.

p.185 'These were little kids . . .': *ibid*.

p.185 'quite unconsciously . . .': *ibid*.

p.185 'I wish all people . . .': 31 Jan. 1936, Caversham.

p.185 'a hopeless misfit . . .': 22 Jan. 1937, p.c.

p.185 'New York and I . . .': 24 Nov. 1936, p.c.

p.185 'Greene grass . . .': to Eva Greene, 14 Dec. 1936, p.c.

p.185 'I long to be in company . . .': 1 Nov. 1936, p.c.

p.186 'yet here I am . . .': 18 Oct. 1936, p.c.

p.186 'My uptown friends . . .': 28 Oct. 1936, p.c.

p.186 'that godforsaken city . . .': 23 Feb. 1937, p.c.

p.186 'We've been fond . . .': FG to Flanagans, n.d., p.c.

p.186 'my heart went out . . .': 9 Nov. 1938, p.c.

p.186 'dark corners': FG to Flanagans, n.d., p.c.

p.187 'My friendship with him . . .': 1 Sept. 1937, p.c.

p.187 'I'm a little frightened . . .': to Eva and Edward Greene, 22 Aug. 1937, p.c.

p.187 'gave me an inferiority complex . . .': *ibid*, 5 Jan. 1938, p.c.

p.187 'the world's most delightful . . .': 10 Aug. 1938, p.c.

p.187 'puerile, ineffective . . .': to Edward Greene, 27 March 1937, p.c.

p.187 'We certainly had doubts . . .': 26 Jan. 1937, Caversham.

p.188 'there has never been . . .': 25 Jan. 1937, Caversham.

p.188 'help in stifling rumour . . .': q. in Mansell, *Let Truth Be Told*, p.34.

p.188 'I could hardly believe . . .': 16 Jan. 1936, Caversham.

p.188 'flabby and uninspired . . .': q. in Briggs, *The Golden Age of Wireless*, p.396.

p.188 'This is serious . . .': q. in Mansell, *op. cit.*, p.36.

p.188 'They do not lump us . . .': 19 April 1936, Caversham.

p.189 'We are facing . . .': q. in Briggs, *op. cit.*, p.407.

p.189 'It will be disastrous . . .': 2 Nov. 1937, Caversham.

p.189 'my brother, Attlee . . .': 22 Jan. 1938, Caversham.

p.190 'There are occasions . . .': 8 June 1938, Caversham.

p.190 'the one place . . .': 13 April 1938, p.c.

p.191 'Your words . . .': 26 April 1938, p.c.

p.191 'in high summer . . .': FG to Eva Greene, 10 Aug. 1938, p.c.

p.191 'I have been thinking of you . . .': 25 Dec. 1938, p.c.

p.191 'The work of the BBC . . .': 9 July 1939, Caversham.

p.191 'the speed and fluency . . .': ibid.

p.192 'extracts from the German . . .': ibid.

p.192 'I shall remain here . . .': 27 Jan. 1939, p.c.

p.192 'legitimate grievances . . .': address to Philadelphia Foreign Policy Association, 12 Nov. 1938, p.c.

p.192 'Ed, you and I . . .': FG to Flanagans, 24 Feb. 1984, p.c.

p.192 'My convictions . . .': 18 Dec. 1939, Caversham.

p.192 'and the prospect of returning . . .': FG to Eva Greene, 8 Sept. 1939, p.c.

p.192 'of the utmost importance . . .': q. in Clarke, op. cit., p.158.

p.192 'What heights and depths . . .': 28 Sept. 1939, p.c.

p.193 'I'm keeping . . .': 23 Oct. 1939, p.c.

p.193 'Men are fighting . . .': 8 Oct. 1940, p.c.

p.193 'part of the war effort . . .': 10 May 1940, p.c.

p.193 'It means . . .': 12 Feb. 1940, p.c.

p.194 'my eventual aim . . .': to Marion Greene, n.d., BL.

p.194 'fierce and dangerous creature': to Marion Greene, 8 Sept. 1936, BL.

p.194 'painful purgatorial . . .': 31 Oct. 1936, Georgetown.

p.194 'the job I once . . .': to Marion Greene, 5 May 1935, BL.

p.194 'drew a principal . . .': Ways of Escape, p.217.

p.195 'Elisabeth's job . . .': to Marion Greene, 27 Nov. 1938, Bodleian.

p.195 'I've been offered . . .': 25 Dec. 1939, Georgetown.

p.195 'The world may . . .': The Old School, p.233.

p.196 'We worked in . . .': q. in Hawtree, Night and Day, p.x.

p.196 'Yes, the pay . . .': n.d., 1937, Georgetown.

p.196 'No matter . . .': Hawtree, op. cit., p.ix.

p.196 'My God no . . .': ibid, p.xi.

p.196 'One doesn't want . . .': 19 July 1937, HRHRC.

p.197 'He was very tall . . .': As I Walked Down New Grub Street, p.100.

p.198 'that little bitch . . .': 16 Jan. 1938, Georgetown.

p.198 'Greene rang . . .': Waugh, 18 Nov. 1937, Diaries, p.426.

p.198 'Graham leapt . . .': Burns, Papa Spy, p.13.

p.198 'somewhat bovine': q. in Thomson, Articles of Faith, p.14.

p.199 'wearing a brown suit . . .': Memoirs of the Forties, p. 15.

p.200 'complete surprise . . .': Articles of Faith, p.147.

p.200 'I find we are changing . . .': Journals 1987–1989, p. 176.

p.200 'This is all very sad . . .': 19 Aug. 1937, Georgetown.

p.201 'improved enormously . . .': 9 Feb. 1938.

p.201 'This is an awful . . .': 13 April 1938, LL, p.92.

p.201 'asking me . . .': ibid.

p.201 'they asked for traces . . .': GG to Jan Dalley, 8 June 1985, Reading.

Chapter 13: Kristallnacht

p.203 'eighty per cent . . .': q. in Rose, Vansittart, p.242.

p.204 'no question of . . .': q. in Pimlott, Labour and the Left in the 1930s, p.117.

p.205 'more and more . . .': q. in ibid, p.121.

p.205 'discussion can be . . .': q. in ibid, p.122.

p.205 'I am bound . . .': 10 Aug. 1936, p.c.

p.205 'not prepared to . . .': 11 Aug. 1936, p.c.

p.206 'Ben Greene's organisation . . .': q. in Pimlott, op. cit., p.149.

p.207 'there is more socialism . . .': q. in ibid., p.116.

p.207 'in which you either . . .': 25 Jan. 1937, p.c.

p.207 'made it clear . . .': ibid.

p.207 'the brutal treatment . . .': BG, 'Socialism and the German Boycott', The Labour Candidate, June 1935.

p.207 'I did indeed feel . . .': statement on Pimlott's Labour and the Left in the 1930s, n.d., p.c.

p.207 'I happen to have . . .': 1 Feb. 1937, p.c.

p.208 'the very greatest regret . . .': 1 October 1938, p.c.

p.208 'Berlin and . . .': *Daily Telegraph*, 9 June 1938.

p.209 'The final elimination . . .': *ibid*, 17 June 1938.

p.209 'more sympathetic . . .': *ibid*, 18 June 1938.

p.209 'Unlike German . . .': *ibid*, 21 June 1938.

p.209 'The anti-Jewish . . .': *ibid*, 22 June 1938.

p.210 'An officially . . .': *ibid*, 11 Nov. 1938

p.210 'the great mass . . .': *ibid*, 14 Nov. 1938.

p.211 'desperate Jews . . .': q. in Smith, *Foley*, p.129.

p.211 'hale, hearty . . .': BG to Clement Attlee, 11 Nov. 1941, NA.

p.211 'Herr Bohle . . .': *Daily Telegraph*, 19 Nov. 1938

p.212 'along the frontier . . .': TS of 'The Great Betrayal', n.d., p.c.

p.212 'I was aware of . . .': *ibid*.

p.212 'said he did not . . .': police interview with BG, n.d. 1940, NA.

p.212 'he thought I was . . .': BG to Clement Attlee, 23 July 1940, NA.

p.212 'You are on this Jewish . . .': *ibid*.

p.212 'a most terrible . . .': BG to Clement Attlee, 11 Nov. 1941, NA.

p.213 'above everything . . .': BG Report to Society of Friends, 19 Dec. 1938, p.c.

p.213 'influential in . . .': BG to Clement Attlee, 11 Nov. 1941, NA.

p.214 'All Jews begged . . .': summary of report to Samuel Hoare, 22 Nov. 1938, p.c.

p.214 'the relief of human need . . .': report by Roger Carter, Aug. 1939, Society of Friends Library.

p.214 'I was in Germany . . .': to Clement Attlee, 11 Nov. 1941, NA.

p.214 'that arrogant young man': BG to Home Office Advisory Committee, 11 Nov. 1941, NA.

p.214 'giving relief . . .': *ibid*.

p.215 'My ideas of relief . . .': 6 March 1939, p.c.

Chapter 14: Peace at Any Price

p.216 'I was prepared . . .': to Home Office Advisory Committee, 24 July 1940, NA.

p.216 'One regarded . . .': to Roderick Young, 28 March 1988, Boston.

p.217 'disliked the . . .': Skidelsky, *Oswald Mosley*, p.345.

p.217 'the jackals . . .': *The New Pioneer*, March 1939.

p.217 'the BCAEC was . . .': Beckett, *The Rebel Who Lost His Cause*, p.156.

p.218 'the founder of the whole show . . .': q. in Griffiths, *Patriotism Perverted*, p.55.

p.218 'a sort of constant . . .': q. in Beckett, *op. cit.*, p.155.

p.218 'always running . . .': *ibid*.

p.218 'one of the loneliest . . .': q. in *ibid*, p.194.

p.218 'the most cruel . . .': *ibid*.

p.218 'the European fascist . . .': Hastings, *The Years of Transition*, p.168.

p.219 'security for . . .': BPP Manifesto, 1939.

p.219 'decided by the committee . . .': q. in Griffiths, *Patriotism Perverted*, p.56.

p.219 'quite a minor . . .': BG to Home Office Advisory Committee, 24 July 1940, NA.

p.219 'why should British . . .': q. in Griffiths, *op. cit.*

p.220 'avoid war and bring . . .': BG to Advisory Committee, *op. cit.*, NA.

p.220 'Ben has written . . .': 16 Feb. 1939, p.c.

p.220 'Ben's pamphlets . . .': 2 May 1939, p.c.

p.220 'I am making plans . . .': 3 Jan. 1939, NA.

p.220 'by dealing with . . .': 6 March 1939, p.c.

p.220 'please don't mention . . .': 7 Feb. 1939, p.c.

p.221 'anyone who lived . . .': McDonald, *A Man of The Times*, p.18.

p.221 'a liability . . .': q. in Cockett, *Twilight of Truth*, p.17.

p.221 'opened letter . . .': 20 Sept. 1938, Georgetown.

p.221 'made clear to . . .': *Daily Telegraph*, 4 May 1939.

p.221 'Herr Hitler will be . . .': q. in Gannon, *The British Press and Germany 1936–39*, p.230.

p.222 'from what I saw . . .': TS of 'Germany 1933-39', Bodleian.

p.222 'large SS man . . .': q. in Tracey, *A Variety of Lives*, p.52.

p.222 'Goebbels was not . . .': HG misc. notes, n.d., Bodleian.

p.223 'more than once . . .': McDonald, *op. cit.*, p.20.

p.223 'the need for the Press . . .': q. in Cockett, *op. cit.*, p.40.

p.223 'Assuming that . . .': q. in TS of Tracey, *op. cit.*

p.223 'Ich komme . . .': *ibid.*

p.224 'no madman had . . .': q. in Griffiths, *op. cit.*, p.57.

p.224 'the huge profits . . .': *ibid.*

p.224 'get in touch . . .': *Peace News*, 21 April 1939.

p.225 'swell the party . . .': 24 Aug. 1939, NA.

p.225 'What utter nonsense!': unpublished item, p.c.

p.225 'the pressure . . .': 31 Oct. 1939, p.c.

p.226 'if we set aside . . .': q. in Cockett, *op. cit.*, p.163.

p.227 'About 150 Britons . . .': *Sunday Express*, 15 Oct. 1939.

p.227 'bluff and treachery': *ibid.*

p.227 'referred to Christ . . .': *Sunday Despatch*, 15 Oct. 1939.

p.227 'look at the record . . .': police notes of interview with BG, n.d., NA.

p.228 'amazed to find . . .': letter to *Sunday Express*, 22 Oct. 1939.

p.228 'just behind . . .': *Berkhamsted Gazette*, 20 Oct. 1939.

p.228 'glanced through . . .': 22 Dec. 1939, p.c.

p.229 'set of gangsters': q. in Simpson, *In the Highest Degree Odious*, p.137.

p.229 'absolute bilge . . .': *ibid.*

p.229 'woolly-headed . . .': *ibid.*

p.229 'we should not forget . . .': q. in Griffiths, *op. cit.*, p.214.

p.229 'particularly distinguished . . .': *Sunday Despatch*, 25 Feb. 1940.

p.229 'for the regeneration . . .': *Northamptonshire Evening Telegraph*, 20 March 1940.

p.230 'an admirer . . .': Berkhamsted police report, 17 May 1940, NA.

p.230 'pro-German . . .': *ibid.*

p.230 'carried out a search . . .': report of 12 July 1940, NA.

p.231 'I have written telling . . .': 8 March 1940, NA.

Chapter 15: The Greenes Go to War

p.234 'advertised for . . .': *Ways of Escape*, p.87.

p.234 'I can see . . .': HCG, 'A Variety of Lives', Bodleian.

p.235 'considering it . . .': 7 April 1939, Georgetown.

p.235 'I miss you so much . . .': 30 Aug. 1939, Bodleian.

p.235 'very lovely . . .': 4 Sept. 1939, Bodleian.

p.235 'I wish one . . .': 12 Nov. 1939, Bodleian.

p.235 'Oh how I wish . . .': 6 Nov. 1939, Bodleian.

p.235 'Don't ever think . . .': 26 Oct. 1939, Bodleian.

p.235 'One good thing . . .': Vivien Greene to GG, 7 Dec. 1939, Bodleian.

p.235 'faint susurrus . . .': 21 Sept. 1939, Bodleian.

p.236 'high heartless . . .': 'Men at Work', *Twenty-One Stories*, p.159.

p.236 'intimations of . . .': *The Infernal Grove*, p.78.

p.237 'stout short figure . . .': q. in Shelden, *Graham Greene*, p.276.

p.237 'Nice for the wife . . .': Vivien Greene, diary, 3 May 1938, Bodleian.

p.237 'I would make . . .': GG to Christopher Hawtree, n.d., Boston.

p.237 'I simply long . . .': n.d., Bodleian.

p.238 'I do hope . . .': 15 Oct. 1940, Bodleian.

p.238 'I've been leading . . .': 16 Dec. 1940, *A Life in Letters*, p.105.

p.238 'I'm glad to say . . .': 18 March 1941, *ibid*, p.107.

p.238 'and he gave . . .': *The Infernal Grove*, p.82.

p.238 'was a kind of . . .': *ibid*, p.104.

p.238 'the whole war . . .': to Mary Pritchett, 18 March 1941, *LL*, p.107.

p.238 'How completely . . .': q. in Shelden, *op. cit.*, p.289.

p.238 'It really was . . .': 18 April 1941, *A Life in Letters*, p.108.

p.239 'makes me sick . . .': n.d., Bodleian.

p.239 'I like this place . . .': 14 June 1939, Bodleian.

p.239 'a dress rehearsal . . .': *ibid.*

p.239 'Don't worry if . . .': 21 Aug. 1939, Bodleian.

p.240 'My last will . . .': *ibid.*

p.240 'Everywhere I saw . . .': 29 Aug. 1939, Bodleian.

p.240 'tall, friendly . . .': *Front Line*, p.13.

p.240 'playing my new game . . .': *Trail Sinister*, p.392.

p.241 'The German military machine . . .': *Daily Telegraph*, 29 Aug. 1939.

p.241 'Are you sure . . .': *Front Line*, p.15.

p.241 'tremendous outburst . . .': *Daily Telegraph*, 3 Sept. 1939.

p.241 'Warsaw is now . . .': *ibid*, 4 Sept. 1939.

p.241 'like most people . . .': *Front Line*, p.31.

p.242 'nightmare retreat . . .': *Trail Sinister*, p.396.

p.242 'slow and decrepit . . .': *ibid.*

p.242 'Safe Rumania . . .': 10 Sept. 1939, Bodleian.

p.242 'between leaving . . .': 12 Sept. 1939, Bodleian.

p.242 'For Christ's sake . . .': *The Three Weeks War in Poland*, p.33.

p.243 'I saw a column . . .': 20 Sept. 1939, Bodleian.

p.243 'under the shock . . .': *ibid.*

p.243 'made suggestions . . .': *The Three Weeks War in Poland*, p.93.

p.243 'found the chauffeur . . .': *Daily Telegraph*, 22 Sept. 1939.

p.244 'extremely skinny': Elisabeth Greene to Marion Greene, 27 June 1942, p.c.

p.244 'dangerously over-confident': unpublished essay by Rodney Dennys, 'The Netherlands 1937–45', p.c.

p.244 'Tell him . . .': *ibid.*

p.244 'There cannot be . . .': *ibid.*

p.245 'In the long run . . .': *ibid.*

p.246 'the scream of sirens . . .': 11 May 1940, Bodleian.

p.246 '"Stukas", . . .': Cox, *Countdown to War*, p.137.

p.247 'Rain, grass . . .': n.d., p.c.

p.248 'an improved device . . .': application for patent, 31 Oct. 1941.

p.249 'You sound as if . . .': 2 Aug. 1941, p.c.

p.249 'Up the airy . . .': n.d., p.c.

p.249 'you are willing . . .': 28 March 1942, p.c.

p.249 'it might be a good idea . . .': 17 Sept. 1942, p.c.

p.250 'becomes an important . . .': *The Lancet*, 6 Dec. 1941.

p.250 'I have more than once . . .': *ibid.*

p.251 'We have considerable . . .': MI5 report, Sept. 1939, NA.

p.251 'a most undesirable . . .': MI5 report initialled TAR, 23 Aug. 1939, NA.

p.251 'relationship with her . . .': memo from H. Parkinson, 15 Oct. 1939, NA.

p.251 'after nearly three years . . .': 12 May 1939, NA.

p.252 'I should be most grateful . . .': memo initialled TAR, 10 Nov. 1939, NA.

p.252 'in view of . . .': 26 March 1941, NA.

p.252 'As a nephew . . .': n.d., NA.

p.252 'Although most reviewers . . .': n.d., NA.

p.252 'quite pro-British': 26 March 1942, NA.

p.253 'a plausible liar . . .': MI5 memo, 1 Jan. 1943, NA.

p.253 'to have had a rough . . .': *ibid.*

p.253 'his brother was not . . .': report by Courtenay Young of MI5, 20 April 1943, NA.

p.253 'How far he is . . .': MI5 memo, 22 Feb. 1945, NA.

p.253 'What the hell . . .': n.d., NA.

p.254 'present myself . . .': *The Infernal Grove*, p.117.

p.254 'sandy-haired . . .': *ibid*, p.113.

p.254 'slouching about . . .': *ibid*, p.136.

Chapter 16: 'We Are All Guilty'

p.256 'The only thing . . .': 7 June 1941, p.c.

p.256 'I am far less . . .': 17 Jan. 1941, p.c.

p.256 'only a symptom . . .': 21 March 1941, p.c.

p.256 'Think what . . .': 15 Jan. 1940, p.c.

p.257 'the most expensive . . .': *Down There on a Visit*, p.160.

p.257 'my half-German cousin . . .': *Diaries*, p.164.

p.257 'nothing noteworthy . . .': *ibid*, p.234.

p.258 'had worked all . . .': *ibid.*

p.258 'long, straggling . . .': *ibid.*

p.258 'could never tire . . .': *ibid*, p.240.

p.259 'there are no "prophets" . . .': 'Trabuco', pub. Sept. 1942.

p.259 'How few there are . . .': 28 Sept. 1941. p.c.

p.259 'the most difficult task . . .': n.d., p.c.

p.259 'Oh what a privilege . . .': diary, 1 Aug. 1942, p.c.

p.259 'wise, gentle . . .': 27 Sept. 1944, p.c.

p.259 'I suppose we'd . . .': to Flanagans, 28 June 1982, p.c.

p.259 'I am not interested . . .': 25 July 1942, p.c.

p.259 'fortune combined . . .': diary, 19 May 1942, p.c.

p.260 'the least I can do . . .': to New York Draft Board, 21 Aug. 1942, p.c.

p.260 'it's absurd . . .': to Eva, n.d., p.c.

p.260 'a real furore . . .': diary, 10 Feb. 1944, *Wartime Chronicle*, p.245.

p.260 'The results were not . . .': *Diaries*, p.265.

p.261 'absolutely fascinated . . .': to Flanagans, 28 June 1982, p.c.

p.261 'He was very attractive . . .': to Flanagans, 21 Sept. 1982, p.c.

p.261 'pure and lovely . . .': 9 Dec. 1944, p.c.

p.261 'remember that God . . .': 30 May 1944, p.c.

p.262 'she won't ever marry . . .': 15 Oct. 1944, p.c.

p.262 'That man will drive . . .': Elena to Flanagans, 20 Sept. 1982, p.c.

p.262 'a much more morbid . . .': to Eva Greene, n.d., p.c.

p.262 'give me the independence . . .': 7 Jan 1945, p.c.

p.263 'the wisest and . . .': to Eva Greene, 27 Sept. 1944, p.c.

p.263 'really shifted . . .': to Flanagans, 28 June 1982, p.c.

p.263 'lovable and strange . . .': 10 Aug. 1945, p.c.

p.263 'He is aloof . . .': *ibid*.

p.263 'a devout attempt . . .': n.d., p.c.

p.264 'I didn't have a devoted . . .': to Flanagans, 21 Sept. 1982, p.c.

p.264 'a very simple . . .': n.d., p.c.

p.264 'more closely again . . .': 15 Feb. 1945, p.c.

p.264 'one of the most moving . . .': *ibid*.

p.264 'I have an ever-deepening . . .': 22 Jan. 1945, p.c.

p.264 'until I am far better . . .': q. in Overy, *The Morbid Age*, p.254.

p.264 'lacking in humility . . .': 22 March 1945, p.c.

p.264 'I need you to help . . .': *ibid*.

p.264 'I had to shake . . .': 21 March 1945, p.c.

p.265 'for the first few years . . .': 28 May 1945, p.c.

p.265 'Our family in some . . .': 4 Oct. 1945, p.c.

Chapter 17: Germany at War

p.266 'I have been through . . .': to Ave Barham, 27 Oct. 1945, p.c.

p.266 'Returning home . . .': 'Early Days', unpublished essay, n.d., p.c.

p.266 'Barbara was always . . .': *A Little of All These*, p.138.

p.266 'the enormous relief . . .': *ibid*, p.139.

p.267 'little house . . .': 'Early Days', p.c.

p.267 'she asked me . . .': to Home Office Advisory Committee, 24 July 1940, NA.

p.267 'You two . . .': unpublished open letter to Rupert Strachwitz, n.d., p.c.

p.267 'for the first time . . .': *ibid*.

p.268 'You're mad . . .': *ibid*.

p.268 'I rather mooched . . .': *ibid*.

p.268 'I sometimes wondered . . .': *ibid*.

p.268 'I simply could not . . .': *ibid*.

p.269 'Mrs Greene is just . . .': *ibid*.

p.269 'genuinely working . . .': 4 Sept. 1939, *The Guy Liddell Diaries*, p.14.

p.269 'a nice and decent man': Marie Vassiltchikov, *Berlin Diaries*, p.165.

p.269 'faithful and loyal friend': open letter, *op. cit.*

p.270 'It was all very haphazard . . .': unpublished essay, 'The Human Touch', n.d., p.c.

p.270 'she does not seem . . .': FG to Eva Greene, 20 Oct. 1940, p.c.

p.270 'I'm very impressed . . .': BG to FG, n.d., p.c.

p.270 'I don't regret . . .': *ibid*.

p.270 'a very pleasant . . .': FG to Eva Greene, 14 Jan. 1943, p.c.

p.271 'I was never . . .': open letter, *op. cit.*, p.c.

p.271 'never doubted . . .': video tape of 'Meine Video Memoiren', n.d., p.c.

p.271 'felt a complete . . .': *ibid*.

p.271 'she thinks I may . . .': FG to Eva Greene, 11 Feb. 1941, p.c.

p.271 'clerical, un-German pig': q. in MacDonogh, 1938, p.117.

p.272 'How interesting . . .': open letter, *op. cit.*, p.c.

p.273 'How are you both . . .': to Ave Barham, 7 May 1944, p.c.

p.273 'went white . . .': BG to Rupert Strachwitz, Dec. 1990, p.c.

p.274 'an incredibly beautiful . . .': Axel von dem Bussche to BG, 15 Nov. 1990, p.c.

p.274 'It seemed to speak . . .': n.d, Boston.

p.276 'One cannot believe . . .': to Ave Barham, 2 Sept. 1945, p.c.

p.276 'Do not worry . . .': to Ave Barham, 18 April 1945, p.c.

Chapter 18: Stitch-Up

p.277 'you were born . . .': 'Reasons for Order', 15 July 1940, NA.

p.277 'Conditions were . . .': statement at Greene family discussion, 2 July 1979, p.c.

p.278 'directed his mind . . .': Simpson, *In the Highest Degree Odious*, p.345.

p.278 'Sir John knew . . .': *ibid*, p.346.

p.278 'seemed to have . . .': 21 April 1940, *Guy Liddell Diaries*, p.82.

p.278 'Intelligence organisations . . .': Simpson, *op. cit.*, p.92.

p.279 'a woman agent . . .': q. in Andrew, *The Defence of the Realm*, p.221.

p.281 'I didn't know German . . .': BG, 'The Great Betrayal', unpublished, n.d., p.c.

p.282 'The lady was . . .': *ibid*.

p.282 'I have never heard . . .': 7 Feb. 1939, p.c.

p.282 'a great personal . . .': statement by Harald Kurtz, n.d., NA.

p.283 'trained in . . .': *ibid*.

p.283 'definitely defeatist . . .': statement by Friedl Gärtner, n.d., NA.

p.284 'If this sudden . . .': q. in Masters, *The Man Who Was M*, p.157.

p.284 'not out to act . . .': q. in *ibid*, p.156.

p.284 'At least it's better . . .': statement by Margaret von Goetz, 31 Aug. 1979, p.c.

p.285 'we were both in tears . . .': *ibid*.

p.285 'difficult patient': statement at Greene family discussion, 2 July 1979, p.c.

p.285 'a small bright room . . .': T.C.P. Catchpool to Leslie Greene, 3 July 1940, p.c.

p.285 'be careful not . . .': 31 Oct. 1940, p.c.

p.286 'an officer took . . .': q. in Simpson, *op. cit.*, p.346.

p.286 'desirous of . . .': 'Reasons for Order', 15 July 1940, NA.

p.287 'substantially accurate . . .': q. in Simpson, *op. cit.*, p.330.

p.287 'I felt very dissatisfied . . .': *ibid*, p.350.

p.287 'He reminded me . . .': *ibid*, p.357.

p.288 'horror-struck': *ibid*.

p.288 'All right . . .': *ibid*.

p.288 'Dear old Ben . . .': statement at Greene family discussion, 2 July 1979, p.c.

p.288 'although I did not share . . .': 8 April 1941, p.c.

p.289 'ardent admirer': statement by Harald Kurtz, n.d., NA.

p.289 'How dare you . . .': statement at Greene family discussion, 2 July 1979, p.c.

p.289 'very smooth . . .': statement by Margaret von Goetz, 31 Aug. 1979, p.c.

p.290 'My God, if . . .': q. in Simpson, *op. cit.*, p.366.

p.290 'This is a trap . . .': *ibid*.

p.290 'Kurtz had been . . .': 21 Oct. 1941, *Liddell Diaries*, p.185.

p.291 'The work is important . . .': q. in Montgomery Hyde, *Norman Birkett*, p.469.

p.291 'The work I do . . .': *ibid*, p.472.

p.291 'more and more come . . .': Hart, *op. cit.*, p.95.

p.291 'is a man who . . .': Hickson to Advisory Committee, 11 Nov. 1941, NA.

p.292 'quite clear that . . .': BG evidence to Advisory Committee, 11 Nov. 1941, NA.

p.292 'the injustices of . . .': *ibid*.

p.292 'and I don't think . . .': proceedings of Advisory Committee, 11 Nov. 1941, NA.

p.292 'severely cross-examined': 18 Jan. 1942, *Liddell Diaries*, p.214.

p.292 'combined deceit . . .': memo, 19 Dec. 1941, NA.

p.292 'what can only ...': 18 Jan. 1942, *Liddell Diaries*, p.214.

p.292 'even if Kurtz's ...': *ibid.*

p.293 'an almost indispensable ...': memo, 23 Dec. 1941, NA.

p.293 'may necessarily ...': to Sir Alexander Maxwell, 6 Jan. 1942, NA.

p.293 'whole business of Greene ...': 18 Jan. 1942, *Liddell Diaries*, p.214.

p.293 'suspend the operation ...': Mr Shepherd of the Home Office to BG, 7 Jan. 1942, p.c.

p.293 'there was undisputed ...': House of Commons, 5 Feb. 1942.

p.294 'he knows her to be ...': memo, 13 April 1943, NA.

p.295 'He was coming over ...': statement by Margaret von Goetz, 1 Feb. 1983, p.c.

p.295 'such an intensity ...': 25 May 1943, p.c.

p.295 'Ben's whole unrest ...': n.d., p.c.

p.295 'It is increasingly ...': 13 June 1944, p.c.

p.296 'his ready humour ...': *The Times*, 23 Dec. 1972

p.296 'buoyant temperament ...': *ibid.*

p.296 'He always saw ...': statement at Greene family discussion, 2 July 1979, p.c.

p.297 'a bad judge ...': Masters, *op. cit.*, p.166.

p.297 'ostensibly devoted ...': MI5 memo, 17 June 1943, NA.

p.297 'a measure which ...': G.R. Mitchell, MI5 memo, 4 Feb. 1945, NA.

p.297 'Greene holds ...': *ibid.*

p.297 'I hope you do not ...': BG, unpublished papers, n.d., p.c.

p.297 'some of his colleagues ...': BG, unpublished papers, n.d., p.c.

p.297 'one of the honestest ...': W.C. Curry to Leslie Greene, 8 Oct. 1940, p.c.

Chapter 19: German Service

p.299 'the calm voice ...': q. in Mansell, *Let Truth Be Told*, p.59.

p.299 'one wasn't allowed ...': *ibid.*, p.70.

p.299 'the BBC's German ...': EH memo, Jan 1940.

p.300 'quick-witted ...': Grisewood, *One Thing at a Time*, p.134.

p.301 'help in stifling ...': q. in Mansell, *op. cit.*, p.34.

p.301 'totalitarian methods ...': q. in Briggs, *The War of Words*, p.9.

p.301 'one knew perfectly well ...': q. in Mansell, *op. cit.*, p.56.

p.302 'if they can admit ...': q. in Briggs, *op. cit.*

p.302 'in a world of poison ...': q. in *ibid*, p.10.

p.303 'variously enslaved ...': Grisewood, *op. cit.*, p.143.

p.303 'completely ignorant ...': q. in Tracey, *A Variety of Lives*, p.78.

p.303 'I couldn't stand ...': *ibid.*

p.304 'much superior ...': Howe, *The Black Game*, p.56.

p.304 'spoke of Crossman ...': Grisewood, *op. cit.*, p.139.

p.304 'this able and ...': diary, 18 Sept. 1941, q. in Howard, *Crossman*, p.85.

p.304 'one of the most versatile ...': *The Infernal Grove*, p.80.

p.304 'there is clearly going ...': 15 April 1942, Pearce (ed.), *Patrick Gordon Walker*, p.109.

p.304 'incompatible': Robert Walmsley, q. in Howe, *op. cit.*, p.95.

p.304 'so funny that ...': q. in Briggs, *op. cit.*, p.394.

p.305 'I spent nearly two years ...': *New Statesman*, 6 Nov. 1962.

p.305 'Herr Hitler, you have ...': *Black Boomerang*, p.16.

p.305 'undermines Hitler ...': *ibid*, p.41.

p.305 'stop gassing': *ibid.*

p.306 'a "black" news ...': *ibid*, p.78.

p.306 'on the basis of which ...': *New Statesman*, 9 Nov. 1962.

p.306 'the car stopped ...': John, *Twice through the Lines*, p.72.

p.307 'Jack is not ...': Young (ed.), *Diaries of Sir Robert Bruce Lockhart*, p.427.

p.307 'a gigantic waste ...': letter to *The Times*, 4 June 1973.

p.307 'Subversive operations ...': *The Times*, 16 May 1973.

p.307 '"black propaganda" seems ...': *The Third Floor Front*, p.26.

p.307 'Judged in terms ...': *New Statesman*, 9 Nov. 1962.

p.308 'nor am I ...': *Black Boomerang*, p.222.

p.308 'genial and Rabelaisian . . .': Robert Walmsley, q. in Howe, *op. cit.*, p.95.

p.308 'very tall, thin . . .': *Inside the BBC*, p.104.

p.308 'burly buccaneering . . .': *The Quest for the Bushmen*, p.21.

p.309 'real leader . . .': q. in Tracey, *op. cit.*, p.79.

p.309 'there was something philistine . . .': q. in *ibid*, p.86.

p.309 'a beast, but . . .': q. in Briggs, *op. cit.*, p.386.

p.309 'I'm sorry, old boy . . .': q. in Mansell, *op. cit.*, p.91.

p.309 'on the ground of . . .': BBC memo, 19 Oct. 1944, Caversham.

p.310 'the talks were terrible . . .': *Black Boomerang*, p.39.

p.310 'a most unpleasant . . .': BBC memo, 23 Jan. 1942, Caversham.

p.311 'Conditions in which . . .': 23 July 1941, *Diaries*, op. cit., p.111.

p.311 'BBC broadcasts . . .': q. in Howe, *op. cit.*, p.236.

p.311 'accusations of . . .': *Propaganda*, p.96.

p.312 'the sincere voices . . .': q in Briggs, *op. cit.*, p.224.

p.312 'listeners at this time . . .': BBC memo 3 Sept. 1940, Caversham.

p.312 'so vulgar . . .': q. in Briggs, *op. cit.*, p.392.

p.312 'one invaluable bait . . .': *Propaganda*, p.98.

p.312 'This is where we do . . .': q. in Briggs, *op. cit.*, p.250.

p.312 'a professed admirer . . .': *The Inner Circle*, p.148.

p.313 'Jamming is really . . .': BBC statement, May 1940, Caversham.

p.314 'hostility is not . . .': q. in Briggs, *op. cit.*, p.155.

p.314 'until Britain is . . .': BBC European Service 'Monthly Intelligence Report', Jan. 1941, q. in Briggs, *op. cit.*, p.388.

p.314 'in Germany civil war . . .': q. in Tracey, *op. cit.*, p.84.

p.315 'quite out of tune . . .': BBC memo, 8 Aug. 1944, Caversham.

p.315 'take refuge in . . .': *New Statesman*, 9 Nov. 1962.

p.315 'it was in the second . . .': q. in Briggs, *op. cit.*, p.626.

p.316 'dead city . . .': HCG, 'Berlin Impressions', 19 Sept. 1945, Caversham.

Chapter 20: Secret Agents

p.317 'Only after recruitment . . .': *Ways of Escape*, p.93.

p.317 'for a brief period . . .': Kim Philby to Norman Sherry, n.d., Boston,

p.318 'After very few sessions . . .': *ibid.*

p.318 'disused police . . .': *Ways of Escape*, p.95.

p.318 'dingy little . . .': 2 April 1942, *A Life in Letters*, p.111.

p.318 'I never quite . . .': 4 May 1942, *ibid*, p.114.

p.318 'my love of Africa . . .': *Ways of Escape*, p.121.

p.319 'one such interrogation . . .': GG to Norman Sherry, 27 Feb. 1991, *A Life in Letters*, p.420.

p.319 'The results of his work . . .': Kim Philby to Norman Sherry, *op. cit.*

p.320 'I didn't at that time . . .': to Norman Sherry, 27 Feb. 1991, p.c.

p.320 'This isn't an ideal . . .': 23 July 1942, LL, p.117.

p.320 'a very nice piece . . .': 28 June 1942, Georgetown.

p.320 'grateful for your . . .': 1 Aug. 1942, Georgetown.

p.320 'His current preoccupation . . .': *Never Judge a Man by his Umbrella*, p.113.

p.320 'I feel it was rather . . .': 30 Nov. 1942, *A Life in Letters*, p.121.

p.321 'when one did go down . . .': 4 Jan. 1943, *ibid*, p.122.

p.321 'quinine and . . .': *ibid.*

p.321 'The Africans at least . . .': *ibid.*

p.321 'This is a quite useless . . .': *ibid.*

p.321 'after the North African . . .': Kim Philby to Norman Sherry, *op. cit.*

p.321 'a large, ugly . . .': *ibid.*

p.322 'bored them into submission . . .': q. in Knightley, *Philby*, p.81.

p.322 'Oh, that was all . . .': *ibid*, p.85.

p.322 'a conscientious but . . .': *The Philby Affair*, p.28.

p.322 'Philby was widely . . .': *Enigma Spy*, p.115.

p.323 'part-time stockbrokers . . .': Trevor-Roper, *op. cit.*, p.32.

p.323 'was liable to . . .': *The Infernal Grove*, p.124.

p.323 'formidable drinker . . .': *op. cit.*

p.323 'You were either . . .': q. in Knightley, *op. cit.*, p.119.

p.324 'worked quietly . . .': Kim Philby to Norman Sherry, *op. cit.*

p.324 'tall, lanky . . .': Cairncross, *op. cit.*, p.118.

p.324 'far closer to . . .': *ibid*, p.121.

p.325 'a question of files . . .': *Ways of Escape*, p.239.

p.325 'more than ever . . .': *The Infernal Grove*, p.187.

p.325 'I can just remember . . .': David R. Hadden '100 Years of Hormonology: A View from No. 1 Wimpole Street' in Journal of the Royal Society of Medicine, July 2005.

p.326 'Philby at one stroke . . .': q. in Knightley, *op. cit.*, p.125.

p.326 'I attributed it . . .': Introduction to *My Silent War*, p.ix.

p.326 'obvious man . . .': Kim Philby to Norman Sherry, *op. cit.*

p.326 'We were very sorry . . .': *ibid.*

p.327 'incredible Victorian . . .': to Marion Greene, n.d., p.c.

p.327 'a dilapidated dump . . .': 9 Sept. 1941, p.c.

p.328 'oppressive, dusty . . .': Barbara Skelton, *Tears Before Bedtime*, Hamish Hamilton, 1987, p.59.

p.328 'hundreds of beggars . . .': 31 Oct. 1941, p.c.

p.328 'impossibly expensive': *ibid.*

p.328 'I feel quite ashamed . . .': *ibid.*

p.328 'slightly repelled . . .': to Marion Greene, 4 March 1942, p.c.

p.328 'tall, slim . . .': Rozanne Colchester to author, 15 Dec. 2009.

p.329 'he's only a bogus . . .': 27 June 1942, p.c.

p.329 'we were fortunate . . .': letter to unnamed recipient, 26 June 1978, p.c.

p.329 'a certain buccaneering . . .': *ibid.*

p.329 'a dear man . . .': Rozanne Colchester, *op. cit.*

p.329 'I made my reputation . . .': to C.J.B. Davy, 12 Dec. 1992, p.c.

p.330 'the key member . . .': J.M. Bruce Lockhart to Rodney Dennys, 24 Jan. 1992, p.c.

p.331 'effectively controlled . . .': letter to unnamed recipient, 26 June 1978, p.c.

p.331 'important and . . .': W.J. Kenyon Jones to Rodney Dennys, 25 Sept. 1991, p.c.

p.332 'rather unattractive . . .': Rodney Dennys to Jean Howard, 21 Aug. 1984, p.c.

p.333 'a long, lean . . .': *The Cat and the Mice*, p.134.

p.333 'Everyone always likes him . . .': 27 June 1942, p.c.

p.333 'Vices: smokes . . .': 27 March 1942, p.c.

p.334 'Elisabeth's engagement . . .': 1 Aug. 1942, Georgetown.

p.334 'I could quite easily . . .': to Marion Greene, 27 June 1942, p.c.

p.334 'I'm sorry things . . .': 15 Oct. 1942, LL, p.120.

p.334 'Graham's friend . . .': 5 Nov. 1942, p.c.

p.334 'that mosquito . . .': letter to unnamed recipient, 26 June 1978, p.c.

p.334 'I hope he hadn't . . .': 9 Nov. 1942, p.c.

p.335 'Luckily I am . . .': 25 July 1943, p.c.

p.335 'Malcolm always . . .': 13 Feb. 1944, p.c.

p.336 'one of the uncomfortable . . .': *ibid.*

p.336 'decadent aristocracy . . .': 7 May 1944, p.c.

p.336 'as vague . . .': 29 Oct. 1944, p.c.

p.336 'Please see that I . . .': 8 June 1944, p.c.

p.336 'to serve in . . .': Foreign Office to Rodney Dennys, 24 Jan. 1947, p.c.

p.336 'while we continued . . .': to C.J.B. Davy, 12 Dec. 1992, p.c.

p.337 'the dying twitches . . .': q. in Bethell, *Spies and Other Secrets*, p.288.

p.337 'very charming . . .': to Richard Greene, 3 April 2003, p.c.

p.337 'the worst traitor . . .': to C.J.B. Davy, 12 Dec. 1992, p.c.

Chapter 21: Scenes from Office Life

p.338 'Have you heard . . .': 18 Aug. 1943, LL, p.128.

p.338 'I'm sorry Graham . . .': to Marion Greene, 25 July 1943, p.c.

p.338 'secure economic base': *The Infernal Grove*, p.236.

p.339 'the luckiest . . .': q. in Holman, *Print for Victory*, p.242.

p.339 'a telephone call . . .': *ibid*.

p.339 'a fervent advocate . . .': *ibid*.

p.339 'a tall, saturnine figure': q. in Thomson (ed.), *Articles of Faith*, p.146.

p.339 'a Counter-Reformation . . .': *ibid*.

p.339 'large, sombrely dressed . . .': *To Keep the Ball Rolling*, p.199.

p.340 'the look of a perennial . . .': *The Infernal Grove*, p.237.

p.340 'Jerrold and I . . .': to Norman Sherry, 11 March 1991, Boston.

p.340 'in her righteous . . .': q. in Shelden, *Graham Greene*, p.434.

p.340 'would settle down . . .': *ibid*.

p.340 'he is, and does . . .': *ibid*.

p.340 'always seemed to him . . .': 16 April 1948,

p.341 'I'm going to be . . .': Oct. 1943, *A Life in Letters*, p.129.

p.341 'let Eyre & Spottiswoode . . .': Rothenstein, *Time's Thievish Progress*, p.166.

p.341 'it was a measure . . .': Kee, introduction to Jonathan Cape edition of *A Crowd Is Not Company*, 1982, p.8.

p.342 'which we badly needed . . .': *Getting to Know the General*, p.21.

p.342 'learnt that . . .': *ibid*.

p.342 'As a publisher . . .': to David Higham, 19 Aug. 1947, Rushden.

p.342 'speaking as a publisher . . .': to Frere, 20 June 1947, Rushden.

p.342 'and from that position . . .': 3 Jan. 1946, Rushden.

p.342 'My own preference . . .': to Frere, 20 June 1947, Rushden.

p.342 'an odd, unhappy . . .': 13 Sept. 1949, unpublished diaries 1948–50, p.c.

p.342 'I think you should . . .': to Norman Sherry, n.d., Boston.

p.343 'a Jekyll and Hyde . . .': 23 Feb. 1948, unpublished diaries 1948–50, p.c.p.249.

p.343 'as I had foreseen . . .': 1 June 1948, unpublished diaries 1948–50, p.c.

p.343 'bloody boring book': Powell, *To Keep the Ball Rolling*. p.201.

p.343 'hilarious': *ibid*.

p.343 'curious lunch . . .': 15 Sept. 1948, Bright-Holmes (ed.), *Like It Was*, p.298.

p.344 'colossal row . . .': Powell, *Journals 1990–1992*, p.106.

p.344 'gathered from Douglas . . .': 25 Oct. 1948, Bright-Holmes (ed.), *Like It Was*, p.304.

p.344 'Graham has no more . . .': *To Keep the Ball Rolling*, p.201.

p.344 'Your case really . . .': 14 Dec. 1948, *LL*, p.162.

p.344 'from the word go . . .': *Journals 1990–1992*, p.105.

p.344 'most of his plans . . .': *Literary Gent*, p.173.

Chapter 22: Hamburg, and a femme fatale

p.345 'Hamburg is a depressing . . .': to Elisabeth Dennys, 21 Oct. 1945, p.c.

p.346 'we tried to demonstrate . . .': q. in TS of Tracey, *A Variety of Lives*.

p.347 'nobody cared . . .': q. in Meehan, *A Strange Enemy People*, p.183.

p.347 'Life in general . . .': 10 Oct. 1946, Bodleian.

p.347 'I enjoyed my rows . . .': q. in TS of Tracey, *op. cit.*

p.348 'some painful surgery . . .': *ibid*.

p.348 'comfortably curled . . .': Clare, *Berlin Days 1946–47*, p.164.

p.348 'Hugh was sitting . . .': *ibid*, p.167.

p.348 'very lovable . . .': q. in Tracey, *op. cit.*

p.349 'There's nothing . . .': 8 March 1946, Bodleian.

p.349 'I think it's time . . .': 1 April 1948, Bodleian.

p.349 'My period . . .': q. in Tracey, *op. cit.*

p.350 'You will fail . . .': *ibid*.

p.350 'gaiety and irreverence': *ibid*.

p.351 'get our audience . . .': q. in Dorril, *MI6*, p.79.

p.351 'took the view . . .': n.d., Caversham.

p.351 'Hugh, how would . . .': q. in Tracey, *A Variety of Lives*, p.126.

p.352 'I love you . . .': 1 Feb. 1944, Bodleian.

p.352 'A.J.P. Taylor . . .': n.d., Bodleian.

p.353 'so belle . . .': q. in Cash, *The Third Woman*, p.12.

p.353 'a perfect milky . . .': *New Statesman*, 19 April 2004.

p.353 'a rather odd . . .': *A Twentieth-Century Life*, p.174.

p.354 'I went to such . . .': 4 Oct. 1948, *Letters of Evelyn Waugh*, p.284.

p.354 'unaffected . . .': 29 Sept. 1948, Davie (ed.), *Diaries of Evelyn Waugh*, p.702.

p.354 'She rampaged . . .': 1 Sept. 1952, Amory (ed.), *Letters of Evelyn Waugh*, p.380.

p.354 'She behaved . . .': 10 June 1960, Amory (ed.), *Letters of Ann Fleming*, p.259.

p.355 'manifestly unsuited . . .': *Time's Thievish Progress*, p.168.

p.355 'thoroughly fed-up . . .': 29 May 1947, Georgetown.

p.355 'in love with a Bacall . . .': to Catherine Walston, 22 Aug. 1947, Georgetown.

p.355 'comforting Vivien . . .': Vivien Greene papers, n.d., Bodleian.

p.356 'He sat on the . . .': diary, 21 Jan. 1980, Bodleian.

p.356 'and I was on the floor . . .': *ibid.*

p.356 'we talked all the time . . .': 29 Sept. 1948, Davie (ed.), *Diaries of Evelyn Waugh*, p.702.

p.356 'I do not know . . .': 12 Feb. 1950, Mosley (ed.), *Letters of Nancy Mitford and Evelyn Waugh*, p.179.

p.356 'both drinkers . . .': 22 Aug. 1951, BL.

p.357 'Mrs Walston . . .': 3 April 1953, Amory (ed.), *Letters of Ann Fleming*, p.126.

p.357 'You know I am . . .': 3 June 1948, Bodleian.

p.357 'Graham, you were . . .': 31 July 1948, Bodleian.

p.357 'unwanted . . .': 'Life', unpublished TS, 1952, Bodleian.

p.358 'a loose American . . .': diary 16 Jan. 1952, Bodleian.

p.358 'What can I say . . .': 3 Jan. 1948, Tulsa.

p.358 'It absolutely . . .': 7 Jan. 1948, Tulsa.

p.358 'Your letter has . . .': 29 June 1948, Tulsa.

p.358 'as Graham was . . .': n.d., Tulsa.

p.358 'is the most experienced . . .': n.d., 1948, Bodleian.

p.359 'a companion spirit': to Catherine Walston, 13 April 1950, Georgetown.

p.359 'How far away Torcello . . .': 8 April 1949, Georgetown.

p.359 'Things have been battering . . .': 20 Aug. 1941, BL.

p.359 'shambling . . .': 11 Jan. 1948, Davie (ed.), *Diaries of Evelyn Waugh*, p.694.

p.359 'like a raddled . . .': 26 Feb. 1949, *Midway on the Waves*, p.157.

p.359 'even then the blue . . .': *Time's Thievish Progress*, p.168.

p.359 'GG thinks of *nothing* . . .': 12 Feb. 1950, Mosley (ed.), *Letters of Nancy Mitford and Evelyn Waugh*, p.179.

p.360 'I never cease . . .': 19 Jan. 1949, Bodleian.

p.360 'I'd so like to say . . .': 16 Jan. 1951, Bodleian.

p.360 'You mustn't feel . . .': 15 Oct. 1962, Bodleian.

p.360 'Graham of course . . .': to Gabriel and Edwina Fielding, n.d., Bodleian.

p.360 'like in that Prior . . .': 9 April 1943, Bodleian.

p.361 'I was the failure . . .': 26 July 1952, Bodleian.

p.361 'How to read . . .': note dated 3 March 1979, Bodleian.

p.361 'hideously unreal . . .': to Father Ivor Daniel, n.d., p.c.

p.361 'I want you to know . . .': draft letter to Dorothy Glover, n.d., Tulsa.

p.361 'No one dares . . .': 11 May 1953, Morgan (ed.), *Backbench Diaries of Richard Crossman*, p.240.

p.361 'My dear, I never . . .': 18 Dec. 1949, Georgetown.

p.361 'the hygienic . . .': 13 April 1950, Georgetown.

p.361 'nerves and gloom': *ibid.*

p.361 'they had at last . . .': Donaldson, *op. cit.*, p.175.

p.362 '*Please* don't . . .': 13 April 1950, Georgetown.

p.362 'nasty shock . . .': to Catherine Walston, 16 Dec. 1975, Georgetown.

p.362 'and by midnight . . .': May 1951, p.c.

p.362 'We drove down . . .': June 1951, p.c.

p.362 'hopelessly . . .': March 1952, p.c.

p.363 'You are the greatest . . .': q. in Sherry, *The Life of Graham Greene*, Vol. 3, p.471.

Chapter 23: Eastern Promise

p.364 'Hugh is off . . .': 16 Aug. 1950, Georgetown.

p.364 'I came into . . .': q. in TS of Tracey, *A Variety of Lives*.

p.365 'the attempt to . . .': *The Third Floor Front*, p.20.

p.365 'wars are not won . . .': Jan. 1951 memo, q. in TS of Tracey, *op. cit.*

p.365 'one of the greatest . . .': q. in Tracey, *A Variety of Lives*, p.134.

p.365 'the underground . . .': *The Third Floor Front*, p.34.

p.366 'there was seldom . . .': *ibid*, p.36.

p.366 'the task of . . .': q. in Tracey, *op. cit.*, p.130.

p.367 'In many parts . . .': *ibid.*

p.367 'fallen completely . . .': to Marion Greene, 6 Nov. 1950, Bodleian.

p.367 'it is an awful . . .': *ibid.*

p.367 'It's over . . .': radio talk 'On Being a Bandit', n.d., Bodleian.

p.367 'The best coup . . .': to GG, 28 March 1951, Boston.

p.367 'one cheerful ruffian . . .': *The Third Floor Front*, p.37.

p.367 'the fifties were . . .': *Ways of Escape*, p.139.

p.367 'I had no employer . . .': *ibid.*

p.368 'I always find . . .': 3 Nov. 1950, Georgetown.

p.368 'overjoyed': to Catherine Walston, 27 Nov. 1950, Georgetown.

p.368 'I haven't even . . .': 7 Dec. 1950, Georgetown.

p.368 'I love you more . . .': *ibid.*

p.368 'the war was like . . .': *Ways of Escape*, p.141.

p.368 'jungle-green . . .': 11 Dec. 1950, Georgetown.

p.368 'I felt utterly . . .': *ibid.*

p.368 'It was a nasty . . .': 16 Jan. 1951, Georgetown.

p.369 'tall, foxy-faced . . .': to Catherine Walston, 25 Dec. 1950, Georgetown.

p.369 'Here he was back again . . .': *ibid.*

p.369 'the dreariest . . .': to Catherine Walston, 28 Aug. 1953, Georgetown.

p.369 'I was rather wistfully . . .': HCG to GG, 3 March 1951, Boston.

p.369 'This is a fascinating . . .': 28 Aug. 1953, Georgetown.

p.369 'my trip to Malaya . . .': 19 March 1953, BL.

p.369 'The spell was . . .': *Ways of Escape*, p.154.

p.369 'no nonsense . . .': to HCG, 26 June 1951, Georgetown.

p.369 'a great soldier . . .': *Memories of Times Past*, Hamish Hamilton, 1988, p.153.

p.370 'very politely . . .': to Catherine Walston, 21 Nov. 1951, Georgetown.

p.370 'very lecherous . . .': *ibid.*

p.370 'bored and irritated . . .': 27 Dec. 1951, Georgetown.

p.370 'What a damned . . .': 21 Nov. 1951, Georgetown.

p.370 'I will go to . . .': q. in Nashel, *Edward Lansdale's Cold War*, p.155.

p.370 'the terrifying weight . . .': *ibid.*

p.370 'complete travesty': *ibid*, p.172.

p.370 'a strangely happy . . .': 15 May 1951, Boston.

p.370 'he seemed like . . .': Elaine Shaplen to HCG, n.d. 1951, Bodleian.

p.370 'sheer hell . . .': *ibid.*

p.371 'a very generous . . .': to Marion Greene, n.d., BL.

p.371 'This is just for you . . .': 8 June 1951, Boston.

p.371 'I liked her . . .': 26 June 1951, Boston.

Chapter 24: Sense and Sensibility

p.372 'What the world needs . . .': 23 Sept. 1945, p.c.

p.372 'a very simple . . .': n.d. 1945, p.c.

p.372 'more in touch . . .': to Eva Greene, 4 Oct. 1945, p.c.

p.373 'Until a man . . .': to Eva Greene, 16 Jan. 1947, p.c.

p.373 'Papa's illness . . .': 22 Sept. 1947, p.c.

p.373 'From Elena . . .': 20 Aug. 1945, p.c.

p.374 'The important thing . . .': to Eva Greene, 14 June 1947, p.c.

p.374 'work of self-knowledge': to Elena Greene, 12 Dec. 1949, p.c.

p.374 'I couldn't have . . .': 14 Jan. 1950, p.c.

p.374 'I am in love . . .': 5 Dec. 1949, p.c.

p.375 'Elena is being . . .': to Eleanor Greene, 17 March 1957, p.c.

p.375 'There isn't . . .': 29 Jan. 1951, p.c.

p.375 'Sometimes . . .': 20 Nov. 1953, p.c.

p.375 'remember being ...': GG to Flanagans, 7 March 1983, p.c.

p.375 'I am forty-two ...': note dated 12 Feb. 1953, p.c.

p.376 'has represented ...': ibid.

p.376 'I feel more ...': 'Notes for Discussion with Berliner', n.d. 1953, p.c.

p.376 'From the moment ...': n.d., p.c.

p.376 'all my life ...': 23 Dec. 1949, p.c.

p.376 'I am not surprised ...': 27 Sept. 1946, p.c.

p.377 'the one place ...': to Elena Greene, 8 Jan. 1952, p.c.

p.377 'immense knowledge ...': ibid.

p.377 'Ben, being Ben ...': to Flanagans, 7 Jan. 1985, p.c.

p.377 'We have so often ...': to Elena Greene, 4 Jan. 1956, p.c.

p.378 'I do not see how ...': 22 Jan. 1956, p.c.

p.378 'got caught in ...': to Elena Greene, 20 Dec. 1950, p.c.

p.378 'Kate is copying ...': to Elena Greene, 1 Feb. 1954, p.c.

p.378 'The children are ...': to Eva Greene, 30 Nov. 1954, p.c.

p.379 'simple, direct ...': to Elena Greene, 1 Feb. 1954, p.c.

p.379 'What a family ...': ibid.

p.379 'suffered not only ...': Preface to The Practice of Endocrinology, p.vi.

p.380 'painstaking ...': obituary in the British Medical Journal.

p.380 'detached outlook ...': obituary in The Times.

p.381 'I can just remember ...': David R. Hadden, '100 Years of Hormonology: A View from No. 1 Wimpole Street' in Journal of the Royal Society of Medicine, July 2005.

Chapter 25: Civil War in Greene Land

p.383 'While satisfying ...': q. in Briggs, The BBC: The First Fifty Years, p.245.

p.383 'Television will be ...': ibid, p.273.

p.383 'fight against ...': ibid, p.276.

p.385 'To seek success ...': ibid, p.300.

p.385 'the one big ...': ibid, p.302.

p.385 'because in doing so ...': q. in Tracey, A Variety of Lives, p.157.

p.386 'nice old boy ...': q. in TS of Tracey, A Variety of Lives.

p.386 'Nobody has called me ...': 12 May 1955, Bodleian.

p.387 'small, birdlike ...': Milne, DG, p.8.

p.387 'her sharp tongue ...': q. in Miall, Inside the BBC, p.139.

p.388 'all the graces ...': q. in Milne, op. cit., p.18.

p.388 'disputed with us ...': ibid, p.25.

p.388 'he's totally insensitive ...': q. in Tracey, op. cit., p.169.

p.388 'a massive ...': Priestland, Something Understood, p.93.

p.388 'tall, massive ...': Miall, op. cit., p.124.

p.388 'the news was a joke ...': Milne, op. cit., p.7.

p.388 'laughably bad': q. in Tracey, A Variety of Lives, p.172.

p.389 'Remember, Priestland ...': ibid, p.94.

p.389 'Kremlin of the BBC ...': q. in Miall, op. cit., p.126.

p.389 'I have never had ...': TS of Tracey, A Variety of Lives.

p.389 'only exists ...': q. in TS of Tracey, A Variety of Lives.

p.389 'Right, we do this': Miall, op. cit., p.110.

p.389 'an icy stare ...': ibid.

p.389 'Hugh was tough ...': q. in Tracey, op. cit., p.177.

p.389 'great charm ...': Miall, op. cit., p.110.

p.390 'largest proportion ...': GG to HG, n.d. 1946, Morgan.

p.390 'You are in fact ...': ibid.

p.390 'I'll send Audrey ...': n.d., BL.

p.391 'Mumma has told me ...': n.d., Morgan.

p.391 'Even if I had ...': 7 Jan. 1955, Morgan.

p.392 'As a great believer ...': n.d., Bodleian.

p.392 'I have just heard ...': 10 Feb. 1958, Georgetown.

p.392 'No one is objecting ...': 18 Feb. 1958, Georgetown.

p.393 'He's a sad ...': q. in Tracey, op. cit., p.147.

p.393 'I am glad that ...': 25 Nov. 1957, Bodleian.

p.393 'I am glad ...': 25 Nov. 1957, Bodleian.

p.393 'I do strongly ...': 9 Jan. 1958, Georgetown.

p.393 'I owe you . . .': n.d., Georgetown.

p.394 'I am very fond . . .': *Daily Mail*, 17 Oct. 1960.

p.395 'I see from . . .': 29 Sept. 1960, Georgetown.

p.395 'I had a letter . . .': 17 April 1959, Boston.

p.395 'Herbert to my surprise . . .': 24 April 1959, Boston.

p.395 'my cousin Barbara . . .': *The Condor and the Crows*, p.x.

p.395 'my escape . . .': to Eva Greene, 4 March 1962, p.c.

p.396 'VG is rubbing . . .': 14 Nov. 1962, p.c.

p.396 'Rudi always gives . . .': to Eva Greene, 11 Jan. 1955, p.c.

p.396 'we talked a lot . . .': to Eva Greene, 5 April 1958, p.c.

p.396 'though when one . . .': to Eva Greene, 8 Aug. 1958, p.c.

p.396 'Remember that . . .': 8 Dec. 1959, Boston.

p.396 'leaving quite . . .': 25 Feb. 1960, p.c.

p.397 'Now suddenly . . .': 8 Dec. 1959, p.c.

p.397 'I had cherished . . .': 8 May 1948, Bodleian.

p.397 'Whatever induced . . .': 8 Jan. 1986, Georgetown.

p.398 'respectful agnostic': q. in Tracey, *op. cit.*, p.398

p.398 'Well, that's all right . . .': q. in *ibid*, p.180.

p.398 'she lost all interest . . .': 25 Sept. 1959, p.c.

p.398 'Perhaps as a Catholic . . .': 21 Sept. 1959, *A Life in Letters*, p.245.

Chapter 26: China Hand

p.399 'I *love* the Chinese . . .': 17 Sept. 1957, p.c.

p.399 'much nicer person': *ibid*.

p.400 'He sees the whole . . .': 30 July 1957, p.c.

p.400 'I expected . . .': *The Wall Has Two Sides*, p.8.

p.400 'They really are . . .': 26 Sept. 1957, p.c.

p.401 'got under the skin . . .': to Elena Greene, 2 Oct. 1957, p.c.

p.401 'released a . . .': 5 Dec. 1957, p.c.

p.401 'the doubt creeps . . .': to Elena Greene, 8 Jan. 1958, p.c.

p.401 'come to the conclusion . . .': 'Free to be Human', *China Now*, Dec. 1972.

p.402 'a certain freshness . . .': q. in Hollander, *Political Pilgrims*, p.314.

p.402 'glorification . . .': *ibid*.

p.402 'allows one . . .': to Flanagans, 13 May 1983, p.c.

p.402 'bonds of common . . .': Marcuse, *Leaves from the Notebook of a China Correspondent*, p.100.

p.403 'the regime's . . .': *ibid*, p.8.

p.403 'Their sources . . .': *ibid*, p.105.

p.403 'a comparative . . .': *ibid*, p.106.

p.403 'I did not ingratiate . . .': *ibid*.

p.403 'his good faith . . .': *ibid*.

p.404 'eyes shining . . .': Suyin, *The House Has Two Doors*, p.279.

p.404 'a growing sense . . .': to Elena Greene, 9 June 1958, p.c.

p.404 'this new development . . .': to Elena Greene, 30 Jan, 1959, p.c.

p.404 'there's no flow . . .': to Elena Greene, 20 Aug. 1959, p.c.

p.404 'I think he got . . .': to Elena Greene, 12 Sept. 1959, p.c.

p.404 'grandeur here . . .': to Elena Greene, 20 June 1960, p.c.

p.405 'why do we never . . .': 14 June 1960, p.c.

p.405 'It is a people's . . .': to Elena Greene,16 July 1960. p.c.

p.405 'if only people . . .': to Elena Greene, 4 Dec. 1960, p.c.

p.406 'He is an exceptionally . . .': to Elena Greene, 24 Dec. 1965, p.c.

p.406 'must not even . . .': 6 Oct. 1963, p.c.

p.406 'Just picture me . . .': 22 Oct. 1963, p.c.

p.406 'this may be . . .': 15 Nov. 1963, p.c.

p.406 'China is now *full* . . .': 18 Nov. 1963, p.c.

p.406 'Oh Lord . . .': to Elena Greene, n.d., p.c.

p.407 'consciously devil . . .': *The Times*, 19 Nov. 1975.

p.407 'Felix's enthusiasm . . .': 20 June 1968, p.c.

p.407 'How CAN . . .': 17 Nov. 1959, p.c.

p.407 'I hope he does not spoil . . .': to Eva Greene, n.d. 1961, p.c.

p.407 'The book is in all . . .': 22 Jan. 1962, Reading.

p.407 'soapiest seller . . .': *Spectator*, Aug. 1965.

p.407 'unbalanced . . .': *Observer*, 1 Aug. 1965

p.408 'what is happening . . .': to Elena Greene, 27 Nov. 1965, p.c.

p.408 'bullying and . . .': *ibid.*

p.408 'I am afraid I can't . . .': 20 Oct. 1966, Reading.

p.408 'tremendous job': to GG, 1 May 1968, Boston.

p.408 'I have never liked . . .': 7 May 1968, Boston.

p.408 'I can't for the life of me . . .': to Graham C. Greene, 22 Oct. 1966, Reading.

p.408 'This is really great . . .': 19 Oct. 1966, Reading.

p.409 'utterly at ease . . .': 27 Feb. 1967, p.c.

p.409 'everyone is . . .': to Anne Greene, 22 Jan. 1967, p.c.

p.409 'I warm to . . .': 20 Dec. 1974, p.c.

p.409 'well-meaning but . . .': to Elena Greene, 25 March 1967, p.c.

p.409 'the best and most . . .': to Flanagans, 12 Feb. 1983, p.c.

p.409 'This is the kind of . . .': 25 March 1967, p.c.

p.410 'It obviously cannot . . .': 27 March 1968, p.c.

p.410 'the sense of incapacity . . .': to Elena Greene, 15 Sept. 1969, p.c.

p.410 'I have never been . . .': to Anne Greene, 22 Jan. 1967, p.c.

p.410 'It is Mao . . .': to Elena Greene, 22 Jan. 1967, p.c.

p.410 'quietly drank . . .': to Elena Greene, 28 July 1972, p.c.

p.411 'everyone, like I have . . .': to Elena Greene, 9 June 1977, p.c.

p.411 'Dear God . . .': to Eva Greene, 27 Jan. 1979, p.c.

p.411 'They can't afford . . .': diary, 28 May 1979, p.c.

p.411 'filled with certainty . . .': to Eva Greene, 17 June 1976, p.c.

p.411 'the coldest . . .': to Eleanor Gamble, 20 March 1933, p.c.

p.411 'You must cast . . .': 7 July 1976, p.c.

p.412 'so anxious . . .': *Guardian*, 12 May 1977.

Chapter 27: Man of Letters

p.413 'Osbert and I . . .': 15 Nov. 1958, Georgetown.

p.413 'I think if I . . .': 4 Feb. 1959, *A Life in Letters*, p.238.

p.413 'a sadistic . . .': GG to David Buttram, 12 Aug. 1973.

p.414 'a few bottles . . .': q. in Hazzard, *Greene on Capri*, p.16.

p.414 'I am not a genius . . .': Cloetta, *In Search of a Beginning*, 67.

p.414 'But what twentieth-century . . .': Gavin Young, *Worlds Apart: Travels in War and Peace*, Hutchinson, 1987, p.294.

p.414 'made the storyteller . . .': *ibid*, p.71.

p.414 'I can re-read . . .': to John Michael Gibson, 20 Oct. 1980, Boston.

p.414 'a very painful . . .': Cloetta, *op. cit.*

p.414 'a reaction against . . .': Mewshaw, *Do I Owe You Something?*, p.139.

p.414 'two of the worst . . .': GG to Elisabeth Dennys, n.d., Boston.

p.414 'intruded herself . . .': Amanda Sanders, 19 May 2003. p.c.

p.415 'either a liar . . .': 13 June 1988, HRHRC.

p.415 'He put words . . .': q. in Lewis, *Anthony Burgess*, p.213.

p.415 'delighted . . .': 27 Sept. 1983, Boston.

p.415 'During my life . . .': Cloetta, *op. cit.*, p.71.

p.415 'Fifty years of . . .': *op. cit.*, p.82.

p.415 'In physiognomy . . .': Hazzard, *op. cit.*, p.10.

p.416 'Ralph is *impossible* . . .': to Yvonne Cloetta, 5 Sept. 1964, Georgetown.

p.416 'The cost of living . . .': letter to *The Times*, 17 April 1951, q. in Hawtree (ed.), *Yours Etc.*, p.112.

p.416 'launched us . . .': Reinhardt, *Memories*, p.56.

p.416 'This could be . . .': *ibid.*

p.417 'I don't believe . . .': *ibid.*

p.417 'and now have . . .': Nov. 1960, Bodleian.

p.418 'in recognition of . . .': letter from GG and John Sutro to *Spectator*, q. in *Yours Etc.*, p.79.

p.418 'Mr G. Greene is . . .': 26 Feb. 1956, q. in Cooper (ed.), *Mr Wu and Mrs Stitch*, p.218.

p.418 'seems to me . . .': 14 May 1964, BL.

p.418 'wasn't going to remain . . .': q. in Lambert, *The Bodley Head*, p.311

p.418 'Priestley was furious . . .': to Lady

Redesdale, 19 May 1957, Mosley (ed.), *Letters of Nancy Mitford*, p.364.

p.419 'genuine warmth . . .': Hill, *The Pursuit of Publishing*, p.68.

p.419 'the cleverest man . . .': *ibid*, p.67.

p.419 'I never once . . .': *ibid*, p.172.

p.420 'It looks as though . . .': 18 May 1961, Georgetown.

p.420 'Heinemann won't . . .': 24 May 1961, Georgetown.

p.420 'this publishing . . .': 6 June 1961, Georgetown.

p.420 'he refused to . . .': Reinhardt, *op. cit.*, p.64.

p.420 'I must in self-protection . . .': 1 June 1961, q. in St John, *William Heinemann*, p.428.

p.420 'the sense of trust . . .': letter to *Observer*, 23 July 1961, q. in *Yours Etc.*, p.107.

p.421 'I have been told . . .': 20 June 1961, HRHRC.

p.421 'They made me . . .': q. in Lambert, *op. cit.*, p.314.

p.421 'steal James Michie . . .': q. in Adamson, *Max Reinhardt*, p.73.

p.421 'saying fairly early . . .': q. in St John, *op. cit.*, p.432.

p.421 'You have been . . .': 16 Oct. 1962, HRHRC.

p.422 'the wonderfully discreet . . .': Euan Cameron, 'A Guiding Light': address to Graham Greene Literary Festival, Berkhamsted, 2005.

p.422 'saw no reason . . .': 4 Sept. 1963, HRHRC.

p.422 'This will get . . .': 2 March 1965, Boston.

p.422 'From my publishing . . .': 21 Sept. 1965, Boston.

p.422 'clings to . . .': *Daily Telegraph*, 10 June 1966, q. in *Yours Etc.*, p.129.

p.423 'I couldn't trust . . .': to HCG, 17 May 1971, Georgetown.

p.423 'They said his new . . .': q. in Hazzard, *op. cit.*, p.46.

p.424 'Easier to change . . .': q. in Korda, *Another Life*, p.318.

p.424 'a tall, lean . . .': *ibid*, p.312.

p.424 'the malevolence . . .': to GG, 19 Nov. 1965, Boston.

p.424 'classic case . . .': q. in Meyer, *Not Prince Hamlet*, p.226.

p.424 'Claud always said . . .': *Figure of Eight*, p.163.

p.424 'one of a minority . . .': *Daily Telegraph*, 20 Aug. 1964, q. in *Yours Etc*, p.112.

p.425 'Hands up . . .': Richard Ingrams to author.

p.425 'you are the only . . .': 22 Jan. 1990, Boston.

p.425 'Having been . . .': 15 Sept. 1990, Boston.

p.425 'most affable . . .': *Oldie*, Oct. 2003.

p.426 'He looks far younger . . .': *20th-Century Characters*, p.208.

p.426 'I hope you have . . .': n.d 1954, Georgetown.

p.426 'If you refuse . . .': 7 May 1964, Amory (ed.), *Letters of Evelyn Waugh*, p.620.

p.426 'Really you old . . .': 14 May 1964, BL.

p.427 'I am not keen . . .': 5 Jan. 1974, Boston.

p.427 'Graham is a master . . .': *Journals 1987–1989*, p.183.

p.427 'I hate biographical . . .': 20 Sept. 1954, Rushton.

p.427 'I never under . . .': to A.S. Frere, 19 June 1959, Rushton.

p.427 'the great point . . .': 5 March 1962, HRHRC.

p.427 'Graham looked . . .': 25 Jan, 1965, *Diaries 1939–60*, p.568.

p.427 'he stooped at . . .': Mewshaw, *op. cit.*, p.138.

p.428 'real horror . . .': *ibid*, p.151.

p.428 'more than fifty . . .': 18 April 1979, Boston.

p.428 'that horrible woman . . .': Mewshaw, *op. cit.*, p.164.

p.429 'in a large . . .': Barbara Skelton, *Weep No More*, Hamish Hamilton, 1989, p.137.

p.429 'tiny carpenter's . . .': GG to Paul Scott, 24 Sept. 1956, HRHRC.

p.429 'This is Graham's room . . .': Euan Cameron, *op. cit.*

p.429 'rather worried . . .': 25 Oct. 1964, Boston.

p.429 'Her foresight . . .': Leopoldo Duran, *Graham Greene: Friend and Brother*, p.182.

p.430 'Everyone is . . .': q. in *Daily Express*, 17 Aug. 1965.

p.430 'another pirate . . .': 27 May 1974, Boston.

p.430 'Today I have been . . .': n.d. 1965, Georgetown.

p.430 'he is more social . . .': 28 Feb. 1966, Mosley (ed.), *Letters of Nancy Mitford and Evelyn Waugh*, p.503.

Chapter 28: Director-General

p.432 'Graham's first . . .': to Eva Greene, 23 July 1959. p.c.

p.432 'It's all very . . .': 28 July 1959, Bodleian.

p.432 'capital choice . . .': *Sunday Pictorial*, 26 July 1959, q. in Briggs, *Competition*, p.319.

p.432 'Greene light . . .': *Daily Mail*, 22 July 1959, q. in Briggs, *ibid*.

p.432 'cold fish . . .': q. in Tracey, *A Variety of Lives*, p.184.

p.432 'the best kind . . .': q. in *ibid*.

p.432 'horrified': 1 July 1959, Stuart (ed.), *Reith Diaries*, p.478.

p.432 'the appointment of . . .': 20 July 1959, *ibid*, p.491.

p.432 'no values . . .': q. in Tracey, *op. cit.*, p.182.

p.433 'a mirror . . .': q. in Briggs, *op. cit.*, p. 317.

p.433 'Democracy rests . . .': q. in Tracey, *op. cit.*, p.196.

p.433 'a core of . . .': q. in *ibid*, p.320.

p.433 'the most effective . . .': q. in Briggs, *op. cit.*, p.387.

p.433 'neutral, unbiased . . .': q. in Tracey, *op. cit.*, p. 234.

p.433 'I realise I am . . .': 15 Aug. 1966, Bodleian.

p.434 'open-hearted . . .': Curran, *A Seamless Robe*, p.321.

p.434 'should have an . . .': q. in Briggs, *op. cit.*, p.379.

p.434 'an engaging . . .': Lusty, *Bound to be Read*, p.246.

p.434 'Hugh lacked . . .': q. in Tracey, *op. cit.*, p.312.

p.434 'He tends . . .': *ibid*.

p.435 'in the end . . .': 27 Feb. 1960, Bodleian.

p.435 'it would be . . .': 31 Dec. 1959, q. in *Reith Diaries*, p.492.

p.435 'Tahu, get out . . .': q. in Briggs. *op. cit.*, p.312.

p.435 'What a splendid . . .': q. in *ibid*, p.297.

p.435 'In the final . . .': Lusty, *op. cit.*, p.216.

p.436 'What a lot of . . .': q. in Briggs, *The BBC: The First Fifty Years*, p.330.

p.436 'taken quiet . . .': Lusty, *op. cit.*, p.244.

p.436 'Although I did . . .': 31 Dec. 1959, q. in Stuart (ed.), *Reith Diaries*, p.492.

p.436 'never wise . . .': Lusty, *op. cit.*, p.216.

p.436 'much deteriorated': 12 May 1960, Stuart (ed.), *Reith Diaries*, p.508.

p.437 'vulgarity and . . .': *ibid*.

p.437 'if I were not . . .': 22 Aug. 1963, *ibid*, p.509.

p.437 'The BBC, particularly . . .': 7 Sept. 1963, *ibid*.

p.437 'I don't think . . .': 1 Jan. 1964, *ibid*.

p.437 'I said I was . . .': 8 Jan. 1964, *ibid*, p.510.

p.437 'I lead . . .': 20 Jan. 1964. *ibid*.

p.437 'the BBC has lost . . .': to Arthur fforde, 18 May 1964, *ibid*, p.514.

p.437 'eclipse, or . . .': 30 March 1964, *ibid*, p.515.

p.437 'more or less . . .': 18 May 1964, *Reith Diaries*, p.516.

p.437 'Don't you think . . .': q. in Briggs, *op. cit.*, p.317.

p.438 'after days of . . .': Milne, *op. cit.*, p.25.

p.438 'I had been directing . . .': *ibid*, p.36.

p.438 'I hope you will not . . .': q. in Briggs, *op. cit.*, p.360.

p.439 'I take my hat . . .': Milne, *op. cit.*, p.38.

p.439 'a pity to spoil . . .': q. in *ibid*, p.39.

p.439 'amateurish in . . .': q. in *ibid*, p.34.

p.439 'subversive anarchist . . .': 4 Dec. 1963, q. in Briggs, *op. cit.*, p.353.

p.439 'Who will rid . . .': *ibid*.

p.439 'I knew that 1964 . . .': q. in Cockerell, *Live from No. 10*, p.99.

p.439 'exaggerated importance . . .': q. in Briggs, *op. cit.*, p.372.

p.440 'Nobody in Britain . . .': Briggs, *op. cit.*, p.324.

p.440 'I long for . . .': 13 Oct. 1964, Bodleian.

p.440 'Thank you . . .': q. in Cockerell, *op. cit.*, p.107.

p.440 'I've often wondered . . .': q. in *ibid*, p.108.

p.441 'Harold Wilson thought . . .': q. in *ibid*, p.113.

p.441 'I fear that . . .': 1 April 1966, Bodleian.

p.441 'even more . . .': q. in Cockerell, *op. cit.*, p.131.

p.442 'We had treated . . .': q. in *ibid*, p.133.

p.442 'this marvellous charm . . .': q. in Tracey, *op. cit.*, p.270.

p.442 'was kind enough . . .': to Tatjana Sais, 18 Nov. 1967, Bodleian.

p.442 'That frightful man . . .': q. in Cockerell, *op. cit.*, p.140.

p.442 'I saw what . . .': q. in Briggs, *op. cit.*, p.561.

p.443 'too sincere . . .': Whitehouse, *A Most Dangerous Woman?*, p.12.

p.443 'propaganda of . . .': *ibid*.

p.444 'She has chosen . . .': 24 May 1967, Bodleian.

p.444 'If you were to ask . . .': q. in Briggs, *op. cit.*, p.309.

p.444 'You're not . . .': Whitehouse, *op. cit.*, p.62.

p.444 'hopeless task . . .': *ibid*.

p.444 'the forces . . .': Lusty, *op. cit.*, p.246.

p.445 'There will be . . .': *ibid*, p.270.

p.445 'You and I . . .': q. in Cockerell, *op. cit.*, p.135.

p.445 'leave the BBC . . .': *ibid*.

p.445 'a disciplinarian . . .': q. in Briggs, *op. cit.*, p.596.

p.445 'So Harold . . .': q. in Cockerell, *op. cit.*, p.135.

p.445 'If I have . . .': 2 April 1968, Bodleian.

p.445 'Wait until . . .': Lusty, *op. cit.*, p.208.

p.445 'It's your own . . .': *ibid*.

p.445 'Charles Hill, sir . . .': Lusty, *op. cit.*, p.250.

p.446 'I hope he will realise . . .': *ibid*.

p.446 'Lord Hill is . . .': *ibid*.

p.446 'Hugh, I am sorry . . .': *ibid*, p. 251.

p.446 'But how can . . .': *ibid*, p.253.

p.446 'sat behind . . .': q. in Hill, *Behind the Screen*, p.72,

p.446 'despicable . . .': to Tatjana Sais, 28 July 1967, Bodleian.

p.446 'had never felt . . .': q. in Briggs, *op. cit.*, p.601.

p.446 'a shocked and . . .': Lusty, *op. cit.*, p.253.

p.446 'an appalling . . .': 27 July 1967, Bodleian.

p.446 'the pettiness . . .': q. in Briggs, *op. cit.*, p.603.

p.446 'Behind the scenes . . .': q. in Tracey, *op. cit.*, p.282.

p.447 'I am on holiday . . .': q. in Lusty, *op. cit.*, p.255.

p.447 'who, I thought . . .': Hill, *op. cit.*, p.74.

p.447 'need convincing . . .': *ibid*, p.78.

p.447 'stood four-square . . .': Lusty, *op. cit.*, p.264.

p.447 'Harold appointed . . .': q. in Cockerell, *op. cit.*, p.136.

p.447 'an almost total . . .': Lusty, *op. cit.*, p.263.

p.447 'aloof . . .': Hill, *op. cit.*, p.78.

p.447 'a great deal of . . .': to Tatjana Sais, 15 Sept. 1967, Bodleian.

p.448 'recognising that . . .': Hill, *op. cit.*, p.80.

p.448 'sealed his fate . . .': Whitehouse, *op. cit.*, p.65.

p.448 'It's one up . . .': Lusty, *op. cit.*, p.263.

p.448 'You matter . . .': 21 Dec. 1966, Bodleian.

p.448 'And then poor Hugh . . .': n.d. 1968, Georgetown.

p.448 'the beer side . . .': 5 April 1967, Bodleian.

p.448 'I went down . . .': 1 April 1964, Bodleian.

p.449 'Last night . . .': 6 Dec. 1966, Bodleian.

p.449 'What I am finding . . .': to Tatjana Sais, 13 Jan. 1967, Bodleian.

p.449 'It will be interesting . . .': 17 Feb. 1967, Bodleian.

p.449 'Not too gloomy . . .': to Catherine Walston, 8 April 1968, Georgetown.

p.449 'What really emerged . . .': 13 Sept. 1967, Bodleian.

p.449 'a woman named . . .': *The Times*, 3 Dec. 1968.

p.449 'wretched Director-General': 1 July 1968, Stuart (ed.), *Reith Diaries*, p.521.

p.449 'I should like . . .': q. in Briggs, *op. cit.*, p.609.

p.449 'and for the first time . . .': to Tatjana Sais, 26 March 1969, Bodleian.

p.449 'for the first time . . .': to Tatjana Sais, 31 March 1969, Bodleian.

p.450 'one of the most . . .': Lusty, *op. cit.*, p.246.

p.450 'the other great D-G': q. in Tracey, *op. cit.*, p.306.

p.450 'A born leader ...': Hill, *op. cit.*, p.142.

Chapter 29: The Old Firm

p.451 'place the film ...': Korda, *Another Life*, p.7.

p.451 'often said that ...': Cloetta, *In Search of a Beginning*, p.118.

p.452 'went to Poland ...': q. in West, *The Quest for Graham Greene*, p.155.

p.452 'we were by ourselves ...': to Yvonne Cloetta, n.d. 1975, Georgetown.

p.452 'I was never ...': 12 Sept. 1982, Boston.

p.452 'I never believed ...': Cloetta, *op. cit.*, p.136.

p.453 'I was flabbergasted ...': q. in Knightley, *Philby*, p.232.

p.453 'I always thought ...': 29 April 1968, Georgetown.

p.454 'shameful ...': Elliott, *With My Little Eye*, p.98.

p.454 'disloyalty is ...': to Elizabeth Bowen, n.d. 1948, LL, p.151.

p.454 'act as the devil's ...': 'The Virtue of Disloyalty', Adamson (ed.), *Reflections*, p.268.

p.454 'a piece of grit ...': *ibid*, p.269.

p.454 'never without bravado': Hazzard, *Greene on Capri*, p.99.

p.454 'I shall be in trouble ...': 9 April 1968, Georgetown.

p.454 'not only because ...': q. in Knightley, *op. cit.*, p.245.

p.454 'I hate to be confused ...': 27 Jan. 1980, Georgetown.

p.455 'you were the two ...': 5 April 1980, Georgetown.

p.455 'if there was anything ...': *Sunday Telegraph*, 10 May 1987.

p.455 'I received ten ...': 13 June 1988, HRHRC.

p.455 'I might have guessed ...': n.d., Boston.

p.455 'The "rise" refers ...': *ibid*.

p.455 'I don't at all ...': 6 March 1979, Boston.

p.456 'a novel free from ...': *Ways of Escape*, p.296.

p.456 'I was very uneasy ...': 19 May 1977, Georgetown.

p.456 '"Maurice" – yes ...': 9 March 1978, Boston.

p.456 'must in no way ...': *The Times*, 4 Sept. 1967, q. in Hawtree (ed.), *Yours Etc*, p.135.

p.456 'Christianity is ...': *The Times*, 22 Sept. 1977, q. in *Yours Etc*, p.138.

p.456 'If I live in a ...': *Evening Standard*, 9 Jan. 1978.

p.457 'Rufa said ...': 24 Sept. 1986, Georgetown.

p.457 'man of sarcastic ...': q. in Knightley, *op. cit.*, p.245.

p.457 'We loved our visit ...': 6 Oct. 1986, Georgetown.

p.457 'They were the most ...': q. in *ibid*, p.234.

p.457 'I told them that ...': q. in *ibid*, p.4.

p.458 'good and loyal friend': 15 May 1988, Georgetown.

p.458 'Prepare yourself ...': Knightley, *A Hack's Progress*, p.232.

p.458 'He would complain ...': Wolf, *Man Without a Face*, p.92.

p.458 'eyes behind ...': Knightley interview with Wolf, *Independent*, 27 Feb. 2008.

p.459 'the hounds of Granada ...': 25 Sept. 1980, Boston.

p.459 'a great friend ...': 20 Nov. 1990, Boston.

p.459 'agreed that the ...': *ibid*.

p.459 'has a suspicious ...': 23 Nov. 1990, Boston.

p.459 'a very charming ...': to Richard Greene, 1 April 2003.

p.459 'the angry exchanges ...': 4 Dec. 1990, Boston.

p.459 'though terminally ...': Cairncross, *The Enigma Spy*, p.184.

p.463 'I learned later ...': Euan Cameron, 'A Guiding Light': address to Graham Greene Literary Festival, Berkhamsted.

p.463 'I do think ...': 17 June 1980, p.c.

p.463 'If I felt ...': q. in letter from Max Reinhardt to Laurence Pollinger, 4 July 1986, HRHRC.

p.463 'Graham, with whom ...': 6 Feb. 1987, q. in Adamson, *Max Reinhardt*, p.161.

p.463 'I have been thinking ...': 10 March 1987, Boston.

p.463 'completely available ...': 16 Feb. 1987, Boston.

p.463 'to pursue the course . . .': 23 March 1987, Reading.

p.464 'pure fantasy': q. in GG letter to *The Times*, 22 March 1987.

p.464 'he himself . . .': *ibid*.

p.464 'one brief letter . . .': *Observer*, 13 March 1988.

p.464 'Uncle Graham . . .': *Observer*, 13 March 1988.

p.464 'I knew, and . . .': Maschler, *Publisher*, p.234.

p.464 'without my knowledge . . .': Reinhardt, *Memories*, p.82.

p.465 'We were scared . . .': q. in de Bellaigue, *British Book Publishing as a Business Since the 1960s*, p.156.

p.465 'The recent flurry . . .': 15 April 1987, Boston.

p.465 'if the new American . . .': letter to *Independent*, 3 June 1987.

p.465 'Before writing . . .': letter to *Independent*, 4 June 1987.

p.465 'I can't bear . . .': *A World of My Own*, p.68.

Chapter 30: Closing Time

p.466 'a vague idea . . .': 21 May 1962, Georgetown.

p.466 'It's a good thing . . .': 27 July 1963, Georgetown.

p.467 'looking through . . .': to GG, 1 Oct. 1969, Boston.

p.467 'I could see . . .': Rankin, *Dead Man's Chest*, p.65.

p.467 'one of the family': *ibid*, p.68.

p.468 'As your brother . . .': 24 Nov. 1962, Bodleian.

p.468 'I have always had . . .': 20 Jan. 1964, p.c.

p.468 'I liked Herbert . . .': Nick Dennys to author.

p.468 'now almost incapacitated . . .': to HCG, 6 Oct. 1965, Bodleian.

p.469 'I am sure . . .': Dr P. M. J. Tomlinson to RG, 29 Nov. 1968, p.c.

p.469 'It was, of course . . .': 22 Nov. 1969, *LL*, p.303.

p.469 'I cannot risk . . .': 30 April 1975, p.c.

p.470 'had been conveniently . . .': John Grigg, *Sunday Telegraph*, 25 Sept. 1977.

p.470 'received abusive . . .': to Cambridge University Press, 26 Jan, 1978, p.c.

p.470 'go too far . . .': 26 Jan. 1978, p.c.

p.471 'if we issue . . .': *ibid*.

p.471 'a huge, open-hearted . . .': n.d., p.c.

p.471 'I do miss . . .': 28 May 1978, p.c.

p.472 'It is a pity that . . .': 28 Nov. 1960, p.c.

p.472 'Elena and Anne . . .': to Eva Greene, 21 May 1970, p.c.

p.472 'unbelievable suffering . . .': 'Thoughts on Becoming Seventy', 22 May 1979, p.c.

p.473 'I'm afraid my Quaker . . .': 7 Oct. 1968, p.c.

p.473 'I know only too . . .': 16 Dec. 1968, p.c.

p.473 'I think they found . . .': 22 Aug. 1969, p.c.

p.473 'It was good . . .': to Catherine Walston, 1 Aug. 1952, Georgetown.

p.473 'You would like him . . .': n.d., p.c.

p.474 'Your book is . . .': 5 Aug. 1981, p.c.

p.474 'I really rather . . .': to HCG, 10 May 1984, Bodleian.

p.474 'Raymond is a very . . .': 6 June 1981, p.c.

p.474 'Please don't . . .': 17 Aug. 1981, p.c.

p.474 'I was glad . . .': 16 June 1989, p.c.

p.474 'little gangster': BG to HCG, 10 May 1984, Bodleian.

p.474 'Poor Raymond . . .': 16 July 1986. p.c.

p.474 'You are the real . . .': 30 Jan. 1975, *LL*, p.333.

p.475 'I was very aware . . .': Annabel Gooch, 'Impressions of My Father', n.d., p.c.

p.475 'What a handsome . . .': Nick Dennys to author.

p.475 'very worried . . .': to Yvonne Cloetta, 10 Aug. 1972, Georgetown.

p.475 'diagnosed it . . .': 23 Dec. 1975, Georgetown.

p.475 'How very stupid . . .': 21 July 1976, Boston.

p.475 'I'm afraid Raymond . . .': 6 May 1981, Georgetown.

p.475 'He was as alert . . .': Gant, 'A memoir of Dr Raymond Greene', n.d., p.c.

p.475 'That was a narrow . . .': Oliver Greene to author.

p.476 'was struck . . .': James Greene, 'Nepotism', n.d., Georgetown.

p.476 'I've got a lot . . .': 1 April 1969, Bodleian.

p.476 'It would be rather . . .': 7 Aug. 1968, Boston.

p.476 'Max, in case . . .': Reinhardt, Memories, p.73.

p.476 'used to have . . .': ibid, p.74.

p.477 'the old relationship . . .': 30 May 1987, Georgetown.

p.477 'small man . . .': Sunday Telegraph, 2 Aug. 1970.

p.478 'Someone called me . . .': 30 Jan. 1975, Boston.

p.478 '14-lb ham . . .': diary, 31 July 1977.

p.478 'the two Grahams . . .': diary, 19 Aug. 1981.

p.479 'Why don't you . . .': q. in Lambert, The Bodley Head, p.325.

p.479 'build the whole . . .': HCG to Tatjana Sais, 30 July 1967, Bodleian.

p.479 'the agonies . . .': ibid.

p.479 'I expect it . . .': 16 June 1984, p.c.

p.479 'cut off the balls . . .': n.d., Georgetown.

p.480 'I felt certain . . .': 6 April 1977, Georgetown.

p.480 'determined that . . .': 3 June 1977, Boston.

p.480 'not intelligent enough . . .': 7 July 1977, Boston.

p.480 'scandal-monger . . .': 3 June 1977, Boston.

p.480 'I don't in the least . . .': 6 April 1977, Georgetown.

p.480 'That poor Sherry . . .': to Catherine Walston, 10 July 1978, Georgetown.

p.480 'Norman Sherry kept . . .': 17 May 1971, Boston.

p.480 'lay off': 7 Jan. 1978, p.c.

p.480 'a nice man . . .': 5 Nov. 1984, A Life in Letters, p.384.

p.481 'distressed by . . .': 25 April 1989, Boston.

p.481 'Yes, Norman . . .': 8 July 1987, Boston.

p.481 'keep Mockler . . .': 30 Oct. 1988, Boston.

p.481 'He has been plaguing . . .': to Julia Stonor, 8 Sept. 1987, p.c.

p.481 'You must know . . .': 7 March 1987, Bodleian.

p.481 'quite ready to read . . .': 3 Oct. 1988, Boston.

p.481 'Really! . . .': 18 April 1989, Boston.

p.481 'I am sorry to think . . .': 16 June 1989, p.c.

p.481 'I think you were right . . .': 26 April 1990, Boston.

p.481 'Understanding your . . .': 3 July 1975, q. in A Life in Letters, p.430.

p.482 'Professor Sherry is . . .': 8 Feb. 1990, Boston.

p.482 'I am glad that . . .': 28 July 1989, p.c.

p.482 'The book is our gift . . .': 1 July 1983, p.c.

p.482 'It is only . . .': 13 May 1983, p.c.

p.482 'human humming . . .': to Flanagans, 7 Feb. 1984, p.c.

p.482 'a tiny niggling . . .': to Flanagans, 6 Feb. 1983, p.c.

p.483 'appropriate for . . .': 16 Aug. 1983, p.c.

p.483 'You seem to find . . .': 7 June 1983, p.c.

p.483 'whether it will be . . .': 7 Sept. 1983, p.c.

p.483 'I do not want . . .': to Tooter Greene, 17 Feb. 1983, p.c.

p.483 'It is complete nonsense . . .': q. in letter from Pat Flanagan to FG, 28 Feb. 1983, p.c.

p.483 'Truth is always . . .': 22 Feb. 1983, p.c.

p.483 'You must, must . . .': 8 March 1983, p.c.

p.484 'has very decided . . .': 17 July 1983, p.c.

p.484 'a sense of inferiority . . .': to Flanagans, 8 March 1983, p.c.

p.484 'Very flashy . . .': 20 Sept. 1965, p.c.

p.484 'I had an affectionate . . .': 16 April 1984, p.c.

p.484 'I am perhaps . . .': to Pat Flanagan, n.d., p.c.

p.484 'Elena, Anne and I . . .': 6 June 1984, p.c.

p.485 'I received a letter . . .': 24 Sept. 1984, p.c.

p.485 'Our two families . . .': 22 Sept. 1984, p.c.

p.485 'We were looking . . .': 27 April 1985.

p.485 'I was very sorry . . .': 23 July 1985.

p.486 'he was more fun . . .': Sarah Greene to author.

p.486 'to see if my brain . . .': q. in Sarah Greene to author.

p.486 'I don't need . . .': 26 Feb. 1987, Georgetown.

p.486 'The death was . . .': 10 March 1987, Georgetown.

p.486 'Moscow and . . .': 26 Feb. 1987, Georgetown.

p.487 'I found Sarah . . .': *ibid.*

p.487 'the intricacies . . .': 'Nepotism', *op. cit.*

p.487 'help you "exorcise" . . .': q. in *ibid.*

p.487 'It will be . . .': 12 April 1979, Georgetown.

p.487 'so far as I can . . .': 'Nepotism', *op. cit.*

p.487 'generous, considerate . . .': *ibid.*

p.487 'I don't suppose . . .': 20 Feb. 1987, Bodleian.

p.487 'never really forgave . . .': 30 May 1987, Georgetown.

p.487 'As I said . . .': 2 March 1987, Georgetown.

p.487 'I imagine you may . . .': 9 March 1987, Georgetown.

p.488 'Poor Hugh . . .': 24 Aug. 1987, Georgetown.

p.488 'was something of . . .': 11 May 1987, Georgetown.

p.488 'expect we'll ever . . .': 30 Sept. 1987, Georgetown.

p.488 'The service was . . .': 13 May 1987, Boston.

p.488 'respectful agnostic': q. in Tracey, *A Variety of Lives*, p.180.

p.489 'I am so sorry . . .': 25 Feb. 1991, Boston.

p.489 'Poor Tooter . . .': 7 Dec. 1990, Boston.

p.489 'My generation . . .': to Amanda Sanders, 25 Feb. 1991, Boston.

p.489 'What a wonderful . . .': 16 Nov. 1990, Boston.

p.489 'The Greenes are going . . .': 4 Dec. 1990.

p.489 'there was something . . .': Hazzard, *Greene on Capri*, p.143.

p.490 'In answer to this . . .': 18 Sept. 1982, Powell, *Journals 1982-1986*, p.36.

p.490 'although I've nothing . . .': The *Tablet*, 23 Sept. 1989.

p.490 'the last title . . .': *Ways of Escape*, p.252.

p.490 'is with lots . . .': q. in David Cesarani, *Arthur Koestler: The Homeless Mind*, p.218.

p.491 'I don't believe . . .': *Tablet*, op. cit.

p.491 'to a certain extent . . .': q. in Duran, *Graham Greene: Friend and Brother*, p.289.

p.491 'I have faith . . .': *ibid.*

p.491 'but I have interpreted . . .': 14 May 1990, p.c.

p.491 'I am afraid . . .': 20 Nov. 1990, p.c.

p.491 'his eyes shining . . .': Yvonne Cloetta to Gillian Sutro, 27 March 1001, Bodleian.

p.491 '"There's nothing . . ."': *ibid.*

p.491 'did not seem to care . . .': *ibid.*

p.491 'Why does it . . .': *ibid.*

Index

www.vintage-books.co.uk